C# Web Services

Building Web Services with .NET Remoting and ASP.NET

Ashish Banerjee

Aravind Corera

Zach Greenvoss

Andrew Krowczyk

Brad Maiani

Christian Nagel

Chris Peiris

Thiru Thangarathinam

D1369264

Wrox Press Ltd. ®

C# Web Services

Building Web Services with .NET Remoting and ASP.NET

Published by Wrox Press Ltd,
Arden House, 1102 Warwick Road, Acocks Green,
Birmingham, B27 6BH, UK
Printed in America
ISBN 1-861004-39-7

Trademark Acknowledgements

Credits

Authors
Ashish Banerjee
Aravind Corera
Zach Greenvoss
Andrew Krowczyk
Brad Maiani
Christian Nagel
Chris Peiris
Thiru Thangarathinam

Technical Architect
Julian Skinner

Technical Editors
Richard Deeson
Daniel Kent
Allan Jones
Adrian Young

Author Agent
Chris Matterface

Project Administrator
Rob Hesketh
Charlotte Smith

Category Manager
Sonia Mullineux

Illustrations
Natalie O'Donnell
Emma Eato

Cover
Chris Morris

Proof Reader
Chris Smith

Technical Reviewers
Ramesh Balaji
Christopher Blexrud
Brandon Bohling
Paul Brazdzionis
Andreas Christiansen
Navin Coutinho
Cristian Darie
Mitch Denny
Stephen Ekpenyong
Slavomir Furman
Brian Hickey
Ben Hickman
Mark Horner
Ron Landers
Don Lee
Gaurav Mantro
Shaun Mcaravey
Jason Montgomery
Kester Neal
Johan Normen
Aruna Panangipally
Maria Pettit
Santosh Ramakrishnan
Scott Robertson
Larry Schoneman
David Schultz
Keyur Shah
Rahul Sharma
Marc Simkin
Srinivas Vignesh R

Index
Bill Johncocks

Production Manager
Liz Toy

Production Coordinator
Emma Eato

About the Authors

Ashish Banerjee

Ashish Banerjee is the Technical Director and CTO (Chief Technical Officer) of Osprey Software Technology (http://www.ospreyindia.com), a 10+ year old software company with development centers in India, the UK and the USA.

He has 14 years of experience in programming and core software technology development. He specializes in telecom software technology. Over the course of this 14 years, he has developed device drivers in both assembler and C, Adverse Drug Reactions Management Systems in C and Oracle on VAX/VMS platform for the USA and the German pharmaceutical industry, designed a super computer's OS and developed a parallelizing compiler. He conducted research work on an Object-Oriented Database in C++, and a Java-based TCP/IP gateway to X.25 Airline reservation systems based on RS6000 clusters. He was a consultant for an EDI extranet application for US Energy. He has also directed research on the Java Advanced Intelligent Network (JAIN).

His recent achievements include a Java-based GSM/SMS mobile commerce gateway for the banking industry, and he has recently designed a Unified Messaging System covering GSM/SMS, e-mail, radio paging, fax, and voice gateways with intercity message routing. He has also architected the International Advertisement Festival (Cannes, France) enterprise intranet and online voting systems.

He guides Masters of Technology-level research and thesis projects for I.E.T.E. (Institute of Electronics and Telecommunications Engineers, found online at http://www.iete.org). He has guided more than 10 postgraduate projects, most of them in the Java telecom software, 3G, and mobile commerce arena.

His areas of professional interests include Telecom, Bioinformatics, and Cryptography. Ashish Banerjee is a Linux and Open Source evangelist.

In his free time he writes about computing and teaches himself Sanskrit.

Aravind Corera

Aravind Corera is an independent software developer who lives and works in Chennai, India, and is currently involved in the design and development of a workflow process automation system. He has been working on Microsoft-based technologies for the past six years, particularly in designing and developing systems based on Microsoft's Component Object Model (COM). Aravind's areas of special interest include Concurrent programming, Distributed Systems, and Transaction Processing Monitors. He holds a degree in Computer Science and Engineering from the Coimbatore Institute of Technology.

Dedicated to my parents who have stood by me, when I needed them most.

Zach Greenvoss

Zach Greenvoss, MCSD, is a Senior Consultant with Magenic Technologies, a Microsoft Gold Certified consulting firm in Northern California. He specializes in middle-tier architecture and implementation, utilizing various technologies including COM+, MSMQ, BizTalk, XML, and the .NET Framework. Before Magenic, Zach worked at the Defense Manpower Data Center in Monterey California, where he developed client-server applications for the Department of Defense.

Zach and his wife, Amanda enjoy globetrotting, caving, gaming, and playing with their two cats. He can be reached at zachg@magenic.com.

I would like to thank my wife Amanda for all her patience, love, and understanding of the time required to both work and write. A special thanks to my parents for always providing an environment in which I could explore my interest in computers and technology. Finally, I am proud to say that I am a CSU Monterey Bay graduate – Go Otters!

Andrew Krowczyk

Andrew Krowczyk is a Senior Software Developer for Zurich North America. He is an MCSD with a Computer Science degree, and is currently wrapping up his Master's degree. At Zurich North America Andrew uses his strong technical skills in Microsoft technologies to develop software that is used in Global company applications. He specializes in COM (+), C++ (C#), VB (VB.NET), ASP (ASP.NET), XML, SQL Server, and related Microsoft technologies. An avid bleeding edge enthusiast, Andrew jumped on the .NET bandwagon right away. He's written several articles for Wrox Press journals such as *ASPToday*, and *C# Today*. He is also a technical reviewer for both journals. Andrew currently resides in the Chicago Suburbs and can be contacted via e-mail at krowczyk@i-netway.com.

I want to thank my wonderful wife Eleanore, for all of her love and support. Without her, I wouldn't be where I'm at today. Thanks for being there Ellie, I love you.

Brad Maiani

Brad Maiani worked throughout the 1980s in the San Francisco Bay Area as a jazz pianist and teacher. A sudden and overwhelming fascination with medieval music led him to graduate school in 1990, where he finished a Ph.D. in Musicology in 1995 with a prize-winning dissertation (on a Gregorian Chant topic, of all things). After teaching music theory for several years at Duke and UNC Chapel Hill, he was faced with a question: pick up the family and move again for another academic gig, or attempt to actually make a living with his lifelong hobby (programming, of course)? The choice was obvious, and he's glad he made it. (So are the kids!)

Brad lives happily with his love Rhonda and their three beautiful children Ryan, Lia, and Tyler, and would be glad to hear from you at bradm@nc.rr.com.

Christian Nagel

Christian Nagel is working as a trainer and consultant for Global Knowledge, the largest independent information technology training provider. Having worked with PDP 11, VMS, and Unix platforms, he looks back on more than 15 years of experience in the field of software development. With his profound knowledge of Microsoft technologies – he's certified as a Microsoft Certified Trainer (MCT), a Solution Developer (MCSD), and a Systems Engineer (MCSE) – he enjoys teaching others programming and architecting distributed solutions. As the founder of the .NET User Group Austria and as an MSDN Regional Director, he is a speaker at European conferences (such as TechEd and VCDC), and is contacted by many developers for consulting and customized courses. You will find Christian's web site at http://christian.nagel.net.

Chris Peiris

Chris Peiris is a systems architect for IT & E-Commerce in Melbourne, Australia. He has designed and developed Microsoft web solutions since 1995. His expertise lies in developing scalable, high-performance web solutions for financial institutions and media groups. Chris will be lecturing "Component Technology" and "Distributed Object Technology" subjects at Monash University, Victoria, Australia. These subjects are based on .Net, COM, DCOM, .Net Remoting, CORBA, Java Beans, and Java RMI. He also writes for several online technical publications and Wrox Press. His core skills are C++, Java, .NET, DNA, MTS, ASP, Site Server, Data Warehousing, WAP, and C++ SQL Server. He can be reached at http://www.chrispeiris.com.

To my father who taught me to conquer,
To my mother who taught me to love at any cost,
To my brother who taught me discipline,
To my friends who taught me to respect,
And to Karen who gave me hope.
To all of you who made my life worthwhile... this is for you.

Thiru Thangarathinam

Thiru works as a Consultant at Spherion Technology Architects, an international technology consulting company in Phoenix, Arizona. He is an MCSD. During the last two years, he has been developing distributed n-tier architecture solutions for various companies using latest technologies such as VB, ASP, XML, XSL, COM+, and SQL Server. When not sitting in front of his computer and writing .NET code, Thiru can be found chatting with his family, listening to Tamil songs and of course reading books. He can be reached via e-mail at ThiruThangarathinam@spherion.com.

I would like to dedicate this book to my father who has been a source of motivation and inspiration for me all along. Special Thanks to Chris for her constant support and being so helpful throughout this project.

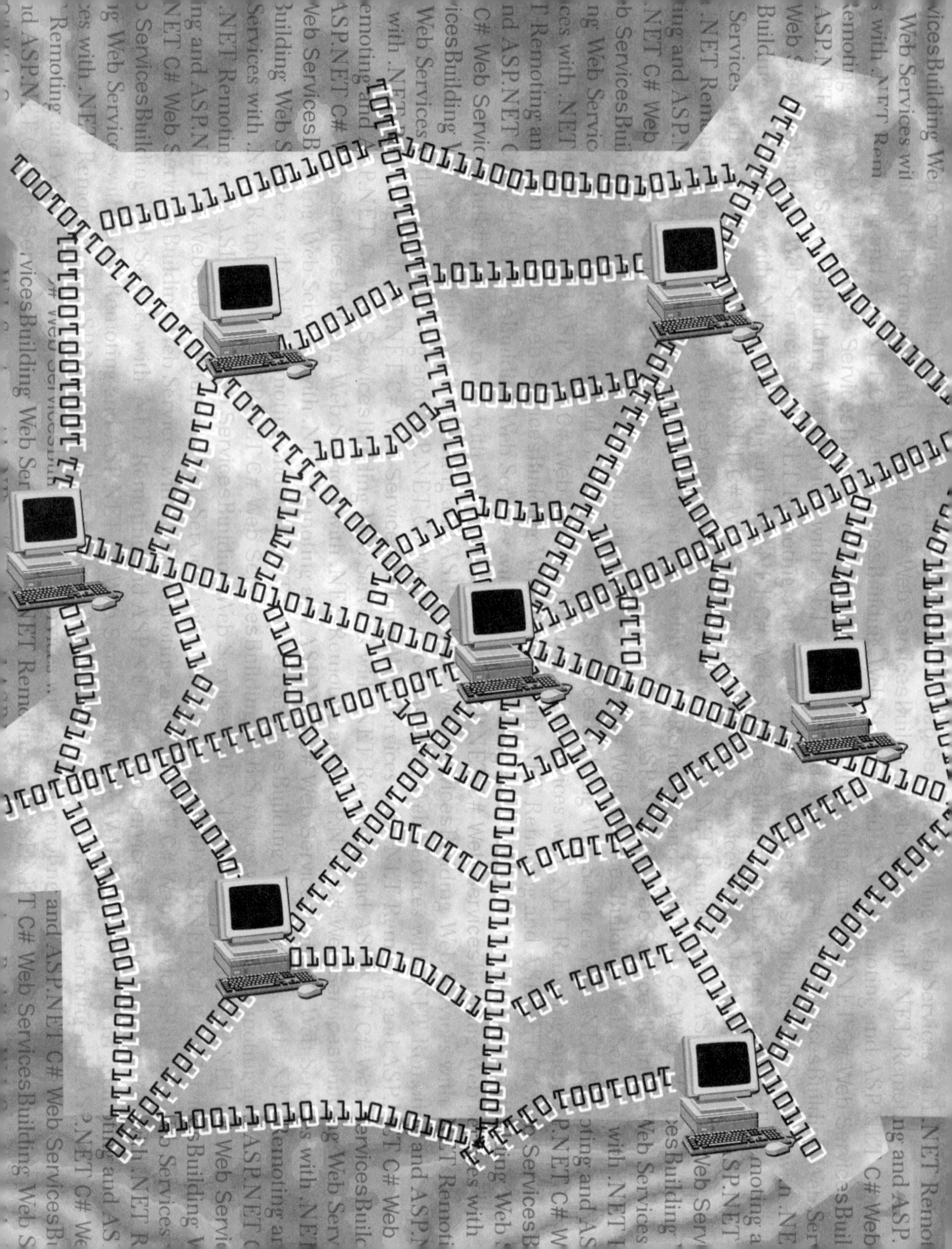

Table of Contents

Table of Contents

Table of Contents

Table of Contents

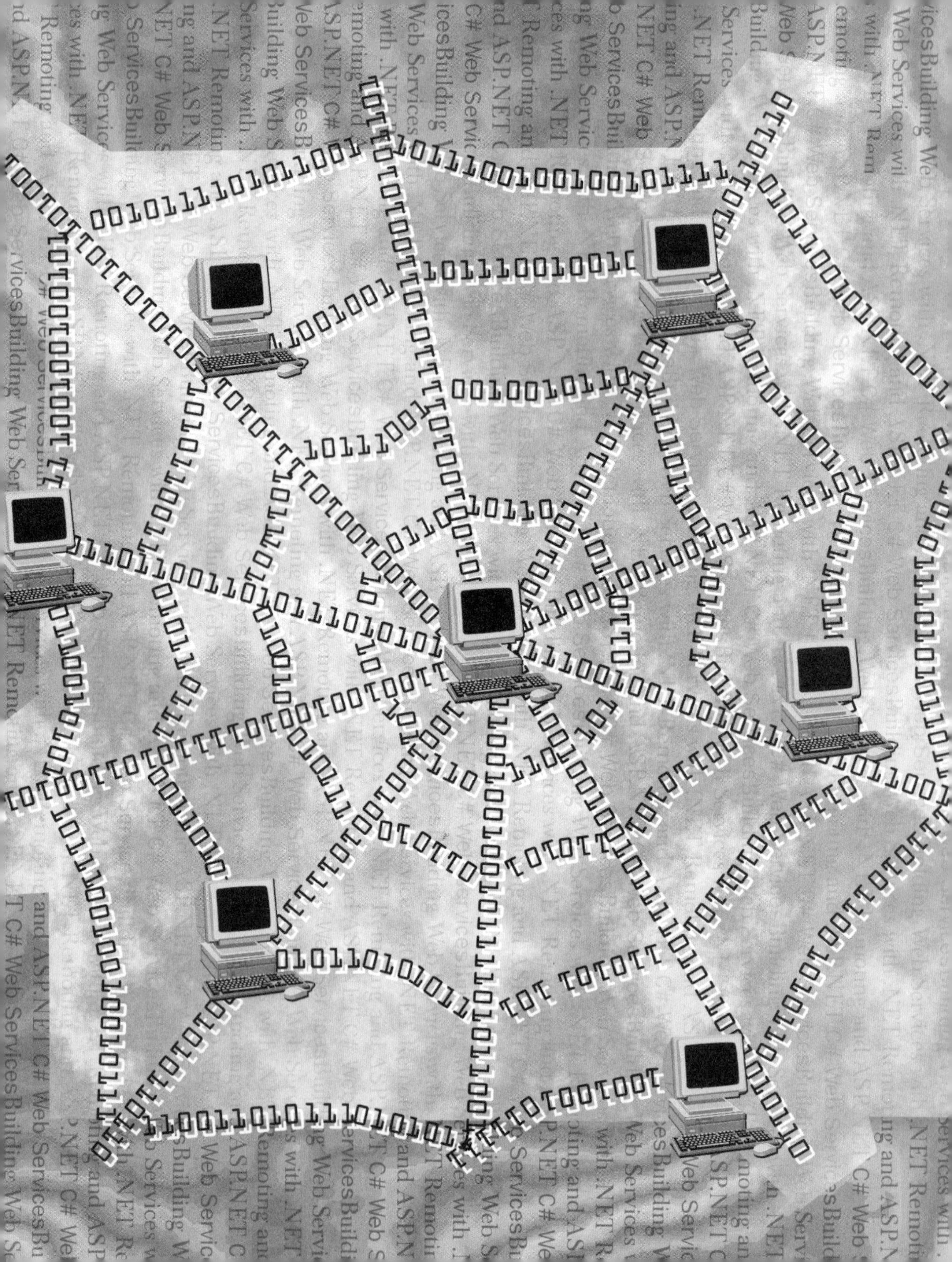

Introduction

What Are Web Services?

Web services are the latest thing in application development, and have attracted the interest of developers working on all platforms. The fundamental concept is simple – web services allow us to make Remote Procedure Calls (RPCs) against an object over the Internet or a network. Web services aren't the first technology to allow us to do this, but they differ from previous technologies in that their use of platform-neutral standards such as HTTP and XML allows us to hide the implementation details entirely from the client. The client needs to know the URL of the service, and the data types used for the method calls, but doesn't need to know whether the service was built in Java and is running on Linux, or is an ASP.NET web service running on Windows.

Microsoft has enthusiastically taken up support for web services in the .NET Framework. In particular, it has provided a number of tools (not least Visual Studio .NET) that make building and accessing web services extremely easy. This book looks at the different ways that we can build web services using C# and the .NET Framework, and at the tools, technologies, and protocols that we will need to work with if we're to take advantage of this vital development.

What Does This Book Cover?

The .NET Framework provides two ways to build web services: **ASP.NET** and **.NET Remoting**. In this book, we will look at both of these methods in detail, providing plenty of example services to show how these will integrate into real applications, and to provide ideas about potential uses for this vital new technology.

We start in **Chapter 1** by looking at what web services are, why they are needed, and how they developed. We also look at some of the benefits that can be gained by using web services, and take a high-level overview of the architecture of a web service.

Chapter 2 looks at the standards and protocols that web services are based on – SOAP and WSDL. It is these standards that allow web services to hide their implementation details, and provide the cross-platform interoperability that is one of the key advantages of web services.

In **Chapter 3**, we start to delve into the specifics of Microsoft's implementations of web services. The Microsoft world provides four ways to build web services (apart from manually creating the SOAP and WSDL files!): ASP.NET and .NET Remoting (which we cover in depth in this book), the VB SOAP Toolkit for exposing COM components as web services, and ATL Server (which provides an easy way to build ISAPI filters, including web services, in unmanaged C++).

We now move on to the core of the book – the sections that will look, in detail, at building web services and web service clients using the tools provided by the .NET Framework. **Chapter 4** demonstrates building an ASP.NET web service. We see how to create, test, debug, and deploy an ASP.NET web service using the example of a credit card validation service.

Now that we've got a web service, we'll need to access it, so **Chapter 5** discusses how to build a client for our new service. There are two ways to do this automatically – using the command-line tool wsdl.exe, and using Visual Studio .NET. This chapter looks at both of these methods of generating ASP.NET web service clients.

The next four chapters deal with .NET Remoting web services. This section starts with an overview of Remoting and the .NET Remoting architecture in **Chapter 6**. Here we introduce the concepts and classes used by the Remoting infrastructure.

Next, in **Chapter 7**, we look at building web services with .NET Remoting and Web Services Anywhere, which is Microsoft's name for web services that use Remoting. .NET Remoting allows us to host our web services in any application – not only IIS – and to use any channel (both a TCP and an HTTP channel are provided), and any format (SOAP and binary formatters are provided).

Now that the concepts of Remoting and Web Services Anywhere have been introduced, we build an example Remoting web service in **Chapter 8**. This chapter uses the example of a pizza delivery company, and uses both the HTTP and TCP channels.

Again, now that we've got a web service, we'll need to build a client application to access it. **Chapter 9** does just this, using the soapsuds.exe utility to create a proxy for the web service, and building web and Windows clients for our service.

The usefulness of web services is obviously limited if we need to know their URLs before they can be accessed. **Chapter 10** looks at Universal Description, Discovery, and Integration (UDDI), which provides a means for us to publish the URLs of our web services and descriptions of their functionality. This allows potential users to find them without having to know their URL in advance.

Chapter 11 looks at an important but little-documented topic – securing web services using the .NET cryptography classes. To demonstrate this, we use a Remoting web service and build a custom channel sink where we apply the encryption/decryption. This concept is developed further in Case Study 2.

Chapter 12 demonstrates an interesting possibility – using a web service to deliver a Windows forms assembly, which can then be instantiated on the client. We use the example of a timesheet application which can be downloaded from our web service and saved locally or run directly. This provides an interesting solution to distribution and versioning problems with desktop applications. We also allow the application's data to be saved to the client, so the application can be run even if no network connection is available.

Finally, to demonstrate some of the possibilities of web services, we look at two **Case Studies**. The first is a flight reservation system built around an ASP.NET web service, and demonstrates how a web service can be integrated into a large web application. The second uses .NET Remoting, and demonstrates how we can build a custom channel sink to implement a cryptography layer that we can plug in to any Remoting web service.

Who Is This Book For?

This book is aimed at experienced developers, who already have some experience of developing or experimenting within the .NET Framework with C#. We also assume some familiarity with ASP.NET and web programming.

What You Need to Use This Book

To run the examples in this book you need to have the following:

❑   Windows 2000 or Windows XP with IIS 5 or later

❑   The .NET Framework SDK Beta 2 or later. The code in this book will not work with .NET Beta 1. Wherever possible, the code has been tested with the Release Candidate.

The complete sourcecode for the examples is available for download from our web site at http://www.wrox.com/Books/Book_Details.asp?isbn=1861004397.

Conventions

We've used a number of different styles of text and layout in this book to help differentiate between the different kinds of information. Here are examples of the styles we used and an explanation of what they mean.

Code has several fonts. If it's a word that we're talking about in the text – for example, when discussing a for (...) loop, it's in this font. If it's a block of code that can be typed as a program and run, then it's also in a gray box:

```
for (int i = 0; i < 10; i++)
{
    Console.WriteLine(i);
}
```

Sometimes we'll see code in a mixture of styles, like this:

```
for (int i = 0; i < 10; i++)
{
    Console.Write("The next number is: );
    Console.WriteLine(i);
}
```

In cases like this, the code with a white background is code we are already familiar with; the line highlighted in gray is a new addition to the code since we last looked at it.

Advice, hints, and background information comes in this type of font.

> **Important pieces of information come in boxes like this.**

Bullets appear indented, with each new bullet marked as follows:

- ❑ **Important Words** are in a bold type font
- ❑ Words that appear on the screen, or in menus like the File or Window, are in a similar font to the one you would see on a Windows desktop
- ❑ Keys that you press on the keyboard like *Ctrl* and *Enter*, are in italics

Customer Support

We always value hearing from our readers, and we want to know what you think about this book: what you liked, what you didn't like, and what you think we can do better next time. You can send us your comments, either by returning the reply card in the back of the book, or by e-mail to feedback@wrox.com. Please be sure to mention the book title in your message.

How to Download the Sample Code for the Book

When you visit the Wrox site, http://www.wrox.com/, simply locate the title through our Search facility or by using one of the title lists. Click on Download in the Code column, or on Download Code on the book's detail page.

The files that are available for download from our site have been archived using WinZip. When you have saved the attachments to a folder on your hard-drive, you need to extract the files using a de-compression program such as WinZip or PKUnzip. When you extract the files, the code is usually extracted into chapter folders. When you start the extraction process, ensure your software (WinZip, PKUnzip, etc.) is set to use folder names.

Errata

We've made every effort to make sure that there are no errors in the text or in the code. However, no one is perfect and mistakes do occur. If you find an error in one of our books, like a spelling mistake or a faulty piece of code, we would be very grateful for feedback. By sending in errata you may save another reader hours of frustration, and of course, you will be helping us provide even higher quality information. Simply e-mail the information to support@wrox.com; your information will be checked and if correct, posted to the errata page for that title, or used in subsequent editions of the book.

To find errata on the web site, go to http://www.wrox.com/, and simply locate the title through our Advanced Search or title list. Click on the Book Errata link, which is below the cover graphic on the book's detail page.

E-Mail Support

If you wish to directly query a problem in the book with an expert who knows the book in detail then e-mail support@wrox.com, with the title of the book and the last four numbers of the ISBN in the subject field of the e-mail. A typical e-mail should include the following things:

- ❑ The **title of the book**, **last four digits of the ISBN**, and **page number** of the problem in the Subject field.

- ❑ Your **name**, **contact information**, and the **problem** in the body of the message.

We *won't* send you junk mail. We need the details to save your time and ours. When you send an e-mail message, it will go through the following chain of support:

- ❑ Customer Support – Your message is delivered to our customer support staff, who are the first people to read it. They have files on most frequently asked questions and will answer anything general about the book or the web site immediately.

- ❑ Editorial – Deeper queries are forwarded to the technical editor responsible for that book. They have experience with the programming language or particular product, and are able to answer detailed technical questions on the subject.

- ❑ The Authors – Finally, in the unlikely event that the editor cannot answer your problem, they will forward the request to the author. We do try to protect the author from any distractions to their writing; however, we are quite happy to forward specific requests to them. All Wrox authors help with the support on their books. They will e-mail the customer and the editor with their response, and again all readers should benefit.

The Wrox Support process can only offer support to issues that are directly pertinent to the content of our published title. Support for questions that fall outside the scope of normal book support is provided via the community lists of our http://p2p.wrox.com/ forum.

p2p.wrox.com

For author and peer discussion join the P2P mailing lists. Our unique system provides **programmer to programmer**™ contact on mailing lists, forums, and newsgroups, all in addition to our one-to-one e-mail support system. If you post a query to P2P, you can be confident that it is being examined by the many Wrox authors and other industry experts who are present on our mailing lists. At p2p.wrox.com you will find a number of different lists that will help you, not only while you read this book, but also as you develop your own applications.

To subscribe to a mailing list just follow these steps:

1. Go to http://p2p.wrox.com/

2. Choose the appropriate category from the left menu bar

3. Click on the mailing list you wish to join

4. Follow the instructions to subscribe and fill in your e-mail address and password

5. Reply to the confirmation e-mail you receive

6. Use the subscription manager to join more lists and set your e-mail preferences

Why this System Offers the Best Support

You can choose to join the mailing lists or you can receive them as a weekly digest. If you don't have the time, or facility, to receive the mailing list, then you can search our online archives. Junk and spam mails are deleted, and your own e-mail address is protected by the unique Lyris system. Queries about joining or leaving lists, and any other general queries about lists, should be sent to listsupport@p2p.wrox.com.

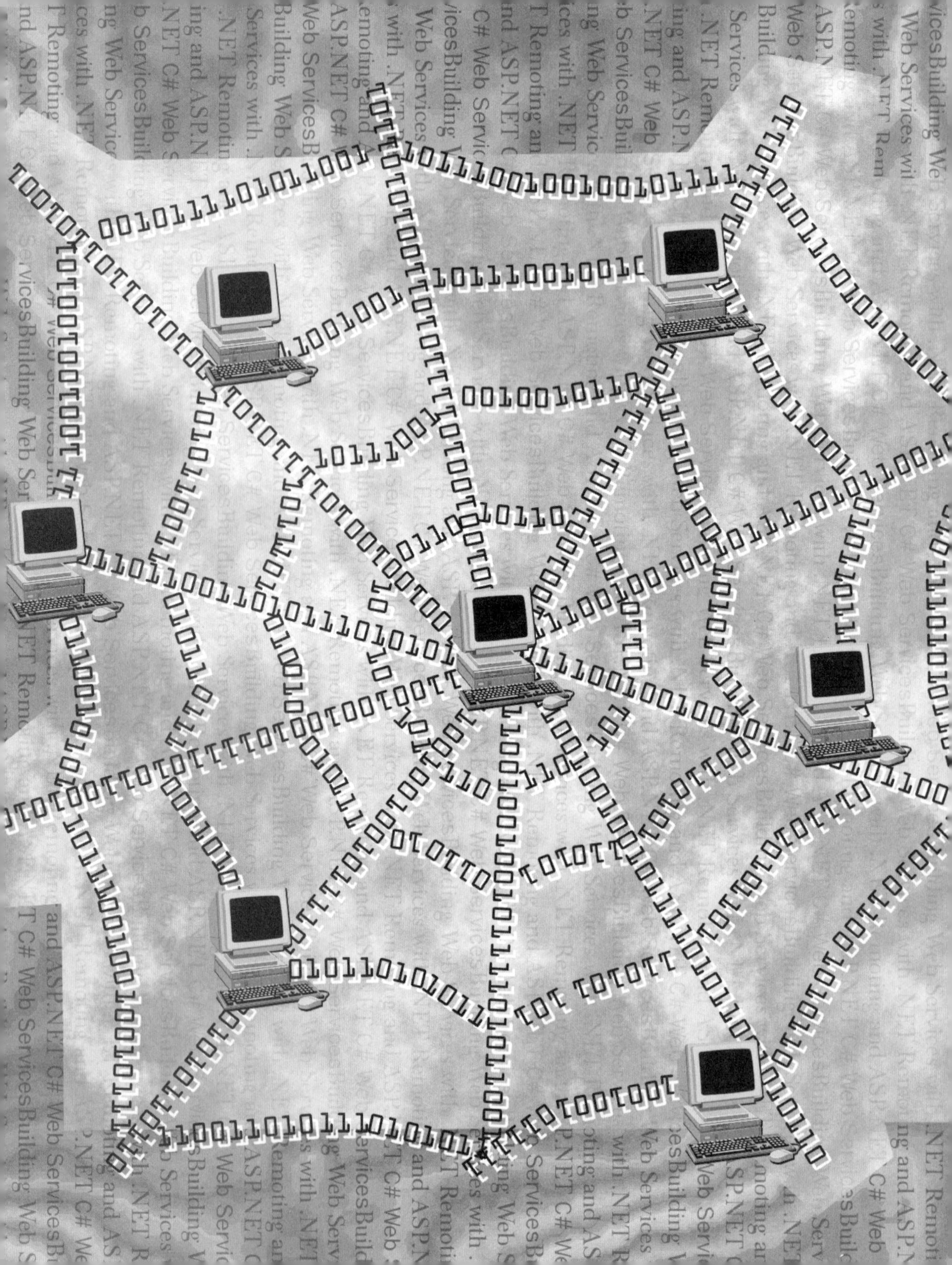

Section One – Getting Started

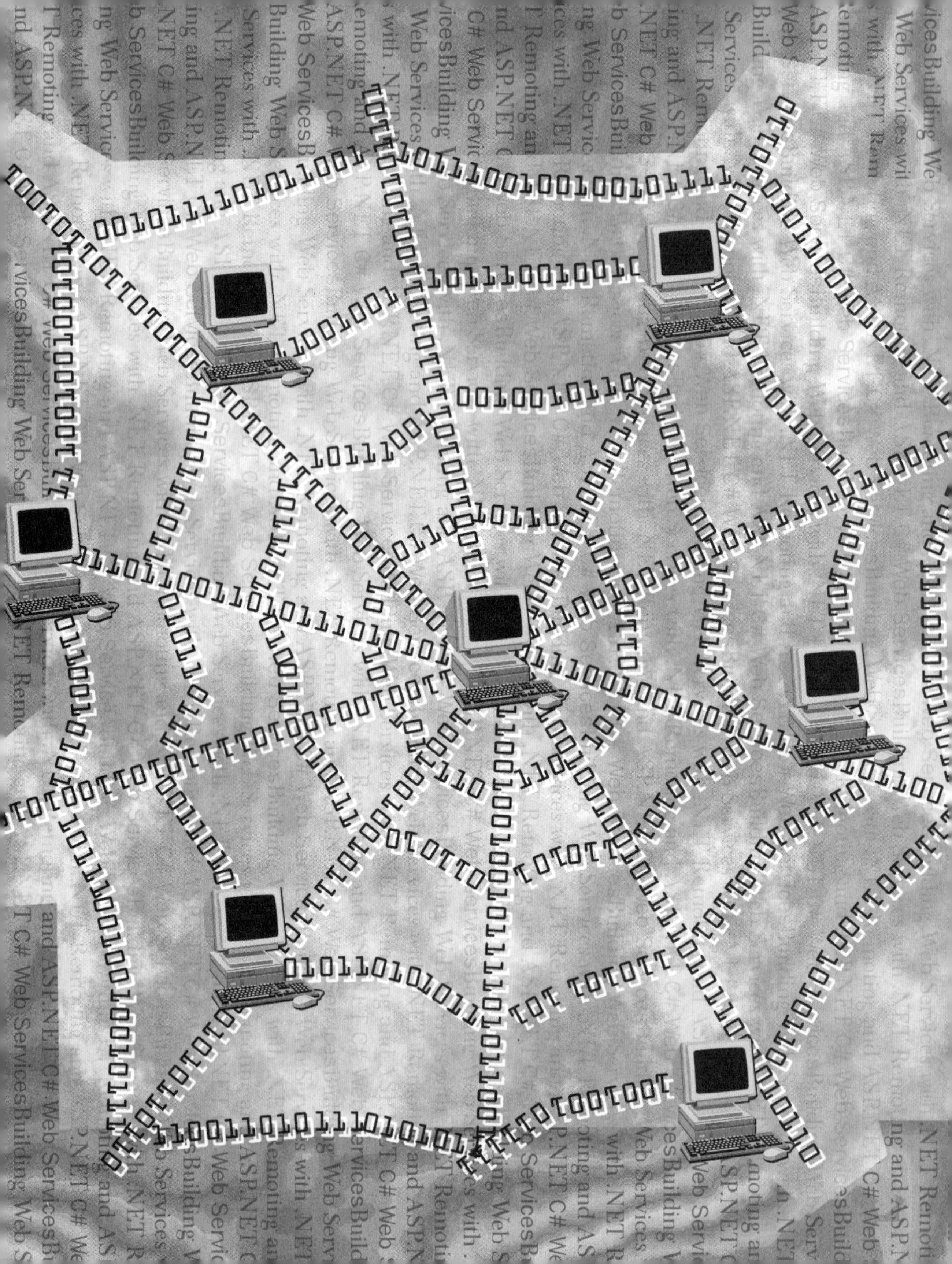

1

What is a Web Service?

If you are reading this book, you must be interested in using web services now or in the near future. Perhaps you are interested in exposing your business to new markets by building external web services for third parties, or perhaps you are considering how to develop software solutions faster and more efficiently using existing web services available on the Internet. Maybe you have no idea what web services are, but you want to understand the new technology that everyone is talking about.

Whatever the reason, this chapter will examine what web services are and why they have generated so much publicity recently. Web services represent a major step in the history of distributed computing, and they have the potential to drastically change the way enterprise software solutions are developed today.

In this chapter, we will look at:

- ❏ How distributed computing began, and how it has evolved into 'software as a service'
- ❏ What web services are and why they are useful
- ❏ The benefits of the web services model
- ❏ The standards that make web services work
- ❏ How web services will be integrated with existing enterprise architectures
- ❏ What the future holds for web services

Let's begin this chapter by taking a step back in time to find out where distributed computing began.

History of Distributed Computing

By examining the history of distributed computing, we can see how web services are a consequence of a natural evolution. Over time, applications have become more loosely coupled and split into multiple components. This has allowed the distribution of an application across many different machines. This way, multiple computers' resources can be used to provide the most resources possible to an application.

The first business use of basic distributed computing involved massive mainframe systems. These expensive computers could handle many users logged into them through dumb terminals. These dumb terminals did not have any processing power of their own – they simply allowed the user access to the resources available on the mainframe computer. The benefit was that these dumb terminals could be located throughout a building, which meant everyone using the mainframe did not have to be physically close to the computer. These machines were also extremely cheap compared to the cost of the mainframe. However, the application itself was still located solely on the central mainframe computer, and was limited to the computing power and resources of this machine.

As computers became cheaper and more powerful, it became a viable option to place them on employees' desktops. This changed the way computers were used, because people now had easy access to relatively powerful machines, so it made sense to use some of that processing power rather than relying on the mainframe server to process every request.

The Client-Server Model

The architecture that grew out of this became known as the **client-server model**. This model involves a central server that contains the database or other central data store that all clients access. The client handles the user-interface screens and some or all of the business logic before sending the data to the server. This frees the server resources to concentrate on data storage and access, while making full use of the resources of the client machines. The client-server model distributes the work of the application across multiple machines, reducing the total load on any single machine.

There are problems with this approach. The major obstacle is the maintenance time required when new applications are shipped out to hundreds or thousands of desktops. The requirements associated with these **fat-client** applications (named because of the amount of resources used on the client machine) are an obstacle to deploying them successfully. If all the correct DLLs and library files are not installed and registered correctly, the application will not function. This is a very frustrating and difficult problem to solve.

These types of applications were also extremely costly in terms of resources required to 'scale up' to a large number of users. They consumed database connections and other server resources in a way that made it difficult to increase the number of client machines without dramatically increasing server power.

The solution to this architectural problem came with the broad acceptance of the World Wide Web. Web applications could now be built so that the only requirement for the client was an internet browser. These applications became known as **thin clients**, because they used far fewer resources on the client machine. Web applications are built using dynamic web pages accessing a database or middle-tier components. In this model, the client machine is used less, because the required resources for HTML pages are much less than for a standard application that runs locally.

However, this model allows for the distribution of the application at the server level. A web server is used to process all HTTP requests, while one or more application servers can be used to run and manage all middle-tier components. A database server contains the actual data store for the application. With so many tiers to the application, the total work is spread across many computers.

There are many benefits to this model, as we have seen from the huge growth in internet companies and applications in the last few years. Clients are no longer forced to install an application locally; applications can be developed for large numbers of people and, when functionality has to be upgraded or replaced, the central web server can be upgraded without ever having to change the client.

While this architecture is often used in building enterprise-level web applications, it is not tied exclusively to web applications. This solution, the n-tier model, is designed to be flexible and able to support any type of user-interface from dynamic web pages, to Visual Basic fat clients to 'PocketPC' devices. The basic components of this architecture are typically similar to those show in the diagram below:

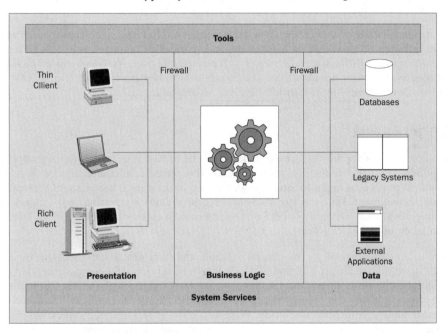

Component Technology

At the same time that the client-server revolution was taking place, interest in component technology was also growing. In the beginning, developers used simple code reuse. This involved sharing common functions and subroutines. This had many problems, one being that if code was not designed very carefully to be portable to another project, it was not very useful and had to be re-implemented or retooled anyway.

When the world moved to an object-oriented programming model, the solution to this problem was going to be the class. Object-oriented programming involved hiding the implementation of a class in private methods and only allowing a client to access the header, or definition file. For enterprise developers this still presented many problems as developers tried to bring classes from one project forward into new ones. They found that compiler name mangling, access to the uncompiled source code, and dependency on a specific programming language made this solution very difficult to achieve.

The next solution lay in components. The concept behind this technology was interface-based programming. A component would publish a well-defined interface that could be used to interact with it. This interface was a contract that was guaranteed to remain in place. Other developers could, therefore, develop using these interfaces, confident that future changes to the component would not break their code.

The component interfaces were in a binary standard, giving developers the choice to use different programming languages for the component and the client. COM, and its distributed cousin, DCOM have done very well in the Microsoft arena. JavaBeans, Java's answer to distributed components, has also been very successful.

Web services are not necessarily going to replace component development; components make a lot of sense in an intranet solution where the environment is controlled, and it does not make sense to expose purely internal objects through a less efficient web service interface. Web services make interoperating easy and effective, but they are not as fast as a binary proprietary protocol such as DCOM. The problem with components lies in distributing them across the Internet.

Into the Present

Most web applications are now built using a tiered model of user interface, components, and database. The components encapsulate the business rules and other specific functionality, as well as all access to the database. We will now begin to look at the next step in the design paradigm of enterprise application development. Web services allow for enterprise-level integration, and support for any device connecting to any server anywhere on the Internet. Web services represent the next major leap in distributed computing technology.

Web services are fundamentally a distributed solution, and their design embraces this by dependence on internet standards such as HTTP and XML. Before web services, if a company created a great COM component for performing some functionality, they could sell and distribute that COM component. Your company might buy this component, install it on every server that needed the functionality, and use the component in your custom solution. With web services this model changes. Now the third-party vendor exposes a web service to provide the functionality previously offered by the COM component. Your company accesses this web service in your custom application, and you no longer need to install any COM components on your servers. As upgrades are made to the functionality of the web service, you have access to them immediately, because the web service is centrally located. Instead of having to redistribute new COM components to all your servers when upgrades are required, nothing has to be done to take advantage of changes in the internal workings of the web service. It avoids the common problem of "DLL Hell" that results from multiple versions of COM components on the same machine, which has plagued COM developers.

This new model now allows for "functionality reuse". This is a fundamentally new concept. It is not interface-based, though it uses many of the concepts related to interfaces. It is not object-oriented, although systems can be built using object-oriented and component-oriented concepts. What functionality-reuse programming allows is the ability to use other systems to perform specific functionality in your application. This allows you to concentrate on the real business problems, while taking advantage of third party expertise and experience in those areas you choose to access via web services. Instead of forcing developers to choose between certain technologies when looking for functionality, web services allow them to choose the correct functionality, not the correct technology. This is because the interface is defined; the application performing the actual functionality can be written in any language. This frees architects and developers by allowing them to choose functionality based solely on the requirements of the system, not the technological constraints.

Web Services

A web service is a piece of functionality exposed through a web interface. This functionality is accessible through standard internet protocols such as HTTP. This means that any client can use the Internet to make **RPC**-like (**Remote Procedure Call**) calls to any server on the Internet and receive the response back as XML. The messages sent back and forth between the client and server are encoded in a special XML dialect called **Simple Object Access Protocol, or SOAP** for short. This protocol defines a standardized way of accessing functionality on remote machines.

The fundamental concept driving web services is that clients and servers can use any technology, any language, and any device. These things are at the discretion of the developer and the medium of the device. It is only the interface that is explicitly defined for each service, so it doesn't matter if the client is a Java servlet, a VB .NET fat client, a Perl CGI application, or a WAP-enabled cell phone. The way they access a web service is the same: SOAP over HTTP. With internet access built into everything these days, all we need to access sophisticated server applications is a basic XML text processor to encode and decode the SOAP messages.

We have seen distributed component technology before. Some examples, such as Distributed COM (DCOM), Common Object Request Broker Architecture (CORBA), and Remote Method Invocation (RMI) for Java, work very well in an intranet environment. These technologies allow components to be invoked over network connections, thus facilitating distributed application development. Each of these works well in a pure environment, but none is very successful at interoperating with the other protocols. Java components cannot be called using DCOM, and COM objects cannot be invoked via RMI. Attempting to use these technologies over the Internet presents an even more difficult problem. Firewalls often block access to the required TCP/IP ports, and because they are proprietary formats both the client and server must be running compatible software.

The advantage of SOAP is that it is sent over HTTP. Most firewalls allow HTTP traffic to give end users the ability to browse the Internet. Web services operate using the same ports in the firewall (port 80 for HTTP and port 443 for HTTPS), allowing server applications to be securely protected while still exposing business functionality via web services. SOAP is not a proprietary protocol; instead, it is an XML standard that defines the messages sent between the client and the web service. Any web service can therefore interact with, and be used from, any technology solution. This increases the ability to distribute systems without relying on a single technology like DCOM, CORBA, or RMI.

Web services are fundamentally for application consumption and not for end users. By exposing a system as a web service, we are allowing third parties to integrate our system's functionality into their custom application. This allows a new approach to developing solutions: instead of designing the required functionality into a system, you can simply access the appropriate web service to perform the required operation. For example, if we are building an e-commerce application, we could use a web service to calculate the correct shipping charges for the customer's shopping basket. Instead of having to create our own custom shipping charge calculator or install and configure a third-party component, we can simply access a shipping and packaging vendor's system via SOAP messages. For the end user, this is a huge benefit because they are provided with consistent and accurate shipping information, instead of separate implementations at every web site they access. As more and more web services are exposed by businesses, application development will involve solving the specific business problems with custom solutions and accessing web services for all infrastructure and non-business-specific problems.

Benefits of Using Web Services

Web services offer a number of benefits for applications that consume third-party web services as well as to those exposing custom web services themselves:

❑ Platform independence

❑ Ubiquitous communication channel

❑ Enterprise interoperability

❑ Functionality reuse

❑ Extension of business

❑ Server neutrality

❑ Secure communications

Let's take a look at each of these in turn.

Platform Independence

As discussed previously, web services can be accessed from any platform that can access the Internet. Any application that has an internet connection can send and receive SOAP messages to and from any web service on the Internet.

Ubiquitous Communication Channel

Web services rely on the Internet as their communication mechanism to operate. The Internet is built on open, standardized protocols such as TCP/IP and HTTP. These are well-established protocols that are supported throughout the Internet. Using the Internet as the communication channel ensures the highest level of access and availability without being locked into a proprietary solution that will not integrate with new systems in the future. Every public web service is available for use because all devices are connected to this extensive and ubiquitous communication channel.

Whether the solution you are deploying is behind a firewall, on a client's desktop, or part of a middle-tier component, it will have access to the external web service. No special software protocols are required on the client machine, making deployment much simpler than distributed component deployment.

Enterprise Interoperability

Web services provide the ability for true enterprise interoperability. In the past few years, we have seen the growth of Business-to-Business (B2B) communication and development. These types of applications involve merging or complementing existing business systems with trading partners and suppliers. Web services allow for the exposing of business functionality via internet standards. Electronic Document Interchange (EDI) has long been used for this same functionality, but implementing it is costly, time-consuming, and not very flexible. Web services allow these processes to be completed via XML and HTTP, both easy-to-use and easily understandable protocols.

Web services are also flexible enough to allow the business to modify and extend the functionality of the web service as business requirements and partners change. This way the company can remain agile and is able to cope with changing business relationships. This is an absolute requirement in today's ever-changing business environment.

Functionality Reuse

Developers can take advantage of functionality implemented by external parties by consuming the web services they expose. This translates to less time developing software that is not related to the specific business problem being solved. Not having to build infrastructure and support services allows the developer to concentrate on providing the best business solution to the problem.

For example, suppose a web service is available that performs a great spelling check on text passed into it. You will never have to write a spell-checking component again: you just need to use the functionality exposed by this web service. In the past, you might have purchased a spell-checking component, and called it remotely. So how is this different, you ask?

The fundamental difference lies in how it is accessed. The component is accessed using proprietary protocols that perhaps don't work on all devices and across all firewalls. With web services, the functionality is available wherever a connection to the World Wide Web is available. The spell-checking functionality is available anywhere. The functionality is exposed, but not the technology. Instead of concentrating on the technology used to implement a solution, we can make choices based on the functionality desired.

Extension of Business

Web services allow a business to extend its relationships and its reach to customers. By allowing third parties to access internal systems via web services, businesses allow their customers to access them in a more integrated, user-centric manner. Businesses can concentrate on their specialty, while easily allowing other applications to use that functionality in their applications. Third parties can develop integrated solutions for customers that combine many related web services offered by vendors. When solutions are packaged into an integrated unit, the user is presented with a better experience, and the vendors drive more business for themselves.

Web services can also be used to extend trading partner relationships. By integrating a supply chain with vendors over web services, business processes can be dynamic and flexible to changing needs and requirements. As new partners are brought in, they can easily integrate into the overall system by using the web services supplied by the company.

Server Neutrality

It does not matter what programming language and server software you use to develop web services. The interface is based on standards, and the messages sent between web services and clients use XML over HTTP. The server can be running UNIX, Windows 2000, Linux, or any other operating system. The software performing the functionality behind the web service can be written in Java, C++, C#, or anything else the development team is comfortable with.

This is a major change from the components of the past, which were written either for the Visual Basic/COM world, or for a Java/JavaBean world. If the exact functionality you desired existed in one world, but not the other, you were forced to use that programming model. With web services, you are no longer forced to choose a programming language based on the third-party functionality desired. This gives the developer of web services great flexibility and opens areas that were once closed. In addition, developers can choose to develop a solution based on their expertise with a programming language – not based on the requirements of the client's machine. This leads to increased productivity and greater developer satisfaction.

Secure Communications

Web services are just as secure as any other web application. The same technology used to secure online commerce sites is used to secure and authenticate web services. Many people are worried that the very advantages that web services provide may also present a major security risk: the ability to make method calls on components over HTTP via standard XML messages. HTTP is allowed through almost all firewalls, so this means that web services can be exposed to the Internet even behind firewalls. This, however, does not mean that hackers can arbitrarily make calls into your protected network using XML-encoded HTTP packets.

You must explicitly create a web service and have it listen to incoming SOAP requests before these packets will do anything. Firewalls can be configured to reject SOAP requests, but SOAP requests for non-existent services will simply generate an HTTP 404 error: resource not found. Once you have built and deployed a web service, you must secure it as you would any other web application. Perhaps only your authenticated trading partners will be allowed to access it, or perhaps you will charge a fee for every access, and log every use of the service.

SSL encryption technology can be used to secure the data in transport; ADSI or LDAP can be used for membership lookup and authentication. The web service can use all the HTTP authentication methods available on the particular server: basic, challenge/response, digest, and so on. In short, web services provide a very secure way to expose functionality on the Web. We will examine security issues and how to address them later in this book.

Standards for Web Services

There have been technologies for exposing and consuming distributed functionality before the advent of web services. DCOM and CORBA are just two examples of this technology. What makes web services so revolutionary and such a change from previous models is the application of true internet standards.

All messages are sent via the HTTP protocol. The messages passing between web services and clients are encoded in XML. How a request for a web service is encoded is specified in the Simple Object Access Protocol, or SOAP for short. This standard, which was developed by a consortium of companies including Microsoft, IBM, DevelopMentor, and Userland Software, is now an official W3C standard under review. SOAP messages are specified in a well-defined XML format. We will study the exact format of this schema in the next chapter.

SOAP makes it possible to access any web service using well-known calls and responses. The actual system residing behind the web service could be a Java program, Windows DNA system, or a legacy mainframe application written in COBOL. As long as they send and receive valid SOAP messages, any system can call them, and they can call any web services on the Internet.

In addition to SOAP there are a handful of standards that are required to make web services a viable solution. The following is a brief list:

❑   XML – (Extensible Markup Language) A standard and unified way to represent data and messages across all web services.

❑   WSDL – (Web Service Description Language) This specifies the interface of the web services: what each method is called and what parameters it accepts and returns. From this document, the valid SOAP messages that can be sent to a web service can be established.

...ry Protocol) This acts as a pointer to all the web services located on a particular ... dynamic discovery of published web services for an organization

...l Description, Discovery and Integration) This acts as a central repository of ...ices. Applications and developers can access the UDDI registry to learn ... are available on the Internet.

...e technologies in depth in the next chapter. For now it is only important to ...ent standard helps to make the entire web services solution workable. The ... each of these technologies in brief:

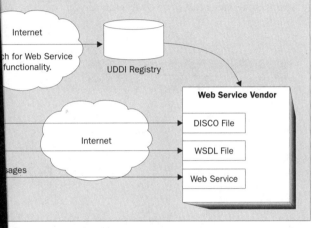

...DDI registry to locate the web service that matches the functionality ...would point the developer to the correct enterprise, and optionally the ... a DISCO document would show what web services are available on the ...nt specifies exactly what methods the web service exposes and the ... The WSDL file is a contract that specifies what SOAP messages to send to ...what messages to expect in return. The SOAP messages themselves are encoded in XML, and contain the method invocation request to the server and the data returned back to the client.

Web Services Architecture

There are two different ways of working with web services. Each has a drastically different architecture and not all solutions will require both to be used. One way to use web services is by exposing them to the outside world to allow access to internal system functionality. The other way to use web services is as a client, or consumer of external web services. In this model, web services are used to access functionality from any tier in an application. This allows the functionality of any distributed system exposed on the Internet to be incorporated into a custom application.

Exposing Web Services

Exposing web services offers new opportunities for businesses. The ability to integrate with external partners and future customers is at last available, easy, and extensive. By exposing services on the Internet, a company allows third parties to build applications that can aggregate multiple services for the end user, thus providing a better overall experience. By exposing a web service, a company is not developing something for end users themselves to experience. A web service is fundamentally built to allow access from other applications. Sending messages and data to this web service provides the ability to extend your business applications in new ways.

An example of how web services can be used to extend your current Windows DNA architecture is shown below:

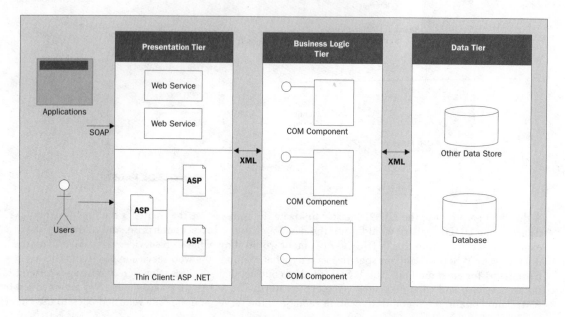

Web services could be thought of as a new form of presentation tier. The strength of the Windows DNA architecture is its flexibility in terms of the ability to move to new user-interfaces. Building an ASP site and a fat client is very simple if you have built your business logic correctly in the middle tier. A web service is simply another way to access your middle-tier business logic. A key difference is that a web service is meant for consumption by an application rather than end users. But web services are still an interface into your system.

The basic principles of interface design apply for web services. The web service can be designed with the necessary granularity for the particular application. It is possible to expose every component in the middle tier as a web service. It is also possible to expose only a few select 'gateway' components that provide the key functionality you wish to expose. These components could then access the entire middle-tier system to perform the functionality required. A broader approach can also be taken by aggregating several systems through a single exposed web service interface.

Ever since Visual Basic allowed the creation of controls by third parties, the development community has seen an explosion in the number of COM objects and third-party controls available. These avoid many of the tedious tasks associated with developing applications and speed up development. We will see companies implement web services for the same reason. For a fee per access, a monthly charge, or perhaps a one-time access fee, third-party developers will expose functionality that other developers will pay to use. This functionality could be anything, and in the next few years we will see this sector expand. Eventually, any service a developer might want will be available easily and efficiently with just a few SOAP calls.

Consuming Web Services

As a developer, you will need to consume web services in the near future. Soon we will have a truly "Programmable Web". A wide range of functionality will be available via open internet standards.

The ability to integrate with business partners and third-party solutions make web services a very powerful technology. Web services can be accessed from any tier of an application. The user-interface layer might use a web service to validate certain specific data, such as country names and phone number formats. The middle tier is where the majority of web service integration takes place. Here business-to-business integration occurs, as web services are called into other business's systems to facilitate data and information sharing. In the data tier, web services could be used to provide some or all of the underlying data of the system. This provides it with a very loosely coupled, distributed architecture that can be reactive to change:

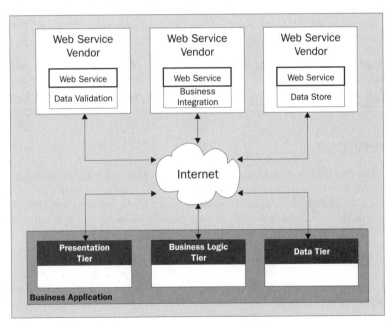

Web services are components of a massively distributed system. In an n-tier application you are limited to the functionality of the middle-tier business objects you build or purchase. With web services, all the functionality on the Internet is open to you as a developer. You are expanding your application, with code you did not have to write, simply by harnessing this functionality.

The Future of Web Services

We are in the beginning of a new era for developing enterprise solutions. Web services will change the way applications are built, and will change the way online business is conducted. At the moment, web services are in their infancy, but in the coming years we will see this technology maturing quickly.

Programmable Web

This term is used in many of Microsoft's press releases and PR materials. As such, many of us would be quick to dismiss it as merely a marketing term. However, the concept behind the 'marketecture' is sound.

The basic idea is that developers will be able to build entire systems by integrating the services and functionality exposed via web services across the Internet. "Any system, any data, any format" will be the mantra. If you, as a developer, need to access a piece of functionality, instead of buying a component or writing it yourself, you will access (and most probably pay for) one of the many web services that offer that functionality. This functionality could be anything from mathematical functions to shipping calculations, to complex invoicing solutions provided by a specific vendor who specializes in the field.

This will enable developers to concentrate on the business problem at hand, and not force them to write the infrastructure and plumbing code that takes up so much time. Using external vendors who concentrate on a specific functionality guarantees that each piece of your total solution is the very best it can be. This same promise was made with object-oriented programming languages, components, rapid-application development tools, and now web services. Time will tell how accurate this prediction will be. Most likely web services will become an integral piece of enterprise solutions, like the previously described technologies have become over time.

The "Programmable Web" refers to the idea that you will be able to access functionality exposed across the Internet from any device connected to the Internet. Enterprise integration and the ability to take advantage of external expertise will make developing enterprise solutions more efficient and provide a more seamless experience for the end user.

.NET My Services

.NET My Services represents a new arena that Microsoft is entering into, as well as a radical change in the way applications will use and access user information. Better known by its former codename, Hailstorm, this is a set of web services that will be offered by Microsoft in late 2002. Collectively, the services offered will allow end users to control their personal information and data, and offer a universal mechanism for web applications, devices, and companies to access this information.

Currently, every application and device is an isolated island of information. The phone number list on a cell phone does not match the phone number list on a user's PDA and mail client. A user's address is entered into hundreds of different web sites and applications, and if they should ever change addresses, updating all these web applications is next to impossible. Each web application and device owns the information fed to it, and users have no control over how that information is used or accessed by other companies.

.NET My Services proposes a solution to this by exposing a set of web services that will manage user information. By storing information in a central location, and protecting that information through Microsoft's Passport authentication service, disparate systems can access the user's information via standard SOAP messages over the Internet. Therefore, a cell phone will have access to the same information a PDA does, and when someone moves, they will only need to update the .NET My Services data store, and all applications and devices that access this will have the updated information.

The Passport service represents the cornerstone of Microsoft's entire .NET My Services initiative. Passport will be used to authenticate and authorize all users and applications when accessing their .NET My Services data store, as well as to provide third-party authentication for custom systems. It will be secured using the Kerberos authentication service. Microsoft knows the success of the .NET My Services initiative rests on user confidence in storing and accessing their data through a web service interface. Microsoft hopes that Passport/Kerberos will give users the confidence that their data is secure.

The .NET My Services web services are important because they are another technology that will enable developers to concentrate on the true business problems and not on infrastructure development. They will manage the storage of user information, sending notifications to .NET My Services-enabled devices, calendaring and task management, and many other user-centric services. Applications can access this data to interact with the user, regardless of the device or application they use. A cell phone will be able to access a user's calendar just as easily as a laptop, because each will simply be accessing a central web service offered by .NET My Services.

Services

The following is a list of .NET My Services services and a brief description of their purpose:

- ❑ .NET Address – Contains address information for a user
- ❑ .NET Profile – Manages user information like name, nickname, special dates, picture, etc
- ❑ .NET Contacts – Contains address book and contact information
- ❑ .NET Location – Electronic and geographical location and meeting information
- ❑ .NET Alerts – Manages notification subscription, management, and routing
- ❑ .NET Inbox – Manages access to items like e-mail and voice mail, including access to existing e-mail systems
- ❑ .NET Calendar – Allows access to the user's calendar and task information
- ❑ .NET Documents – Stores a user's documents for retrieval from any device
- ❑ .NET ApplicationSettings – Maintains various application-specific settings
- ❑ .NET FavoriteWebSites – Contains a list of favorite web sites
- ❑ .NET Wallet – Manages credit cards, receipts, coupons, and other transaction records
- ❑ .NET Devices – Contains settings for the various .NET My Services-enabled devices a user has
- ❑ .NET Services – Contains information about what services a user has
- ❑ .NET Usage – A report containing information on how much a user accesses the .NET My Services services

Issues

Many people are concerned about the privacy implications of .NET My Services. By allowing a single company (Microsoft) to control all of a user's information, many people worry that Microsoft could abuse the information stored in .NET My Services. People are also worried that storing information in a single company presents a single point of failure for virus attacks or data loss. In addition, companies and malicious users need to be kept from accessing a user's personal information stored in .NET My Services. If this model is to work, all of a user's information must be located in .NET My Services – but does this expose the user to potential privacy risks?

Microsoft's response to these concerns has been to illustrate that .NET My Services is fundamentally user-centric. The users themselves control who has access to their private information, and for how long. Therefore, if a user wants to allow a web application to access .NET My Services to get their address and contact information, they would explicitly allow the application to access their .NET My Services data store for that purpose only. Part of the benefit of .NET My Services is the control end users will have over their personal information. They will be able to control who has access to their information, for how long and, to a limited extent, what they do with the information.

Microsoft has also said it will not mine information from .NET My Services or sell advertising based on information stored in the services. It will act like any other vendor or application when wishing to access a user's information; explicit permission must be obtained from the user before Microsoft has access to the data.

Microsoft is committed to providing .NET My Services at 24/7 availability. Microsoft runs some of the most heavily used sites on the World Wide Web, and they will use the experience and architecture from these sites in its attempts to create truly robust and enterprise-level availability for .NET My Services.

The Future of .NET MY Services

.NET My Services is going to be a business opportunity for Microsoft; most services are not going to be free. End users will pay to store their information in .NET My Services, and developers and companies will pay to access that information. It is unknown if the development community and the end user community are willing to pay for centralized storage and access to their personal information. Whatever the outcome of .NET My Services, however, it does represent a first step in the direction of software as a service. We will see more companies offering web services, with the benefits that we have discussed. .NET My Services is just the tip of the iceberg.

Summary

This chapter has covered what web services are, and what they offer to the enterprise developer. We have examined how we arrived at this point in development history, and why web services are needed to move forward. We examined how web services can benefit a company, from the standpoint of both exposing and consuming services. We also looked at the future of web services and how they relate to Microsoft's vision for the future of application development.

The rest of this book will concentrate on how we actually build and consume web services. Hopefully, this chapter gives you a solid background in understanding where this technology is coming from, and why it is important.

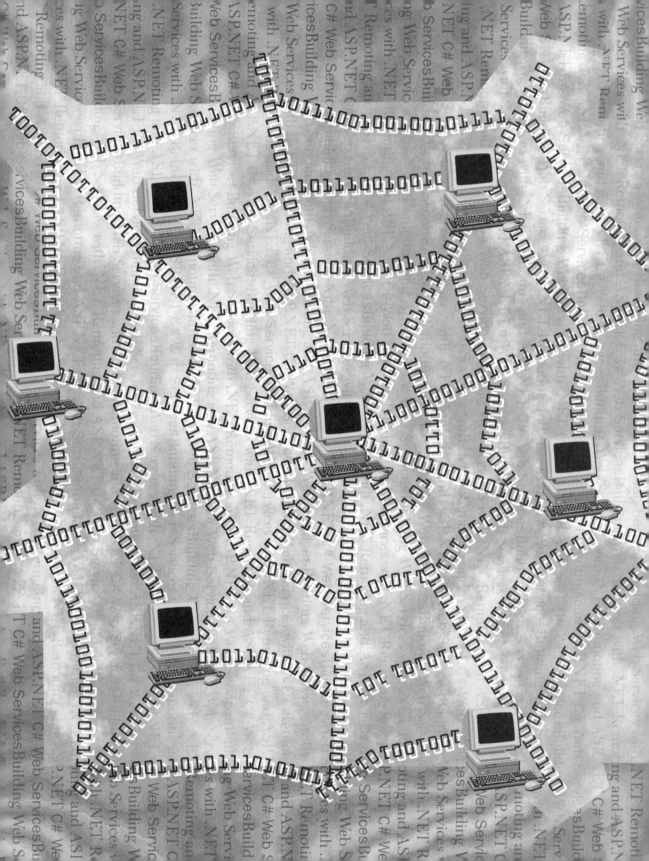

2

Web Service Protocols

In the last chapter we examined what web services are and why they will be an important technology for developing enterprise applications. In this chapter we will look at the standards and protocols that enable any system to interoperate using web services. Strong standards are vital if web services are to fulfil the promise of cross-platform interoperability. We will now examine these standards and learn how they work.

In this chapter we will cover:

- ❑ The XML protocols that web services use to interoperate
- ❑ The SOAP message format and how it serializes data
- ❑ The WSDL standard and how it defines the interface of a web service
- ❑ The DISCO format and how it is used to enable discovery of web services
- ❑ How the UDDI registry serves as a central repository for web services

Let's begin this chapter by finding out what SOAP is.

SOAP

Simple Object Access Protocol (SOAP) is the core protocol for web services. It is an XML standard used to call remote methods on a server hosting a web service. SOAP specifies both the format of the method request and the format of the parameters passed in the message. SOAP contains a set of serialization rules enabling the sending and receiving of the correct information. SOAP does not specify anything about how the methods themselves are implemented – it only defines how clients should communicate with them.

The SOAP standard explicitly states that HTTP is not the only transport method that can be used to send SOAP messages. SOAP is merely the format of the messages; they can be sent via any messaging system desired. It is even conceivable to create an SMTP-based SOAP solution, but for this book we will concentrate mostly on sending and receiving SOAP messages over HTTP. Using the simple and stateless HTTP protocol provides for tremendous scalability as well as the ability to pass through existing firewall software unimpeded. It is also available for almost all devices and systems, therefore enjoying the advantage of cross-platform support.

The SOAP standard allows any device or application to expose and consume web services. The SOAP messages are well defined; if both the client and server send valid SOAP messages, each can be written in different languages and reside on completely different systems. The server could be a J2EE web service and the client could be a .NET Windows Forms application. SOAP acts as the neutral protocol for them to communicate.

Most implementations of SOAP do not require the developer ito have an intimate knowledge of the protocol itself. It is much like HTTP – you can easily develop web pages without worrying about the specifics of HTTP headers and POST/GET commands. For example, Microsoft's Visual Studio .NET hides the actual SOAP calls behind a proxy class and makes the creation and consumption of a web service seem as simple as utilizing a local object. This ease of use is great, but sometimes it is necessary to roll up our sleeves and really understand the underlying technology. To do this with web services requires an understanding of SOAP.

The SOAP specification was originally published as version 0.9 in early 1999. It was continually revised throughout 1999, with version 1.0 appearing in November of that year. This version gained wide acceptance and many implementations were released based on this standard. In April 2000, SOAP version 1.1 was released and submitted to the W3C for review. This implementation has gained widespread popularity and is the current industry standard. We will be examining the SOAP specification v1.1 in this chapter. The W3C has recently released a SOAP 1.2 Working Draft specification, but it is still early in the standardization process. Version 1.2 will go through an extensive review process before being released as a W3C Recommendation. For the latest information about the SOAP specification, see the W3C web site: http://www.w3.org/2000/xp/.

Format

SOAP is an XML specification. All SOAP messages are inherently encoded in XML. SOAP uses both schemas and namespaces extensively, and understanding these is crucial to understanding the SOAP specification. For detailed information on these topics, please see the Wrox Press book, *Professional XML 2nd Edition*, ISBN 1-861005-05-9.

A SOAP message can be one of three types. These types are:

❑ **Method call**

❑ **Response message**

❑ **Fault message**

A method call is a request for a method invocation on a remote server. It contains the name of the method to invoke as well as any parameters required for the method. A response message is returned from the web service with the result(s) of the method call. A fault is a special type of response message generated if the remote object throws an exception or otherwise generates an error; this message is returned to the client as a fault message. Note that a SOAP fault message can only be generated if the actual remote server is contacted and invoked. If the error lies in the transport, the client will receive a transport-specific error. In the case of HTTP this would be some form of standard HTTP error.

A basic SOAP message has the format:

```
<SOAP-ENV:Envelope
              xmlns:SOAP-ENV="http://schemas.xmlsoap.org/soap/envelope/">
   <SOAP-ENV:Header>
      <!-- Transaction-specific header details -->
   </SOAP-ENV:Header>
   <SOAP-ENV:Body>
      <!-- Transaction-specific elements -->
   </SOAP-ENV:Body>
</SOAP-ENV:Envelope>
```

All SOAP messages follow the same format. All of the information is contained within a SOAP `Envelope` element. Inside this element there is always a `Body` element, and optionally a `Header` element. Each of these elements is scoped to a specific SOAP namespace.

Note that all elements specific to the SOAP specification (Envelope, Header, and Body) are scoped to the namespace `http://schemas.xmlsoap.org/soap/envelope/`. The namespace prefix is defined within the `Envelope` element using the namespace declarative `xmlns`. The prefix given to represent the namespace in this example is `SOAP-ENV`. This is a commonly used prefix, as it is the one used in the SOAP specification, but it is by no means the required prefix. Namespace prefixes are only placeholders for the complete namespace; the crucial information is the full namespace.

Scoping all elements to a specific SOAP namespace allows developers to include elements within a SOAP message that would otherwise be duplicates. The SOAP specification makes heavy use of XML namespaces for this very reason. Almost every element included in a SOAP message must be explicitly namespace qualified. This ensures that no two elements will be confused with one another. Therefore, even if another `Body` element is included within the message somewhere, as long as each is prefixed with the correct namespace the web service will understand which element to examine for the true payload.

Let's take a brief look at each of the elements of a SOAP message in turn.

Envelope

All SOAP messages are encased within an `Envelope` element. This will always be the outermost or top element for any SOAP message sent or received. Within an `Envelope` element there will always be a single `Body` element. Optionally, there can be a single `Header` element, but if so it must be first element in the envelope. There can be additional user-defined elements besides `Header` and `Body`, but these must follow the `Body` tag. Like all elements in a SOAP message, any additional elements or attributes must be qualified by a namespace.

Header

The SOAP `Header` element is used to send meta-information about the SOAP message. This information is not necessarily part of the method call, but may include transaction information, the caller's identity, or other 'out-of band' data. The uses for this depend on the particular web service application.

The SOAP specification allows for a `mustUnderstand` attribute to be included in any element within the `Header`. The web service receiving this SOAP message must be able to process the element marked with the `mustUnderstand` attribute, or else it must not handle the SOAP request. If the server cannot process or understand the marked element it will return a fault message indicating this. This way a client can ensure the server will be able to process and interpret the vital information passed in the `Header`. The possible values for this attribute are '0' for false and '1' for true, with the default being '0.' Here is an example of using the `Header` to pass the ID of the client to the web service for security purposes:

```
<SOAP-ENV:Envelope
    xmlns:SOAP-ENV="http://schemas.xmlsoap.org/soap/envelope/">
    <SOAP-ENV:Header>
        <MYNS:CallerID
            xmlns:MYNS="My URI"
            SOAP-ENV:mustUnderstand="1">
            WroxDomain/KayR
        </MYNS:CallerID>
    </SOAP-ENV:Header>
    <SOAP-ENV:Body>


                    <!-- Call information -->

    </SOAP-ENV:Body>
</SOAP-ENV:Envelope>
```

In this example, we use the Header to pass the identity of the client to the server. Note that we use a namespace to qualify all elements and tags not specific to the SOAP specification. The following line creates the namespace prefix:

```
xmlns:MYNS="My URI"
```

In a production application the actual namespace would be a Universal Resource Identifier (URI) created from your company's domain name, GUID, or other unique qualifier. This ensures the namespace is unique across all XML documents and that name collisions do not occur. A URI needs to be unique when multiple XML schemas are used together, to ensure that elements scoped to that URI can be interpreted correctly.

The SOAP-ENV:mustUnderstand attribute is set to '1' to tell the web service it must process the CallerID element or not process this SOAP message at all. Note that this is scoped to the SOAP specification's namespace with the SOAP-ENV prefix. This is because the mustUnderstand element is defined in the SOAP specification, and needs to be declared as such.

Body

The Body element will always be present in a SOAP message, and contains the heart of the message. The type of message being sent determines what is located within the Body element itself. For a SOAP method call, it contains the serialized method invocation request with the name of the method and each parameter serialized in XML format. The format of the serialized parameters is very important because all systems must agree on how data is sent back and forth. For a response message back from a web service the Body element contains the returned data in the same XML data format. If an error occurred and a fault message is returned, the Body element contains the fault and error information.

Let's look at an example of a series of calls on a particular web service. We will examine what the three different forms of SOAP messages look like for a fictitious web service. Our web service adds two numbers together and returns the result. The method on the server looks like this:

```
int AddNumbers(int nNum1, int nNum2);
```

The SOAP request to this web service would look like this:

```
<SOAP-ENV:Envelope
    xmlns:SOAP-ENV="http://schemas.xmlsoap.org/soap/envelope/">
    <SOAP-ENV:Body xmlns:addNum="Some-URI">
        <addNum:AddNumbers>
            <nNum1>5</nNum1>
            <nNum2>10</nNum2>
        </addNum:AddNumbers>
    </SOAP-ENV:Body>
</SOAP-ENV:Envelope>
```

The request for the web service is serialized in the Body element itself. Again, note the use of the namespace qualifier. In this case, the namespace would come from the WSDL file used to determine the interface of the web service and the format of the SOAP messages to construct. We will examine this protocol in the next section. The name of the method must be qualified, but the parameters need not be; it is assumed they are qualified by the enclosing method element.

The method request is encoded as a qualified element with each of the parameters contained as a separate sub-element. The names of the elements are determined by the method and parameter names, as specified in the WSDL file. We will examine the SOAP serializing format in detail in the next section, "*Data Types and SOAP Serialization.*"

The response to this SOAP request, coming from the web service itself, would look like this:

```
<SOAP-ENV:Envelope
    xmlns:SOAP-ENV="http://schemas.xmlsoap.org/soap/envelope/">
    <SOAP-ENV:Body xmlns:addNum="Some-URI">
        <addNum:AddNumbersResponse>
            <return>15</return>
        </addNum:AddNumbersResponse>
    </SOAP-ENV:Body>
</ SOAP-ENV:Envelope>
```

As you can see, the web service responded with the return value from the method. This was enclosed within the Body element, and is qualified with the namespace prefix. The response element is formed with the name of the method concatenated with "Response". The name of the response element could be specified differently in the WSDL file; however, this is how the SOAP specification encodes responses; it is how .NET encodes responses, and it is how most other vendors do it as well. This element contains the return data and any serialized custom data members.

If the method call were not successful, we would receive a SOAP fault message from the web service. This is composed of a single Fault element within the Body element. The Fault element itself can contain four sub-elements:

- ❑ faultcode – This is a qualified string specifying what type of error occurred. This field is not meant for human consumption, but is there to provide applications a mechanism for identifying the error for other applications.

- ❑ faultstring – This is a human-readable string describing the cause of the error. Both this element and faultcode are mandatory for all fault messages.

- ❑ faultactor – This specifies what server the error occurred on. This can be very useful in a situation where the SOAP message is passed between multiple web services.

❑ detail – This element contains application-specific error information. This will generally contain sub-elements that contain error messages and application-specific error conditions from the web service. Every sub-element must be qualified with a specific user-defined namespace. This ensures all elements are unique within the document.

If we sent two numbers to our web service that were outside of the range of its ability to manipulate, it would generate the following SOAP fault message:

```
<SOAP-ENV:Envelope
    xmlns:SOAP-ENV="http://schemas.xmlsoap.org/soap/envelope/">
    <SOAP-ENV:Body xmlns:addNum="Some-URI">
        <SOAP-ENV:Fault>
            <faultcode>SOAP-ENV:Server</faultcode>
            <faultstring>Application Error</faultstring>
            <faultactor>http://addnumwebservice.domain.com</faultactor>
            <detail xmlns:addNum="Some-URI">
                <addNum:Message>Overflow - Parameters too large
                </addNum:Message>
                <addNum:ErrorCode>1234</addNum:ErrorCode>
            </detail>
        </SOAP-ENV:Fault>
    </SOAP-ENV:Body>
</SOAP-ENV:Envelope>
```

You can see that the message returned is a SOAP fault message reporting an error to the client. The client can use this message to report to the end user why there was an error, and/or log the error and perform other processing. The fault mechanism provides a unified method of sending error conditions to the client regardless of how errors are generated internally to the web service. This assists interoperability by standardizing the way error conditions and exceptions are communicated between systems.

Data Types and SOAP Serialization

How data is serialized in a SOAP message is vitally important. Data must be serialized both for method parameters and for data returned from successful method calls. All systems must agree on a standard way to represent data types, so the SOAP specification explicitly states how each type of data is serialized in a SOAP message. The end result is that any data can be transformed into a valid SOAP message and sent over HTTP to a web service or back to a client. The majority of the serialization rules come from the XML Schema standard.

As an example, suppose we have a method with the following signature that computes the tax for an order:

```
float GetTax(string Name, int OrderNumber, float TotalCost);
```

The SOAP message sent to this web service looks like this:

```
<SOAP-ENV:Envelope
    xmlns:SOAP-ENV="http://schemas.xmlsoap.org/soap/envelope/"
    xmlns:xsi="http://www.w3.org/2001/XMLSchema-instance">
    <SOAP-ENV:Body xmlns:getTax="Some-URI">
        <getTax:GetTax>
            <Name xsi:type="string">Amanda</Name>
            <OrderNumber xsi:type="integer">111</OrderNumber>
            <TotalCost xsi:type="float">7.06</TotalCost>
        </getTax:GetTax>
    </SOAP-ENV:Body>
</SOAP-ENV:Envelope>
```

Note that we are now using a new namespace: http://www.w3.org/2001/XMLSchema-instance. This is the namespace used to qualify data types in the XML Schema specification. This namespace explicitly types each parameter as a specific data type. The xsi:type attribute specifies the variable type based on the data types available in the XML Schema specification. Each parameter encoded in a SOAP message has a specific data type associated with it. Note that when the xsi:type attribute is not included, the element type is defaulted to a string.

The XML Schema specification lists many of the common data types that are available in most programming languages. The following is a list of some of the common data types used; for the complete list see the XML Schema specification itself located at http://www.w3.org/TR/xmlschema-2/.

- ❑ string
- ❑ boolean
- ❑ float
- ❑ int
- ❑ dateTime
- ❑ binary

Here is another example. On the server the method signature is this:

```
void SomeMethod(int nIntIn, float fFloatIn, boolean bBoolIn, string strIn);
```

The serialized SOAP Body element would be formatted like this:

```
<SOAP-ENV:Body xmlns:xxx="Some-URI">
    <xxx:SomeMethod>
        <nIntIn xsi:type="int">1</nIntIn>
        <fFloatIn xsi:type="float">3.1415</fFloatIn>
        <bBoolIn xsi:type="boolean">true</bBoolIn>
        <strIn xsi:type="string">Hello World</strIn>
    </xxx:SomeMethod>
</SOAP-ENV:Body>
```

Again, note how the method name becomes a qualified element in the Body element. Inside, each parameter is listed as a typed element.

This would obviously be very simple if all method calls were this trivial. To be a truly robust and flexible standard, however, SOAP must be able to serialize complex method calls with any parameters. One common example is a method that accepts an object. There needs to be a way to serialize an object into an XML format so the receiving web service can utilize that object. SOAP uses a very simple format for serializing complex data objects. Basically, the name of the object is used as the outermost element, with each data element contained in a typed sub-element. Therefore, if we have the following object:

```
public struct book
{
    public string Author;
    public string Title;
    public float Price;
}
```

It would be serialized in a SOAP message like this:

```
<Book>
    <Author xsi:type="string">William Shakespeare</Author>
    <Title xsi:type="string">Macbeth</Title>
    <Price xsi:type="float">19.95</Price>
</Book>
```

To see how this is used in a real SOAP message, let's look at another example. We need to call the following method on a remote web service:

```
boolean BuyBook(Book aBook);
```

Here is the SOAP message required to call the remote web service, with the serialized object in the message:

```
<SOAP-ENV:Envelope
    xmlns:SOAP-ENV="http://schemas.xmlsoap.org/soap/envelope/"
    xmlns:xsi="http://www.w3.org/2001/XMLSchema-instance">
    <SOAP-ENV:Body xmlns:bookStore="Some-URI">
        <bookStore:BuyBook>
            <Book>
                <Author xsi:type="string">William Shakespeare</Author>
                <Title xsi:type="string">Macbeth</Title>
                <Price xsi:type="float">19.95</Price>
            </Book>
        </bookStore:BuyBook>
    </SOAP-ENV:Body>
</SOAP-ENV:Envelope>
```

In this example, the Book object is serialized into XML format. The data members are represented as child elements of the root class element. The SOAP processor on the server side will be able to read this packet of information and recreate the Book object with the supplied data. It will then make the call to the BuyBook method using the reconstructed object.

SOAP also allows for the serialization of arrays. Suppose we need to call a web service with the following signature:

```
void SortArray(int[] nArray);
```

The SOAP message to send to this web service would look like this:

```
<SOAP-ENV:Envelope
    xmlns:SOAP-ENV="http://schemas.xmlsoap.org/soap/envelope/"
    xmlns:SOAP-ENC="http:// schemas.xmlsoap.org/soap/encoding/"
    xmlns:xsi="http://www.w3.org/2001/XMLSchema/instance">
    <SOAP-ENV:Body xmlns:sort="Some-URI">
        <sort:SortArray>
            <SOAP-ENC:Array SOAP-ENC:arrayType="xsi:int[5]">
                <SOAP-ENC:int>3</SOAP-ENC:int>
                <SOAP-ENC:int>1</SOAP-ENC:int>
                <SOAP-ENC:int>4</SOAP-ENC:int>
                <SOAP-ENC:int>1</SOAP-ENC:int>
                <SOAP-ENC:int>5</SOAP-ENC:int>
            </SOAP-ENC:Array>
```

```
        </sort:SortArray>
     </SOAP-ENV:Body>
  </SOAP-ENV:Envelope>
```

SOAP encodes arrays by wrapping them in a `SOAP-ENC:Array` element. This element must contain a `SOAP-ENC:ArrayType` attribute that specifies what data type the array is composed of as well as the number of elements contained in the array. Inside of the `SOAP-ENC:Array` element are the individual array items as separate elements, with the qualified type of the data as each element name.

The SOAP specification gives many more rules and standards for representing data in a SOAP message. There is a series of rules for serialization, and we have only touched on the most basic forms. More advanced forms of serialization involve multi-reference values, where a single data element is referenced from multiple places within the SOAP message using `XPointer` syntax. This saves space in the SOAP message, as a single value can be used multiple times in the same message. The basic concepts we have seen here are the core needed to understand how SOAP serializes messages.

Hopefully this overview has given you a better understanding of how SOAP messages are built and how web services communicate. Remember that in most situations these messages will be transparent to the developer, just as the format of a DCOM call is transparent. SOAP is the underlying messaging infrastructure that enables web services to communicate between any systems.

SOAP Over HTTP

HTTP provides the advantages of scalability and interoperability throughout the Internet, with all the benefits we examined in the last chapter.

Sending the SOAP messages we have examined over HTTP is not difficult. Most requests on a web server will be sent via a HTTP `Post` command, with the SOAP message in the HTTP payload itself. The requirements for a SOAP packet sent via HTTP are:

❑ The `Content-type` must be declared as `text/xml`.

❑ An additional `SOAPAction` HTTP header must be included. The value is a URI describing the web service this SOAP packet is requesting.

The `SOAPAction` header is included to allow firewalls to process incoming SOAP messages quickly without forcing them to process the entire XML payload. This value can be anything – the web service provider determines the format. Clients discover the correct setting in the WSDL file, as we will see in the next section. If the firewall is configured to allow SOAP calls to pass through, this header can be used to discover quickly and easily if this is a valid SOAP message. Firewalls can also be configured to reject SOAP messages by using this header to screen HTTP packets coming into their network.

Here is a full example of an HTTP message sent to a web service:

```
POST /GetQuote.aspx HTTP/1.1
Host: www.randomnameserver.com
Content-Type: text/xml; charset="utf-8"
Content-Length: nnn
SOAPAction: "uri:RandomNameServer#GetName"
<SOAP-ENV:Envelope
    xmlns:SOAP-ENV="http://schemas.xmlsoap.org/soap/envelope/"
```

```
        xmlns:xsi="http://www.w3.org/1999/XMLSchema/instance/">
        <SOAP-ENV:Body xmlns:name="Some-URI">
            <name:GetRandomQuote/>
        </SOAP-ENV:Body>
    </SOAP-ENV:Envelope>
```

This HTTP packet is sent to the fictitious URL: http://www.randomnameserver.com/GetQuote.aspx. The web service invoked is the `GetRandomQuote` service, which accepts no parameters. The `SOAPAction` header specifies the unique URI of the web service. The web server receiving the SOAP message interprets this value and passes the SOAP message to the appropriate web service. Note the complete HTTP `POST` packet of information required to send a valid SOAP message. If the request is successfully received and processed by the server, the full HTTP response from the server will look like this:

```
HTTP/1.1 200 OK
Content-Type: text/xml; charset="utf-8"
Content-Length: nnn
<SOAP-ENV:Envelope
    xmlns:SOAP-ENV="http://schemas.xmlsoap.org/soap/envelope/"
    xmlns:xsi="http://www.w3.org/1999/XMLSchema/instance/">
    <SOAP-ENV:Body xmlns:name="Some-URI">
        <name:GetRandomQuoteReponse>
            <return>A joy shared is a joy doubled.</return>
        </name:GetRandomQuoteReponse>
    </SOAP-ENV:Body>
</SOAP-ENV:Envelope>
```

You can see the HTTP response packet sent to the client contains both the HTTP headers and the full SOAP response message. It is a successful call, so the HTTP return code is 200 – OK.

If an error occurs in the processing of a web service the HTTP response code returned is 500 – Internal Server Error. This lets the client know immediately that the SOAP message contained in the HTTP packet is a fault message indicating failure. The `Fault` element is mandatory and a SOAP HTTP server must pack it with information about the error and return it to the client along with the HTTP 500 error code. If the random quote server returns a fault, it would look like this:

```
HTTP/1.1 500 Internal Server Error
Content-Type: text/xml; charset="utf-8"
Content-Length: nnn
<SOAP-ENV:Envelope
    xmlns:SOAP-ENV="http://schemas.xmlsoap.org/soap/envelope/">
    <SOAP-ENV:Fault>
        <SOAP-ENV:Fault>
            <faultcode>SOAP-ENV:Server</faultcode>
            <faultstring>Server Error</faultstring>
            <detail>
                <message>No more quotes today</message>
            </detail>
        </SOAP-ENV:Fault>
    </SOAP-ENV:Body>
</SOAP-ENV:Envelope>
```

WSDL

SOAP is a standard that defines how the messages sent to a web service are to be formatted and encoded. This standard allows any device to request any service because of the standardization of the messages sent between them. How do you know what messages to send to the server? How can you tell what methods a particular web service exposes, and what parameters it accepts?

One option is external documentation. This documentation would need to specify what methods are exposed and what the parameters are for each method. This documentation would be difficult and costly to maintain and update. The greatest weakness of this approach is the varied forms of documentation each web service vendor would produce. Clients would be forced to interpret and understand widely differing documentation styles and formats.

The Web Service Description Language, WSDL, provides a better solution. This language is designed to describe a web service and all of its methods. This is done in XML, so all systems can understand and interpret the information. In a WSDL document, all of the parameters and method names of a web service are specified, including the location of the web service itself. The end result is that valid SOAP messages required for a specific web service can be generated and sent to that web service. The biggest advantage is that WSDL is a standardized protocol, just like SOAP, so any system can interpret the web service's methods and understand what SOAP messages to generate and send.

Many implementations of web services, including .NET, use the published WSDL file to create a proxy object that communicates with the external web service. This local proxy object mimics the method calls available on the web service, allowing developers to work with a local object instead of writing SOAP messages. Internally the proxy object creates and formats the correct SOAP messages to send to the web service. .NET provides the tool wsdl.exe to create a proxy object given a WSDL document location. Visual Studio .NET also provides this ability directly within the IDE. The Microsoft SOAP Toolkit also allows web services to be invoked via a local object dynamically. We will examine this technology in the next chapter.

There are also numerous tools to create the WSDL file defining a web service. ASP.NET provides the ability to dynamically generate WSDL documents for any exposed web service by simply passing a WSDL command as part of the querystring. For example: http://www.mywebservice.com/math.aspx?WSDL. This is very convenient because the WSDL document is automatically generated by the .NET runtime, ensuring it is accurate and updated. The SOAP Toolkit provides a tool to generate a WSDL document for a COM object, allowing any existing COM object to be exposed as a web service.

Note that the specification makes it clear that SOAP is not the only message protocol that can be used. WSDL is extensible, and new bindings can be added to a web service to allow for messages to be sent via multiple protocols. The specification provides binding information for SOAP, HTTP GET and POST, and MIME, but we will cover SOAP because of its widespread acceptance and standardization. See the WSDL specification for information on the other formats.

Many contract languages emerged while web services were developing. The most prevalent have been: Service Description Language (SDL), SOAP Contract Language (SCL), and Network Accessible Services Specification Language (NASSL). As stated in the specification, WSDL consolidates the concepts in each of these previous languages, and is intended to be a unifying standard. Many of the previous standards were vendor-specific, while WSDL is a multi-vendor, universal standard. This gives it great strength as no one company controls it, therefore interoperability is easier between different implementations.

Format

Like SOAP, WSDL is an XML standard. WSDL is a very verbose, complex standard used to describe the methods and operations of a web service. In most implementations WSDL files are used primarily for application and developer tool consumption. These allow for the creation of client-side proxy objects that generate the correct SOAP messages and send them to the web service destination. We will examine this use for WSDL later.

The WSDL standard is interesting in that it enables any network service to be described, not just web services. This means that in addition to SOAP web services, any network service that requires formatted data to be sent and returned can be defined. You could design an entire custom messaging solution and use WSDL to define the interfaces. Because of this flexibility, a WSDL document contains abstract definitions for a service followed by protocol-specific (in our case SOAP-specific) implementation details.

To begin with, let's take a look at the basic format of a WSDL document. It is an XML document composed of the following five major sections. The name and description of each section is summarized below. We will look at each section in detail after examining an actual WSDL document.

- ❑ types – This section defines the different custom data types used throughout the document.

- ❑ message – This is an abstract representation of the logical messages that the service accepts and returns.

- ❑ portType – This is a list of abstract operations that roughly translate to the method signatures of the web service. It defines the logical messages that each operation accepts and returns.

- ❑ binding – This defines the message format and protocol for each specific portType. This section defines what protocols, like SOAP, this web service can interpret and understand to communicate.

- ❑ service – This section defines the physical address of the web service, with a set of named ports that refer to specific addresses.

Here is an example of a WSDL file for a very simple web service. The example is taken directly from the WSDL specification and only consists of a single method: GetTradePrice. The web service accepts a ticker symbol and a time value, and returns the stock price at that time for that equity. We will look at the different sections of it, and how it relates to building the required SOAP messages used to communicate with the web service. The complete WSDL specification is located on the W3C's Web site: http://www.w3.org/TR/wsdl. Let's take a look at the entire file and then examine each of its individual pieces:

```xml
<?xml version="1.0"?>
<definitions name="StockQuote"
        targetNamespace="http://example.com/stockquote.wsdl"
        xmlns:tns="http://example.com/stockquote.wsdl"
        xmlns:xsd="http://www.w3.org/2000/10/XMLSchema"
        xmlns:xsd1="http://example.com/stockquote.xsd"
        xmlns:soap="http://schemas.xmlsoap.org/wsdl/soap/"
        xmlns="http://schemas.xmlsoap.org/wsdl/">
    <message name="GetTradePriceInput">
        <part name="tickerSymbol" element="xsd:string"/>
        <part name="time" element="xsd:timeInstant"/>
    </message>
    <message name="GetTradePriceOutput">
        <part name="result" type="xsd:float"/>
    </message>
```

```
        <portType name="StockQuotePortType">
            <operation name="GetTradePrice">
                <input message="tns:GetTradePriceInput"/>
                <output message="tns:GetTradePriceOutput"/>
            </operation>
        </portType>
        <binding name="StockQuoteSoapBinding" type="tns:StockQuotePortType">
            <soap:binding style="rpc"
                          transport="http://schemas.xmlsoap.org/soap/http"/>
            <operation name="GetTradePrice">
                <soap:operation soapAction="http://example.com/GetTradePrice"/>
                <input>
                    <soap:body use="encoded"
                               namespace="http://example.com/stockquote"
                               encodingStyle=
                               "http://schemas.xmlsoap.org/soap/encoding/"/>
                </input>
                <output>
                    <soap:body use="encoded"
                               namespace="http://example.com/stockquote"
                               encodingStyle=
                               "http://schemas.xmlsoap.org/soap/encoding/"/>
                </output>
            </operation>>
        </binding>
        <service name="StockQuoteService">
            <documentation>My first service</documentation>
            <port name="StockQuotePort" binding="tns:StockQuoteSoapBinding ">
                <soap:address location="http://example.com/stockquote"/>
            </port>
        </service>
    </definitions>
```

All WSDL documents must be contained within a `definitions` element. This helps to clarify that WSDL is a set of definitions about a web service:

```
<?xml version="1.0"?>
<definitions name="StockQuote"
            targetNamespace="http://example.com/stockquote.wsdl"
            xmlns:tns="http://example.com/stockquote.wsdl"
            xmlns:xsd="http://www.w3.org/2000/10/XMLSchema"
            xmlns:xsd1="http://example.com/stockquote.xsd"
            xmlns:soap="http://schemas.xmlsoap.org/wsdl/soap/"
            xmlns="http://schemas.xmlsoap.org/wsdl/">
```

As you can see, the `definitions` element also contains a `name` attribute that denotes the name of this WSDL file and serves as a form of documentation. Also, note the abundance of namespace declarations within the document. These are used to keep each element in the document unique, so every element is qualified to reference the correct namespace.

Types

The `types` element of the WSDL file contains any special or compound data types the web service utilizes. Here, the serialized objects and arrays are defined for reference later in the document. This way data types can be defined once and referenced multiple times in the document.

The WSDL file we are examining does not have a `types` element, as it does not use any custom data types. As we will see in the next section it only uses a `string`, a `timeInstant`, and a `float`, each defined in the XML Schema language as an intrinsic data type. The `timeInstant` data type is an XML Schema type used for representing time.

However, in a different document, the `types` section might look something like this:

```
<types>
    <schema targetNamespace="http://example.com/stockquote/schema"
            xmlns="http://www.w3.org/2000/10/XMLSchema">
        <complexType name="TimePeriod">
            <all>
                <element name="startTime" type="xsd:timeInstant"/>
                <element name="endTime" type="xsd:timeInstant"/>
            </all>
        </complexType>
        <complexType name="ArrayOfFloat">
            <complexContent>
                <restriction base="soapenc:Array">
                    <attribute ref="soapenc:arrayType"
                               wsdl:arrayType="xsd:float[]"/>
                </restriction>
            </complexContent>
        </complexType>
    </schema>
</types>
```

This is from a different example in the WSDL specification. This web service is similar to our example, except that the method accepts a stock ticker as a `string` and a custom `TimePeriod` structure containing a start and end time. The web service then returns an array of `floats` giving the stock prices for that equity for the specified time period.

The `types` element contains the definitions for both the input structure and the return array. These are encoded in the XML Schema language used to define data types. This should look familiar from our discussion of SOAP serialization, as this is very similar in format. The structure is broken down into its different elements, and the name and data type explicitly defined for each. The array is likewise defined using XML Schema encoding rules.

Message

This section defines the abstract messages that this web service can accept and return. For most web services these messages will translate to the input and output parameters of a single method. Each message is broken into parts, each of which is a different data type. The reason for this extra level of abstraction is that WSDL can be used to define other services that accept data beside web services.

Here is the message section from our example:

```
<message name="GetTradePriceInput">
    <part name="tickerSymbol" element="xsd:string"/>
    <part name="time" element="xsd:timeInstant"/>
</message>
<message name="GetTradePriceOutput">
    <part name="result" element="xsd:float"/>
</message>
```

This web service defines two message formats. One is the input message and the other is the output message. Each is composed of the individual data types as its various parts. We will see later how WSDL maps this abstract message definition to a concrete SOAP implementation.

The format for the part element is very simple. It consists of a mandatory name attribute, which is used to reference this part element later in the document. In addition, an element attribute or a type attribute can be included. The element attribute is used to refer to a qualified SOAP or XML Schema data type, as the example shows. The type attribute is used to reference a previously defined custom data type in the types section of this WSDL file.

portType

The portType section defines an operation as a set of messages beginning and ending with the web service. This is functionally identical to an exposed method on an object. It can accept data and return data in specific formats. In fact, the portType defines operations, which are the method calls available for a particular web service. Again, this is kept abstract to enable WSDL to be used to define other network services and not just web service methods. Each operation contains definitions for the input messages and output messages. Note that both do not need to be present for a valid operation.

Here is our example WSDL file's portType section:

```
<portType name="StockQuotePortType">
    <operation name="GetTradePrice">
       <input message="tns:GetTradePriceInput"/>
       <output message="tns:GetTradePriceOutput"/>
    </operation>
</portType>
```

The only operation defined for this web service is GetTradePrice. This operation accepts and returns a message. These messages have been defined previously in the message section, and are referenced here. This is useful, because we do not have to define the potentially complex input parameters in this location. The WSDL format splits each section apart, allowing for more precise definitions that reference other sections.

The tns prefix used to qualify the message names is a common namespace prefix referring to the local document. You will note the full namespace represented by this prefix is the URL of this particular WSDL document. Therefore an application processing this document would know to look for GetTradePriceInput and GetTradePriceOutput messages within this same WSDL file. This convention is used throughout the WSDL document to refer to earlier defined elements and data types.

Binding

The binding section defines a specific message format for each portType in the WSDL document. There can be multiple bindings for any given portType. This contains the first physical implementation details in the file, as it describes what protocol can be used to communicate with this web service, and is intended to 'bind' a particular protocol to the message and operation definitions we have seen previously in this document.

Let's see how this works in our sample:

```
<binding name="StockQuoteSoapBinding" type="tns:StockQuotePortType">
    <soap:binding style="rpc"
                  transport="http://schemas.xmlsoap.org/soap/http"/>
    <operation name="GetTradePrice">
```

```
            <soap:operation soapAction="http://example.com/GetTradePrice"/>
            <input>
                <soap:body use="encoded"
                            namespace="http://example.com/stockquote"
                            encodingStyle=
                            "http://schemas.xmlsoap.org/soap/encoding/"/>
            </input>
            <output>
                <soap:body use="encoded"
                            namespace="http://example.com/stockquote"
                            encodingStyle=
                            "http://schemas.xmlsoap.org/soap/encoding/"/>
            </output>
        </operation>>
    </binding>
```

This section only has a SOAP binding: this will allow us to construct SOAP messages to send to this web service. The first line gives the name of this binding section, for documentation purposes. The type attribute references the portType element this binding is defining. Again, note the use of the tns prefix to represent the local document's namespace. This section will provide SOAP implementation details for each operation defined in the portType section.

The binding element is next, and is a required element in the binding section. The namespace used to qualify the element determines what protocol is bound to this web service. By using the soap namespace declaration it signifies the binding is a SOAP implementation. The element also contains several attributes that provide more implementation details for the specified protocol. For SOAP, the style attribute's value can be rpc or document, which determines the format of the SOAP messages sent. The transport attribute specifies how the SOAP messages will be sent to this web service. Use the URI value http://schemas.xmlsoap.org/soap/http to utilize HTTP. Other URIs may be used to define other transport protocols.

Next is the operation element, which references a specific operation in the portType section. For each operation in the portType section, SOAP specific details are provided for messages sent in and out. The soapAction attribute of the soap:operation element defines what the soapAction HTTP header must be when messages are sent to this web service. Inside the input and output elements the soap:body element simply specifies that the previously defined messages must be encoded and passed in as SOAP messages. It also specifies the namespaces used and how data is to be encoded in the messages themselves.

Service

Finally, we're in the service section. We already know what operations this web service supports, and exactly what format of messages to send to it. The only missing piece of information is where to actually send the messages themselves. This last section declares this:

```
<service name="StockQuoteService">
    <documentation>My first service</documentation>
    <port name="StockQuotePort" binding="tns:StockQuoteSoapBinding ">
        <soap:address location="http://example.com/stockquote"/>
    </port>
</service>
```

This section contatins a collection of `port` elements. Each port specifies a specific endpoint or address to communicate with this web service. There must be at least one port for each binding, but there can be many. The `service` element therefore defines all the different addresses that can be used to communicate with this web service.

This example has only a single port element, which refers to the `StockQuoteSoapBinding` through the name attribute. The `soap:address` element is used to specify this is an endpoint for SOAP messages. The only possible attribute for this element is the `location` attribute specifying where to send messages to.

SOAP Messages

We have now examined the entire WSDL document in detail. Let's construct a sample SOAP exchange based on the information gleaned from the WSDL document, because this the very purpose of WSDL.

By examining the WSDL file we know that the only format available for us is SOAP. This is because we have examined the `binding` section and found only the SOAP binding listed for this web service. Therefore we know we are gong to be constructing SOAP messages to communicate with this web service.

We start with the standard SOAP envelope:

```
<SOAP-ENV:Envelope
    xmlns:SOAP-ENV="http://schemas.xmlsoap.org/soap/envelope/"
    xmlns:xsi="http://www.w3.org/2001/XMLSchema-instance">
</SOAP-ENV:Envelope>
```

We also know we are going to need a `Body` element, which contains our method request for the remote web service. We look to the `portType` section to determine the operation name: `GetTradePrice`. This is the name of the remote method we are invoking:

```
<SOAP-ENV:Envelope
    xmlns:SOAP-ENV="http://schemas.xmlsoap.org/soap/envelope/"
    xmlns:xsi="http://www.w3.org/2001/XMLSchema-instance">
    <SOAP-ENV:Body>
        <GetTradePrice>
        </GetTradePrice>
    </SOAP-ENV:Body>
</SOAP-ENV:Envelope>
```

We know from the binding section that the input for this method is SOAP-encoded. We look to the `portType` section to get the names of the messages for this method. This references the `message` section, which defines the individual elements of the method call. Note that in some WSDL files the `message` section will then reference the `types` section for data type information. We also use the data type information provided in this section for each of the parameters in the method call. We now have almost all the information needed to construct our SOAP packet:

```
<SOAP-ENV:Envelope
    xmlns:SOAP-ENV="http://schemas.xmlsoap.org/soap/envelope/"
    xmlns:xsi="http://www.w3.org/2001/XMLSchema-instance">
    <SOAP-ENV:Body>
        <GetTradePrice>
            <tickerSymbol xsi:type="string">MSF</tickerSymbol>
            <time xsi:type="timeInstant">09:33AM</time>
        </GetTradePrice>
    </SOAP-ENV:Body>
</SOAP-ENV:Envelope>
```

However, if you remember from the last section on SOAP, all elements in a SOAP message must be fully namespace qualified. Therefore we need to qualify the GetTradePrice element with a namespace. Where does this namespace come from? The binding section provides the namespace used for the input calls of this operation. Therefore, our final SOAP message looks like this:

```
<SOAP-ENV:Envelope
    xmlns:SOAP-ENV="http://schemas.xmlsoap.org/soap/envelope/"
    xmlns:xsi="http://www.w3.org/2001/XMLSchema-instance">
    <SOAP-ENV:Body xmlns:e="http://example.com/stockquote">
        <e:GetTradePrice>
            <tickerSymbol xsi:type="string">MSF</tickerSymbol>
            <time xsi:type="timeInstant">09:33AM</time>
        </e:GetTradePrice>
    </SOAP-ENV:Body>
</SOAP-ENV:Envelope>
```

If we send this to the HTTP address specified in the service section, we will be successfully communicating with the web service. Remember that the SOAPAction HTTP header must be set to the soapAction attribute specified in the binding section. This enables the firewall to monitor incoming SOAP packets.

The structure of the response from the web service can also be determined from the WSDL file, in much the same way. The response is very simple in this case, and only consists of a single float value:

```
<SOAP-ENV:Envelope
    xmlns:SOAP-ENV="http://schemas.xmlsoap.org/soap/envelope/"
    xmlns:xsi="http://www.w3.org/2001/XMLSchema-instance">
    <SOAP-ENV:Body xmlns:e="http://example.com/stockquote">
        <e:GetTradePriceReponse>
            <result xsi:type="float">25.25</result>
        </e:GetTradePriceReponse>
    </SOAP-ENV:Body>
</SOAP-ENV:Envelope>
```

Client Proxies

While very useful for describing web services, WSDL is not a very user-friendly protocol. Look at how much WSDL it takes to define a relatively simple web service. As web services provide more methods and more complex parameters, the WSDL document gets more and more difficult to manage and understand.

Fortunately, WSDL is generally not meant for end-user consumption. Most implementations of SOAP provide some form of developer tool that can read a WSDL file and generate a client-side object that communicates with the specified web service. This provides many benefits for the developer. By interacting with a local component, we gain the abstraction of simply working with another object, and can make the same calls to it as to any other object. All the details of SOAP messages and formatting are hidden away inside the implementation of this client-side object.

Most SOAP and web services vendors are utilizing WSDL in this manner. The ability to provide a local object that communicates with the web service transparently is becoming standard in any web service implementation. Microsoft's Visual Studio .NET uses this approach, as do the Microsoft SOAP Toolkit and ATL Server.

DISCO

The DISCO protocol is used to discover web services located on a particular domain. Of all the protocols and formats we will look at, this is the least concrete. Microsoft is the driving vendor behind this protocol but even so, its implementation differs from its documentation.

The basic idea is to provide a single location for clients to locate all of the exposed web services in an enterprise. Therefore a company would have a DISCO file located on its web server. A potential client examines this DISCO file and learns where the WSDL files are located for every web service this company exposes. This is obviously useful, but when the UDDI registry is introduced into the picture, the DISCO protocol's usefulness is brought into question. As you will see in the next section, UDDI is a central repository for locating available web services on the Internet. In most cases, the UDDI registry will point to the specific WSDL document required to utilize the web service. This obviously cuts the DISCO protocol out of the picture.

However, the DISCO protocol is well suited for both dynamic discovery and for interrogating all the possible web services on an unknown domain. Only time will tell is this is a useful feature for web services.

Format

The DISCO format is extremely simple, which makes sense since it is basically a collection of pointers to WSDL files. The following is an example of a DISCO document:

```xml
<?xml version="1.0" ?>
<disco:discovery xmlns:disco="http://schemas.xmlsoap.org/disco">
    <disco:contractRef ref="http://MyWebServer/UserName.asmx?WSDL"/>
    <disco:discoveryRef ref="SomeFolder/default.disco"/>
</disco:discovery>
```

Everything in this document is contained within a `discovery` element, which is qualified to the `http://schemas.xmlsoap.org/disco` namespace. Inside this there are two possible elements: a `contractRef` and a `discoveryRef` element. The `contractRef` element refers to a WSDL document that specifies the interface, or contract, for a web service. The `discoveryRef` element references another discovery document like this one. This way a single file can link to other DISCO documents. By examining all of these elements, exposed web services can be interrogated and understood.

UDDI

Universal Description, Discovery, and Integration, or UDDI, is a registry used to store business information and publish services. With UDDI, potential clients can search for and find web services exposed by any registered business. The UDDI registry itself exposes several web services to allow any client to search the registry using standard SOAP messages. UDDI registries can be accessed from Microsoft (http://uddi.microsoft.com/) and IBM (http://www-3.ibm.com/services/uddi/).

The UDDI registry is intended to be the yellow pages of the new Internet. It is where businesses list their services, and developers go to locate and shop for available services. In the new model of the Programmable Web, UDDI will be how services are marketed and discovered. UDDI will be extensively covered in Chapter 10. There we will examine how search messages can be sent to the registry, and how businesses can register their web services.

Summary

This chapter covered the various protocols used by web services to allow disparate systems to communicate and interoperate with each other. We covered the SOAP, WSDL, and DISCO protocols, looking at the exact format of the XML messages of each protocol. We also introduced the UDDI registry system.

Web services operate by utilizing well-known XML protocols to facilitate communication between themselves and their clients. This chapter has examined these protocols and their message formats. These protocols are very low level, and very often you will not have to worry about SOAP messages and WSDL documents. However, understanding the formats and how the messages themselves are constructed will enable you to develop better, more efficient web service applications.

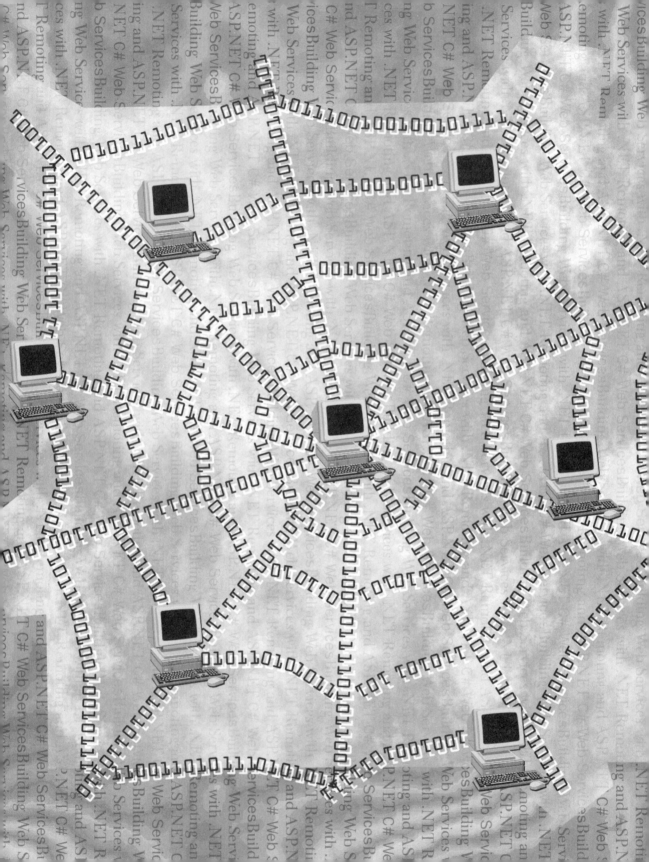

3

Web Services and the .NET Framework

In the last two chapters, we examined what web services offer to both developers and architects of enterprise applications. We also looked at the standards and technologies that allow web services to interoperate regardless of the platforms they are running on. We are now going to examine the options that Microsoft has made available for developers of web service applications.

Not all of these technologies utilize the .NET Framework but examining each of them will provide a good overview of the technological options available from Microsoft. These are by no means the only technological solutions available for developing and consuming web services. This is merely meant as a primer on the current Microsoft technologies.

By their very nature web services are interoperable with other implementations. While other vendors' web services technologies will operate differently and use different languages, the SOAP and WSDL interfaces crucial to web service communication will remain the same. Therefore, using Microsoft products will not prevent you from using external web services created with other technologies.

We will also cover how web services fit into the .NET Framework and how .NET is built around the fundamental concept of software as a service. The .NET Framework enables the creation and consumption of web services in a fast and efficient manner. This allows novice web service developers to create sophisticated solutions utilizing web services today.

In this chapter we will cover the following topics:

❑ The SOAP Toolkit and how it can be used to expose standard COM components as web services using existing languages and technologies

❑ ASP.NET and the .NET Framework and how they enable developers to create sophisticated web service applications quickly and efficiently

❑ .NET Remoting and its role as the .NET replacement for DCOM

❑ What ATL Server is and how it is useful for C++ developers

❑ How web services are tightly integrated into the .NET Framework

The SOAP Toolkit

The SOAP Toolkit was available long before the .NET Framework and Visual Studio .NET. The Toolkit is meant to provide an easy route into developing and consuming web services. It enables developers to utilize their existing COM programming skills to create fully SOAP-compatible web services with minimal effort and coding.

It is important to remember that the SOAP Toolkit does not use the .NET Framework, nor is it in any way connected to it. We are not going to cover the SOAP Toolkit in great detail but we will examine its fundamentals so you can understand how it works and why it was created.

You can download the SOAP Toolkit from http://msdn.microsoft.com/soap. The installation routine is very simple. It installs the core SOAP Toolkit's COM objects, the WSDL Generator that enables any COM object to be exposed as a web service, and a Trace Utility to monitor and debug incoming SOAP calls on a server.

Overview

The Toolkit enables a developer to expose any standard COM or COM+ object as a SOAP-compatible web service. This is a very powerful technique, as the COM object can be written in the language of your choice with existing tools that developers are comfortable working with. No new skills are needed to expose this web service to the world. Any client will be able to access and utilize the COM component via SOAP over HTTP.

Clients can also consume web services using the SOAP Toolkit. The Toolkit provides a local proxy object to abstract all communication with the external web service. Developers work with this proxy as if it were an internal component. The Toolkit object creates and sends valid SOAP messages to the external web service and handles serializing the data types and processing the response messages. Client developers utilize existing COM skills to work with and consume the proxy object, which exposes the functionality of the web service while hiding away the SOAP/HTTP transactions.

Exposing Web Services

The SOAP Toolkit enables developers to expose any COM object as a valid web service. The web service itself conforms to the SOAP specification version 1.1 that we examined in the last chapter, and can serialize and deserialize data types and method requests appropriately. This also means any client application on any system can communicate with the exposed COM object by sending and receiving valid SOAP messages. This is accomplished with the standards we discussed in the last chapter: SOAP and WSDL.

The SOAP Toolkit includes the WSDL Generator, a tool that generates WSDL documents that fully describe the exposed COM objects for clients. This tool also generates a WSML document; this is a Web Service Meta Language document, and it is a Microsoft-only standard. WSML is an XML-based language used to map incoming SOAP requests to the actual COM object methods. With this document, the SOAP Toolkit's infrastructure can map the SOAP calls to the correct method calls. In addition to the object and method names, this document also describes the order and format of the parameters to map from the SOAP messages to the COM methods. Any COM object can be exposed in this manner. If the WSDL Generator cannot process a custom data type it will still generate the WSDL and WSML files. The developer would then have to modify these files by hand before exposing the COM object.

Once the WSDL and WSML files are created and the COM object is loaded and deployed correctly, it can be exposed as a web service. The SOAP Toolkit allows web services to be published with an ISAPI listener or an ASP page listener. The ISAPI listener hooks into Internet Information Services (IIS) and interprets all incoming SOAP requests. It compares these against the loaded WSDL and WSML files. If there is a match, the WSML file is used to load the correct COM object. The listener then uses the SOAP Toolkit's deserialization object to deserialize the SOAP message. It can then call the correct COM method, passing in the data parameters and objects from the SOAP message. The ASP page does this same process in VBScript code, allowing the developer to customize the events and perform any special logging or communication features that are required.

The following diagram shows how the SOAP Toolkit interprets incoming SOAP messages and invokes the COM object's method:

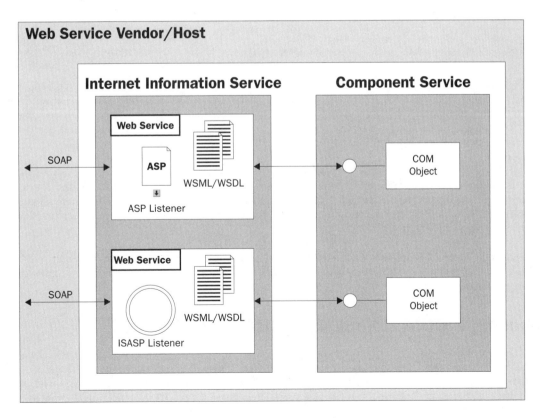

The ISAPI filter or ASP page listener interprets the incoming SOAP message. Each of the interface options, ISAPI and ASP, processes the SOAP message, and examines the internal list of WSML files to see if it is a valid SOAP request for this server. If it is, the information in the WSML document is used to instantiate the correct COM object. Using the information in the WSDL file and SOAP message, the method on the COM object corresponding to the SOAP request is called with the correct parameters. The response from the COM object is packaged and serialized into a SOAP response and sent back to the caller to be interpreted.

Consuming Web Services

The SOAP Toolkit provides a client-side object that interprets and processes exposed WSDL documents on the Internet. The object dynamically queries a WSDL document, and takes on the methods of the remote web service, becoming a proxy for the external web service. The local object handles the SOAP messaging and HTTP calls, forwarding these to the external service.

Therefore, if an external web service exposed the following method as a simple web service:

```
void GetSalesTax(string State, string Zip);
```

Instead of generating the complex SOAP messages we examined in the last chapter, the following VBScript code can be used with the SOAP Toolkit to utilize this web service:

```
Set SoapClient = CreateObject("MSSOAP.SoapClient")
Call SoapClient.mssoapinit("http://www.mathserver.com/Math.wsdl")

MsgBox (SoapClient.GetSalesTax ("CA", "93933"))
```

The `SoapClient` object is created like any standard COM object. The `mssoapinit()` method accepts the location of the WSDL file, as well as several optional parameters specifying exactly what service and port to reference in the WSDL document. Recall from the last chapter that a single WSDL document can contain several services and ports for messages to be sent to. If one of these parameters is missing, the first service or port listed in the referenced WSDL document is used.

After the `mssoapinit()` method has been called, the web service methods are exposed as methods on the instantiated `SoapClient` object. In this example, the `GetSalesTax()` method is called like a standard COM method would be called. Internal to this method, a SOAP message is generated and the parameters serialized into the format we examined in the last chapter. This message is sent via HTTP to the location specified in the WSDL document.

Since the `SoapClient` object is a standard COM component located on the client's machine, any language used to develop COM-enabled applications can be used to interact with and consume external web services via this object.

Exposing a COM Object with the SOAP Toolkit

To illustrate how the SOAP Toolkit works, we will walk through the creation of a simple Visual Basic 6 COM object and show how to expose it as a web service. This will demonstrate how existing programming experience in Visual Basic can be used to develop web service applications today. We are using Visual Basic 6 because it is the fastest way to create a simple COM object for demonstration purposes. The same principles would apply to any COM object created in any language.

First create a new Visual Basic ActiveX DLL Project. Change the name of the `Class1` object to `MathComponent` and add the following code to the file:

```
Public Function AddNumbers(ByVal nNum1 As Integer, ByVal nNum2 As Integer) _
                          As Integer
   AddNumbers = (nNum1 + nNum2)
End Function
```

Compile this project to a DLL file called `Math.dll`. This COM object simply adds two numbers together and returns the result, like our example web service in the last chapter. Obviously this is a very simple COM object, but the purpose of this example is to demonstrate the SOAP Toolkit in action, not to create a fully featured COM library.

We need to create the WSDL and WSML files. Clients use the WSDL file to understand the methods this web service exposes and what protocols can be used to communicate with it. The WSML file is used to map incoming messages to the correct methods in the component. Remember that WSML files are solely used by the SOAP Toolkit – they are not a standard used for other web services or .NET web services. To create these files, we will run the SOAP Toolkit's WSDL Generator.

Through a simple wizard interface, this application enables you to select the DLL file you wish to expose as a web service. The following is the screen for selecting the correct DLL and giving the web service a name:

Once you have selected the DLL file, you are asked to select the individual component(s) you wish to expose from that DLL, and you are even given the option to individually select the methods to expose. This provides very fine control over the structure of the web service. Methods can be created that are only accessible internally while others are publicly accessible as web services. The public COM methods are only accessible as web services if these steps are carried out. This screen looks like this:

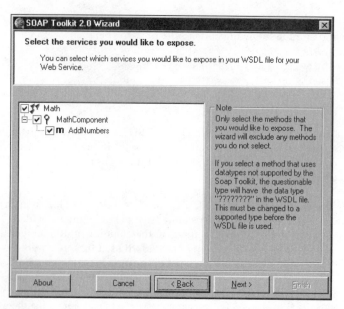

By checking the checkbox next to AddNumbers, we have selected the only method exposed by our COM object. Note that if the WSDL Generator tool cannot understand how to serialize a data type it will leave it up to the developer to add the custom code into the WSDL document. This would involve leveraging the WSDL skills we learned in the last chapter and writing the XML Schema code in the WSDL document for each of the troublesome custom data types.

Once these steps are done, you must select the location where you will deploy the web service. This is saved to the WSDL file so that clients accessing this file know where to send SOAP requests. Also specified is the type of listener: ASP or ISAPI and the XSD Schema namespace type to support. The screen for this step looks like this:

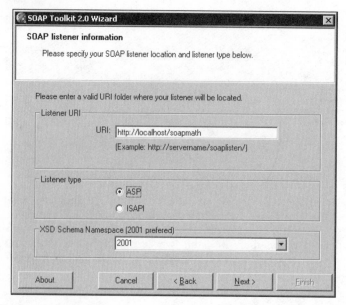

The listener URI is the location of the web service for clients to access and send messages to this service. Note that this does not have to be on the same machine used to run the WSDL Generator. The XSD Schema Namespace option relates to what version of the W3C XML Schema standard your SOAP web service will support. There are three versions of the XSD namespace in effect: 1999, 2000, and 2001. The WSDL file produced can conform to any of these three standards, but it is recommended to utilize the latest (2001) unless your web service must be compatible with a legacy SOAP implementation. For the majority of web service applications, choose the most current XSD namespace.

The choice of the listener is important. You have a choice between ASP and ISAPI. If the ISAPI listener is chosen, the default mapping, as defined in the WSML file, is used for incoming SOAP messages and the developer does not have to do any more work to enable clients to access this component as a web service. In addition, the ISAPI listener is a compiled DLL, providing significant performance advantage over the ASP listener. If an ASP listener is used, an ASP file is generated to perform the mapping between the SOAP message and the actual component. This option only needs to be chosen if custom logging or notification must be performed when incoming SOAP calls are accepted. The ASP file itself can be modified to perform these custom actions. The ASP listener generated for our Math component is shown below:

```
<%@ LANGUAGE=VBScript %>
<%
Option Explicit
On Error Resume Next
Response.ContentType = "text/xml"
Dim SoapServer
If Not Application("MathInitialized") Then
    Application.Lock
    If Not Application("MathInitialized") Then
        Dim WSDLFilePath
        Dim WSMLFilePath
        WSDLFilePath = Server.MapPath("Math.wsdl")
        WSMLFilePath = Server.MapPath("Math.wsml")
        Set SoapServer = Server.CreateObject("MSSOAP.SoapServer")
        If Err Then SendFault "Cannot create SoapServer object. " & _
                        Err.Description
        SoapServer.Init WSDLFilePath, WSMLFilePath
        If Err Then SendFault "SoapServer.Init failed. " & Err.Description
        Set Application("MathServer") = SoapServer
        Application("MathInitialized") = True
    End If
    Application.UnLock
End If
Set SoapServer = Application("MathServer")
SoapServer.SoapInvoke Request, Response, ""
If Err Then SendFault "SoapServer.SoapInvoke failed. " & Err.Description

Sub SendFault(ByVal LogMessage)
    Dim Serializer
    On Error Resume Next
    ' "URI Query" logging must be enabled for AppendToLog to work
    Response.AppendToLog " SOAP ERROR: " & LogMessage
    Set Serializer = Server.CreateObject("MSSOAP.SoapSerializer")
    If Err Then
        Response.AppendToLog "Could not create SoapSerializer object. " & _
                        Err.Description
        Response.Status = "500 Internal Server Error"
    Else
        Serializer.Init Response
        If Err Then
```

```
        Response.AppendToLog "SoapSerializer.Init failed. " & _
                      Err.Description
        Response.Status = "500 Internal Server Error"
    Else
        Serializer.startEnvelope
        Serializer.startBody
        Serializer.startFault "Server", "The request could not be " & _
            "processed due to a problem in the server. Please contact " & _
            " the system administrator. " & LogMessage
        Serializer.endFault
        Serializer.endBody
        Serializer.endEnvelope
        If Err Then
            Response.AppendToLog "SoapSerializer failed. " & Err.Description
            Response.Status = "500 Internal Server Error"
        End If
    End If
    End If
    Response.End
End Sub
%>
```

We will not cover this file in depth, as this is not the intent of this example. The heart of the file lies in these two lines:

```
Set SoapServer = Application("MathServer")
SoapServer.SoapInvoke Request, Response, ""
```

This gets the `SoapServer` component loaded from the `Application` cache, and invokes the current SOAP request via the `SoapInvoke()` method. This method performs the mapping of the SOAP message (loaded in the `Request` ASP object) and the method call on the component. The ASP file itself contains a lot of other code involving loading the `SoapServer` object and handling errors.

Lastly, the wizard asks for a location to save the generated WSML and WSDL files. This is a very simple process and, once it is done, you have a fully featured web service ready to deploy to your web server. Clients from all over the Internet will then be able to utilize your component via standard HTTP and SOAP messages.

The SOAP Toolkit produces a WSDL document and a WSML document. The WSDL document describes the exposed COM object as an external web service. We examined this protocol in detail in the last chapter. If you examine the other document produced, the WSML file, you will see another XML document in a similar format to WSDL. WSML describes the relationship between an exposed web service and the actual COM object methods implementing the web service. The WSML document produced by our example is shown below:

```
<?xml version='1.0' encoding='UTF-8' ?>
<!-- Generated 09/16/01 by Microsoft SOAP Toolkit WSDL File Generator, Version
1.02.813.0 -->
<servicemapping name='MathCOM'>
    <service name='MathCOM'>
        <using PROGID='proMath.MathComponent' cachable='0'
               ID='MathComponentObject' />
        <port name='MathComponentSoapPort'>
            <operation name='AddNumbers'>
                <execute uses='MathComponentObject' method='AddNumbers'
dispID='1610809344'>
```

```
                    <parameter callIndex='1' name='nNum1' elementName='nNum1'/>
                    <parameter callIndex='2' name='nNum2' elementName='nNum2'/>
                    <parameter callIndex='-1' name='retval' elementName='Result'/>
                </execute>
            </operation>
        </port>
    </service>
</servicemapping>
```

Each `service`, `port`, and `operation` node in the original WSDL document is referenced in this document. Each provides information as to the specific COM object to instantiate and what method to invoke on that object. It also specifies the arguments to pass to the method and the order to pass them in. You will probably never have to create or modify a WSML document on your own, but it helps to see what is happening behind the scenes.

To install this web service, open up the Internet Information Services Console and create a new virtual directory. Call it `soapmath`, since this is what we put in the WSDL file via the Toolkit's wizard. Point the virtual directory to the location containing the newly generated files, including the WSML and WSDL files and the ASP page.

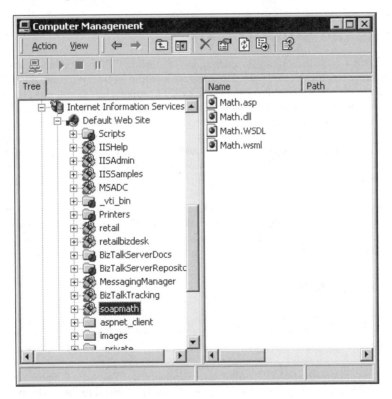

The WSDL and WSML files need to be located in a virtual directory in IIS so clients can access them and discover the web service. If the ASP option is chosen, the generated ASP file must be placed in the same location as well. Clients can now send SOAP messages to the web server. These calls are intercepted by the ISAPI filter or ASP listener and sent to the appropriate method on the component as specified by the WSML file.

The COM object must be registered on the web server. In a development environment this will probably be the same machine you are working on, but when the web service is deployed don't forget to register the COM object or its local proxy on the web server. Once this has been completed, the COM object is exposed to the world as a web service. Any client using any SOAP-enabled device can access the AddNumbers() method via SOAP and HTTP messaging. To prove this, let's create a VBScript client to call the web service, using the SOAP Toolkit's client-side object.

Add the following code to a text file and save it as SoapClient.vbs:

```
Set MathService = CreateObject("MSSOAP.soapclient")

MathService.mssoapinit("http://localhost/soapmath/math.wsdl")

MsgBox(MathService.AddNumbers(10,5))
```

Clicking on this file in Windows will cause the web service to be called and the response echoed back via a message box. This illustrates how the SOAP client object works, as well as proving our exposed COM object is accessible as a web service. The SOAP Toolkit enables the creation of web service applications with existing technology and tools.

When to Use the SOAP Toolkit

The SOAP Toolkit is a great technology for making use of existing COM components and exposing them to the world as web services. It can also be used to integrate external web services into an existing COM-enabled application, such as a Visual Basic 6, ASP 3, or MFC application. If you must continue to develop or support applications using these technologies, this is the tool to use. The SOAP Toolkit will provide the ability to utilize functionality developed and deployed on any machine with any technology anywhere on the Internet. This impressive power can be accessed using the same tools that developers are familiar with today. This tool also enables developers to begin using C# and the .NET Framework on new projects, while still utilizing their old COM components and services through SOAP Toolkit-enabled web services. This way, old investments are not lost but development can continue using the new, more powerful .NET toolset.

We covered the SOAP Toolkit in this chapter because we are not going to cover it again in this book. If you are in a .NET environment, or planning on moving to one soon, there is no need for the SOAP Toolkit. If you plan on developing enterprise-level web service applications, the .NET Framework and the extensive suite of tools in Visual Studio .NET provide the best option.

Summary of the SOAP Toolkit

The SOAP Toolkit is a very useful tool for developers who wish to explore web services but do not want to migrate to the .NET platform. Using the SOAP Toolkit enables developers to build web service applications using the same technology and languages they have been using to create COM components and applications.

Another useful thing about the SOAP Toolkit is its extensibility. The SOAP Toolkit exposes both a high-level API and a low-level API. So far we have primarily referred to the high-level API. Working with this layer is very simple as the SOAP messages and interfaces are very far removed from the developer. However, if custom serialization or custom processing of messages must be performed, the SOAP Toolkit allows developers to utilize the low-level API to facilitate these operations. This low-level API exposes objects for working directly with SOAP messages and HTTP packets. This flexibility in working with web services and SOAP make the SOAP Toolkit a very powerful tool.

The biggest disadvantage to using the SOAP Toolkit is the fact that it is not a .NET solution. For some this will be its greatest strength, but those of you reading this book to discover how to develop web services in C# will not, I assume, be in this crowd. The SOAP Toolkit is a great tool for developing web service applications using 'classic' COM-based languages.

ASP.NET

ASP.NET is a set of components and services layered on top of the .NET Framework. By using ASP.NET to develop web services, developers gain the use of the extensive class library included with the Framework. This provides all of the base functionality for working with SOAP messages and processing WSDL files. ASP.NET also provides a rich runtime environment for hosting web services that alleviates much of the work involved in setting up and deploying web service applications. ASP.NET is the way to create web services in the .NET Framework.

All of the advantages of .NET are available to the developer of ASP.NET web services. By using ASP.NET on top of the .NET Framework, developers gain the benefits of the existing stateless ASP model that provides very scalable performance, as well as access to the intrinsic ASP objects: `Application`, `Context`, `Server`, `Session`, `Site`, and `User`. These objects have been rewritten for the .NET Framework and can be used from ASP.NET to provide functionality for web applications to manage state and store settings and objects in the global and user cache.

Exposing Web Services

ASP.NET WebForm applications are much like 'standard' ASP 3 applications. They consist of a set of `.aspx` files that contain the application code, logic, and the web site's various web pages. One of the major differences between the two is that ASP.NET pages are compiled, unlike standard ASP pages that are composed of interpreted VBScript code. ASP.NET applications have full access to all the namespaces and classes of the .NET Framework, and can utilize all of them to create richly featured applications. The `.aspx` pages reside in Internet Information Services, which works with the Common Language Runtime to instantiate and run the compiled .NET code.

ASP.NET web services are based on all as the same concepts of ASP.NET WebForm applications, except they expose no user interface. Instead, they expose public functionality via methods with WSDL and SOAP interfaces. They are still composed of .NET compiled code, and still reside in IIS, giving the system administrator all the same options for securing and monitoring web services as they have for other web applications in IIS.

Web services are located in `.asmx` files, and contain special attributes that define them as web services. The .NET code can be located directly inside these files, or they can reference external assemblies containing the actual components exposed. The second is the practice performed by Visual Studio .NET automatically, and as such you will see it the most often. In the next chapter we will examine this concept in detail.

ASP.NET also provides developers with additional benefits. One is the ability to automatically generate WSDL and DISCO documentation. One of the major benefits of .NET code is that it is self-describing. This is achieved through the process of reflection and the extensive metadata stored in assemblies. ASP.NET uses these tools to generate WSDL files dynamically, based on the web service's interface. Therefore, as a web service is developed and changed, there is no need to manually update and replace WSDL files. ASP.NET handles this with the automatic and dynamic generation of WSDL and DISCO files. It also generates a test page that enables quick testing of web services through a web browser without having to write client access code.

Namespaces

All of the .NET Framework namespaces are available to ASP.NET web service applications. The following four namespaces are specifically designed to support developers in building web services solutions:

- ❑ `System.Web.Services` – This namespace contains the `WebService` class, which developers can inherit from to gain access to the intrinsic ASP.NET objects. This namespace also contains the `WebMethod` attribute that enables .NET components to be exposed as external web services.

- ❑ `System.Web.Services.Description` – This contains classes that enable you to create and consume WSDL files. In the majority of web service applications this will not have to be done by the developer; Visual Studio .NET handles most of the low-level details.

- ❑ `System.Web.Services.Discovery` – This enables developers to create and manipulate DISCO files. We will discuss this namespace and its uses later in the book.

- ❑ `System.Web.Services.Protocols` – This namespace contains the classes used to communicate with web services. These can be in SOAP, HTTP, or MIME as defined in the SOAP specification.

Consuming Web Services

Consuming web services is not an ASP.NET-specific technology. Any .NET language and application can be used as a client for external web services. A key aim in the development of .NET is to make consuming and utilizing web services very easy and powerful. By doing this, Microsoft hopes to make web services a viable programming model for all developers.

Like the SOAP Toolkit, Visual Studio .NET creates a client-side proxy object to manage and abstract all communication with the external web service. This client-side object is based on the remote web service's WSDL file. The object is created in the same .NET language as the project. It can then be used like any other .NET object. Calls to it are translated to SOAP messages and sent via HTTP to the remote web service. As with the SOAP toolkit, this provides a level of abstraction for the developer in that they do not have to worry about the details of SOAP and HTTP messaging and serialization.

Visual Studio .NET provides a very easy and convenient method for locating and consuming external web services. From the IDE, one can directly access the UDDI registry and search for a web service based on the functionality or business type desired. This tight integration with the available tools for web services makes Visual Studio .NET a great tool for developing web service applications. Visual Studio .NET also allows developers to specify a web server address. This server will be dynamically queried for available web services. Therefore, if a web service is implemented on a particular server, it can be utilized, even if it is not registered with UDDI. Having Visual Studio .NET so tightly integrated with the UDDI registry makes discovering web services easier and more efficient than finding the desired functionality in third-party components or applications. We will be covering UDDI in more depth later in this book.

.NET Remoting

.NET Remoting represents the next generation of distributed component technologies. As such, it supersedes DCOM in the .NET Framework. .NET Remoting enables .NET components to be exposed and utilized from a client machine as if the component was local, in a similar fashion to the client-side proxies we have discussed already. This can be done exactly as with DCOM, proprietary binary TCP/IP method calls being made to the components. The power of .NET Remoting is in its ability to be used over any messaging layer (such as SOAP) and protocol (such as HTTP or TCP/IP). SOAP and HTTP can be used to consume an external .NET component. This is obviously similar toASP.NET web services but .NET Remoting provides a richer interface, enabling subscription to events, allocation and deallocation of objects, and other services that one can do with standard distributed object systems. Web services only allow for single method calls to be requested. The downside to .NET Remoting is that it is not standardized, and is a Microsoft-only implementation.

.NET Remoting is built on a layered model, with each layer replaceable by custom code created by a developer. Therefore, new messaging, transport, and communication protocols can be implemented and plugged in as needed. Currently, only binary and SOAP messaging protocols are included in the .NET Framework.

.NET Remoting components can use COM+ component services to provide transactional, highly available components to their clients.

We will cover .NET Remoting in Section Three of this book.

When to Use .NET Remoting

The ability to instantiate and call components via the SOAP and HTTP standards is very powerful, and provides developers with the ability to build distributed object-oriented systems. Unlike most web services, components exposed as a Remoting object can retain state and act like standard distributed components, while still providing the ability to be invoked and instantiated using SOAP and HTTP.

For distributed objects that require better performance than HTTP provides, such as in an intranet environment and between tiers, using Remoting objects with the TCP/IP protocol is the best choice. This uses a proprietary call format to serialize method calls into a binary format and transport them to the remote component. While the ubiquity and interoperability of SOAP are lost, the performance and security of the binary protocol could be very useful in certain environments. Components exposed in this manner closely resemble DCOM objects.

The power of Remoting lies in its extensibility. While only shipping with the SOAP and binary formatters, the .NET Framework allows developers to create custom formatters and plug them into the serialization process. This flexibility is very powerful, and allows developers to create customized, robust distributed systems easily and effectively.

ATL Server

ATL Server is a tool designed to allow C++ developers to expose and consume web services. It provides C++ programmers with the power and flexibility of web services with the same interfaces and technology as ATL itself. The ATL Server application is an extension of the ISAPI filter interface, and can perform custom processing and replacement of tags in generated HTML code. The goal of ATL Server is to provide an easy to-use tool for a C++ developer that is still as powerful and as fully featured as ISAPI filters.

ATL Server also provides the ability to create C++ client objects that interact with external web services. Like the other technologies we have examined, the exposed WSDL document is used to create a client object that is accessed and manipulated like any other local object. This object is created in C++ and manages the creation and processing of all SOAP messages. It also handles the sending of appropriate HTTP packets and processing of response codes.

As this technology is obviously intended for C++ developers exclusively, we will not be covering it in this book. It will be covered in a future Wrox book on C++ .NET.

When to Use ATL Server

ATL Server is a tool designed for developers who need the most power and control for their web service applications. ATL Server allows developers to build a web service in C++ as an ISAPI filter, giving the developer maximum control over performance and scalability. This tool, like the SOAP Toolkit for Visual Basic, will also create a client object, allowing C++ applications to access a remote web service by simply calling a local proxy.

Of course, this power comes at a cost. Like ATL itself, ATL Server is a very complicated technology, and can only be used effectively by a seasoned C++ developer. Used incorrectly, it can result in memory leaks, severe consumption of server resources, and overwriting important information in memory. The performance gains are significant, but these need to be weighed against the benefit of developing in a more forgiving environment like the .NET Framework. The productivity gains of the .NET Framework must also be considered versus the complexity of working with C++. The strengths and weaknesses of your development teams must be carefully assessed, and the needs and requirements of your application must also be considered.

Summary

We have seen many different ways of building web service applications, and it may seem overwhelming at first. The choice of which development tool to use for creating a web service depends on the task at hand and the preference of the developer. This chapter has provided a broad overview of the Microsoft tools for developing web service applications. We examined the SOAP Toolkit and how it enables developers to create and consume web services without the use of the .NET Framework. This can be useful for developers not able or unwilling to migrate; however .NET provides a rich set of features for developing web service applications. We introduced ASP.NET as the easiest route to building web services in the .NET Framework.

We also introduced .NET Remoting and how this can be used to distribute any .NET component. This remote component can be accessed from any device via any transport protocol. Microsoft provides SOAP and TCP/IP protocols in the .NET Framework. However, the Remoting architecture is fully extensible and can be reworked and extended to include other protocols and formats. We also briefly looked at the ATL Server technology, for completeness. Because this is a C++ technology we will not cover it in this book but it is important to understand all the options that Microsoft offers for web service development.

Web services are a powerful new development model, as important as the shift to component development. They represent a fundamental change in the way applications are developed and will enable the creation of more sophisticated applications and distributed systems. Throughout the rest of this book we will examine exactly how to develop these applications, and how to make use of the tools Microsoft provides.

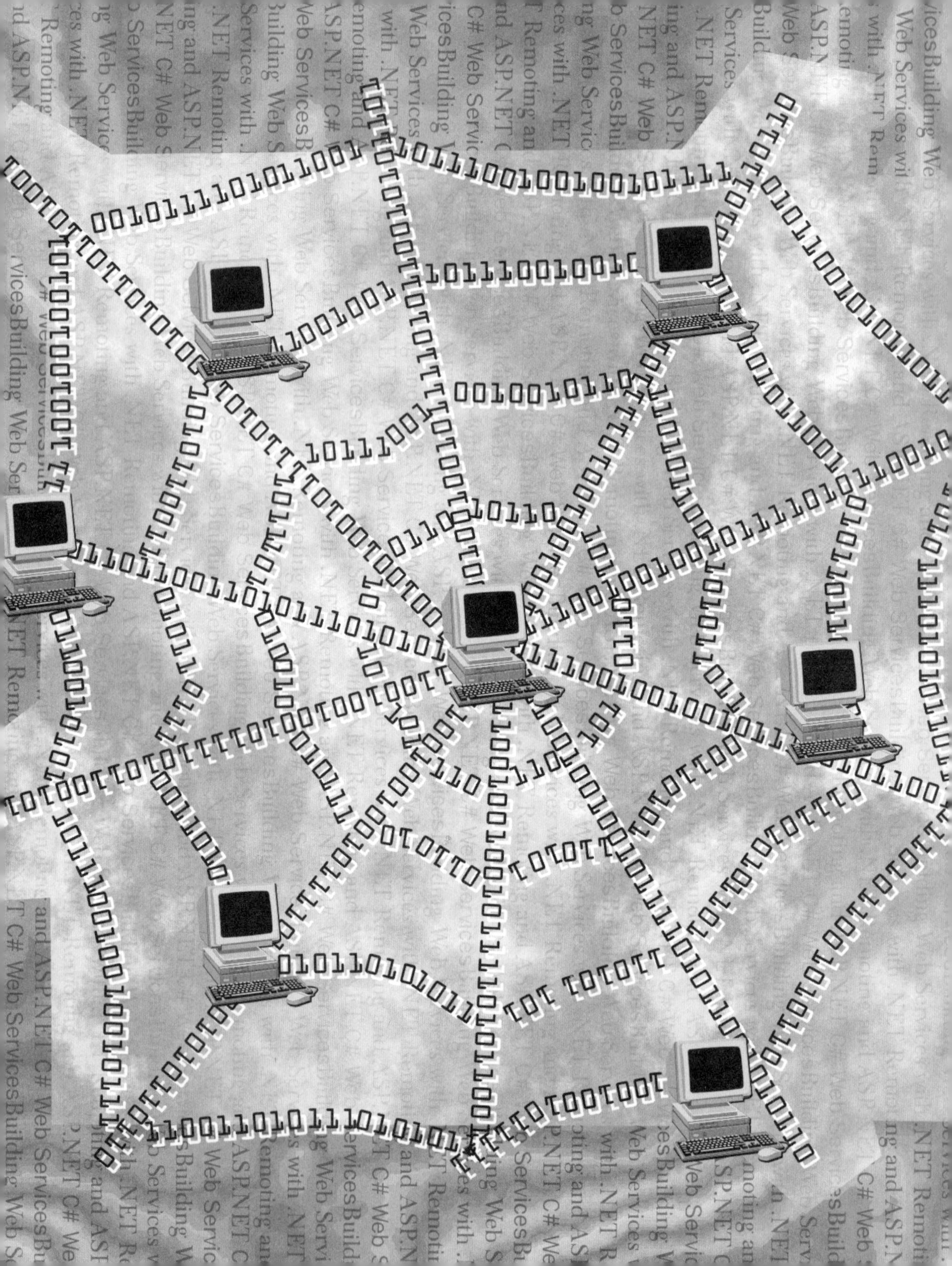

Section Two – ASP.NET Web Services

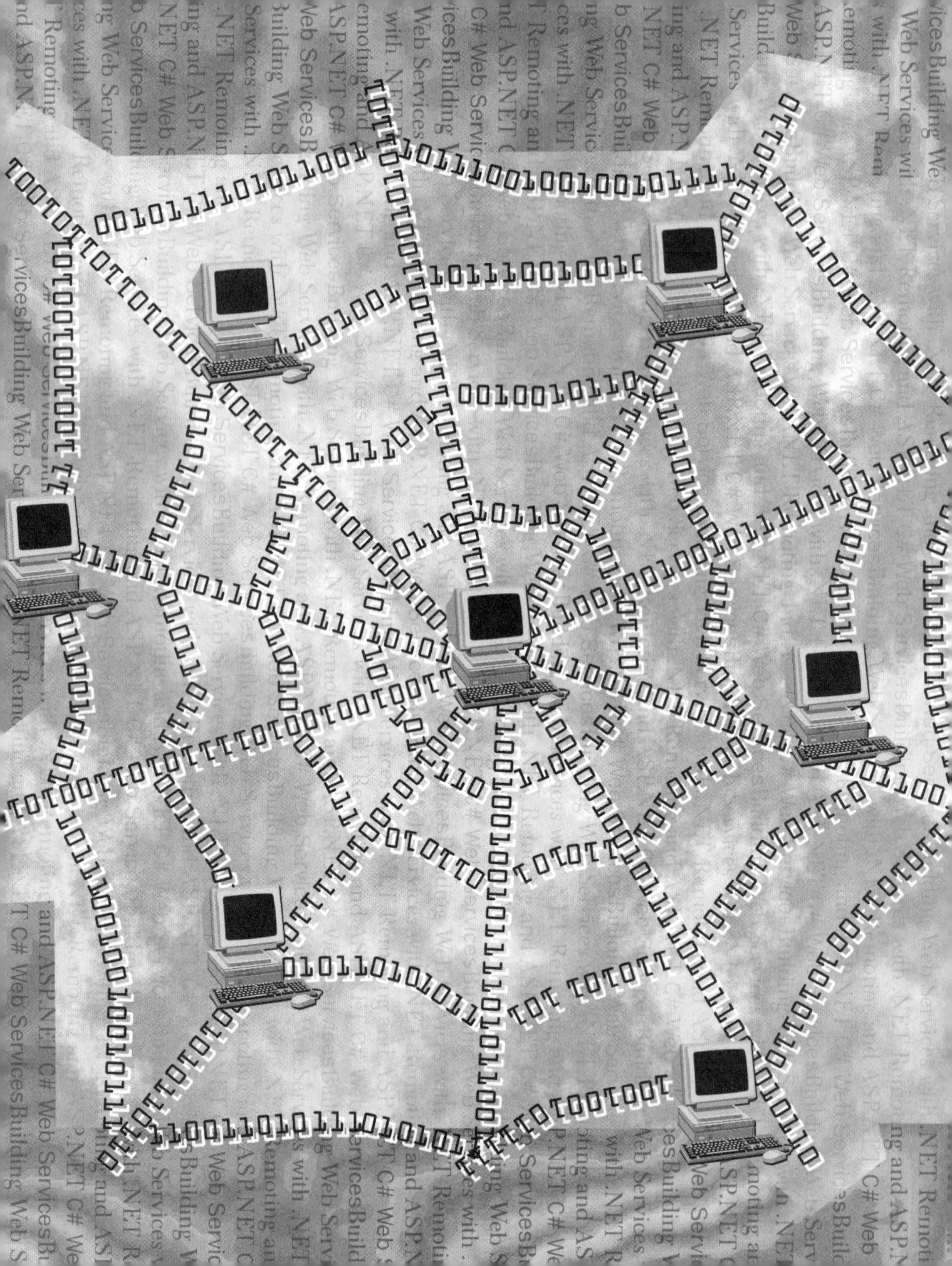

4

Building an ASP.NET Web Service

Since the inception of the Internet, the real underlying principle has been the distribution and sharing of data. Connecting businesses that handle data with businesses that provide services to manipulate that data is an important part of the modern world of commerce. More and more information is available every day, and every day businesses share increasing amounts of data. As broadband becomes widely established, the true allure of distributed computing comes to light. Everyone in commerce – partners, suppliers, distributors, and consumers alike – are benefiting from and relying on networked data access.

One of the problems that arise from this type of environment is that of interoperability between different systems. Before the global push for web services, interoperability was generally seen as a particularly difficult problem to tackle. Data could be transferred with rather unpolished systems built on SOAP (Simple Object Access Protocol) or simple HTML and POST requests. In some cases, the use of remote objects could be implemented through DCOM (Distributed Component Object Model).

Web services are poised to achieve much more than the simple transfer of data between organizations, and have the potential to allow real-time distributed programming logic to be integrated into applications. With XML-based SOAP and HTTP, the web services model has two of the key building blocks of the Internet as its foundation stones, promising broad support for the technology and ease of integration into existing systems. In this chapter, we are going to cover the essentials of building an ASP.NET web service, both with and without the Visual Studio .NET IDE.

Overview of ASP.NET Web Services

For those of you who don't already have a good idea of what a web service is and why you'd want to use one, the term 'web service' describes a general model for building applications that naturally integrate with communication over the Internet. If you have a general idea of how DCOM (Distributed Component Object Model) or Remote Method Invocation works, then you already have a picture of what web services aim to achieve.

Briefly, at the simplest level a web service uses SOAP and HTTP to make business logic available to remote consumer applications over HTTP so that such applications can freely invoke methods of your centralized business objects:

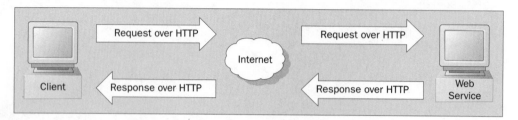

As you can see in the above figure, a client request is passed using SOAP over HTTP via the Internet. The web service sends its response to the client application as a SOAP message over HTTP. Both the request and response SOAP messages are primarily XML-based, containing essential information in their **XML payload**. The elegance of this solution is that, where interoperability is concerned, web services can greatly reduce the pain of getting different systems to communicate by facilitating the negotiation of communication boundaries. As long as the client application can generate the XML required for a SOAP request and interpret the XML within the SOAP response, it is in a position to communicate with a web service.

Now that we have a good idea of the underlying principles that apply to web services in the .NET world, we shall look at the actual protocols that work together to make it all happen seamlessly.

Web Service Protocols

In previous Microsoft architectures, proprietary protocols were really the limiting factor in giving a variety of clients access to remote method invocations. For example, the DCOM protocol consisted of a proprietary communication protocol with a method request layer sitting on top. The idea of the web service initiative is to remove the limitations that restrict clients and come up with a more generally acceptable method of accessing remote services. As we now know, SOAP and HTTP are the most important underlying technologies behind calling a web service.

> *You may also hear the term "Wire Format" mentioned when talking about web service protocols. This term comes from the notion of sending and receiving data across the "wire" or connection. In actuality it refers to the underlying communication protocols used in sending data from point A to point B.*

SOAP

SOAP (Simple Object Access Protocol) is a method of exchanging structured XML-based information over the Internet. Simplicity is the primary goal of the SOAP protocol, and takes precedence over functionality, resulting in a very straightforward protocol with minimal built-in functionality. Despite this, the framework that the protocol defines is both extensible and modular, making it a very powerful and flexible message transport system. For more detailed information about the SOAP protocol, see the W3C Recommendation at http://www.w3.org/TR/SOAP.

It is interesting to note that the SOAP protocol specification is not tied to HTTP, and may use any transport protocol capable of carrying SOAP envelopes from one point to another. This includes such protocols as SMTP, FTP, or disk storage.

However, it is clear that for SOAP to be really useful, it should use a widely used and accepted transport protocol, and thus HTTP is the typical first choice. SOAP in the web services world leverages the existing architecture of the Internet, so access is only limited by the client's ability to support basic iternet communication standards.

The SOAP Protocol Specification

When we look at the actual SOAP protocol specification, we see that it is split into four main areas:

❑ **Envelope** – The mandatory SOAP envelope encapsulates data. The SOAP envelope defines a SOAP message and is the most basic object exchanged between SOAP processors.

❑ **Data Encoding Rules** – This part of the SOAP specification defines optional data encoding rules for describing application defined data types, as well as a model for serializing objects.

❑ **Message Exchange Model** – This part of the SOAP specification defines a request/response pattern for exchange of data messages. Although SOAP is based on an RPC-type mechanism, it doesn't mandate a particular message exchange pattern.

❑ **Binding** – The fourth part of the SOAP specification describes a binding between SOAP and the transport protocol. This part of the specification is optional, as we already know that other mechanisms are quite acceptable for the transportation of the SOAP envelope.

The diagram below shows the basic structure of a SOAP message:

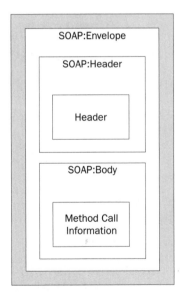

What does this mean to the developer? Well for most of us, it's probably simpler to look at how SOAP is used in web services, where a SOAP request is made up of the following XML elements:

❑ **Envelope** – Defines the content of the message

❑ **Header** – (Optional) Contains header information

❑ **Body** – Contains call and response information

Simple SOAP Request Example

Let's consider a simple SOAP request to find the price of bananas. In its most basic form, such a request would resemble something like this:

```
<SOAP-ENV:Envelope>
    <SOAP-ENV:Body>
        <GetPrice>
            <Item>Bananas</Item>
        </GetPrice>
    </SOAP-ENV:Body>
</SOAP-ENV:Envelope>
```

> The namespace prefix used for SOAP elements depends on how the namespace is referenced. Here, we've used **SOAP-ENV**, as in **<SOAP-ENV:Envelope>**, although you will find alternatives in use. For example, in WSDL documents, **S** is generally used, for instance **<S:Envelope>**

As you can see, the SOAP envelope is an XML element that contains certain information related to the request. One thing to keep in mind is that, strictly speaking, the envelope tag should be scoped with the SOAP envelope URI:

```
<SOAP-ENV:Envelope
    xmlns:SOAP-ENV="http://schemas.xmlsoap.org/soap/envelope/">
```

Before we go any further, let's list the basic syntax rules for SOAP messages:

- ❑ Must be encoded using XML
- ❑ Must have a SOAP envelope
- ❑ Can have an optional SOAP header
- ❑ Must have a SOAP body
- ❑ Must use the SOAP envelope namespaces
- ❑ Must use the SOAP encoding namespace
- ❑ Must not contain a DTD reference
- ❑ Must not contain XML processing instructions

The next two code snippets show the actual output of the SOAP request and response for a sample .NET remoted call to illustrate the contents of real SOAP request and response messages.

Soap Request

The example below is a hypothetical SOAP request to a web service that returns pricing information about an item. As you can see, we are requesting the price of a "Banana":

```
POST /Server.PriceWatcher.remote HTTP/1.1
User-Agent: Mozilla/4.0+(compatible; MSIE 6.0; Windows 5.0.2195.0;
    MS .NET Remoting; MS .NET CLR 1.0.2914.16 )
```

```
SOAPAction: "http://schemas.microsoft.com/clr/nsassem/Server.PriceWatcher/
    Server#GetPrice"
Content-Type: text/xml; charset="utf-8"
Content-Length: 498
Expect: 100-continue
Connection: Keep-Alive
Host: localhost

<SOAP-ENV:Envelope xmlns:xsi="http://www.w3.org/2001/XMLSchema-instance"
    xmlns:xsd="http://www.w3.org/2001/XMLSchema"
    xmlns:SOAP-ENC="http://schemas.xmlsoap.org/soap/encoding/"
    xmlns:SOAP-ENV="http://schemas.xmlsoap.org/soap/envelope/"
    xmlns:pw="http://schemas.microsoft.com/clr/nsassem/Server.PriceWatcher/
    Server"
    SOAP-ENV:encodingStyle="http://schemas.xmlsoap.org/soap/encoding/">

    <SOAP-ENV:Body>
        <pw:GetPrice id="ref-1">
            <id>Banana</id>
        </pw:GetPrice>
    </SOAP-ENV:Body>

</SOAP-ENV:Envelope>
```

As you can see, the above SOAP request starts with HTML header type information listing information such as the `Content-Type` and `Content-Length`. There is also a `SOAPAction` header, which gives the URL for the web service followed by a pound sign (#) and the name of the web method, `GetPrice`. If we look further down the request, we come to the XML format SOAP envelope itself. There are a lot of XML namespace declarations in the initial `<Envelope>` tag, including the standard `xsd` XML Schema (XSD) namespace, `SOAP-ENV` mentioned before, and the `pw` namespace for web method elements. Within the `<Envelope>` element is a SOAP `<Body>` element, which describes what the request is for: to retrieve the price of a banana.

The SOAP message will be processed by the remote web service code, which bundles up the result of its computations as a SOAP response to return to the client application that initiated the call. The SOAP response we would expect to receive for this sample call would resemble the document reproduced next.

Soap Response

```
HTTP/1.1 100 Continue

HTTP/1.1 200 OK
Content-Type: text/xml; charset="utf-8"
Server: MS .NET Remoting, MS .NET CLR 1.0.2914.16
Content-Length: 782

<SOAP-ENV:Envelope xmlns:xsi="http://www.w3.org/2001/XMLSchema-instance"
    xmlns:xsd="http://www.w3.org/2001/XMLSchema"
    xmlns:SOAP-ENC="http://schemas.xmlsoap.org/soap/encoding/"
    xmlns:SOAP-ENV="http://schemas.xmlsoap.org/soap/envelope/"
    SOAP-ENV:encodingStyle="http://schemas.xmlsoap.org/soap/encoding/"
    xmlns:sv="http://schemas.microsoft.com/clr/nsassem/Server/Server"
    xmlns:pw="http://schemas.microsoft.com/clr/nsassem/Server.PriceWatcher/
    Server">

    <SOAP-ENV:Body>
```

```
        <pw:GetPriceResponse id="ref-1">
            <return href="#ref-4"/>
        </pw:GetPriceResponse>
        <sv:ItemInfo id="ref-4">
            <Id>Banana</Id>
            <Price id="ref-5">2.00</Price>
        </sv:ItemInfo>
    </SOAP-ENV:Body>

</SOAP-ENV:Envelope>
```

HTTP

HTTP is the transfer protocol used in the vast majority of web requests. For the purposes of this discussion of web services, it's not necessary to fully understand the inner workings of the HTTP protocol, which is the basic form of internet communication. However, we shall look at HTTP GET and POST operations, as these can be used as alternatives to SOAP when calling a web service.

HTTP-GET and HTTP-POST are two standard HTTP-based approaches for encoding and passing parameters to remote machines as name-value pairs. A basic request consists of HTTP request headers that specify what the client wants from the server. The server responds with one or more HTTP response headers that, if the operation was successful, usually include the requested data.

It is interesting to note that parameters are passed in the form of UUencoded text. This text is appended to the URL (as the **querystring**) for HTTP-GET, and as part of the HTTP request message in the case of HTTP-POST.

System.Web.Services.Protocols

The .NET Framework provides a namespace that contains classes defining the protocols available for the transmission of data between ASP.NET web service clients and the actual web services themselves. This is the System.Web.Services.Protocols namespace.

The following table lists the names and descriptions of the classes found within it:

Class Name	Purpose
HttpGetClientProtocol	The client proxy for ASP.NET web services using HTTP-GET derives from this class.
HttpMethodAttribute	Apply to a web service client when using HTTP-GET or HTTP-POST to set the types for serializing the parameters sent to a web service method, and for parsing the response returned. This class cannot be inherited.
HttpPostClientProtocol	The client proxy for ASP.NET web services using HTTP-POST derives from this class.
HttpSimpleClientProtocol	The base class for communicating with a web service over HTTP. Both HttpGetClientProtocol and HttpPostClientProtocol are derived from it.

Class Name	Purpose
HttpWebClientProtocol	ASP.NET web service clients that use HTTP require a proxy class deriving indirectly or directly from HttpWebClientProtocol for calling the web service.
MatchAttribute	This class represents the attributes of a match. It may not be inherited.
SoapClientMessage	Contains the data of SOAP messages sent or received by a web service client at a specific SoapMessageStage for a web service method.
SoapDocumentMethod Attribute	An optional attribute for a web service method to change the format of the SOAP messages exchanged with a web service method.
SoapDocumentService Attribute	An optional attribute of a web service to set the default format of SOAP messages exchanged with web service methods exposed by the web service.
SoapException	The exception thrown when a web service method is called over SOAP and the request fails for some reason.
SoapExtension	In ASP.NET, SOAP extensions are derived from this class.
SoapExtensionAttribute	Override in a derived class to create a custom SOAP extension to apply to a web service method.
SoapHeader	Override in a derived class to specify the contents of the SOAP header.
SoapHeaderAttribute	Apply to a web service or a web service client to specify a SOAP header the web service or web service client should process. This class may not be inherited.
SoapHeaderCollection	A collection of SoapHeader objects.
SoapHeaderException	The exception thrown when processing of the SOAP header fails for a web service method called via SOAP.
SoapHttpClientProtocol	The client proxy for ASP.NET web services using SOAP derives from this class.
SoapMessage	Embodies the data contained in a SOAP request or SOAP response at some specific SoapMessageStage.
SoapRpcMethodAttribute	An optional attribute for a web service method that changes the format of SOAP communication with that web service method.
SoapRpcService Attribute	An optional attribute for a web service that changes the default format of SOAP communication with that web service's methods.
SoapServerMessage	Encapsulates the data contained in a SOAP message sent to, or received from, a web service method at some specific SoapMessageStage.

Table continued on following page

Class Name	Purpose
SoapUnknownHeader	Encapsulates the data in a SOAP header that was not recognized by the web service or web service client that received it. This class may not be inherited.
WebClientProtocol	The base class that all ASP.NET web service client proxies derive from.

As you can see, this namespace contains quite a few classes. We are particularly interested in the WebClientProtocol class, so let's take a closer look at it now.

The WebClientProtocol Class

In the world of ASP.NET web services, the WebClientProtocol class specifies the base class for all ASP.NET web service client proxies. This is important, because a client can't easily access a web service without a proxy to go through. A **proxy** is simply a "passthrough" object that implements the communication protocols needed to actually make the call. In essence, it acts as a middleman between your code and the web service. When we build a web service client using ASP.NET, we must create a proxy class derived from WebClientProtocol for the particular web service that we intend to call.

Luckily for us, it is unnecessary to manually create a proxy class in most cases, as wsdl.exe will create a proxy class using the WSDL service description of the web service in question. The wsdl.exe utility is covered in its own section later in the chapter. In some cases, we might want to use some of the properties of the WebClientProtocol class when developing our web service clients. For example, many of the properties can be used to set up and initialize the WebRequest object that is used when making a web request. Here is a quick look at some of the important properties available on the class:

Public Properties	Description
ConnectionGroupName	Associates a request to a named connection group, or returns the name of the group if already set.
Credentials	Contains security credentials required for web service client authentication.
PreAuthenticate	Set to true to enable pre-authentication, where the WWW-authenticate header is sent to the server with each request. If false, the header is only sent on the first request.
RequestEncoding	Specifies the character encoding for client requests to the web service.
Timeout	Specifies how long a web service client should allow a synchronous web service request to complete before throwing an error.
URL	Contains the base URL of the web service requested by the client.

Web Service Architecture

Now that we know about the underlying protocols and how a web service operates, let's take a little look at the "big picture"; the underlying architecture of all web services. To do this, we can extend our previous example to show how we could make a call to the PriceWatcher web service to get the current price of a banana.

There are three key aspects of the web service architecture that must be available to clients if they are to be able to make use of a service:

❑ There must be a discovery mechanism to locate useable web services. Think of this as the equivalent of looking through the Yellow Pages for a phone number.

❑ There must be a service description defining the purpose of available services. When we've found a phone listing, how do we get a full description of the service offered?

❑ There must be standard wire formats for communication between the client and the web service. In other words, what information will we need when we call the phone number?

The diagram below depicts the web service architecture at a fairly high level, showing (I hope) that the core infrastructure is relatively straightforward:

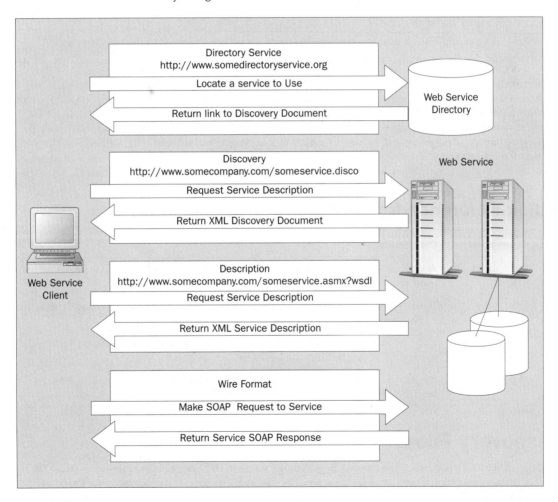

The four basic steps in discovering and calling a web service shown in the above figure are:

1. The Directory Phase

   Client application uses a directory service to locate a service to use.

   Directory Service returns a link to the selected service's discovery document.

2. The Discovery Phase

   Client application uses the link returned to request the service's discovery document.

   Web service returns its discovery document in XML format.

3. The Service Description Request

   Client application requests the service description from the information provided in the discovery document.

   Web service returns the service description in XML format.

4. Calling the Web Service

   Client application uses the service description to make a request to the web service.

   Web service returns its response in XML format.

One important thing to note is that in general, the Directory, Discovery, and Description phases of the above diagram are completed by the developer during coding of the web service client. Usually, the developer will know in advance the service their application will use, and so can determine all the information required to call the web service at compile time. Very often, you will be able to use the description (WSDL) document accompanying a web service to automatically build a proxy library DLL that the client can use for making calls to the web service. This will be discussed in more in depth as we learn more about consuming ASP.NET web services in Chapter 5.

Quick Reference for Architecture Components

Component	Description
Directory	A web service directory is a centralized repository of web services provided by third parties, much like a Yellow Pages for web services.
Discovery	"Discovering a web service" is the process of locating the service description for a given web service.
Description	The service description is required to use a particular web service. It defines the methods and interactions the web service supports.
Wire Format	As previously discussed, SOAP is the key protocol, or wire format, for web service communication.

Discovery Files

So, web service discovery is the process by which we locate Web Services Description Language (WSDL) documents describing a particular web service. The discovery process provides a way for consumer applications to learn that a web service exists and allows the consumer to find the associated WSDL document. These files are created when you initiate a new web service project, The discovery of web services is covered in details in Chapter 10.

The Service Description

The service description, sometimes called the **WSDL contract**, is undoubtedly the most important piece of information that a web service can provide (with the exception of the actual coding logic!). The WSDL document permits client applications to determine the **web methods** exposed by a given web service.

WSDL is an XML-based description language that has been submitted to the World Wide Web Consortium (http://www.w3.org). Its purpose is to describe network services as a set of endpoints operating on messages containing either document-oriented or procedure-oriented information. The W3C site contains more detailed information about the WSDL 1.1 specification if you require it.

We need to know a few things about how WSDL relates to web services. Principally, we need to know how to read and understand WSDL documents. We need to know how to create documents, and we need to know how .NET web services use WSDL documents.

Viewing a WSDL Document

Viewing an actual WSDL document is as simple as typing in the URL of the web service in question, with the parameter ?WSDL appended to the end. For example, to view the WSDL document associated with our CreditVerify sample web service, we would type the following in a browser window:

http://localhost/nonide/wsCreditVerify.asmx?WSDL

The browser would then display the following XML document:

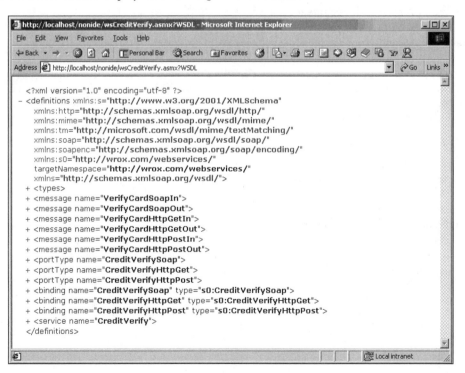

The WSDL specification states that WSDL documents define services as collections of network endpoints, or ports. The main elements of a WSDL document are:

- ❑ <definitions> – namespace definitions used in this WSDL file

- ❑ <types> – a container for data type definitions using some type system (XSD)

- ❑ <message> – an abstract, typed definition of the data being communicated

- ❑ <portType> – an abstract set of operations supported by one or more endpoints

- ❑ <binding> – a concrete protocol and data format specification for a particular port type

- ❑ <port> – a single endpoint defined as a combination of a binding and a network address

- ❑ <service> – a collection of related endpoints

The wsdl.exe Utility

Given a WSDL description file, an XML Schema file, or a discovery document (with a .disco or .discomap extension) for a web service, the wsdl.exe command-line utility can automatically produce a class, the **client proxy class**, that .NET client applications can use to consume that web service. As long as your PATH environment variable includes the .NET executables and programs directory, wsdl.exe is fairly simple to use, requiring the URL of the web service as a parameter:

```
wsdl http://localhost/nonide/wsCreditVerify.asmx
```

or a file path to the WSDL document itself:

```
wsdl c:\Inetpub\wwwroot\nonide\wsCreditVerify.wsdl
```

The client proxy class produced can then be compiled to create an assembly for making calls to the web service from client applications. We explore this further in Chapter 5. The class is generated as C# source code by default, but you can change this using the /language command-line option before the WSDL file location. For example, to generate a Visual Basic .NET proxy class, use:

```
wsdl /language:VB http://localhost/nonide/wsCreditVerify.asmx
```

By default, the proxy class is saved with a name derived from the web service name, such as CreditVerify.cs. Use the /out option to give an alternative filename for the created code:

```
wsdl /out:wsCCCheck.cs http://localhost/nonide/wsCreditVerify.asmx
```

When you are connecting to a server that requires authentication, you can specify the server's domain name, the user name, and the password as required:

```
wsdl http://localhost/nonide/wsCreditVerify.discomap /n:CreditVerifyProxy
     /out:CreditVerifyProxy.cs  /domain:WROX /username:TestUser
     /password=passme
```

You can also set the protocol to use. The default is SOAP, but you can also specify HttpGet, HttpPost, or any custom protocol that is defined in the configuration file:

```
wsdl http://localhost/nonide/wsCreditVerify.discomap /n:CreditVerifyProxy
/out:CreditVerifyProxy.cs /protocol:HttpGet
```

As well as creating client proxy classes from WSDL files, wsdl.exe can produce a client proxy class directly from an existing web service that does not have a WSDL file already. You just need to specify the location of the web service with ?WSDL appended on the end:

```
wsdl http://localhost/nonide/wsCreditVerify.asmx?WSDL
```

The complete list of options available for wsdl.exe is given in the following table:

Command line option	Purpose
/appsettingurlkey: *key* or /urlkey: *key*	Specifies the configuration key for reading the default value for the URL property when generating code.
/appsettingbaseurl: *baseurl* or /baseurl: *baseurl*	Indicates the base URL to use when resolving the URL fragment. The URL fragment is determined by converting the URL from this argument to the URL in the WSDL document. You must specify the /appsettingurlkey option to use this feature.
/d[omain]: *domain*	Indicates the domain name to use when connecting to a server that requires authentication.
/l[anguage]: *language*	Indicates the language to use when generating the proxy class. Either CS (C#; default), VB (Visual Basic), or JS (JScript).
/n[amespace]: *namespace*	Indicates the namespace for the generated proxy or template. The global namespace is used by default.
/nologo	Prevents Microsoft's graphic appearing on start up.
/o[ut]: *filename*	Indicates a file to contain the proxy code generated by wsdl.exe. The default file name derives from the web service name. Generated datasets are stored in separate files.
/p[assword]: *password*	Indicates the password for servers that require authentication.
/protocol: *protocol*	Indicates the protocol that the proxy will implement. Either SOAP (the default), HttpGet, HttpPost, or a custom protocol given in the configuration file.
/proxy: *URL*	Provides the URL of the proxy server to use for HTTP requests. The system proxy setting is used by default.

Table continued on following page

Command line option	Purpose
/proxydomain: *domain* or /pd: *domain*	Gives the domain for connecting to proxy servers that require authentication.
/proxypassword: *password* or /pp: *password*	Indicates the password for connecting to proxy servers that require authentication.
/proxyusername: *username* or /pu: *username*	Indicates the user name for connecting to proxy servers that require authentication.
/server	Causes wsdl.exe to generate an abstract class for a web service based on the WSDL files, as opposed to creating client proxy classes.
/u[sername]: *username*	Indicates the user name for connecting to servers that require authentication.
/?	Outputs the command syntax and options available.

How .NET Uses WSDL Documents

As you may remember, web service clients rely on the information provided by a WSDL document to properly request service methods across the wire. To illustrate this, open wsCreditVerify.wsdl from the source code foe this chapter and take a look at the types section of the document:

```xml
<types>
    <s:schema attributeFormDefault="qualified" elementFormDefault="qualified"
    targetNamespace="http://wrox.com/webservices/">
        <s:element name="VerifyCard">
            <s:complexType>
                <s:sequence>
                    <s:element minOccurs="1" maxOccurs="1" name="sCardNumber"
                        nillable="true" type="s:string" />
                    <s:element minOccurs="1" maxOccurs="1" name="sCardType"
                        nillable="true" type="s:string" />
                </s:sequence>
            </s:complexType>
        </s:element>
        <s:element name="VerifyCardResponse">
            <s:complexType>
                <s:sequence>
                    <s:element minOccurs="1" maxOccurs="1" name=
                        "VerifyCardResult" nillable="true" type="s:string" />
                </s:sequence>
            </s:complexType>
        </s:element>
```

```
            <s:element name="string" nillable="true" type="s:string" />
        </s:schema>
    </types>
```

This tells us that there is one publicly accessible method, called `VerifyCard`. It also tells us that this method requires two input parameters, `sCardNumber` and `sCardType`, and produces one return value, of type `string`.

Creating a Credit Card Validation Web Service

In this section, we shall create a web service to be consumed by an ASP.NET application to verify credit card numbers. The benefit of such a service would be that your application wouldn't have to know anything about the underlying algorithm that performs the actual verification of the credit card numbers. The algorithm and C# code presented are based on the ANSI X4.13 LUHN formula (also known as the modulus 10 or mod 10 algorithm). This algorithm is provided as an example only and may not validate all types of credit card numbers accurately. For our purposes, it provides us with some nice sample code to dive into as we learn how to create ASP.NET web services.

We will look at how to create this web service with and without the Visual Studio .NET IDE. Firstly, let's draw up a schematic representation of the flow of information in a typical call to the web service that we intend to build:

ASP.NET Web Service Data Types

Before we jump in and start knocking our web service together, let's take a moment to talk about the data types available in ASP.NET web services. As you know, all programming languages provide various data types for storing data.

Web services in ASP.NET support many different data types that can all be encoded and serialized into XML. The table below lists the primitive data types supported by web services (the data types outlined in the XML Schema Definition (XSD)) and their C++ and CLR equivalents. This serves simply to illustrate the different data type representations.

It is interesting to note that the types available for use are limited by the binding protocol used. As discussed earlier, HTTP operations such as `GET` and `POST` are limited to name-value pairs. SOAP however allows for more sophisticated structures to be encoded and serialized as XML, such as classes and directed graphs:

Web Service Data-type	CLR Data-type	C++ Data-type
boolean	Boolean	bool
byte		char, __int8
double	Double	double
datatype		struct
decimal	Decimal	
enumeration	Enum	enum
float	Single	float
int	Int32	int, long, __int32
long	Int64	__int64
Qname	XmlQualifiedName	
short	Int16	__int16, short
string	String	BSTR
timeInstant	DateTime	
unsignedByte		unsigned __int8
unsignedInt	UInt32	unsigned __int32
unsignedLong	UInt64	unsigned __int64
unsignedShort	UInt16	unsigned __int16

Creating a Web Service Without the Visual Studio .NET IDE

Web services can easily be developed with or without the Visual Studio .NET IDE. The only prerequisite is the installation of the Microsoft .NET Framework.

An ASP.NET web service resides in a text file with a .asmx extension. You may include all your web service's code in this file, or alternatively place the code in a separate C# file (with a .cs extension) and reference it in the .asmx file with a CodeBehind attribute. The .asmx file itself is the main entry point for every consumer client application that accesses your web service.

To start out, open up your favorite text editor (such as Notepad). We shall be putting all our business logic in a separate C# file (as discussed above), but we still need an .asmx page to reference it. Visual Studio .NET can automatically create this file for us, but in this instance we've chosen to do it ourselves. Enter the following line into your text editor:

```
<%@ WebService Language="C#" CodeBehind="wsCreditVerify.asmx.cs"
    class="CreditVerifyWebService.CreditVerify" %>
```

Save this file as `wsCreditVerify.asmx`. That's all there is to the `.asmx` file in this case, as we are simply using it as an entry point to our service, and the code will reside in a separate `.cs` file.

So now let's start on the `wsCreditVerify.asmx.cs` file. The first few lines contain the namespace references our web service requires. We'll need `System` and `System.Text` for the conversion and text manipulation we're doing, and the `System.Web.Services` namespace is also very important, as this is what we derive our web service from:

```
using System;
using System.Web;
using System.Web.Services;
using System.Text;
```

Next, we need to declare a namespace for our web service, which we've already used in the `class` attribute in the `wsCreditVerify.asmx` file: the `CreditVerifyWebService` namespace. The namespace will be used by consumer applications that call our web service and instantiate objects:

```
namespace CreditVerifyWebService
{
```

At this time, we are also going to define our `CreditVerify` class (the class given in the `class` attribute of the `.asmx` file), deriving it from `System.Web.Services.WebService`.

The `WebService` attribute, inside the square brackets above the class definition below, designates this class as a web service, and is discussed in its own section later in the chapter. Notice the namespace declaration, which is very important. By default, web services generated by Visual Studio .NET use the `http://tempuri.org` namespace, which takes its name from "temporary URI". A web service's WSDL document describes web-callable endpoints, and uses an XML namespace to uniquely identify these endpoints. It is advisable to change this from `tempuri.org` so that publicly consumable web services are distinguished from other web services that use `tempuri.org`:

```
namespace CreditVerifyWebService
{
    [WebService(Namespace="http://wrox.com/webservices/")]
    public class CreditVerify : System.Web.Services.WebService
    {
```

The next piece of code defines the publicly available method of the web service that can be called by a client application. As you can see, it is designated with the `WebMethod` attribute, which makes the method publicly viewable and callable by remote consumer applications. As well as this attribute, methods that are to be exposed by the web service must also be declared `public`. The `VerifyCard` method in turn calls the private `CheckCCNumber` method:

```
[WebMethod(Description="Verifies a credit card number and type")]
public string VerifyCard(string sCardNumber, string sCardType)
{
    return CheckCCNumber(sCardNumber,sCardType);
}
```

The private method `CheckCCNumber` is just an ordinary C# method. For simplicity, I will discuss only the parts of the code that pertain to the sample web service we are building. First, we declare appropriate local variables and also force the incoming `sCardType` to upper case:

```
private string CheckCCNumber(string sCardNumber,string sCardType)
{
    string sType, sLength, sPrefix, sNumber, sResult;
    bool bPrefixValid, bLengthValid;
    long lResult, lQSum, lSum;
    int ch;
    sType = sCardType.ToUpper();
```

The next section of code sets up the appropriate credit card number prefixes and lengths based on the incoming card type. For example, a sCardType of "M" denotes MasterCard, and we then know that the card length must be 16 digits, and the acceptable prefixes are 51, 52, 53, 54, and 55. Some of the common credit card types recognized by the web service include "V", Visa, "M", MasterCard, "A", American Express, and "D", Discover:

```
switch (sType)
{
    case "V":
        sLength = "13;16";
        sPrefix = "4";
        break;
    case "M":
        sLength = "16";
        sPrefix = "51;52;53;54;55";
        break;
    case "A":
        sLength = "15";
        sPrefix = "34;37";
        break;
    case "C":
        sLength = "14";
        sPrefix = "300;301;302;303;304;305;36;38";
        break;
    case "D":
        sLength = "16";
        sPrefix = "6011";
        break;
    case "E":
        sLength = "16";
        sPrefix = "2014;2149";
        break;
    case "J":
        sLength = "15;16";
        sPrefix = "3;2131;1800";
        break;
    default:
        sLength = "";
        sPrefix = "";
        break;
}
```

The above switch statement gives us the correct number length and prefix information for supported card types. Next, we remove non-numeric characters and validate the lengths and prefixes using a neat construct based on a foreach statement with the .Split method of the string class:

```
sNumber = TrimToDigits(sCardNumber);
bPrefixValid = false;
bLengthValid = false;
foreach(string s in sPrefix.Split(';'))
```

```
{
   if((sNumber.IndexOf(s)) == 0)
      bPrefixValid = true;
}
foreach(string y in sLength.Split(';'))
{
   if(Convert.ToString(sNumber.Length) == y)
      bLengthValid = true;
}
```

The next section of code determines if the credit card passed into the web service is valid according to the Luhn algorithm. I've added some comments to make what's going on a little clearer:

```
//set the result value to 0

lResult = 0;

//if the prefix is valid, add one to the result value

if(bPrefixValid == true)
   lResult += 1;

//if the length is valid, add two to the result value

if(bLengthValid == true)
   lResult += 2;

//set the sum and quotient sum values to 0

lQSum = 0;
lSum = 0;

//loop through the digits in the credit card number

for(int z=1; z == (sNumber.Length - 1); z++)
{
   //convert each substring (digit) to an integer number

   ch = Convert.ToInt32(sNumber.Substring(sNumber.Length - z + 1, 1));

   //if the modulus operation is 0

   if(z % 2 == 0)
   {
      lSum = 2 * ch;
      lQSum += lSum % 10;
   }

   //if the sum is greater than 9, increment the quotient sum
   //otherwise add the digit to the quotient sum

   if(lSum > 9)
      lQSum ++;
   else
      lQSum += ch;
}
```

```
//now finish up the checks

if(lQSum % 10 != 0)
   lResult += 4;

if(sLength == "")
   lResult += 8;
```

After these computations, we can interpret the lResult value and determine the validity of the credit card number according to its type. By passing lResult through a switch statement, we can assign a pertinent message to the return string:

```
switch(lResult)
{
   case 0:
      sResult = "CARD IS OK";
      break;
   case 1:
      sResult = "WRONG CARD TYPE";
      break;
   case 2:
      sResult = "WRONG LENGTH";
      break;
   case 3:
      sResult = "WRONG LENGTH AND CARD TYPE";
      break;
   case 4:
      sResult = "WRONG CHECKSUM";
      break;
   case 5:
      sResult = "WRONG CHECKSUM AND CARD TYPE";
      break;
   case 6:
      sResult = "WRONG CHECKSUM AND LENGTH";
      break;
   case 7:
      sResult = "WRONG CHECKSUM, LENGTH AND CARD TYPE";
      break;
   case 8:
      sResult = "UNKNOWN CARD TYPE";
      break;
   default:
      sResult = "GENERAL FAILURE";
      break;
}

//return the output

return (sResult);
}
```

The last code we need is the TrimToDigits method that eliminates any non-numeric characters from the credit card number passed into the web service. We use the System.Text encoding class to encode each character into its ASCII value and make sure the value is within the proper range:

```
private string TrimToDigits(string tstring)
{
   string s, ts;
```

```
string ch;
   s = "";
   ts = tstring;
   for(int y = 0; y < ts.Length; y++)
   {
       ch = ts.Substring(y, 1);
       ASCIIEncoding AE = new ASCIIEncoding();
       byte[] Converted = AE.GetBytes(ch);
       if(Converted[0] >= 48 && Converted[0] <= 57)
       {
           s += ch;
       }
   }
   return (s);
}
```

That's all the functionality that our web service needs to encapsulate, but before we can use the C# code-behind file, we must compile it to a DLL. You can do this from the command line using .NET's csc.exe compiler. Once that is done, create a bin subdirectory in the folder that contains the web service files, and place the DLL in there. Now we need to make the directory containing all the code files accessible to IIS, by setting it up as an IIS virtual directory.

Creating an IIS Virtual Directory

First, open up the Internet Services Manager (Control Panel | Administrative Tools | Internet Services Manager). Right-click on Default Web Site in the left hand-pane, and select New | Virtual Directory from the Action menu.

This initiates a wizard for creating the new IIS directory. The steps to take to set up the virtual directory are very straightforward. At the welcome message for the Virtual Directory Creation Wizard, click Next to move on. Enter the alias when prompted by the next dialog – this is the name of our virtual directory, nonide – and click Next again. Now either browse to the folder that contains the code to place in the new virtual directory, or type its path directly if you know it. Click Next to move to the final stage of the wizard. Make sure the Read and Run scripts (such as ASP) boxes are selected, and click Next to complete the setup process.

Now open your web browser and navigate to http://localhost/nonide/wsCreditVerify.asmx. Requesting this page that we've just created causes ASP.NET to compile our web service and display an information page for it. If you've input the code correctly, you should see the following:

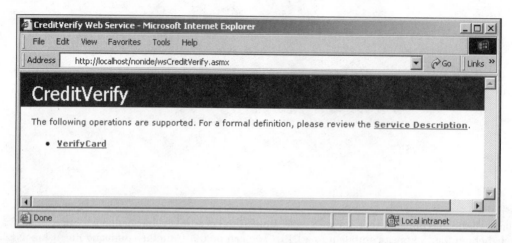

This page details all the web methods exposed by our web service – just the `VerifyCard` method in this case. There is also a **Service Description** link, which displays the web service's WSDL document. Click the `VerifyCard` link to open the **Test** page for the web method:

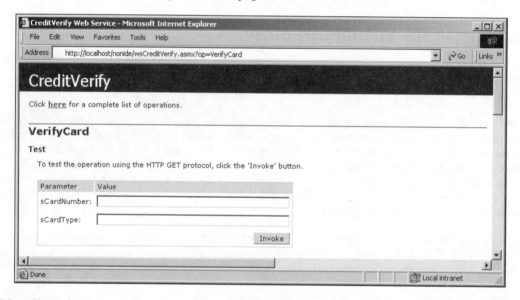

We will use the above page in the section on testing web services later in the chapter, but now we'll talk a bit more about the `WebService` and `WebMethod` attributes that we've already touched on.

The WebService Attribute

Although not required for a web service to be published and consumed, the `WebService` attribute can be very useful. With this attribute, you can do such things as:

❑   Specify a name for the web service that isn't restricted by the CLR (Common Language Runtime) rules for runtime identifiers. This name will be used in the Service Description and Service Help pages.

❑ Change the default XML namespace before the web service is made public (from http://tempuri.org).

❑ Set a descriptive message for the web service.

```
[WebService(Name="Credit Card Number Verification Service")]

[WebService(Namespace="http://wrox.com/webservices")]

[WebService(Description="This is a web service that validates credit card
            numbers and types.")]
```

The WebMethod Attribute

Attaching the WebMethod attribute to a public method of a C# class indicates that the method should be exposed as part of the web service. Properties of the WebMethod attribute allow further configuration to alter the web service method behavior.

Taking a look at the member properties of the attribute, we find the following:

❑ **BufferResponse** – This attribute enables the buffering of responses for a web service method. When true (default), ASP.NET buffers the entire response before sending it to the client. When false, ASP.NET buffers the response in chunks of 16 Kb. The main reason for turning off buffering is the need to handle large amounts of data. Either way, data is always buffered; this flag just tells the application how much data is to be buffered before being sent.

It is interesting to note that ASP.NET disables SOAP extensions for web service methods that aren't buffered. This could have an impact on your web service.

```
[WebMethod(BufferResponse=false)]
```

❑ **CacheDuration** – This property enables caching of the results for the web service method. ASP.NET will cache results for each unique parameter set. 0 (default) disables the caching of results. The duration is calculated in seconds.

```
[WebMethod(CacheDuration=60)]
```

❑ **Description** – This property simply supplies a description for the web service's help page. The default value is an empty string.

```
[WebMethod(Description="This method checks the validity of CC numbers.")]
```

❑ **EnableSession** – This property enables session state for the web service method. Once enabled, the web service can access session state information through the HTTPContext.Current.Session or WebService.Session property. The default value is false.

```
[WebMethod(EnableSession=true)]
```

❑ **MessageName** – This property allows the web service to uniquely identify overloaded methods using an alias.

```
public class aService : System.Web.Services.WebService
{
    [WebMethod(MessageName="SubtractDoubles")]
    public double Subtract(double dValOne, double dValTwo)
    {
        return dValOne - dValTwo;
    }
    [WebMethod(MessageName="SubtractIntegers")]
    public int Subtract(int iValOne, int iValTwo)
    {
        return iValOne - iValTwo;
    }
}
```

❑ **TransactionOption** – This property allows the web service method to participate as the root object of a transaction. There are only two possible behaviors for a web service in this respect. It may either not participate in a transaction, or it can create a new transaction. By default, the value is `TransactionOption.Disabled`. The possible values for non-participation are `Disabled`, `NotSupported`, and `Supported`. The possible values for creating a new transaction are `Required` and `RequiresNew`.

To enable transaction support, you must reference `System.EnterpriseServices.dll` in your code. This DLL contains the information for COM+ services. You can also use the `SystemEnterpriseServices.ContextUtil` class to call the `SetComplete()` and `SetAbort()` methods.

Then, add this line to the "using" section:

```
using System.EnterpriseServices;
```

and set the transaction option:

```
[WebMethod(TransactionOption=TransactionOption.RequiresNew)]
```

Creating a Web Service with Visual Studio .NET

Creating a web service with the Visual Studio .NET environment is quick and easy. With a few mouse clicks, Visual Studio .NET will set up all the appropriate development files and create a shell service for you. It also sets up the IIS directory for the web application. Another benefit of Visual Studio .NET is that you can debug the service quite easily with its integrated debugging tools. In this section, we are going to create the same web service as in the previous section, except that we are going to use the IDE to simplify construction and explore some of the handy features that Visual Studio .NET offers web services developers.

The first thing that we want to do is select File | New | Project. Select Visual C# Projects and highlight the ASP.NET Web Service template. Name your web service CreditVerifyIDE. Visual Studio .NET indicates that it will create the project at http://localhost/CreditVerifyIDE, saving us the step of creating the IIS directory:

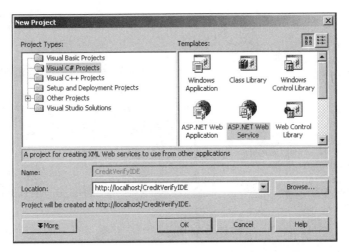

If you wish, you can change the location using the **Browse...** button, for instance if you are deploying on a remote computer. Click **OK** and Visual Studio .NET will set up our project:

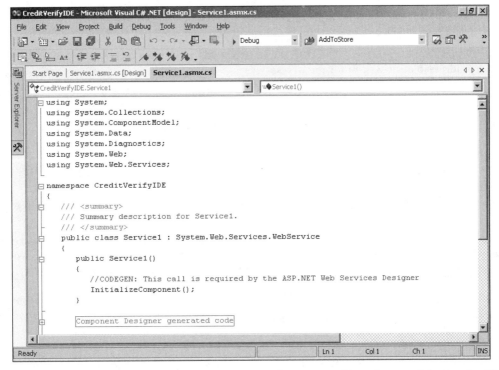

As you can see, the `Service1.asmx.cs` file is created automatically with some default code. The `.asmx` file does exist, but since it all it does is set the `CodeBehind` attribute, the IDE hides the file and just shows the `.asmx.cs` code that powers our web service. You'll notice that right-clicking on the `.asmx` file in **Solution Explorer** and selecting **View Code** takes us to the `.asmx.cs` file too. Now let's change the name of the class and method that we are exposing, as well as the `.asmx` file. Change both of these to `CreditVerify` and `VerifyCard` respectively:

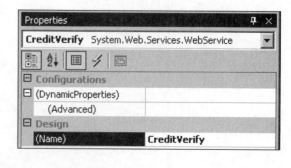

Note the files generated by the IDE that appear in the Solution Explorer window:

❑   AssemblyInfo.cs – A project information file containing metadata about the assemblies in the project, such as name, version, and culture information.

❑   CreditVerify.asmx – Contains the WebService processing directive and serves as the addressable entry point for the web service

❑   CreditVerify.asmx.cs – This file contains the code-behind class for the web service. The Code View for CreditVerify.asmx also displays the contents of this file.

❑   CreditVerifyIDE.vsdisco – An XML-based file containing URLs for resources providing dynamic discovery information for the web service.

❑   global.asax – A file for handling application-level events. Resides in the root directory of the ASP.NET application.

❑   web.config – An XML-based file that contains configuration information for ASP.NET resources.

There are other files that won't show up in the Project Explorer, unless you click the Show All button. These files are located in the root directory of the web service directory structure, so in this case these files would be located in the c:\inetpub\wwwroot\CreditVerifyIDE\ directory:

❑   CreditVerify.asmx.resx – XML based resource file for the CreditVerify.asmx file

❑   Global.asax.cs – Code behind the Global.asax file

❑   Global.asax.resx – Resource file for the Global.asax page

❑   Licenses.licx – Contains licensing information for the project

❑   CreditVerifyIDE.csproj – The project file for the project that contains configuration and build settings, and keeps a list of files associated with the project

❑   CreditVerifyIDE.csproj.webinfo – Contains the path to the project on the development server

The `CreditVerify.asmx.cs` file generated by Visual Studio .NET contains some code that we won't need for our web service. In particular, some of the `using` namespace references can be removed, as we won't actually need them in our service. We just need the following:

```
using System;
using System.Web;
using System.Web.Services;
using System.ComponentModel;
using System.Text;
```

You'll also notice that a constructor, a `Dispose()` method, and a sample `HelloWorld()` method have been created. The `HelloWorld` method is there for example purposes, so remove it if you wish.

We will just reuse the code we've already developed, rather than starting something from scratch, so copy all the code from the `NonIDE` example into the Visual Studio .NET Editor.

That's about all that's needed to be able to fire up the web service. Click on the **Debug | Start** menu option. A web browser window should appear, showing a `CreditVerify.asmx` help page looking identical to the previous one created without the IDE.

In the next section, we discuss the process of testing the web service. We shall use the Visual Studio .NET IDE for this task, as it offers some very nice debugging tools.

Testing Web Services

At this point, we are able to test the web service using the information page that appears when we open the `.asmx` page for the service in a browser. We can also debug the service by running it in the Visual Studio .NET IDE using the debugging aids that the environment provides.

Testing the Service from a Browser

As we've already seen, pulling up the `.asmx` page in a web browser will display a help page along with detailed information about each of the web methods that your service exposes. Let's take a look at the `VerifyCard` information page:

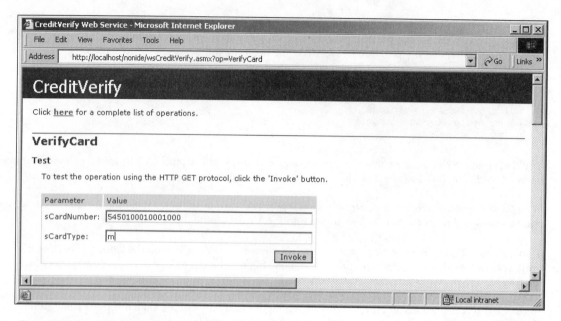

Entering information in the sCardNumber and sCardType input boxes and hitting Invoke will call the web service using HTTP-GET. This is a quick and easy way to check the behavior of the web methods exposed by a web service. If we press Invoke after typing in a valid credit card number, we should see the following page:

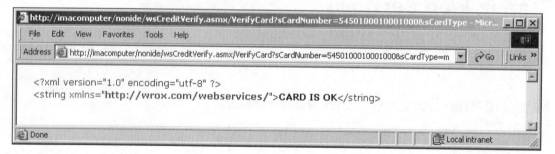

This page shows the SOAP response, consisting of just the string returned by the web method.

Debugging with the IDE

Debugging with the IDE is very similar to debugging any other Visual Studio .NET application. Once the project is loaded in the IDE, you can start a debugging session by clicking Debug | Start (or alternatively hitting *F5*). This launches a web browser session and loads the .asmx file. You can set breakpoints in the IDE to interrupt execution at certain points within the web service:

```
        private string CheckCCNumber(string sCardNumber,string sCardType)
        {
            string sType, sLength, sPrefix,sNumber, sResult;
            bool bPrefixValid, bLengthValid;
            long lResult, lQSum, lSum;
            int ch;

            sType = sCardType.ToUpper();

            switch (sType)
            {
```

To debug a call to a web service from the client application end requires a slightly different setup. In this case, we need to enable ASP.NET debugging for the client application. This information will pertain more to the consumer applications discussed in Chapter 5, but we shall briefly cover the settings here.

To enable ASP.NET debugging in a C# application, follow this procedure:

1. In Solution Explorer, select the **C# project** (for example `WebService1`)

2. Right-click and select **Properties**

3. Select **Configuration Properties**, and click on **Debugging**

4. Set **Enable ASP.NET Debugging** to **True** under the **Debuggers** heading

With these settings in place, you'll notice that when you start debugging the client application, the debugger attaches itself to the application and to the ASP.NET worker process, `aspnet_wp.exe`. When the client application makes a SOAP call to a web service, the debugger tracks the call so you can follow the call stack chain right up to the web service process itself.

Examining and Modifying the SOAP Response

When we deal with SOAP in ASP.NET web services, we have the option of modifying the SOAP response that the web service sends to the client application. One of the main issues when developing a web service is determining how the XML within the SOAP request is to be encoded. For example, we can use an XSD schema to define a strict XML document, or use the encoding rules outlined in the SOAP specification. By default, ASP.NET web services use XSD schemas.

First off, why would we even want to change formatting? The SOAP specification states that the contents of SOAP messages sent to and from a web service follow XML formatting rules. It doesn't however specify the encoding format of that XML. ASP.NET web services give developers a way of altering the encoding formats manually. One instance where we might need to do this would be if a web service requires a certain parameter encoding scheme that requires us to change the default encoding format to comply with the web service when we call it.

There are two types of modifications that we can make. We can modify the format of parameters passed within the SOAP request (Parameter Encoding), and we can modify the encoding of the SOAP Body itself (SOAP Body Encoding). We'll cover both of these below.

Parameter encoding is an important issue to understand. When making calls to a web service, we exchange parameter data between the lient and the web service inside the SOAP request or response objects. Parameter encoding will impact on the look of the resulting XML document.

Parameter Encoding

WSDL defines two encoding styles for parameters:

❑ Literal

❑ Encoded

The following examples demonstrate how to specify both Literal parameter encoding and Encoded parameter encoding, as well as showing the XML payload of the resulting SOAP response.

Literal Parameter Encoding

```
//apply SoapDocumentMethodAttribute

[System.Web.Services.Protocols.SoapDocumentMethodAttribute(
    "http://www.wrox.com/GetAddress",
    RequestNamespace="http://www.wrox.com/",
    ResponseNamespace="http://www.wrox.com",
    Use=System.Web.Services.Description.SoapBindingUse.Literal)]
public string GetAddress(string Client){
```

```
//resulting XML payload of the SOAP response

<?xml version="1.0" encoding="utf-8"?>
<SOAP-ENV:Envelope xmlns:xsi="http://www.w3.org/2001/XMLSchema-instance"
            xmlns:xsd="http://www.w3.org/2001/XMLSchema"
            xmlns:SOAP-ENV="http://schemas.xmlsoap.org/soap/envelope/">

    <SOAP-ENV:Body>
        <GetAddress xmlns="http://www.wrox.com">
            <address>
                <Street>123 Oak Street</Street>
                <City>Chicago</City>
                <Zip>60018</Zip>
            </address>
        </GetAddress>
    </SOAP-ENV:Body>

</SOAP-ENV:Envelope>
```

Encoded Parameter Encoding

```
//apply a SoapDocumentMethodAttribute OR SoapRpcMethodAttribute

[System.Web.Services.Protocols.SoapDocumentMethodAttribute(
    "http://www.wrox.com/GetAddress",
    RequestNamespace="http://www.wrox.com/",
```

```
        ResponseNamespace="http://www.wrox.com",
        Use=System.Web.Services.Description.SoapBindingUse.Encoded)]
public string GetAddress(string Client){
```

```
//resulting XML payload of SOAP response

<?xml version="1.0" encoding="utf-8"?>
<SOAP-ENV:Envelope xmlns:xsi="http://www.w3.org/2001/XMLSchema-instance"
    xmlns:xsd="http://www.w3.org/2001/XMLSchema"
    xmlns:SOAP-ENV="http://schemas.xmlsoap.org/soap/envelope/"
    xmlns:SOAP-ENC="http://schemas.xmlsoap.org/soap/encoding/"
    xmlns:tns="http://www.wrox.com"
    xmlns:tnsTypes="http://www.wrox.com/encodedTypes"
    xmlns:wsdl="http://schemas.xmlsoap.org/wsdl/" >

    <SOAP-ENV:Body SOAP-ENV:encodingStyle=
    "http://schemas.xmlsoap.org/soap/encoding">
      <tnsTypes:GetAddress>
         <address href="#1" />
      </tnsTypes: GetAddress>
      <tnsTypes:Address id="1">
         <Street id="2">string</Street>
         <City id="3">string</City>
         <Zip id="4">string</Zip>
      </tnsTypes:Address>
    </SOAP-ENV:Body>

</SOAP-ENV:Envelope>
```

SOAP Body Formatting

In WSDL, there are two defined styles for how a web service method can be formatted within the Body element of a SOAP request or response. In most cases, we would use the Document style encoding method:

❑ **RPC** (Remote Procedure Call) – The <Body> element is formatted according to the SOAP specification for RPC-style SOAP. All parameters are wrapped within a single element that takes its name from the web service method, and each element within represents the parameter of the same name.

❑ **Document** – The <Body> element is encoded following an XSD schema. The service description for the web service must define an XSD schema for SOAP requests to and SOAP responses from the web service method. Clients must pass SOAP messages that conform to the specifications of the defined XSD schemas.

ASP.NET web services support both the Document and RPC encoding styles. Document is the default.

Document Encoding Style

To specify a Document encoding style, first apply a SoapDocumentMethodAttribute to the method in the proxy class:

```
//apply SoapDocumentMethodAttribute
[System.Web.Services.Protocols.SoapDocumentMethodAttribute(
   "http://www.wrox.com/GetAddress",
```

```
              RequestNamespace="http://www.wrox.com/",
              ResponseNamespace="http://www.wrox.com",
              Use=System.Web.Services.Description.SoapBindingUse.Literal)]
       public string GetAddress(string Client){
```

An XSD schema must then be defined within the service description to define the structure of the SOAP request and response:

```
<s:element name="GetAddress">

   <s:complexType>
      <s:sequence>
         <s:element minOccurs="1" maxOccurs="1" name="Client"
         nillable="true" type="s:Address" />
      </s:sequence>
   </s:complexType>

</s:element>

<s:complexType name="Address">

   <s:sequence>
      <s:element minOccurs="1" maxOccurs="1" name="Street" nillable="true"
      type="s:string" />
      <s:element minOccurs="1" maxOccurs="1" name="City" nillable="true"
      type="s:string" />
      <s:element minOccurs="1" maxOccurs="1" name="Zip" nillable="true"
      type="s:string" />
   </s:sequence>

</s:complexType>
```

Based on the XSD schema defined in the service description, the XML for a SOAP request would be as follows. Notice how the file follows the schema:

```
<?xml version="1.0" encoding="utf-8"?>
<SOAP-ENV:Envelope xmlns:xsi="http://www.w3.org/2001/XMLSchema-instance"
                   xmlns:xsd="http://www.w3.org/2001/XMLSchema"
                   xmlns:SOAP-ENV="http://schemas.xmlsoap.org/soap/envelope/">

   <SOAP-ENV:Body>
      <GetAddress xmlns="http://www.wrox.com">
         <Client>
            <Street>string</Street>
            <City>string</City>
            <Zip>string</Zip>
         </Client>
      </GetAddress >
   </SOAP-ENV:Body>

</SOAP-ENV:Envelope>
```

RPC Encoding Style

To specify RPC-style encoding, we need a SoapRpcMethodAttribute before the method declaration:

```
//RPC style on supports Encoded parameter encoding style, there is no USE
//property

[System.Web.Services.Protocols.SoapRpcMethodAttribute(
    "http://www.wrox.com/Rpc",
    RequestNamespace="http://www.wrox.com",
    ResponseNamespace="http://www.wrox.com")]
public GetAddress Rpc(string Client) {
```

With the RPC method, the XSD schema is not defined in the service description:

```
<?xml version="1.0" encoding="utf-8"?>
<SOAP-ENV:Envelope xmlns:xsi="http://www.w3.org/2001/XMLSchema-instance"
    xmlns:xsd="http://www.w3.org/2001/XMLSchema"
    xmlns:SOAP-ENV="http://schemas.xmlsoap.org/soap/envelope/"
    xmlns:SOAP-ENC="http://schemas.xmlsoap.org/soap/encoding/"
    xmlns:tns="http://www.wrox.com"
    xmlns:tnsTypes="http://www.wrox.com/encodedTypes"
    xmlns:wsdl="http://schemas.xmlsoap.org/wsdl/">

    <SOAP-ENV:Body SOAP-ENV:encodingStyle=
    "http://schemas.xmlsoap.org/soap/encoding/">
        <tns:Rpc>
            <client TARGET="_self" HREF="#1" />
        </tns:Rpc>
        <tnsTypes:Address id="1">
            <Street id="2">string</Street>
            <City id="3">string</City>
            <Zip id="4">string</Zip>
        </tnsTypes:Address>
    </SOAP-ENV:Body>

</SOAP-ENV:Envelope>
```

As you can see, we can change the way that SOAP requests and responses are generated by the web service using the properties and coding methods described above.

State Management in Web Services

Although stateless web application designs provide easier scalability in high-capacity, load-balanced environments, ASP.NET web services allow you to use the Application and Session state objects provided by IIS. Your web service will have access to these objects when deriving from the WebService class. In this section, we will discuss the simple settings that allow web services to access Application and Session.

Accessing and Using the Application Object

Any class deriving from the WebService class automatically has access to the Application object without need for special calls or settings. For example, if we wanted to store an application-level variable that allowed us to set a custom timeout value in minutes, we could use this code:

```
Application["appCustomTimeOut"] = 15;
```

Reading the application variable is also quite easy:

```
int iTimeOut;
iTimeOut = Application["appCustomTimeOut"];
```

Accessing and Using the Session Object

The `Session` object, on the other hand, requires specific code to enable it for use within web services. To use the `Session` object within a web method, set the `EnableSession` property of the `WebMethod` attribute to `true`:

```
[WebMethod(EnableSession = true)]
```

Setting this property allows us to access session state within the method. To set a variable, use the following format:

```
Session["SomeSessionVariable"] = "SomeValue";
```

To retrieve a variable, use this:

```
string sSessionVal;
sSessionVal = Session["SomeSessionVariable"];
```

Session state can then be accessed and used just as from any other ASP.NET application.

Deploying and Configuring Web Services

The process of deploying a web service involves copying the `.asmx` file and any required assemblies to the web server where it is to be deployed. Note however that you do not need to copy assemblies that are part of the Microsoft .NET Framework.

If, for example, we were deploying the `CreditVerify` web service used earlier, we would create a virtual directory as previously discussed and copy over the necessary files. The directory structure might look somewhat like this:

```
\inetpub
    \wwwroot
        \CreditVerify
            CreditVerify.disco
            CreditVerify.asmx
            Web.config (optional)
            \Bin
                any other assemblies needed (none in this case)
```

The Web.Config File

The `Web.Config` file contains specific information related to ASP.NET web settings. An in-depth discussion of every configuration section is beyond the scope of our current discussion, so we will concentrate on the section that pertains to the behavior of web services: the `<webServices>` element.

The `<webServices>` section controls settings for web services. As you may or may not know, the `Web.Config` file is an XML document, and all tags and attributes (sometimes called subtags) are case-sensitive and must follow the rules of well-formed XML. For configuration tags and attribute names, the first character is lowercase and the first character of subsequent concatenated words is uppercase (a casing often called **camel case**). For attribute values that are members of enumerations, the first character is uppercase and the first character of subsequent words is uppercase (sometimes called **Pascal case**). Exceptions are `true` and `false`, which are lowercase.

The following XML shows the available settings for the `<webServices>` tag within the `<system.web>` element:

```
<configuration>
  <system.web>
    <webServices>
      <protocolTypes>
        <add type="System.Web.Services.
          Protocols.SoapServerProtocol" />
        <add type="System.Web.Services.
          Protocols.HttpServerProtocol" />
        <add type="System.Web.Services.
          Protocols.DiscoveryServerProtocol" />
      </protocolTypes>
      <returnWriterTypes>
        <add type="System.Web.Services.Protocols.XmlReturnWriter" />
      </returnWriterTypes>
      <parameterReaderTypes>
        <add type="System.Web.Services.
          Protocols.HtmlFormParameterReader" />
        <add type="System.Web.Services.
          Protocols.UrlParameterReader" />
      </parameterReaderTypes>
      <protocolReflectorTypes>
        <add type="System.Web.Services.
          Description.SoapProtocolInfoReflector" />
        <add type="System.Web.Services.
          Description.HttpPostProtocolInfoReflector" />
        <add type="System.Web.Services.
          Description.HttpGetProtocolInfoReflector" />
      </protocolReflectorTypes>
      <mimeReflectorTypes>
        <add type="System.Web.Services.
          Description.XmlMimeInfoReflector" />
        <add type="System.Web.Services.
          Description.FormInfoReflector" />
      </mimeReflectorTypes>
      <protocolImporterTypes>
        <add type="System.Web.Services.
          Description.SoapProtocolInfoImporter" />
        <add type="System.Web.Services.
          Description.HttpPostProtocolInfoImporter" />
```

```
            <add type="System.Web.Services.
             Description.HttpGetProtocolInfoImporter" />
        </protocolImporterTypes>
        <mimeImporterTypes>
            <add type="System.Web.Services.
             Description.XmlMimeInfoImporter" />
            <add type="System.Web.Services.
             Description.FormInfoImporter" />
        </mimeImporterTypes>
        <protocolInfoTypes>
            <add type="System.Web.Services.
             Description.SoapProtocolInfo" />
            <add type="System.Web.Services.
             Description.HttpGetProtocolInfo" />
            <add type="System.Web.Services.
             Description.HttpPostProtocolInfo" />
        </protocolInfoTypes>
        <mimeInfoTypes>
            <add type="System.Web.Services.Description.HtmlFormInfo" />
            <add type="System.Web.Services.Description.XmlMimeInfo" />
            <add type="System.Web.Services.Description.AnyMimeInfo" />
        </mimeInfoTypes>
        <referenceResolverTypes>
            <add type="System.Web.Services.Discovery.DiscoveryResolver" />
            <add type="System.Web.Services.Discovery.ServiceResolver" />
            <add type="System.Web.Services.Discovery.SchemaResolver" />
        </referenceResolverTypes>
        <discoverySearchPatternTypes>
            <add type="System.Web.Services.Discovery.ServiceSearchPattern"
             />
        </discoverySearchPatternTypes>
        <soapExtensionTypes>
        </soapExtensionTypes>
        <soapExtensionReflectorTypes>
        </soapExtensionReflectorTypes>
        <soapExtensionImporterTypes>
        </soapExtensionImporterTypes>
        <sdlHelpGenerator href="DefaultSdlHelpGenerator.aspx" />
      </webServices>
    </system.web>
</configuration>
```

The <webServices> section follows the typical configuration file format for ASP.NET, where settings are nested within a <system.web> tag. For precise details on the ASP.NET configuration runtime, check out the articles on Microsoft's developer site at msdn.microsoft.com.

Summary

In this chapter we've developed a simple ASP.NET web service both manually using a standard text editor (such as Notepad), and from Visual Studio .NET's IDE. We've also looked at the basics of WSDL notation – the XML file format that provides the service description for web services.

I hope that you are now starting to understand the power and versatility of the web services model, and the potential it has to simplify tasks that, at best, have been awkward up to now, by providing standard ways of serializing data passed to and received from a web service. WSDL is an exciting component of this model and plays a very important and integral part when using web services from an application. WSDL describes every aspect of interaction with a web service in such a way that an application can programmatically determine exactly how to send it requests, and interpret its responses. We're now ready to move on to look at how to code client applications that consume web services, and we shall do this in the next chapter.

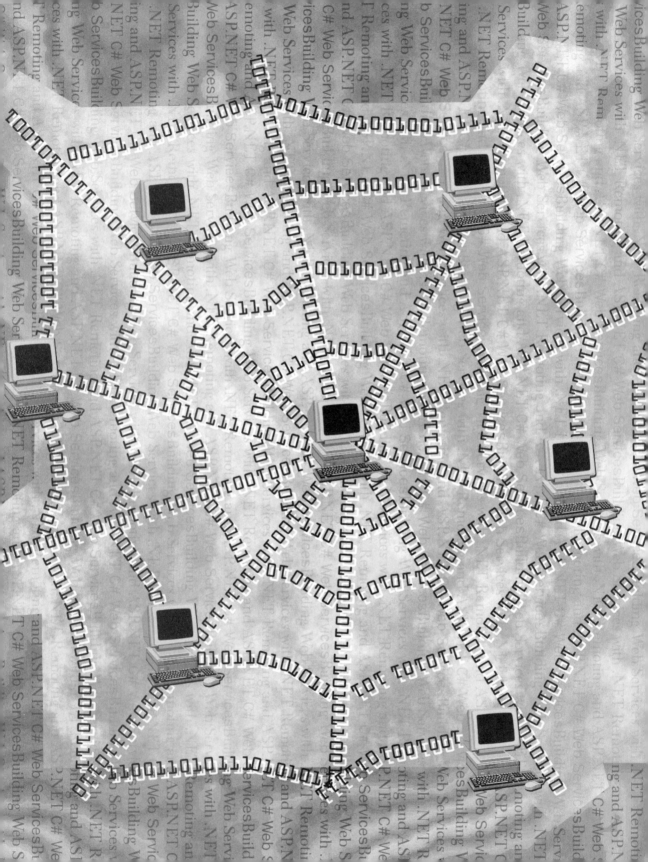

Consuming ASP.NET Web Services

Now that we've covered the basics of creating a web service, let's begin to examine the process of discovering and using web services. By now, you should have a good idea of the potential impact that web services will have on the way that applications in the future will be written. Coupled with the expansion of broadband internet connectivity, web services are likely to herald greater and greater decentralization of programming logic. Applications could become much richer as advanced features become available over the Internet. Clients could easily access remote data via SOAP calls and use business logic residing anywhere in the world quickly and simply, regardless of the platform they are running on.

In this chapter, we shall explore how client applications communicate with web services. We'll then move on to how a consumer application could discover a web service and access the WSDL document that describes it. From there, we'll move on to the methods for creating a proxy class for accessing a web service. Finally we'll build both a C# Windows Form and a console application to access the credit card validation web service from Chapter 4 using techniques described in this chapter, so it's a good idea to make sure that you've got that example running before you proceed.

How do Clients Communicate with Web Services?

As discussed previously, there are two ways to access an ASP.NET web service: via HTTP-GET or HTTP-POST, or via the preferred (and richer) SOAP method. Determining which to use depends on what you wish to accomplish. If your client application is unable to use SOAP, but can handle HTTP commands, you'd probably want to use the HTTP method. .NET makes it quite easy to use web services via SOAP, and generates a proxy class that makes access to the web service transparent by hiding the actual SOAP implementation from the developer. This makes accessing a remote service as simple as using code in a local DLL file. We discuss the issue of proxies later in the chapter.

There are three key steps necessary for an application to consume a web service for the first time:

1. Discovery of the available web methods

2. Creating a proxy for the web service (when using SOAP)

3. Calling the web service's methods

Calling a Web Service with HTTP

Perhaps the most basic way to call a web service is by simple HTTP methods such as HTTP-POST. The web service returns its response as an XML document, which must be parsed by the client to extract the data it contains. This parsing could be accomplished using the DOM object provided by IE 5 and above.

Note that HTTP methods only support simple data types (int, string, enum, array) and return data in the form of a simple XML document.

The following HTML code snippet shows a call to a hypothetical web service that subtracts parameter b from parameter a:

```
<HTML>
    <BODY>
        <FORM action="http://wrox.com/SubtractService.asmx/Subtract"
                method="POST">
            <INPUT name="a"></INPUT>
            <INPUT name="b"></INPUT>
            <INPUT type="submit" value="Submit"></INPUT>
        </FORM>
    </BODY>
</HTML>
```

The typical response if parameter a were 5 and b were 3 would be something like this XML file:

```
<?xml version="1.0" encoding="utf-8" ?>
<int xmls=http://tempuri.org/>2</int>
```

In general, if your application is only going to use simple data types, one of the two HTTP methods might be preferable to SOAP, as they avoid the overhead of having to go through the client proxy.

Calling a Web Service with SOAP

Consuming web services using SOAP is fairly straightforward once you have the WSDL document defining the web service's interfaces. The consumer application generally needs to know the signatures of the methods exposed by the web service at compile time. .NET can generate a special **proxy class** that encapsulates these details for the compiler to access web methods through it. The proxy class handles all communication between client and web service. It packages the SOAP request for HTTP, and marshals the SOAP-encoded response to the return the data type expected by the application.

As discussed in the previous chapter, .NET comes with a utility called wsdl.exe that can retrieve the WSDL document for a web service and automatically generate an appropriate proxy class from it.

The following figure depicts the flow of data when this class is used to access a web service:

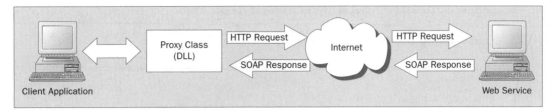

We will cover the wsdl.exe application in greater detail later in the chapter.

Discovering ASP.NET Web Services

Most developers already know the web service they intend to use by the time they start building an application. However, what if you want to find out what types of web services are available? What if there was a web service "Search Engine" that would allow developers to locate web services? For example, think of how the Window's Registry allows you to find components locally on your machine. Could this same concept be applied as a method to find remote components for use?

UDDI

Luckily for us, such a thing does indeed exist. Web services directories are a sort of cataloging system, providing central locations where web service providers can publish information about the web services they offer. The **UDDI** (**Universal Description, Discovery, and Integration**) specifications outline standards for publishing and discovering information.

UDDI defines XML Schemas that provide four different types of information about web services that together allow software developers to learn about and consume web services:

- ❑ Business Information
- ❑ Service Information
- ❑ Binding Information
- ❑ Service-Specific Information

The UDDI Business Registry is an organization that allows businesses to locate information about web services programmatically. The UDDI Registry publishes information gathered from web service providers to assist in the consumption of those services. For further information about the UDDI Registry, go to their site at http://www.uddi.org.

The disco.exe Tool

The disco.exe tool gives developers a way to retrieve WSDL descriptions for services on remote machines. There are several ways that the disco.exe utility can be used. The following list gives examples of how it can be used, followed by the command-line syntax that will perform each task:

❑ Output discovered documents to current directory:

```
Disco http://localhost/nonide/wsCreditVerify.asmx?WSDL
```

❑ Output discovered documents to alternate directory:

```
Disco http://localhost/nonide/wsCreditVerify.asmx?WSDL /out:SomeDirectory
```

❑ Discovery using `.disco` document:

```
Disco http://localhost/nonide/wsCreditVerify.disco
```

❑ Discovery using URL only:

```
Disco http://localhost/nonide/
```

Alternatively, you could use something like this if you know a site exposes web services:

```
Disco http://www.wrox.com
```

❑ Discovery when authentication is needed:

```
Disco http://www.wrox.com/ /domain:wrox /username:TestUser /password:passme
```

❑ Help:

As with most command-line programs, the `/?` switch displays usage info:

```
Disco /?
```

Discovering Web Services using Visual Studio .NET

Discovering and using new web services with Visual Studio .NET is very simple. Microsoft provides a specialized web reference browser to aid in adding web references to any .NET application. To launch the browser, load up Visual Studio .NET and start a new C# Windows Application.

Adding a Web Reference in Visual Studio .NET

From the menu bar, click Project | Add Web Reference. You will see the following screen:

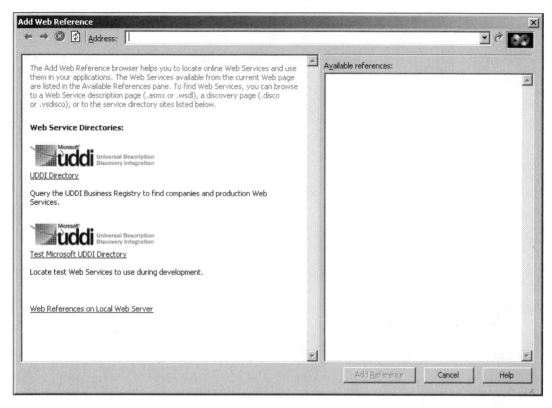

Note the address box at the top where you can enter a URL for any of the following types of pages to retrieve Service Contract information:

- ❏   .asmx
- ❏   .wsdl
- ❏   .disco
- ❏   .vsdisco

By default, links are provided to the Microsoft UDDI Directory and the Test Microsoft UDDI Directory. The former allows you to query the UDDI Business Registry to find companies and production web services, while the latter allows you to locate test web services to use during the development process.

Also, note the link to **Web References on Local Web Server**. If we click on that link, we can view details of the `default.vsdisco` file for our local machine. As you may remember, this file contains discovery information for local web services. The left-hand pane shows the actual contents of the `.vsdisco` document. Links to the `.vsdisco` documents for the web services referenced in the `default.vsdisco` file appear in the right-hand pane. There should at least be the two web services from Chapter 4 there; one created with the Visual Studio .NET IDE, and the other without. Let's click on one of these links to see what else we can learn:

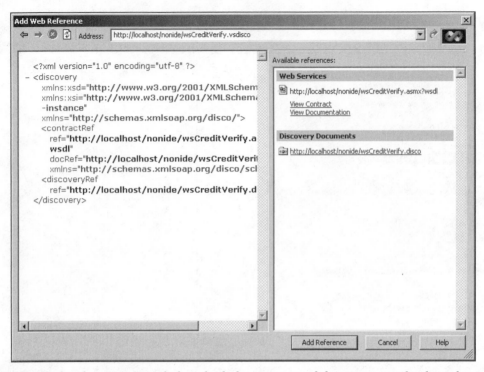

Now the right-hand pane contains links to both the contract and documentation for the web service. The View Contract link takes us to a screen showing the WSDL file for the web service, and the View Documentation link brings up the main information page for the web service shown below:

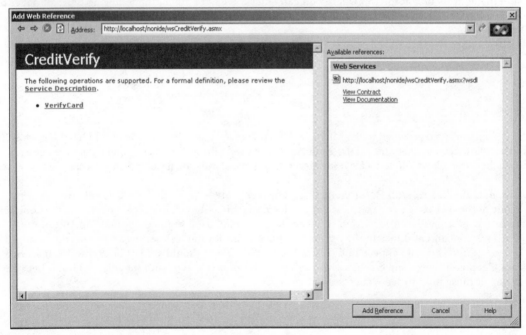

We've seen this screen already of course – it's the exact same screen that you get when you simply open the `.asmx` file in a regular web browser, and it also lets you view information about specific methods and test them just as we did in Chapter 4. While we're here, click the Add Reference button for either web service so that we can use it in the project later.

To recap the process of adding a web reference to your application:

1. On the Project menu, click Add Web Reference.

2. In the Address box of the Add Web Reference dialog, type the URL to the `.disco` or `.wsdl` file you would like to access. Click the Go button to retrieve discovery information.

3. When the discovery document is retrieved, select the web service from the Available References box.

4. Click Add Reference to add a web reference for that web service.

Viewing and Using the WSDL Document

Take a look at the WSDL document for the web service developed in the previous chapter, by typing http://localhost/nonide/wsCreditVerify.asmx?WSDL in your browser:

Among other things, this document tells us that the web service exposes a method called `VerifyCard`, but how do we call and use this method in code? In the next few sections we will discuss how to use the methods described in the WSDL document by creating a proxy class.

A proxy class is nothing more than an "intermediary" between your code and the web service. A proxy is needed to abstract away all of the implementation details in regards to making the actual SOAP or HTTP requests to the web service. This way, making a call to a web service method is as simple as creating an instance of the proxy class and making the calls through it. The proxy class itself handles the actual calls to the web service.

Creating the Proxy

There is always more than one way to do the same thing, be it skinning a cat as in the old adage, or creating a web service proxy class. Altogether, there are three different ways to create the proxy class. Firstly, you could code it by hand, but it would be a tedious task and, as both the `wsdl.exe` utility and the Visual Studio .NET IDE can create it for us, we shall focus on these two methods.

Using wsdl.exe

In the previous chapter, we outlined the `wsdl.exe` utility along with the parameters for calling it. Now let's use it to create a client proxy class for our `CreditVerify` web service. `wsdl.exe` isn't difficult to use and it very effectively takes all the hard work out of creating a proxy class.

First make sure the .NET directories appear in your Windows PATH environment variable, and start up a command prompt window. We can create a proxy class with any of the following files:

❑ With the `.asmx` file as the parameter:

```
wsdl http://localhost/CreditVerifyIDE/wsCreditVerify.asmx
    /n:CreditVerifyProxy /out:CreditVerifyProxy.cs
```

❑ With the `.wsdl` document as the parameter:

```
wsdl http://localhost/nonide/wsCreditVerify.asmx?wsdl /n:CreditVerifyProxy
    /out:CreditVerifyProxy.cs
```

❑ With the `.discomap` file as the parameter:

```
wsdl http://localhost/nonide/wsCreditVerify.discomap /n:CreditVerifyProxy
    /out:CreditVerifyProxy.cs
```

All three of the above calls would generate an identical proxy class `CreditVerifyProxy.cs` that abstracts the SOAP implementation details for calling the web service.

Using csc to Compile the Proxy Class

By compiling the proxy class into a DLL assembly, we can reference and use it in applications, or we could add the class to a project and use it that way. A C# command-line compiler, `csc.exe`, is provided with Visual Studio .NET, and this is how we would use it to compile our proxy class:

```
csc /target:library /r:System.dll; System.Web.dll; System.Web.Services.dll;
    System.Data.dll; System.Xml.dll CreditVerifyProxy.cs
```

Using the Compiled Proxy DLL Assembly

We can use the compiled client proxy assembly quite easily in an application. The easiest way is to simply include the namespace with a `using` statement like this:

```
using CreditVerifyProxy;
```

We could then create an instance of the proxy class in the application with the following code:

```
//Create an instance of the CreditVerify class defined in the Proxy Class
CreditVerify cv = new CreditVerify();
```

We could now access the methods from the `CreditVerify` class through the `cv` object.

Details of the Generated Proxy Class

`wsdl.exe` produces a single source file, however the proxy class that this file contains exposes both synchronous and asynchronous versions of each web service method. In total, there are three different methods for each of the available web service methods.

For instance, the method `VerifyCard()` from our previously discussed web service has the following methods in its proxy class: `VerifyCard()`, `BeginVerifyCard()`, `EndVerifyCard()`. The first of these, `VerifyCard()`, calls the web method synchronously. As you've probably guessed, `BeginVerifyCard()` and `EndVerifyCard()` are for asynchronous calls. These are highlighted in the `CreditVerifyProxy()` class generated by `wsdl.exe` below:

```
namespace CreditVerifyProxy {
    using System.Diagnostics;
    using System.Xml.Serialization;
    using System;
    using System.Web.Services.Protocols;
    using System.Web.Services;

    [System.Web.Services.WebServiceBindingAttribute(Name="CreditVerifySoap",
     Namespace="http://wrox.com/webservices/")]

    public class CreditVerify :
        System.Web.Services.Protocols.SoapHttpClientProtocol {

[System.Diagnostics.DebuggerStepThroughAttribute()]
  [System.Web.Services.Protocols.SoapDocumentMethodAttribute(
   "http://wrox.com/webservices/VerifyCard",
   RequestNamespace="http://wrox.com/webservices/",
   ResponseNamespace="http://wrox.com/webservices/",
   Use=System.Web.Services.Description.SoapBindingUse.Literal,
      ParameterStyle =
      System.Web.Services.Protocols.SoapParameterStyle.Wrapped)]

      public string VerifyCard(string sCardNumber, string sCardType) {
          object[] results = this.Invoke("VerifyCard", new object[] {
            sCardNumber,
```

113

```
            sCardType});
        return ((string)(results[0]));
    }
    [System.Diagnostics.DebuggerStepThroughAttribute()]

    public System.IAsyncResult BeginVerifyCard(string sCardNumber,
        string sCardType, System.AsyncCallback callback,
        object asyncState) {
        return this.BeginInvoke("VerifyCard", new object[] {
            sCardNumber,
            sCardType}, callback, asyncState);
    }
    [System.Diagnostics.DebuggerStepThroughAttribute()]

    public string EndVerifyCard(System.IAsyncResult asyncResult) {
        object[] results = this.EndInvoke(asyncResult);
        return ((string)(results[0]));
    }
}
}
```

We'll look more at calling a web service asynchronously later in the chapter. While we're looking at this file, notice that the code begins with some namespace declarations, and references important namespaces such as `Web.Services.Protocols`, and `Xml.Serialization`. These namespaces are required for making calls over the Internet to the actual endpoint where the web service is deployed.

Also note the `WebServiceBindingAttribute`, which sets the binding used by proxy calls to the web service. In this case, we see that it is the SOAP protocol:

```
[System.Web.Services.WebServiceBindingAttribute(Name="CreditVerifySoap",
Namespace="http://wrox.com/webservices/")]
public class CreditVerify : System.Web.Services.Protocols.SoapHttpClientProtocol {
```

Each proxy class method contains the network invocation and marshaling code to invoke and receive a response from the web service method. As we already know, the default is to use SOAP requests and responses. The proxy class also marshals method arguments to and from the CLR (Common Language Runtime) as necessary.

Automatic Proxy Creation Using Visual Studio .NET

Visual Studio .NET is a very powerful tool, so it's not surprising that it lets us do the same tasks as `wsdl.exe`, but from the cozy world of the IDE. In fact, we've already set up our application to use the proxy class. Remember when we added the web reference to the project? Visual Studio .NET transparently generated the proxy class as soon as we added it, although there are a few things that we need to do in order to access the proxy.

First, we ought to rename the web reference to something more meaningful. By default, the web reference is given the name of the referenced server, or localhost when referencing a service on your own machine as in this case. Let's call our web reference CreditVerifyProxy:

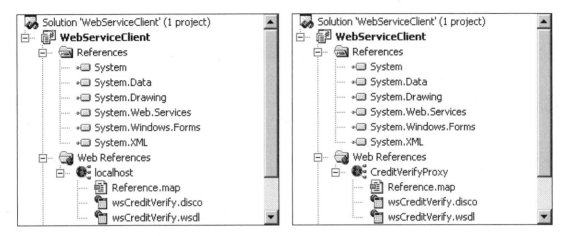

Using a meaningful name helps make our code more readable, as this is the namespace that Visual Studio .NET uses for accessing the web service in question. Now we're all set to use the newly created proxy class in an application. We know our namespace is now called CreditVerifyProxy, so creating an instance of the class requires just the following code in a C# application:

```
CreditVerifyProxy.CreditVerify cv = new CreditVerifyProxy.CreditVerify();
```

Accessing a method of the web service through the proxy object is now just as straightforward:

```
string result = cv.VerifyCard(sCardNumber, sCardType);
```

Behind the scenes, Visual Studio .NET takes care of the proxy DLL compilation and so on. In this case, Web References.CreditVerifyProxy.wsCreditVerify.cs.dll is the temporary file created by Visual Studio .NET for the project to access the web service. It is compiled from the generated class called wsCreditVerify.cs, which is also automatically generated when you first make the web reference selection.

Synchronous vs. Asynchronous Calls

Let's look at the two ways to make calls to web methods discussed earlier: synchronous (program waits for the call to complete before continuing), or asynchronous (program continues execution while the call continues in the background).

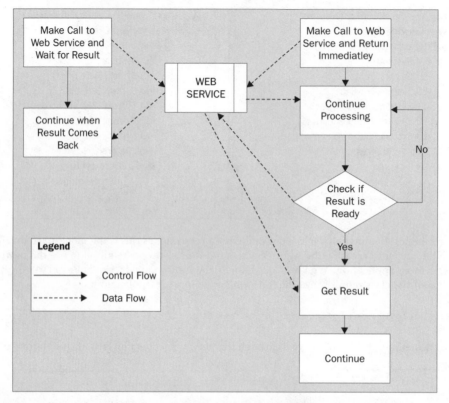

Synchronous calls are the standard mechanism that people tend to use by default. Calling a web service asynchronously is more sophisticated, and warrants a closer look.

Since the wsdl.exe utility generates asynchronous methods automatically, we don't need to write extra code in the web service application in order to handle asynchronous calls. This holds true even if only a synchronous implementation of a web service method is provided by the developer.

The .NET Framework Design Pattern

There is an underlying design pattern for asynchronous calls throughout the .NET Framework: a Begin method and an Endmethod initiate and terminate asynchronous processing respectively. wsdl.exe generates both of these two methods:

❑ Begin<WebServiceMethodName> – Tells the web service to start processing the call, but return immediately. Instead of returning the data type specified by the web service call, a type implementing the IAsyncResult interface is returned.

❑ End<WebServiceMethodName> – Tells the web service to return the results of a web method initiated previously.

The IAsyncResult interface contains an AsyncWaitHandle property of type WaitHandle. This common interface allows your client application to wait on the call and be signaled with "any" or "all" semantics (such as WaitHandle.WaitOne, WaitAny, and WaitAll). For example, if you want your client application to wait asynchronously for one web method, call WaitOne for the processing of that web service to complete.

There are two mechanisms commonly used for making asynchronous web method calls:

1. Using synchronization objects

2. Callbacks

Let's take a look at each of these in turn.

The Synchronization Object

The synchronization object allows us to make a call to a web service method (using the Begin<METHODNAME> method), and then continue processing. At a later point in the program, we can call the End<METHODNAME> method, passing in the synchronization object to get the results of the call. This way we can continue program flow inside a function, rather than leaving it as is the case with callbacks:

```
// Asynchronously invoke the VerifyCard Method, no callback
// In this example, we'll assume that more processing is taking place
// inbetween the call and the checking of the result (see comment)

using System;
using System.Runtime.Remoting.Messaging;
using CreditVerifyProxy;

class TestSyncObject
{
    public static void Main()
    {
        string CCNum = "5459000011112222";
        string CCTyp = "M";
        CreditVerify cv = new CreditVerify();

        // Performs action but does not return the data
        IAsyncResult ar = cv.BeginVerifyCard(CCNum,CCTyp,null,null);

        // Wait for the asynchronous operation to complete
        ar.AsyncWaitHandle.WaitOne();

        // Do some more processing here
        // Wait until something happens before continuing

        // Get the result
        string result;

        // Get the result from the above call
        result = cv.EndVerifyCard(ar);

        // Dump result
        Console.Write(result);
    }
}
```

So, nothing too complicated about synchronization objects – what about callbacks?

Callback

In essence, the asynchronous callback is the .NET equivalent of a delegate. It works by setting up a separate method that is called when the asynchronous operation completes. The calling application can continue processing other tasks until the callback function is called. This signifies that processing has completed, and the application can act appropriately. This differs from using a synchronization object in that that we can't control when to check the web method to see if it has finished and has the results we need. In the callback scenario, it is done automatically as soon as the web method completes.

```
// Invoking method using asynchronous callback.

using System;
using System.Runtime.Remoting.Messaging;
using CreditVerifyProxy;

class TestCallback
{
    public static void Main()
    {
        string CCNum = "5459000011112222";
        string CCTyp = "M";

        // Create a new instance of the CreditVerify proxy class
        CreditVerify cv = new CreditVerify();

        // Instantiate an asynchronous callback object and set its
        // callback function (the VerifyCallBack function below)
        AsyncCallback cb = new AsyncCallback(
                        TestCallback.VerifyCardCallback);

        // Now we call the asynchronous BeginVerifyCard method and then
        // in essence, "wait" until something else happens, or someone
        // hits a key to quit
        IAsyncResult ar = cv.BeginVerifyCard(CCNum,CCTyp,cb,cv);

        Console.Write("Press Key to Quit.");
        intStopChar = Console.Read();
    }

    public static void VerifyCardCallback(IAsyncResult ar)
    {
        // When the web service method returns, it will automatically
        // call this method
        CreditVerify cv = (CreditVerify) ar.AsyncState;
        string result;

        // Now call the EndVerifyCard method to get the results of the call
        result = cv.EndVerifyCard(ar);

        // Output results
        Console.Write(result);
    }
}
```

Callbacks vs. Synchronization Objects

Which you use will depend on the situation you face. If you would rather control when to check whether the asynchronous call has completed, then use synchronization objects. If it is more appropriate to structure your code so that calls can be made and the result handled by a special function invoked as soon as the method completes (which will interrupt whatever task the calling application is processing), then callbacks would better suit your needs.

Either way, calling a web method asynchronously from a client application is a relatively painless procedure with the automated features of Visual Studio .NET.

Now we have covered the basics of generating a proxy and instantiating objects to access the web service from a client application, let's put it into practice by developing a client application for our credit card validation web service.

Creating a Web Service Client

Web services can be consumed in many ways. They can be utilized and consumed by many different types of clients. They can be called from any web-based application, as well as from other web services. In fact, not all consumers of web services are client-based at all. Many are server-based applications and services that gather and process data through remote web services.

Here are two types of web service calls:

End user to web service – This the model we shall implement in the sample application in this section. The client application communicates with a web service directly over the Internet (via the proxy) to access information or processing that is not available locally to the client.

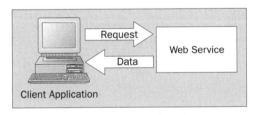

Web service to web service – A good example of this scenario would be a stock price application. You might have a client application (or web page) that provides users with information related to their stocks. The application could query a web service written by your company to obtain this information for them. Your company, however, uses a third-party web service for the actual stock information. In this case, your web service is making calls to another web service to get its information. Note that the consumer application doesn't have to be .NET-based – it can be any application capable of making calls to the web service and interpreting the SOAP/XML response.

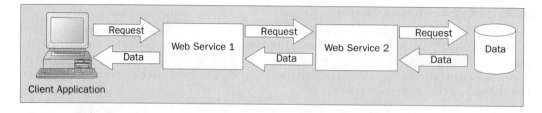

Building a Sample Client in C#

We are going to build a Windows application in C# that verifies a credit card number by consuming our credit card validation web service. I assume that you already know how to create a C# Windows application in Visual Studio .NET, so create one as usual, and call it WebServiceClient. Add a web reference to the CreditVerify web service that we wrote and discussed in Chapter 4 by following the same steps as before:

1. Open up the Add Web Reference dialog from the Project menu.

2. Type in the URL for one of the following file types: .asmx, .vsdisco, .disco, or .wsdl. Alternatively, browse to find the web service.

3. Add the web reference for CreditVerify.

4. Rename the web reference something more appropriate, such as CreditVerifyService.

Now we can use the web service in the application, Let's create the form that our client will use, and place the following controls on it, named as indicated:

❑ TextBox – **txtCardNumber** – *for inputting the credit card number*

❑ ComboBox – **cboType** – *for selecting the type of credit card*

❑ Label – **lblStatus** – *for displaying the message returned by the web service*

❑ Button – *for submitting the data to the web service*

Also place some descriptive labels, to make it look something like this:

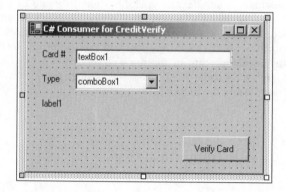

We need to set up a few items for the Type combo box, including Visa, Master Card, Discover, and American Express. You can add these programmatically or through the Items dialog in the Properties window of Visual Studio .NET.

Using the Web Service in Code

Since we've already added the web reference to the web service, we can readily access it from code. In our test C# consumer application, we are going to place code in the click event for the Verify Card button to take the information input by the user and pass it to the VerifyCard method for validation.

Double-click the Verify Card button in the Visual Studio .NET designer, and insert the following code:

```
string sCardNumber = "";
string sCardType = "";

//just put the text from the textbox into a variable
sCardNumber = txtCardNumber.Text;

//switch on the selected combo box item
switch(cboType.Text)
{
    case "Visa":
        sCardType = "V";
        break;
    case "Master Card":
        sCardType = "M";
        break;
    case "Discover":
        sCardType = "D";
        break;
    case "American Express":
        sCardType = "A";
        break;
}

//Create an instance of the Proxy Class
CreditVerifyProxy.CreditVerify  cv = new CreditVerifyProxy.CreditVerify();

//just set the text of the label on the form to the result of the call
lblStatus.Text = cv.VerifyCard(sCardNumber,sCardType);
```

This is the code that creates an instance of the CreditVerify class from CreditVerifyProxy:

```
CreditVerifyProxy.CreditVerify cv = new CreditVerifyProxy.CreditVerify();
```

Once we have the proxy class instance, we can make calls just as if we were calling the web methods of the web service direct, without having to worry about SOAP and HTTP:

```
lblStatus.Text = cv.VerifyCard(sCardNumber,sCardType);
```

Overleaf is an example of the output from testing the application on a number that is too long and has incorrect start digits for the card type. Note that I have changed the font and color of the status label:

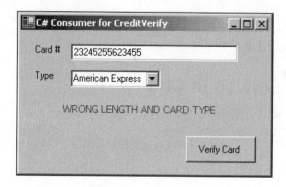

Debugging the Consumer

Debugging the consumer application is just like debugging any other Visual Studio .NET application. The only difference is that calls to web methods are sent over the wire, so you must have internet access available when debugging. If, on the other hand, you are developing both the web service and client application on the same machine, the web service must be installed and running in IIS for it to be accessible to the client, and for debugging to work.

Debugging web services themselves was examined in Chapter 4, but if we want to step directly from our client application into the web service code, we must first explicitly enable ASP.NET debugging for the project.

Setting up ASP.NET Debugging

Perform the following steps in the client application to set up ASP.NET debugging:

1. In Solution Explorer, select the WebServiceClient item:

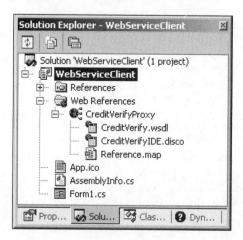

2. Right-click and select Properties, or View | Property Pages from the menu. You will see the following property page dialog box:

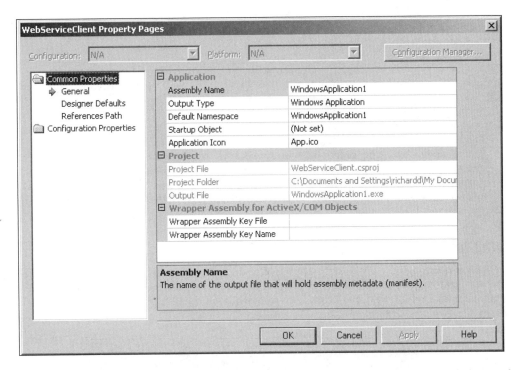

3. Click on Configuration Properties | Debugging to get to the next screen, and change the Enable ASP.NET Debugging value in the Debuggers section to True:

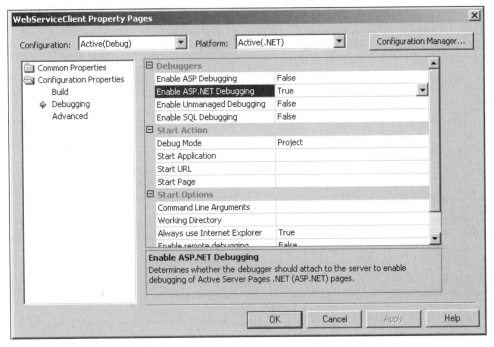

4. Click OK to apply the changes. Now we'll be able to debug the web service calls from the client application.

ASP.NET debugging attaches the client application to the ASP.NET worker process, `aspnet_wp.exe`. When the consumer makes a call to the web service, the debugger can track the SOAP call and follow the call stack chain into the web service.

> This debugging feature will only work for web services that you are running locally on your machine. Debugging cannot work over a network, so you cannot debug by stepping into web services hosted on a remote machine (such as for a third-party web service provider). Debugging a client application that uses a remote web service is just like testing an application that calls third-party libraries, where you don't have access to the codebase.

Stepping into the Web Service

I'll quickly run through the process of stepping in to the web service call now that ASP.NET debugging is enabled for the client. First, we need to start up our web service project in a separate instance of the Visual Studio .NET IDE. Set a file breakpoint somewhere in the `CheckCCNumber` web method, and go to Build | Configuration Manager... to make sure that the web service is set to run in debug mode:

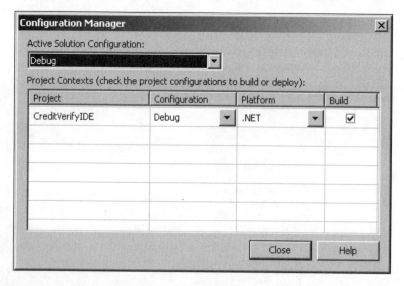

Now, start the web service by clicking Debug | Start. The service should start up and pop up an Internet Explorer window that displays the information page, which we can safely ignore. We are going to use our client application to query the web service.

Switch to the client C# project, and verify that it has a web reference for the web service currently running in debug mode in the other Visual Studio .NET instance.

In most cases, this should already be the case. As long as the IIS virtual directory hasn't changed, you should be all set to go.

Let's set a file breakpoint in our client application right before the call to the web service. Now start the client, also in debug mode, and wait for it to reach the breakpoint we just set:

```
//just set the text of the label on the form to the result of the call
lblStatus.Text = cv.VerifyCard(sCardNumber,sCardType);
```

Now use the usual step into function key (*F11*) to step into the web service call.

Inside the Web Service Call

Once we step into the web service from the client application, we're immediately switched over to the instance of Visual Studio .NET where the web service is running. Let's have a look at what's going on in both the web service and the consumer.

In the Web Service:

```
private string CheckCCNumber(string sCardNumber,string sCardType)
{
    string sType, sLength, sPrefix,sNumber, sResult;
    bool bPrefixValid, bLengthValid;
    long lResult, lQSum, lSum;
    int ch;

    sType = sCardType.ToUpper();

    switch (sType)
    {
        case "V":
            sLength = "13;16";
            sPrefix = "4";
            break;
        case "M":
```

The web service IDE has stopped at the breakpoint that we set in the CheckCCNumber web method. Some useful information is displayed in the top of the IDE window:

```
= /% /% /% /% ▾
Hex 🔲 ▾ ▾  Program [1692] aspnet_wp.exe: ▾ Thread [932] <No Name> ▾ Stack Frame webservice1.dll!CreditVerifyWeb ▾ ▾
editVerify.asmx.cs*                                                              ◁ ▷ ✕  Solution E
```

These boxes tell us that the web service is attached to the `aspnet_wp.exe` process as mentioned previously, and also let us view **Thread** and **Stack Frame** details.

In the Consumer:

```
namespace WebServiceClient.CreditVerifyProxy {
    using System.Diagnostics;
    using System.Xml.Serialization;
    using System;
    using System.Web.Services.Protocols;
    using System.Web.Services;


    [System.Web.Services.WebServiceBindingAttribute(Name="CreditVerifySoap", Namespace="http://wrox.com/webservices/")]
    public class CreditVerify : System.Web.Services.Protocols.SoapHttpClientProtocol {

        [System.Diagnostics.DebuggerStepThroughAttribute()]
        public CreditVerify() {
            this.Url = "http://localhost/CreditVerifyIDE/CreditVerify.asmx";
        }


        [System.Diagnostics.DebuggerStepThroughAttribute()]
        [System.Web.Services.Protocols.SoapDocumentMethodAttribute("http://wrox.com/webservices/VerifyCard", RequestNam
        public string VerifyCard(string sCardNumber, string sCardType) {
            object[] results = this.Invoke("VerifyCard", new object[] {
                        sCardNumber,
                        sCardType});
            return ((string)(results[0]));
        }
```

The consumer has halted inside the `VerifyCard` method within the web service proxy class. The **Call Stack** information given in the IDE running the client application is worth noting here:

This window shows that the call stack jumps from the `WebServiceClient.exe` process to `system.web.services.dll`. Also note that the first step after `WebServiceClient.exe` is to call the `SoapHttpClientProtocol:Invoke` method.

We are now free to look at a host of data items and parameters using the **Watch** and **Variables** windows for both the consumer and the web service.

Visual Studio .NET's tools for debugging web services and consumer applications are very powerful and easy to use, making our job as developers of complex web services and clients that much easier.

Things to Keep in Mind

As with any technology, best practices evolve steadily over time with each new triumph and failure. However, there are a few key things to note about consumer applications in general:

❑ **Handle cases when the server is unavailable** – Because web services are hosted on remote machines, there is a chance that the service will become unavailable at some time or another. An important area to consider when choosing a web service provider is that of Service Level Agreements – will the provider guarantee that the web service won't suffer outages for long enough to seriously curtail the usefulness of your application? In any case, you must make provisions for the fact that the service may not be available.

❑   **Be efficient about the number of requests for dynamic data** – This is a key area when dealing with web services. Requests for data are made to remote systems over the Internet, so data lookups and operations could be significantly more expensive than with a non-distributed software development model.

❑   **Read the SOAP, UDDI, and WSDL specifications** – Familiarity with the key components and protocols related to web services will aid in better understanding of the technology, and hence better design, both when providing web services and consuming them. They can be found at:

SOAP	– http://www.w3.org/TR/SOAP/
WSDL	– http://www.w3.org/TR/wsdl/
UDDI	– http://www.uddi.org
WEBSERVICES.ORG	– http://www.webservices.org/

❑   **Cache data from the service where possible** – Rather than repeatedly requesting the same data, cache the data in the consumer. Data retrieval is much more costly with web services.

❑   **Ensure the data network has surplus bandwidth** – Reduce the chance that your own network could be the bottleneck and possible failure point.

Summary

In this chapter we have covered various topics related to the consumption of ASP.NET web services. Perhaps you are already being overwhelmed with ideas for powerful additions you will be able to make to your client applications through the web services model!

In the first part of the chapter we looked at calling web services with HTTP-GET, HTTP-POST, and SOAP methods, and how to discover web services and reference them in applications. We also examined some important details about proxies and how we use them to consume web services.

We finished up with web service debugging techniques, and picked out some key points to remember when writing and consuming web services.

Section Three – .NET Remoting

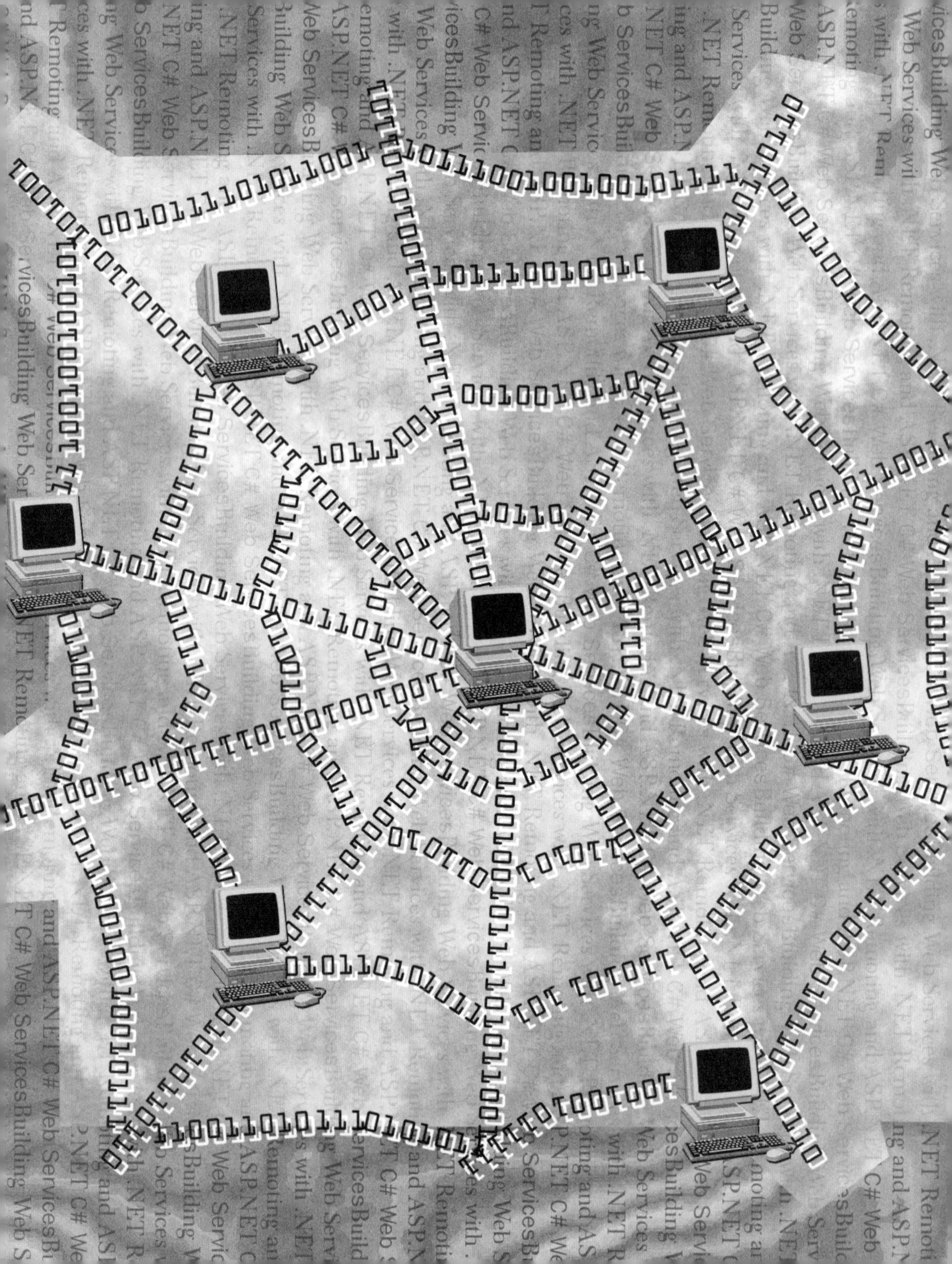

6

.NET Remoting Architecture

In the last few chapters, we have seen how ASP.NET web services can be created and used. ASP.NET web services require the ASP.NET runtime as hosting environment. Using .NET Remoting directly, we can host a web service in any application we want. .NET Remoting allows much more flexibility because different transport protocols may be used, we can get a performance increase with different formatting options, and it's possible to host the server in different application types.

The next four chapters will deal with .NET Remoting. In this chapter, we will look at the architecture of .NET Remoting, and go into detail in the following areas:

- ❑ What is .NET Remoting?
- ❑ .NET Remoting Fundamentals
- ❑ Object Types
- ❑ Activation
- ❑ Marshaling
- ❑ Asynchronous Remoting
- ❑ Call Contexts

The next chapter will show different application types, transport protocols, and formatting options, and Chapters 8 and 9 will show an example of using .NET Remoting. Let's begin the chapter with a look at .NET Remoting.

> *As with the previous chapters, the code for the examples in this chapter can be downloaded from* http://www.wrox.com.

What is .NET Remoting?

.NET Remoting is the replacement for DCOM. As we have seen in the last chapters, ASP.NET web services are an easy-to use-technology to call services across a network. ASP.NET web services can be used as a communication link with different technologies, for example to have a COM or a Java client talk to web services developed with ASP.NET. As good as this technology is, however, it is not fast and flexible enough for some business requirements in intranet solutions, and ASP.NET web services requires the ASP.NET runtime. With .NET Remoting we get **Web Services Anywhere** that can run in every application type.

Web Services Anywhere

The term "Web Services Anywhere" means that web services can not only be used in any application, but any application can offer web services. ASP.NET web services require the IIS to run; web services that make use of .NET Remoting can run in any application type: console applications, Windows Forms applications, Windows services, and so on. These web services can use **any transport** with **any payload encoding**.

In the next chapter we will talk about when and how to use .NET Remoting with different transports (TCP and HTTP) and about different payload encoding mechanisms (SOAP and binary).

CLR Object Remoting

The next part of .NET Remoting that we need to be aware of is **CLR Object Remoting.** With CLR Object Remoting we can call objects across the network, as if they were being called locally.

With CLR Object Remoting we have:

- ❑ **Distributed Identities** – Remote objects can have a distributed identity. If we pass a reference to a remote object, we will always access the same object using this reference.

- ❑ **Activation** – Remote objects can be activated using the new operator. Of course, there are other ways to activate remote objects, as we will see later.

- ❑ **Lease-Based Lifetime** – How long should the object be activated on the server? At what time can we assume that the client no longer needs the remote object? DCOM uses a ping mechanism that is not scalable to internet solutions. .NET Remoting takes a different approach with a lease-based lifetime that is scalable.

- ❑ **Call Context** – With the SOAP header, additional information can be passed with every method call that is not passed as an argument.

We will cover all of these CLR Object Remoting features in detail later on in this chapter.

.NET Remoting Fundamentals

The methods that will be called from the client are implemented in a remote object class. In the figure opposite we can see an instance of this class as the Remote Object. Because this remote object runs inside a process that is different from the client process – usually also on a different system – the client can't call it directly. Instead the client uses a **proxy**. For the client, the proxy looks like the real object with the same public methods. When the methods of the proxy are called, **messages** will be created. These are serialized using a **formatter** class, and are sent into a **client channel**. The client channel communicates with the server part of the channel to transfer the message across the network. The **server channel** uses a **formatter** to deserialize the message, so that the methods can be dispatched to the **remote object**:

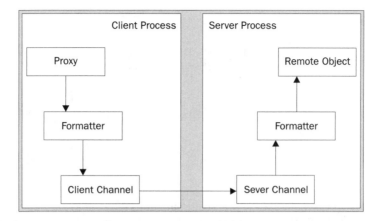

In the simplest case, we have to create a remote object class and instantiate a channel for a .NET Remoting application. The formatter and the proxy will be supplied automatically. The architecture is very flexible in that different formatters and channels can be used. We cover the use of the TCP and HTTP channels, and the SOAP and binary formatters in the next chapter.

In the next section we'll start with the simplest case to develop a remoting object, server, and client. In this section we will not go into the details of the remoting architecture, as we will cover this later after we've finished a simple client and server.

Remote Object

A remote object is implemented in a class that derives from `System.MarshalByRefObject`. `MarshalByRefObject` defines methods for lifetime services that will be described later when we use the leasing features. A remote object is confined to the application domain where it is created. As we already know, a client doesn't call the methods directly; instead a proxy object is used to invoke methods on the remote object. Every public method that we define in the remote object class is available to be called from clients.

> *What is an **application domain** ? Before .NET, processes were used as a security boundary so that one process couldn't crash another process because it used private virtual memory. With the help of the managed environment of .NET, the code of an application can be checked, and there's no way to crash the process. To reduce the overhead with different processes, the concept of an application domain was introduced with .NET. Multiple applications can run in the same process without influencing each other if they are called within different application domains. If one of these applications throws an exception that isn't handled, only the application domain is terminated, and not the complete process. To invoke a method in an object running in a different application domain, .NET remoting must be used.*

The following code sample shows a simple remote object class, and the code for this simple example can be found in the `SimpleTest` folder of the code download for this chapter, which is available from http://www.wrox.com. The method `Hello()` is declared public to make it available for a remoting client:

```
// MyRemoteObject.cs

using System;
namespace Wrox.Samples
{
```

```
public class MyRemoteObject : System.MarshalByRefObject
{
    public MyRemoteObject()
    {
        Console.WriteLine("Constructor called");
    }
    public string Hello()
    {
        Console.WriteLine("Hello called");
        return "Hello, .NET Client!";
    }
}
}
```

> **It is useful to implement the class of the remote object in a different assembly from that of the remote server itself. This assembly can then be used in different server applications, and the client application can use it to get the metadata needed to build the proxy.**

We build the assembly MyRemoteObject from the class MyRemoteObject as follows:

```
csc /t:library /out:MyRemoteObject.dll MyRemoteObject.cs
```

Server

The remote object needs a server process where it will be instantiated. This server has to create a channel and put it into listening mode so that clients can connect to this channel. In this chapter, we will use simple console applications as hosting servers, and in the next chapter we will look at the different application types.

Server Configuration File

The server channel can be configured programmatically or by using a configuration file.

> **Using configuration files for remoting clients and servers has the advantage that the channel and remote object can be configured without changing a single line of code and without the need to recompile. Another advantage is that the remoting code we have to write is very short.**
>
> **Specifying the options programmatically has the advantage that we could get to the information during runtime. One way to implement this can be that the client uses a directory service to locate a server that has registered its long running objects there.**

Configuration files have the advantage that the channel, endpoint name, and so on, can be changed without changing a single line of code and without doing a recompile. We will use configuration files first before we look at what happens behind the scenes when doing the configuration programmatically.

For versioning and probing of assemblies, we can have application configuration files with the same name as the executable, but with a `.config` file extension, such as `SimpleServer.exe.config`. The .NET Remoting configuration can be put into a different file or the same file. We have to read the .NET Remoting configuration explicitly, so it doesn't matter from a programming viewpoint. From the administrator viewpoint it would be useful to put the .NET Remoting configuration inside the same file as this can be used to configure the channel with the .NET Admin tool.

When the client connects to the remote object it needs to know the URI of the object, that is, the name of the host where the remote object is running, the protocol and port number to connect to, the name of the server, and the name of the remote object. Such a connection string can look like this:

```
tcp://localhost:9000/SimpleServer/MyRemoteObject
```

With the exception of the host name we have to specify all these items in the configuration file.

In the following configuration file, `SimpleServer.exe.config`, all of the remoting configurations must be added as child elements to `<system.runtime.remoting>`. The `<application>` element specifies the name of the server with the name attribute. The application offers a service and requires the configureation of channels for the service. Correspondingly we have the `<service>` and `<channels>` elements. The service that is offered from the application must be listed as a child of `<service>`. This is the remote object itself. The remote object is specified with the `<wellknown>` element.

The remoting framework uses the information to create an object from the type specified. For instantiating the object the framework requires the name of the assembly to know where the type of this object can be loaded from. We can set this information with the XML attribute `type`. `type="Wrox.Samples.MyRemoteObject, MyRemoteObject"` defines that the type of the remote object is `MyRemoteObject` in the namespace `Wrox.Samples`, and it can be found in the assembly `MyRemoteObject`. The `mode` attribute is set to `SingleCall`. We will talk later about all the different object types and modes. With `objectURI` we set the endpoint name of the remote object that will be used from the client.

The name of the assembly is often confused with the name of the file in which the assembly is stored. The assembly name is `MyRemoteObject`, while the file of the assembly is `MyRemoteObject.dll`. With method calls where an assembly name is needed as argument, never use the file extension.

In the `<channels>` section we define the channels that will be used from the server. There are already some channels defined in the machine configuration file `machine.config` that we can use from our applications. Such a predefined channel can be referenced using the `ref` attribute of the `<channel>` element. Here we reference the predefined server channel using the TCP protocol: `tcp server`. We have to assign the port of this channel with the `port` attribute, as the server must have a well-known port number that the client must be aware of:

```
<configuration>
    <system.runtime.remoting>
        <application name="SimpleServer">
            <service>
                <wellknown
                    mode="SingleCall"
                    type="Wrox.Samples.MyRemoteObject, MyRemoteObject"
                    objectUri="MyRemoteObject" />
```

```
            </service>
            <channels>
                <channel ref="tcp server" port="9000" />
            </channels>
        </application>
    </system.runtime.remoting>
</configuration>
```

Machine.config

We can find predefined channels in the machine-wide configuration file `machine.config`. This configuration file is in the directory `%SystemRoot%\Microsoft.NET\Framework\<vx.x.x>\CONFIG`.

Six channels are predefined in this file, as we can see in the following XML segment. The `id` attribute defines the identifier of the channel that can be used with the `ref` attribute as we have done in the application configuration file to reference the `tcp server` channel. The `type` attribute defines the class and assembly name of the channel. With the `id` we can easily guess the protocol that is used by channel. The `id` also if the channel can be used on the client or server side. The `http` and `tcp` channels include both client and server functionality:

```
    <channels>
        <channel
            id="http"
            type="System.Runtime.Remoting.Channels.Http.HttpChannel,
            System.Runtime.Remoting,
            Version=1.0.3300.0, Culture-Neutral,PublicKeyToken-b77a5c561934e089" />
        <channel
            id="http client"
            type="System.Runtime.Remoting.Channels.Http.HttpClientChannel,
            System.Runtime.Remoting,
            Version=1.0.3300.0, Culture-Neutral,PublicKey Token-b77a5c561934e089" />
        <channel
            id="http server"
            type="System.Runtime.Remoting.Channels.Http.HttpServerChannel,
            System.Runtime.Remoting,
            Version=1.0.3300.0, Culture-Neutral,PublicKey Token-b77a5c561934e089" />
        <channel
            id="tcp"
            type="System.Runtime.Remoting.Channels.Tcp.TcpChannel,
            System.Runtime.Remoting,
            Version=1.0.3300.0, Culture-Neutral,PublicKey Token-b77a5c561934e089" />
        <channel
            id="tcp client"
            type="System.Runtime.Remoting.Channels.Tcp.TcpClientChannel,
            System.Runtime.Remoting,
            Version=1.0.3300.0, Culture-Neutral,PublicKey Token-b77a5c561934e089" />
        <channel
            id="tcp server"
            type="System.Runtime.Remoting.Channels.Tcp.TcpServerChannel,
            System.Runtime.Remoting,
            Version=1.0.3300.0, Culture-Neutral,PublicKey Token-b77a5c561934e089" />
    </channels>
```

Starting the Channel

All the server has to do is read the configuration file and activate the channel. This can be done with a single call to the static method `RemotingConfiguration.Configure()`.

Here the server is implemented in a console application. `RemotingConfiguration.Configure()` reads the configuration file `SimpleServer.exe.config` to configure and activate the channel. The creation of the remote object and communication with the client is done by the remoting infrastructure; we just have to make sure that the process doesn't end. We do this with `Console.ReadLine()` that will end the process when the user enters the return key:

```
// SimpleServer.cs

using System;
using System.Runtime.Remoting;
namespace Wrox.Samples
{
   class SimpleServer
   {
      static void Main(string[] args)
      {
         RemotingConfiguration.Configure("SimpleServer.exe.config");
         Console.WriteLine("Press return to exit");
         Console.ReadLine();
      }
   }
}
```

We compile the file `SimpleServer.cs` to a console application:

```
csc /target:exe SimpleServer.cs
```

> We have to either copy the assembly of the remote object class to the directory of the server executable, or make a shared assembly and install it in the global assembly cache. The compiler doesn't complain that we are not referencing it because we didn't use the type **MyRemoteObject** in our server application. But the class will be instantiated from the remoting framework by reading the configuration file, so the assembly must be in a place where it can be found. If you get the **exception System.Runtime.Remoting. RemotingException: cannot load type Wrox.Samples.MyRemoteObject** while running the client application, remember this issue.

Client

Creating the client is as simple as creating the server. Here we will create a client using a configuration file.

Client Configuration File

The client configuration file `SimpleClient.exe.config` uses the XML `<client>` element to specify the URL of the server using `protocol://hostname:port/application`. In this example we use `tcp` as the protocol, and the server runs on `localhost` with the port number `9000`. The application name of the server is defined with the `name` attribute of the `<application>` element in the server configuration file.

The `<wellknown>` element specifies the remote object we want to access. As in the server configuration file, the `type` attribute defines the type of the remote object and the assembly. The `url` attribute defines the path to the remote object. Appended to the URL of the application is the endpoint name `MyRemoteObject`. The channel that is configured with the client can again be found in the configuration file `machine.config`, but this time it is the client channel:

```
<configuration>
    <system.runtime.remoting>
        <application name="SimpleClient">
            <client url="tcp://localhost:9000/SimpleServer">
                <wellknown
                    type="Wrox.Samples.MyRemoteObject, MyRemoteObject"
                    url =
                    "tcp://localhost:9000/SimpleServer/MyRemoteObject"
                />
            </client>
            <channels>
                <channel ref="tcp client" />
            </channels>
        </application>
    </system.runtime.remoting>
</configuration>
```

Client Application

As in the server, we can activate the client channel by calling `RemotingConfiguration.Configure()`. Using configuration files we can simply use `new` to create the remote object. Next we call the method `Hello()` of this object:

```
// SimpleClient.cs

using System;
using System.Runtime.Remoting;
namespace Wrox.Samples
{
    class SimpleClient
    {
        static void Main(string[] args)
        {
            RemotingConfiguration.Configure("SimpleClient.exe.config");
            MyRemoteObject obj = new MyRemoteObject();
            Console.WriteLine(obj.Hello());
        }
    }
}
```

We can compile the client to a console application as we've done before with the server:

csc /target:exe /reference:MyRemoteObject.dll SimpleClient.cs

The assembly of the remote object must also be copied for the client application as well, but here it is clearer as we have to reference it explicitly in the compiler command.

Running the Server and the Client

Let's take a step back to look at the files we created so far. This table helps to summarize the files and assemblies and their purposes:

Class	Source File	Assembly File	Description
MyRemote Object	MyRemote Object.cs	MyRemote Object.dll	Remote object class. We offer the Hello() method.
SimpleServer	Simple Server.cs	Simple Server.exe	The server creates and registers a server channel. We use the configuration file SimpleServer.exe.config to configure the channel and the remote object.
SimpleClient	Simple Client.cs	Simple Client.exe	The client application. The configuration file SimpleClient.exe.config defines how to connect to the remote object.

Starting the server and then the client we get the following output from the client:

This is the output screen from the server. We can see that the constructor of the remote object is called twice. The remoting infrastructure instantiates the remote object once before the client activation takes place:

As we have seen it was an easy task to build a simple client and server: create a remote object class, and implement a client and a server. If we are using configuration files, only one remoting call is necessary to read the configuration file and start the channel.

There's a lot more that is provided by .NET remoting. In the next section we will look at more of the terms of this architecture, and discuss all the sub-namespaces and their purpose.

More .NET Remoting

As we have seen it was an easy task to build a simple client and server. We created a remote object that will run on the server, and registered a channel using a configuration file. For simple remoting applications that's all what is needed, but a lot more is possible with .NET Remoting. Let us discuss some terms of the architecture:

❑ **Remote Objects**

As we have seen now, a remote object class must derive from the class `MarshalByRefObject`. Calling this object across application domains requires a proxy. .NET Remoting supports two types of remote objects: **well-known** and **client-activated**. For **well-known** objects a URI is used for identification. The client uses the URI to access such objects, which is why they are called well-known. For well-known objects we have two modes: **SingleCall** and **Singleton**. With a `SingleCall` object, the object is created new with every method call; it is a **stateless** object. A `Singleton` object is created only once. `Singleton` objects share state for all clients.

The other object type that is supported with .NET Remoting is **client-activated**. This object type uses the type of the class for activation. The URI is created dynamically behind the scenes and returned to the client. In further calls to the remote object this URI is used automatically to call methods in the same instance that was created. Client-activated objects are **stateful**.

❑ **Activation**

Well-known `SingleCall` objects are not created at the time when the client invokes the new method. Instead, they are created with every method call. They could also be called server-activated. Client-activated objects are created at the time when the client instantiates the object; that's why they are called client-activated. In both cases the client gets a **proxy** of the remote object. We have to differentiate a transparent proxy from a real proxy. The **transparent proxy** is created dynamically using the metadata of the remote object class. At proxy creation the methods and arguments of the public methods of the remote object are read from the metadata, and the proxy makes these methods available to the client. For the client the transparent proxy looks like the remote object class, but instead it calls methods of the **real proxy** to send the method calls across the network.

❑ **Marshaling**

The process when data is sent across application domains is called marshaling. Sending a variable as argument of a remote method, this variable must be converted so that it can be sent across application domains. We differentiate two kinds of marshaling: Marshal-by-value (MBV) and Marshal-by-reference (MBR). With **Marshal-by-value** the data is serialized to a stream, and this stream is sent across. **Marshal-by-reference** creates a proxy on the client that is used to communicate with the remote object.

❑ **Interception**

To fully understand the remoting architecture we have to discuss interception. With interception we can put some functionality into the method call chain. For example, if we call a method of an object, the interception layer could catch the call to convert the method call, or do some logging. Interception is used in every part of the call chain with .NET remoting.

For interception **sink** objects are used. A sink can perform some actions with messages it receives, for example conversions or logging. Sinks are connected in sink chains; one sink passes the message to the next sink. We can differentiate formatter sinks, custom channel sinks, and transport sinks. **Formatter sinks** transform the messages into a message stream. The **transport sink** is the last sink in the chain in the client to send the message into the channel, and the first sink in the server to receive the message. Transport sinks are built into the channel. With **custom channel sinks** the interception mechanism can be used to add custom functionality to read and write the data received and implement logging, add additional headers, or to redirect messages, for example.

Now that we are more familiar with remoting terms we can look into the classes of the remoting namespace.

System.Runtime.Remoting Namespace

If we use configuration files, only one remoting call is necessary to read the configuration file and start the channel. The only class we used from the System.Runtime.Remoting namespace was Remoting Configuration. Instead of using configuration, files the channel startup can be done programmatically. Before we do this let's get an overview of the classes that can be found in the remoting namespaces.

The System.Runtime.Remoting namespaces are contained in the assemblies mscorlib and System.Runtime.Remoting:

❑ In the namespace System.Runtime.Remoting some utility classes such as RemotingConfiguration and RemotingServices can be found. RemotingConfiguration is used to read configuration files and to get information about the registered channels; RemotingServices is used to publish remote objects.

❑ System.Runtime.Remoting.Activation: The channel uses the class RemotingDispatcher to dispatch method calls to the remote object. In this namespace, we can also find some interfaces for the activation of remote objects: IActivator, IConstructionCallMessage, and IConstructionReturnMessage.

❑ The namespace System.Runtime.Remoting.Channels has base classes for channels, and channel registration. An important class in this namespace is ChannelServices. This utility class can be used to register and to unregister a channel with the methods RegisterChannel() and UnRegisterChannel(), and it is also used to dispatch messages into a channel using SyncDispatchMessage() or AsyncDispatchMessage().

❑ With the .NETF we get two channel types: TCP and HTTP. The TCP channels can be found in the namespace System.Runtime.Remoting.Channels.Tcp, where as the HTTP channels are in System.Runtime.Remoting.Channels.Http. In the next chapter we will look into the differences between these channels.

❑ The System.Runtime.Remoting.Contexts namespace not only has classes for the context management inside an application domain, but also defines IContribute<XX> interfaces to intercept remoting calls.

❑   The lifetime of remote stateful objects is defined by a leasing mechanism. The namespace `System.Runtime.Remoting.Lifetime` defines the classes `LifetimeServices` and `ClientSponsor`, and the interfaces `ISponsor` and `ILease`.

❑   The namespace `System.Runtime.Remoting.Messaging` defines some interfaces for messages, such as `IMessage`, `IMethodCallMessage`, and `IMethodReturnMessage`. Method calls are converted to messages that are passed between message sinks. Message sinks are interceptors that can change messages before they are passed into the channel.

❑   The soapsuds tool converts assembly metadata to WSDL. The classes that help with these actions can be found in the namespaces `System.Runtime.Remoting.Metadata` and `System.Runtime.Remoting.MetadataServices`. We will use the soapsuds tool in Chapter 9.

❑   The namespace `System.Runtime.Remoting.Proxies` contains classes that control and provide proxies.

The classes in the `System.Runtime.Remoting.Services` namespace provide services to the remoting framework. The class `EnterpriseServicesHelper` provides remoting functionality for COM+ services, `RemotingService` can be used to access ASP.NET properties like `Application`, `Session`, and `User` for web services running in Internet Information Services. `RemotingClientProxy` is a base class for a proxy that is generated from the soapsuds utility, and `TrackingServices` provides a way to register tracking handlers.

Let's look in more detail at how to use the .NET Remoting architecture.

Remote Objects

With remote objects we have to differentiate between **well-known** objects and **client-activated** objects.

> **Well-known objects are stateless; client-activated objects hold state.**

If we use client-activated objects that hold state we should bear in mind that every call across the network takes time. It is not a good idea to use properties to set some state of the remote object. Instead, it would be much faster to use method calls with more arguments and so use fewer calls that are sent across the network. With COM it was said that a COM object could similarly be used locally, or across the network. The reality showed that if a COM object was implemented with properties to be easy to use from the client, it was not efficient on the network, and if it was efficient on the network it was not easy to use from a scripting client. With .NET we already have the advantage that remote object classes must derive from `MarshalByRefObject`, and such objects should implemented in a way that is efficient when used across the network. Classes that don't derive from `MarshalByRefObject` can never be called across the network.

Well-Known Objects

For **well-known** objects, the client must know the endpoint of the object – that's why they are called well-known. The endpoint is used to identify the remote object. In contrast to that, with **client-activated** objects the type of the class is used to activate the remote object.

Instead of using a configuration file as we have done earlier to register a channel and define a well-known object, we can do this programmatically. To get the same result as with the configuration file we have to do some more coding steps:

- ❑ Create a server channel
- ❑ Register the channel in the .NET remoting runtime
- ❑ Register a well-known object

Removing the configuration file and the call to `RemotingConfiguration.Configure()`, the implementation of the server can look like the following sample. In the configuration file we specified the TCP Server channel in the `<channels>` section. Here, we create an instance of the class `TcpServerChannel` programmatically, and define `9000` as listening port in the constructor.

Next we register the channel in the .NET Remoting runtime with the static method `ChannelServices.RegisterChannel()`. `ChannelServices` is a utility class to help with channel registration and discovery.

Using the `RemotingConfiguration` class we register a well-known object on the server by calling `RegisterWellKnownServiceType()`. The helper class `WellKnownServiceTypeEntry` can be used to specify all the values that are required for well-known objects that are registered on the server. Calling the constructor of this class we specify the type of the remote object `MyRemoteObject`, the endpoint name `SimpleServer/MyRemoteObject`, and the mode that is one value of the enumeration `WellKnownObjectMode: SingleCall`:

```
// SimpleServer.cs

using System;
using System.Runtime.Remoting;
using System.Runtime.Remoting.Channels;
using System.Runtime.Remoting.Channels.Tcp;
namespace Wrox.Samples
{
   class SimpleServer
   {
      static void Main(string[] args)
      {

         // Create and register the server channel

         TcpServerChannel channel = new TcpServerChannel(9000);
         ChannelServices.RegisterChannel(channel);

         // Register the remote object type and endpoint

         WellKnownServiceTypeEntry remObj = new
            WellKnownServiceTypeEntry(
               typeof(MyRemoteObject),
               "SimpleServer/MyRemoteObject",
               WellKnownObjectMode.SingleCall);
         RemotingConfiguration.RegisterWellKnownServiceType(remObj);
         Console.WriteLine("Press return to exit");
         Console.ReadLine();
      }
   }
}
```

With the compilation of the server we now have to reference the assembly of the remote object as the type is used in our code:

143

```
csc /target:exe /reference:MyRemoteObject.dll SimpleServer.cs
```

Nothing has really changed with the server and the remote object, so we can use the same client application we created earlier to communicate with the new server. To complete the picture, we will change the client code as can be seen below:

```csharp
// SimpleClient.cs

using System;
using System.Runtime.Remoting;
using System.Runtime.Remoting.Channels;
using System.Runtime.Remoting.Channels.Tcp;
namespace Wrox.Samples
{
    class SimpleClient
    {
        static void Main(string[] args)
        {

            // Create and register the client channel

            TcpClientChannel channel = new TcpClientChannel();
            ChannelServices.RegisterChannel(channel);

            // Register the name and port of the remote object

            WellKnownClientTypeEntry entry = new WellKnownClientTypeEntry(
                typeof(MyRemoteObject),
                "tcp://localhost:9000/SimpleServer/MyRemoteObject");
            RemotingConfiguration.RegisterWellKnownClientType(entry);
```

Now a client channel from the class `TcpClientChannel` is instantiated and registered. We use the `WellKnownClientTypeEntry` class to define the remote object. In contrast to the server version of this class, the complete path to the remote object must be specified here as we have to know the server name in the client, but the mode is not specified because this is defined from the server. The `RemotingConfiguration` class is then used to register this remote object in the remoting runtime.

As we saw earlier, the remote object can be instantiated with the new operator. To demonstrate that a well-known object gets activated with every method call, the method `Hello()` is now called five times in a for loop:

```csharp
            MyRemoteObject obj = new MyRemoteObject();
            for (int i=0; i < 5; i++)
                Console.WriteLine(obj.Hello());
        }
    }
}
```

Running this program we can see in the output of the server (see screenshot opposite) that a new instance of the remote object is not created by calling the new operator in the client code, but with every method call instead. Well-known objects could also be called **server-activated** objects as compared to client-activated objects. With client-activated objects a new object gets instantiated on the server when the client invokes the new operator:

```
Visual Studio.NET Command Prompt - simpleserver
D:\Pro C# Web Services\SimpleServer\bin\Debug>simpleserver
Press return to exit
Constructor called
Constructor called
Hello called
Constructor called
Hello called
Constructor called
Hello called
Constructor called
Hello called
Constructor called
Hello called
```

One important fact that we should remember with well-known objects:

> **A well-known object doesn't have state. A new instance is created with every method call.**

Activator.GetObject

Instead of using the `new` operator to instantiate remote objects, we can use the `Activator` class. Behind the scenes in the implementation of the `new` operator this class is used not only for remote but also for local object instantiations. For well-known objects the static method `GetObject()` returns a proxy to the remote object.

Using `Activator.GetObject()` instead of the `new` operator we no longer need to register the well known client type, because the URL to the remote object must be passed as argument to the `GetObject()` method:

```
// Create and register the client channel

TcpClientChannel channel = new TcpClientChannel();
ChannelServices.RegisterChannel(channel);
MyRemoteObject obj = (MyRemoteObject)Activator.GetObject(
    typeof(MyRemoteObject),
    "tcp://localhost:9000/SimpleServer/MyRemoteObject");
```

Whether we use the `new` operator or the `Activator.GetObject()` method is just a matter of choice. The `new` operator is easier to use and hides the fact that we deal with remote objects. `GetObject()` is nearer to the reality as the name of this method clearly shows that a new object does not get instantiated. We already know that with both versions when we use well-known objects a proxy is returned, and no connection to the server happens at this time.

Singletons

Well-known objects can be in `SingleCall` mode or `Singleton`. With the `SingleCall` mode an object is created with every method call; with a `Singleton` only **one** object is created in all. `Singleton` objects can be used to share information between multiple clients.

Using a configuration file the only change that must be done to the server is setting the mode attribute of the <wellknown> element to Singleton:

```
<wellknown
    mode="Singleton"
    type="Wrox.Samples.MyRemoteObject, MyRemoteObject"
    objectUri="MyRemoteObject" />
```

Without using a configuration file, the enumeration WellKnownObjectMode.SingleCall has to be replaced with WellKnownObjectMode.Singleton:

```
WellKnownServiceTypeEntry remObj = new WellKnownServiceTypeEntry(
    typeof(MyRemoteObject),
    "SimpleServer/MyRemoteObject",
    WellKnownObjectMode.Singleton);
RemotingConfiguration.RegisterWellKnownServiceType(remObj);
```

No changes are required for the client.

Multiple threads are used on the server to fulfill concurrent requests from clients. We have to develop this remote object in a thread-safe manner. For more about thread issues see the Wrox book Professional C#.

> One more aspect of singletons that must be thought of is scalability. A **Singleton** object can't be spread across multiple servers. If scalability across multiple servers may be needed, don't use singletons.

Client-Activated Objects

Unlike well-known objects, client-activated objects can have state. A client-activated object is instantiated on the server when the client creates it, and not with every method call.

> We can define properties in a client-activated object. The client can set values and get these values back, but we should be aware that every call across the network takes time. For performance reasons, it is better to pass more data with a single method call instead of doing multiple calls across the network.

Configuration Files

For client-activated objects the **server configuration file** must set the tag <activated> instead of <wellknown>. With the <activated> tag, only the type attribute with the class and assembly name must be defined. It is not necessary to define a URL for the remote object because it will be instantiated by its type. For well-known objects, a URL is required, but client-activated objects use the type for activation. The .NET Runtime automatically creates a unique URL to the remote object instance for client-activated objects. The URL that we defined for well-known objects is not unique for a single instance, but because a well-known instance is newly created with every method call a unique URL is not required:

```
<configuration>
    <system.runtime.remoting>
        <application name="SimpleServer">
            <service>
                <activated type="Wrox.Samples.MyRemoteObject,
                           MyRemoteObject" />
            </service>
            <channels>
                <channel ref="tcp server" port="9000" />
            </channels>
        </application>
    </system.runtime.remoting>
</configuration>
```

The client configuration file requires a similar change:

```
<configuration>
    <system.runtime.remoting>
        <application name="SimpleClient">
            <client url="tcp://localhost:9000/SimpleServer">
                <activated
                    type="Wrox.Samples.MyRemoteObject, MyRemoteObject" />
            </client>
            <channels>
                <channel ref="tcp client" />
            </channels>
        </application>
    </system.runtime.remoting>
</configuration>
```

Using the same code for the server and the client that we used before with the old configuration files, the constructor of the remote object is just called once for every calling of the new operator. Calling methods doesn't create new objects.

RemotingConfiguration

As we have seen before with well-known objects, we can register client-activated objects programmatically too. The server has to call RemotingConfiguration.RegisterActivatedServiceType(), and the client RemotingConfiguration.RegisterActivatedClientType() if we want to create and register the remote object programmatically. Similar to using the configuration file we have to set the type of the remote object using this method.

Non-default Constructor

With client-activated remote objects, it is possible to use a non-default constructor. This is not possible with well-known objects because a new object is created with every method call. We'll change the class MyRemoteObject in the file MyRemoteObject.cs to demonstrate non-default constructors and keeping state with client-activated remote objects:

```
public class MyRemoteObject : System.MarshalByRefObject
{
    public MyRemoteObject(int state)
    {
        Console.WriteLine("Constructor called");
        this.state = state;
```

```
        }
        private int state;
        public int State
        {
            get
            {
                return state;
            }
            set
            {
                state = value;
            }
        }
        public string Hello()
        {
            Console.WriteLine("Hello called");
            return "Hello, .NET Client!";
        }
    }
```

Now, in `SimpleClient.cs` we can invoke the constructor using the `new` operator as can be seen in this example:

```
RemotingConfiguration.Configure("SimpleClient.exe.config");
MyRemoteObject obj = new MyRemoteObject(333);
int x = obj.State;
Console.WriteLine(x);
```

Activator.CreateInstance

Instead of using the `new` operator, we can create client-activated objects with the `Activator` class. Well-known objects have to be created with the `GetObject()` method; client-activated objects require the method `CreateInstance()` because here the remote object really is instantiated on request of the client. With the method `CreateInstance()` it is also possible to invoke non-default constructors.

The following code example shows a client without a configuration file. The channel is created and registered as before. With `Activator.CreateInstance()` we instantiate a client-activated remote object. This method accepts activation attributes. One of these attributes must be the URL to the remote server. The class `System.Runtime.Remoting.Activation.UrlAttribute` can be used to define the URL of the remote object that is passed to the `CreateInstance()` method.

> *We can also use overloaded versions of `CreateInstance()` that don't accept activation arguments if we use a configuration file or the utility class `RemotingConfiguration` to define the URL to the remote object.*

The second argument of `CreateInstance` allows passing arguments to the constructor. To allow a flexible number of arguments, this parameter is of type `object[]` where we can pass any data type. In the `MyRemoteObject` class we now have a constructor that accepts a single `int` value, so we create an object array with one element, and assign an `int` value to that element of the array. The `attrs` array that is also an object array also has only one element. This is a `URLAttribute` where we pass the URL to the remote object to the constructor of this class. Both arrays are passed into the `CreateInstance()` method together with the type of the remote object to create the remote object in the right place using the appropriate constructor:

```
// SimpleClient.cs

using System;
using System.Runtime.Remoting;
using System.Runtime.Remoting.Channels;
using System.Runtime.Remoting.Channels.Tcp;
using System.Runtime.Remoting.Activation;

namespace Wrox.Samples
{
    class SimpleClient
    {
        static void Main(string[] args)
        {
            TcpClientChannel channel = new TcpClientChannel();
            ChannelServices.RegisterChannel(channel);
            object[] constr = new object[1];
            constr[0] = 333;
            object[] attrs = {
                    new UrlAttribute("tcp://localhost:9000/SimpleServer") };
            MyRemoteObject obj = (MyRemoteObject)Activator.CreateInstance(
                    typeof(MyRemoteObject), constr, attrs);
            int x = obj.State;
            Console.WriteLine(x);
        }
    }
}
```

Lease-Based Lifetime

A well-known single-call object can be garbage-collected after the method call of the client because it doesn't hold state. This is different for long-lived objects, which means both client-activated and well-known singleton objects. If the remote object is deactivated before the client stops using it, the client will get a RemotingException that the object has been disconnected with the next method call that is made from the client. The object has to be activated as long as the client needs it. What if the client crashes and if it cannot inform the server that the object is not needed any more? Microsoft's DCOM technology used a ping mechanism where the client regularly pings the server to inform it that the client is still alive and which objects it needs, but this is not scalable to internet solutions. Imagine thousands or millions of continuous ping requests going through the server. The network and the server would be loaded unnecessarily. .NET Remoting uses a **lease-based lifetime mechanism** instead. Comparing this mechanism to cars, if we lease a car we do not hear anything from the leasing company for months after the lease was instantiated. The object also remains activated until the lease time runs out with the .NET Remoting leasing facility.

> If the exception RemotingException: **Object <URI> has been disconnected or does not exist at the server** occurs, this may be because of an expired lease time.

There are some ways in which we can influence leasing times of objects. One way is to use configuration files, and another way is to do it programmatically for the server, the remote object, or in the client. Let us look at what can be configured first.

The remote object has a maximum time to lease which is defined with the LeaseTime option. If the client does not need the remote object for this time period, the object will be deactivated. Every time the client invokes a method with the remote object the leasing time **is incremented** by a value that is defined with RenewOnCallTime.

Sponsor

Let's compare.NET Remoting leasing again with the leasing of cars. If someone pays for the lease of the car, they are a sponsor. We have sponsors with .NET Remoting, too. If we don't want to rely on the client to invoke methods to extend the lifetime, we can use a **sponsor**. Using a sponsor is a good way to have long-running objects where we don't know how long the object will be needed for, or when the time intervals at which the client makes calls to the object are unforeseeable. The sponsor can **extend** the lease of the remote object. If the leasing time is expired, the sponsor is asked if it extends the lease. The default time until a call to a sponsor is timed out is defined with the SponsorshipTimeout option. If that time is reached, another sponsor can be asked. The option LeaseManagerPollTime defines the time the sponsor has to return a lease time extension.

The default values for the lease configuration options are listed in this table:

Lease Configuration	Default Value (seconds)
leaseTime	300
renewOnCallTime	120
sponsorshipTimeout	120
leaseManagerPollTime	10

LifetimeServices

There are several methods available to change the options for lifetime services. With the System.Runtime.Remoting.Lifetime.LifetimeServices class we can set default leasing time options that are valid *for all objects in the application domain* using static properties of this class.

Configuration Files

We can also write the lifetime configuration in the application **configuration file** of the server. This way this configuration is valid *for the complete application*. For the application configuration file we have the <lifetime> tag where leaseTime, sponsorshipTimeout, renewOnCallTime, and pollTime can be configured using attributes:

```
<configuration>
   <system.runtime.remoting>
      <application name="SimpleServer">
         <lifetime
            leaseTime = "15M"
            sponsorshipTimeOut = "4M"
            renewOnCallTime = "3M"
            pollTime = "30S" />
      </application>
   </system.runtime.remoting>
</configuration>
```

Overriding InitializeLifetimeService

Setting the lifetime options in the configuration file is useful if we want to have the same lifetime management for all objects of the server. If we have remote objects with different lifetime requirements, it would be better to set the lifetime for the object programmatically. In the remote object class we can override the method `InitializeLifetimeService()` as we can see in the following example. The method `InitializeLifetimeService()` of the base class `MarshalByRefObject` returns a reference to the `ILease` interface that can be used to change the default values. Changing the values is only possible as long as the lease has not been activated, so that's why we check for the current state to compare it with the enumeration value `LeaseState.Initial`. We set the `InitialLeaseTime` to the very short value of one minute and the `RenewOnCallTime` to 20 seconds so that we soon see the results of the new behavior in the client application:

```csharp
// MyRemoteObject.cs

using System;
using System.Runtime.Remoting.Lifetime;
namespace Wrox.Samples
{
    public class MyRemoteObject : System.MarshalByRefObject
    {
        public MyRemoteObject(int state)
        {
            Console.WriteLine("Constructor called");
            this.state = state;
        }
        public override object InitializeLifetimeService()
        {
            ILease lease = (ILease)base.InitializeLifetimeService();
            if (lease.CurrentState == LeaseState.Initial)
            {
                lease.InitialLeaseTime = TimeSpan.FromMinutes(1);
                lease.RenewOnCallTime = TimeSpan.FromSeconds(20);
            }
            return lease;
        }
        private int state;
        public int State
        {
            get
            {
                return state;
            }
            set
            {
                state = value;
            }
        }
        public string Hello()
        {
            Console.WriteLine("Hello called");
            return "Hello, .NET Client!";
        }
    }
```

I'm changing the client code a little bit so that we can see the effects of the lease time. After the remote object is created, we do a loop five times to call the helper method DisplayLease() before we sleep for 20 seconds. The method DisplayLease() gets the ILease interface of the remote object by calling the method GetLifetimeService(). No exception is thrown if the object that is returned from GetLifetimeService() is not a ILease interface. This can be the case if the remote object is a well-known type that doesn't support the leasing mechanism. Calling the property CurrentLeaseTime we access the actual value of the lease to display it in the console.

```csharp
// SimpleClient.cs

using System;
using System.Runtime.Remoting;
using System.Runtime.Remoting.Lifetime;
using System.Threading;
namespace Wrox.Samples
{
    class SimpleClient
    {
        static void Main(string[] args)
        {
            try
            {
                RemotingConfiguration.Configure("SimpleClient.exe.config");
                MyRemoteObject obj = new MyRemoteObject(33);
                for (int i=0; i < 5; i++)
                {
                    DisplayLease("In loop: " + i, obj);
                    Thread.Sleep(20000);
                }
                Thread.Sleep(30000);
                obj.Hello();
            }
            catch(RemotingException ex)
            {
                Console.WriteLine(ex.Message);
            }
        }
        public static void DisplayLease(string s, MarshalByRefObject o)
        {
            ILease lease = o.GetLifetimeService() as ILease;
            if (lease != null)
            {
                Console.WriteLine(s + " - remaining lease time: " +
                        lease.CurrentLeaseTime);
            }
        }
    }
}
```

Running the client application we now see the displays from the loop. The initial lifetime of the remote object is nearly 60 seconds because we have set the InitialLeaseTime property to one minute. The lifetime is reduced with the following loops. Starting with loop number two, the lifetime remains constant with 20 seconds. This is because we have set RenewOnCallTime property to 20 seconds. Every time we ask for the current value of the lifetime we do a new call on the remote object, so the lease time is set to 20 seconds. After we exit the loop we wait another 30 seconds, and this time the remote object is already garbage-collected because the lifetime has been exceeded, so we get a RemotingException the next time we call a method:

```
Visual Studio .NET Command Prompt                                    _ □ X

D:\books\c# web services\code\chap06\lifetime>simpleclient
In loop: 0 - remaining lease time: 00:00:59.9599424
In loop: 1 - remaining lease time: 00:00:39.9511712
In loop: 2 - remaining lease time: 00:00:19.9899856
In loop: 3 - remaining lease time: 00:00:19.9899856
In loop: 4 - remaining lease time: 00:00:20
Object </4de2a5cd_8eba_488a_9f88_1efa150b25f5/13.rem> has been disconnected or d
oes not exist at the server.

D:\books\c# web services\code\chap06\lifetime>_
```

ClientSponsor

The third option to change the values for the lifetime services is by implementing a sponsor. A sponsor for an Indy cart team gives money to the team, so that the team can do its job. This is similar to remoting: a sponsor extends the lifetime of an object so that the object can do its job. Without a sponsor, the client would have to make method calls on the remote object to keep it alive.

The .NET Remoting runtime uses the ISponsor interface to extend the lifetime of remote objects using sponsoring. ISponsor defines the method Renewal(), which is called by the .NET remoting infrastructure to extend the lease time of the current object. This method has the following signature:

```
TimeSpan Renewal(ILease lease);
```

With the lease argument we can read the current configuration and the actual status of the lease time; with the return value we have to define the additional lease time for the object.

The class ClientSponsor provides a default implementation for a sponsor. ClientSponsor implements the interface ISponsor. ClientSponsor also derives from MarshalByRefObject, so it can be called across the network:

ClientSponsor Properties and Methods	Description
RenewalTime	This property defines the time that is used to extend the leasing time of the remote object.
Register()	With this method we can register a specified remote object with the sponsor, so that the sponsor answers requests for this object. The challenge with this method is that it must be called in the process of the remote object, because it adds the managed object to the sponsor table of this process.
Unregister()	Sponsorship is canceled. Unregister() removes the remote object from the sponsor table.
Renewal()	Renewal() is the method that is called by the runtime to extend the lifetime.
Close()	Close() clears the list of objects managed with this sponsor.

ClientSponsor Example

A useful place to put the sponsor is in the client process as shown in the next diagram. This has the advantage that the sponsor will not extend the lifetime of the remote object when the client is not reachable:

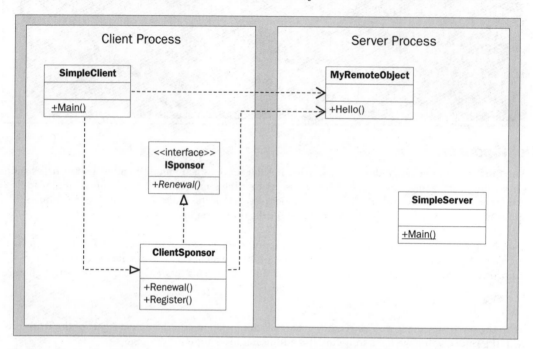

The client must create an instance of the ClientSponsor class, and call the Register() method where the remote object must be registered. As a result of this registration, the remoting runtime calls the Renewal() method that is defined with the ISponsor interface to renew the lifetime.

To demonstrate the calls to the sponsor in action I have created a MySponsor class that derives from ClientSponsor in the client application. The only thing that this class should do differently from the base class is answering Renewal() requests and writing **Renew called** to the console.

> *Renewal() is not declared virtual in the base class so we have to add an implements declaration of the ISponsor interface and implement this method explicitly. After writing "Renew called" to the console we just return the renewal time value that is defined by the RenewalTime property of the client sponsor.*

```
// SimpleClient.cs

// ...

public class MySponsor: ClientSponsor, ISponsor
{
    TimeSpan ISponsor.Renewal(ILease lease)
    {
        Console.WriteLine("Renewal called");
        return this.RenewalTime;
    }
}
```

The following code example shows the `Main()` method of the client that creates a sponsor and sets the `RenewalTime` of the sponsor:

```
// SimpleClient.cs

// ...

static void Main(string[] args)
{
    RemotingConfiguration.Configure("SimpleClient.exe.config");
    MyRemoteObject obj = new MyRemoteObject(333);
    MySponsor sponsor = new MySponsor();
    sponsor.RenewalTime = TimeSpan.FromMinutes(2);
    sponsor.Register(obj);
```

The sponsor is a remote object created in the client process. Here, the server acts as a client when doing the renewal, and the client acts as server when the sponsor is called. To support this, the channel for the client must support a client and a server channel, and the same is also true for the channel running on the server.

To see the sponsor in action we'll add a `for` loop to the `Main()` method in the file `SimpleClient.cs`. The time to sleep is longer than the configured `RenewalTime`, so we should see calls to the sponsor:

```
for (int i=0; i < 20; i++)
{
    DisplayLease("In loop: " + i, obj);
    obj.Hello();
    Thread.Sleep(25000);
}
```

We have to change the configuration files and use the `TcpChannel` instead of the `TcpClientChannel` in the client configuration file `SimpleClient.exe.config`, because this channel has the functionality of both a client and server channel. If we start both the client and server application on the same system, we also have to configure a different port. Here I'm using port 9002, so we can run the application on a single system:

```
<channels>
    <channel ref="tcp" port="9002" />
</channels>
```

The server configuration file `SimpleServer.exe.config` needs a similar change:

```
<channels>
    <channel ref="tcp" port="9000" />
</channels>
```

Running the Example

The console output of the client application in the screenshot overleaf lists the lease times of the remote object. The first line shows a lease time value that is near to 60 seconds; this was the initial lease time. 25 seconds later the second iteration of the loop happened. The garbage collection doesn't happen immediately after the time 0 is reached, so the remote object was lucky that the lease time was extended twice to 20 seconds after a wait (loops 2 and 3), but the `Renewal()` method still wasn't called. Before loop 4, the `Renewal()` method was called for the first time, and here the lease was extended to the value that the sponsor supports, 2 minutes. The lease time again is decremented, before `Renewal()` is called again before loop 10:

```
Visual Studio .NET Command Prompt                                    _ □ X
D:\books\c# web services\code\chap06\sponsor>simpleclient
In loop: 0 - remaining lease time: 00:00:59.9499280
In loop: 1 - remaining lease time: 00:00:34.9439712
In loop: 2 - remaining lease time: 00:00:20
In loop: 3 - remaining lease time: 00:00:20
Renewal called
In loop: 4 - remaining lease time: 00:01:58.6180128
In loop: 5 - remaining lease time: 00:01:33.6120560
In loop: 6 - remaining lease time: 00:01:08.6060992
In loop: 7 - remaining lease time: 00:00:43.6001424
In loop: 8 - remaining lease time: 00:00:20
In loop: 9 - remaining lease time: 00:00:20
Renewal called
In loop: 10 - remaining lease time: 00:01:58.6079984
In loop: 11 - remaining lease time: 00:01:33.6020416
In loop: 12 - remaining lease time: 00:01:08.5960848
In loop: 13 - remaining lease time: 00:00:43.5901280
In loop: 14 - remaining lease time: 00:00:20
In loop: 15 - remaining lease time: 00:00:20
Renewal called
In loop: 16 - remaining lease time: 00:01:58.6280272
In loop: 17 - remaining lease time: 00:01:33.6220704
In loop: 18 - remaining lease time: 00:01:08.6161136
In loop: 19 - remaining lease time: 00:00:43.6101568
```

Remote Object Types Summary

We have now seen the types of the remote objects and their purpose. Let's summarize the features of these objects in the following table.

Object Type	Time of Object Activation	State	Leasing
Well-known `SingleCall`	With every method call	Stateless	No
Well-known `Singleton`	Only once with the first method call	State shared for all clients	Yes
Client-Activated	When the client instantiates the remote object	State	Yes

Activation

So far we have seen different object types and how these remote objects can be activated using the `new` operator and the `Activator` class. Depending whether the object type is a well-known object or a client-activated object we can use `GetObject()` or `CreateInstance()`. Let us look further into the client side to see what happens on the client that we can also make use of.

RemotingServices.Connect

Instead of using the `new` operator or the `Activator` class it is also possible to use the static method `Connect()` of the class `RemotingServices` for well-known objects. This method doesn't really instantiate the connection as we maybe would assume from its name. A connection is not needed at this point, but all the information passed here will be used to build up the connection when the first method call is made.

In this code example below, we create a proxy by calling `RemotingServices.Connect()`. This method requires the type of the remote object as we have seen with the `Activator` class, and the URL string to the remote object:

```
static void Main(string[] args)
{
    RemotingConfiguration.Configure("SimpleClient.exe.config");
    MyRemoteObject obj =
        (MyRemoteObject)RemotingServices.Connect(
        typeof(MyRemoteObject),
        "tcp://localhost:9000/SimpleServer/MyRemoteObject");
```

Error Messages

If the connection string that is used with the `Connect()` method is wrong, we get an error the first time that a remote method is called.

The possible error messages we can get are listed here:

❏ SocketException: No such host is known.

This error message occurs when the host name cannot be resolved.

❏ SocketException: No connection could be made because the target machine actively refused it.

If the specified port number is incorrect or the server is not started, we will get this error message.

❏ RemotingException: Object <Name> has been disconnected or does not exist at the server.

This error message occurs if the name of the endpoint is incorrectly specified, or when the leasing time has expired when using a client-activated object.

Proxy

`RemotingServices.Connect()` defines the connection and **creates a proxy**. No matter which options are used to create remote objects, it is always a proxy that is created and returned by the creation methods. The proxy looks just like the real object as it has the same public methods; but the proxy just converts the method call to a message so that it can be sent across the network.

We actually create two objects in this case: the **transparent proxy** and the **real proxy**. The transparent proxy is the one used by the client. It looks like the remote object with the same public methods. This proxy is created dynamically by reading the metadata of the assembly from the remote object. The transparent proxy itself uses the real proxy to create messages from method calls. The transparent proxy is an instance of the class `System.Runtime.Remoting.Proxies.__ TransparentProxy`. This class is internal to the `mscorlib` assembly, so we cannot derive custom proxies from it, and we won't find it in the MSDN documentation.

In the picture below we can see that the client uses the __TransparentProxy. The transparent proxy has the method Hello() because this method is available from the remote object. The transparent proxy creates an object that implements the interface IMessage to pass it to the Invoke() method of the RealProxy. IMessage contains the method name and parameters that can be accessed through the property IMessage.Properties. The real proxy transforms this into an IMethodCallMessage and sends it to the remote object through the channel.

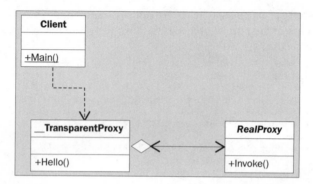

With the utility class RemotingServices we can check if the object really is a proxy to the remote object and not the remote object itself with the static method IsTransparentProxy(). The method RemotingServices.GetRealProxy() returns a reference to the RealProxy class:

```
MyRemoteObject obj = new MyRemoteObject();
if (RemotingServices.IsTransparentProxy(obj))
{
    Console.WriteLine("a transparent proxy!");
    RealProxy proxy = RemotingServices.GetRealProxy(obj);
}
```

An example where the method IsTransparentProxy() returns false is the case where the remote object is instantiated locally in the application domain. This would be the case if we do a new of the remote object class inside the server application. No proxy is needed for the server, of course, because it won't need to invoke the object on a different system.

Messages

The proxy deals with messages. All message objects implement the interface IMessage. IMessage contains a dictionary of the method name and parameters that can be accessed through the property IMessage.Properties.

In the namespace System.Runtime.Remoting.Messaging more message interfaces and classes are defined. The interfaces are specialized versions for passing and returning methods for example IMethodMessage, IMethodCallMessage, and IMethodReturnMessage. These interfaces have specialized properties that give faster access to method names and parameters. With these interfaces, it is not necessary to deal with the dictionary to access this data.

Marshaling

Marshaling is the term used when an object is converted so that it can be sent across the network (or across processes or application domains). Unmarshaling creates an object from the marshaled data.

With **marshal-by-value (MBV)** the object is serialized into the channel, and a copy of the object is created on the other side of the network. The object to marshal is stored into a stream, and the stream is used to build a copy of the object on the other side with the unmarshaling sequence. **Marshaling-by-reference (MBR)** creates a proxy on the client that is used to communicate with the remote object. The marshaling sequence of a remote object creates an `ObjRef` instance that itself can be serialized across the network.

Objects that are derived from `MarshalByRefObject` are always marshaled by reference – as the name of the base class says. To marshal a remote object the static method `RemotingServices.Marshal()` is used.

`RemotingServices.Marshal()` has these overloaded versions:

```
public static ObjRef Marshal(MarshalByRefObject obj);
public static ObjRef Marshal(MarshalByRefObject obj, string objUri);
public static ObjRef Marshal(MarshalByRefObject obj, string objUri,
        Type requestedType);
```

The first argument `obj` specifies the object to marshal. The `objUri` is the path that is stored within the marshaled object reference; it can be used to access the remote object. The `requestedType` can be used to pass a different type of the object to the object reference. This is useful if the client using the remote object shouldn't use the object class but an interface that the remote object class implements instead. In this scenario the interface is the `requestedType` that should be used for marshaling.

ObjRef

With all these `Marshal()` methods an `ObjRef` is returned. The `ObjRef` is serializable because it implements the interface `ISerializable`, and can be marshaled by value. The `ObjRef` knows about the location of the remote object: the host name, the port number, and the object name. `RemotingServices.Unmarshal()` uses the `ObjRef` to create a proxy that will be used by the client.

Passing Objects

With methods of remote objects we can pass basic data types and classes that we define. Whether an object is passed by value or by reference depends on the class declaration, as we will see next. We will add two methods to the class `MyRemoteObject` that return objects of class A and B. Class A will be serializable and passed using MBV to the client, B will be remotable and passed using MBR.

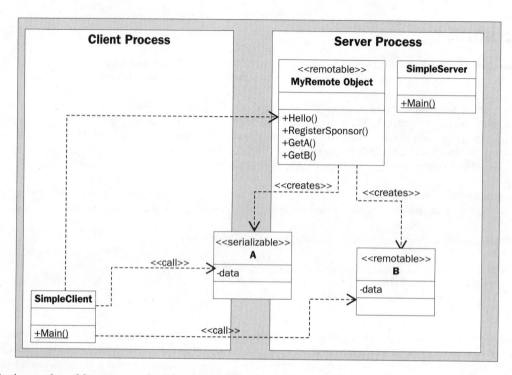

Let's start by adding two methods to the remote object class `MyRemoteObject` in the file `MyRemoteObject.cs` that returns objects of class `A` and `B` with the methods `GetA()` and `GetB()`. We will create the classes `A` and `B` in the next section:

```
// MyRemoteObject.cs

using System;

namespace Wrox.Samples
{
    public class MyRemoteObject : System.MarshalByRefObject
    {
        public MyRemoteObject()
        {
            Console.WriteLine("MyRemoteObject constructor called");
        }

        // serialized version

        public A GetA()
        {
            return new A(11);
        }

        // remote version

        public B GetB()
        {
            return new B(22);
        }
```

```
      public string Hello()
      {
         Console.WriteLine("Hello called");
         return "Hello, .NET Client!";
      }
   }
}
```

Marshal-By-Value

To create a class that will be serialized across the network, the class must be marked with the attribute [Serializable]. Objects of these classes don't have a remote identity, as they are marshaled to a stream before they're sent to the channel, and unmarshaled on the other side.

We add class A to the file MyRemoteObject.cs. This class has a field of type int that is also serializable. If a class is marked serializable, but has a reference to a class that is not serializable, the exception SerializationException will be thrown when marshaling this class. The class A defines the read-only property Data where the value of the field data is returned:

```
[Serializable]
public class A
{
   private int data;
   public A(int data)
   {
      Console.WriteLine("Constructor of serializable class A called");
      this.data = data;
   }
   public int Data
   {
      get
      {
         Console.WriteLine("A.Data called");
         return data;
      }
   }
}
```

Marshal-By-Reference

A class that should be called remotely is derived from MarshalByRefObject. We have used this class already for our remote object.

We add class B also to MyRemoteObject.cs. This class is similar to class A with the exception that it is not marked serializable; instead it derives from the class MarshalByRefObject. When we pass class B across the network, a proxy will be created.

Behind the scenes, RemotingServices.Marshal() is called to create an ObjRef, this object reference is sent across the channel, and with RemotingServices.Unmarshal() this object reference is used to create a proxy:

```
public class B : MarshalByRefObject
{
   private int data;
```

```
      public B(int data)
      {
         Console.WriteLine("Constructor of remotable class B called");
         this.data = data;
      }
      public int Data
      {
         get
         {
            Console.WriteLine("B.Data called");
            return data;
         }
      }
   }
}
```

Client Example

The server is the same as we have created previously. It is entirely our choice whether we create the channel programmatically or with a configuration file, and whether we use a well-known or a client-activated object.

In the client we can now call the new methods of the remote object class. Let us change the Main() method in the file SimpleClient.cs to call the newly created remote methods:

```
static void Main(string[] args)
{
   RemotingConfiguration.Configure("SimpleClient.exe.config");
   MyRemoteObject obj = new MyRemoteObject();
   obj.Hello();
   A a = obj.GetA();
   int a1 = a.Data;
   B b = obj.GetB();
   int b1 = b.Data;
}
```

The remote object class, the server, and the client can be compiled as we saw earlier. When we start the server and the client, we get the console output of the server. B is a remote class, so B.Data is called on the server as we can see here:

In the client console window we can see the Console.WriteLine() output of the A class because this class was serialized to the client.

Passing objects of classes that are neither marked **[Serializable]** nor derived from **MarshalByRefObject** will generate the exception System.Runtime.Serialization. SerializationException: The type typename is not marked as serializable.

Sending MBR Objects to the Server

Sending marshal-by-value objects from the client to the server is very similar to sending them in the other direction, but what about sending a remotable object to the server? How does the server come back to the client?

Instead of showing the derivation of MarshalByRefObject in this picture, I've introduced a stereotype <<remotable>> to make it easier to read. We can see <<remotable>> as indicatng inheritance from MarshalByRefObject. The MBR class B will be instantiated from the client, and passed with the method SetB() to the remote object MyRemoteObject. The remote object will use the object that was instantiated on the client across the network:

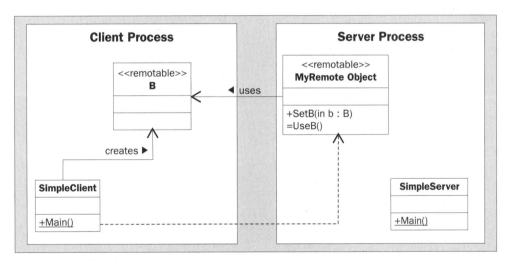

Let's add two methods to the remote object class in the file MyRemoteObject.cs. With the method SetB() the client can pass a remotable object of type B to the server. The method SetB() accepts an object of class B. In the last section we created class B so that it derives from MarshalByRefObject, so the object will not be copied but a proxy will be created instead. The method SetB() stores the reference to the proxy of B in the field b. The method UseB() uses the field b to call the property Data and passes the value returned to the client.

163

```
public class MyRemoteObject : System.MarshalByRefObject
{
    public MyRemoteObject()
    {
        Console.WriteLine("MyRemoteObject Constructor called");
    }
    private B b;
    public void SetB(B b)
    {
        Console.WriteLine("SetB called");
        this.b = b;
    }
    public int UseB()
    {
        Console.WriteLine("UseB called");
        return b.Data;
    }

// ...
```

> One important thing to note here is that the class **MyRemoteObject** now has state.
> Using this class as a well-known object would result in **b** being set to **null** with every
> method call, so **UseB()** wouldn't work. This remote object class can only be used in
> client-activated object configurations.

The client can be changed to call the remote object. In the client code, we create a new instance of the class B and initialize it with the value 44. While obj is instantiated remotely with the new operator, b is created locally because the class B is not listed in the client configuration file, but the class MyRemoteObject is. Accessing the Data property merely performs a local call:

```
// SimpleClient.cs

class SimpleClient
{
    static void Main(string[] args)
    {
        RemotingConfiguration.Configure("SimpleClient.exe.config");
        MyRemoteObject obj = new MyRemoteObject(333);
        obj.Hello();
        B b = new B(44);

        // This is a local call!

        int b1 = b.Data;
```

When calling SetB() with MyRemoteObject, we pass a reference to b to the server. Because B is derived from MarshalByRefObject a reference can be passed. Next we call the UseB() method where this reference is used within the server. The remote object will try to access the object that is running in the client process:

```
        // Pass a reference to the object running in the client
        // to the server
```

164

```
        obj.SetB(b);

        // Use the object in the client from the server

        b1 = obj.UseB();
```

To run this application we have to use a bi-directional channel. Because the client application now has to act both as a client to call methods in the remote object, and as a server where the instance b is invoked from the server, we must use the `TcpChannel` that can do both. If we use the wrong channel, the result will be a `RemotingException` with the following error message:

> The remoting proxy has no channel sinks which means either the server has no registered server channels that are listening, or this application has no suitable client channel to talk to the server.

Be sure to specify a reference to the channel `tcp` in both the client and server configuration files as we did earlier instead of `tcp client` and `tcp server`.

Running the server and client application, we get this output in the client:

The first time we see the output of the `B.Data` is when we access this property locally. The second output we see is when a method of the object running in the client is invoked from the server by calling `obj.UseB()` in the client application.

Tracking Services

A great feature for analyzing a running application is Tracking Services. This service can be used to observe the marshaling process of MBR objects. Indeed it can be very simply activated: we have only to create a tracking handler and register this handler with the utility class `TrackingServices`.

Tracking Handler

A tracking handler implements the interface `ITrackingHandler`. This interface defines three methods that are called by the remoting infrastructure when marshaling and unmarshaling occurs:

ITrackingHandler methods	Description
MarshaledObject,	This method is called when an MBR object is marshaled
UnmarshaledObject	This method is called when an MBR object is unmarshaled
DisconnectedObject	DisconnectedObject() is called when an MBR object is disconnected, for example when the lease time of an client-activated object expires

The class MyTrackingHandler is implemented in the assembly MyTrackingHandler that is available both for the client and the server to make this tracking available both for clients and servers. This class implements the interface ITrackingHandler, so we have to implement the methods MarshaledObject(), UnmarshaledObject(), and DisconnectedObject(). We use the URI property of the ObjRef that is passed to output the path to the object; in addition, we output the type of the marshaled object. With the first argument, it would also be possible to access the properties of the object to marshal:

```
// MyTrackingHandler.cs
using System;
using System.Runtime.Remoting;
using System.Runtime.Remoting.Services;

namespace Wrox.Samples
{
    public class MyTrackingHandler: ITrackingHandler
    {
        public void MarshaledObject(object obj, ObjRef or)
        {
            Console.WriteLine();
            Console.WriteLine("The object " + or.URI + " is marshaled");
            Console.WriteLine("Type: " + or.TypeInfo.TypeName);
        }
        public void UnmarshaledObject(object obj, ObjRef or)
        {
            Console.WriteLine();
            Console.WriteLine("The object " + or.URI + " is unmarshaled");
            Console.WriteLine("Type: " + or.TypeInfo.TypeName);
        }
        public void DisconnectedObject(object obj)
        {
            Console.WriteLine(obj.ToString() + " is disconnected");
        }
    }
}
```

Register Tracking Handler

Both in the server and in the client application, in the files SimpleClient.cs and SimpleServer.cs, we can create a new instance of the MyTrackingHandler class and register it with the tracking service:

```
static void Main(string[] args)
{
    RemotingConfiguration.Configure("SimpleServer.exe.config");
    TrackingServices.RegisterTrackingHandler(new MyTrackingHandler());
```

Running the Program

We run the application with a client that will:

1. Create the remote object MyRemoteObject

2. Call the method obj.GetB() to return the MBR object of class B to the client

3. Call the method obj.SetB() to pass the MBR object of class B to the server

We can see the output in the following screenshots. The first picture shows the server output where MyRemoteObject and B are marshaled, and with the call to SetB(), B is unmarshaled. The last line of the output shows that the lease time of the remote object expired, so it was disconnected:

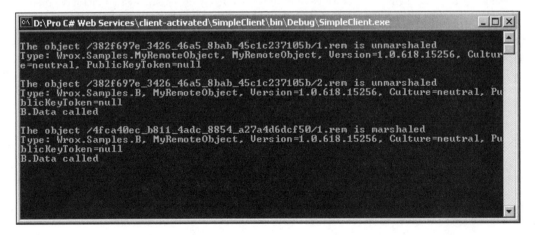

In the client output MyRemoteObject and B are unmarshaled before the call to SetB(), where B is marshaled:

Asynchronous Remoting

Calling remote methods across the network can take some time. We can call the methods asynchronously, which means that we start the methods, and during the time the method call is running on the server we can do some other tasks on the client. .NET Remoting can be used asynchronously in the same way as local methods.

Calling Local Methods Asynchronously

One way to do this is to create a thread that makes the remote call while another thread answers users' requests or does something else. It is a lot easier, however, to do it with the built-in support provided in the .NET Framework in the form of **delegates**. With delegates, threads are created automatically, and we don't have to do it ourselves.

First, let us look at an asynchronous example without calling remote methods.

In the sample class `AsyncLocal` we can see the `LongCall()` method, which takes some time to process. We want to call this method asynchronously:

```
using System;
using System.Threading;
namespace Wrox.Samples
{
    class AsyncLocal
    {
        public void LongCall()
        {
            Console.WriteLine("LongCall started");
            Thread.Sleep(5000);
            Console.WriteLine("LongCall finished");
        }
```

To make this method asynchronous we have to declare a **delegate**. The delegate must have the same signature and return type as the method that should be called asynchronously. The method `LongCall()` accepts no arguments and has a `void` return type, and the same is true for the defined delegate `LongCallDelegate`. With the keyword `delegate` the C# compiler creates a class that is derived either from `Delegate` or from `MulticastDelegate`, depending whether there is a return type or not. We can see this generated class by opening the generated assembly with the `ildasm` utility:

```
        private delegate void LongCallDelegate();
        public AsyncLocal()
        {
        }
```

In the `Main()` method we can now create a new instance of the class `LongCallDelegate`, and pass `obj.LongCall`. The constructor of the delegate class requires the target as an argument. We can look at the delegate as a type-safe, object-oriented function pointer. The object itself is passed with the method name of the function to the constructor:

```
        static void Main(string[] args)
        {
            AsyncLocal obj = new AsyncLocal();
            LongCallDelegate d = new LongCallDelegate(obj.LongCall);
```

Now we can start the method by calling `BeginInvoke()` on the delegate. Visual Studio .NET does not display this method with the IntelliSense feature because it is not available at the time of programming this method call; instead, it will be created as soon as we compile the project. The compiler creates three methods for the delegate class: `Invoke()`, `BeginInvoke()`, and `EndInvoke()`. `Invoke()` can be used to call the method synchronously, whereas `BeginInvoke()` and `EndInvoke()` are used to call the method asynchronously.

`BeginInvoke()` has two arguments in addition to the arguments that are declared with the delegate. With the first argument, an `AsyncCallback` delegate can be passed to this method. With the asynchronous callback, we can define a method with an `IAsyncResult` argument that will be called when the method is finished. In this sample, we pass `null` with both arguments, and put the returned reference to `IAsyncResult` into the variable `ar`:

```
IAsyncResult ar = d.BeginInvoke(null, null);
```

The method call is started asynchronously. We can now doing something else in the main thread at the same time:

```
Thread.Sleep(1000);
Console.WriteLine("Main running concurrently");
```

As soon as we want to be sure that the asynchronous method completed (maybe we need some result from this method), the reference to the `IAsyncResult` interface can be used. With the `IAsyncResult` interface, we can check if the method is finished by checking the `IsCompleted` property. We can wait until the method completes by using the `AsyncWaitHandle` property and call `WaitOne()`. `WaitOne()` is a blocking call that waits until the method that belongs to the `IAsyncResult` is finished:

```
    ar.AsyncWaitHandle.WaitOne();
    if (ar.IsCompleted)
        d.EndInvoke(ar);
    Console.WriteLine("Main finished");
      }
   }
}
```

Calling Remote Methods Asynchronously

The same programming model used for local calls can also be used for remote calls. We will extend the remoting example by using some arguments and return values with a remote method.

First, we extend the remote object class `MyRemoteObject` with the long-running method `LongTimeAdd()`. Nothing else changes with the server:

```
// MyRemoteObject.cs

// ...

    public int LongTimeAdd(int val1, int val2, int ms)
    {
        Thread.Sleep(ms);
        return val1 + val2;
    }
```

In the client program, we have to declare a delegate with the same parameters as the `LongTimeAdd()` method:

```
// SimpleClient.cs

// ...
```

```
class SimpleClient
{
    private delegate int LongTimeAddDelegate(int val1, int val2,
            int ms);
```

In the Main() method after creating the remote object we create a instance of the delegate and pass the method LongTimeAdd to the constructor:

```
static void Main(string[] args)
{
    RemotingConfiguration.Configure("SimpleClient.exe.config");
    MyRemoteObject obj = new MyRemoteObject();
    LongTimeAddDelegate d = new LongTimeAddDelegate(obj.LongTimeAdd);
```

The remote method can now be started asynchronously with the BeginInvoke() method of the delegate class. Instead of two arguments BeginInvoke() now has five arguments – the first three arguments are the ones that are passed to the remote method. Here we pass the values 3 and 4 to add with a sleep time of 100 ms. The method BeginInvoke() will return immediately; we can do some other stuff in the main thread:

```
IAsyncResult ar = d.BeginInvoke(3, 4, 100, null, null);
Console.WriteLine("LongTimeAdd started");
```

To get the result that is returned with the method LongTimeAdd() we have to wait until the method is completed. This is done using ar.AsyncWaitHandle.WaitOne(). Calling the delegate method EndInvoke() we get the result that is returned from LongTimeAdd():

```
ar.AsyncWaitHandle.WaitOne();
if (ar.IsCompleted)
{
    Console.WriteLine("LongTimeAdd finished");
    int result = d.EndInvoke(ar);
    Console.WriteLine("result: " + result);
}
```

Callbacks with Delegates

.NET Remoting supports two types of callbacks: with remote objects that are passed to the server, and with delegates. Using a delegate we can pass a AsyncCallback delegate when calling the method BeginInvoke() to have a callback when the asynchronous remote method completes. We have to define a method that has the same signature and return type that the delegate AsyncCallback defines. The delegate AsyncCallback is defined with this signature in the assembly mscorlib:

```
public delegate void AsyncCallback(IAsyncResult ar);
```

We implement the method LongTimeAddCallback that has the same signature and return type. The implementation of this method is similar to how we handled the asynchronous method in the last code sample. It doesn't matter if the method is implemented as a class method or an instance method. We only need access to the delegate that is used to start the remote method. To make the delegate available to the static method we'll now declare d as static member variable:

```
private delegate int LongTimeAddDelegate(int val1, int val2, int ms);
private static LongTimeAddDelegate d;
public static void LongTimeAddCallback(IAsyncResult ar)
{
    if (ar.IsCompleted)
    {
        Console.WriteLine("LongTimeAdd finished");
        int result = d.EndInvoke(ar);
        Console.WriteLine("result: " + result);
    }
}
```

In the Main() method, we have to create a new instance of the AsyncCallback delegate and pass a reference to the function that should be called asynchronously. With the BeginInvoke() method we pass the instance of the AsyncCallback so that the method LongTimeAddCallback() will be invoked when the remote method LongTimeAdd() completes:

```
static void Main(string[] args)
{
    RemotingConfiguration.Configure("SimpleClient.exe.config");
    MyRemoteObject obj = new MyRemoteObject();
    d = new LongTimeAddDelegate(obj.LongTimeAdd);
    AsyncCallback cb =
                new AsyncCallback(SimpleClient.LongTimeAddCallback);
    IAsyncResult ar = d.BeginInvoke(3, 4, 3000, cb, null);
    Console.WriteLine("LongTimeAdd started");
```

One Way

If a remote method doesn't return a result to the client we can call the method in a **fire-and-forget** style: we call the method asynchronously, but there is no requirement to wait for the method to complete. With .NET Remoting such a method is called **OneWay**: data is sent to the server, but none is returned.

A one way method must be declared with the OneWay attribute in the remote object class. The attribute class OneWayAttribute is part of the namespace System.Runtime.Remoting.Messaging. We add the TakeAWhile() method to the RemoteObjectClass:

```
[OneWay]
public void TakeAWhile(int ms)
{
    Console.WriteLine("TakeAWhile started");
    Thread.Sleep(ms);
    Console.WriteLine("TakeAWhile completed");
}
```

In the client the one way method TakeAWhile() can be called like a synchronous method, but it will be completed asynchronously. The method call will return immediately:

```
MyRemoteObject obj = new MyRemoteObject();
obj.TakeAWhile(5000);
```

If a synchronous method of a remote object throws an exception this exception will be propagated to the client. This is different with OneWay methods:

> If a **OneWay** method throws an exception this exception will not be propagated to the client.

Call Contexts

Client-activated objects can hold state. For this kind of object we must hold state on the server. Well-known objects are stateless. Every time we call a method a new object gets instantiated on the server. We have to pass all the data that we need on the server with every method call, but it is not necessary to pass the data with method arguments. If, for example, a user ID is needed with every method call to the remote object, the **call context** can be used.

The call context flows with the logical thread and is passed with every remote method call. A logical thread is started from the calling thread and flows through all method calls that are started from the calling thread, and passes through different contexts, different application domains, and different processes.

The CallContext class is a utility class in the namespace System.Runtime.Remoting.Messaging. We can add data to the context with CallContext.SetData(), and reading the data can be done with CallContext.GetData().

> We cannot pass basic data types with the context, but only objects of classes that implement the interface **ILogicalThreadAffinative**.

A class that can be passed with the call context must implement the interface ILogicalThreadAffinative. This interface doesn't define a single method; it is just a marker to the .NET Remoting runtime. A logical thread can spawn multiple physical threads as such a call can cross process boundaries, but it is bound to a flow of method calls. Implementing the interface ILogicalThread
Affinative in a class means that objects of this class can flow with the logical thread. Additionally, the class is marked with the Serializable attribute, so that the object can be marshaled into the channel. The class UserName defines a LastName and FirstName property that will flow with every method call:

```
[Serializable]
public class UserName : ILogicalThreadAffinative
{
    public UserName()
    {
    }
    private string lastName;
    public string LastName
    {
        get
        {
            return lastName;
        }
        set
        {
            lastName = value;
        }
    }
    private string firstName;
    public string FirstName
    {
        get
        {
            return firstName;
        }
```

```
            set
            {
                firstName = value;
            }
        }
    }
```

In the client program we can create a `UserName` object that will be passed with the remote method `Hello()`. `CallContext.SetData()` assigns the `UserName` object to the call context:

```
RemotingConfiguration.Configure("SimpleClient.exe.config");
MyRemoteObject obj = new MyRemoteObject();
UserName user = new UserName();
user.FirstName = "Christian";
user.LastName = "Nagel";
CallContext.SetData("User", user);
obj.Hello();
```

In the remote object we can read the call context by calling `CallContext.GetData()`. For the context name "User" a `UserName` object was passed, so we can cast the return value of `GetData()` to `UserName`:

```
public string Hello()
{
    Console.WriteLine("Hello called");
    UserName user = (UserName)CallContext.GetData("User");
    if (user != null)
    {
        Console.WriteLine("context passed from {0} {1}",
                user.FirstName, user.LastName);
    }
    return "Hello, Client!";
}
```

Summary

In this chapter we have covered the .NET Remoting architecture. We looked into the parts of a client / server application using:

- ❏ The remote object that derives from `MarshalByRefObject`

- ❏ A channel that is used for the communication between client and server (we used the TCP channels)

- ❏ The proxy that is used by the client to create messages that are marshaled into the channel

.NET Remoting applications can make use of application configuration files where we can specify channels and remote objects, or all of this can be done programmatically.

.NET Remoting supports both stateful and stateless solutions with client-activated and well-known objects. Stateful objects have a leasing mechanism that is scalable to solutions with thousand of clients. We saw how to pass call contexts to the server.

In the next chapter we will look in more detail at the different channels and formatters that come with the framework, and consider some application scenarios that will illustrate how this technology can be used.

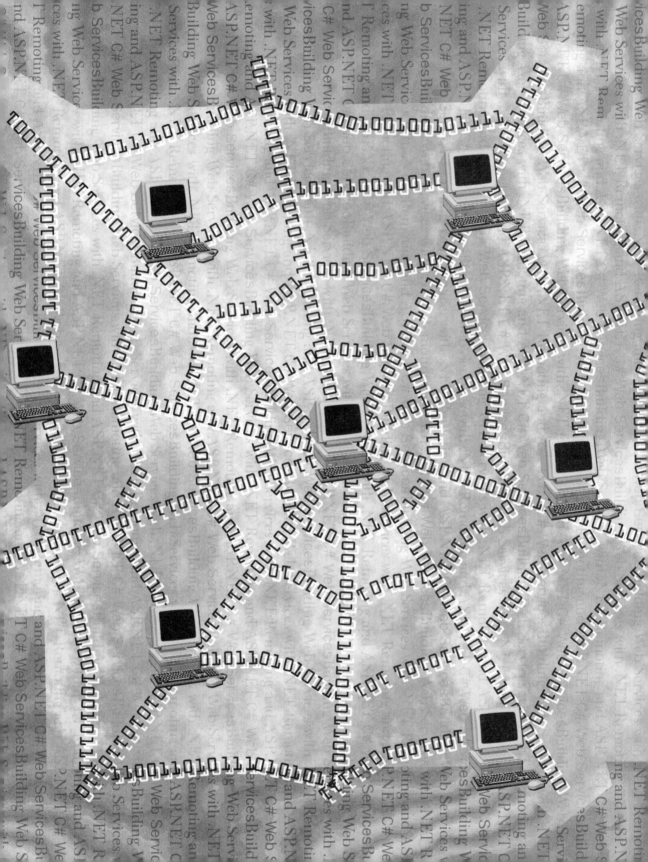

7

Web Services Anywhere

With .NET Remoting, the service can be hosted in any **application type** such as console applications, Windows Forms applications, and so on. Web Services Anywhere doesn't only mean that any application types can be used – it also means that the web service can use any **transport** and any **payload**.

In the last chapter, we discussed the architecture of .NET Remoting, and how channels and formatters fit into it. In this chapter we will look at the application types, transport protocols, and payloads.

The predecessor of .NET Remoting, DCOM, uses the TCP/IP protocol with a DCOM-specific format for data sent between client and server. It's possible to configure other transport protocols such as SPX or NetBEUI, but it is not possible to change how the data is formatted without going to the core.

.NET Remoting allows complete flexibility with both the transport protocol and the formatting options. We can change the transport and formatters independently of one another. Out of the box, we get a TCP channel, an HTTP channel, and SOAP and binary formatters.

In this chapter, we'll be looking at different application types, and at the channels and the formatters that are available with the .NET framework. Particularly we will look at:

- ❑ Application Scenarios
- ❑ Hosting Servers
- ❑ Channels
- ❑ Formatters

As with the previous chapter, the code contained in this chapter can be downloaded from http://www.wrox.com.

Application Scenarios

Web services can be used anywhere with .NET remoting. You can create solutions in intranet environments that replace DCOM, create solutions that include communication with supplier companies using different technologies (including non-Windows platforms), and build a peer-to-peer solution where a Windows Forms application hosts a server and client channel, for example. Let's look into some application scenarios.

XML Web Services

XML web services are used to communicate across the Internet and to enable communication with different technologies such as CORBA and Java. XML web services use SOAP to format method calls. We can use ASP.NET web services as we have seen in Chapters 4 and 5, but we can also use .NET Remoting in this particular scenario. In this case, the server can be hosted in IIS as with ASP.NET web services, but it can equally be hosted in other application types:

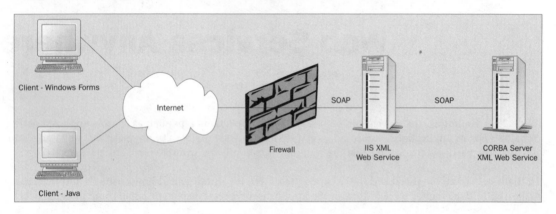

In the diagram above you can see two web services. One is running in the IIS, and another is running in a CORBA Server. With XML web services, different platforms can be used for communication. The server application running on the IIS uses the web service of the CORBA server, and itself offers a service for other clients. The web service that is offered from the IIS Server is used by a Windows Forms client and a Java client across the Internet.

Web Services with Binary Formatters

If both the client and server are created as a .NET application we can use the binary formatter instead of the SOAP formatter. The binary formatter has performance advantages against the SOAP formatter. In this chapter, we will concentrate on the architectural differences between theses formatters. In intranet solutions, we can also use the TCP channel instead of the HTTP channel. The TCP channel has some performance advantages.

> *Some people think that a web service can be used from any platform and any operating system. This is not always the case, and obviously this is not the case with binary formatters. Using binary formatters you are bound to the .NET Framework for both the server and the client. When talking about web services that can be used from any platform, the term **XML web service** should be used.*

Peer-to-Peer Web Services

.NET Remoting can also be used in peer-to-peer scenarios. With peer-to-peer solutions, a system is both a client and a server. We only have the requirement that a server is registered in a central service. A Windows service application running on a server system can be used for this requirement. All client systems can ask the server for running services to contact the peer system directly:

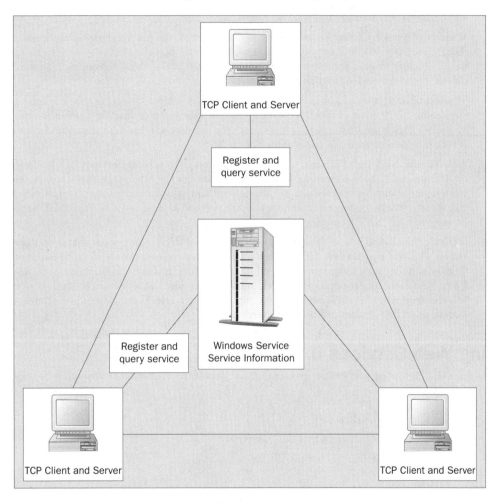

In the diagram above you can see multiple PCs communicating. A central information database is used at application startup to register a service running on the PC, and to get the information about where other services can be found. After application startup, the central server is not needed any more. The PCs can communicate as peers because every one of these has both a client and a server implemented. Napster and Windows Messenger are examples of such a service.

If these PCs offer an XML web service, this can be used over the Internet. If a binary protocol is used, efficient communication within the intranet environment is possible.

Hosting Servers

ASP.NET web services are hosted in Internet Information Services. .NET Remoting web services can be hosted in several different application types:

❑   We can use a **Windows Service** to host the .NET Remoting server. This has the advantage that the server can be started automatically when the system first boots. In the next chapter, we will implement a Windows Service to host a .NET Remoting server.

❑   **Windows Forms** applications or **console** applications can be used as hosting environments for .NET Remoting. A client application can host a remote object so that the server can call it back. For peer-to-peer solutions we can also make use of the .NET Remoting technology to offer services from Windows Forms applications.

There is nothing special about creating a channel and remote objects in this kind of application. In the last chapter, we used console applications as hosting environments; using Windows Forms applications is very similar. We can also use configuration files or create the server programmatically in this instance.

❑   As with ASP.NET web services, we can use **Internet Information Services** as a hosting environment for .NET Remoting web services. This has the advantage that the server is started automatically, and we can use the functionality that is offered by this runtime. It also has some restrictions, however. In this chapter, we will look at how the ASP.NET runtime can be used to host .NET Remoting web services.

❑   It is also possible to host a .NET Remoting server in a .NET component that is configured within a **COM+ application**. Using this application type allows the .NET component to use COM+ services such as transactions and object pooling, but the component can be accessible from .NET remoting instead of DCOM. Windows XP has a new feature that offers web services from COM+ applications by simply selecting a checkbox. Behind the scenes, this feature of COM+ makes use of .NET Remoting.

Hosting Web Services in ASP.NET

To build a .NET Remoting server that uses the infrastructure from Internet Information Services and ASP.NET we must:

❑   Create a virtual web directory

❑   Create a remote object class in a DLL assembly

❑   Configure the remote object in the file `Web.config`.

Let's take a look at each of these steps in turn.

Create a Virtual Web Directory

A virtual directory in IIS can be created using the Internet Services Manager administrative utility with the menu Action | New | Virtual Directory, or by right-clicking the mouse button on a folder you want to share, selecting Sharing in the context menu, and choosing the tab Web Sharing. The Alias that must be entered in the first screen of the resultant wizard specifies the application name that is used to access the remote object, and the Directory string specifies the physical directory where the configuration file of the server application must be found.

We will create a virtual directory called IISHosting for the purposes of this example.

Remote Object Class

The remote object class must be placed inside a component library. The assembly must be put into the `bin` directory of the web application:

```csharp
// MyRemoteObject.cs

using System;
namespace Wrox.Samples
{
   public class MyRemoteObject : MarshalByRefObject
   {
      public MyRemoteObject()
      {
      }
      public string Hello()
      {
         return "Hello, Client";
      }
   }
}
```

We can compile this file to a library and put it into the `bin` directory:

```
csc /target:library /out:bin/MyRemoteObject.dll MyRemoteObject.cs
```

Server Configuration File

The configuration file must be named `web.config` and must be put into the root directory of the web application. With the exception of the file name, it looks very similar to the server configuration files we used in the last chapter, but there are some important differences:

❑   The `<application>` tag may not have a `name` attribute because the virtual web directory already defines the name of the application

❑   Channel information is not needed because an HTTP channel is already present from the ASP.NET runtime

In this configuration file, we define a well-known object. The URI to the object is `MyRemoteObject.soap`. The extension `soap` is often used for objects that use the SOAP formatter, while `rem` can be used for objects that use the binary formatter:

```xml
<configuration>
   <system.runtime.remoting>
      <application>
         <service>
            <wellknown
               mode="SingleCall"
               type="Wrox.Samples.MyRemoteObject, MyRemoteObject"
               objectUri="MyRemoteObject.soap" />
         </service>
      </application>
   </system.runtime.remoting>
</configuration>
```

Client

If you use a configuration file for the client that specifies the URL to the web application with the url attribute of the `<client>` tag, the url attribute of the `<wellknown>` tag specifies the path to the remote object. The difference between this and the client configuration files we used in the last chapter is that we now use the HTTP channel, and we can ignore the port number as long as the web application is running with the default port number 80.

In this client configuration file we specify a connection to a well-known object with the type `Wrox.Samples.MyRemoteObject` in the assembly `MyRemoteObject`. The URL to the remote object is `http://localhost/IISHosting/MyRemoteObject.soap`. Here `IISHosting` is the name of the virtual web directory, and `MyRemoteObject.soap` is the URI of the remote object that we defined in the server configuration file:

```
<configuration>
   <system.runtime.remoting>
      <application name="SimpleClient">
         <client url="http://localhost/IISHosting">
            <wellknown
               type="Wrox.Samples.MyRemoteObject, MyRemoteObject"
               url="http://localhost/IISHosting/MyRemoteObject.soap" />
         </client>
         <channels>
            <channel ref="http client" />
         </channels>
      </application>
   </system.runtime.remoting>
</configuration>
```

The client is again implemented in a console application. We read the client configuration file to configure and to start the channel. The instance of the remote object is created with the new operator:

```csharp
// Client.cs

using System;
using System.Runtime.Remoting;
namespace Wrox.Samples
{
   class SimpleClient
   {
      static void Main(string[] args)
      {
         RemotingConfiguration.Configure("Client.exe.config");
         MyRemoteObject obj = new MyRemoteObject();
         Console.WriteLine(obj.Hello());
      }
   }
}
```

When compiling the client with this command, we have to reference the file `MyRemoteObject.dll` for the metadata of the class `MyRemoteObject`. The assembly `MyRemoteObject` must be also available at runtime in the directory of the client because the metadata information is needed to build a proxy at runtime:

```
csc /target:exe /r:MyRemoteObject.dll Client.cs
```

With the remote object configured to run in ASP.NET, it isn't necessary to create our own server and start it. The World Wide Web Publishing Service (the service of IIS) is already started, and the ASP.NET runtime checks the configuration file `web.config` to automatically start and register the channel.

Restrictions

We always have to create a server application that creates and registers a channel when using console, Windows Forms, or other such application types to host remoting objects. In the last chapter, we always created the server as a console application type where we started the channel. If we use the ASP.NET runtime instead, there's the advantage that we don't have to write a server process. It is also not necessary to start the hosting process manually, because the World Wide Web Publishing Service is automatically started.

Hosting remote objects in the ASP.NET runtime also has some disadvantages. Only well-known objects are supported in the ASP.NET runtime, which means that you can't hold state in the remote object. The reason for this is that the runtime can be restarted automatically, and the state would be lost. In addition to that, we are restricted to the SOAP formatter, which is less efficient than the binary formatter.

Using ASP.NET Features

.NET Remoting can run in any application type. This gives us the advantage that we can use the services that are offered from the specific application types. Hosting the remoting server in IIS means that we can use ASP.NET features. The class `RemotingService` (don't confuse it with `RemotingServices`) in the `System.Runtime.Remoting.Services` namespace has some properties that you may know from ASP.NET. The properties of the class `RemotingService` are listed in this table:

Property	Description
Application	The `Application` property gives access to the `HttpApplicationState`. You can store data that can be accessed from all clients.
Context	The `Context` property returns the `HttpContext`. With this you can read HTTP-specific information about the request. This is not only the query string that is passed from the client application, but also some HTTP header information like client languages, application name, etc. that can be sent by the client application.
Server	The `Server` property returns the `HttpServerUtiltity` that provides helper methods to Web requests.
Session	`Session` returns the `HttpSessionState` that can be used to store data across different requests from the same client. As you already know, the remoting objects that can run in the IIS server are well-known, and so stateless. You can use the session to store some state.
User	The `User` property returns a reference to the `IPrincipal` interface. With this and the `IIdentity` interface you can read the name of the user.

Application Object

So let's try to use the `Application` property with the remote object. With the `Application` property of the `RemotingService` class we use a facility of ASP.NET with which we can create variables that are shared across multiple clients. The `Application` property returns an object of type `HttpApplicationState` which is a collection of all shared variables in the web application.

To demonstrate that we can indeed use ASP.NET facilities, we will use this `Application` property to display a usage count. The method `UsageCount()` should increment a count variable every time it is called and return the actual value back to the client.

To have the `Application` property available, our class `MyRemoteObject` must derive from `RemotingService`. `RemotingService` derives from `MarshalByRefObject`, so the object is remotable. The method `UsageCount()` uses the indexer of the `Application` property to access the value that is stored in the collection with the name `UsageCount`. When the method is called for the first time, this item is not stored in the collection of the `Application` property. In this case, the indexer returns `null`. With the `if` statement, we check for this to add the new item `UsageCount` to the `Application` property with the `Add()` method of `HttpApplicationState`. In the `else` sequence, we use the returned value from the `Application` property to write it into the variable `count`, and to set the incremented value to the `Application` property:

```csharp
// MyRemoteObject.cs

using System;
using System.Runtime.Remoting.Services;
namespace Wrox.Samples
{
    public class MyRemoteObject : RemotingService
    {
        public MyRemoteObject()
        {
        }
        public int UsageCount()
        {
            int count = 1;
            object o = Application["UsageCount"];
            if (o == null)
            {
                Application.Add("UsageCount", count);
            }
            else
            {
                count = (int)o;
                Application["UsageCount"] = ++count;
            }
            return count;
        }
    }
}
```

In the client application we can now call the `UsageCount()` method to get a new value every time this method is called.

User Authentication

We can authorize users for our web service simply by using an ASP.NET runtime feature: user authentication. Let's add user identification to the web service to read this information from with the `RemotingService` class. The ASP.NET services use the same configuration file as we have used for the remote object: `web.config`. For authentication and authorization we have to add the `<system.web>` element to the `<configuration>` section. Authentication and authorization uses sub-elements of `<system.web>`. We set the authentication mode to `Windows` to make use of the Windows authentication, and with the `authorization` section we define which users are allowed to use the service. Here the user `chris` from the domain `sentinel` may use the service, and access will be denied for all other users. Note that you'll have to alter the values stated here to the values on your own system to get this example to work:

```
<configuration>
    <system.web>
        <authentication mode="Windows" />
        <authorization>
            <allow users="sentinel\chris" />
            <deny users="*" />
        </authorization>
    </system.web>
    <system.runtime.remoting>
        <application>
            <service>
                <wellknown
                    mode="SingleCall"
                    type="Wrox.Samples.MyRemoteObject, MyRemoteObject"
                    objectUri="MyRemoteObject.soap" />
            </service>
        </application>
    </system.runtime.remoting>
</configuration>
```

We add another method to the MyRemoteObject class: The method Hello() should greet the user by name. The property User of the class RemotingService returns a reference to the IPrincipal interface. This interface has the property Identity that itself returns the user name with the property Name:

```
// MyRemoteObject.cs

using System;
using System.Runtime.Remoting.Services;
namespace Wrox.Samples
{
    public class MyRemoteObject : RemotingService
    {
        public MyRemoteObject()
        {
        }
        public int UsageCount()
        {
            int count = 1;
            object o = Application["UsageCount"];
            if (o == null)
            {
                Application.Add("UsageCount", count);
            }
            else
            {
                count = (int)o;
                Application["UsageCount"] = ++count;
            }
            return count;
        }
        public string Hello()
        {
            if (User.Identity == null)
                return "no identity";
            string name = User.Identity.Name;
            return "Hello " + name;
        }
    }
}
```

We denied all users access to our web service (with the exception of the user listed in the `allow` section of the configuration file), so the client application must pass the `username` and `password` to the service. If the user of the client application is not authorized, we get a `WebException` with this message: **The remote server returned an error: (401) Unauthorized.**

The `username` and `password` for the user can be set using the channel sink properties. We can get to these properties with the `GetChannelSinkProperties()` method of the `ChannelServices` utility class. This method returns an `IDictionary` with all property names and values. We change the `Main()` method in the file `client.cs` to display all names and values of these properties in a `foreach` loop. After this, username, password, and domain are set to new values before the remote method `Hello()` is called. With an authorized user the method `Hello()` will now be called successfully:

```
// Client.cs

using System;
using System.Collections;
using System.Runtime.Remoting;
using System.Runtime.Remoting.Channels;
namespace Wrox.Samples
{
    class SimpleClient
    {
        static void Main(string[] args)
        {
            RemotingConfiguration.Configure("Client.exe.config");
            MyRemoteObject obj = new MyRemoteObject();
            IDictionary props = ChannelServices.GetChannelSinkProperties(obj);
            foreach (string key in props.Keys)
            {
                Console.WriteLine(key + ": " + props[key]);
            }
            Console.WriteLine();
            props["username"] = "chris";
            props["password"] = "somesecret";
            props["domain"] = "sentinel";
            Console.WriteLine(obj.Hello());
        }
    }
}
```

When we run the client application we can see the properties that are associated with the channel: username, password, domain, preauthenticate, proxyname, proxyport, timeout, and allowautoredirect. All these values are initialized to their default values, so authentication wouldn't take place. After changing the username, password, and domain to the relevant values, the string `Hello SENTINEL\chris` (or equivilant) is returned from the server:

SoapHttpClientProtocol

One way to pass the `username` and `password` values is by using the channel sink properties. This technique has the disadvantage that we must know how the properties must be named, and if we do it incorrectly the compiler can't check it. We will detect this while running the application.

There is, however, a better way. Instead of using the remote object with the `new` operator (or the `Activator` class) we can use the class `SoapHttpClientProtocol` instead.

The .NET Remoting Server with the HTTP channel supports the WSDL protocol as an ASP.NET web Service does. You can look at the WSDL information of the service with a browser using the URL http://localhost/IISHosting/MyRemoteObject.soap?wsdl. In contrast to ASP.NET web services, we don't get a test page when using the URL string without ?wsdl.

You can read more about WSDL in Chapter 2.

The screenshot below shows the output that is generated from the HTTP channel by accessing the WSDL information:

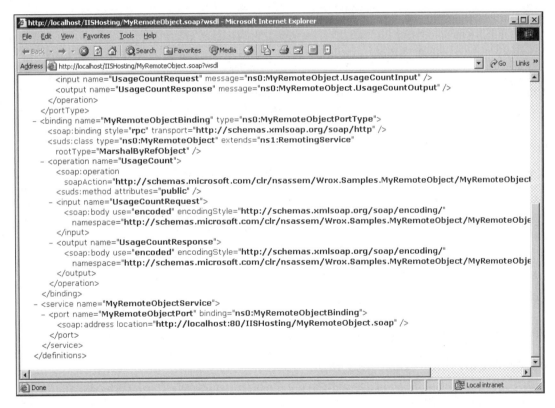

The `WSDL.exe` utility creates a proxy class that derives from `SoapHttpClientProtocol` by accessing the WSDL information that is delivered by the server. With the following command, the file `MyRemoteObject.cs` is created, and this can be used from within the client application:

```
wsdl http://localhost/IISHosting/MyRemoteObject.soap?wsdl
/out:MyRemoteObject.cs
```

With the generated class, the `Credentials` of the user can be passed with a property of this class.

The `wsdl` utility was covered in Chapter 5. You can read more about securing web services in Chapter 11.

Channels

For communication between a client and a server, a channel is used. The channel sends a message using a transport protocol. With the first release of the .NET Framework we get a TCP and an HTTP channel. The HTTP channel uses the HTTP protocol and so can easily be used across firewalls, whereas the TCP channel uses the TCP protocol and is more efficient for intranet solutions.

You can also implement a custom channel that uses a different protocol. Some time after the release of the .NET Framework, other channels such as an SMTP channel will become available, and will provide functionality to send and to receive e-mails by calling methods. Another useful channel could be one that uses Message Queuing as a transport protocol to give an abstraction layer for the `System.Messaging` classes. This would allow us to call methods instead of having to create messages for the message queue. Currently, we have to create messages that are sent to the Message Queue with `System.Messaging`, but it would be easier if it were possible to invoke methods instead. The COM+ Queued Components service adds an abstraction layer to Message Queuing that allows it to invoke methods, and messages are created by a recorder, but the COM+ service has the disadvantage that it needs to implement the COM interface `IPersistStream` to pass a .NET class with such a method. A remoting channel using Message Queuing could make such an abstraction layer easier to use for .NET clients.

IChannel Interface

All channels implement the interface `IChannel`, so common to all channels are the properties that are defined with the channel: a name, a `priority`, and the method `Parse()`. The name can be used to identify the channel. You already know the names of some predefined channels that are defined in the file `machine.config`: `tcp`, `tcp client`, `tcp server`, `http`, `http client`, and `http server`. We used these channels in Chapter 6.

You can use more than one channel in the same server by adding a second channel to the application configuration file. If the server supports both a TCP and an HTTP channel, it can be reached in two ways. The client can then choose either the TCP or the HTTP channel to connect to the server.

The **channel priority** is used to order the channels. On the client side, the channel with the higher priority is chosen first to connect to the server. If the connection with the higher priority channel fails, the runtime tries to connect with the next channel.

Configuration File – Setting Properties

We can define the properties of a channel in the configuration file. We already discussed this in the last chapter, but here we'll look at using these files to set channel properties in more detail.

The properties that a channel supports depend upon the type of the channel. For a custom channel, custom properties can be defined. Every channel must support the properties `name` and `priority`, because these properties are defined in the `IChannel` interface. The HTTP and TCP channels also support the property `port` to define a listening port number.

The following example shows a server configuration file where the application starts two channels that are referenced within the `<application>` element. The channels themselves are declared outside the `<application>` element in the `<channels>` declaration where the port, priority, and name are set as attributes of the `<channel>` tag. In the channel declaration, we create the channel with the id "high prio http", set its priority to 20 and its name to High Priority HTTP Channel. Similarly, the channel with the id "my tcp" has priority 11 and the name "My TCP Channel". Both of these channels are referenced in the `<application>` section by using the ref attribute. As you can see with the channel my tcp, we can override the channel properties in the application section as here the priority is changed to 24:

```
<configuration>
    <system.runtime.remoting>
        <application name="SimpleServer">
            <channels>
                <channel ref="high prio http" />
                <channel ref="my tcp" priority="24" port="9001" />
            </channels>
        </application>
        <channels>
            <channel id="high prio http"
                type="System.Runtime.Remoting.Channels.Http.HttpChannel,
                    System.Runtime.Remoting,
                    Version=1.0.3300.0,Culture=neutral,PublicKeyToken=b77a5c561934e089"
                port="9000"
                priority="20"
                name="High Priority HTTP Channel" />
            <channel id="my tcp"
                    type="System.Runtime.Remoting.Channels.Tcp.TcpChannel,
                    System.Runtime.Remoting,
                    Version=1.0.3300.0,Culture=neutral,PublicKeyToken=b77a5c561934e089"
                    priority="11"
                    name="My TCP Channel" />
        </channels>
    </system.runtime.remoting>
</configuration>
```

In the C# code, we read and start the channel by calling the static method `RemotingConfiguration.Configure()`.

Sometimes we would like to know at runtime what channels are configured and running. The `ChannelServices` class supports this task. We can query all channels that are registered in the remoting runtime with the property `RegisteredChannels`. This property returns an array of channels that we use to output the `ChannelName` and `ChannelPriority`:

```
static void Main(string[] args)
{
    RemotingConfiguration.Configure("SimpleServer.exe.config");
    IChannel[] channels = ChannelServices.RegisteredChannels;
    foreach (IChannel channel in channels)
    {
        Console.WriteLine(channel.ChannelName +
                " - Priority: " + channel.ChannelPriority);
    }
    Console.WriteLine("Press return to exit");
    Console.ReadLine();
}
```

In the output of the console application, we can see both channels that we configured in the application configuration file:

Channel Constructor – Setting Properties

Instead of using the configuration file we can also set the properties of a channel programmatically. The constructors of the `TcpChannel` and the `HttpChannel` allows passing a class that implements the `IDictionary` interface. The `ListDictionary` class implements `IDictionary`, so we can set the properties of the channel by creating a `ListDictionary` and adding property names and values to the dictionary. This dictionary can be passed to the constructor of the channel. Besides this dictionary, we also have to pass formatter sink providers. A formatter sink provider is a factory class to create formatter sinks. We will talk about these later:

```
BinaryClientFormatterSinkProvider clientSinkProvider =
    new BinaryClientFormatterSinkProvider();
BinaryServerFormatterSinkProvider serverSinkProvider =
    new BinaryServerFormatterSinkProvider();
ListDictionary properties = new ListDictionary();
properties.Add("Name", "My TCP Channel");
properties.Add("Priority", "20");
TcpChannel channel =
    new TcpChannel(properties, clientSinkProvider, serverSinkProvider);
```

IChannelReceiver Interface

Besides the interface `IChannel`, the channel must also implement the interface `IChannelReceiver`, the `IChannelSender` interface, or both of them. The server is the receiving part where methods will be invoked, so the server must implement the `IChannelReceiver` interface. The classes `TcpServerChannel`, `HttpServerChannel`, `TcpChannel`, and `HttpChannel` implement this interface.

The `IChannelReceiver` interface defines the methods to start and to stop the listening of the channel, `StartListening()` and `StopListening()`, and a method that returns all URLs of the objects that are using this channel: `GetUrlsForUri()`.

IChannelSender Interface

The `IChannelSender` interface must be implemented from the client part. It provides sending functionality to the channel, so the `TcpClientChannel` and `HttpClientChannel` implement this interface. `TcpChannel` and `HttpChannel` are both client and server in a single class, so these classes implement this interface too.

This interface defines a single method: `CreateMessageSink()`. The client calls this method to create a channel message sink that delivers messages to the channel. The sink returned from this method is either a `BinaryClientFormatterSink` or a `SoapClientFormatterSink`. We will look at these formatters soon, and discuss when each one should be used.

TCP Channel

The TCP protocol is a connection-oriented protocol. The diagram below shows the sequence during a TCP communication. The server creates a listening socket and waits for clients to connect to it. The listening socket must have a port number known to the client. The client creates a socket that can have any available port number. The client uses the port number of the server to connect to the server process, and passes its own port number to the server. The server can use this port number to send some data to the client. The client receives the data, and sends some data to the server. The sending and receiving can go on until the connection is closed:

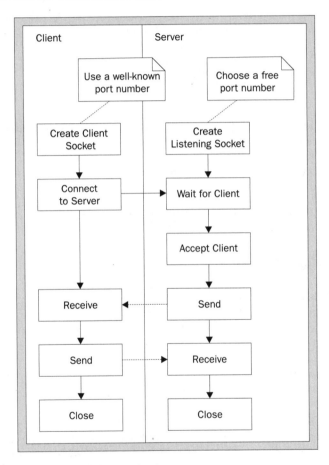

System.Runtime.Remoting.Channels.Tcp

The namespace `System.Runtime.Remoting.Channels.Tcp` defines three classes: `TcpClientChannel`, `TcpServerChannel`, and `TcpChannel`. `TcpChannel` is both a sending and a receiving channel.

HTTP Channel

The HTTP channel uses the HTTP protocol. Of course, the HTTP protocol also uses the TCP protocol. Let's look at the layers in these protocols:

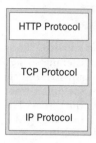

The lowest level protocol in the graphic above, the **Internet Protocol** (IP) uses Internet addresses such as 16.187.112.125 to connect two hosts. With TCP we can connect to a specific process on a host because here port numbers are used to identify a network service. HTTP is an application-layer protocol that itself uses TCP. With HTTP, commands are defined and are sent as requests across the network using the TCP protocol. The server can interpret these predefined commands to send an HTTP response.

HTTP Protocol

The HTTP protocol defines **request messages** (client to server) and **response messages** (server to client). A message consists of a request command, a message header, and a message body. Some examples of request commands: GET, HEAD, and POST. Message headers are used to send cookies, client application identifications, timeouts of documents, etc. The message body includes the data that is built up by the formatter, such as the SOAP request that itself includes an envelope and a body.

The HTTP 1.1 protocol is defined with RFC 2068. You can read this RFC document at http://rfc.net/rfc2068.html.

System.Runtime.Remoting.Channels.Http

The channels HttpClientChannel, HttpServerChannel, and HttpChannel are defined in exactly the same way as the TCP channels in the namespace System.Runtime.Remoting.Channels.Http. In addition to these three channels, this namespace has the classes HttpRemotingHandler and HttpRemotingHandlerFactory. These two classes are used for .NET Remoting servers configured within IIS by the ASP.NET runtime to forward HTTP requests to the HTTP channel.

Formatters

What the message that is sent across a channel looks like depends upon the formatter. A channel has an associated formatter. Let's look at the remoting sequence from the client when the client invokes a method on the proxy. The proxy sends the messages to a formatter that in turn is responsible for converting the messages to a format that can be sent across the network. With .NET Remoting we get two formatting types: binary and SOAP formatters. The SOAP formatter can be used to communicate with different technologies, whereas the binary formatter is useful for fast and efficient communication between .NET applications. You can also write your own formatters to create a different data representation. One example for a custom channel would be to create a message format that can be read from a COM object without the necessary SOAP transformation. A different formatter could be used to format messages as e-mails, which are sent using the SMTP channel.

The default formatter for the TCP channel is the binary formatter, and the default formatter for the HTTP channel is the SOAP formatter, but this can be changed as we will soon see.

Serialization

A formatter implements the interface `IRemotingFormatter`. `IRemotingFormatter` derives from `IFormatter`. This interface is not only used for remoting, but is also used to serialize object trees into files. `IFormatter` defines the properties `Binder`, `Context`, and `SurrogateSelector`. `Binder` defines a `SerializationBinder` that does type lookups using reflection during deserialization. The `Context` defines a `StreamingContext` that is used to define what fields can be ignored during serialization depending whether the serialization is across processes, across machines, or in files. With the property `SurrogateSelector`, it can be specified if another object should handle the serialization process instead. `IFormatter` also defines the methods `Serialize()` and `Deserialize()`. `Serialize()` is used to serialize an object tree into a stream, `Deserialize()` uses the stream to build an object tree of it. The interface `IRemotingFormatter` overloads the methods `Serialize()` and `Deserialize()` with an additional argument to pass header information.

Binary Formatter

The binary formatter serializes an object tree in a binary format that is native to .NET. This format is efficient if the size of the data created is small. It doesn't compress the data as this would take more CPU cycles to fulfill the request, but it would be possible to add a compression sink that does this work. It is not necessarily the fastest solution to send compressed data across the network because compression needs a lot of CPU cycles.

The binary formatter has the disadvantage that it can be used only in a solution where both the client and the server are written with .NET as other technologies do not understand this format. The SOAP protocol can be used instead for communication with different technologies.

SOAP Formatter

The SOAP formatter serializes an object tree in the SOAP format. SOAP uses XML syntax. This format is useful to communicate with different platforms like DCOM, Java RMI, and CORBA that also offer SOAP conversions.

You can read more about SOAP in Chapter 2.

Comparing Formatter Results

To see the differences between formatters in action we will use the formatters to write a serialized object to a file instead of writing it to the channel. In the first example we'll create a serializable class `Employee` in the file `SerializeObject.cs`. This class is marked with the `Serializeable` attribute, so that this class can be serialized to streams. We implement only an `int` and a `string` property to see the serialization effects easily:

```
using System;
using System.IO;
using System.Runtime.Serialization;
using System.Runtime.Serialization.Formatters.Binary;
using System.Runtime.Serialization.Formatters.Soap;

[Serializable]
class Employee
{
```

```
    public Employee()
    {
    }
    private int id;
    public int Id
    {
        get
        {
            return id;
        }
        set
        {
            id = value;
        }
    }
    private string name;
    public string Name
    {
        get
        {
            return name;
        }
        set
        {
            name = value;
        }
    }
}
```

We'll add a `Main` method to this class and create an instance of the `Employee` class, and assign some values to the properties:

```
public static void Main()
{

    // create the object to serialize

    Employee e = new Employee();
    e.id = 987654321;
    e.Name = "John Doe";

    // ...
```

With the binary formatter, the object will be serialized to the file `Demo.rem`. The binary formatter is created with the default constructor; then we set the `Context` property to a `StreamingContext` for cross-machine marshaling. With cross-machine marshaling we can compare the result with the marshaling size for remoting scenarios. A `FileStream` object is created to serialize the object with the `Serialize()` method of the `BinaryFormatter` class into a file:

```
    // use a binary formatter

    BinaryFormatter formatter1 = new BinaryFormatter();
    formatter1.Context =
        new StreamingContext(StreamingContextStates.CrossMachine);
    FileStream stream1 = new FileStream("Demo.rem", FileMode.Create);
    formatter1.Serialize(stream1, e);
    stream1.Close();
```

We use the SOAP formatter in a similar way. The only things that change are the filename and the formatter. To use the class `SoapFormatter` we have to reference the assembly `System.Runtime.Serialization.Formatters.Soap`. The binary formatter can be found in the core assembly `mscorlib`:

```
        // use the SOAP formatter

        SoapFormatter formatter2 = new SoapFormatter();
        formatter2.Context =
            new StreamingContext(StreamingContextStates.CrossMachine);
        FileStream stream2 = new FileStream("Demo.soap", FileMode.Create);
        formatter2.Serialize(stream2, e);
        stream2.Close();
    }
```

To compile the program to a console application, type the following at the command line:

```
csc /target:console SerializeObject.cs
```

After we start the application, two files are generated. The binary file `Demo.rem` has a size of 145 bytes, but the SOAP formatted file `Demo.soap` is 660 bytes long. This is a big difference for such a small object.

Binary Format

The binary file `Demo.rem` cannot be read with Notepad or any other text editor, but we can read the data with the binary editor of Visual Studio .NET. Opening the file with Visual Studio .NET automatically starts the binary editor. In the picture below you can see that the data stored is information about the assembly of the serialized object, the class and member variable names, and the data. With the binary format, the size can be very small:

SOAP Format

Now open the file `Demo.soap`. Being 660 bytes in size, it is four times larger than the binary file. We can see the SOAP `Envelope` around the SOAP `Body`. In the SOAP `Body` the fields `id` and `name` can be seen with the data inside the `<a1:Employee>` element. Of course, the bigger size is due to the XML format:

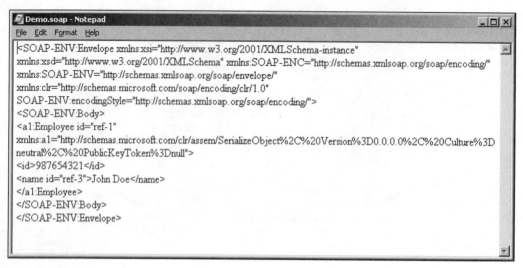

Using the SOAP formatter to send data across the network can result in more network packets transferred.

Comparing DataSets with Binary and SOAP Formatters

What about the size differences of larger objects that get serialized? Is the SOAP format still four times larger than the binary format? DataSets are often sent across a channel, so it would be interesting to compare these.

This demo program creates a DataSet object that is filled with all employees from the NorthWind sample database that comes with SQL Server. The query is SELECT * FROM employees to make a big result set. The same code we used earlier to serialize this object can be used to create the files:

```
// create the object to serialize

DataSet ds = new DataSet("DemoSet");
string connString = "user id=sa;password=sa;" +
    "initial catalog=northwind;data source=localhost";
SqlConnection conn = new SqlConnection(connString);
SqlDataAdapter adapter = new SqlDataAdapter(
    "SELECT * FROM employees", conn);
adapter.Fill(ds);
```

Comparing the sizes of the resulting files may at first surprise us. The binary file has a size of 269,998 bytes, but the SOAP file is only a few bytes larger at 274,238 bytes. The reason that the SOAP format is not much bigger is that the DataSet implements the interface ISerializable and thereby controls its own serialization. This means that binary data is stored within the SOAP body.

What do we learn from these results, comparing a binary to a SOAP serialization? The difference depends whether you use the standard serialization with the [Serialization] attribute, or custom serialization is selected by implementing the ISerializable interface. For the serialization of big objects or object trees that implement standard serialization using the [Serializable] attribute, the binary formatter is more efficient than the SOAP formatter. On the other hand, if the object uses custom serialization by implementing the ISerializable interface, the SOAP format can be efficient, too. Using custom serialization with the SOAP protocol, however, we lose the advantage of communicating with other technologies.

Channels and Formatters

How is the formatter associated with the channel? As you already know, the binary formatter is the default for the TCP channel, and the SOAP formatter is the default for the HTTP channel. .NET Remoting is flexible, so this can be changed. Maybe you have to cross a firewall with a pure .NET solution. The HTTP channel has the advantage of being easy to use over a firewall, but because both the client and server are using .NET technologies, the binary formatter would be the most efficient.

The formatter cannot be assigned directly to the channel. We must instead use formatter sink providers and formatter sinks.

A channel is associated with a formatter sink provider. The formatter sink provider is a factory class that creates formatter sinks. In the last chapter we have seen that a sink processes messages. This is exactly the same for formatter sinks. A formatter sink processes messages with the help of a formatter class.

Let's look at the SOAP classes for formatter sink providers, formatter sinks, and formatters in the diagram below. The client channel has an associated channel sink provider that implements the interface `IClientChannelSinkProvider`. The SOAP provider is implemented in the class `SoapClientFormatterSinkProvider` (the binary version of the class that implements this interface is `BinaryClientFormatterSinkProvider`, but this class is not shown in the diagram). The sink provider creates channel sinks that implement the interface `IClientChannelSink`. `SoapClientFormatterSink` not only implements the interface `IClientChannelSink`, but also the interfaces `IClientFormatterSink` and `IMessageSink`, too. With the methods of the `IMessageSink` interface the formatter sink can process messages synchronously and asynchronously. For message processing, the `SoapClientFormatterSink` uses the `SoapFormatter` that we already know:

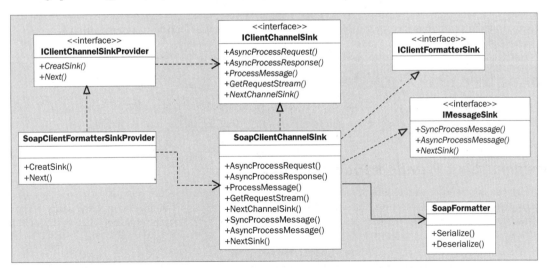

The server side looks very similar to the client side. The server channel has an associated `IServerChannelSinkProvider`. The class that implements the `IServerChannelSinkProvider` creates an object of a class that implements `IServerChannelSink`. The `SoapServerFormatterSink` again uses the `SoapFormatter`:

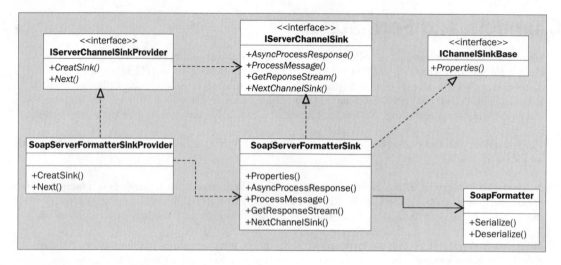

What are the advantages of this architecture?

❑ The channel has an associated interface with the name I<XXX>ChannelSinkProvider, where <XXX> is the name of the channel. By using an interface, we can assign any provider to the channel that implements this interface.

❑ Looking into this interface we not only see a method to create a sink, but also the property Next. More than one sink provider can be assigned to a single channel, so one provider after another can be used to create sinks that will be connected together to process a message.

A custom sink provider can be implemented to do logging, or IP filtering to accept only certain IP addresses, for example.

Formatter Sink Provider

To summarize what we have seen before, a formatter sink provider is associated with a channel. A formatter sink provider creates a formatter and connects that formatter to the channel. Let's look into how we can assign a different sink provider to a channel.

Assigning Sink Providers Programmatically

With the constructor of a channel, we can assign a provider other than the default with the channel. It is not possible to set the sink provider after the channel is constructed. The following code sample shows how the binary formatter provider can be associated with the HTTP client channel. As a result of this the BinaryFormatter is used with this HTTP channel:

```
BinaryClientFormatterSinkProvider sinkProvider =
    new BinaryClientFormatterSinkProvider();
HttpClientChannel channel = new HttpClientChannel(
    "my client channel", sinkProvider);
```

Predefined Sink Providers

The machine-wide configuration file `machine.config` not only defines some channels as we have seen in Chapter 6, but also some formatter sink providers, too. The formatter sink providers are grouped into client providers and server providers. The client providers with the id `soap` and `binary` are the default providers for the `tcp` and `http` channels. For the server we have a `soap`, a `binary`, and a `wsdl` provider. The only really new provider is the `wsdl` provider. You know the WSDL syntax already from Chapter 2, but in Chapter 9 we will look at the result of the WSDL provider for .NET Remoting that can be used when creating client applications:

```
<configuration>
   <system.runtime.remoting>
      <channelSinkProviders>
         <clientProviders>
            <formatter
            id="soap" type=
            "System.Runtime.Remoting.Channels.SoapClientFormatterSinkProvider,
            System.Runtime.Remoting,
            Version=1.0. 3300.0,Culture=neutral,PublicKeyToken=b77a5c561934e089" />
               <formatter
                  id="binary" type=
            "System.Runtime.Remoting.Channels.BinaryClientFormatterSinkProvider,
            System.Runtime.Remoting,
            Version=1.0. 3300.0,Culture=neutral,PublicKeyToken=b77a5c561934e089" />
            </clientProviders>
            <serverProviders>
               <formatter
            id="soap" type= "
            "System.Runtime.Remoting.Channels.SoapServerFormatterSinkProvider,
            System.Runtime.Remoting,
            Version=1.0. 3300.0,Culture=neutral,PublicKeyToken=b77a5c561934e089" />
               <formatter
            id="binary" type=
            "System.Runtime.Remoting.Channels.BinaryServerFormatterSinkProvider,
            System.Runtime.Remoting,
            Version=1.0. 3300.0,Culture=neutral,PublicKeyToken=b77a5c561934e089" />
               <provider
            id="wsdl" type=
            "System.Runtime.Remoting.MetadataServices.SdlChannelSinkProvider,
            System.Runtime.Remoting,
            Version=1.0. 3300.0,Culture=neutral,PublicKeyToken=b77a5c561934e089" />" />
            </serverProviders>
         </channelSinkProviders>
      </system.runtime.remoting>
</configuration>
```

Using Configuration Files for Sink Providers

This example shows how the SOAP formatter provider can be assigned to the TCP channel. To do this you only have to add the `<serverProviders>` section as child of the `<channel>` tag:

```
<configuration>
   <system.runtime.remoting>
      <application name="SimpleServer">
         <service>
            <wellknown
               mode="SingleCall"
```

```
              type="Wrox.Samples.MyRemoteObject, MyRemoteObject"
              objectUri="MyRemoteObject.rem" />
      </service>
      <channels>
         <channel ref="tcp server" port="9000">
            <serverProviders>
               <formatter ref="soap" />
            </serverProviders>
         </channel>
      </channels>
    </application>
  </system.runtime.remoting>
</configuration>
```

Summary

With .NET Remoting, web services can be used in Windows Forms applications, Windows Services, ASP.NET, and so on. By using a service in IIS, we can take advantage of some ASP.NET features by using the `RemoteService` class.

We can communicate with TCP or HTTP channels with a binary or a SOAP formatter. Using the TCP channel with the binary formatter, we can have fast communication that not only replaces DCOM, but can also talk to Java and CORBA solutions with the SOAP formatter.

.NET Remoting has an extremely flexible architecture in that channels and formatters can be replaced independently, and multiple providers can be attached to a channel.

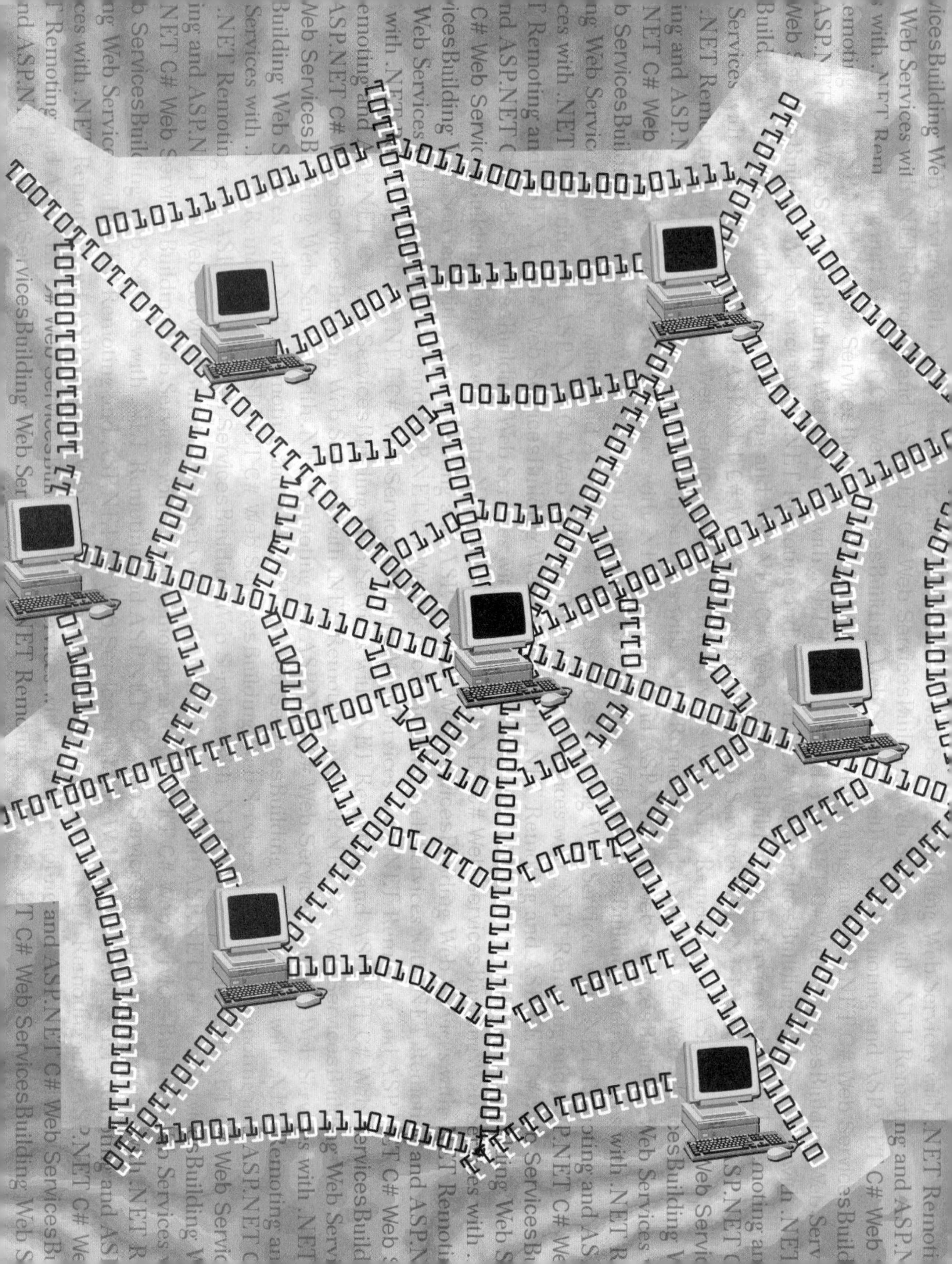

8

Building a Web Service with .NET Remoting

.NET Remoting provides a flexible and extensible framework for objects to communicate with each other seamlessly, even when they are living in different application domains, in different processes, and on different machines. In the last two chapters, we saw that the .NET Remoting architecture consisted of the following parts:

❑   Well-known and client-activated remote object types to support both stateless and stateful remote objects

❑   HTTP channels to easily communicate across the Internet, and TCP channels for fast communication

❑   SOAP formatters for communication with other technologies, and binary formatters for efficient communication in a .NET-only environmen.

In both this and the next chapter we will build on the knowledge gained in the previous two chapters to implement and use two web services with .NET Remoting.

Both web services are logically related (they are complementary parts of one Web Pizza delivery service) and are running inside the same process. One web service uses an HTTP channel and will be available from the Internet; the other web service uses a TCP channel. We want one channel to be available from the Internet, but the other will only be accessed over an intranet.

The service will read and write to a database, so we will also look at how to implement and call stored procedures, and how to create `DataSet` objects and pass them across the network.

We will also look into implementing event handlers using .NET Remoting to make callbacks from the server to the client that is connected via the TCP channel.

Introducing Our Pizza Delivery Example

The application in this chapter is a pizza store that supplies pizzas ordered over the Web. The goal of this application is not only to make it possible for customers to order pizzas directly, but also to allow the partner company bulk order via other user interfaces designed by the partner company.

For both the customer and the sales partner, the web service should allow the user to obtain a list of available pizzas with their toppings, and (obviously) to order pizzas.

Use Case Diagram

In this use case diagram we will focus only on the parts that will be implemented in this chapter – the Web Pizza Delivery system. The main actors shown here (the *Order Application* and the *Sales Application*) are systems outside the scope of the web services that we will write. These applications will be implemented in the next chapter; these are the clients of the two web services we are going to write.

The order application actor instantiates the use case *Order a Pizza*. In this use case, the order is written to the database, and another use case is used to inform the sales application that a new order arrived:*Inform about Pizza Order*. Here, we will use the event mechanism of .NET Remoting to pass this information to the sales application.

The sales application uses another use case to deliver the pizza (*Deliver Pizza*). We set the order to be delivered in this use case. The only thing we do here is set a flag in the database; we will not look into ways of delivering the pizza to the customer:

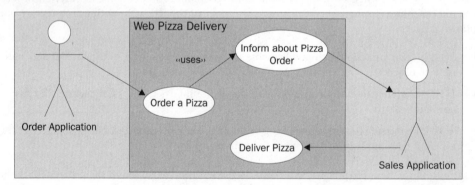

Deployment

The next diagram shows a broad overview of the deployment of the completed application.

The ASP.NET client application will be used to order pizzas via the Web. This application can be hosted in a different network. Using an HTTP channel for communication with the Pizza Web Service host running the **Pizza Order Web Service** makes it easy for a security administrator to open the ports used with this service in the firewall.

The Windows Forms client connects to the **Pizza Delivery Web Service** that is running on the same host as the Pizza Order Web Service. This client application will receive events when a new order arrives. It is also possible to administrate the pizza database from this application, as well as setting the 'delivered' flag of a pizza order.

In the next chapter we will implement both the Windows Forms and the ASP.NET client applications, but in this chapter we will concentrate on implementing two web services that will run on the Pizza Web Service host:

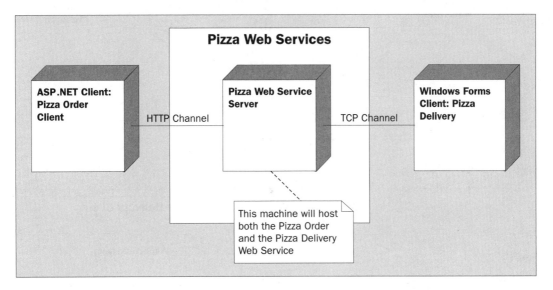

Assemblies

The components diagram overleaf shows all of the assemblies in this solution. The remote object classes are implemented in the PizzaService assembly. This assembly depends on the PizzaData assembly that has the class PizzaDB to connect to the database to query and update pizza orders. The PizzaOrder assembly will have a PizzaOrder class that can be serialized for use on both the client and the server. The Web client application represented in the WebPizzaOrder assembly creates an instance of the PizzaOrder class to pass a method of the remote object to the web service.

PizzaServer is the assembly of a Windows service application. We will use a Windows service as the hosting process for the remote object class so that it can be started automatically when booting the system.

The PizzaService assembly has classes for both the PizzaOrderService and the PizzaDeliveryService service. Both the HTTP and TCP channels will be available from this assembly.

The dashed lines between the assemblies indicate the dependencies; for example, the PizzaServer assembly is dependent on the PizzaService assembly. This dependency means that the PizzaService assembly must be compiled before the PizzaServer service can be built.

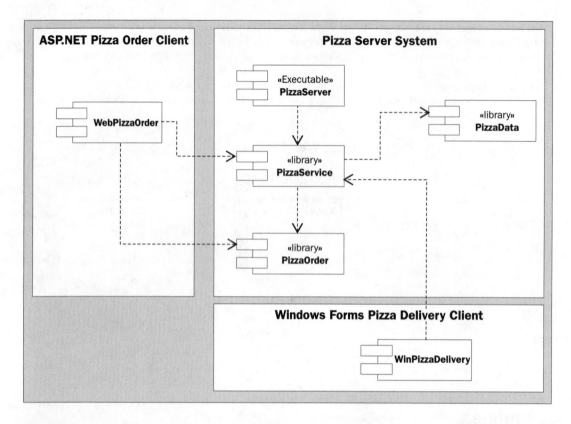

Classes

The class diagram shows the methods, properties, and relationships of the classes of the two web services. The only class that connects to the database is `PizzaDB`. This class has some methods to perform queries and call stored procedures. This class will be used from both service classes: `PizzaOrderService` and `PizzaDeliveryService`. `PizzaOrderService` supports the HTTP channel; `PizzaDeliveryService` will be accessible with the TCP channel. `PizzaOrder` and `PizzaOrderDetail` are serializable classes that can be passed by value across the network. `PizzaOrder` has an aggregation relationship with `PizzaOrderDetail` because `PizzaOrder` includes one or multiple `PizzaOrderDetails`:

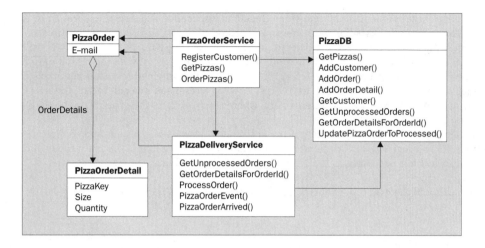

Ordering a Pizza

Let's start with the implementation of the first part – the Pizza Order web service. The default sequence when a pizza is ordered is shown in the diagram below. The client application here is the ASP.NET web client that will use the HTTP channel to connect to the remote object `PizzaOrderService`. `PizzaDB` is the class that is our connection to the database. This class reads the pizza order information from the database, and writes orders and customer information to it:

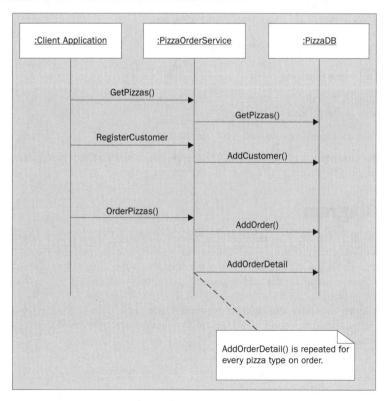

The "Order a Pizza" sequence is started when the client application requests the pizzas from the web service. The web service uses the GetPizzas() method of the PizzaDB class to return a DataSet to the client. If the user is not already registered in the database, RegisterCustomer() is called. The web service invokes the AddCustomer() method of the PizzaDB class to write the customer to the database. Next, the pizzas can be ordered with OrderPizzas(). With a single order, multiple pizzas can be requested for delivery, so a single call to OrderPizzas() results in one call to AddOrder() and possible multiple calls to AddOrderDetail() where every pizza of the order is written to the database.

The sequence looks a little bit different if the customer is already registered, and in the case where the customer doesn't register. The implementation of the web service that is the main focus of this chapter, however, so it is not necessary to look in detail into these sequences.

Later we will add the event mechanism already discussed to this sequence.

Data Services

First we'll implement the data tier of our pizza service. We'll use Microsoft SQL Server for the database, and so we'll use the SQL managed provider classes. We could also choose a different database instead and use the OLE DB or ODBC managed provider. We will not look more closely than is necessary at the database classes, however, nor discuss the functionality because the main focus is on web services in this chapter, so database classes are of secondary importance.

Data-Centric .NET Programming with C# , *published by Wrox Press (ISBN: 1-861005-92-X), contains more information about the classes in the* System.Data *namespace.*

For the implementation of the data tier we will:

❑   Create a Pizza database

❑   Create the Pizzas, Customers, PizzaOrders, and PizzaOrderDetails tables and enter some data to the Pizzas table

❑   Create stored procedures to add, retrieve, and update records in the tables

❑   Build the component library PizzaData with the class PizzaDB that calls the stored procedures and returns a DataSet for the pizzas

Database Diagram

The database just has four tables as the database diagram opposite shows. The Customers table stores the information needed for customers. All information needed to display the pizzas can be found in the Pizzas table. PizzaId is a unique key for the pizza, Name is the name of the pizza, and additionally we have Topping that shows all the add-ons to the pizza, and a Price.

A single PizzaOrder can have multiple PizzaOrderDetails. The PizzaOrder is associated with the Customer using a unique e-mail address, and for every pizza type on the order we have a record in the PizzaOrderDetails table:

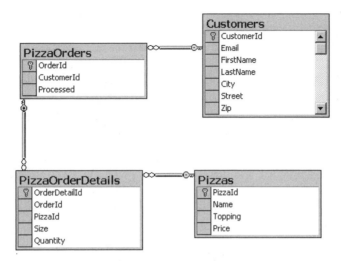

The `Pizzas` table is also filled with some data as is shown in the picture below. The other tables will be filled when we are running the program:

	Name	Topping	Price
	Four Cheeses	Mozzarella, Cheddar, Edam, Parmesan Cheeses	6,95
	Genovese	Artichoke, Ham, Romano Cheese	6,95
	Hawaiian	Ham and Pinapple	6,95
	Margherita	Tomato Sauce and Mozarella Cheese	5,95
	Rustica	Ricotta, Mozzarella, Salami, Prosciutto	6,95
	Spinocolli	Spinach, Brocolli, Mushroom, Garlic	7,95
	Vegetarian	Mushroom, Green Peppers, Onion, Sliced Tomato	6,95
▶			

Stored Procedures

To write the data to the database we use stored procedures: `AddCustomer()`, `AddPizzaOrder()`, `AddPizzaOrderDetail()`, `UpdatePizzaOrderToBeProcessed()`, `GetPizzas()`, `GetPizzaOrders()`, `GetOrderDetailsForOrderId()`, and `GetUnprocessedOrders()`. We will only look at the source code of a few of these stored procedures, because the others don't differ much from this pattern.

`AddPizzaOrderDetail()` is used to add a pizza order to the `PizzaOrderDetails` table. This stored procedure requires the parameters `OrderId`, `PizzaId`, `Size`, and `Quantity` passed to it, and returns the `OrderDetailId` that is automatically created from the database with an identity seed of 1. `@@Identity` is a predefined Transact SQL keyword that returns the identifier. The SQL statement `INSERT INTO` is used to insert the values of the parameters to the table `PizzaOrderDetails`:

```
CREATE PROCEDURE dbo.AddPizzaOrderDetail
    (
        @Orderid INTEGER,
        @PizzaId CHAR(5),
        @Size INTEGER,
```

```
            @Quantity INTEGER,
            @OrderDetailId INTEGER OUTPUT
    )
AS
    SET NOCOUNT ON;
    INSERT INTO PizzaOrderDetails
    (
        Orderid,
        PizzaId,
        Size,
        Quantity
    )
    VALUES
    (
        @Orderid,
        @PizzaId,
        @Size,
        @Quantity
    );

    SELECT @OrderDetailId = @@Identity;
    RETURN
```

AddCustomer() and AddPizzaOrder() are implemented similarly as they use an INSERT INTO SQL statement, too.

UpdatePizzaOrderToBeProcessed() uses a SQL UPDATE statement. This stored procedure is used to change the Processed column of an order that is going to be delivered with the SQL UPDATE statement. A single parameter (the OrderId) is passed with this procedure. With the WHERE clause in the UPDATE statement, the record corresponding to the OrderId is selected, and the Processed field is updated to 1:

```
CREATE PROCEDURE dbo.UpdatePizzaOrderToBeProcessed
    (
        @OrderId int
    )
AS
    SET NOCOUNT ON
    UPDATE PizzaOrders
        SET Processed = 1
        WHERE Id = @OrderId
    RETURN
```

The stored procedure GetPizzas() uses a simple SELECT statement to return the fields PizzaId, Name, Topping, and Price of all records of the Pizzas table:

```
CREATE PROCEDURE dbo.GetPizzas
AS
    SET NOCOUNT ON
    SELECT PizzaId, [Name], Topping, Price
        FROM Pizzas
    RETURN
```

GetPizzaOrders() uses two tables in the SELECT statement to return information for the order and the customer to the caller. We define the link between the tables PizzaOrders and Customers with the WHERE condition:

```
CREATE PROCEDURE dbo.GetPizzaOrders
AS
    SET NOCOUNT ON
    SELECT OrderId, PizzaOrders.CustomerId, Customers.FirstName,
        Customers.LastName, Customers.Email
      FROM Customers, PizzaOrders
      WHERE PizzaOrders.CustomerId = Customers.CustomerId
    RETURN
```

Data Access Component

To access the database, we use a component library with the generated assembly PizzaData and the class PizzaDB in the namespace PizzaService. We use the managed SQL provider to access the SQL Server database.

In the constructor of the class PizzaDB we get the connection string from the application configuration file and store it in the field dsn. Instead of hard-coding this string into the program, we use an application configuration file instead. The method ConfigurationSettings.AppSettings.Get() reads the application configuration file to return the value for the key that is passed with the argument:

```
// PizzaData.cs

using System;
using System.Data;
using System.Data.SqlClient;
using System.Configuration;

namespace PizzaService
{
    public class PizzaDB
    {
        private string dsn;

        public PizzaDB()
        {
            dsn = ConfigurationSettings.AppSettings.Get("ConnectionString");
            if (dsn == null)
                throw new ConfigurationException("No database configuration");
        }
```

The application configuration file needs an <appSettings> section with the key ConnectionString. The name of the file must be the name of the executable that will load the library assembly of the PizzaDB class (the hosting server) followed by the file extension .config – that is, if the server is called PizzaService.exe then the name of the configuration file must be PizzaService.exe.config.

In this configuration file you have to change the username and password to an account that has access to the Pizza database:

```
<configuration>
  <appSettings>
    <add key="ConnectionString" value="Data Source=localhost;
        Initial Catalog=Pizza;User id=myuser;Password=mypassword;" />
  </appSettings>
</configuration>
```

The method `GetPizzas()` in the class `PizzaDB` returns a `DataSet` that contains all pizzas in the database. With the `SqlConnection` class we use the connection string that was passed with the constructor of the `PizzaDB` class. In the constructor of the adapter we pass the name of the stored procedure and the connection object to fill the `DataSet` with the `Fill()` method:

```
public DataSet GetPizzas()
{
    SqlConnection connection = new SqlConnection(dsn);
    string commandText = "GetPizzas";
    SqlDataAdapter adapter = new SqlDataAdapter(commandText,
        connection);
    DataSet ds = new DataSet("Pizzas");
    adapter.SelectCommand.CommandType = CommandType.StoredProcedure;
    adapter.Fill(ds);

    return ds;
}
```

`GetUnprocessedOrders()` is similar to `GetPizzas()`. This method returns a data set consisting of only the orders that are not processed; this is handled by checking the records in the stored procedure `GetUnprocessedOrders` with `WHERE Processed = 0`. This method will be used from the class `PizzaDeliveryService`:

```
public DataSet GetUnprocessedOrders()
{
    SqlConnection connection = new SqlConnection(dsn);
    string commandText = "GetUnprocessedOrders";
    SqlDataAdapter adapter = new SqlDataAdapter(commandText,
        connection);
    DataSet ds = new DataSet("Orders");
    adapter.SelectCommand.CommandType = CommandType.StoredProcedure;
    adapter.Fill(ds);
    return ds;
}
```

`GetOrderDetailsForOrderId()` takes an order id as argument, and creates a `SqlDataAdapter` object that uses a command object to call a stored procedure where the argument `orderId` can be passed. The stored procedure returns records that are used to fill the `DataSet`:

```
public DataSet GetOrderDetailsForOrderId(int orderId)
{
    SqlConnection connection = new SqlConnection(dsn);

    // Create command to call stored procedure

    SqlCommand command = new SqlCommand("GetOrderDetailsForOrderId",
        connection);
    command.CommandType = CommandType.StoredProcedure;
    SqlParameter paramOrderId = new SqlParameter("@OrderId", orderId);
    command.Parameters.Add(paramOrderId);

    // Create SqlDataAdapter and fill the DataSet

    SqlDataAdapter adapter = new SqlDataAdapter();
    adapter.SelectCommand = command;
    DataSet ds = new DataSet("OrderDetails");
    adapter.Fill(ds);
```

One of the methods that call a stored procedure to write new entries to the database is `AddOrderDetail()`. To call a stored procedure that doesn't return records, we can call the `ExecuteNonQuery()` method of the `SqlCommand` class. The `CommandType` property of this command must be set to the enumeration value `CommandType.StoredProcedure`. The property `CommandText` defines the name. Every parameter that must be passed to the stored procedure must be added as a `SqlParameter` to the command object. `SqlParameter` maps the variable to the parameter name of the stored procedure. For parameters that are returned from the stored procedure, the `SqlParameter.Direction` property has to be set to `ParameterDirection.Output`. The default value for this property is `ParameterDirection.Input`. After calling the stored procedure we can use the output variable `paramId` to access the returned value from the stored procedure and return it to the calling method:

```
public int AddOrderDetail(int orderid, string pizza,
    int size, int qty)
{
    SqlConnection connection = new SqlConnection(dsn);
    SqlCommand command = new SqlCommand();
    command.Connection = connection;
    command.CommandType = CommandType.StoredProcedure;
    command.CommandText = "AddPizzaOrderDetail";
    SqlParameter paramOrderId = new SqlParameter("@OrderId", orderid);
    command.Parameters.Add(paramOrderId);
    SqlParameter paramPizzaId = new SqlParameter("@PizzaId", pizza);
    command.Parameters.Add(paramPizzaId);
    SqlParameter paramSize = new SqlParameter("@Size", size);
    command.Parameters.Add(paramSize);
    SqlParameter paramCount = new SqlParameter("@Quantity", qty);
    command.Parameters.Add(paramCount);
    SqlParameter paramId = new SqlParameter("@Id", SqlDbType.Int);
    paramId.Direction = ParameterDirection.Output;
    command.Parameters.Add(paramId);
    connection.Open();
    command.ExecuteNonQuery();
    connection.Close();
    return (int)paramId.Value;
}
```

The methods `AddOrder()`, `UpdateOrderToBeProcessed()`, and `AddCustomer()` are implemented in a similar way, so we will not list these methods here.

> *To be sure that these classes are functional I'm creating test applications before using them from the web service itself. Such a test application is simply a console application that calls the methods of the `PizzaDB` class to write some sample values to the database, and to read some values back.*

PizzaOrder Assembly

The `PizzaOrder` assembly has the classes `PizzaOrder` and `PizzaOrderDetail`. These classes have an aggregation relationship – `PizzaOrderDetail` is contained in the `PizzaOrder` class. The client will create instances of these classes to order a pizza and pass them to the remote object. So, because both the client and the remote object require access to these classes, these classes are separated in their own assembly `PizzaData` with the namespace `PizzaService`.

PizzaOrderDetail

The class `PizzaOrderDetail` represents an order line of the complete pizza order. This class only has some properties that can be mapped to the `PizzaOrderDetails` table: `PizzaKey` is a unique identifier for the pizza; `PizzaSize` defines one of three available sizes, and `Quantity` the number pizzas ordered from the same type. The class is marked with the `[Serializable]` attribute so that it can be marshaled across the network:

```
// PizzaOrderDetail.cs

using System;
namespace PizzaService
{
    [Serializable]
    public class PizzaOrderDetail
    {
        public PizzaOrderDetail()
        {
        }
        private string pizzaKey;
        public string PizzaKey
        {
            get
            {
                return pizzaKey;
            }
            set
            {
                pizzaKey = value;
            }
        }
        public enum Size { Large, Medium, Small };
        private Size pizzaSize;
        public Size PizzaSize
        {
            get
            {
                return pizzaSize;
            }
            set
            {
                pizzaSize = value;
            }
        }
        private int quantity;
        public int Quantity
        {
            get
            {
                return quantity;
            }
            set
            {
                quantity = value;
            }
        }
    }
}
```

PizzaOrder

The `PizzaOrder` class (which is also serializable) collects all order lines in an `ArrayList`. Members of this class must be serializable, too. This is the case with `ArrayList` and all items in the list. `PizzaOrder` represents a complete order that can include different pizzas. The method `AddOrderDetail()` is used to add pizzas to the order. The property `Email` associates the order with a customer:

```csharp
// PizzaOrder.cs

using System;
using System.Collections;
namespace PizzaService
{
    [Serializable]
    public class PizzaOrder
    {
        public PizzaOrder()
        {
        }
        private ArrayList orderDetails = new ArrayList();
        public ArrayList OrderDetails
        {
            get
            {
                return orderDetails;
            }
        }
        public void AddOrderDetail(PizzaOrderDetail item)
        {
            orderdetails.Add(item);
        }
        private string email;
        public string Email
        {
            get
            {
                return email;
            }
            set
            {
                email = value;
            }
        }
    }
}
```

Pizza Order Web Service

With the classes `PizzaDB` and `PizzaOrder`, we have the foundations to start implementing the web service itself. The remote object class `PizzaOrderService` accepts remote calls from a remoting client, and uses the class `PizzaDB` to read from and write to the database. `PizzaOrderService` is implemented in a separate assembly `PizzaService`. It is not necessary to install this assembly on the client machine because the client only needs the metadata of this assembly, but there's a good reason not to put this remote object class directly in the assembly of the hosting server. Using a separate assembly for the remote object class allows us to use this remote object from different hosting servers easily.

The class `PizzaOrderService` is put into the namespace `PizzaService`.

MarshalByRefObject

PizzaService derives from MarshalByRefObject so that this class can be called remotely, and the client can use a proxy to communicate with it:

```
// PizzaOrderService.cs

using System;
using System.Data;
using System.Configuration;
namespace PizzaService
{

    /// <summary>
    /// Remote object class to order Pizzas
    /// </summary>

    public class PizzaOrderService : MarshalByRefObject
    {
        public PizzaOrderService()
        {
        }
```

Error Handling

If something goes wrong, we want to return a useful error message to the client. We can do this by throwing an exception in the server code. A good design guideline is not throwing exceptions of type Exception, because this way the client cannot differentiate the exception types. We also don't want to propagate the complete error information of the SqlException class to the client. Instead, we create a new class that derives from Exception and call it PizzaServiceException. Exceptions of this type should be sent across the channel (and so be marshaled by value), so we must add the [Serializable] attribute. We want to pass a string describing the error in the constructor, so we add the constructor with the string argument. We don't need additional initialization because all features we need are already available in the Exception class, and we can call the base class constructor in the initializer list. For serialization and deserialization we need additional constructors: the default constructor is required for SOAP serialization, and the constructor with the SerializationInfo and the StreamingContext is used for deserialization to the client:

```
// PizzaServiceException.cs

using System;
using System.Runtime.Serialization;
namespace PizzaService
{
    [Serializable]
    public class PizzaServiceException : Exception
    {
        // default constructor required for serialization

        public PizzaServiceException()
        {
        }
        public PizzaServiceException(string message) : base(message)
        {
        }
```

```
        // constructor required for deserialization

        protected PizzaServiceException(SerializationInfo info,
            StreamingContext context) : base(info, context)
        {
        }
    }
}
```

We put the `PizzaServiceException` class into the separate assembly `PizzaServiceException` and compile this into the file `PizzaServiceException.dll` because this allow us to install and use this assembly on both the client and the server independently.

Remote Methods

The method `GetPizzas()` returns a `DataSet` that holds all pizzas of the database. We use the method `GetPizzas()` of the data access class `PizzaDB`. In the case of a `SqlException` if the database is not working we throw a `PizzaServiceException`:

```
public DataSet GetPizzas()
{
    DataSet ds = null;
    try
    {
        PizzaDB data = new PizzaDB();
        ds = data.GetPizzas();
    }
    catch (SqlException ex)
    {
        throw new PizzaServiceException("Database exception: " +
            ex.Number);
    }
    return ds;
}
```

`OrderPizzas()` is another method of `PizzaOrderService` that is available for a remoting client. This method accepts a `PizzaOrder` as an argument. We created the class `PizzaOrder` earlier with the attribute `[Serializable]`, so `PizzaOrder` objects can be passed across the network to the remoting object.

`OrderPizzas()` creates a `PizzaDB` component like `GetPizzas()`, adds a new pizza order to the database with `AddOrder()`, and adds order details with `AddOrderDetail()` for every pizza type that is found in the `PizzaOrder` instance.

> Remember that it is not allowed to keep state in a well-known `SingleCall` object as a new instance gets created with every method call. So we are not allowed to put the `PizzaDB` object in a member variable to reuse it.

Writing an order to the database requires that the e-mail address must already be registered in the `Customers` table because there's a relationship between the `Order` and the `Customers` tables. If this is not the case, a `SqlException` will be thrown. We catch this exception and throw a `PizzaServiceException` to the client instead:

```
public void OrderPizzas(PizzaOrder order)
{

    // Use the database component to add an order

    try
    {
        PizzaDB data = new PizzaDB();
        int orderid = data.AddOrder(order.Email);
        foreach (PizzaOrderDetail item in order.OrderDetails)
        {
            data.AddOrderDetail(orderid, item.PizzaKey,
                (int)item.PizzaSize, item.Quantity);
        }
    }
    catch (SqlException ex)
    {
        throw new PizzaServiceException("Database Exception: " +
            ex.Number + " Email not registered?");
    }
}
```

RegisterCustomer() is the third method that can be used from the client. This method uses the PizzaDB class to write a new customer to the database:

```
public void RegisterCustomer(string email, string firstName,
    string lastName, string city, string street,
    string zip, string phone)
{
    // Use the database component to add a customer
    try
    {
        PizzaDB data = new PizzaDB();
        data.AddCustomer(email, firstName, lastName, city, street,
            zip, phone);
    }
    catch (SqlException ex)
    {
        throw new PizzaServiceException("Database Exception: " +
            ex.Number + " Customer already registered?");
    }
}
```

Test Server

Now we need a hosting server. Before implementing a Windows service to host the pizza service, a simple console application for testing is good enough. This way it is also easier to debug the application, and it is not a lot of work. If the solution doesn't work with the console application it will not work as a Windows service.

The test server is a simple console application, PizzaServerTest, that reads the remoting configuration file to activate the remote channel and the remote object, and calls Console.ReadLine() so that the server doesn't exit:

```
// PizzaServerTest.cs

using System;
using System.Runtime.Remoting;
using System.Configuration;
namespace PizzaServerTest
{
   class TestServer
   {
      static void Main(string[] args)
      {
         RemotingConfiguration.Configure("PizzaService.config");
         Console.WriteLine("Press return to exit");
         Console.ReadLine();
      }
   }
}
```

Configuration File

The configuration file `PizzaService.config` defines the channel and the endpoint name of the remote object. Because the channel should be reached across the Internet, the HTTP server channel that is predefined in the file `machine.config` is used. If you don't have a web server running on your machine you can configure the server to run on port 80. Here, I'm using port 9000 because this port is not used on my PC.

The remote object is defined as a well-known type. The mode `SingleCall` defines that a new object is created with every method call. Objects of this object type can be destroyed after a method call so we don't hold unnecessary resources for a client on the server.

The URI that can be used to access this object as is shown here: http://servername:9000/PizzaService /PizzaOrderService.soap. We use the `.soap` extension to mark that the SOAP formatter is used for this remote object. As we know from Chapter 6, the SOAP formatter is the default formatter for the HTTP channel:

```
<configuration>
   <system.runtime.remoting>
      <application name="PizzaService">
         <service>
            <wellknown mode="SingleCall"
               type="PizzaService.PizzaOrderService, PizzaService"
               objectUri="PizzaOrderService.soap" />
         </service>
         <channels>
            <channel ref="http server" port="9000" />
         </channels>
      </application>
   </system.runtime.remoting>
</configuration>
```

PizzaDeliveryService Web Service

The second web service that we are going to implement for the Pizza Delivery solution is the one that will be used in the intranet from the Windows client. It shouldn't be possible to use the HTTP channel to access the second remote object `PizzaDeliveryService`, but the object is coupled with the `PizzaOrderService` object such that the `PizzaOrderService` object should invoke a method in the `PizzaDeliveryService` object. This means that all clients that register events in `PizzaDeliveryService` are informed when a new pizza order arrives. We will implement this event feature later after implementing the methods that will be invoked directly from the Windows client.

Deliver Pizzas – Sequence

Looking again at the use case diagram we had earlier when we started this project, we have the Sales Application actor that starts the Deliver Pizza use case. Until now, we haven't discussed this sequence in detail, because this is the action that we have to implement in the second web service.

The sequence diagram below shows the communication of the Windows client application with the Pizza Delivery web service. The client application will call `GetUnprocessedOrders()` from the Web service to display all pizza orders that are not processed. The class `PizzaDeliveryService` calls the method with the same name from `PizzaDB` to get a `DataSet` that in turn is returned to the client. Next the client can call `GetOrderDetailsForOrderId()` to get the pizza information from a selected order. Here again a `DataSet` is returned. When delivering an order, `ProcessOrder()` gets called which updates the database by calling the method `UpdateOrderToBeProcessed()`:

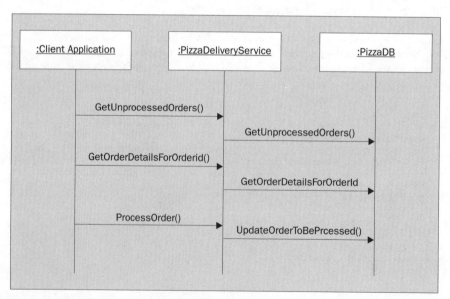

PizzaDeliveryService – Remote Object Class

Similarly to the `PizzaOrderService` class we created earlier, `PizzaDeliveryService` must derive from `MarshalByRefObject`. We create a new source file `PizzaDeliveryService.cs`, but put it in the same assembly as the other remote object, `PizzaService`:

```
// PizzaDeliveryService.cs

using System;
using System.Runtime.Remoting;
using System.Data;
using System.Configuration;
namespace PizzaService
{
    public class PizzaDeliveryService : MarshalByRefObject
    {
```

The methods in the `PizzaDB` that will be used from this class are already implemented, so writing the methods of `PizzaDeliveryService` is an easy task. In all of these methods, we simply create a `PizzaDB` object to call one method as we have seen in the sequence diagram:

```
public DataSet GetUnprocessedOrders()
{
    PizzaDB data = new PizzaDB();
    return data.GetUnprocessedOrders();
}
public DataSet GetOrderDetailsForOrderId(int orderId)
{
    PizzaDB data = new PizzaDB();
    return data.GetOrderDetailsForOrderId(orderId);
}
public void ProcessOrder(int orderId)
{
    PizzaDB data = new PizzaDB();
    data.UpdateOrderToBeProcessed(orderId);
    return;
}
```

Two Channels for Two Remote Objects

The challenging task starts now: `PizzaOrderService` is available via an HTTP channel, but to connect to `PizzaDeliveryService` we should use a TCP channel. It is easy to configure multiple channels for a remote object with a configuration file: the channel must be added to the <channels> section, and the client can choose the channel to connect to the remote object. The scenario is different here, however. We don't want to allow connections to the `PizzaDeliveryService` over the HTTP channel. This class should only be used from the intranet.

The first idea I had about this was to add a second <application> section that is used for the second remote object, but this doesn't work as only one application element is allowed in the <system.runtime.remoting> section.

The second idea was to use two configuration files, and to call `RemotingConfiguration.Configure()` a second time. The second call to `Configure()` results in an exception because the application name was already set.

So the conclusion of my tests is:

> It is not possible to use multiple application sections in a single application domain. The architecture of .NET Remoting allows just one remoting application per application domain.

We have to find a different way to implement different channels for different objects inside a process. My third idea was to create a new application domain with a different configuration file for each domain.

Creating an Application Domain

We already discussed application domains in Chapter 6, but here we have a real use for them. One way to use two different channels for the two services would be to run inside different processes, and to use a TCP channel for communication between them, but the challenge here is that both services should run inside the same process. We can create a second application domain to make different objects available to different channels.

We'll use the `TestServer` that we implemented previously and extend it to start the second remote channel in a new application domain. In the `Main()` method of this console application, we create a new application domain using `AppDomain.CreateDomain()`, and create an instance of `DeliveryMain`. The constructor of the `DeliveryMain` class configures the second service with the file `PizzaDeliveryService.config`:

```
class TestServer
{
    static void Main(string[] args)
    {
        RemotingConfiguration.Configure("PizzaOrderService.config");
        AppDomain deliveryDomain = AppDomain.CreateDomain("Delivery");
        ObjectHandle oh = deliveryDomain.CreateInstance(
            "PizzaServerTest", "PizzaServerTest.DeliveryMain");
        Console.WriteLine("Press return to exit");
        Console.ReadLine();
    }
}
class DeliveryMain
{
    public DeliveryMain()
    {
        RemotingConfiguration.Configure("PizzaDeliveryService.config");
    }
}
```

Configuration File

The configuration file `PizzaDeliveryService.config` is shown here:

```
<configuration>
    <system.runtime.remoting>
        <application name="PizzaDeliveryService">
            <service>
                <wellknown mode="Singleton"
                    type="PizzaService.PizzaDeliveryService,
                    PizzaService"
                    objectUri="PizzaDeliveryService.bin" />
            </service>
            <channels>
                <channel ref="tcp" port="9001" />
            </channels>
        </application>
    </system.runtime.remoting>
</configuration>
```

The remote object for the Pizza Delivery service is configured as `Singleton` because here we want to have state, but this state should also be shared for all clients. Unlike the ASP.NET clients that are used for ordering pizzas, we don't expect that many clients for the delivery of `Pizzas`.

The `objectUri` that defines the endpoint to the remote object has the `bin` extension to indicate that we will use the binary formatter. With the TCP channel we use here the binary formatter is the default.

Supporting Events

Now the really challenging task starts. The service `PizzaDeliveryService` should call an event handler in the Windows client application to inform the client application when a new order arrives. The challenging part in this is that this event should be invoked from the `PizzaOrderService` that is running in a different application domain from the `PizzaDeliveryService`.

Order a Pizza Sequence with Events

The sequence diagram to order a pizza we have seen earlier is extended with the event mechanism: calling the `OrderPizza()` method of the `PizzaOrderService` should not only add the order to the database, but should also call `PizzaOrderArrived()` in the `PizzaDeliveryService` object. This in turn should call the event handler in the Windows client application that is shown in the right of this diagram:

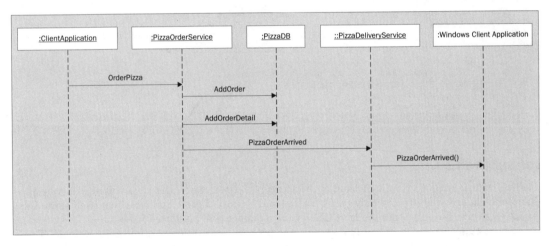

To implement events we must:

❑ Define a delegate that specifies the parameters of the method that will be called in the client application

❑ Declare a event that makes it easy for the client application to register an event handler

❑ Invoke the event to inform the client when a new pizza order arrives

Let's look at this in more detail.

Delegates and Events for PizzaDeliveryService

We have to add a delegate to the file `PizzaDeliveryService.cs`. The delegate `PizzaOrderEvent` defines the arguments of the handler that the client must implement. A good idea would be to pass the `PizzaOrder` object when a new order arrives. The parameter must be serializable to be passed to the client application; this is the case with `PizzaOrder`. `PizzaOrder` is the type of the second parameter with the `PizzaOrderEvent` delegate. The first parameter is the sender of the event to make it possible for the receiving method to get the information about the event publisher. This is a convention that should be used with events.

To make it easy for the Windows client application to register an event handler we declare an event of type `PizzaOrderEvent` in the class `PizzaDeliveryService`. This way the Windows client application can use the += operator to add an event handler:

```
// PizzaDeliveryService.cs

using System;
using System.Runtime.Remoting;
using System.Data;
using System.Configuration;
namespace PizzaService
{
    public delegate void PizzaOrderEvent(object sender, PizzaOrder order);

    /// <summary>
    /// PizzaDeliveryService for singleton remote objects
    /// </summary>

    public class PizzaDeliveryService : MarshalByRefObject
    {
        public event PizzaOrderEvent OrderArrived;
        public PizzaDeliveryService()
        {
        }

//...
```

Invoking the Event

Calling `OrderArrived()` in a method of the `PizzaDeliveryService` class will now invoke all handlers that are registered for this event. This would be easy if the Windows client itself started the event sequence, but this is not the case. The event sequence will be started from the `PizzaOrderService` that is running in the same process but a different application domain. The TCP channel shouldn't be used for communication with the `PizzaDeliveryService` because it incurs unnecessary overhead if used inside an application domain.

The sequence diagram shown opposite gives a good overview of how the client will get informed when a new order arrives. When the `OrderPizzas()` method in the `PizzaOrderService` class is called, we call the method `PizzaOrderArrived()` in the `PizzaDeliveryServiceHelper` class. This method in turn calls `PizzaOrderArrived()` in the `PizzaDeliveryService` class, which sends the event to the Windows client application.

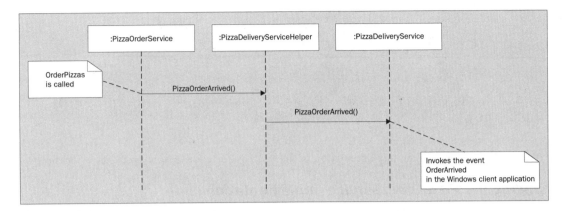

The `PizzaDeliveryService` object is configured as a `Singleton`, which means that all remote clients using the object will get a reference to the same instance. Only one object will be created for all clients using it across a channel. The `PizzaOrderService` class is not using the `PizzaDeliveryService` across the TCP channel, so the `Singleton` doesn't apply to the `PizzaOrderService`. We can solve this dilemma by adding a static member to the class `PizzaDeliveryService` that references an object of this class. The static member referencing the Singleton is called `singleton`. This static variable is initialized in the constructor of the class that will be invoked when the remote object is created:

```
public class PizzaDeliveryService : MarshalByRefObject
{
    public event PizzaOrderEvent OrderArrived;
    protected static PizzaDeliveryService singleton = null;
    public PizzaDeliveryService()
    {
        singleton = this;
    }
}
```

By creating a static method `PizzaOrderArrived()` in the class `PizzaDeliveryService`, it will be possible to invoke all registered event handlers with a call to the defined event `OrderEvent()`. This method will be called from the `PizzaOrderService` class. There's the useful side effect here that, because this method is not an instance method, it will not be available for .NET remoting clients. These clients shouldn't call this method anyway.

It could happen that no Windows client has yet created the first instance of the `PizzaDeliveryService` class, when an ASP.NET client orders pizzas. This is why we check if `singleton` is still `null` before invoking the event:

```
public static void PizzaOrderArrived(PizzaOrder order)
{
    if (singleton != null)
        singleton.OrderArrived(singleton, order);
}
```

Static methods cannot be called in a different application domain; a static method will be invoked in the application domain of the caller. To avoid this problem, we create a helper class with a instance method that can be called across application domains, and invokes the static method `PizzaDeliveryService.PizzaOrderArrived()`:

```
public class PizzaDeliveryServiceHelper : MarshalByRefObject
{
    // method will be passed to be called from the PizzaService

    public void PizzaOrderArrived(PizzaOrder order)
    {
        PizzaDeliveryService.PizzaOrderArrived(order);
    }
}
```

Now we have to change the implementation of the `PizzaOrderService` class to allow for this.

Changing the PizzaOrderService Implementation

The `PizzaOrderService` class has to invoke a method on the `PizzaDeliveryService` class that must be passed to the `PizzaService` class. Again, we declare a delegate with the same arguments:

```
// PizzaOrderService.cs

//...

namespace PizzaService
{
    public delegate void OrderReceived(PizzaOrder order);

    /// <summary>
    /// Remote object class to order Pizzas
    /// </summary>

    public class PizzaOrderService : MarshalByRefObject
    {

//...
```

Additionally to that, we create an instance of the delegate, and add a static method `RegisterOrderReceivedHandler()` which assigns the passed handler to the delegate:

```
private static OrderReceived orderReceived = null;
public static void RegisterOrderReceivedHandler(OrderReceived handler)
{
    orderReceived = handler;
}
```

Now we can change the implementation of `OrderPizzas()` to invoke the `orderReceived()` method in the `PizzaDeliveryService` class in the file `PizzaDeliveyService.cs`:

```
public void OrderPizzas(PizzaOrder order)
{
    // use the database component to Add a order
    PizzaDB data = new PizzaDB();
    int orderid = data.AddOrder(order.Email);

    foreach (PizzaOrderDetail item in order.OrderDetails)
    {
```

```
        data.AddOrderDetail(orderid, item.PizzaKey,
            (int)item.PizzaSize, item.Quantity);
    }

    if (orderReceived != null)
    {
        orderReceived(order);
    }
}
```

Assigning the Delegate

The job of the hosting server of the web services is to assign the function that must be called in the `PizzaDeliveryService` class to the delegate of the `WebService` class. We will change our test server to do this task. Until now, the test server only created a second application domain and configured the channels and remote objects with the configuration files.

The sequence diagram shown overleaf makes this complex scenario easier to understand. The two big rectangles represent the different application domains: the application domain for the Pizza Order service, and the application domain for the Pizza Delivery service. Both application domains are running inside the same process. In the rectangles of these application domains we can see the communication between the objects for the initialization process:

❑   The `TestServer` creates an object of the class `DeliveryMain` inside the Delivery application domain. We have implemented this already for the second web service.

❑   Next, the `TestServer` needs the event handler to pass it to the `PizzaOrderService`. For this task `GetDeliveryHandler()` of the `DeliveryMain` class gets called. This method creates a new instance of the class `PizzaDeliveryServiceHelper` and returns the method `PizzaOrder Arrived` to the `TestServer`. The `TestServer` passes this method to the `PizzaOrderService` in the `PizzaOrderService.RegisterOrderReceivedHandler()` method.

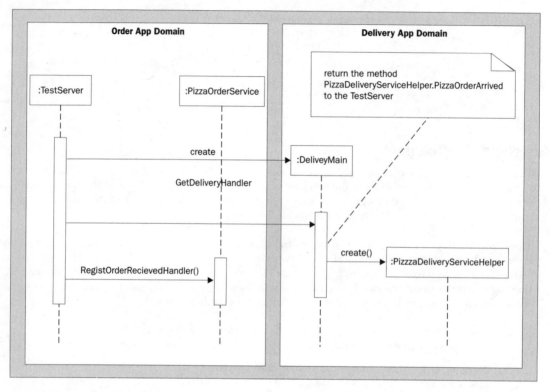

Let's step into the implementation. The `DeliveryMain` class will now be invoked across application domains, so it must derive from `MarshalByRefObject`. The method `GetDeliveryHandler()` creates a new instance of the helper class `PizzaDeliveryServiceHelper`, and returns a delegate to the `PizzaOrderArrived` method of this helper class:

```
class DeliveryMain : MarshalByRefObject
{
    public DeliveryMain()
    {
        RemotingConfiguration.Configure("PizzaDeliveryService.config");
    }
    public OrderReceived GetDeliveryHandler()
    {
        PizzaDeliveryServiceHelper helper =
            new PizzaDeliveryServiceHelper();
        return new OrderReceived(helper.PizzaOrderArrived);
    }
}
```

The class that is running in the first application domain of the server now unwraps the `ObjectHandle` that is returned. It does this when creating an instance in the delivery domain to call the method `GetDeliveryHandler()` to pass the delegate to the `PizzaOrderService`:

```
class TestServer
{
    static void Main(string[] args)
    {
        RemotingConfiguration.Configure("PizzaOrderService.config");
        AppDomain deliveryDomain = AppDomain.CreateDomain("Delivery");
        ObjectHandle oh = deliveryDomain.CreateInstance("PizzaServerTest",
            "PizzaServerTest.DeliveryMain");
        DeliveryMain delivery = (DeliveryMain)oh.Unwrap();

        // call GetDeliveryHandler in the other app domain

        PizzaOrderService.RegisterOrderReceivedHandler(
            delivery.GetDeliveryHandler());
        Console.WriteLine("Press return to exit");
        Console.ReadLine();
    }
}
```

In the next chapter, we will implement the Windows client application whose only job in regard to these events is to implement a sink class and register a sink object in the PizzaDeliveryService class.

Windows Service

When the service is running in the console application, we can change the hosting server to a Windows service. Using a Windows service has the advantage that the service can be automatically started at boot-time, and a configured account can be used to run it.

Using the Visual Studio .NET project **Windows Service** automatically creates a handler when the service is started and stopped.

We can configure the remoting channel using a configuration file using the OnStart() method that is called when the service is started. Creating a second application domain to configure a second remote object can be done in the same way that we did it earlier with the console application server:

```
protected override void OnStart(string[] args)
{
    RemotingConfiguration.Configure("PizzaService.config");
}
```

OnStop() is called when the service is stopped. We should stop the running channels. If the channels are configured using a configuration file, we can get the registered channels with the help of the utility class ChannelServices.

RegisteredChannels() returns an array of all channels that are registered in the runtime. Unregistering the channel with the UnregisterChannel() method stops a channel.

```
protected override void OnStop()
{
    IChannel[] channels = ChannelServices.RegisteredChannels;
    foreach (IChannel channel in channels)
    {
        ChannelServices.UnregisterChannel(channel);
    }
}
```

After adding the code to start and stop the channels, we can add service installers to install and configure the service application. With the service installers, the service can be installed using the installutil command-line utility, or a Windows installer package.

Summary

In this chapter, we have created two web services. The service PizzaOrderService is available over an HTTP channel and uses the SOAP formatter; PizzaDeliveryService uses a TCP channel and the binary formatter and is meant to be used in an intranet. With this service, we can order pizzas by writing orders to the database. With the service PizzaDeliveryService it is not only possible to process an order, but a client can also register its interest to be informed when new orders arrive.

We have seen that events can be used across the network as if they were located locally, but in this chapter an additional complexity was added because different application domains were used for these two services. This was because it is not allowed to put objects that require different channels in the same application domain. Over the course of this chapter, we have seen how an object can be marshaled across different application domains.

In the next chapter we implement an ASP.NET and a Windows client application that use the services we built in this chapter.

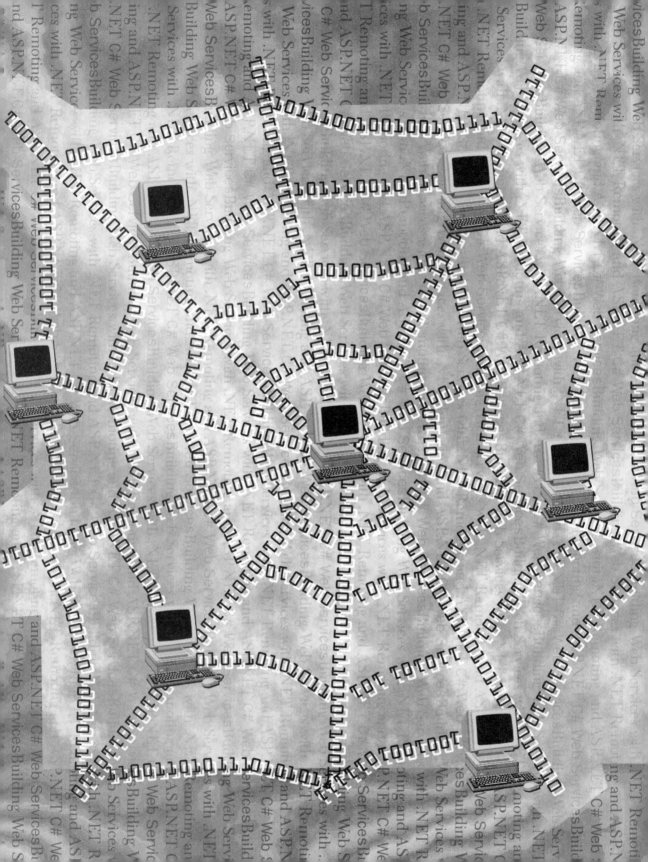

9

Building a .NET Remoting Client

In this chapter, we will implement two .NET Remoting clients. One client will use the ASP.NET functionality and connect using an HTTP channel; the second will be implemented as a Windows Forms client and will use a TCP channel.

For the HTTP channel, we will use **soapsuds** and discuss the features of this utility to create the meta data required for the client application's proxy.

In the ASP.NET application, we will use a Web Forms data grid control to display all available pizzas returned from the PizzaService, and make it possible to place pizza orders.

The Windows application will use a Windows Forms data grid control to display all open orders. From this application we can view and process the open orders. This application will also implement an **event sink** to get up-to-the-minute information for newly arrived orders that will be called from the PizzaDelivery web service.

Web Services

In the last chapter we implemented two web services. The PizzaService web service is available using an HTTP channel. It can easily be configured to be called across the Internet. The PizzaServiceDelivery web service uses a TCP channel.

Let's review the methods that are available from these services by looking at a class diagram of the upcoming solution:

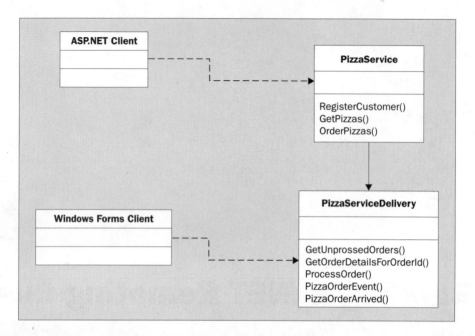

The PizzaService web service supports the methods RegisterCustomer(), GetPizzas(), and OrderPizzas(). A new customer can register their personal data with RegisterCustomer(). If the customer is already registered, they can immediately use GetPizzas() to get a list of all available pizzas and OrderPizzas() to place a new order that is written to the database.

The PizzaServiceDelivery web service will be used from a TCP channel. GetUnprocessedOrders() returns all orders that are not delivered. GetOrderDetailsForOrderId() returns all pizzas in a single order, and ProcessOrder() should be used for orders that are delivered to the customer.

The event PizzaOrderEvent can be used from the Windows client to register an event handler to get up to the minute information about new orders. The PizzaService class uses the class method PizzaOrderArrived() to pass information about new orders.

Let's begin by implementing the ASP.NET client.

ASP.NET Client

The ASP.NET client uses a simple user interface, which can be seen in the following screenshot. There are some labels, a text box to enter the e-mail address, a grid control, a submit button, and a hyperlink. The hyperlink points to a registration page that can be used if the customer's e-mail address is not already registered.

Web Pizza Order

If you already registered with Web Pizza, you can order your Pizzas here. If you didn't register, register here!   Registration

E-Mail: [   ]

Pizza	Topping	Select for Order	Quantity
Databound	Databound	☐	1
Databound	Databound	☐	1
Databound	Databound	☐	1
Databound	Databound	☐	1
Databound	Databound	☐	1

[Send Order]   Error Message

When the page is loaded, the grid will be filled with Pizzas, and the user will be able to select the pizzas to order and enter a quantity. If the user hasn't previously registered their e-mail address, the following form must be completed before placing an order:

Web Pizza Order

Registration

First Name: [   ]

Last Name: [   ]

Email: [   ]

City: [   ]

Street: [   ]

ZIP Code: [   ]

Phone Number: [   ]

[Register]

Error Message

Web.Config

The configuration file of an ASP.NET application is `Web.config`. Unlike with console applications, the section `<system.runtime.remoting>` is read automatically by the ASP.NET runtime to configure a channel and a remote object. It is not necessary to call `RemotingConfiguration.Configure()` explicitly as we have done earlier. All we have to do is write a remoting entry to `Web.config`, as we can see here:

```
<system.runtime.remoting>
    <application>
        <client url="http://localhost:9000/PizzaService">
            <wellknown type="Wrox.Pizza.Service.PizzaService, PizzaService"
                url="http://localhost:9000/PizzaService/PizzaService.soap" />
        </client>
        <channels>
            <channel ref="http client" />
        </channels>
    </application>
</system.runtime.remoting>
</configuration>
```

In the `<client>` section we specify the URI to the well-known remote `PizzaService` object

Remoting Services and WSDL

Like with ASP.NET web services, remoting services that use the HTTP channel and the SOAP formatter also offer WSDL information. You can use a web browser (as shown in the screenshot opposite) to obtain the WSDL information by passing the URL to the remote object appended with a `?wsdl`. For our remoting Web service I'm using the URL http://localhost:9000/PizzaService/PizzaService.soap?wsdl.

The WSDL feature of .NET remoting only differs from that for ASP.NET Web Services in not offering help and test pages:

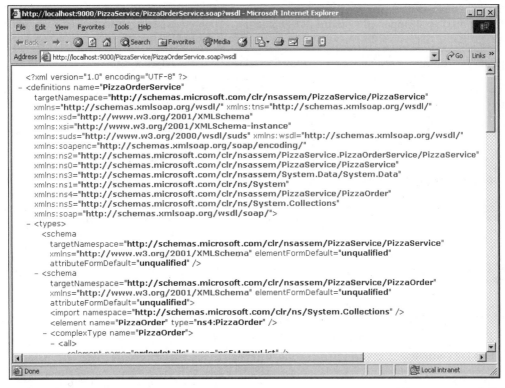

Similarly to ASP.NET Web services, we can use the wsdl.exe utility for .NET remoting with HTTP channels. However, as we've already discussed this tool when we covered ASP.NET web services, we'll move directly on to cover the use of the soapsuds tool instead.

Soapsuds Utility

With soapsuds, we can create a proxy by using the metadata of the remote object. This generated proxy can be used to access the remote object across the network.

If we access the WSDL information from a remote server that requires authentication, we have several options for authentication . If the remote server can be accessed through a proxy server, we can also configure this server with soapsuds command-line options:

Option	Short version	Description
-domain:domainname	-d:domainname	If the server where we access the WSDL information requires authentication, we can pass the username, password, and domain name with the options -u, -p, and -d
-username:user	-u:username	
-password:password	-p:password	
-httpproxyname:proxyserver	-hpn:proxyserver	If we use a proxy server to access the remote server, the options -hpn and -hpp can be used to specify server name and port number
-httpproyport:port	-hpp:port	

With `soapsuds`, we can use assemblies directly to read the metadata, or we can access the WSDL information that is supported from the HTTP channel. The `soapsuds` options for input are listed here:

Options for Input	Short Version	Description
`-inputassemblyfile:filename`	`-ia:filename`	With `-ia`, the metadata of an assembly is read to generate a proxy
`-types:type1, assembly`		If you want to create specific classes from an assembly, the option `-types` can be used
`-inputschemafile:schema`	`-is:schema`	If you already have a schema file, this can be used as input source
`-inputdirectory:directory`	`-id:directory`	You can specify a different input directory to read the assembly from with `-id`
`-urltoschema:schema`	`-url:schema`	With `-url` we can read the WSDL information from a running server

The `soapsuds` options that influence the generated output are here:

Options for Output	Short Version	Description
`-generatecode`	`-gc`	Proxy classes with C# sourcecode are generated using this option. We can add these classes to our client assembly.
`-outputassemblyfile:filename`	`-oa:filename`	Instead of generating C# sourcecode, an assembly that can be referenced from the client assembly is generated with `-oa`.
`-proxynamespace:namespace`	`-pn:namespace`	By default, the generated code is in the same namespace as the server code. You can change the namespace of the generated code with the `-pn` option. If you use a different namespace for the client-generated proxy, you also have to change the configuration file of the remoting client to reflect the newly assigned namespace in the type declaration.
`-strongnamefile:filename`	`-sn:filename`	If you generate an assembly with the `-oa` option, it is also possible to create a shared one. With the `-sn` option, a key file can be referenced to create a strong name for the assembly.

Options for Output	Short Version	Description
`-nowrappedproxy`	`-nowp`	By default a proxy class is generated that invokes the remote object across the channel. With the option `-nowp` the generated methods are empty and do not call the remote object.
`-wrappedproxy`	`-wp`	
`-outputdirectory:directory`	`-od:directory`	`-od` specifies the output directory. The default output directory is the current directory.
`-outputschemafile:schema`	`-os:schema`	If you want a schema file created, you can use the `-os` option to specify the file name.
`-sdl`		The default option `-wsdl` generates a WSDL schema. With `-sdl` the SDL schema can be generated.
`-wsdl`		

Creating a Proxy Using soapsuds

For the HTTP channel we will use the `soapsuds` utility to create a proxy class using the running server.

The command:

```
soapsuds -url:http://localhost:9000/PizzaService/PizzaService.soap?wsdl -gc
```

creates C# source files from the metadata of the remote object. The option `-url` requires the path to the remote object that returns the WSDL information. Be sure to append `?wsdl` so that the schema describing the methods of the remote object is returned. The option `-gc` generates C# sourcecode.

The `soapsuds` utility generates two source files for our service: `PizzaService.cs` and `PizzaOrder.cs`. The generated code for the remote object class resides in the source file `PizzaService.cs`. Let's look into this file:

```
namespace Wrox.Pizza.Service {
using System;
using System.Runtime.Remoting.Messaging;
using System.Runtime.Remoting.Metadata;
using System.Runtime.Remoting.Metadata.W3cXsd2001;
[SoapType(XmlNamespace =
"http://schemas.microsoft.com/clr/nsassem/Wrox.Pizza.Service/PizzaService",
XmlTypeNamespace =
"http://schemas.microsoft.com/clr/nsassem/Wrox.Pizza.Service/PizzaService")]
    public class PizzaService :
        System.Runtime.Remoting.Services.RemotingClientProxy
    {
```

The namespace that is generated is the same as the original `PizzaService` class. The namespace that is included is `System.Runtime.Remoting.Metadata`, which defines some SOAP attributes. The SOAP attributes such as `[SoapType]`, `[SoapMethod]`, and `[SoapField]` are used to control the SOAP wire format.

With the `wsdl.exe` utility (which we discussed in Chapter 5), the proxy class derives from `SoapHttpClientProtocol`. With soapsuds, the proxy class derives from `RemotingClientProxy` instead.

In the constructor of the `PizzaService` class, we configure the proxy. The `ConfigureProxy()` method of the `RemotingClientProxy` class accepts the type and URI of the remote object class. A transparent proxy is then generated, and this will be referenced using the protected field `_tp`:

```
// Constructor

public PizzaService()
{
    base.ConfigureProxy(this.GetType(),
        "http://192.168.0.16:9000/PizzaService.soap");
    System.Runtime.Remoting.SoapServices.PreLoad(
        typeof(Wrox.Pizza.PizzaOrder));
}
```

All public methods of the remote object class are created for the proxy class, too. The implementation just calls the same method of the transparent proxy:

```
// Class Methods


    [SoapMethod(SoapAction =
"http://schemas.microsoft.com/clr/nsassem/Wrox.Pizza.Service.PizzaService/
    PizzaService#GetPizzas")]
    public System.Data.DataSet GetPizzas()
    {
        return ((PizzaService) _tp).GetPizzas();
    }
    [SoapMethod(SoapAction =
"http://schemas.microsoft.com/clr/nsassem/Wrox.Pizza.Service.PizzaService/
    PizzaService#OrderPizzas")]
    public void OrderPizzas(Wrox.Pizza.PizzaOrder order)
    {
        ((PizzaService) _tp).OrderPizzas(order);
    }
    [SoapMethod(SoapAction =
"http://schemas.microsoft.com/clr/nsassem/Wrox.Pizza.Service.PizzaService/
    PizzaService#RegisterCustomer")]
    public void RegisterCustomer(String email, String firstName,
        String lastName, String city, String street, String zip,
        String phone)
    {
        ((PizzaService) _tp).RegisterCustomer(email, firstName,
            lastName, city, street, zip, phone);
    }
    }
}
```

The `OrderPizzas` method requires a `Wrox.Pizza.PizzaOrder` class. This class is also generated automatically by the `soapsuds` utility. `PizzaOrder` can be found in the file `PizzaOrder.cs`. Instead of public properties, public fields are automatically generated by the utility:

```
namespace Wrox.Pizza {
using System;
using System.Runtime.Remoting.Messaging;
using System.Runtime.Remoting.Metadata;
using System.Runtime.Remoting.Metadata.W3cXsd2001;

    [Serializable, SoapType(XmlNamespace =
        "http://schemas.microsoft.com/clr/nsassem/Wrox.Pizza/PizzaOrder",
        XmlTypeNamespace =
        "http://schemas.microsoft.com/clr/nsassem/Wrox.Pizza/PizzaOrder")]
    public class PizzaOrder
    {

        // Class Fields

        [SoapField(Embedded=true)]
        public System.Collections.ArrayList orderdetails;
        public String email;
    }
}
```

With the client application we need both the `PizzaOrder` class and `PizzaOrderDetail`. The `AddOrderDetail` method is not created with the `soapsuds` tool, so we will not use this generated class in the client. Instead, we will use the `PizzaOrder` assembly that we created in Chapter 8.

Creating an Assembly Using Soapsuds

Instead of creating C# source files, we can create assemblies using the following syntax:

```
soapsuds -url:http://localhost:9000/PizzaService/PizzaService.soap?wsdl
         -oa:PizzaService.dll
```

The generated code is the same as we have seen with the C# source files, but we get an assembly instead.

Filling the DataGrid

After adding the soapsuds-generated file `PizzaService.cs` and the assembly `PizzaOrder` to the ASP.NET client application, we can fill the `DataGrid` and pass order requests to the web service.

Page_Load Event

The proxy class `PizzaService` (which was created in the file `PizzaService.cs`) has a useful role when communicating with the remote object. We create the proxy in the `Page_Load` event handler in the file `PizzaOrder.aspx.cs` that is called when the page is loaded. We check if the page is initially loaded by examining the `PostBack` flag.

After creating the proxy with the `PizzaService` constructor, we can call `GetPizzas()` to obtain a `DataSet` that contains all available pizzas. With the data binding technology, the data grid is associated with the data source. How the `PizzaListDataGrid` displays the pizzas must be defined with grid-templates. We will show this in the next section:

```
        private void Page_Load(object sender, System.EventArgs e)
        {
           if (!Page.IsPostBack)
           {
              Wrox.Pizza.Service.PizzaService service =
                 new Wrox.Pizza.Service.PizzaService();
              DataSet ds = service.GetPizzas();

              PizzaListDataGrid.DataSource = ds.Tables[0];
              PizzaListDataGrid.DataBind();
           }
        }
```

DataGrid Templates

The `System.Web.UI.WebControls.DataGrid` class provides some templates that can be added to the `aspx` page for defining the display of multiple rows.

The `<asp:BoundColumn>` elements directly associate a column of the grid with a field of the data source. In our example, the second column of the grid is bound to the `Topping` field in the record of the `DataSet`.

`<asp:TemplateColumn>` elements are more powerful, in that the layout of this column can be completely customized by adding other elements. The first column of the grid specifies the header text `Pizza`, and a child `<ItemTemplate>`. In the `<ItemTemplate>` element of the first column, we can see two `<asp:Label>` elements. The first label element is only used to read the identity of the selected pizzas when the order is submitted. `DataBinder.Eval(Container.DataItem, "Id")` associates this label with the `Id` column of the `Pizzas` record. This label is not displayed. The second label displays the name of the pizza.

The third column displays a checkbox where the user can select a pizza to order. This checkbox is not associated with the data source. The ID of this checkbox, `Select`, will be used to obtain the selection value.

Because the user can not only select a pizza to order, but also order more than one of the selected pizzas, the forth column displays a textbox. The user can enter the quantity of pizzas in here. The initial value in this textbox is 1 as we can assume that, mostly, only one pizza will be ordered. The identifier `Quantity` will be used to get the value of this field:

```
<asp:datagrid id="PizzaListDataGrid" style="Z-INDEX: 106;
                  LEFT: 54px; POSITION: absolute; TOP: 234px"
                  runat="server" AutoGenerateColumns="False">
   <HeaderStyle Font-Bold="True"></HeaderStyle>
   <Columns>
      <!-- 1st column -->
      <asp:TemplateColumn HeaderText="Pizza">
         <ItemTemplate>
            <asp:Label ID="PizzaID" Runat="server" Text=
               '<%# DataBinder.Eval(Container.DataItem, "Id") %>'
               Visible="false" />
            <asp:Label ID="PizzaName" Runat="server" Text=
               '<%# DataBinder.Eval(Container.DataItem, "Name") %>'
               />
         </ItemTemplate>
      </asp:TemplateColumn>
      <!-- 2nd column -->
```

```
        <asp:BoundColumn DataField="Topping" HeaderText="Topping" />
        <!-- 3rd column -->
        <asp:TemplateColumn HeaderText="Select for Order">
            <ItemTemplate>
                <center>
                    <asp:CheckBox ID="Select" Runat="server" />
                </center>
            </ItemTemplate>
        </asp:TemplateColumn>
        <!-- 4th column -->
        <asp:TemplateColumn HeaderText="Quantity">
            <ItemTemplate>
                <center>
                    <asp:TextBox ID="Quantity" Runat="server"
                        Columns="2" Width="20px">1</asp:TextBox>
                </center>
            </ItemTemplate>
        </asp:TemplateColumn>
    </Columns>
</asp:datagrid>
```

Starting the page in a browser will display the pizzas that are returned from the web service in the database, as we can see in the screenshot below. The only thing left to do (apart from the registration) is to write a handler for the submit button:

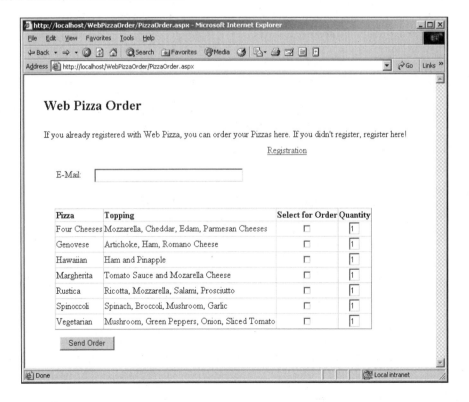

Submit Handler

In the click event handler of the submit (**Send Order**) button, we order all requested pizzas via the web service. We create a new `PizzaOrder` object locally on the client. To allow this, the `PizzaOrder` assembly must be referenced, and the namespace `Wrox.Pizza` must be included. The `EMail` property is set to the e-mail address that is entered in the `TextEmail` textbox.

We then loop through all items in the data grid. `PizzaListDataGrid.Items[i]` returns a `DataGridItem` from the current row. As you will remember, we have a check box in the third column that can be identified with the `Select` ID. Instead of stepping to the third column and the children inside this column, we can search the control by using the `FindControl()` method of the `DataGridItem` to get to a reference to a control returned.

`PizzaListDataGrid.Items[i].FindControl("Select")` returns the `CheckBox` control of this row. We use this checkbox to verify if the pizza was chosen for an order; if not then we continue with the next row in the `for` loop.

If the pizza was selected, we read the quantity and the pizza key in the same way that we accessed the checkbox element. For every selected pizza, we create a new `PizzaOrderDetail` object that is added to the `PizzaOrder`.

Both `PizzaOrder` and `PizzaOrderDetail` can be serialized, so we can pass the `PizzaOrder` to the web service with the method `OrderPizzas()`:

```csharp
private void ButtonSubmitOrder_Click(object sender,
    System.EventArgs e)
{
    PizzaOrder order = new PizzaOrder();
    order.EMail = TextEmail.Text;
    for(int i=0; i < PizzaListDataGrid.Items.Count; i++)
    {
        CheckBox selected = (CheckBox)
            PizzaListDataGrid.Items[i].FindControl("Select");
        if (selected.Checked)
        {
            TextBox txtQty = (TextBox)
                PizzaListDataGrid.Items[i].FindControl("Quantity");
            Label labelKey = (Label)
                PizzaListDataGrid.Items[i].FindControl("PizzaId");
            PizzaOrderDetail item = new PizzaOrderDetail();
            item.PizzaKey = labelKey.Text;
            item.Quantity = Convert.ToInt32(txtQty.Text);
            order.AddOrderDetail(item);
        }
    }
    PizzaService service = new PizzaService();
    service.OrderPizzas(order);
    Response.Redirect("OrderCompleted.aspx");
}
```

We can now request a lot of pizzas with a single order as can be seen in the screenshot opposite. Pressing the **Send Order** button will process the order, and if successful, `OrderCompleted.aspx` is the next page that we'll see.

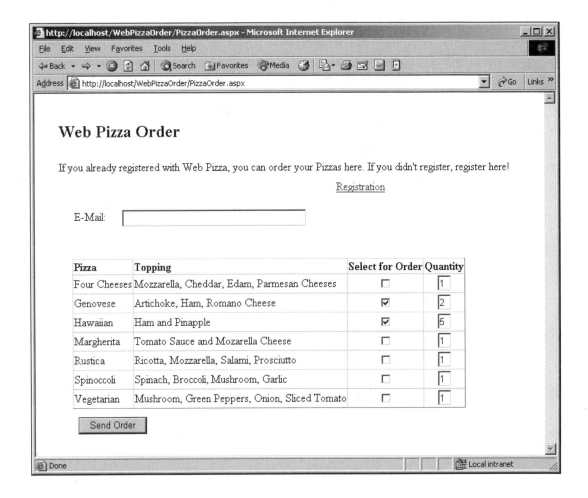

Windows Forms Client

The second client we are creating is the one that uses the TCP channel. This client will be created as a Windows application using Windows Forms.

User Interface

The user interface of this client has two grid controls, three buttons, and some labels as can be seen in the following screenshot showing the design. The first grid control (dataGridOpenOrders) will display all of the orders that have not been processed at this time. The second grid control (dataGridSelectedOrder) will display all of the pizzas in the order selected by the first control.

Pressing the Refresh button will reload the open orders from the web service. The Process button will be clicked when the selected order is delivered. Here, the web service will be used to mark the order as processed.

The label **NEW ORDER** is not visible by default. This label will show up when a new order arrives. We will use events across the network to get this behavior:

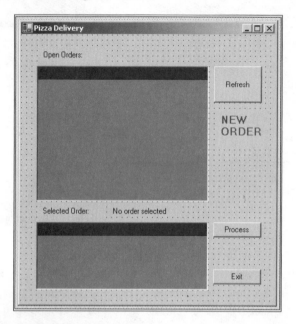

Client Channel Configuration

The Windows client will use the TCP channel to connect to the PizzaServiceDelivery web service; again we use a configuration file to configure the channel:

```
<configuration>
    <system.runtime.remoting>
        <application name="Client">
            <client url="tcp://localhost:9001/PizzaServiceDelivery">
                <wellknown type="Wrox.Pizza.Service.PizzaServiceDelivery,
                    PizzaService"
url="tcp://localhost:9001/PizzaServiceDelivery/PizzaServiceDelivery.rem" />
                                                        </client>
            <channels>
                <channel ref="tcp" port="9003" />
            </channels>
        </application>
    </system.runtime.remoting>
</configuration>
```

The client will supply an event handler that will be called from the remote service. We also have to assign a port number that is not already used from a different application. In this instance, we'll be using the port number 9003.

The configuration file is loaded in the `Main()` method of the Windows application:

```
[STAThread]
static void Main()
{
    RemotingConfiguration.Configure("PizzaDelivery.exe.config");
    Application.Run(new FormDelivery());
}
```

This web service uses a TCP channel and the binary formatter, so we can't use the soapsuds utility to generate a client proxy. We need a different way to make the metadata of the remote service assembly available, so we add a reference to the assembly `PizzaService` to the client application.

Implementing the Windows Event Handlers

To get the open orders from the web service, we create a protected helper method `RefreshOrders()`. We call the `GetUnprocessedOrders()` method of the web service to get a `DataSet` of all open orders. By assigning the table of this `DataSet` to the `DataSource` property of the data grid, the data binding mechanism is activated to display all elements of the data set in the grid control:

```
protected void RefreshOrders()
{
    try
    {
        dataGridOpenOrders.BeginInit();
        PizzaServiceDelivery delivery = new PizzaServiceDelivery();
        DataSet ds = delivery.GetUnprocessedOrders();
        dataGridOpenOrders.DataSource = ds.Tables[0];
    }
    finally
    {
        dataGridOpenOrders.EndInit();
    }
    labelNewOrderArrived.Visible = false;
}
```

The `RefreshOrderDetails()` method is somewhat similar to `RefreshOrders()`. We still call the web service, but this time we call the `GetOrderDetailsForOrderId()` method instead, and use data binding with the second grid control. We have to pass an order ID to this method, which can be read from the first grid control:

```
protected void RefreshOrderDetails()
{
    try
    {
        dataGridSelectedOrder.BeginInit();

        // get order id of the selected order

        int row = dataGridOpenOrders.CurrentCell.RowNumber;
        int orderId = (int)dataGridOpenOrders[row, 0];
        PizzaServiceDelivery delivery = new PizzaServiceDelivery();
        DataSet ds = delivery.GetOrderDetailsForOrderId(orderId);
        dataGridSelectedOrder.DataSource = ds.Tables[0];
```

```
            selectedOrder = orderId;
            labelOrderId.Text = selectedOrder.ToString();
        }
        finally
        {
            dataGridSelectedOrder.EndInit();
        }
    }
```

The call to both refresh methods is added to the constructor of the form class so that the grids immediately display the order information at program start:

```
public FormDelivery()
{
    try
    {

        //
        // Required for Windows Form Designer support
        //

        InitializeComponent();
        RefreshOrders();
        RefreshOrderDetails();
    }
    catch (Exception ex)
    {
        MessageBox.Show(ex.Message, "Error",
            MessageBoxButtons.OK, MessageBoxIcon.Error);
    }
}
```

In case the remote server is not available, we catch the exception with a `try...catch` block. The default error message if the server is not running is displayed below.

`RefreshOrders()` is also called in response to the click event of the **Refresh** button. The code for this event handler is shown here. Because such a remote call can take some time, the cursor is changed to a wait cursor during the method call:

```
private void buttonRefresh_Click(object sender, System.EventArgs e)
{
    Cursor currentCursor = Cursor.Current;
    try
    {
        Cursor.Current = Cursors.WaitCursor;
        RefreshOrders();
    }
    catch (Exception ex)
    {
```

```
            MessageBox.Show(ex.Message, "Error",
               MessageBoxButtons.OK, MessageBoxIcon.Error);
         }
         finally
         {
            Cursor.Current = currentCursor;
         }
      }
```

`RefreshOrderDetails()` will be called when the user clicks in the first grid control to select a order:

```
      private void DataGridOpenOrders_Click(object sender,
         System.EventArgs e)
      {
         Cursor currentCursor = Cursor.Current;
         try
         {
            Cursor.Current = Cursors.WaitCursor;
            RefreshOrderDetails();
         }
         catch (Exception ex)
         {
            MessageBox.Show(ex.Message, "Error",
               MessageBoxButtons.OK, MessageBoxIcon.Error);
         }
         finally
         {
            Cursor.Current = currentCursor;
         }
      }
```

Process the Selected Order

The selected order will be processed in the `Click` event handler of the **Process** button. Here we call the `ProcessOrder()` method of the web service. After processing a order, `RefreshOrders()` is called again so that the processed order is not displayed in the order list:

```
      private void buttonProcess_Click(object sender, System.EventArgs e)
      {
         Cursor currentCursor = Cursor.Current;
         try
         {
            PizzaServiceDelivery delivery = new PizzaServiceDelivery();
            delivery.ProcessOrder(selectedOrder);

            RefreshOrders();
            dataGridSelectedOrder.DataSource = null;
         }
         catch (Exception ex)
         {
            MessageBox.Show(ex.Message, "Error",
               MessageBoxButtons.OK, MessageBoxIcon.Error);
         }
         finally
         {
            Cursor.Current = currentCursor;
         }
      }
```

Running the Client Application

When the client application is running, all orders are displayed in the first grid control as soon as the application is started. All order details for a single order are displayed in the second grid control as soon as the order is selected. Pressing the Process button removes the order from the open order list. Note that the e-mail addresses are all non-functional, for obvious reasons:

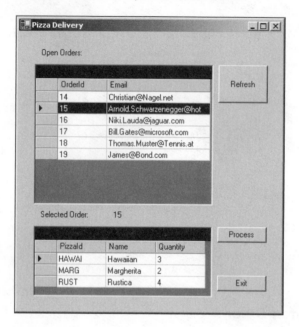

Adding Event Handling

Up to this point, we've used only the client part of the channel in the client application. We simply called the web service as we did previously with the ASP.NET application. However, we also want to be informed when a new order arrives with the Windows client. The label NEW ORDER should show up as soon as a new order arrives.

To do this, we also have to add some code to the server so that the server fires the event. In the client, we also have to implement an event handler.

Creating a Sink Class

For the sink class, we create a separate DLL assembly called OrderArrivedSink. The sink class must derive from MarshalByRefObject, because this class will be called across the network. An instance will be created on the client, and it will be called from the server. The method OrderArrived() must have the same signature and return type as the delegate we have defined in Chapter 8.

The [OneWay] attribute declares the method as a fire-and-forget method because the server will not get a return value. This method will be called asynchronously. We discussed this in Chapter 6.

In the method that is called by the server, we set a flag so that the NEW ORDER label is visible. A reference to this label is passed inside the constructor of this class:

```
using System;
using System.Runtime.Remoting.Messaging;
using Wrox.Pizza;
namespace Wrox.Pizza.Client
{
    public class OrderArrivedSink : MarshalByRefObject
    {
        private System.Windows.Forms.Label labelNewOrderArrived;
        public OrderArrivedSink(System.Windows.Forms.Label label)
        {
            labelNewOrderArrived = label;
        }
        [OneWay]
        public void OrderArrived(object sender, PizzaOrder order)
        {
            labelNewOrderArrived.Visible = true;
        }
    }
}
```

Registering a Sink Object

In the Windows client application, we have to reference the assembly of the sink class. The OrderArrived() method of the sink class should be registered in the server as soon as the client starts.

In the FormDelivery constructor, we can create a new OrderArrivedSink object and pass the label that should be made visible when the event arrives. The PizzaServiceDelivery remote object supports the event OrderArrived to be called across the network. A new delegate instance (PizzaOrderEvent) is assigned to this event using the += operator. The argument of the delegate constructor is the OrderArrived method of the sink object, because this will be called from the server. The delegate itself will be passed by value across the network to the server because it implements ISerializable, but the argument of the delegate will be passed by reference. Remember that the sink derives from MarshalByRefObject:

```
        private OrderArrivedSink sink = null;
        public FormDelivery()
        {
            try
            {

                //
                // Required for Windows Form Designer support
                //

                InitializeComponent();
                RefreshOrders();
                RefreshOrderDetails();

                // register sink

                sink = new OrderArrivedSink(labelNewOrderArrived);
                PizzaServiceDelivery delivery = new PizzaServiceDelivery();
                delivery.OrderArrived += new PizzaOrderEvent(sink.OrderArrived);
            }
```

```
            catch (Exception ex)
            {
               MessageBox.Show(ex.Message, "Error",
                  MessageBoxButtons.OK, MessageBoxIcon.Error);
            }
         }
```

Now, when we add a new order with the ASP.NET client application, the NEW ORDER label will be made visible until the Refresh button is clicked again.

Summary

In this chapter, we have created ASP.NET and Windows Forms clients for a HTTP and a TCP channel. We used the soapsuds utility to create a proxy using the metadata of the HTTP channel. For TCP channels, this utility cannot be used as it is based on SOAP information. We referenced the assembly of the service to create the proxy for the Windows Forms client.

With both clients, we used configuration files to configure the channel. It is not necessary to load the configuration file explicitly with ASP.NET applications because this is done automatically from the ASP.NET runtime. However, the configuration has to be put into Web.config. Windows Forms applications require an explicit call to RemotingConfiguration.Configure().

We have also seen that events can be called across the network, and that the implementation is not very different from using local events. We only have to check that the sink can be called remotely by deriving the sink class from MarshalByRefObject, and to configure the correct channels that send and receive on both sides of the network.

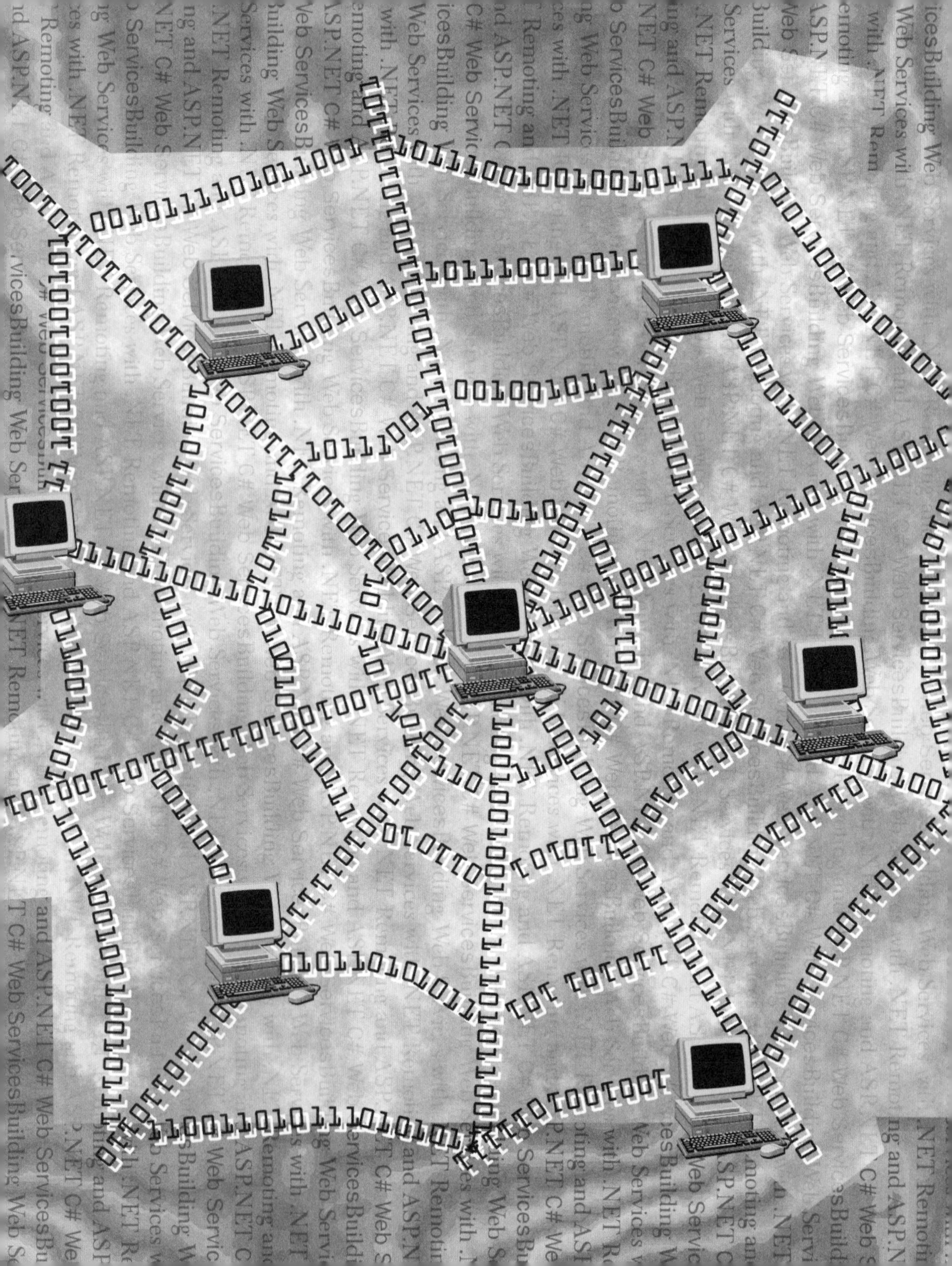

Section Four – Advanced Topics

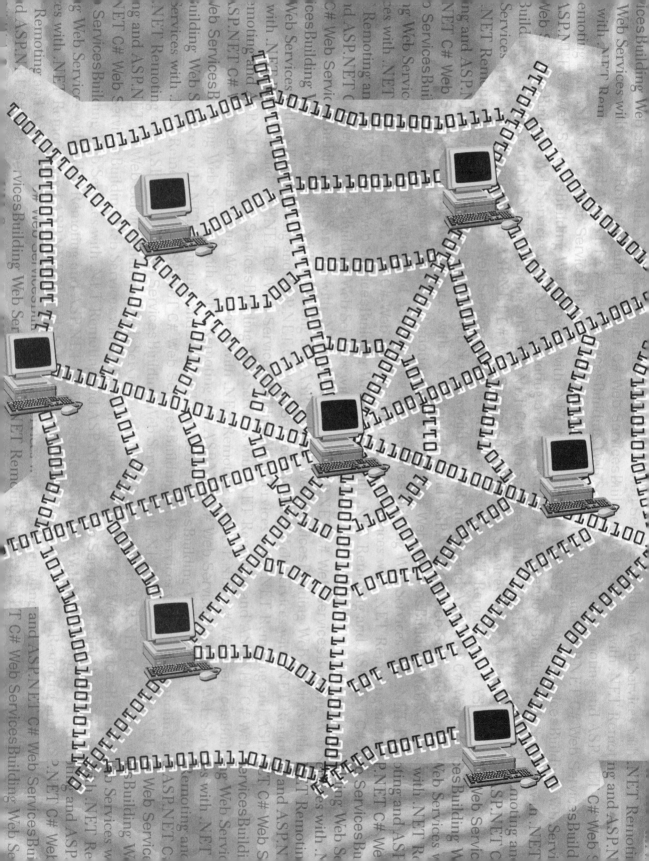

Universal Description, Discovery, and Integration (UDDI)

Do you remember the early days of the Internet? Do you remember the boring text browsers and the tedious socket programming? Since then the world has changed a lot. The Internet is a household commodity now.

What makes the greatest research tool known to mankind so powerful? The answer is the searching mechanisms. It does not matter how many new web pages get added every day if our clients cannot find them. There are millions of web pages on the Internet, but some pages are never visited by any user. What would the Internet be without search engines like Yahoo or Google?

The next generation of web programming will be heavily based on web services. There will be numerous web services that aim to add value to products and services. How will a potential B2B online order publisher find a web service that is compatible with its system? Is there a way to find out what web services IBM offers? Can I publish and promote my web service so that other people can benefit from my hard labor?

It seems obvious that we need to create a registry of web services. This registry will contain details about businesses and the services they offer. This is the essence of UDDI.

What is UDDI?

UDDI stands for Universal Description, Discovery, and Integration. UDDI is an industry standard agreed by a number of software vendors headed by Microsoft, IBM, and Ariba. UDDI involves the shared implementation of a web service based on the UDDI specifications. The UDDI Business Registry is an internet directory of businesses and the applications they have exposed as web services for trading partners and customers to use. UDDI was mainly developed to:

❑ Facilitate the discovery of web services

❑ Define how web services interact over the Internet

❑ Share the web service information in a global registry

Web Services Discovery Mechanism

Web service discovery is the process of locating, or discovering, one or more Web Services Description Language (WSDL) documents that describe a particular web service.

1. A web service client will locate a service using a web services directory (UDDI). The UDDI will have a link to the discovery document of the web service.

2. An XML discovery (DISCO) file will be returned to the client when a request is made for the discovery document. The DISCO files are explained in the next section.

3. The discovery file will have the service description information (WSDL file links). The WSDL files will describe the services in XML format. The web service consumers can create proxy objects using the WSDL file and start using the web service.

What are DISCO Files?

The discovery (DISCO) specification defines an algorithm for locating service descriptions. If web service clients know the location of the service description (WSDL file), they can bypass the discovery process.

A published `.disco` file, which is an XML document that contains links to other resources describing the web service, enables programmatic discovery of a web service. The following example shows the structure of a discovery document:

```
<?xml version="1.0" ?>
<disco:discovery xmlns:disco="http://schemas.xmlsoap.org/disco"
                 xmlns:wsdl="http://schemas.xmlsoap.org/disco/wsdl">
   <wsdl:contractRef ref="http://MyWebServer/webService.asmx?WSDL"/>
</disco:discovery>
```

The `.disco` file contains links (URLs) to resources that provide discovery information for a web service. This example clearly mentions the location of the WSDL contract. If the URLs are relative, they are assumed to be relative to the location of the discovery document. However, a web site that implements a web service need not support discovery. Another site, such as a UDDI directory, could be responsible for describing the service. Alternatively, there may be no public means of finding the service, such as when you create it for private use.

UDDI Building Blocks

The core of the UDDI technology is the UDDI registry. This registry is a collection of information on all the registered web services. The information on web services falls into three general categories:

❑ **White pages information** – this is general information about the web service. For example URL for web services, Company name, address etc. This information is similar to white pages phone book information.

❑ **Yellow pages information** – the category system is similar to regular yellow pages categories. The categorization is done by standards bodies. These categories are based on standard taxonomies. For example, Microsoft is classified under "NAICS (North American Industrial Classification System) : Software Publisher".

❑ **Green pages information** – the green pages describe the services offered by the web service. This is the key part for discovering the potential of the web service. This section will list all public interfaces and discovery mechanisms to find associated web services.

Here are the services offered by Microsoft, as listed in the uddi.microsoft.com registry:

Services

Click on service name to see the full service details:

Name	Description	Service Key
UDDI Web Sites	UDDI Registry Web Sites	86e46aad-82a5-454f-8957-381c2f724d6f
UDDI Web Services	UDDI SOAP/XML message-based programmatic web service interfaces.	33c3d124-e967-4ab1-8f51-d93d95fac91a
Home Page	Corporate Home Page	17b29861-2f33-402c-98f0-fd16cf5b8e9c
Online Shopping	This site is designed to help you easily learn about and order Microsoft® software and hardware and Microsoft Press® titles that can enhance your computing.	491e8f93-e90f-42e3-a048-726744453659
Microsoft Developer Network	MSDN, the Microsoft Developer Network, is the essential resource for developers. MSDN developer programs make it easy to find timely, comprehensive development resources, including software subscription programs, technical information, Web sites, and conf	4de36949-e757-4de1-a3bd-b3f1d4350325
Technet	TechNet provides in depth "how-to" technical information on Microsoft products as well as a chance to interact with peers — and Microsoft. You can access forums for sharing best practices with others and provide feedback directly to Microsoft regarding fu	f9d39c6f-aa09-4c5c-bc7b-6b26b0ba016d
Volume Licensing Select Program	The select program for volume licensing user guide for the Select CD application.	367df918-7d5e-4b00-8cf6-afe56367c2d6
Electronic Business Integration Services	EBIS EDI information	bd9b1a10-4668-42e9-ac69-d3da905c314d
Web services for smart searching	These services provide support for smarter resolution of mistyped URLS for web sites.	a97ef39e-853b-47bd-985a-1eb0fab7d342

It is important to note that UDDI is a registry in the sense that it contains entries that direct users to resources outside it. The data contained in UDDI is relatively lightweight; as a registry, its task is to provide network addresses to the resources – schemas, interface definitions, endpoints. These data structures reside in other locations.

Also, it is important to note that UDDI has been designed in a highly normalized fashion. Therefore it is not bound to any technology. In other words, a UDDI registry entry can contain any type of resource, whether that resource is XML-based or not. For example, the UDDI registry could contain information about a business's EDI system and its DCOM interface or a service that uses the fax machine as its primary communication mechanism. The point here is that, while UDDI itself uses XML to represent the data it stores, it allows for other kinds of technology to be registered. This design decision was made to ensure that UDDI is an infrastructure that endures and does not become outdated as technology moves forward.

Accessing UDDI on the Web

Both Microsoft and IBM have set up UDDI registries that can be searched through their web-based interfaces. This manual method is the simplest way to perform a UDDI search.

❑ The IBM UDDI web interface can be found at http://www-3.ibm.com/services/uddi/find

❑ The Microsoft UDDI web interface can be found at http://uddi.microsoft.com/

In addition to allowing searches, both of these web-based interfaces allow businesses and services to be registered.

Accessing UDDI Programmatically

As UDDI registries are themselves web services, we can interact with UDDI at both design time and run time to discover technical data about a business's services, so that those services can be invoked and used. This will allow us to tightly integrate our applications with UDDI.

The UDDI Data Structures

Obviously, for a system designed to act as a large-scale registry of businesses, the structures used to store the data are very important. The UDDI data structures have been designed with flexibility in mind; they allow a wide range of business situations to be represented. They have also been designed to ensure that related information in the registry can be easily linked.

The individual facts about a business, its services, technical information or even information about specifications for services are kept separate, and are accessed individually by way of unique identifiers, or keys. A UDDI registry assigns these unique identifiers when information is first saved, and these identifiers can be used later as keys to access the specific data instances on demand.

Each unique identifier generated by a UDDI registry takes the form of a Universally Unique ID (UUID).

A UUID is a hexadecimal string that has been generated according to an algorithm that prevents any two UUIDs from ever being the same.

A UUID looks something like this:

```
AEAC8990-2891-3894-DEC1-AEF97501DD1B
```

UDDI has 4 main data structures, each of which is represented as an XML element.

❑ Business information is stored in a businessEntity element

❑ Service information is stored in a businessService element

❑ Binding information is stored in a bindingTemplate element

❑ Specifications for the services offered are stored in a tModels element

Storing Business Information

You only need a `businessEntity` element to publish data within a UDDI repository. The other data elements are optional.

During the discovery phase, the `businessEntity` element serves as a handle to retrieve pertinent information about a company. A `businessEntity` element contains the following types of information:

❑ Company name

❑ Business description and industry codes such as NAICS and UNSPSC (the Universal Standard Products and Services Classification)

❑ The products and services offered

❑ The geographical location the company serves

The `businessEntity` element uses the following elements to store the company information:

❑ `name` – stores the name of the company. This is a required attribute.

❑ `description` – stores a text description of the business.

❑ `contacts` - stores a set of `contact` elements, which each hold the contact information of someone within the business.

❑ `categoryBag` - stores data categorized on industry type (based on NAICS), product type (based on UNSPSC), service type, and geography.

❑ `IdentifierBag` – stores industry codes, for instance D&B number, which uniquely identify the `businessEntity`.

`categoryBag` and `IdentifierBag` are structures that group entities. With the help of these structures we can drill down into business information on given variables (for example, according to geography).

Here is an example of a simple `businessEntity` element:

```
<businessEntity businessKey="434554F4-6E17-1342-EA41-36E642531DA0" operator="">
    <name>Chris Peiris Personal Web Site</name>
    <description xml:lang="en">A non comercial web site for educational
                purposes</description>
    <contacts>
        <contact>
            <description xml:lang="en">Systems Architect</description>
            <personName>Chris Peiris</personName>
            <phone>613 414238903</phone>
            <email>chris_peiris@yahoo.com</email>
            <address>
                <addressLine>ITE Level 11</addressLine>
                <addressLine>No. 25 Bligh St. Sydney</addressLine>
            </address>
        </contact>
    </contacts>
</businessEntity>
```

Note the UUID stored in the `businessKey` attribute of the `businessEntity` element. As we mentioned before, these UUIDs allow us to refer to a particular entity within UDDI, safe in the knowledge that there can be no ambiguity.

Storing Service Information

Service information deals with technical and business descriptions. It is stored in the `businessService` element. Each web service has one or more technical web descriptions. These technical descriptions include information that allows clients to communicate with the service. This could be:

❑ URLs or addresses to communicate to child web services

❑ Configuration options on the host web server

❑ Prerequisite web services that should run before this web service

❑ Load balancing information on the host web server

Information about invoking a web service is stored in an element called `bindingTemplate`. The `bindingTemplate` "binds" technical and business data to a web service. So what information do we bind? We need to know all the technical information that we require for seamless integration of the web service. For example, for a purchase order web service, we may need to answer the following questions:

❑ What is the format of our purchase orders?

❑ Are they in a specific XML format geared towards online transactions such as OBI (Open Buying on Internet)?

❑ What are the security requirements for accessing purchase orders?

The `businessService` and `bindingTemplate` data structures go hand in hand. Here is an example of those structures:

```
<businessService businessKey="434554F4-6E17-1342-EA41-36E642531DA0"
serviceKey="AEAC8990-2891-3894-DEC1-AEF97501DD1B">

  <name>Sample electronic invocing system</name>

  <description xml:lang="en">
    This is a custom built invoicing system. OBI (Open Buying on the Internet)
    XML standard is used transfer data between 2 different business entities.
  </description>

  <bindingTemplates>
    <bindingTemplate bindingKey="FE542889-EE4B-2348-2345-AEFC3901223A"
    serviceKey="AEAC8990-2891-3894-DEC1-AEF97501DD1B">

    <description xml:lang="en">Sample Invoicing Template</description>

    <accessPoint URLType="http">http://www.test_bindingtemplate3.com</accessPoint>

    <tModelInstanceDetails>
      [tModel Data goes here]
    </tModelInstanceDetails>
    </bindingTemplate>
  </bindingTemplates>
</businessService>
```

The `businessService` element contains the key of the service entity and also the key for the business it belongs to.

```
<businessService businessKey="434554F4-6E17-1342-EA41-36E642531DA0"
serviceKey="AEAC8990-2891-3894-DEC1-AEF97501DD1B">
```

The `name` and `description` elements then add some information about the service

```
<name>Sample electronic invocing system</name>

<description xml:lang="en">
   This is a custom built invoicing system. OBI (Open Buying on the Internet)
   XML standard is used transfer data between 2 different business entities.
</description>
```

The `bindingTemplates` element contains the `bindingTemplate` elements. Each contains its own key and the key of the service it belongs to in order that the service can still be referenced if the `bindingTemplate` element is separated from the rest of the `businessService`:

```
<bindingTemplates>
    <bindingTemplate bindingKey="FE542889-EE4B-2348-2345-AEFC3901223A"
    serviceKey="AEAC8990-2891-3894-DEC1-AEF97501DD1B">
```

We use the description element to describe the binding template and, in this case, we use the `accessPoint` element to provide information on how the service is accessed:

```
        <description xml:lang="en">Sample Invoicing Template</description>
        <accessPoint URLType="http">http://www.test_bindingtemplate3.com</accessPoint>
```

We could have used a `hostingRedirect` element, in place of `accessPoint`, to redirect requests for information to another `bindingTemplate`. Either `accessPoint` or `hostingRedirect` must be included. This roughly translates to "Tell clients how to access your service or point them in the direction of another binding template."

In the `tModelInstanceDetails` element, we would include details of the technology models that apply to this service. Technology models are covered in the next section.

Technology Models

UDDI draws a distinction between abstraction and implementation with its concept of the technology model. The `tModel` structure represents technical fingerprints, interfaces, and abstract types of meta data. Binding templates are the concrete implementation of one or more `tModels`. Inside a binding template, we register the access point for a particular implementation of a `tModel`. `tModels` can be published separately from binding templates that reference them. For example, a standards body or industry group might publish the canonical interface for a particular use case. Several businesses could then write implementations to this interface. Accordingly, each of those businesses' implementations would refer to that same `tModel`.

Each `tModel` also gets a unique identifier to help companies, and more importantly other applications, to find it. The `tModels` represent all the integration information required to consume a web service. Different service providers can easily build a software product to consume the web service as long as the tModels are compatible.

A useful example of how UDDI and WSDL relate can be found by looking at the UDDI web service itself. The UDDI API is a SOAP-based XML API defined by an XML schema (http://www.uddi.org/schema/2001/uddi_v1.xsd) and corresponding WSDL files for inquiry (http://www.uddi.org/wsdl/inquire_v1.wsdl) and publishing (http://www.uddi.org/wsdl/publish_v1.wsdl). If you examine these WSDL files, you will discover they do not have a `<service>` element identified; in other words, no endpoints are provided.

261

These two WSDL files have been registered in UDDI as `tModels`. The `uddi-org:publication` WSDL is defined as follows in UDDI:

```
<tModelDetail generic="1.0" operator="Microsoft Corporation" truncated="false"
xmlns="urn:uddi-org:api">
  <tModel tModelKey="uuid:64c756d1-3374-4e00-ae83-ee12e38fae63"
  operator="www.ibm.com/services/uddi" authorizedName="0100000M99">

    <name>uddi-org:publication</name>

    <description xml:lang="en">
      UDDI Publication API - Core Specification
    </description>

    <overviewDoc>
      <description xml:lang="en">
        This tModel defines the publication API calls for interacting
        with the UDDI registry.
      </description>
      <overviewURL>http://www.uddi.org/wsdl/publish_v1.wsdl</overviewURL>
    </overviewDoc>

    <categoryBag>
      <keyedReference tModelKey="uuid:c1acf26d-9672-4404-9d70-39b756e62ab4"
        keyName="types" keyValue="specification" />
      <keyedReference tModelKey="uuid:c1acf26d-9672-4404-9d70-39b756e62ab4"
        keyName="types" keyValue="xmlSpec" />
      <keyedReference tModelKey="uuid:c1acf26d-9672-4404-9d70-39b756e62ab4"
        keyName="types" keyValue="soapSpec" />
      <keyedReference tModelKey="uuid:c1acf26d-9672-4404-9d70-39b756e62ab4"
        keyName="types" keyValue="wsdlSpec" />
    </categoryBag>
  </tModel>
</tModelDetail>
```

As with other UDDI elements, each `tModel` has a unique key associated with it. We also define the UDDI registry that contains the master copy of this technology model, in the operator attribute. The identity of the individual that created this `tModel` is included in the `authorizedName` attribute.

```
<tModel tModelKey="uuid:64c756d1-3374-4e00-ae83-ee12e38fae63"
  operator="www.ibm.com/services/uddi" authorizedName="0100000M99">
```

The `categoryBag` element is used to hold references to information that will help to categorize this technology model. In this case, we use `keyedReference` elements to reference other technology models.

```
<categoryBag>
  <keyedReference tModelKey="uuid:c1acf26d-9672-4404-9d70-39b756e62ab4"
    keyName="types" keyValue="specification" />
  <keyedReference tModelKey="uuid:c1acf26d-9672-4404-9d70-39b756e62ab4"
    keyName="types" keyValue="xmlSpec" />
  <keyedReference tModelKey="uuid:c1acf26d-9672-4404-9d70-39b756e62ab4"
    keyName="types" keyValue="soapSpec" />
  <keyedReference tModelKey="uuid:c1acf26d-9672-4404-9d70-39b756e62ab4"
    keyName="types" keyValue="wsdlSpec" />
</categoryBag>
```

The most important categorization defines this `tModel` as being of type "`wsdlSpec`". By following these conventions, tools can be written which can search UDDI and find only `tModels` that are categorized a certain way.

The Microsoft UDDI SDK

Microsoft has provided a Software Developers Kit for UDDI. It is available from its web site by searching for "UDDI".

The SDK provides a local UDDI registry that can be used for testing applications. It also provides APIs for both Visual Studio 6 and Visual Studio .NET. For the purposes of this book, we are obviously more interested in the API for Visual Studio .NET.

Using the Send Tool

We can use the "Send.exe" utility that is included with the SDK to send requests and data to a UDDI registry. This is useful for testing a UDDI installation.

In order to use Send.exe, we must provide the full XML for the SOAP we wish to send to the registry. The following code is a request to search a UDDI registry for businesses called "Microsoft"

```
<?xml version='1.0' encoding='UTF-8'?>
<Envelope xmlns='http://schemas.xmlsoap.org/soap/envelope/'>
<Body>
    <find_business generic='2.0' xmlns='urn:uddi-org:api'>
        <name>Microsoft</name>
    </find_business>
</Body>
</Envelope>
```

If we are using the local UDDI registry, here is the syntax to request the search. (Assuming the XML data is in file called search.xml)

Send.exe http://localhost/udd/inquire.asmx search.xml

If we want to send the request to the Microsoft UDDI registry, we would use:

Send.exe http://uddi.microsoft.com/inquire search.xml

Using the SDK With C#

The Microsoft UDDI SDK includes an assembly, Microsoft.UDDI.dll, that allows us to easily access the UDDI API from within our .NET projects.

Of course, in order to use the namespaces contained in the assembly, we need to add a reference to Microsoft.UDDI.dll (It is installed with the SDK, under the VS7 folder)

We also need to add appropriate using statements to our C# files, in order that we can conveniently access the classes we need to use:

```
using Microsoft.Uddi;
using Microsoft.Uddi.Api;
using Microsoft.Uddi.Business;
using Microsoft.Uddi.Service;
using Microsoft.Uddi.Binding;
using Microsoft.Uddi.ServiceType;
```

Note that we will not always need to use all of these namespaces but we often need several of them to complete an operation.

We will be covering some simple requests to a UDDI registry. More complex requests can, of course, be made. The UDDI API specification is a good place to start if you need more details. Each method call in the specification is implemented in the Microsoft UDDI SDK as a wrapper for .NET.

Making an Inquiry

Requesting a search of a UDDI registry is known as making an inquiry.

A general process for discovery, lookup, and invocation is:

❑ Send an inquiry to a UDDI registry to locate a businessEntity element for the appropriate business offering web services

❑ Locate matching businessService elements to identify all the web services offered by a businessEntity

❑ Select a bindingTemplate element to retrieve the address of the web service and tModel element to ensure technical compatibility between the systems

Finding a Business

Searching for a business is the most basic type of UDDI inquiry. We achieve this using the find_business UDDI method. This has the following form in XML:

```
<find_business [maxRows="nn"] generic="2.0" xmlns="urn:uddi-org:api_v2">
  [<findQualifiers/>]
  [<name/><name/>...]
  [<discoveryURLs/>]
  [<identifierBag/>]
  [<categoryBag/>]
  [<tModelBag/>]
</find_business>
```

The findQualifiers element allows us to alter the behavior of the search. For instance, adding the following element inside the findQualifiers element would force the search to be case-sensitive:

```
<findQualifier>caseSensitiveMatch</findQualifier>
```

The name element contains a business name we wish to search for.

identifierBag, categoryBag, and tModelBag allow us to search for elements that contain specific references in them.

There are more details on the XML formatting of UDDI inquiry requests in the UDDI API specification.

The UDDI query find_business is represented in .NET by the class FindBusiness. The general rule is that UDDI queries are represented by classes that share the same name, once the underscore has been removed and the normal capitalization rules applied.

The following code will search the Microsoft UDDI registry for companies called "Microsoft":

```
Inquire.Url = "http://uddi.microsoft.com/inquire";
FindBusiness fb = new FindBusiness();
fb.MaxRows = 100;
fb.FindQualifiers.Add("sortByNameAsc");
fb.Name = "Microsoft";
BusinessList bl = fb.Send();
```

First we set the static member, Inquire.Url to the location of the UDDI registry inquiry service:

```
Inquire.Url = "http://uddi.microsoft.com/inquire";
```

We then create a new instance of the FindBusiness class:

```
FindBusiness fb = new FindBusiness();
```

We set some properties of the instance, to define search options.

```
fb.MaxRows = 100;
fb.FindQualifiers.Add("sortByNameAsc");
fb.Name = "Microsoft";
```

Finally, we populate a BusinessList object with the results of the inquiry by sending the request:

```
BusinessList bl = fb.Send();
```

BusinessList is a class that, as you would expect, stores a set of businesses returned by the inquiry. The SDK provides classes to represent each type of UDDI data type and sets of objects of those data types. We can access the details returned by the query as follows:

```
foreach(BusinessInfo b in bl.BusinessInfos)
{
   Console.WriteLine(b.name);
}
```

We loop through the BusinessInfo objects that are contained in BusinessList.BusinessInfos, extracting the name of each.

Once we have located a business, we will most likely want to extract more details about it. We can do this by using the get_businessDetail UDDI query, which is implemented in .NET as the class GetBusinessDetail. We must provide the query with the unique key of the business we want details for.

The following code uses a business key from a BusinessInfo object, b, that might already have been created with a find_business query:

```
GetBusinessDetail gbusinessDetails = new GetBusinessDetail();
gbusinessDetails.BusinessKeys.Add(b.BusinessKey);
BusinessDetail businessDetails = gbusinessDetails.Send();
```

The BusinessDetail object contains a set of BusinessEntity objects in its BusinessEntities member. We can therefore output the authorized names (remember, these are the identities of the individuals who add the entries to the registry) with the following code:

```
foreach(BusinessEntity e in d.BusinessEntities)
{
   Console.WriteLine(e.AuthorizedName);
}
```

Finding a service

The find_service query call returns a serviceList message that contains services that match the conditions specified in the arguments. The find_sevice query has the following format:

```
<find_service businessKey="uuid_key" " [maxRows="nn"] generic="2.0
xmlns="urn:uddi-org:api_v2" >
   [<findQualifiers/>]
   [<name/> [<name/>]...13 ]
   [<categoryBag/>]
   [<tModelBag/>]
</find_service>
```

The elements in find_service should be familiar from find_business. This query works very similarly to find_business aside from having less options and finding individual services rather than whole businesses.

find_service is represented by the .NET class FindService. We can therefore retrieve and output the names of all the services that are offered by a particular business using code such as this:

```
// (we already have a BusinessInfo object, b)

FindService fs = new FindService();
fs.BusinessKey  = b.BusinessKey;
ServiceList sList = fs.Send();

foreach(ServiceInfo s in sList)
{
   Console.WriteLine(s.name);
}
```

There are, of course many more possibilities than we have covered in this brief introduction. As we mentioned earlier, each query in the UDDI API Specification is implemented as a .Net class, allowing a wide range of queries to be constructed.

Publishing to UDDI

The Publishing API allows the following activities:

❑　Registration of new business and services

❑　Deletion of existing services of businesses

❑　Management of security on the business data (UDDI registry-specific)

The Publisher API is intended for software programmers or Independent Software Vendors (ISVs) who would like to publish their web services to a UDDI node.

UDDI Security

As the publishing API allows users to manipulate the data held in a UDDI registry, it requires a security model to ensure that users can only change appropriate data.

The authentication model for a UDDI registry is specified by the registry operator. The UDDI 2.0 specification suggests having an authentication model but does not specify or recommend any particular technology.

For instance, Microsoft could have applied any of the following authentication models to its test registry (test.uddi.microsoft.com):

❑   Normal cookie-based authentication

❑   Clear text user name/password authentication

❑   Windows integrated authentication

❑   Microsoft passport authentication

In fact, Microsoft chose to implement its Passport technology to provide security.

Authentication tokens are required for all publisher API calls. You can obtain the authentication token by invoking the get_authToken() UDDI method. Each UDDI operator can have its own system for generating authentication tokens so tokens from one registry cannot be used with another.

The get_authToken method is used to obtain an authentication token unless the registry provides some other method for getting a token:

```
<get_authToken generic="2.0" xmlns="urn:uddi-org:api_v2"
userID="someLoginName"
cred="someCredential" />
```

The cred attribute is the password or other credential that validates the user's identity.

Saving Information to UDDI

Saving Information About a Business

We can add or update information about a business to a UDDI registry by using the save_business UDDI method. The method contains the authentication token necessary to perform the operation and one or more businessEntity elements, in the following format:

```
<save_business generic="2.0" xmlns="urn:uddi-org:api_v2" >
  <authInfo/>
  <businessEntity/> [<businessEntity/>...]
</save_business>
```

For example, the following request would update the details of a business:

```
<?xml version="1.0" encoding="UTF-8"?>
<Envelope xmlns="http://schemas.xmlsoap.org/soap/envelope/">
  <Body>
    <save_business generic="1.0" xmlns="urn:uddi-org:api">
      <authInfo>udditest</authInfo>
      <businessEntity businessKey="434554F4-6E17-1342-EA41-36E642531DA0"
        operator="">
        <name>Chris Peiris Personal Web Site</name>
        <description xml:lang="en">
          A non comercial web site for educational purposes
        </description>
        <contacts>
          <contact>
            <description xml:lang="en">Systems Architect</description>
            <personName>Chris Peiris</personName>
            <phone>613 414238903</phone>
            <email>chris_peiris@yahoo.com</email>
            <address>
              <addressLine>ITE Level 11</addressLine>
              <addressLine>No. 25 Bligh St. Sydney</addressLine>
            </address>
          </contact>
        </contacts>
      </businessEntity>
    </save_business>
  </Body>
</Envelope>
```

You will notice that the authentication token is only "udditest":

```
<authInfo>udditest</authInfo>
```

The test account with UDDI SDK (udditest) has a blank password. There would be an extra password tag in a practical implementation.

We can use the "Send.exe" utility to enter this XML data into the UDDI registry. If we are using the local UDDI registry, here is the syntax to register the business (Assuming the XML data is in file called save_business.xml):

Send.exe http://localhost/udd/publish.asmx save_business.xml

If we want to create a new entry in the UDDI registry rather than update existing data, we simply send the request without UUID values for the elements we wish to create. For instance, in the previous request we could replace

```
<businessEntity businessKey="434554F4-6E17-1342-EA41-36E642531DA0"
        operator="">
```

with:

```
<businessEntity businessKey="" operator="">
```

to have the registry create a new businessEntity.

The save_business method is implemented in .NET as the SaveBusiness class. This class is used in a similar way to the query classes we saw earlier. We create an instance of the class, populate it with data (this often involves creating other UDDI objects to insert into it), and finally use the Send method to make the request:

```
//assuming we have already populated a BusinessEntity object, be

Publish.User = "udditest";
Publish.Password = "";
Publish.Url = "http://localhost/uddi/publish.asmx";

SaveBusiness s = new SaveBusiness();
s_b.BusinessEntities.Add(be);
BusinessDetail bd = s.Send();
```

Saving a Service

The save_service method adds or updates one or more businessService elements. Its format is very similar to save_business:

```
<save_service generic="2.0" xmlns="urn:uddi-org:api_v2" >
<authInfo/>
<businessService/> [<businessService/>…]
</save_service>
```

Here is an example of a request to update the details of a service:

```
<?xml version="1.0" encoding="UTF-8"?>
<Envelope xmlns="http://schemas.xmlsoap.org/soap/envelope/">
  <Body>
    <save_service generic="1.0" xmlns="urn:uddi-org:api">
      <authInfo>udditest</authInfo>
      <businessService businessKey="434554F4-6E17-1342-EA41-36E642531DA0"
        serviceKey="AEAC8990-2891-3894-DEC1-AEF97501DD1B">

        <name>Sample electronic invoicing system</name>
        <description xml:lang="en">
            This is a custom built invoicing system. OBI (Open Buying on the
            Internet) XML standard is used transfer data between 2 different
            business entities.
        </description>
        <bindingTemplates>
          <bindingTemplate
              bindingKey="FE542889-EE4B-2348-2345-AEFC3901223A"
              serviceKey="AEAC8990-2891-3894-DEC1-AEF97501DD1B">
            <description xml:lang="en">Sample Invoicing Template</description>
            <accessPoint URLType="http">
               http://www.test_bindingtemplate3.com
            </accessPoint>

            <tModelInstanceDetails>
              <tModelInstanceInfo
                 tModelKey="uuid:E31A569A-AEFF-4468-BA4D-2BF22FE4ACEE">
                 <description xml:lang="en">
                    tModel for  Individual Customers
```

```
                    </description>
                    <instanceDetails>
                      <description xml:lang="en">
                        The system is optimized to deal with small
                        volume customers to save resources.
                      </description>
                      <overviewDoc>
                        <description xml:lang="en">
                           Indivial Customer tModel Overviw
                        </description>
                        <overviewURL>
                          http://www.test_tmodel.com/instancedetails/overview.htm
                        </overviewURL>
                      </overviewDoc>
                      <instanceParms>
                        http://www.test_tmodel.com/instanceparms.htm
                      </instanceParms>
                    </instanceDetails>
                  </tModelInstanceInfo>

                <tModelInstanceInfo
                    tModelKey="uuid:E51A569A-AEFF-4468-BA4D-2BF22FE4ACEE">
                    <description xml:lang="en">
                      tModel for  Load Balacing on the Web Farm
                    </description>
                    <instanceDetails>
                    <description xml:lang="en">
                       This system uses Microsoft Network Load Balancing.
                    </description>
                     <overviewDoc>
                       <description xml:lang="en">
                         MS Network Load Balacing tModel Overviw
                       </description>
                       <overviewURL>
                          http://www.test_tmodel.com/instancedetails/overview.htm
                       </overviewURL>
                     </overviewDoc>
                     <instanceParms>
                       http://www.test_tmodel.com/instanceparms.htm
                     </instanceParms>
                    </instanceDetails>
                  </tModelInstanceInfo>

               </tModelInstanceDetails>
            </bindingTemplate>
          </bindingTemplates>
        </businessService>
      </save_service>
    </Body>
  </Envelope>
```

We give both the UUID for the service we want to update and the UUID for the business this service belongs to:

```
<businessService businessKey="434554F4-6E17-1342-EA41-36E642531DA0"
  serviceKey="AEAC8990-2891-3894-DEC1-AEF97501DD1B">
```

We then go on to give the data for the service. This service has one binding template that contains two technology models.

The save_service method is implemented in .NET with the SaveService class, which is used in the same way as SaveBusiness.

The save_binding method is also very similar in format to save_business:

```
<save_binding generic="2.0" xmlns="urn:uddi-org:api_v2" >
<authInfo/>
<bindingTemplate/> [<bindingTemplate/>…]
</save_binding>
```

This method is implemented in .NET by the SaveBinding class.

Saving a Technology Model

The save_tModel UDDI method adds or updates one or more tModel elements. As you would expect, it is similar in structure to the other methods we have seen:

```
<save_tModel generic="2.0" xmlns="urn:uddi-org:api_v2" >
  <authInfo/>
  <tModel/> [<tModel/>…]
</save_tModel>
```

The following example request shows how save_tModel is used to update the details of a technology model:

```
<?xml version="1.0" encoding="UTF-8" ?>
<Envelope xmlns="http://schemas.xmlsoap.org/soap/envelope/">
  <Body>
    <save_tModel generic="1.0" xmlns="urn:uddi-org:api">
      <authInfo>udditest</authInfo>
      <tModel operator="" tModelKey="uuid:E31A569A-AEFF-4468-BA4D-2BF22FE4ACEE">
        <name>Individual Customer tModel</name>
        <description xml:lang="en">
          This model uses simple algorithms to save CPU processing time
        </description>
        <overviewDoc>
          <description xml:lang="en">tModel Technical Spec</description>
          <overviewURL>
            http://test.uddi.org/tmodels/TEST_tModel3/overview.htm
          </overviewURL>
        </overviewDoc>
        <identifierBag>
          <keyedReference keyName="chrispeiris.com" keyValue="2000"/>
        </identifierBag>
      </tModel>
      <tModel operator="" tModelKey="uuid:E41A569A-AEFF-4468-BA4D-2BF22FE4ACEE">
        <name>Corporate Customer tModel</name>
        <description xml:lang="en">
          This model uses complex algorithms.
        </description>
        <overviewDoc>
```

```
                  <description xml:lang="en">tModel Technical Spec</description>
                  <overviewURL>
                    http://test.uddi.org/tmodels/TEST_tModel3/overview.htm
                  </overviewURL>
               </overviewDoc>
               <identifierBag>
                  <keyedReference keyName="chrispeiris.com" keyValue="2000"/>
               </identifierBag>
            </tModel>

            <tModel operator="" tModelKey="uuid:E51A569A-AEFF-4468-BA4D-2BF22FE4ACEE">
               <name>MS Load Balancing tModel Data</name>
               <description xml:lang="en">
                  The web farm is load balanced using this Microsoft technology.
               </description>
               <overviewDoc>
                  <description xml:lang="en">tModel Load Balancing Spec</description>
                  <overviewURL>
                    http://test.uddi.org/tmodels/TEST_tModel3/overview.htm
                  </overviewURL>
               </overviewDoc>
               <identifierBag>
                  <keyedReference keyName="chrispeiris.com" keyValue="2000"/>
               </identifierBag>
            </tModel>

        </save_tModel>
    </Body>
</Envelope>
```

You can see that this example request updates the details of three separate technology models. The details of each are given, according to the structure of the tModel element.

This method is implemented in .NET by the class SaveTModel.

Removing Information from UDDI

Sometimes we need to remove out of date information from a UDDI registry, rather than updating it with new data. The UDDI API provides a set of methods that remove entities from UDDI.

Deleting a Business

The delete_business API call is used to remove one or more business registrations and all direct contents from a UDDI registry:

```
<delete_business generic="2.0" xmlns="urn:uddi-org:api_v2" >
   <authInfo/>
   <businessKey/>
    [<businessKey/> ...]
</delete_business>
```

Deleting a Service

The `delete_service` API call is used to remove one or more previously `businessService` elements from the UDDI registry and from its containing `businessEntity` parent:

```
<delete_service generic="2.0" xmlns="urn:uddi-org:api_v2" >
  <authInfo/>
  <serviceKey/>
  [<serviceKey/> …]
</delete_service>
```

Deleting A Technology Model

The `delete_tModel` API call is used to logically delete one or more `tModel` structures. Logical deletion hides the deleted `tModel` from `find_tModel` result sets but does not actually remove it:

```
<delete_tModel generic="2.0" xmlns="urn:uddi-org:api_v2" >
  <authInfo/>
  <tModelKey/> [<tModelKey/> …]
</delete_tModel>
```

Deleting a Binding Template

The `delete_binding` API call causes one or more instances of `bindingTemplate` data to be deleted from the UDDI registry:

```
<delete_binding generic="2.0" xmlns="urn:uddi-org:api_v2" >
  <authInfo/>
  <bindingKey/> [<bindingKey/> …]
</delete_binding>
```

Summary

In this chapter, we have taken a brief look at the developing technology of UDDI. We have seen:

❑   That UDDI is a multi-vendor standard for building registries of businesses and services

❑   That UDDI registries can be accessed through their own interfaces or through a standard API

❑   That the Microsoft UDDI SDK allows us to programmatically access UDDI in C#

❑   The data structures that UDDI uses to store information about businesses and services

❑   The queries that we can use to extract data from UDDI registries

❑   The format of the requests that we can use to add, update, or remove UDDI data

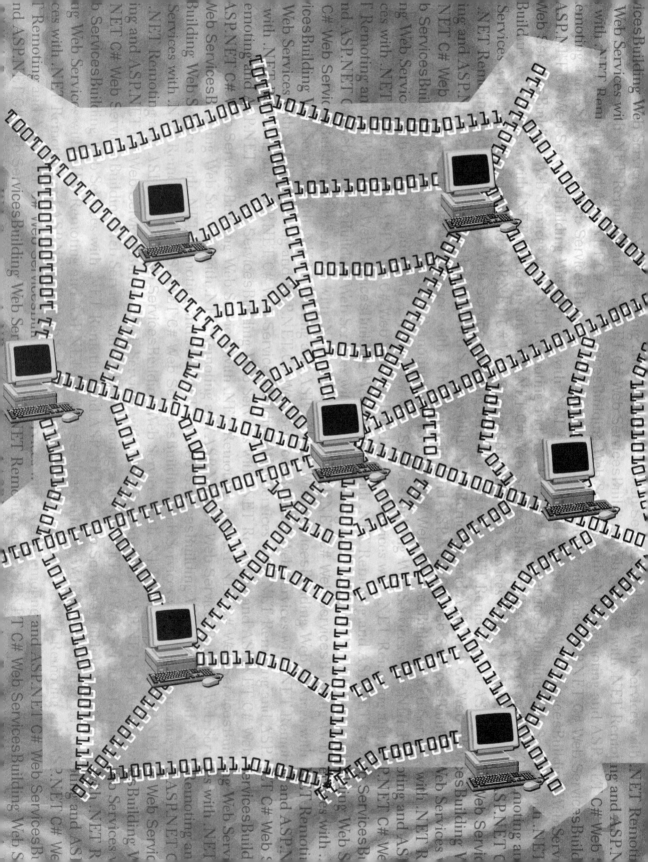

11

.NET Security and Cryptography

This chapter will cover the basics of security and cryptography and show you how to integrate this into your web services with the minimum of fuss. We'll begin this chapter with a brief discussion of the .NET Framework's security architecture, because this will have an impact on the solutions that we may choose to implement for our web services.

Cryptography is, however, the cornerstone of .Net web services security model, so we cover cryptography from the .NET Framework's reference point. This will show specific techniques for designing application-layer security along with some code examples.

From there, we'll move on to discuss the basis of cryptography, and how to implement it. We'll cover the following areas in this discussion:

- ❑   Hash algorithms
- ❑   SHA
- ❑   MD5
- ❑   Secret Key Encryption
- ❑   Public Key Cryptography Standard
- ❑   Digital Signatures
- ❑   Certification
- ❑   Secure Sockets Layer communications

We'll then extend our discussion in this area by creating a credit card example, which will transmit credit card details from the client to the server. We'll take advantage of the .NET Remoting architecture and transmit our data using a secure custom message sink using an XOR function. Later in the chapter, we'll expand this example to take advantage of key-based encryption techniques.

As always, the code for this chapter is available for download from http://www.wrox.com.

First, however, let's take a look at what web service security actually is, and why we need it.

Web Service Security

The need to secure our web services can never be over-emphasized. Web services are built to be accessed by users, so they will always be vulnerable to **DOS** (**Denial of Service**) attacks, unauthorized access attempts, and break-in attempts by vandals or hackers whose motives may vary from plain snooping to stealing financial data. Hackers may also attempt to disrupt your web services by corrupting the data or program files if they gain access to your server. You also need to secure your server against worms and viruses lurking on the Internet to ensure that your service will remain usable.

Although exposing your web service over the Internet carries the highest risk, intranets are also vulnerable to external attacks. In most cases, intranets have some segments running over wireless networks or may tunnel through other service providers (for example, using the Internet). Intranets made accessible to telecommuters through RAS (Remote Access Server) may also find this is used as an avenue by an external intruder to launch an attack on the intranet.

Web services can also be delivered over mobile networks to WAP-enabled mobile phones or similar devices having mobile IP access over GPRS, so these will also need to be protected. Except for when noted otherwise, all discussions in the following sections will be valid for such mobile network-delivered web services.

.Net Security Overview

The .NET framework provides two basic types of security models:

❑ Code Access Security

❑ Role-based Security

Code access security protects your server against malicious code or codes compromised by virus or intentional modification while being transported over Internet, whereas role-based security lets the web service determine the access and trust level of the user or the user agent acting on behalf of the user.

User authentication also logically falls within role-based security. However, due to its special significance, we'll devote a separate section to this topic. Both role-based and code access security use the same underlying architecture and APIs within the .NET framework. The core security infrastructure is implemented in `Mscorlib.dll` in the `System.Security` namespace. Each namespace extends these core classes to provide specific functionality. Let's discuss the API in more detail.

.Net Security Framework API

In this section, we will deal with the basics of the .Net security infrastructure. Specific security models relating to code access, authentication, and role-based security will be dealt with in their own sections.

> We will not cover this subject in detail in this chapter. For more information about this subject, please see *Professional C#*, published by Wrox Press (ISBN 1-861004-99-0).

Before we delve into this, though, let's take a look at the permission objects that underpin these security mechanisms.

Permission Objects

The CLR (Common Language Runtime) uses permission objects to represent permissions while enforcing the security model, manifested by the interface `System.Security.IPermission`:

```
// other-src/PermTest.cs

using System;
using System.Security;
using System.Net;
using System.Text.RegularExpressions;
public class PermTest
{
    public static void Main(string [] args)
    {
        WebPermission wp = new WebPermission();
        wp.AddPermission(NetworkAccess.Connect, new Regex(".*\\.uddi\\.org"));
        wp.AddPermission(NetworkAccess.Accept,
                        new Regex("orders\\.partner\\.com"));
        SecurityElement secEle = wp.ToXml();
        Console.WriteLine(secEle);
    }
}
```

The above console application example code will produce an XML formatted output which can be stored in a file by redirecting the console output. The `SecurityElement` produces a lightweight representation of security objects in XML format. This class is marked as `sealed`, and therefore cannot be extended. The output of the captured file is reproduced below:

```
<IPermission class="System.Net.WebPermission, System, Version=1.0.2411.0,
Culture=neutral, PublicKeyToken=b77a5c561934e089" version="1">
    <ConnectAccess>
        <URI uri=".*\.uddi\.org"/>
    </ConnectAccess>
    <AcceptAccess>
        <URI uri="orders\.partner\.com"/>
    </AcceptAccess>
</IPermission>
```

The `System.Net.WebPermission` class extends the `System.Security.CodeAccessPermission` abstract class, which in turn implements the interface `System.Security.IPermission`.

The `System.Net.WebPermission` class controls an application's right to access a URL or to serve a URI to the Internet.

`System.Net.WebPermission` defines two permissions: `accept` and `connect`. `accept` grants the application object the right to accept an incoming connection from another computer or Application Domain, whereas `connect` grants the application the right to initiate a connection to another Application Domain.

Code Access Security

The .NET Framework provides a security mechanism called **Code Access Security**. It protects computer systems from malicious mobile code, allows downloaded code to run safely, and protects trusted code from intentionally or accidentally compromising security.

Code Access Security identifies the executable codes, and grants access rights to resources based on such criteria as zone of origin (Internet, intranet, or local machine), digital signature and software developers' certificates.

Knowledge about Code Access Security comes into play while writing secure class libraries. There are two key concepts:

❑ Security Demand

❑ Security Overrides

Let's take a look at each of these in more detail.

Security Demand

Security Demand allows your class library to insist that the other classes calling your instance or static methods should have a set of permissions specified by you. You can either place the demands as attributes or can write codes explicitly.

The code below lets you place a file I/O permission demand on the caller of the method, using attributes:

```
[FileIOPermissionAttribute(SecurityAction.LinkDemand, Unrestricted=true)]
public string File2String(string fname)
```

The same end could be achieved by a different means, such as:

```
public string File2String(string fname)
{
    FileIOPermission fip = new FileIOPermission(PermissionState.Unrestricted);
    fip.Demand();

    //Read from the file and convert to string
}
```

The `Demand` method call triggers the runtime (CLR) to walk the caller stack and check the permission demanded for all the callers in the call hierarchy. A `SecurityException` is thrown if any of the callers in the call hierarchy do not have the demanded permissions.

Security Overrides

Security Overrides allow you to override the code permission explicitly. For example, while calling a third-party class library that may be implementing financial formulae, you might wish to switch off the file I/O permission temporarily:

```
FileIOPermission fip = new FileIOPermission(PermissionState.None);

fip.Deny();
Calc noTrust = new Calc();
long algo = noTrust.Compute();
fip.RevertDeny();
```

The above code switches off the file permissions (by calling `Deny` method) before dealing with a useful but an untrustworthy class. The permissions are switched on afterwards by calling the method `RevertDeny` of the permissions object.

The above technique helps prevent a type of attack called "Lure Attacks" or "Trojan Horse Attacks".

> In most cases the default .NET Framework security settings are adequate. Before incorporating Code Access Security, ensure that you are not duplicating work. The most likely condition of use is when you wish to incorporate custom permissions in your class library.

Role-Based Security

Role-based security allows your code to grant or deny permissions based on who the user is, or perhaps what their role in your organization is. Even if your code enjoys full trust from the Code Access Security perspective, your code will have same restrictions as that of the user trying to run it.

Role-based security finds applications in the financial domain. For example, a manager may be allowed to process a database table containing daily transactions but may be unable to access or modify another set of business logic objects dealing with pending stock.

The `System.Security.Principal.IPrincipal` interface represents the concept of a **Principal**. Principals define the security context. Roles are then associated with Principals. Applications implementing role-based security grant access rights based on the roles associated with the Principal. The `System.Security.Principal.IIdentity` interface represents the concept of an **Identity**, which encapsulates the user information being validated.

The implementation mechanism for role-based security is similar to that of Code Access Security. In this case, the `PrincipalPermission` object represents the identity and role that a particular principal class must possess in order to execute. You can either create a declarative permission using attributes or explicitly write a code to support it:

```
[PrincipalPermissionAttribute(SecurityAction.Demand, Name="Tom",
                              Role = "Teller")]
public class Locker
```

The following code fragment enforces role-based permission through programming:

```
String id1 = "Tom";
String role1 = "Teller";
PrincipalPermission PrincipalPerm1 = new PrincipalPermission(id1, role1);

String id2 = "Alice";
String role2 = "Supervisor";
PrincipalPermission PrincipalPerm2 = new PrincipalPermission(id2, role2);

(PrincipalPerm1.Union(PrincipalPerm2)).Demand();
```

The above code states that only the roles of `Teller` or `Supervisor` can access the rest of the code. A `SecurityException` is raised if this demand is not met.

Security Tools

Microsoft provides many security tools in its .NET SDK. Most of these tools are console-based utility applications. These can be used to help implement the security processes outlines above. We won't be discussing the use of these tools in great detail, however – as with the previous topics, please see *Professional C#* for more details about them.

There are two groups of tools provided with the SDK:

Permissions and Assembly Management Tools

Program Name	Function
Caspol.exe	Stands for Code Access Security Policy tool. Lets you view and modify security settings.
Signcode.exe	File signing tool, lets you digitally sign your executable files.
Storeadm.exe	Administration tool for isolated storage management. Restricts code access to filing system.
Permview.exe	Displays assembly's requested access permissions.
Peverify.exe	Checks if the executable file will pass the runtime test for type safe coding.
Secutil.exe	Extracts a public key from a certificate and puts it a usable format, in your source code.
Sn.exe	Creates assemblies with strong names. That is, digitally signed namespace and version info.

Certificate Management Tools

Program Name	Function
Makecert.exe	Creates a X.509 certificate for testing purposes.
Certmgr.exe	Assembles certificates into a CTL (Certificate Trust List). Can also be used for revoking.
Chktrust.exe	Validates a signed file containing data, its PKCS#7 hash and a X.509 certificate.
Cert2spc.exe	Creates an SPC (Software Publisher Certificate) from an X.509 certificate.

Custom Tools

There may be specific circumstances that will require us to develop special purpose tools. As programmers, we may be called upon by the system administrators to design specific tool kits to help secure the web services, detect attacks, or develop counter-attack devices.

One of the popular counter-attack techniques that are fast becoming popular is known as a "Honey Trap". Honey traps derive their name from the traps used by bear trappers. These consisted of a snare attached to a pot of honey to attract the bear. Similar techniques are used by the **Trackers** (the name given to those who try to prevent hackers) to trap the hackers. It is used as a second line of defense, because it is only after the internet server is broken into that this trap can be useful.

A directory is created with an obvious name such as `Credit Cards Directory` to attract the vandal once they break into the system. Any activity regarding this directory causes an alert to be sent to the system administrator.

The code snippet below exploits the functionality of the `FileSystemWatcher` class, provided in the .NET Framework, to handle file system events:

```
FileSystemWatcher watcher = new FileSystemWatcher();
watcher.Path= target;
watcher.NotifyFilter = NotifyFilters.FileName | NotifyFilters.LastAccess
watcher.Changed += new FileSystemEventHandler(OnChanged);
watcher.EnableRaisingEvents = true;
```

Now that we understand the way that the .NET Framework implements its security features, let's take a look at the security layers that affect web services.

Web Service Security Layers

Web Services can be secured at three levels, each of which corresponds to an OS layer described in the following table:

OS Layer	Security Type	Comments
Application Layer	HTTP Authentication, Cryptography	Programmer applied techniques.
TCP	SSL (Secure Sockets Layer)	Requires minimum or no programming efforts.
IP	IP Security (IPSec)	Transparent to programmers, but limited to Windows 2000 and Unix machines. Ideal for LAN and WAN.

In the next few paragraphs we will briefly touch upon each of the security techniques, before going into some detail on cryptography.

IP Security

IP Security is an Internet standard for securing Internet data traffic at the IP layer, and it is specified broadly by RFC 1825 (http://www.ietf.org/rfc/rfc1825.txt). IP Security operates at IP level and therefore is transparent to the programmer. This protocol operates by adding two headers to the IP packets; one for **authentication** and the other for **encryption**.

Authentication mechanisms assure the receiver of the data that the claimed sender is indeed the actual sender. Encryption techniques, on the other hand, ensure data confidentiality by scrambling the data being protected in a predetermined manner.

The IP Security architecture allows for a wide range of security mechanisms to achieve authentication and encryption. This often creates incompatibilities among competing platforms and implementations. The security based on this model is therefore best suited for securing LAN and WAN based web applications, where all the machines taking part in the communication are controlled by a unified system administration.

Another limitation of this model is that there is no standard way for programmers to ensure that their applications only run on IP Security based systems, which means that this layer could easily be bypassed.

TCP Layer Security

TCP layer security is popularly known as **SSL** (Secure Sockets Layer). SSL was invented by Netscape (now a part of AOL) to provide a transparent encryption layer for HTTP.

This is the security mechanism widely relied upon to ensure the integrity of HTTP-based communication. The .Net Framework is based upon SOAP over HTTP, so it too depends on SSL for ensuring data integrity.

We will revisit this topic in a little later on in this chapter when we discuss cryptography, because this is an encryption-based system.

Application Layer Security

.Net Framework provides the HTTP authentication mechanism specified in RFC 2617. It provides for a username and password-based authentication mechanism. As hinted above, the HTTP layer depends on SSL for its encryption needs.

The abstract RemotingClientProxy class found in the namespace System.Runtime.Remoting.Services provides three properties: Domain, Username, and Password. These support the HTTP authentication process. The soapsuds tool extends this abstract RemotingClientProxy class while generating proxies pointing to web services:

```
PassTest hi = new PassTest(); // soapsuds generated proxy
if(hi is RemotingClientProxy) {
   RemotingClientProxy proxy = (RemotingClientProxy)hi;
   proxy.Url = "http://localhost:8000/Test/PassTest.soap";
   proxy.Username = "test";
   proxy.Password =  "secret";
}
```

Another way of protecting your web data from snooping is to write your own security channel sinks, which is how we'll be approaching the problem later in this chapter. Yet another way to secure the web services data integrity is to use cryptographic techniques, encapsulated within the application objects. This is what we'll discuss in this next section.

Cryptography Basics

Rather than being a general exposition of cryptography, this section is meant to familiarize you with basic techniques required to deal with .Net security and protecting your web services through encryption. The three building blocks we need are hashing algorithms, secret key encryption, and an understanding of the Public Key Cryptographic System (PKCS).

Hashing algorithms digest long sequences of data into short **footprints**, the most popular being 64 bit hash keys. The two most popular hashing algorithms are SHA (Secured Hash Algorithm) and MD5 (Message Digest version 5). These hash keys are used for signing digital documents – in other words, the hash is generated and encrypted using a **private key**.

Secret key encryption is commonly used to protect data through passwords and pass phrases (long phrases that would be difficult to guess). Secret key encryption is suitable for situations where the encrypted data needs to be accessed by the same person who protected it.

Public Key Cryptography is most widely used in protecting data through encryption. It is also used for digital signatures. Public Key Cryptography is based on asymmetric keys. This means that you always have a pair of keys. One is known to all and is called the **public key**. The other key of the pair is kept secret and is known only to the owner. This is called the **private key**. If we use the public key to encrypt data, it can only be decrypted using the corresponding private key of the key pair, and vice versa.

The Public Key is known to all, so any one can decrypt the information! However, the private key is known only to the owner, so this process acts as a **digital signature**. In other words, if the public key decrypts the message, we know that the sender was the owner of the private key. As hinted in the previous paragraph, rather than encrypting the whole document using the private key, a hash algorithm is used to digest the data into a compact form, and this is then encrypted using the private key. The result of this process is called the **digital signature** of the digital document.

If the data is encrypted using the public key, it can then only be decrypted by the corresponding private key, which means that only the owner of the private key will be able to read the unencrypted data.

The cryptographic namespace of .Net Framework is `System.Security.Cryptography`.

Hash Algorithms

Hash algorithms are also called **one-way functions**. This is because of their mathematical property of non-reversibility. The hash algorithms reduce a stream of large binary strings into a fixed length binary byte array. This fixed length binary array is used for computing digital signatures as explained above. We will cover digital signatures in more detail in the next few subsections.

To verify a piece of information, the hash is recomputed and compared against a previously computed hash value. If both the values match, the data has not been altered. The cryptographic hashing algorithms map a large stream of binary data to a much shorter fixed length, so it is theoretically possible to have two different documents having the same hash key.

Although, in theory, it is possible that two documents may have the same MD5 hash key and a different check sum, it is computationally impossible to create a forged document having the same hash key as the original hash value. Take the case of a virus attack on an executable code. In the late 80s the state-of-art was to create a check sum or a CRC (Cyclic Redundancy Check) as a protection measure against accidental or malicious damage to the code integrity.

The virus makers drew cunning designs to create viruses that added padding code to the victim's files so that the checksum and CRC remained unchanged in spite of the infection. However, using MD5 hash values, this kind of stealth attack is rendered unfeasible.

Windows Meta Files (WMF), still use check sums in the file header. For example, the .NET Framework class System.Drawing.Imaging.WmfPlaceableFileHeader has a read/write property of type short called Checksum. However, due to ease of computation, checksum is used as a cheap mode of protection against accidental damage rather than against malicious attacks.

Here is a simple program to calculate a checksum:

```
// other-src/Checksum.cs

using System;
using System.IO;
public class Checksum
{
```

The method below computes the checksum:

```
public static ushort compute(Stream strm)
{
    long sum = 0;
    int by;
    while((by = strm.ReadByte())!= -1)
      sum = (((by % 0xff) + sum) % 0xffff);
    return ((ushort)(sum % 0xffff));
}
```

This is the entry point for the program. Here, we check to see if we've received the correct argument from the command line to run the program, and stop the program if we haven't:

```
public static void Main(string [] args)
{
    if(args.Length != 1)
    {
        Console.WriteLine("usage: Checksum <file name>");
        Environment.Exit(1);
    }
```

First, we open the file for which the check sum is to be computed:

```
        FileStream fs = File.OpenRead(args[0]);
```

We then compute the checksum and close the file, and then output the result to the screen:

```
        ushort sum = compute(fs);
        fs.Close();
        Console.WriteLine(sum);
    }
}
```

Compile this program with:

csc Checksum.cs

and run it with:

Checksum <filename>

Due to their unsafe nature, checksum and CRC are sometimes called as poor cousins of cryptographic hash algorithms. We will now look into classes provided by the .NET Framework to cater to cryptographic-grade algorithms.

Cryptographic Hash Algorithms

The abstract class `HashAlgorithm` represents the concept of cryptographic hash algorithms within the .NET Framework. The framework provides seven classes that extend `HashAlgorithm` abstract class. These are:

❑ `MD5CryptoServiceProvider` (extends abstract class `MD5`)

❑ `SHA1CryptoServiceProvider` (extends abstract class `SHA1`)

❑ `SHA256Managed` (extends abstract class `SHA256`)

❑ `SHA384Managed` (extends abstract class `SHA384`)

❑ `SHA512Managed` (extends abstract class `SHA512`)

❑ `HMACSHA` (extends abstract class `KeyedHashAlgorithm`)

❑ `MACTripleDES` (extends abstract class `KeyedHashAlgorithm`)

The last two classes belong to a class of algorithm called **keyed hash algorithms**. The keyed hashes extend the concept of cryptographic hash with the use of a shared secret key. This is used for computing the hash of a data transported over an unsecured channel.

Displayed below is an example of computing a hash value of a file:

```
// other-src/TestKeyHash.cs

using System;
using System.IO;
```

285

```
using System.Security.Cryptography;
using System.Text;
using System.Runtime.Serialization.Formatters.Soap;
public class TestKeyHash
{
    public static void Main(string[] args)
    {
        if(args.Length != 1)
        {
            Console.WriteLine("usage TestKeyHash <file name>");
            Environment.Exit(1);
        }
}
```

Here, we create the object instance of the .NET SDK framework class, with a salt (a random secret to confuse a potential snooper):

```
byte[] key = Encoding.ASCII.GetBytes("My Secret Key".ToCharArray());
HMACSHA1 hmac = new HMACSHA1(key);
FileStream fs = File.OpenRead(args[0]);
```

The next four lines compute the hash, convert the binary hash into a printable base 64 format, close the file, and then print the base 64-encoded string as the result of hashing to the screen:

```
byte[] hash = hmac.ComputeHash(fs);
string b64 = Convert.ToBase64String(hash);
fs.Close();
Console.WriteLine(b64);
    } // END: main
}
```

The code can be compiled at the command line using the following:

csc TestKeyHash.cs

To execute the code, give the following command at the console prompt:

TestKeyHash TestKeyHash.cs

This should produce the output:

M3TvTQLzNNKIDu4ViB8nbKtXa0A=

The above example uses an instance of the HMACSHA1 class. The output displayed is a Base64 encoding of the binary hash result value. Base64 encoding is widely used in MIME and XML files formats to represent binary data. To recover the binary data from a Base64 encoded string, we could use the code fragment given below:

```
byte[] orig = Convert.FromBase64String(b64);
```

The XML parser, however, does this automatically. We will come across this in later examples.

SHA

SHA-1 is a block cipher and operates on a block size of 64 bits. However, the subsequent enhancements of this algorithm have bigger key values, thus increasing the value range and therefore enhancing the cryptographic utility. We must note that the bigger the key value sizes, the longer it takes to compute the hash. Moreover, for relatively small data files, smaller hash values are more secure. To put it another way, the hash algorithm's block size should be less than or equal to the size of the data itself.

The hash size for the SHA1 algorithm is 160 bits. Here is how to use it, which is similar to the HMACSHA1 code discussed earlier:

```
// other-src/TestSHA1.cs

using System;
using System.IO;
using System.Security.Cryptography;
using System.Text;
using System.Runtime.Serialization.Formatters.Soap;
public class TestSHA1
{
    public static void Main(string[] args)
    {
        if(args.Length != 1)
        {
            Console.WriteLine("usage TestSHA1 <file name>");
            Environment.Exit(1);
        }
        FileStream fs = File.OpenRead(args[0]);
        SHA1 sha = new SHA1CryptoServiceProvider();
        byte[] hash = sha.ComputeHash(fs);
        string b64 = Convert.ToBase64String(hash);
        fs.Close();
        Console.WriteLine(b64);
    } // END: main
}
```

The .NET framework provides bigger key size algorithms as well, namely SHA256, SHA384 and SHA512. The numbers at the end of the name indicate their block size.

The class SHA256Managed extends the abstract class SHA256, which in turn extends the abstract class HashAlgorithm. The Forms Authentication module of ASP.NET security (System.Web.Security.Forms AuthenticationModule) uses SHA1 as one of its valid formats to store and compare user passwords.

MD5

MD5 stands for Message Digest version 5. It is a cryptographic, one way hash algorithm. The MD5 algorithm competes well with SHA. MD5 is an improved version of MD4, devised by Ron Rivest of RSA fame. In fact, FIPS PUB 180-1 states that SHA-1 is based on similar principals to MD4. The salient features of this class of algorithms are:

❑   It is computationally unfeasible to forge an MD5 hash digest

❑   MD5 is not based on any mathematical assumption such as the difficulty of factoring large binary integers

❑   MD5 is computationally cheap, and therefore suitable for low latency requirements

❑   It is relatively simple to implement

The MD5 is the de facto standard for hash digest computation, due to the popularity of RSA.

The .NET Framework provides an implementation of this algorithm through the class MD5CryptoServiceProvider in the System.Security.Cryptography namespace. This class extends the MD5 abstract class, which in turn extends the abstract class HashAlgorithm. This class shares a common base class with SHA1, so the examples previously discussed can be modified easily to accommodate this:

```
FileStream fs = File.OpenRead(args[0]);
MD5 md5 = new MD5CryptoServiceProvider();
byte[] hash = md5.ComputeHash(fs);
string b64 = Convert.ToBase64String(hash);
fs.Close();
Console.WriteLine(b64);
```

Secret Key Encryption

Secret key encryption is arguably the earliest cryptographic technique because it predates the invention of modern digital computers. The most famous of these was the Enigma encryption device invented by Arthur Scherbius in the early 1900s. It was used by the Germans in the Second World War. This device gave nightmares to the Allies and the first valve-based digital computer was built to decipher the Enigma encrypted messages. Apart from its historical value, it still finds a place in the .NET Framework due to the speed of computation compared to the Public Key Cryptography System (PKCS), which we'll discuss later.

Secret key encryption is widely used to encrypt data files using passwords. The simplest technique is to seed a pseudo random number using a password, and then encrypt the files with an XOR operation using this pseudo random number generator. We'll take a deeper look at the XOR function later when we discuss our credit card example.

The .NET Framework represents the secret key by an abstract base class SymmetricAlgorithm. Four concrete implementations of different secret key algorithms are provided by default:

❑ DESCryptoServiceProvider (extends abstract class DES)

❑ RC2CryptoServiceProvider (extends abstract class RC2)

❑ RijndaelManaged (extends abstract class Rijndael)

❑ TripleDESCryptoServiceProvider (extends abstract class TripleDES)

Let's explore the SymmetricAlgorithm design. As will be clear from the example code below, two separate methods are provided to access encryption and decryption. Here is a console application program that encrypts and decrypts a file given a secret key:

```
// other-src/SymEnc.cs

using System;
using System.Text;
using System.IO;
using System.Security.Cryptography;
public class SymEnc
{
    public static void Main(string[] args)
    {
        if(args.Length != 4)
            UsageAndExit();
```

Here, we compute the index of the algorithm that we'll use:

```
int algoIndex = int.Parse(args[0]);
if(algoIndex < 0 || algoIndex >= algo.Length)
    UsageAndExit();
```

We open the input and output files (the file name represented by `args[3]` is the output file, and `args[2]` is the input file):

```
FileStream fin = File.OpenRead(args[2]);
FileStream fout = File.OpenWrite(args[3]);
```

We create the symmetric algorithm instance using the .Net Framework class `SymmetricAlgorithm`. This will use the algorithm name indexed by the `args[0]` parameter. After this, we'll set the key parameters, and display them on screen for information:

```
SymmetricAlgorithm sa = SymmetricAlgorithm.Create(algo[algoIndex]);
sa.IV = Convert.FromBase64String(b64Keys[algoIndex]);
sa.Key = Convert.FromBase64String(b64IVs[algoIndex]);
Console.WriteLine("Key " + sa.Key.Length);
Console.WriteLine("IV " + sa.IV.Length);
Console.WriteLine("KeySize: " + sa.KeySize);
Console.WriteLine("BlockSize: " + sa.BlockSize);
Console.WriteLine("Padding: " + sa.Padding);
fout.SetLength(0);
```

At this point, we check to see which operation is required, and execute the appropriate static method:

```
if(args[1].ToUpper().StartsWith("E") )
    Encrypt(sa,fin, fout);
else
    Decrypt(sa,fin, fout);
}
```

Here is where the encryption itself takes place:

```
public static void Encrypt(SymmetricAlgorithm sa, Stream fin, Stream fout)
{
    ICryptoTransform trans = sa.CreateEncryptor();
    byte[] buf  = new byte[2048];
    CryptoStream cs = new CryptoStream(fout,trans,
                                       CryptoStreamMode.Write);
    int len;
    while((len = fin.Read(buf,0, buf.Length))>0)
    {
        cs.Write(buf,0,len);
    }
    cs.Close();
    fin.Close();
}
```

Here's the decryption method:

```
public static void Decrypt(SymmetricAlgorithm sa, Stream fin, Stream fout)
{
    ICryptoTransform trans =  sa.CreateDecryptor();
    byte[] buf  = new byte[2048];
    CryptoStream cs = new CryptoStream(fin,trans, CryptoStreamMode.Read);
    int len;
    while((len = cs.Read(buf,0, buf.Length))>0)
    {
        fout.Write(buf,0,len);
    }
    fin.Close();
    fout.Close();
}
```

This next method prints usage information:

```
public static void UsageAndExit()
{
  Console.Write("usage SymEnc <algo index> <D|E> <in> <out> ");
  Console.WriteLine("D =decrypt, E=Encrypt");
  for(int i=0; i < algo.Length; i++)
     Console.WriteLine("Algo index: {0} {1}", i, algo[i]);
  Environment.Exit(0);
}
```

The static parameters used for object creation are indexed by args[0]. How we arrive at these magic numbers will be discussed later:

```
private static string[] algo = { "DES", "RC2","Rijndael","TripleDES"};
private static string [] b64Keys =
{
    "U0SF45LK98A="
    ,"6u9T53ZI08lh3OsAbCiwIw=="
    ,"hHftT57BsGRh51mZ7oM1/HjqsQv9GMzqFzlJIEvHhXU="
    ,"GciNE/Kl0IFsssUfP+qftCVYzQyqayxX"
};
private static string [] b64IVs =
{
    "h4Mcpbv2Ae8="
    ,"DLYVm/FTW6Y="
    ,"Eib9uK4vUQQiWUYFDDN3BA=="
    ,"FmPGvz4v9PI="
};
}
```

After compilation, this program can encrypt and decrypt using all four of the symmetric key implementations provided by the .NET Framework. The secret keys and their initialization vectors (IV) have been generated by a simple code generator, which we will examine shortly.

The commands given below encrypt and decrypt files using DES algorithm. With the first command, we take a text file, 1.txt, and use the DES algorithm to create an encrypted file called 2.bin. The next command decrypts this file back and stores it into 3.bin.

```
SymEnc 0 E 1.txt 2.bin
SymEnc 0 D 2.bin 3.bin
```

The first parameter of the SymEnc program is an index to the string array, which determines the algorithm to be used:

```
private static string[] algo = { "DES", "RC2","Rijndael","TripleDES"};
```

The string defining the algorithm is passed as a parameter to the static Create method of the abstract class SymmetricAlgorithm. This class has an abstract factory design pattern:

```
SymmetricAlgorithm sa = SymmetricAlgorithm.Create(algo[algoIndex]);
```

To encrypt, we get an instance of the ICryptoTransform interface by calling the CreateEncryptor method of the SymmetricAlgorithm class extender:

```
ICryptoTransform trans = sa.CreateEncryptor();
```

Similarly, for decryption, we get an instance of the ICryptoTransform interface by calling the CreateDecryptor method of the SymmetricAlgorithm class instance:

```
ICryptoTransform trans = sa.CreateDecryptor();
```

We use the class CryptoStream for both encryption and decryption. However, the parameters to the constructor differ. For encryption we use:

```
CryptoStream cs = new CryptoStream(fout,trans, CryptoStreamMode.Write);
```

Similarly, for decryption we use:

```
CryptoStream cs = new CryptoStream(fin,trans, CryptoStreamMode.Read);
```

We call the Read and Write methods of the CryptoStream for decryption and encryption respectively. For generating the keys we use a simple code generator, listed below:

```
using System;
using System.IO;
using System.Text;
using System.Security.Cryptography;

public class SymKey
{
    public static void Main(string[] args)
    {
        StringBuilder keyz = new StringBuilder();
        StringBuilder ivz =  new StringBuilder();

        keyz.Append("private static string [] b64Keys = \n{\n");
        ivz.Append("private static string [] b64IVs = \n{\n");
```

For each of the algorithms, we generate the keys and IV:

```
for(int i=0; i < algo.Length; i++)
{
    SymmetricAlgorithm sa = SymmetricAlgorithm.Create(algo[i]);
    sa.GenerateIV();
    sa.GenerateKey();
    string comma = (i==0)?"":",";
    keyz.AppendFormat("{0}\"{1}\"\n",comma,
                      Convert.ToBase64String(sa.Key));
    ivz.AppendFormat("{0}\"{1}\"\n",comma,
                      Convert.ToBase64String(sa.IV));
}
```

Here, we print or emit the code:

```
    keyz.Append("\n};\n");
    ivz.Append("\n};\n");
    Console.WriteLine(keyz.ToString());
    Console.WriteLine(ivz.ToString());
}
```

The algorithm names for symmetric keys used by .NET SDK are given the correct index values here:

```
    private static string[] algo = { "DES", "RC2","Rijndael","TripleDES"};
}
```

The above program creates a random key and an initializing vector for each algorithm. It converts the binary data into Base 64 encoding using the public instance method `ToBase64String` of the class `Convert`. Kerberos, the popular network authentication protocol supported by Windows 2000 and all of the Unix flavors, uses secret key encryption for implementing security.

In this next section we will look into public key encryption.

PKCS

The Public Key Cryptographic System is a type of asymmetric key encryption. This system uses two keys, one private and other public. The public key is widely distributed whereas the private key is kept secret. One cannot derive or deduce the private key by knowing the public key, so the public key can be safely distributed.

The keys are different, yet complementary. That is, if you encrypt data using the public key, only the owner of the private key can decipher it, and vice versa. This forms the basis of PKCS encryption.

If the private key holder encrypts a piece of data using their private key, any person having access to the public key can decrypt it. The public key, as the name suggests, is available publicly. This property of the PKCS is exploited along with a hashing algorithm, such as SHA or MD5, to provide a verifiable digital signature process.

The abstract class `System.Security.Cryptography.AsymmetricAlgorithm` represents this concept in .NET Framework. Two concrete implementations of this class are provided by default:

- ❑ `DSACryptoServiceProvider` – which extends the abstract class `DSA`
- ❑ `RSACryptoServiceProvider` – which extends the abstract class `RSA`

DSA (Digital Signature Algorithm) is specified by NIST (National Institute of Standards and Technology) see FIPS PUB 186-2 issued on 27 January 2000. The original DSA standard was, however, issued by NIST, way back in August 1991. DSA cannot be used for encryption and is good only for digital signatures. We will discuss digital signatures in more detail in the next subsection.

RSA algorithms can also be used for encryption as well as digital signatures. RSA is the de facto standard and has much wider acceptance than DSA. RSA is a tiny bit faster than DSA as well.

RSA algorithm is named after its three inventors R. Rivest, A. Shamir, and L. Adleman. It was patented in USA, but the patent expired on 20th September 2000. RSA can be used for both digital signature and data encryption. It is based on the assumption that large numbers are extremely difficult to factor. The use of RSA for digital signatures is approved within the FIPS PUB 186-2 and defined in ANSI X9.31 standard document.

To gain some practical insights into RSA implementation of the .NET Framework, consider the code given below:

```
// other-src/TestRSAKey.cs

using System.Security.Cryptography.Xml;
public class TestRSAKey
{
    public static void Main(string [] args)
    {
        RSAKeyValue rsa = new RSAKeyValue();
        string str = rsa.Key.ToXmlString(true);
        System.Console.WriteLine(str);
    }
}
```

The above code creates a pair of private and public key and prints it out on the console in XML format. To compile the above code, simply open a console session, run `corvar.bat` (if necessary) to set the .NET SDK paths, and compile the program by typing the following command:

csc TestRSAKey.cs

This should produce a file called `TestRSAKey.exe`. Execute this program and redirect the output to a file such as `key.xml`:

TestRSAKey > key.xml

The file `key.xml` contains all the private and public members of the generated RSA key object. You can open this XML file in Internet Explorer 5.5 or above. If you do so, you will notice that the private member variables are also stored in this file. The binary data representing the large integers is encoded in `Base64` format.

The program listed above uses an `RSAKeyValue` instance to generate a new key pair. The class `RSAKeyValue` is contained in the `System.Security.Cryptography.Xml` namespace. This namespace can be thought of as the XML face of the .NET cryptographic framework. It contains a specialized, lightweight implementation of XML for the purpose of cryptography, and the model allows XML objects to be signed with a digital signature.

The `System.Security.Cryptography.Xml` namespace classes depend upon the classes contained in the `System.Security.Cryptography` namespace for the actual implementation of cryptographic algorithms.

The `key.xml` file, generated by redirecting the output of the C# test program `TestRSAKey`, contains both private and public keys. However, we need to keep the private key secret while making the public key widely available. Therefore we need to separate out the public key from the key pair.

Here is the program to do it:

```
using System;
using System.IO;
using System.Security.Cryptography.Xml;
using System.Security.Cryptography;
using System.Text;

public class TestGetPubKey
{
    public static void Main(string [] args)
    {
        if(args.Length != 1)
        {
            Console.WriteLine("usage: TestGetPubKey <key pair xml>");
            Environment.Exit(1);
        }
        string xstr = File2String(args[0]);
```

The code below creates an instance of the RSA implementation and re-initializes the internal variables through the XML-formatted string:

```
        RSACryptoServiceProvider rsa = new RSACryptoServiceProvider();
        rsa.FromXmlString(xstr);
        string x = rsa.ToXmlString(false);
        Console.WriteLine(x);
    }// END: Main

    /* NO error checking is used to retain clearity.*/

    public static string File2String(string fname)
    {
        FileInfo finfo = new FileInfo(fname);
        byte[] buf = new byte[finfo.Length];
        FileStream fs = File.OpenRead(fname);
        fs.Read(buf, 0, buf.Length);
        return (new ASCIIEncoding()).GetString(buf);
    }
}
```

The above program is logically similar to `TestRSAKey.cs`, except that it has to read the key file and pass a different parameter in the `ToXmlString` method.

The cryptography classes use a lightweight XML implementation, thus avoiding the elaborate ritual of parsing the fully-formed generic XML data containing serialized objects. This has another advantage of speed because it bypasses the DOM parsers.

To compile the code listed above, type:

```
csc TestGetPubKey.cs
```

This should produce the `TestGetPubKey.exe` file. Run this file giving `key.xml` as the name of the input file, and redirect the program's output to `pub.xml`. This file will contain an XML-formatted public key. The binary data, basically binary large integers, is `Base64` encoded. You may recall that `key.xml` contains both the public and private key pairs, and was generated by redirecting the output of `TestRSAKey.exe`. The following line will redirect `key.xml`'s public key to `pub.xml`:

```
TestGetPubKey key.xml > pub.xml
```

Now, lets write a program to test the encrypt and decrypt features of the RSA algorithm:

```
// other-src/TestCrypt.cs

using System;
using System.IO;
using System.Security.Cryptography.Xml;
using System.Security.Cryptography;
using System.Text;
public class TestCrypt
{
    public static void Main(string [] args)
    {
        if(args.Length != 4)
        {
            Console.WriteLine("usage: TestCrypt <key xml> <E|D> <in> <out>");
            Console.WriteLine(" E= Encrypt, D= Decrypt (needs private key)");
            Environment.Exit(1);
        }
```

Here, we read the public or private key into memory:

```
        string xstr = File2String(args[0]);
```

We create an instance of an RSA cryptography service provider and initialize the parameters based on the XML lightweight file name passed in `args[0]`:

```
        RSACryptoServiceProvider rsa = new RSACryptoServiceProvider();
        rsa.FromXmlString(xstr);
```

We display the key file name:

```
        Console.WriteLine("Key File: "+args[0]);
        string op = "Encrypted";
```

We read the input file and store it into a byte array:

```
        /* Read the input file fully */

        byte[] inbuf = new byte[(new FileInfo(args[2])).Length];
```

```
        byte[] outbuf = null;
        FileStream fs = File.OpenRead(args[2]);
        fs.Read(inbuf,0, inbuf.Length);
        fs.Close();
```

We either encrypt or decrypt depending on the args[1] option:

```
        if(args[1].ToUpper().StartsWith("D"))
        {
            op = "Decrypted";
            outbuf = rsa.Decrypt(inbuf, false);
        }
        else
            outbuf = rsa.Encrypt(inbuf, false);
```

We'll write back the result in the output buffer into the file, and display the result:

```
        /* Write back to output file */

        fs = File.OpenWrite(args[3]);
        fs.Write(outbuf,0,outbuf.Length);
        fs.Close();
        Console.WriteLine(op+ " input ["+args[2]+"] to output ["+args[3]+"]");

    }// END: Main
```

Here's a helper method to read the file name passed as an argument and convert the content to string:

```
    /* NO error checking is used to retain clarity.*/

    public static string File2String(string fname)
    {
        FileInfo finfo = new FileInfo(fname);
        byte[] buf = new byte[finfo.Length];
        FileStream fs = File.OpenRead(fname);
        fs.Read(buf, 0, buf.Length);
        fs.Close();
        return (new ASCIIEncoding()).GetString(buf);
    }
}
```

The above test program encrypts or decrypts a short file depending on the parameters supplied to it. It takes four parameters; the XML formatted private or public key file, option E or D standing for encrypt or decrypt options respectively and input and output file names.

The above program can be compiled with the following command:

csc TestCrypt.cs

The above command will produce a TestCrypt.exe file. To test the encrypt and decrypt functions, we'll create a small plain text file called plain.txt. The content of this single line is reproduced here.

```
Hello World!
```

Recall that we have also created two other files `key.xml` and `pub.xml`. The file `key.xml` contains a key pair and `pub.xml` contains the public key extracted from the file `key.xml`.

Let's encrypt the plain text file `plain.txt`. To do so use the command given below:

```
TestCrypt pub.xml E plain.txt rsa.bin
```

Note that we have used the public key file to encrypt it. You can type the output on the console, but this won't make any sense to us because it contains binary data. You could use a binary dump utility to dump out the file's content. I use a homegrown C# utility, `Bin2Hex` which I have included in the sourcecode download. Run it with this command:

```
Bin2Hex rsa.bin
```

If you execute the above command you will notice that the total number of bytes is 128 compared to the input of 13 bytes. This is because the RSA is a block cipher algorithm and the block size equals the key size, so the output will always be in multiples of the block size. You may wish to re-run the above examples with larger files to see the resulting encrypted file length.

Let us now decrypt the file to get back the original text back. Use the following command to decrypt:

```
TestCrypt key.xml D rsa.bin decr.txt
```

Note that we used the `key.xml` file, which contains the private key, to decrypt. That's because we use the public key to encrypt and private key to decrypt. In other words, anyone may send encrypted documents to you if they know your public key, but only you can decrypt the message. The reverse is true for digital signatures, which we will cover in the next section.

Digital Signature Basics

Digital signature is the encryption of a hash digest (for example MD5 or SHA-1) of data using a private key. The digital signature can be verified by decrypting the hash digest and comparing it against a hash digest computed from the data by the verifier.

As noted earlier, the private key is known only to the owner, so the owner can sign a digital document by encrypting the hash computed from the document. The public key is known to all, so anyone can verify the signature by recomputing the hash and comparing it against the decrypted value, using the public key of the signer.

The .NET Framework provides DSA and RSA digital signature implementations by default. We will consider only DSA, as RSA was covered in the previous section. Both of the implementations extend the same base class, so all programs for DSA discussed below will work for RSA as well:

We will go through the same motions of producing a key pair and a public key file and then sign and verify the signature:

```
// other-src/GenDSAKeys.cs

using System;
using System.Security.Cryptography;
using System.Text;
```

297

```
public class GenDSAKeys
{
   public static void Main(string[] args)
   {
      DSACryptoServiceProvider dsa = new DSACryptoServiceProvider();
      string prv = dsa.ToXmlString(true);
      string pub = dsa.ToXmlString(false);
      FileUtil.SaveString("dsa-key.xml", prv);
      FileUtil.SaveString("dsa-pub.xml", pub);
      Console.WriteLine("Created dsa-key.xml and dsa-pub.xml");
   }
}
```

The above code generates two XML-formatted files dsa-key.xml and dsa-pub.xml, containing private and public keys respectively. Before we can run this, however, we need to create the FileUtil class used to output our two files:

```
// other-src/FileUtil.cs

using System.IO;
using System.Text;
public class FileUtil
{
   public static void SaveString(string fname, string data)
   {
      SaveBytes(fname, (new ASCIIEncoding()).GetBytes(data));
   }
   public static string LoadString(string fname)
   {
      byte[] buf = LoadBytes(fname);
      return (new ASCIIEncoding()).GetString(buf);
   }
   public static byte[] LoadBytes(string fname)
   {
      FileInfo finfo = new FileInfo(fname);
      byte[] buf = new byte[finfo.Length];
      FileStream fs = File.OpenRead(fname);
      fs.Read(buf, 0, buf.Length);
      fs.Close();
      return buf;
   }
   public static void SaveBytes(string fname, byte[] data)
   {
      FileStream fs = File.OpenWrite(fname);
      fs.SetLength(0);
      fs.Write(data,0, data.Length);
      fs.Close();
   }
}
```

The following code signs the data:

```
// other-src/DSASign.cs

using System;
using System.IO;
using System.Security.Cryptography;
using System.Text;
```

```
public class DSASign
{
    public static void Main(string [] args)
    {
        if(args.Length != 3)
        {
            Console.WriteLine("usage: DSASign <key xml> <data> <sign>");
            Environment.Exit(1);
        }
        string xkey = FileUtil.LoadString(args[0]);
        FileStream fs = File.OpenRead(args[1]);
```

The DSA provider instance is created and the private key is reconstructed from the XML format using the following two lines of code:

```
        DSACryptoServiceProvider dsa = new DSACryptoServiceProvider();
        dsa.FromXmlString(xkey);
```

The next line signs the file:

```
        byte[] sig = dsa.SignData(fs);
        fs.Close();
        FileUtil.SaveString(args[2], Convert.ToBase64String(sig));
        Console.WriteLine("Signature in {0} file",args[2]);
    }
}
```

To verify the signature, we'll use the following sample code:

```
// other-src/DSAVerify.cs

using System;
using System.IO;
using System.Security.Cryptography;
using System.Text;
public class DSAVerify
{
    public static void Main(string [] args)
    {
        if(args.Length != 3)
        {
            Console.WriteLine("usage: DSAVerify <key xml> <data> <sign>");
            Environment.Exit(1);
        }
        string xkey = FileUtil.LoadString(args[0]);
        byte[] data = FileUtil.LoadBytes(args[1]);
        string xsig = FileUtil.LoadString(args[2]);
        DSACryptoServiceProvider dsa = new DSACryptoServiceProvider();
        dsa.FromXmlString(xkey);
        bool verify = dsa.VerifyData(data, Convert.FromBase64String(xsig));
        Console.WriteLine("Signature Verification is {0}", verify);
    }
}
```

The actual verification is done using the highlighted code fragment.

The next four commands listed below compile the two source files, followed by the signing and verification process:

```
csc DSASign.cs FileUtil.cs
csc DSAVerify.cs FileUtil.cs
DSASign dsa-key.xml DSASign.cs sig.txt
DSAVerify dsa-pub.xml DSASign.cs sig.txt
```

There are many helper classes within the `System.Security.Cryptography`, `System.Security.Cryptography.Xml` namespace, which provide many features to help deal with digital signatures and encryption and, at times, provide overlapping functionality. Therefore, there is more than one way of doing the same thing. This chapter does not endeavor to cover all of the classes exhaustively; our aim is to equip you to deal with the .NET security issues pertaining to C# web services.

X.509 Certificates

X.509 is a public key certificate exchange framework. A public key certificate is a digitally signed statement by the owner of a private key, trusted by the verifier (usually a certifying authority) that certfies the validity of the public key of another entity. This creates a trust relationship between two unknown entities. This is an ISO standard specified by the document ISO/IEC 9594-8. X.509 certificates are also used in SSL (Secure Socket Layer), which is covered in the next section.

There are many certifying authority services available over Internet. VeriSign (http://www.verisign.com) is the most popular one. This company was also founded by the RSA trio themselves. You can also run your own Certificate Authority (CA) service over an Intranet using Microsoft Certificate Server.

The Microsoft .NET Framework SDK also provides tools for generating certificates for testing purposes.

```
makecert -n CN=Test test.cer
```

The above command generates a test certificate. You can view it by clicking on the `test.cer` file from the Windows Explorer.

From the same screen, you could also install this certificate on your computer.

Three classes dealing with X.509 certificates are provided in the .NET Framework in the namespace System.Security.Cryptography.X509Certificates. Here is a program that loads and manipulates the certificate created above:

```
// other-src/LoadCert.cs

using System;
using System.Security.Cryptography.X509Certificates;
public class LoadCert
{
    public static void Main(string[] args)
    {
        if(args.Length != 1)
        {
            Console.Write("usage loadCert <cert file> ");
            Environment.Exit(0);
        }
        X509Certificate cert = X509Certificate.CreateFromCertFile(args[0]);
        Console.WriteLine("hash= {0}",cert.GetCertHashString());
        Console.WriteLine("effective Date= {0}",cert.GetEffectiveDateString());
        Console.WriteLine("expire Date= {0}",cert.GetExpirationDateString());
        Console.WriteLine("Isseued By= {0}",cert.GetIssuerName());
        Console.WriteLine("Issued To= {0}",cert.GetName());
        Console.WriteLine("algo= {0}",cert.GetKeyAlgorithm());
        Console.WriteLine("Pub Key= {0}",cert.GetPublicKeyString());
    }
}
```

The static method CreateFromCertFile loads the certificate file and creates a new instance of the class X509Certificate.

The next section deals with SSL, which uses X.509 certificates for establishing the trust relationship.

Secure Sockets Layer

SSL (Secure Sockets Layer) protocol provides privacy and reliability between two communicating applications over the Internet. SSL is built over the TCP layer. In January 1999, IETF (Internet Engineering Task Force) adopted an enhanced version of SSL 3.0 and called it TLS, which stands for Transport Layer Security. TLS is backwardly-compatible with SSL, and is defined in RFC 2246. However, the name SSL stayed due to wide acceptance of this Netscape protocol name.

SSL provides connection-oriented security and has the following four properties:

❑ Connection is private and encryption is valid for that session only.

❑ Symmetric key cryptography, like DES, is used for encryption. However, the session secret key is exchanged using public key encryption.

❑ Digital Certificates are used to verify each other's identities by the communicating entities.

❑ Secure hash functions, like SHA and MD5, are used for message authentication code (MAC).

The SSL protocol sets the following goals for itself:

❑ **Cryptographic security**: SSL uses symmetric key for session and public key for authentication

❑ **Interoperability**: Interoperates between different OS and programming languages

❑ **Extensibility**: Adds new protocols for encrypting data are allowed within SSL framework

❑ **Relative efficiency**: Reduces computation and network activity by using caching techniques

The following is a simplified discussion of the SSL algorithm sequence:

Two entities communicating using SSL protocols must each have a public-private key pair, optionally with digital certificates validating their respective public keys.

At the beginning of a session, the client and server exchange information to authenticate each other. This ritual of authentication is called the **Handshake Protocol**. During this, a session id, the compression method and the cipher suite to be used are negotiated. If the certificates exist, they are then exchanged. Although certificates are optional, either the client or the server may refuse to continue with the connection and end the session in the absence of a certificate.

After receiving each other's public keys, a set of secret keys based on a randomly generated number is exchanged by encrypting it with each other's public keys. After this, the application data exchange can commence. The application data will be encrypted using a secret key, and a signed hash of the data is sent to verify the data integrity.

Microsoft implements the SSL client in the .NET framework classes. However, the server side SSL can be used by deploying your service through the IIS web server.

The code fragment given below can be used to access SSL-protected web servers from the.NET platform:

```
WebRequest req = WebRequest.Create("https://www.microsoft.com");
WebResponse result = req.GetResponse();
```

Note that above URL starts with "**https**", which signals the WebRequest class to use SSL protocol. Interestingly, the same code is useful for accessing unsecured URLs as well.

Presented below is a utility class for accessing a secured URL. It takes care of the minor details such as encoding. This class has a utility design pattern. Utility design pattern classes have all static methods and no instance of the class can be created. System.IO.File class is also an example of a utility design pattern class:

```
// other-src/WebStreamUtil.cs

using System;
using System.Net;
using System.IO;
using System.Text;

// Gets a URL (http or https) and creates a stream.
// Has utility design pattern, with no instance allowed.

public class WebStreamUtil
{
    private WebStreamUtil() {} // No instances allowed
```

The following code creates a stream object using UTF-8 encoding. This is the most widely used default encoding:

```
public static Stream Create(string url)
{
    return Create(url, "utf-8");
}
```

We create a stream object from a URL and given encoding format:

```
public static Stream Create(string url, string encod)
{
```

Using the .NET SDK WebRequest object, we create an HTTP-secured request object and get its response stream:

```
WebRequest req = WebRequest.Create(url);
WebResponse result = req.GetResponse();
Stream ReceiveStream = result.GetResponseStream();
```

We create an encoding instance from the .NET Framework object Encoding:

```
Encoding enc = System.Text.Encoding.GetEncoding(encod);
```

Here, we'll create the stream reader:

```
StreamReader sr = new StreamReader( ReceiveStream, enc);
```

We read the stream fully – the entire web page or serialized object is read into the memory:

```
Char[] cbuf = new Char[256];
int len;
StringBuilder build = new StringBuilder();
while((len = sr.Read(cbuf, 0, cbuf.Length)) > 0)
{
    string tmp = new string(cbuf, 0, len);
    build.Append(tmp);
}
sr.Close();
```

We'll create a stream object from the strings read into memory:

```
byte[] byt = (new ASCIIEncoding()).GetBytes(build.ToString());
return new MemoryStream(byt);
    }
    public static int MaxContentLength = 16384; // 16k
}
```

The usage pattern of the utility class, demonstrated above, is simply calling the static `Create` method with the URL of the web service. A test program to demonstrate the use of this class is displayed below:

```
using System;
using System.IO;
public class GetWeb
{
    public static void Main(string[] args)
    {
        if(args.Length != 1)
        {
            Console.WriteLine("usage: GetWeb url");
            Console.WriteLine("example: GetWeb https://www.microsoft.com");
            Environment.Exit(0);
        }
        MemoryStream ms = null;;
        try
        {
            ms = (MemoryStream) WebStreamUtil.Create(args[0]);
        } catch(Exception x) {
            Console.WriteLine(x.StackTrace );
            Console.WriteLine("Bad URL: {0}",args[0]);
        }
        if(ms != null)
          ms.WriteTo(Console.OpenStandardOutput());
    }
}
```

The above console application gets a secured (SSL protected) URL and displays the content on the standard output. To compile the code, give the following command:

```
csc GetWeb.cs WebStreamUtil.cs
```

The utility class `WebStreamUtil` is compiled in, together with the main program. However, you would normally create a separate DLL file in production scenarios.

Encrypting your Web Service Data

Given infinite time and resources, any security technology can be broken into. This is true for both physical sources and the Internet. Any safe in this world can be broken into by thieves, given enough resources and enough time. However, the law of diminishing returns is used to secure our worldly possession and digital data. The trick is to make a locking device which cannot be broken into within the timeframe that the asset is unattended or the data has any value. Alternatively, we could have an asset that could be unlocked without the key, but only by using resources whose deployment cost would outstrip the benefit of breaking in.

Another obvious method of protecting your physical assets and digital data is not to keep it in unsafe places. For example, if you are an ASP (Application Service Provider) and your clients subscribe to your services on a monthly basis, why would you need to keep your customers' credit card information online?

Let us take a hypothetical scenario of an ASP (Application Service Provider) providing a pay-per-view service. The client of this online service can pay a nominal amount of, say, 90 cents to read an article of interest, or listen to the online jukebox for a fee of 10 cents per song. The web service would consolidate these micro payments, much like telecom operators bill their customers on a per-call basis, and collect a consolidated monthly figure by charging the customer's credit card.

The user, however, has to provide the credit card details online once, while registering. Assuming that the credit card details travel safely over SSL, we now need to worry about its safety once the details are in our possession. Using the basic cryptographic techniques we learned in the previous section, you can devise a simple security system.

In this simple technique, the credit card details, collected from the user over SSL, are encrypted using a public key (whose private key is not held at the web server!) and stored in a secure SQL database as BLOBs (Binary Large Objects). This database is replicated on a machine that runs behind a firewall and also has a non routable IP address. Credit card verification software, running behind the firewall, has the private key embedded in its code. Therefore, there is only one piece of code that needs to know this, and only this piece of software decrypts it for the purpose of verification and charging. You could then advertise on your web site that the clients' credit cards are "untouched by human eyes".

SET Secure Electronic Transaction Protocol is specified jointly by MasterCard and Visa. SET is published as open specification for the industry and is the de facto standard. The SET specification comes in four documents and can be downloaded from the Visa web site. Three gateway interfaces are provided, namely TCP sockets, HTTP, and SMTP (Simple Mail Transfer Protocol). However, the protocol is flexible and extensible enough to cater for Mobile Commerce platforms such as NBS (Narrow Band Socket, an industry standard for bandwidth-challenged mobile wireless devices) and WAP transfer protocol layer (basically UDP, if the lower layer is IP).

SET does not require SSL for transport. This is because of the application-layer protocol-level security.

We will first begin by writing our own encryption channel sink, to protect a sample Credit Card Validation system. After we've done this, we will revisit the example and incorporate encryption within the application object itself to make it more secure and robust.

Credit Card Validation Example

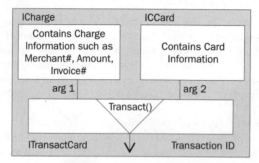

The Credit Card Validation sample simulates a Credit Card transaction. Its design can be abstracted into three interfaces: `ICCard`, `ICharge` and `ITransactCard`. These three interfaces are found in the `Card.cs` file found in the `card` subdirectory of the chapter source files that are available as part of the code download for this chapter.

The diagram above depicts the relationship between the interfaces visually. The interface `ITransactCard` represents the transaction validation process through its `Transact` method, which takes two parameters. The first parameter is the interface `ICharge` that contains information related to the charge such as merchant ID, amount, and invoice number. The second parameter is the `ICCard` interface, which represents the information contained by the physical credit card, such as card number, card holder's name, zip code, etc. A partial listing of `Card.cs` is given below.

The enumeration below defines the types of cards that we might expect:

```
public enum CardTypes : short {Undefined, Visa, Master, Amex, Discovery}
```

The interface `ICCard` represents the concept of the physical credit card:

```
public interface ICCard
{
    string CardNumber      {get;set;}
    string HolderName      {get;set;}
    string ZipCode         {get;set;}
    DateTime ExpiryDate    {get;set;}
    CardTypes CType        {get;set;}

}
```

The interface below contains information related to a charge that is placed on the credit card during a transaction:

```
public interface ICharge
{
    string MerchantId    {get;set;}
```

```
       double Amount        {get;set;}
       string CurrencyName {get;set;}
       string InvoiceRef    {get;set;}
    }
```

The interface defines the transaction, and will be implemented by web services to simulate a credit card transaction. The next method IsValid provides a means of checking the validity of a credit card, without transacting on it:

```
    public interface ITransactCard
    {
        long Transact(ICharge charge, ICCard card);
        bool IsValid(ICCard card);
    }
```

The class listed below implements the interface ICCard:

```
    [Serializable]
    public sealed class SimpleCCard : ICCard
    {
        public string CardNumber
        {
            get {return cardNumber;}
            set {cardNumber = value;}
        }
        public string HolderName
        {
            get {return holderName;}
            set {holderName = value;}
        }
        public string ZipCode
        {
            get {return zipCode;}
            set {zipCode = value;}
        }
        public DateTime ExpiryDate
        {
            get {return expDt;}
            set {expDt = value;}
        }
        public CardTypes CType
        {
            get {return ctyp;}
            set {ctyp = value;}
        }
        private DateTime expDt;
        private CardTypes ctyp = CardTypes.Undefined;
        private String cardNumber = null;
        private String holderName = null;
        private String zipCode = null;
    } // END: class SimpleCCard
```

The class listed below implements the interface ICharge:

```
    [Serializable]
    public class SimpleCharge : ICharge
    {
```

```
        public string MerchantId
        {
            get {return merchantId;}
            set {merchantId = value;}
        }

        public double Amount
        {
            get {return amount;}
            set {amount = value;}
        }

        public string CurrencyName
        {
          get {return curn;}
          set {curn = value;}
        }
        public string InvoiceRef
        {
            get {return invref;}
            set {invref = value;}
        }
        private String merchantId = null;
        private double amount = 0;
        private string invref = null;
        private string curn = null;
    } // END: SimpleCharge
```

There are other interfaces and classes defined in the file Card.cs. We'll take a look at these in detail later because they will be the part of the more advanced version of this credit card validation system that we'll create at the end of this chapter.

We can compile Card.cs using the following console command:

csc /t:library Card.cs

The above command produces the file Card.dll. This file is used by both the client and the server codes.

The server-side code is contained in the file SimpleTransact.cs. The class SimpleTransact implements the interface ITransactCard and inherits from System.MarshalByRefObject, which is the base class from which well-known Singleton or Single Call web services must extend:

```
using System;
namespace Wrox.ProCSharpWebServices.Chapter11.Card.Service
{
    public class SimpleTransact: MarshalByRefObject, ITransactCard
    {
        public SimpleTransact()
        {
            Console.WriteLine(" SimpleTransact created");
        }
```

The next method provides the simulation of a credit transaction for this example and returns a random number as a transaction identifier:

```
public virtual long Transact(ICharge charge, ICCard card)
{
    long ret = 0;
    try
    {
        Console.WriteLine("Card = {0}", card.CardNumber);
        Console.WriteLine("Amount = {0}", charge.Amount);
        ret = (new Random()).Next();
    }
    catch(Exception z)
    {
        Console.WriteLine(z.StackTrace);
        Console.WriteLine("Invalid Private Key, so cant read");
    }
    return ret;
}
```

The following method always returns `true`. For now, we'll ignore the `catch` part of the code. We will deal with it in the advanced portion of the study:

```
public virtual bool IsValid(ICCard card)
{
    try
    {
        Console.WriteLine("Card = {0}", card.CardNumber);
    }
    catch(Exception )
    {
        Console.WriteLine("Invalid Private Key, so cant read");
    }
    return true;
}
    }
}
```

We'll compile this file as follows:

csc /t:library SimpleTransact.cs /r:Card.dll

This brings us to the server. This uses a file `DirectHost.cs` containing the `DirectHost` class. It is a part of the .NET SDK and provides a simple platform to run web services from the command line. Essentially, all this class does is to register the services using the `RemotingConfiguration.Configure` method:

```
RemotingConfiguration.Configure(args[i+1])
```

The file `DirectHost.cs` can be compiled into `DirectHost.exe` with the following command:

csc DirectHost.cs

This brings us to the client-side code. We'll create a utility class called `TransactCard`. This class contains a static method called `Transact` that takes three parameters (the URL of the web service, an `ICCard` instance, and an `ICharge` instance). It uses these parameters to perform the transaction as shown in the code listing overleaf:

```
using System;
using System.IO;
using System.Security.Cryptography;
using System.Text;
using System.Runtime.Serialization.Formatters.Soap;
using System.Runtime.Remoting;
using System.Runtime.Remoting.Channels;
using Wrox.ProCSharpWebServices.Chapter11.Card;
public class TransactCard
{
    private TransactCard(){} // DO NOT Allow any instance.
    public static long Transact(String url, ICCard card, ICharge charg)
    {
```

The static method of the .NET Framework `Activator.GetObject` is called to get the remote reference of the `ITransactCard` object instance:

```
ITransactCard txn =
        (ITransactCard)Activator.GetObject(typeof(ITransactCard),url);
```

Here, we call the remote web service through a transparent proxy provided by the above method call to `GetObject`:

```
        return txn.Transact(charg, card);
    }
    public static void SetValues(ICCard card, ICharge charge)
    {
        try
        {
            card.CardNumber = "1234567812340000"; // invalid card number
            card.HolderName = "Phantom";
            card.ZipCode = "Dankali 1";
            card.ExpiryDate = DateTime.Now;
            card.CType = CardTypes.Visa;
        }
        catch(Exception x)
        {
          Console.WriteLine(x.StackTrace);
        }
        Console.WriteLine("After seting card values");
        try
        {
            charge.Amount = 10000.0;
            charge.CurrencyName = "USD";
            charge.InvoiceRef = "INV001";
            charge.MerchantId = "11111111";
        }
        catch(Exception x1)
        {
            Console.WriteLine(x1.StackTrace);
        }
        Console.WriteLine("After seting charge values");
    }
}
```

The remainder of this program sets the values that we'll use for the card and the charge information. We won't compile this file just yet, though. Let's consider the remainder of the client-side code first.

`SimpleCardClient.cs` contains the class `SimpleCardClient`. This contains the static `Main` method, which will be the client-side entry point. The file is listed below, along with comments:

```
using System;
using System.IO;
using System.Security.Cryptography;
using System.Text;
using System.Runtime.Serialization.Formatters.Soap;
using System.Runtime.Remoting;
using System.Runtime.Remoting.Channels;
using System.Runtime.Remoting.Channels.Http;
using Wrox.ProCSharpWebServices.Chapter11.Card;
public class SimpleCardClient
{
    public static void Main(string[] args)
    {
```

We register the HTTP Channel:

```
if(args.Length == 0)
    ChannelServices.RegisterChannel(new HttpChannel());
else
    RemotingConfiguration.Configure(args[0]);
```

Here, we create instances of the `SimpleCCard` and `SimpleCharge`, which represent the concepts of the credit card and the charge respectively:

```
ICCard card = new SimpleCCard();
ICharge charge = new SimpleCharge();
```

We initialize these objects with some test values, to perform the simulated transaction:

```
TransactCard.SetValues(card, charge);
```

The `Transact` method has been explained above; it will contact the web service and perform the transaction, before it returns the transaction ID:

```
try {
    long txnId = TransactCard.Transact(URL,card, charge);
    Console.WriteLine("Sucess {0}", txnId);
}
catch(Exception ex)
{
    Console.WriteLine(ex.StackTrace);
    for(Exception nxt = ex.InnerException; nxt != null;
        nxt = nxt.InnerException)
    {
        Console.WriteLine("*** Inner Exception ***");
        Console.WriteLine(nxt.StackTrace);
        Console.WriteLine(nxt.Message);
    }
    Console.WriteLine(ex.Message);
}
}
```

This line sets the URL of the web service that we'll be using:

```
      private static String URL =
              "http://localhost:8000/Transact/SimpleTransact.soap";
  }
```

Now, we'll compile these files using the following command line syntax:

```
csc SimpleCardClient.cs TransactCard.cs /r:Card.dll
```

The above command compiles the client and creates the executable file `SimpleCardClient.exe`.

Now let's try to protect our transaction web service from snooping by any unauthorized entity. We shall implement protection of our service through a password-based encryption mechanism. Essentially we will develop a Security Channel and fit it at both the client and server end through configuration files:

Note that we won't be covering the creation of this security channel and the associated message sinks in this chapter. For more information, please see Case Study 2, which will provide more information on the subject.

We'll base our data scrambling and unscrambling algorithm on a simple mechanism called XOR. XOR is a binary bit operator available with all modern programming languages as a standard operator.

We'll illustrate this with an example. If A, B, and C represent three binary numbers, then:

```
A XOR B = C
C XOR B = A
```

If B is a secret value shared by the sender and receiver, then the sender wanting to send the binary message A can XOR it with B and send the resulting scrambled data C. On receiving scrambled data C that we know has been XOR operated with B, the receiver can XOR C with B and recover the original plain text. Any person who is a potential snooper would not be able to make sense of the scrambled data C without prior knowledge of the scrambling agreement and the shared secret value B. The following diagram depicts the XOR operation graphically:

```
        Binary                              Hex

        11000000011111111111101110          COFFEE

          10010001101000101 0110            123456
        110100101100101110111000            D2CBB8

          10010001101000101 0110            123456
        11000000011111111111101110          COFFEE


                                      = XOR operator
```

The shared secret value must be at least as long as the data that is being scrambled. This is, however, not a very practical thing to achieve because of the size of the necessary shared secret value.

Instead, we rely on a simple password that can be remembered and easily stored (in safe places). This shared secret password is then used to seed a pseudo-random number generator. These give the illusion of generating a sequence of random numbers, but when they are given the same seed (or initializing value) the same sequence will be generated. We can use a .NET Framework class called PasswordDeriveBytes for this purpose.

The logic is contained in the file XorCrypt.cs, which is listed below:

```csharp
using System;
using System.IO;
using System.Security.Cryptography;
public class XorCrypt
{
```

The constructor takes a password and uses the PasswordDeriveBytes class to generate a sequence of random numbers using the GetBytes method:

```csharp
public XorCrypt(string passwd)
{
    rand = new PasswordDeriveBytes(passwd,SALT);
    xorBuf = rand.GetBytes(LEN);
    count = 0;
}
```

The method below encrypts or decrypts an input stream into an output stream. The same method serves both functions because XOR is a symmetric operation:

```csharp
public void XorStream(Stream inx, Stream outx)
{
    int b;
    while((b = inx.ReadByte()) != -1)
        outx.WriteByte(crypt((byte)b));
}
```

Here, the actual XOR operation takes place:

```
public byte crypt(byte b) {
    byte by = b;
    by ^= xorBuf[count++];
    if(count >= xorBuf.Length) {
        xorBuf = rand.GetBytes(LEN);
        count = 0;
    }
    return by;
}
```

The internal parameters are defined here. The salt is a random sequence to add noise to the algorithm, thus making the random sequence harder to guess:

```
private static byte[] SALT = {0xC0,0xFF,0xE};
private byte [] xorBuf = null;
private const int LEN = 4096;
private int count;
private PasswordDeriveBytes rand;
}
}
```

We now have to fit this encryption utility into a channel sink. To do this we'll need to create a SOAP wrapper around the encrypted output. We need a SOAP wrapper because the HTTP Channel expects only serialized objects to pass through the channel, and will try to de-serialize the response to see if an exception was encountered. We have created a utility called CryptHelper contained in the file XorHelper.cs. This file is listed below:

```
using System;
using System.Text;
using System.Collections;
using System.IO;
using System.Reflection;
using System.Runtime.Remoting.Channels;
using System.Runtime.Remoting.Channels.Http;
using System.Runtime.Remoting.Messaging;
using System.Runtime.Remoting.Metadata;
using System.Diagnostics;
using System.Runtime.Serialization;
using System.Runtime.Serialization.Formatters.Soap;
namespace Wrox.CSharpWebServices.Chapter11
```

The structure below is the SOAP wrapper:

```
[Serializable]
public struct CryptData
{
    public byte[] cipherValue;
}
```

The utility class contains some useful methods used by both client and server channel sinks:

```
internal class CryptHelper
{
```

The encryption method scrambles the data and wraps it in the SOAP wrapper:

```
public static MemoryStream Encrypt(String secret, Stream inx)
{
    CryptData data = new CryptData();
    data.cipherValue = XorStream(secret, SafeCopy(inx)).ToArray();
    MemoryStream outx = new MemoryStream();
    SoapFormatter soap = new SoapFormatter();
    soap.Serialize(outx, data);
    outx.Position = 0;
    return outx;
}
```

This decryption method unscrambles the data by unwrapping the SOAP cover from the scrambled data, and then performing an XOR operation on it to recover the original plain text:

```
public static MemoryStream Decrypt(String secret, Stream inx)
{
    MemoryStream iny = SafeCopy(inx);
    SoapFormatter soap = new SoapFormatter();
    CryptData data = (CryptData)soap.Deserialize(iny);
    return XorStream(secret, new MemoryStream(data.cipherValue));
}
```

The `SafeCopy` method creates a copy of the stream. This is required because the HTTP Channel-supplied stream is forward only and read-once:

```
public static  MemoryStream SafeCopy(Stream responseStream)
{
    MemoryStream resStream = new MemoryStream();
    StreamWriter sw = new   StreamWriter(resStream);
    StreamReader sr = new StreamReader(responseStream);
    String line;
    while ((line = sr.ReadLine()) != null)
    {
        sw.WriteLine(line);
    }
    sw.Flush();
    resStream.Position = 0;
    return resStream;
}
```

This method uses the secret password supplied during channel construction (through the configuration file, which we'll discuss shortly) to create a `XorCrypt` object instance and use its `XorStream` method to XOR the input for scrambling and unscrambling the data:

```
public static MemoryStream XorStream(String secret, Stream inx)
{
    XorCrypt xoro = new XorCrypt(secret);
    MemoryStream outx = new MemoryStream();
```

```
            xoro.XorStream(inx, outx); // actual encryption done in this method
            outx.Flush();
            outx.Position = 0;
            return outx;
        }
    }
```

Before we compile this, we'll create the client and server portion of the channel sink in the file `XorSink.cs`:

```
using System;
using System.Text;
using System.Collections;
using System.IO;
using System.Reflection;
using System.Runtime.Remoting.Channels;
using System.Runtime.Remoting.Channels.Http;
using System.Runtime.Remoting.Messaging;
using System.Runtime.Remoting.Metadata;
using System.Diagnostics;
using System.Runtime.Serialization;
using System.Runtime.Serialization.Formatters.Soap;
namespace Wrox.CSharpWebServices.Chapter11
{
    public class XorClientSinkProvider : IClientChannelSinkProvider
    {
        private IClientChannelSinkProvider next = null;
        private String secret = "UNKNOWN";
        public XorClientSinkProvider()
        {
        }
```

The shared secret value is stored in the configuration file as an attribute, and passed as a dictionary entry during construction:

```
        public XorClientSinkProvider(IDictionary d, ICollection c)
        {
            string pass = (string) d["secret"];
            if(pass != null && pass.Length > 0)
                secret = pass;
        }
```

The client sink gets created here:

```
        public IClientChannelSink CreateSink(IChannelSender channel, String url,
                                             Object remoteChannelData)
        {
            IClientChannelSink nextSink = null;
            if (next != null)
            {
                nextSink = next.CreateSink(channel, url, remoteChannelData);
                if (nextSink == null)
                {
                    return null;
                }
            }
            return new XorClientSink(nextSink, secret);
        }
```

```
      public IClientChannelSinkProvider Next
      {
         get
         {
            return next;
         }
         set
         {
            next = value;
         }
      }
   }
internal class XorClientSink : IMessageSink, IClientChannelSink,
                                   IChannelSinkBase
{
   private IClientChannelSink nextSink;
   private String secret;
```

The constructor receives the secret password, indirectly, from the configuration file:

```
      public XorClientSink( IClientChannelSink nextSink, String secret)
      {
         this.nextSink = nextSink;
         this.secret = secret;
         Console.WriteLine("Ctor [{0}]", secret);
      }
```

We ignore the asynchronous method calls. These are translated in the `ProcessMessage` method call, where we place our hook:

```
      public IMessageCtrl AsyncProcessMessage(IMessage msg,
                                              IMessageSink replySink)
      {
         return NextSink.AsyncProcessMessage(msg,replySink);
      }
      public void AsyncProcessRequest(IClientChannelSinkStack sinkStack,
                                   IMessage msg, ITransportHeaders headers,
                                   Stream stream)
      {
         nextSink.AsyncProcessRequest(sinkStack, msg, headers, stream);
      }
      public void AsyncProcessResponse(IClientResponseChannelSinkStack
                                 sinkStack, object state,
                                 ITransportHeaders headers, Stream stream)
      {
         nextSink.AsyncProcessResponse(sinkStack,state,headers,stream);
      }
      public Stream GetRequestStream( IMessage msg,ITransportHeaders headers )
      {
         Stream ret = null;
         if(nextSink != null)
            ret = nextSink.GetRequestStream(msg,headers);
         return ret;
      }
```

The client side first encrypts the message request stream and then decrypts the response stream. This process is reversed at the server end:

```
public void ProcessMessage(IMessage msg,ITransportHeaders
                          requestHeaders,
                          Stream requestStream,
                          out ITransportHeaders responseHeaders,
                          out Stream responseStream )
{
    MemoryStream reqStream = CryptHelper.Encrypt(secret, requestStream);
    nextSink.ProcessMessage(msg,requestHeaders, reqStream ,
                         out responseHeaders, out responseStream);
    responseStream = CryptHelper.Decrypt(secret, responseStream);
}
```

The next method gets translated in the ProcessMessage method call:

```
public IMessage SyncProcessMessage(IMessage msg)
{
    IMessage rmsg = NextSink.SyncProcessMessage(msg);
    return msg;
}
public IDictionary Properties
{
    get
    {
        return prop;
    }
}
private Hashtable prop = new Hashtable();
public IClientChannelSink NextChannelSink
{
    get {return nextSink;}
}
public IMessageSink NextSink
{
    get
    {
        IMessageSink ret = null;
        for(IClientChannelSink nxt = nextSink; nxt != null;
            nxt = nxt.NextChannelSink)
        {
            if(nxt is  IMessageSink)
            {
                ret = (IMessageSink) nxt;
                break;
            }
        }
        return ret;
    }
}
}// END: XorClientSink
```

Here, we'll construct our server's channel sink:

```
public class XorServerChannelSinkProvider : IServerChannelSinkProvider
{
    private IServerChannelSinkProvider next = null;
```

```
                    private String secret = "UNKNOWN";
                    public XorServerChannelSinkProvider()
                    {
                    }
```

The attribute secret contains the secret password. We collect this and pass it while constructing the channel sink:

```
            public XorServerChannelSinkProvider(IDictionary d,
                                                 ICollection providerData)
            {
                string pass = (string) d["secret"];
                if(pass != null && pass.Length > 0)
                    secret = pass;
            }
            public void GetChannelData(IChannelDataStore channelData)
            {
            }
```

The server channel sink gets created here:

```
            public IServerChannelSink CreateSink(IChannelReceiver channel)
            {
                IServerChannelSink nextSink = null;
                if (next != null)
                {
                    nextSink = next.CreateSink(channel);
                }
                return new XorServerChannelSink(nextSink,secret);
            }
            public IServerChannelSinkProvider Next
            {
                get
                {
                    return next;
                }
                set
                {
                    next = value;
                }
            }
        } //END: class XorrServerChannelSinkProvider
        internal class XorServerChannelSink :  IServerChannelSink
        {
            private IServerChannelSink nextSink = null;
            private String secret;
            public XorServerChannelSink(IServerChannelSink nextSink, String secret)
                    : base()
            {
                this.nextSink = nextSink;
                this.secret = secret;
                Console.WriteLine("Ctor [{0}]", secret);
            }
```

The unscrambling of the request is the reverse of the process that took place at the client side. The response stream is scrambled back before sending to the client:

```
public ServerProcessing ProcessMessage(IServerChannelSinkStack
                                    sinkStack, IMessage requestMessage,
                                    ITransportHeaders requestHeaders,
                                    Stream requestStream,
                                    out IMessage msg,
                                    out ITransportHeaders responseHeaders,
                                    out Stream responseStream)
{
    MemoryStream reqStream = CryptHelper.Decrypt(secret,requestStream);
    sinkStack.Push(this, null);
    ServerProcessing processing =
            nextSink.ProcessMessage(sinkStack, requestMessage, requestHeaders,
                                    reqStream, out msg,
                                    out responseHeaders,
                                    out responseStream);
    sinkStack.Pop(this);
    responseStream = CryptHelper.Encrypt(secret, responseStream);
    return processing;
}
public void AsyncProcessResponse(IServerResponseChannelSinkStack
                                    sinkStack, Object state,
                                    IMessage msg, ITransportHeaders headers,
                                    Stream stream)
{
    sinkStack.AsyncProcessResponse(msg, headers, stream);
}
public Stream GetResponseStream(IServerResponseChannelSinkStack
                                    sinkStack, Object state,
                                    IMessage msg, ITransportHeaders headers)
{
    return null; //the soap formatter creates a mem chunk stream on null
}
public IServerChannelSink NextChannelSink
{
    get
    {
        return nextSink;
    }
}
public IDictionary Properties {get { return prop; }}
private Hashtable prop = new Hashtable();
} //END: class XorServerChannelSink
} //END: Namespace
```

And now we are ready to compile our sink, using the command given below:

csc /t:library XorSink.cs XorHelper.cs XorCrypt.cs

This should generate the `XorSink.dll` file. There is a batch file called `compile1.bat`, which compiles all of the files needed for this portion of the sample

Now we need to set the server-side configuration file, in order to register our channel sink.

```
<configuration>
  <system.runtime.remoting>
    <application name="Transact">
      <service>
        <wellknown mode="SingleCall" type =
            "Wrox.ProCSharpWebServices.Chapter11.Card.Service.SimpleTransact,
```

```
            SimpleTransact" objectUri="SimpleTransact.soap" />
        </service>
        <channels>
          <channel port="8000"
                 type="System.Runtime.Remoting.Channels.Http.HttpChannel,
                 System.Runtime.Remoting, publicKeyToken = b77a5c561934e089,
                 version = 1.0.3300.0, culture = neutral">
            <serverProviders>
              <provider secret="my secret" type =
                "Wrox.CSharpWebServices.Chapter11.XorServerChannelSinkProvider,
                XorSink" />
              <formatter type =
                "System.Runtime.Remoting.Channels.SoapServerFormatterSinkProvider,
                System.Runtime.Remoting, publicKeyToken = b77a5c561934e089,
                version = 1.0.3300.0, culture = neutral"/>
            </serverProviders>
          </channel>
        </channels>
      </application>
    </system.runtime.remoting>
</configuration>
```

The above file is called `DirectHost1.exe.config`. Our server side channel sink declaration is highlighted.

The client-side configuration file is called `SimpleCardClient1.exe.config`. It is listed below, with our client channel specifics highlighted:

```
<configuration>
  <system.runtime.remoting>
    <application>
      <channels>
        <channel type="System.Runtime.Remoting.Channels.Http.HttpChannel,
                 System.Runtime.Remoting" >
          <clientProviders>
            <formatter type =
            "System.Runtime.Remoting.Channels.SoapClientFormatterSinkProvider,
            System.Runtime.Remoting" />
            <provider secret="my secret" type =
                "Wrox.CSharpWebServices.Chapter11.XorClientSinkProvider,
                XorSink" />
          </clientProviders>
        </channel>
      </channels>
    </application>
  </system.runtime.remoting>
</configuration>
```

We are now ready to run this sample. Both the client and the web service are run from the command line. We start the server with:

```
DirectHost -cfg DirectHost1.exe.config
```

The client can then be run with the following command:

```
SimpleCardClient SimpleCardClient1.exe.config
```

The client prints out the transaction ID, and the server prints out the card and the charge details on screen. Let's now move on to enhance this example to make use of key-based encryption techniques.

Enhancing the Credit Card Validation Sample

We will now consider an application-specific means of protecting the sensitive data. This technique is similar to SET, because the application is not dependent on underlying layers for encryption. The programmer is in direct control of the encryption methodology, but the design is transparent to the other parts of the application.

The idea is to create a design whereby a class of objects can act as one-way secure storage for the client. The server should be able to both read and write the properties of the objects. This can be achieved if we use a key pair. The client side would only have the public key whereas the server side would have both sides of the key pair:

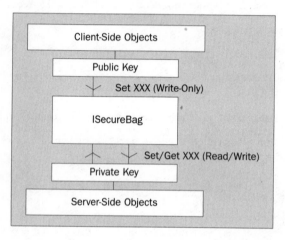

The above abstract concept is provided by the `ISecureBag` interface in the file `Card.cs`:

```
public interface ISecureBag
{
    RSA Key {get; set;}
}
```

A concrete implementation of the above interface is provided by the class below. The `SecureBag` class is `Serializable`. It holds the key for encrypting and decrypting the data within the object at run time. Classes that extend it can use the services for encryption and, if they have a private key, they can decrypt the data as well. The important information (such as the credit card number) is not kept in clear text – even in the memory – during run time. This avoids the possibility of a **core dump** attack. In this kind of attack a memory snapshot is taken to gain access to unencrypted information residing in the runtime memory space:

```
[Serializable]
public class SecureBag : ISecureBag
{
```

Here we set the RSA property methods:

```
public virtual RSA Key
{
    get
```

```
        {
            CheckPubKey();

            return rsa;
        }
        set
        {
            rsa = value;
            pubxml = rsa.ToXmlString(false); // public key portions
        }
    }
}
```

This is a helper method for decryption to be used by the classes inheriting this method to decrypt their secured properties and data members:

```
    protected string DecryptString(byte[] encr)
    {
        if(rsa == null)
            throw new ApplicationException("No Private key defined");
        string ret = null;
        if(encr != null)
        {
            byte [] decrp =
                    ((RSACryptoServiceProvider) rsa).Decrypt(encr, false);
            ret = (new ASCIIEncoding()).GetString(decrp);
        }
        return ret;
    }
```

Here, we provide a helper method to store sensitive data members in encrypted format:

```
    protected  byte[] EncryptString(string val)
    {
        CheckPubKey();
        return ((RSACryptoServiceProvider) rsa).Encrypt((new
                ASCIIEncoding()).GetBytes(val), false);
    }
```

If the public key object is NULL, we create it from the in-memory XML string:

```
    protected void CheckPubKey()
    {
        if(rsa == null)
        {
            if(pubxml == null)
                throw new ApplicationException("No Public key defined");
            rsa = new RSACryptoServiceProvider();
            rsa.FromXmlString(pubxml);
        }
    }
    private string pubxml = null;
```

We do not serialize the RSA object for security reasons:

```
    [ NonSerialized ]
    protected RSA rsa = null;
} // END: class SecureBag
```

The CCard class implements the ICCard interface while extending the SecureBag class:

```
[Serializable]
public sealed class CCard : SecureBag, ICCard
{
```

Encrypted members are not saved in memory in plain text:

```
public string CardNumber
{
    get
    {
        return DecryptString(encCardNumber);
    }
    set
    {
        encCardNumber = EncryptString(value);
    }
}
```

The cardholder's name is also encrypted, as is the zip code:

```
public string HolderName
{
    get
    {
        return DecryptString(encHolderName);
    }
    set
    {
        encHolderName = EncryptString(value);
    }
}
public string ZipCode
{
    get
    {
        return DecryptString(encZipCode);
    }
    set
    {
        encZipCode = EncryptString(value);
    }
}
```

These object members need not be protected with encryption:

```
public DateTime  ExpiryDate
{
    get
    {
        return expDt;
    }
    set
    {
        expDt = value;
    }
```

```
    }
    public CardTypes CType
    {
        get
        {
            return ctyp;
        }
        set
        {
            ctyp = value;
        }
    }
    private DateTime expDt;
    private CardTypes ctyp = CardTypes.Undefined;
    private byte [] encCardNumber = null;
    private byte [] encHolderName = null;
    private byte [] encZipCode = null;
} // END: class CCard
```

Similarly, the class `Charge` implements the interface `ICharge` to implement the public key encrypted data security:

```
[Serializable]
public sealed class Charge : SecureBag, ICharge
{
```

The merchant's ID is encrypted as follows:

```
    public string MerchantId
    {
        get
        {
            return DecryptString(encMerchantId);
        }
        set
        {
            encMerchantId = EncryptString(value);
        }
    }
```

The amount is also encrypted, but the remaining members aren't:

```
    public double Amount
    {
        get
        {
            return Convert.ToDouble(DecryptString(encAmount));
        }
        set
        {
            string str = Convert.ToString(value);
            Console.WriteLine("Charge Amt = {0}",str);
            encAmount = EncryptString(str);
        }
    }
```

```
            public string CurrencyName
            {
                get { return curn; }
                set { curn = value; }
            }
            public string InvoiceRef
            {
                get { return invref; }
                set { invref = value; }
            }
            private byte[] encMerchantId = null;
            private byte[] encAmount = null;
            private string invref = null;
            private string curn = null;
        } // END: class Charge
```

Let us now consider the implementation of the embedded storage of public and private keys within a class object. The class `KeyMan` provides a base implementation of this functionality. As seen from the code below, the keys are converted to `Base64` encoded strings and embedded into a `private static String` member instance:

```
using System.Security.Cryptography;
using System;
using System.Text;
public class KeyMan : MarshalByRefObject
{
    public KeyMan() {}
    public KeyMan(string b64)
    {
        k = b64;
    }
    public RSA Key
    {
        get
        {
            RSA rsa = new RSACryptoServiceProvider();
            byte[] by = Convert.FromBase64String(k);
            string pubxml = (new ASCIIEncoding()).GetString(by);
            rsa.FromXmlString(pubxml);
            return rsa;
        }
    }
    private string k = null;
}
```

The public key is embedded within the `PubKey` class. What looks like a random string in the code below is actually the `Base64` encoded public key:

```
public class PubKey : KeyMan
{
    public PubKey(): base(sk) {}
    private static string sk =
"PFJTQUtleV ... UI8L0V4cG9uZW50PjwvUlNBS2V5VmFsdWU+DQo=";
}
```

The `PrvKey` class (which contains the private key) is similar.

Both of these `Base64` encoded keys were generated from `key.xml` and `pub.xml` by passing them through the code given below. The XML files themselves are the products of the previous examples discussed in the above section on RSA keys:

```
using System;
public class ToBase64
{
    public static void Main(string[] args)
    {
        if(args.Length != 1)
        {
            Console.WriteLine("usage ToBase64 <file name>");
            Environment.Exit(0);
        }
        byte[] targ = FileUtil.LoadBytes(args[0]);
        Console.WriteLine(Convert.ToBase64String(targ));
    }
}
```

The output of the above code was captured by redirecting the standard output to a file.

The web service code for our simulated transaction is provided by the class `SecureTransact` which extends `SimpleTransact` (refer to the earlier part of this example at the beginning of this chapter). The file `SecureTransact.cs` is listed below:

```
using System;
using Wrox.ProCSharpWebServices.Chapter11.Card;
namespace Wrox.ProCSharpWebServices.Chapter11.Card.Service
{
    public class SecureTransact :SimpleTransact
    {
```

We create an instance of the private key encapsulation object in its constructor:

```
        public SecureTransact()
        {
            Console.WriteLine(" SecureTransact created");
            key = new PrvKey();
        }
        public SecureTransact(KeyMan prvKey)
        {
            key = prvKey;
        }
```

The overridden method maintains compatibility with the previous example stage, so it checks if the objects passed as parameters implement the `ISecureBag` interface. If `true` then we set the private key so that we can read the object values. Recall that secure bag objects need a private key to be able to provide read functionality. After this, we call the base method:

```
        public override long Transact(ICharge charge, ICCard card)
        {
            if(charge is ISecureBag)
```

```
        ((ISecureBag)charge).Key = key.Key;
    if(card  is ISecureBag)
        ((ISecureBag)card).Key = key.Key;
    return base.Transact(charge, card);
}
```

Here, we set the private key if the argument implements `ISecureBag` interface, and then we default to the base method:

```
public override bool  IsValid(ICCard card)
{
    if(card  is ISecureBag)
        ((ISecureBag)card).Key = key.Key;
    return base.IsValid(card);
}
private KeyMan key;
}
```

The compilation is accomplished using the command:

```
csc /t:library SecureTransact.cs SimpleTransact.cs PrvKey.cs KeyMan.cs
    /r:Card.dll
```

The client can access the above service remotely by following these steps:

❑ Construct the `Ccard` and `Charge` objects

❑ Set their `Key` property with the public key of the web service

❑ Create or get the instance of the remote service object

❑ Call the method `Transact` on this remote object

The client file is listed below:

```
public class SecureCardClient
{
    public static void Main(string[] args)
    {
```

This registers the HTTP Channel. We do not need any configuration file here:

```
        ChannelServices.RegisterChannel(new HttpChannel());
```

Here, we create the encapsulating public key object and set the `Key` property members of the `SecureBag` extenders:

```
        KeyMan k = new PubKey(); // public key can also be remoted!
        CCard card = new CCard();
        card.Key = k.Key;
        Charge charg = new Charge();
        charg.Key = k.Key;
```

Now, we set the values for our charge and card. Note that we have write-only access on the client side:

```
        TransactCard.SetValues(card, charg);
```

This calls the remote method through the helper class. This was discussed earlier in the chapter:

```
      try {
          long txnId = TransactCard.Transact(URL,card, charg);
          Console.WriteLine("Sucess {0}", txnId);
      }
      catch(Exception ex)
      {
          Console.WriteLine(ex.StackTrace);
          for(Exception nxt = ex.InnerException; nxt != null;
              nxt = nxt.InnerException)
          {
              Console.WriteLine("*** Inner Exception ***");
              Console.WriteLine(nxt.StackTrace);
              Console.WriteLine(nxt.Message);
          }
          Console.WriteLine(ex.Message);
      }
    }
    private static String URL =
                      "http://localhost:8000/Transact/SecureTransact.soap";
}
```

The client code is compiled as follows:

```
csc SecureCardClient.cs TransactCard.cs  PubKey.cs KeyMan.cs /r:Card.dll
```

The batch file compile2.bat provided compiles all of the files needed for this portion of the example.

All that remains now is to set the configuration files to reflect the changes that we've made. The server-side configuration file DirectHost2.exe.config is given below:

```
<configuration>
  <system.runtime.remoting>
    <application name="Transact">
      <service>
        <wellknown mode="Singleton" type =
            "Wrox.ProCSharpWebServices.Chapter11.Card.Service.SecureTransact,
            SecureTransact" objectUri="SecureTransact.soap" />
      </service>
      <channels>
        <channel port="8000" type =
                "System.Runtime.Remoting.Channels.Http.HttpChannel,
                System.Runtime.Remoting, publicKeyToken = b77a5c561934e089,
                version = 1.0.3300.0, culture = neutral" />
      </channels>
    </application>
  </system.runtime.remoting>
</configuration>
```

We execute this service with the following command:

```
DirectHost -cfg DirectHost2.exe.config
```

The client code is simply executed by running the SimpleCardClient.exe file. The client prints the transaction ID and the server prints the card and the charge details. We now directly control the encryption at the application object level. The programmer is in direct control and need not depend on the deployment staff for success in securing the application security and data sensitivity policies.

Summary

Web services will be pervasive, and so will need security measures. All three security layers (namely: IPSec, SSL, and application-layer security) will be needed to implement a safe Internet.

In a nutshell, then, we have three security mechanisms available to us:

- ❑ Depend on SSL and other built-in mechanisms
- ❑ Devise Channel-layer security
- ❑ Devise application-specific security

Each option needs to be evaluated in terms of the level of security provided, overheads incurred by the security mechanism, and the service operators' security needs and perception of the threat.

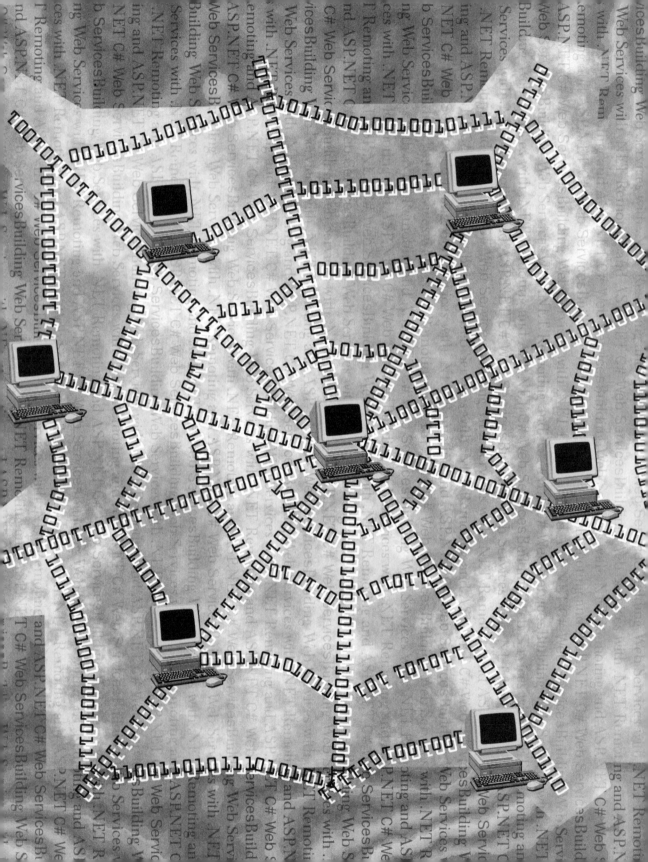

12

Web Services as Application Plug-Ins

You've just been asked to do the impossible. Yesterday.

Due to a sensitive personnel issue, customers at the facilities division of the university you work for are clamoring for a custom application. The shop managers there have long been keeping handwritten records of the specific tasks they send their employees out to do, noting a description of each job, who was sent to do it, what day they were to go, and how long the managers thought the job should take to complete. Recently, an employee who had been out for some time for an injury was applying for additional workman's compensation time, and as justification for his request he mentioned a particular job he had been on prior to his injury that involved quite a bit of lifting. This aggravated his back injury initially, and as a result he's convinced that his earlier, slight accident is why it is taking longer to heal than his doctors initially advised.

The problem is that the shop managers are certain he wasn't *on* the job he claims to have initially strained his back on, but the handwritten record that would prove their case is missing. Not only is the particular shop manager in the doghouse for losing his records, but higher management is in a snit as well (since they're supposed to know about sensitive personnel issues...). Thus, they want a desktop application written, which will be installed on all shop managers' desktop machines to help them manage, sort, and update their data. Additionally, the upper management wants access to this same data, and as I said at the outset, they want it yesterday.

We're going to build a Windows application that maintains this timesheet data, which will allow for the entry of weekly projected records as well as the sorting and searching of the data as a whole. The primary purpose of our Windows application, then, is to help managers track their daily tasks. More to the point of the present book, we'll enable the delivery of our application through a web service, and allow for an automated and seamless upgrade process when our application is updated. If revisions to the code are made, the application can be recompiled and the newer class library can be placed on the network in one place, without bothering users with a personal visit for the re-installation of our application. When first loaded, the smaller client application will first check to see that the version of the file on the client is up-to-date with the server version. If it is not, the presumption is that the timesheet application has been updated in some way, and we'll provide functions to deliver the newer version of the DLL to the client without intervention from the IT department, thus automating the upgrade process. Finally, we'll also provide the ability to store an XML representation of our data on the client (so that the application can be used even when the network is inaccessible).

There are four steps we need to take to achieve this:

❑   Build a Windows application to manage our timesheet data

❑   Change that application's output type to a class library, so the resulting DLL can be managed by a web service

❑   Build a web service that automates the delivery of our DLL

❑   Finally, build a small client application that will serve as the portal to our web service, and allow for client-side options that will enable our users to work even if the network and database are unavailable

Designing the GUI

We'll therefore start by designing the timesheet application as a straightforward Windows application. We'll develop and test this as we would any other Windows application, before recompiling it as a DLL and exposing it via a web service. We aren't going to look in detail at the process of designing the database or the GUI, because our concern here is primarily with exposing the application as a web service and accessing data, which may come either directly from the database server or from the local XML copy on the client.

Drawing our Form

We'll begin by creating a Windows application project in Visual Studio .NET (as we'll see, this will ultimately be compiled as a class library). The form will be used for three main purposes – entering data into the database, searching the database, and displaying the data – so we'll design a form with three main sections – a number of textboxes and combo boxes for entering a new record in the database; a section where we can enter or choose values to search for; and a DataGrid for displaying the results of our searches. We'll also add a calendar control, so the user can select a date range for particular jobs, and a set of radio buttons that allow the user to select the field to sort by:

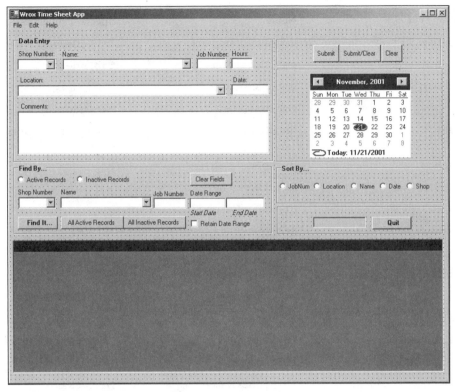

Duplicating the form I created should be a simple matter of dragging and dropping controls, as long as your form's dimensions are approximately the same as mine (832 x 692 pixels).

The table below shows the particular controls we'll use, as well as their respective names and any special property settings:

Control Type	Name	Special Properties
Button	btnActiveRecords	TabIndex=15
Button	btnClear	TabIndex=24
Button	btnClearFinds	TabIndex=14
Button	btnFind	TabIndex=25
Button	btnInactiveOnly	TabIndex=16
Button	btnQuit	TabIndex=18
Button	btnSubmit	TabIndex=8
Button	btnSubmitClear	TabIndex=9
CheckBox	chkDateRange	
ComboBox	cmboFindByName	TabIndex=11

Table continued on following page

Control Type	Name	Special Properties
ComboBox	cmboFindShopNum	TabIndex=10
ComboBox	cmboLocation	TabIndex=5
ComboBox	cmboName	TabIndex=1
ComboBox	cmboShopNum	TabIndex=0
DataGrid	dataGrid1	AlternatingBackColor= LightBlue
GroupBox	groupBox1	
GroupBox	groupBoxBtns	
GroupBox	groupBoxCalendar	
GroupBox	groupBoxData	
GroupBox	groupBoxFind	
GroupBox	groupBoxSortBy	
Label	lblComments	Text="Comments:"
Label	lblDate	Text="Date:"
Label	lblDRange	Text="Date Range"
Label	lblEndDate	Text="End Date"
Label	lblFindByName	Text="Name"
Label	lblFindJobNum	Text="Job Number"
Label	lblFindShopNum	Text="Shop Number"
Label	lblHours	Text="Hours"
Label	lblJobNum	Text="Job Number"
Label	lblLocation	Text="Location:"
Label	lblName	Text="Name:"
Label	lblShopNum	Text="Shop Number:"
Label	lblStartDate	Text="Start Date"
MainMenu	mainMenu1	
MenuItem	menuItem1	
MenuItem	menuItem2	
MenuItem	menuItem3	
MenuItem	menuItem4	
MenuItem	menuItem5	
MenuItem	menuItem6	

Control Type	Name	Special Properties
MenuItem	menuItem7	
MenuItem	menuItem8	
MenuItem	menuItem9	
MonthCalendar	monthCalendar1	
RadioButton	radioButton1	Text="JobNum"
RadioButton	radioButton2	Text="Location"
RadioButton	radioButton3	Text="Name"
RadioButton	radioButton4	Text="Date"
RadioButton	radioButton5	Text="ShopNum"
RadioButton	rbtnActiveOnly	Text="Active Records"
RadioButton	rbtnInactiveOnly	Text="Inactive Records"
TextBox	txtComments	
TextBox	txtDate	
TextBox	txtEndDate	
TextBox	txtFindByJobNum	
TextBox	txtHours	
TextBox	txtJobNum	
TextBox	txtRecordsFound	Enabled=False
TextBox	txtStartDate	

When your form is arranged visually to your liking, save it as frmTimeSheets.cs (we use this VB-style name in order to distinguish this file from the later version that we'll compile into a DLL).

Writing the Code

Now that we've completed the GUI design, we can start to write our actual code. There are three principal sections to our code. Firstly, we will need to populate the DataGrid and the combo boxes when the form originally loads; next, we will write the code to allow the user to update the database; and finally, we need to allow the user to search through the data and display the results.

Starting Up

First, we'll configure some initial settings. We'll start by adding the using directives to include the namespaces we'll be using, and then declare the namespace for our application as Wrox.ProCSharpWebServices. Chapter12. Next, the class frmTimeSheets is declared, which inherits from System.Windows. Forms.Form. Then come the auto-generated declarations of the controls we've placed on the form:

337

```
using System;
using System.Drawing;
using System.Collections;
using System.ComponentModel;
using System.Windows.Forms;
using System.Data;
using System.Data.SqlClient;

namespace Wrox.ProCSharpWebServices.Chapter12
{
    /// <summary>
    /// Summary description for frmTimeSheets.
    /// </summary>
    public class frmTimeSheets : System.Windows.Forms.Form
    {
        private System.Windows.Forms.DataGrid dataGrid1;
        private System.Windows.Forms.GroupBox groupBoxData;
        private System.Windows.Forms.Label lblShopNum;
        private System.Windows.Forms.ComboBox cmboShopNum;
        private System.Windows.Forms.Label lblName;


        ...
```

Now we'll add a few fields of our own, at the end of the auto-generated list. One of these, `private string orderBy`, will assist us when we generate our search strings. We'll also create `DataSet` (`ds`) and `SqlConnection` (`con`) objects, as well as a string (`source`) for our connection to SQL Server. Finally, we'll set up the path where our application will ultimately reside (`appPath`), as well as a boolean value (`useLocalData`) to indicate whether or not the local XML representation of the data that we'll be creating is in use (set to `false` at startup):

```
private string orderBy;
DataSet ds = new DataSet();
static string source = "Data Source=hucbaldlt;Initial Catalog=Shops;" +
                                         "User ID=sa;Password=";
SqlConnection con = new SqlConnection (source);
static string appPath = Environment.GetFolderPath
                  (Environment.SpecialFolder.ProgramFiles) + "\\TimeSheet";
bool useLocalData = false;
```

For simplicity's sake, we've hard-coded the database connection details into the application and used the sa username. In a live application, we would obviously not connect as sa (to restrict the level of access for each user), and we would either supply connection details separately (for example, in a configuration file), or oblige users to enter their username and password.

Now we'll give the form constructor some startup settings (just in case, we'll place them in a `try` block). Since the default data to return to the grid will be the records that represent active workers (as opposed to those who are no longer on the job), we'll set the `rbtnActiveOnly.Checked` property to `true` upon startup. Next, we call three methods:

❑   `FillDataSet()` fills our `DataSet` with records from SQL Server.

❑   `GetAllData()` will grab all the records from the `DataSet` and display them in the `DataGrid`.

❑   `LoadCombos()` will populate the various combo boxes with the appropriate selections (we'll examine the code for these methods shortly).

The final three lines of the `try` block grab a date from the `monthCalendar` control, format a string, and place that string in the `txtDate` textbox. In the unlikely event of trouble (think positively!), the `catch` block provides an apology and a specific error message:

```
public frmTimeSheets() // Constructor
{
    InitializeComponent();

    try
    {
        rbtnActiveOnly.Checked = true;
        FillDataSet();
        LoadCombos();
        GetAllData();
        DateTime d = monthCalendar1.SelectionStart;
        string dateStr = d.Month + "/" + d.Day + "/" + d.Year;
        txtDate.Text = dateStr;
    }
    catch(Exception ex)
    {
        MessageBox.Show("There was an error starting up. This straightforward" +
                " message tells why:\n\n" + ex.ToString(), "I Can't Get Started");
    }
}

protected override void Dispose( bool disposing )
{
    // Standard Windows Forms code...
}

#region Windows Form Designer generated code.

[STAThread]
static void Main()
{
    Application.Run(new frmTimeSheets());
}
```

Populating the DataSet

Because we want to limit the number of connections we make to the database, and because the final application will need to be able to take data either from the local XML file or from the database server, we will load the data into a `DataSet` and provide search and filter facilities against that, rather than re-querying the database every time we want a fresh view of the data.

The first method fired in our constructor obtains the data to populate this `DataSet`. We'll use a single main `DataTable` to hold the data that we'll display in our `DataGrid`. However, we'll need to access the primary key columns of several tables if we want to update the database, so we'll populate a few more `DataTables` that won't be visisble to the user. After calling the `Open()` method on our `SqlConnection` object, we create a `SqlDataAdapter`, passing it a `SELECT` string and a reference to our connection to SQL Server; finally, we call its `Fill()` method to populate the `DataSet`. We then reset the `SelectCommand` and fill the other `DataTables`.

If the database is unavailable, we will provide a means to read that data from the client side via an XML file (see the `if` portion of the `catch` clause, where the `DataSet`'s `ReadXml()` method is called). Finally, if the database is unavailable and the XML file doesn't exist on the client, we bow out gracefully:

```
private void FillDataSet()
{
    try
    {
        con.Open();
        SqlDataAdapter da = new SqlDataAdapter("SELECT Name, JobNumber, " +
                "ShopNumber, JobLocation, theDate, Hours, Active, Comments " +
                                              " FROM AllData", con);
        da.Fill(ds, "AllData");

        da.SelectCommand.CommandText = "SELECT JobLocation, IDJobLocation " +
                                                        "FROM JobLoc";
        da.Fill(ds, "JobLoc");

        da.SelectCommand.CommandText = "SELECT IDJobNum, JobNumber FROM JobNum";
        da.Fill(ds, "JobNum");

        da.SelectCommand.CommandText = "SELECT Name, IDWorker FROM Worker";
        da.Fill(ds, "Worker");

        da.SelectCommand.CommandText = "SELECT ShopNumber, IDShopNumber FROM " +
                                                        "ShopNum";
        da.Fill(ds, "ShopNum");

        con.Close();
    }
    catch (Exception ex)
    {
        MessageBox.Show(ex.Message);
        if (File.Exists(appPath + "\\TimesheetData.xml"))
        {
            this.ds.ReadXml(appPath + "\\TimesheetData.xml");
            useLocalData = true;
            MessageBox.Show("Can't connect to the database - using local copy " +
                        "of the data.", "Connection error", MessageBoxButtons.OK,
                                                MessageBoxIcon.Warning);
        }
        else
        {
            throw new Exception("Can't connect to database or local data cache" +
                                                "\n\n" + ex.ToString());
        }
    }
}
```

Loading the Form Controls with Data

The LoadCombos() method does what its name implies, and populates our five combo boxes. By referencing the Rows collection of our DataSet's Table (at index 0), we can loop through that collection's contents using the foreach keyword. We don't want to add repeated entries to the boxes, so we use the ComboBox class's FindString() method, which simply returns a zero-based index of the first occurrence of the string we're looking for. If no item is found (that is, the entry hasn't already been added to the combo box), -1 is returned. We use this as a flag to call the Add() method of the combo box's Items collection, passing in the name of the database column we want each populated with. (We only need to loop through three times, since two pairs of our combo boxes share the same data.) When all is complete, we set the Sorted property of each to true to sort the entries in the combo box, and call the Update() method to actually display the data required:

```csharp
private void LoadCombos()
{
    try
    {
        foreach (DataRow dr in ds.Tables[0].Rows)
        {
            if (cmboShopNum.FindString(dr["ShopNumber"].ToString()) == -1)
            {
                cmboShopNum.Items.Add(dr["ShopNumber"]);
                cmboFindShopNum.Items.Add(dr["ShopNumber"]);
            }

            if (cmboName.FindString(dr["Name"].ToString()) == -1)
            {
                cmboName.Items.Add(dr["Name"]);
                cmboFindByName.Items.Add(dr["Name"]);
            }

            if (cmboLocation.FindString(dr["JobLocation"].ToString()) == -1)
            {
                cmboLocation.Items.Add(dr["JobLocation"]);
            }
        }

        cmboShopNum.Sorted = true;
        cmboShopNum.Update();
        cmboFindShopNum.Sorted = true;
        cmboFindShopNum.Update();
        cmboName.Sorted = true;
        cmboName.Update();
        cmboFindByName.Sorted = true;
        cmboFindByName.Update();
        cmboLocation.Sorted = true;
        cmboLocation.Update();
    }
    catch(Exception ex)
    {
        MessageBox.Show("Something is amiss, but never fear. This helpful " +
                "message from Microsoft will surely clarify.\n\n" + ex.ToString(),
                                        "Error! Comboboxes Hosed");
    }
}
```

In addition to LoadCombos(), a second function was called upon startup in our form's constructor: GetAllData(). Calling GetAllData() allows our application to begin life with a populated DataGrid.

GetAllData() works like this: for a bit of GUI interaction, we'll set the cursor to an hourglass (to show the user that a bit of work is being done; we'll turn it back to an arrow when we've retrieved the data). Next, we declare a string (select), which will be used to evaluate whether the user wants to view records pertaining to active or inactive workers; we set that string within if ... else statements. Notice that the Boolean field indicating whether an entry is still active is interpreted differently depending on whether the data is taken directly from the database (in which case, it will be represented as a numeric bit) or from the XML file (where it will take the form of a string). We therefore use the ternary operator to set the select string to the appropriate value based on the useLocalData field.

In order to filter our data in the `DataSet`, we will use a `DataView` object (`dv`), and we will populate our `DataGrid` with this. We instantiate this with a reference to the `DataTable` in our `DataSet` (since we're only working with a single table, we set the index to 0), we set its `RowFilter` property to the `select` string. Then, we set its `Sort` property via the `GetRadioButton()` method, which simply checks to see which of the form's radio buttons is selected in the **Sort By** group box. All that remains is to set the data binding of our `DataGrid` to the `DataView` object we've just created. We also set the `Cursor` property of the form back to an arrow, and fill the `txtRecordsFound` textbox with a message relaying the number of records we found:

```
protected void GetAllData()
{
    try
    {
        this.Cursor = Cursors.WaitCursor;
        string select = "";
        if (rbtnInactiveOnly.Checked)
            select = useLocalData ? "Active='False'" : "Active=0";
        else // Default is active records only
            select = useLocalData ? "Active='True'" : "Active=1";

        DataView dv = new DataView(ds.Tables[0]);
        dv.RowFilter = select;
        dv.Sort = GetRadioButton();
        dataGrid1.SetDataBinding(dv, "");
        this.Cursor = Cursors.Arrow;
        txtRecordsFound.Text = dv.Count + " record(s) found";
    }
    catch(Exception ex)
    {
        MessageBox.Show("I guess I'm not perfect yet. Here's one of my flaws:" +
                                    "\n\n" + ex.ToString(), "Whoops...");
    }
}
```

Handling Form Events

Before we move on, there are some rather mundane GUI operations to take care of. Specifically, we're going to add code to the `Click` event handlers for our buttons, and to the `DateChanged` handler for the `monthCalendar`.

First, we'll provide responses to our **All Active Records** and **All Inactive Records** buttons' `Click` events. Here we just manually reset the appropriate radio button to select active or inactive records and then request the data by calling the `GetAllData()` method:

```
private void btnInactiveOnly_Click(object sender, System.EventArgs e)
{
    try
    {
        rbtnInactiveOnly.Checked = true; // Reset the Inactive Only radiobtn
        GetAllData();
        LoadCombos();
    }
    catch(Exception ex)
    {
        MessageBox.Show("Sorry, but something slipped. Hope this helps...\n\n" +
                                    ex.ToString(), "Trouble in Paradise");
    }
```

```
    }

    private void btnActiveRecords_Click(object sender, System.EventArgs e)
    {
        try
        {
            rbtnActiveOnly.Checked = true; // Reset the Active Only radiobtn
            GetAllData();
            LoadCombos();
        }
        catch(Exception ex)
        {
            MessageBox.Show("Blast! There was an error, and this is all I know " +
                                    "about it:\n\n" + ex.ToString(), "Danger!");
        }
    }
```

The code for our "clear" buttons is also very simple. We'll deal with two of them now (leaving the Submit/Clear button for later). The primary Clear routine will fire on a click of the upper right-hand corner button:

```
    private void btnClear_Click(object sender, System.EventArgs e)
    {
        cmboShopNum.Text = "";
        cmboName.Text = "";
        txtJobNum.Text = "";
        txtHours.Text = "";
        cmboLocation.Text = "";
        txtComments.Text = "";
    }
```

This simply inserts an empty string in all the textboxes and combo boxes on the form.

The code for the Clear Fields button (btnClearFields) is only slightly more complex. It works in tandem with the Retain Date Range checkbox (chkDateRange). Users will often perform multiple searches on a specific date range (such as "What work did all the shops do in the first two weeks of July in the last five years?"). Clicking the Retain Date Range checkbox will allow them to select a date range only once in the course of a session if they so desire. To make this work, of course, the btnClearFields click event needs to check to see if the start and end dates are to be retained or cleared along with the other "find" text and combo boxes. First, we respond directly to the button's Click event, sending the request to the ClearFinds() method:

```
    private void btnClearFields_Click(object sender, System.EventArgs e)
    {
        ClearFinds();
    }
```

ClearFinds() works like this: if the Checked property of chkDateRange returns true, then only cmboFindShopNum, cmboFindByName, and txtFindByJobNum are cleared, but whatever is in the txtStartDate and txtEndDate textboxes is retained. Otherwise, these two textboxes are sent empty strings as well:

```
    private void ClearFinds()
    {
        if (chkDateRange.Checked)
```

```
    {
        cmboFindShopNum.Text = "";
        cmboFindByName.Text = "";
        txtFindByJobNum.Text = "";
    }
    else
    {
        cmboFindShopNum.Text = "";
        cmboFindByName.Text = "";
        txtFindByJobNum.Text = "";
        txtStartDate.Text = "";
        txtEndDate.Text = "";
    }
}
```

There is also a short routine to ease the entry of start and end dates for the user, which relies on our monthCalendar control. The date selected by a user's click on the calendar is accessed via the monthCalendar1.SelectionStart property. We assign that date to a DateTime type we'll call d:

```
private void monthCalendar1_DateChanged(object sender,
                              System.Windows.Forms.DateRangeEventArgs e)
{
    DateTime d = monthCalendar1.SelectionStart;
```

Before we place a date string in one of the appropriate textboxes, we need to determine their collective state (that is, which box will receive the date string is determined by whether one or both contain a string when the user clicks the calendar). If the txtStartDate textbox is empty, then it will be the one filled. Using the Month, Day, and Year properties of our DateTime object d (and some judiciously placed slashes), we concatenate a string that looks like a genuine date:

```
    if (txtStartDate.Text == "")
    {
        string dateStr = d.Month + "/" + d.Day + "/" + d.Year;
        txtStartDate.Text = dateStr;
    }
```

If the txtEndDate textbox already contains a string, then we can presume the user is initiating a new date range. If this is the case, we empty the txtEndDate textboxes and insert the user's selected date in txtStartDate:

```
    else if (txtEndDate.Text.Length > 0)
    {
        txtEndDate.Text = "";
        string dateStr = d.Month + "/" + d.Day + "/" + d.Year;
        txtStartDate.Text = dateStr;
    }
```

If neither of these conditions are true, then the StartDate box must be full and the EndDate must be empty, so we'll insert our new date string in the EndDate textbox:

```
    else
    {
        string dateStr = d.Month + "/" + d.Day + "/" + d.Year;
        txtEndDate.Text = dateStr;
    }
```

Adding Data to the Database

Our form has two buttons that allow the addition of new records to the database (btnSubmit and btnSubmitClear). Essentially, both these buttons will perform the same task when clicked upon: the only difference will be the way the form is re-drawn after the new data is submitted to SQL Server. Clicking on the btnSubmitClear button will perform two tasks:

❑ Submit data entered on the form to the database

❑ Clear all the textboxes and combo boxes on the form, leaving a clean slate for the user to begin the entry of a new record

We'll separate these tasks into two methods, NewRecord() and ClearAll():

```
private void btnSubmitClear_Click(object sender, System.EventArgs e)
{
    NewRecord();
    ClearAll();
}
```

We'll begin with ClearAll(), since it's by far the easier of the two. We need only insert empty strings into each of the combo boxes and textboxes on the data entry portion of our form:

```
private void ClearAll()
{
    cmboShopNum.Text = "";
    cmboName.Text = "";
    txtJobNum.Text = "";
    txtPhase.Text = "";
    txtHours.Text = "";
    cmboLocation.Text = "";
    txtComments.Text = "";
}
```

There are more elegant ways to accomplish this, particularly when there are a large number of controls to clear. With only seven text boxes, though, this will do just fine.

Managers will often enter multiple time data records for a single employee in one session. Therefore, it makes sense to have a button that will perform exactly the same task as btnSubmitClear, but will retain the employee name and shop number after a record has been submitted to the database (so they don't have to be manually selected again from the combo boxes). All we need to do to accomplish this is to store the contents of the shop number and name combo boxes in two temporary variables before we call NewRecord() and ClearAll(), and plug those variables back in after these functions have completed their respective tasks:

```
private void btnSubmit_Click(object sender, System.EventArgs e)
{
    // Grab the state of the shopNum and Name combos, so we can plug
    // their contents back after LoadCombos() fires
    string tempShopNum = cmboShopNum.Text;
    string tempName = cmboName.Text;
    NewRecord();
    ClearAll();
    cmboShopNum.Text = tempShopNum;
    cmboName.Text = tempName;
}
```

Helper Methods for NewRecord()

Now for `NewRecord()`. After entering the signature, we'll begin by anticipating a possible user error, as well as plan for second helper method that will grab primary keys from our database's various tables (which we will then insert in their proper locations as foreign keys). Let's write the `NoBlanks()` and `GetPrimaryKey()` methods first before diving in completely with `NewRecord()`.

The NoBlanks() Method

Regarding the more "defensive" of our two helper functions, we're going to say that our form's location data and comments may be left blank if desired, but that all of the remaining elements on the data entry portion of the form must contain valid entries. Using the logical OR operator (||), we can test for blank entries quite easily. If any are found to be empty, we'll display a message box to that effect and return `false` back to the `NewRecord()` function that called `NoBlanks()`. If all is well, we'll get on with it and return `true`:

```
private bool NoBlanks()
{
    if (cmboShopNum.Text == "" || cmboName.Text == "" ||
        txtJobNum.Text == "" || txtHours.Text == "" || txtDate.Text == "")
    {
        MessageBox.Show("The Shop Number, Name, Job Number, Phase, Hours and " +
                        "Date fields can't be blank.", "More Data Required");
        return false;
    }
    else
    {
        return true;
    }
}
```

The GetPrimaryKey() Method

The next method we need retrieves the primary key for a row from one of our subsidiary `DataTables` in the `DataSet`, and is appropriately enough called `GetPrimaryKey()`. First, we'll declare four member variables: an `int` (pk) that will be the key we're searching for (initialized to 0); a string `strSelect`, which we'll use to hold the `DataView` filter that we'll use to search for our keys; and finally another string `pkColumn`, which will store the name of the primary key column for each table:

```
private int GetPrimaryKey (string tableRequest, string data)
{
    int pk = 0;
    string strSelect = "";
    string pkColumn = "";
```

Next, we'll concoct a `switch` statement, which will evaluate which table is being requested (tracked by `tableRequest`), and concatenate a filter string accordingly, using the data passed in from the form's various textboxes and combo boxes. We'll also store the name of the primary key column for that table:

```
switch (tableRequest)
{
    case "Worker":
        strSelect = "Name='" + data + "'";
        pkColumn = "IDWorker";
        break;
```

```
        case "JobNum":
           strSelect = "JobNumber=" + data;
           pkColumn = "IDJobNum";
           break;

        case "JobLoc":
           strSelect = "JobLocation='" + data + "'";
           pkColumn = "IDJobLocation";
           break;

        case "ShopNum":
           strSelect = "ShopNumber=" + data;
           pkColumn = "IDShopNumber";
           break;
    }
```

In other words, if our form's cmboName had "Smith, John" in it when the following call was made:

```
    GetPrimaryKey("Worker", cmboName.Text);
```

... then our function simply looks to the Worker table and gets the primary key for the record whose Name column contains 'Smith, John'.

We can now go out and actually search our DataSet for those keys. This will complete our GetPrimaryKey() method, and allow us to return to the NewRecord() method that will call it. This is just a matter of creating a new DataView for the appropriate table in the DataSet, applying the filter to it, and then retrieving the value for the primary key column from the first row in the filtered DataView. We cast this to an int, as all our primary keys have integer values:

```
    try
    {
        DataView dv = new DataView(ds.Tables[tableRequest]);
        dv.RowFilter = strSelect;
        pk = (int)dv[0][pkColumn];
        return pk;
    }
    catch(Exception ex)
    {
        MessageBox.Show("There was an internal error while grabbing a " +
                   "primary key. The " + tableRequest + " you requested " +
                   "can't be found in the database. Call the help desk " +
                   "and read this to them very slowly:\n\n" +
                   ex.ToString(), "Couldn't get a primary key from " +
                   tableRequest);
        pk = 0;
        return pk;
    }
```

The NewRecord() Method

Now that we've written the helper methods, we can write NewRecord() itself. Our first task is to provide for the fact that our client *might* be using the XML copy of the data we're going to make available (for when the database isn't accessible). If this is the case, then the data cannot be updated, only read. Remembering our Boolean useLocalData variable that we set at the beginning of our code, one small routine to accomplish this might look like:

```
private void NewRecord()
{
    if (useLocalData)
    {
        MessageBox.Show("Using local copy of data - can't update the " +
                        "data source.", "Update error", MessageBoxButtons.OK,
                                        MessageBoxIcon.Warning);
        return;
    }
```

Next, we call our `NoBlanks()` method, and return from the method if the user hasn't filled in all the fields:

```
    if (NoBlanks() != true)    // Required data not specified by user
        return;
```

Now we can get the primary keys:

```
    int pkWorker = GetPrimaryKey("Worker", cmboName.Text);
    int pkJobNum = GetPrimaryKey("JobNum", txtJobNum.Text);
    int pkJobLoc = GetPrimaryKey("JobLoc", cmboLocation.Text);
    int pkShopNum = GetPrimaryKey("ShopNum", cmboShopNum.Text);
    if (pkWorker == 0 || pkJobNum == 0 || pkJobLoc == 0 || pkShopNum == 0)
        return; // Couldn't find the primary key!
```

We store the primary key values in four local `int` variables. The values that get assigned to these variables will be the foreign keys that actually get inserted into our database when the user clicks `btnSubmit` or `btnSubmitClear`.

Since it is the `Schedule` table that will hold the data we're about to submit to the database, we create a SQL string (`strSql`) that selects all of its columns. Next, we create a `SqlDataAdapter` (passing in our SQL string and the active connection to the database), and use it to fill a new table in our `DataSet`. We then call the `NewRow()` method on our new `DataTable`; as you might expect, this adds a new empty row to the table:

```
    string strSql = "SELECT WorkerID, ShopNumberID, theDate, JobLocationID, " +
                            "JobNumID, Phase, Hours, Comments FROM Schedule";
    SqlDataAdapter da = new SqlDataAdapter(strSql, con);
    da.Fill(ds, "Schedule");
    DataRow dr = ds.Tables["Schedule"].NewRow();
```

Next, we set the values of our new row using a combination of the items entered on the form by the user and the results of our `GetPrimaryKey()` calls:

```
    dr["WorkerID"] = pkWorker;
    dr["ShopNumberID"] = pkShopNum;
    dr["theDate"] = "'" + txtDate.Text + "'";
    dr["JobLocationID"] = pkJobLoc;
    dr["JobNumID"] = pkJobNum;
    dr["Phase"] = txtPhase.Text;
    dr["Hours"] = txtHours.Text;
    dr["Comments"] = txtComments.Text;
```

We can now add this row to the `DataTable`, and update the database. In order to insert a new record into the database, we will need an `InsertCommand`. To get ADO.NET to generate one for us automatically, we need to instantiate a `SqlCommandBuilder`, passing our `SqlDataAdapter` into its constructor:

```
ds.Tables["Schedule"].Rows.Add(dr);
SqlCommandBuilder cmdBuilder = new SqlCommandBuilder(da);
```

We're now ready to submit our data to the database with the help of the `SqlDataAdapter`'s `Update()` method: (passing in our `DataSet` and the name of the table we want to be affected). If this succeeds, we'll also add a new `DataRow` to the `AllData` table in our `DataSet`, so that the new entry will be displayed on the client as well as saved to the server:

```
try
{
    da.Update(ds, "Schedule");

    dr = ds.Tables[0].NewRow();
    dr["Name"] = cmboName.Text;
    dr["ShopNumber"] = cmboShopNum.Text;
    dr["theDate"] = "'" + txtDate.Text + "'";
    dr["JobLocation"] = cmboLocation.Text;
    dr["JobNumber"] = txtJobNum.Text;
    dr["Hours"] = txtHours.Text;
    dr["Comments"] = txtComments.Text;
    dr["Active"] = 1;
    ds.Tables[0].Rows.Add(dr);
}
catch (Exception ex)
{
    MessageBox.Show("Sorry, there was an error adding a record. The only " +
                    "explanation I can offer is:\n\n" + ex.ToString(),
                                "Who Wrote This Code, Anyway?");
}
```

To stop our update taking over the processor entirely (and halting any other processes that might be going on at the time), we'll call `Application.DoEvents()`. Next, we need to commit the data changes we just sent to the database to our in-memory representation of that database (the `DataSet`). This is accomplished by the `AcceptChanges()` method. Finally, `LoadCombos()` and `GetAllData()` are called so that our combo boxes and `DataGrid` reflect our new entry:

```
Application.DoEvents(); // Don't take over
ds.AcceptChanges();

LoadCombos();
GetAllData();
}
```

Data Access Methods

Now that our form is drawn and populated with some startup data, and we have the code written that allows shop managers to enter new records, we need routines for searching the database. What we want is a flexible searching mechanism, one that can respond to multiple types of queries that will consist of varying numbers of search parameters based upon the state of the forms at the time the request is made. Enter `GetFindData()`, which returns a formatted search string to a `DataView` object (to which our `DataGrid` is bound).

Writing GetFindData()

First, we need to choose a set of parameters that our function will expect to receive when called:

Type	Name	Description
bool	blnActive	Checks to see if the "active records only" radio button is selected
string	strShopNum	The shop number to search for
string	strName	The employee name to search for
string	strJobNum	The job number to search for
string	strLocation	The location to search for
string	strStartDate	The start of the date range to select records from
string	strEndDate	The end of the date range to select records from
string	strOrderBy	The parameter to order the entire search by

Our first task will be to create a search string, which will be modified by our function based upon the parameters it is sent. Since our `DataGrid`'s `DataBinding` will be set to a `DataView` object, our string will be formatted according to the needs of the `DataView.RowFilter` property. This `RowFilter` simply expects name-value pairs separated by `"And"`, with those values placed in quotes. One thing to note is that if we're using the XML representation of the data, we'll need to format the start and end date strings in the "sortable" ISO format before comparing them to the dates in the XML document:

```
public string GetFindData (bool blnActive,
                           string strShopNum,
                           string strName,
                           string strJobNum,
                           string strLocation,
                           string strStartDate,
                           string strEndDate)
{
   string strSelect;
   if (blnActive == false)
      strSelect = "Active = 'false'";
   else     // Default is active records only
      strSelect = "Active = 'true'";

   if (strShopNum != "")
      strSelect += " AND ShopNumber = '" + strShopNum + "'";

   if (strName != "")
      strSelect += " AND Name = '" + strName + "'";

   if (strJobNum != "")
      strSelect += " AND JobNumber = '" + strJobNum + "'";

   if (strLocation != "(Unspecified)" && strLocation != "")
      strSelect += " AND JobLocation = '" + strLocation + "'";
```

```
      if (useLocalData)
      {
         DateTime startDate = Convert.ToDateTime(strStartDate);
         strStartDate = startDate.ToString("s");

         DateTime endDate = Convert.ToDateTime(strEndDate);
         strEndDate = endDate.ToString("s");
      }

      strSelect = " theDate >= '" + strStartDate + "' AND theDate <= '" +
                                          strEndDate + "' AND " + strSelect;

      return strSelect;
   }
```

Next, we want to sort the data on the basis of which of our form's radio buttons are selected. For this, we'll need a small helper function, which will simply evaluate which of the radio buttons is selected and return the name(s) of the column(s) to sort by. We'll use this string to set the DataView's Sort property:

```
   private string GetRadioButton()
   {
      orderBy = "Name";
      if (radioButton1.Checked)
         orderBy = "JobNumber, Name";

      if (radioButton2.Checked)
         orderBy = "JobLocation, Name";

      if (radioButton3.Checked)
         orderBy = "Name";

      if (radioButton4.Checked)
         orderBy = "theDate, Name";

      if (radioButton5.Checked)
         orderBy = "ShopNumber, Name";

      return orderBy;
   }
```

Finally, let's write a short method (appropriately called FillGrid()) to fill our DataGrid with the response to a call to GetFindData(). First, we create strSearch by calling GetFindData() and passing it the state of our form's contents (and offer a way out in case nonsense is returned). Then, a DataView object is created by passing in a reference to the table in our DataSet. Next, the RowFilter property of our DataView is set to the string we received at the outset of the method, and the DataView's Sort property is adjusted according to the results of a call to GetRadioButton(). Lastly, we bind our DataGrid to the DataView object, and post the number of records found in the txtRecordsFound textbox. Naturally, we wrap all this in a try block, and provide a catch in the unlikely event of error:

```
   private void FillGrid()
   {
      string strSearch = GetFindData(rbtnActiveOnly.Checked,
                               cmboFindShopNum.Text,
                               cmboFindByName.Text,
                               txtFindByJobNum.Text,
                               cmboLocation.Text,
```

351

```
                                         txtStartDate.Text,
                                         txtEndDate.Text);

        if (strSearch == "")
        {
            MessageBox.Show("There was an error while working on your search. " +
                                        "Sorry.", "Find Error: Seek Help");
            return;
        }
        try
        {
            DataView dv = new DataView(ds.Tables[0]);
            dv.RowFilter = strSearch;
            string orderBy = GetRadioButton();
            dv.Sort = orderBy;

            dataGrid1.SetDataBinding(dv, "");
            txtRecordsFound.Text = dv.Count + " record(s) found";
        }
        catch(Exception ex)
        {
            MessageBox.Show("I haven't the foggiest notion what happened. " +
                        "Try this:\n\n" + ex.ToString(), "Problems, Problems");
        }
    }
```

Lastly, let's write the code to manage a user's click on the btnFind button. Ultimately, of course, it is this event that will actually fire the FillGrid() method (which itself is the caller of GetFindData()). Apart from calling this method, we'll set the Enabled property of our button to false while FillGrid() is doing its work, and then turn that same property to true once all is finished:

```
private void btnFind_Click(object sender, System.EventArgs e)
{
    btnFind.Enabled = false; // A slight indication that work is being done
    FillGrid();
    btnFind.Enabled = true; // Turn the light back on
}
```

It's time for a test run. Press *F5* and you should be presented with a reasonable approximation of the following:

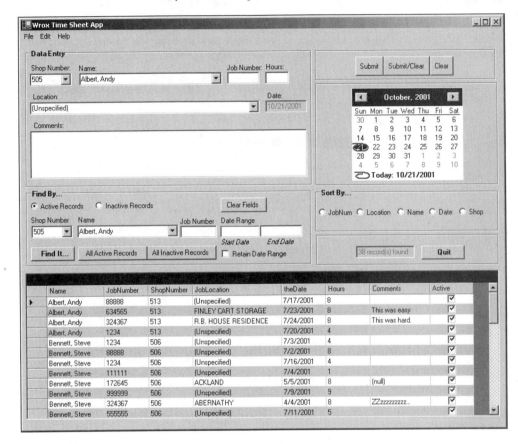

Versioning and Distribution Concerns

At this point, we have a fully functioning application that resides in a standard `.exe` file. This `.exe` is a completely standalone entity: no special installation procedures are required to distribute it to those for whom it is intended for daily use. It could even be "mass mailed" to those in your university who require it.

As the inevitable feature requests start trickling in, however, a classic problem arises: how do we minimize the hassle of distributing upgraded versions of our application, and ensure that all users are employing the most current version of our work with a minimum of intervention on our part?

It can be done, if we take our code and re-compile it as a C# class library. In this format (and with some clever casting), our application can be delivered to clients as a `byte[]` array. Once on the client, the `Form` object that encapsulates our code can be instantiated and run, with the same effect as a quick double-click on an `.exe` file. More to the point, we can provide a method that will first check to see that the DLL exists on the client, and automate its delivery if it is not. Finally, this same method can check to see that the version on the client is not older than the master version that we'll park on the network. If the client is out of date, we can deliver the upgraded version automatically.

Creating a Class Library from our WinForm Code

We'll begin transforming our `.exe` into a DLL file simply by changing the project output type of our project. Right-click on the project in Solution Explorer and select **Properties**. In the project's property pages, select **Class Library** from the drop-down list of output types, and ensure that the name of the assembly is set to **TimeSheet**:

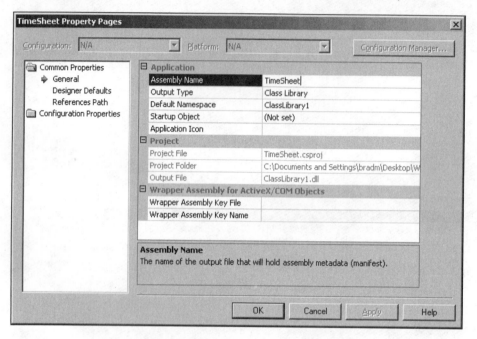

Now, press *F5* to compile our new class library. The `TimeSheet.dll` file which is generated is the file that we'll use to distribute our application, so it will need to be placed in a more exposed location. I selected the directory `C:\Program Files\TimeSheet`, as we can access the `Program Files` folder through the `Environment.GetFolderPath()` method.

Now, let's build a web service to expose this file to the outside world.

Making the Web Service

For our needs, the creation of our web service couldn't be much easier. We will expose our assembly and the data through a simple ASP.NET web service with only two methods. Add a new C# ASP.NET web service project named `PlugInService` to your solution. We'll be using .NET's file-handling classes to load our DLL, and the ADO.NET `SqlClient` data provider to access the data, so we need to add `using` directives for these namespaces:

```
using System.Data;
using System.Diagnostics;
using System.Web;
using System.Web.Services;
using System.IO;
using System.Data.SqlClient;
```

Building the Web Service

The first of the service's two methods will be called `GetPlugIn()`, and will return the raw data of the `TimeSheet.dll` file as a `byte` array.

Next, we create a `FileStream` object by calling the `File.Open()` static method (again provided from the `System.IO` namespace). We only need read access, so we'll set the `FileMode` parameter to `FileMode.Open`. We put the DLL in a subdirectory under the `Program Files` folder, so we'll use the `Environment`'s `GetFolderPath()` method to find the right location:

```
[WebMethod]
public byte[] GetPlugIn()
{
    string appPath = Environment.GetFolderPath
                    (Environment.SpecialFolder.ProgramFiles) + "\\TimeSheet";
    FileStream appStream = File.Open(appPath + "\\TimeSheet.dll",
                                                    FileMode.Open);
```

We're going to expose the assembly as a `byte` array, so we'll declare an array named `appData`, and set its size to be the `Length` property of the `appStream` object we just created:

```
    byte[] appData = new byte[appStream.Length];
```

Next, we iterate through the file stream, calling its `ReadByte()` method until we reach the end of the stream. This method returns an `int` rather than a `byte`, so we need to cast the return value to a `byte` before adding it to our array:

```
    for (long index = 0; index < appStream.Length; index++)
        appData[index] = (byte)appStream.ReadByte();
```

When we've reached the end of the loop, all that remains is to close the `appStream` and return the byte array `appData` to the method that called it. Doing so, we're handing the caller the raw bytes of our `TimeSheet.dll`:

```
    appStream.Close();
    return appData;
}
```

To complete our web service, we need one more method. This method will return an XML-formatted string representation of our data to the client for use when the database is unavailable. This will allow the locally saved copy of our application to be used, even if a network connection is unavailable. We begin by establishing a connection to SQL Server, creating a `SqlDataAdapter` that requests all the data from our `AllData` view, and using it to fill a `DataSet`. To generate an XML string from a `DataSet` is extremely easy – we just call its `WriteXml()` method to populate a `StringWriter`, then call the `ToString()` method of this class to convert this to a string. The real work, in other words, takes place in only three lines of code (the last three)!

```
[WebMethod]
public string GetData()
{
    SqlConnection cn = new SqlConnection("Data Source=hucbaldlt;" +
                            "Initial Catalog=Shops;User ID=sa;Password=");
    cn.Open();
```

```
        SqlDataAdapter da = new SqlDataAdapter("SELECT Name, JobNumber, " +
                    "ShopNumber, JobLocation, theDate, Hours, Active, Comments " +
                                                        "FROM AllData ", cn);

        DataSet ds = new DataSet();
        da.Fill(ds, "AllData ");

        cn.Close();

        StringWriter sw = new StringWriter();
        ds.WriteXml(sw);
        return sw.ToString();
    }
```

That completes the code for our web service! Test it by selecting **Build and Browse** from the **File** menu:

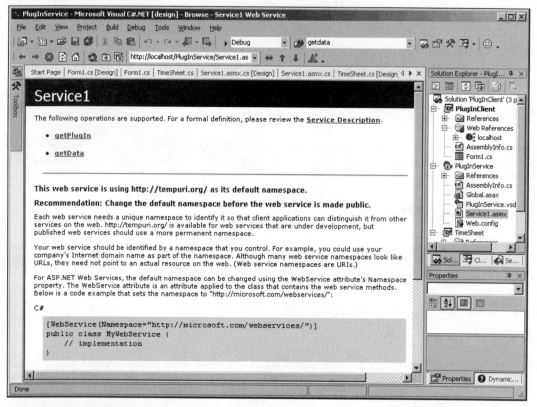

If you've managed to get this far, you can rest assured that our service has compiled successfully. Since it doesn't provide any "visible" functions, what remains is to build a client that can consume the work it does, and make its purpose known.

Building a Windows Client

For our final project, we only need a small Windows application that will provide access to our `TimeSheet.dll` file, and which will ensure that the version on the client is up-to-date with the version we'll place on the network.

Add a new C# Windows Application project named `PlugInClient` to the solution. Once your blank form appears, set its `Text` property to `"WROXWinForm Client"`, and drop four buttons onto it, giving them the names `btnRun`, `btnInstall`, `btnRunLocal`, and `btnSaveData`. If you wish, drop a `mainMenu` component on the form and provide **File**, **Edit**, and **Help** menus. Size the buttons however you wish, and set their `Text` properties to reflect the following screenshot:

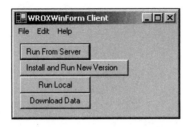

Finally, switch to code view and add the following `using` directives at the top of the file:

```
using System.IO;
using System.Reflection;
```

We will declare two static string variables as fields of the class that will point to the locations we'll provide for our DLL file. The first will be the local version (that is, the one that resides on the client in the `Program Files\TimeSheet` directory). We'll call this `appPath`:

```
static string appPath = Environment.GetFolderPath
                    (Environment.SpecialFolder.ProgramFiles) + "\\TimeSheet";
```

The second location for our DLL will be its place on our intranet, which, of course, can be anywhere we choose. This will allow us to place updated versions of our code in a single location; we'll shortly write a routine that will check the network version against the age of the client's file and download the newer code if necessary.

```
// Any intranet location
static string serverPath = "F:\\TimeSheet\\TimeSheet.dll";
```

Next, we need to provide a function that will fire during the `Form_Load` event which will adjust the way the form appears based upon the presence or absence of the `TimeSheet.dll` file on the client, and which will make sure that the client version is as new as the network file if it is found to be present locally.

We begin by instantiating two `FileInfo` objects. One, `fiClient`, will represent the user's `Program Files\TimeSheet` directory (which is where we'll expect the local version of our `TimeSheet.dll` to reside, and where we'll put it if it doesn't). The second, `fiServer`, will represent the network path of the external version of the file, which is always presumed to be the latest version (moreover, this is the location where we would place any upgraded versions of our code in the future). For both `FileInfo` objects, we simply pass in the appropriate paths as parameters, using the strings we just created:

```
private void CheckVersion()
{
    try
    {
        FileInfo fiClient = new FileInfo(appPath + "\\TimeSheet.dll");
        FileInfo fiServer = new FileInfo(serverPath);
```

357

We'll always allow the data to be saved to the client, but we'll check the status of the client and server versions of the assembly to decide which of the other buttons to display. The `FileInfo` class has an `Exists` property, which will allow us to see if `TimeSheet.dll` already exists on the client when our form loads. If it doesn't, then the only one of the other three form buttons we want shown is the one marked Install and Run New Version:

```
if(fiClient.Exists == false)
{
    btnInstall.Show();
    btnRun.Hide();
    btnRunLocal.Hide();
}
```

Similarly, we want to make sure that the client DLL is not older than the server version. Again, a `FileInfo` property allows for this easily (specifically `LastWriteTime`):

```
else if (fiServer.LastWriteTime > fiClient.LastWriteTime)
{
    btnRun.Hide();
    btnRunLocal.Hide();
    btnInstall.Show();
}
```

Again, we would want only the Install and Run New Version button to appear in this particular case, so the client can get a newer copy of the DLL for future use.

Finally, if the DLL exists on the client and it is up-to-date with the network version, we want to hide the Install button when the form is loaded. We accomplish this with an `else` clause:

```
    else
    {
        btnInstall.Hide();
    }
}
catch (Exception ex)
{
    MessageBox.Show("All is lost. I cannot run the CheckVersion() function. " +
                "Don't shoot the messenger.\n\n" + ex.ToString(),
                "Who Wrote This Code, Anyway?");
}
```

We want this method to fire whenever the form is loaded, so we'll call it from within the `Form_Load` event handler:

```
private void Form1_Load(object sender, System.EventArgs e)
{
    CheckVersion();
}
```

All that remains is for us to provide four short methods, one for each of our buttons' `click` events. Three of these will rely upon our web service, so we need to add a web reference to it in our client application. In the Add Web Reference wizard, enter the URL that points to the web service (for example, http://localhost/PlugInService/Service1.asmx):

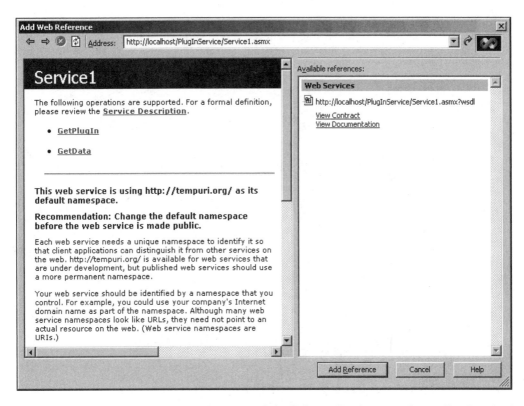

Now, simply click the **Add Reference** button, and the Solution Explorer window will reflect the fact that a web reference to our service has been added to our client application.

Now we're ready to write our four final methods (which are surprisingly short). The first, `GetDll()`, is the one we'll call if the client doesn't have the DLL locally, or if the local version is out of date. We begin by instantiating an instance of our web service. Next, we create a `byte[]` array, and fill it with the results of our service's `GetPlugIn()` method:

```
private void GetDll()
{
    try
    {
        this.Cursor = Cursors.WaitCursor;
        localhost.Service1 plugInService = new localhost.Service1();
        byte[] appData = plugInService.GetPlugIn();
```

This downloads the raw data for our DLL from the server; we'll save this locally so it can be run again as desired. We therefore call `File.Open()` again to create a `FileStream` object, passing in a string parameter giving the file's ultimate destination, as well as particular `FileMode` (here `OpenOrCreate`) and `FileAccess` settings (here `Write`, since we're writing out a new file on the client):

```
        FileStream appStream = File.Open(appPath + "\\TimeSheet.dll",
                                FileMode.OpenOrCreate, FileAccess.Write);
```

359

Finally, we call the `FileStream`'s `Write()` method, passing it the `byte[]` array returned by our web service (`appData`), the index with which to begin (`0`), and to end (which the `appData.Length` property happily provides). When all is complete, we close the file, and release any other resources that may be associated with our `FileStream` object:

```
        appStream.Write(appData, 0, appData.Length);
        appStream.Close();

        this.Cursor = Cursors.Arrow;
    }
    catch (Exception ex)
    {
        MessageBox.Show("A problem occured while firing the GetDll() " +
                    "function. I suspect the problem is as follows: \n\n" +
                    ex.ToString(), "Who Wrote This Code, Anyway?");
    }
}
```

The `ReadDll()` method allows the client to read the DLL directly from the network location where we've chosen to park it. We begin just as we did with `GetDll()`, by instantiating a version of our web service, and creating a `byte[]` array by calling our service's `GetPlugIn()` function:

```
private void ReadDll()
{
    try
    {
        this.Cursor = Cursors.WaitCursor;

        localhost.Service1 plugInService = new localhost.Service1();
        byte[] appData = plugInService.GetPlugIn();
```

Now, we'll create a new `Assembly` object by calling the `Assembly.Load()` method, passing in the `appData byte[]` array we just received from our web service:

```
        Assembly plugInAssembly = Assembly.Load(appData);
```

Finally, with a bit of creative casting, we'll instantiate a `Form` object from the DLL data just passed into our assembly. Casting the `plugInAssembly` we just created to a `Form`, we call the `Assembly`'s `CreateInstance()` method. This method requires a string providing the fully qualified name of the form we want an instance of. Last but not least, we set our newly created form's `Visible` property to `true`, and call its `Activate()` method:

```
        Form plugInForm = (Form)plugInAssembly.CreateInstance
                            ("WROXTimeSheetsWinForms.frmTimeSheets");
        plugInForm.Visible = true;
        plugInForm.Activate();

        this.Cursor = Cursors.Arrow;
    }
    catch (Exception ex)
    {
        MessageBox.Show("Instead of doing what it was SUPPOSED to do, " +
                    "the ReadDll() function did THIS: \n\n" + ex.ToString(),
                    "Egregious Error Ensued");
    }
}
```

The third method to add to our client application will presume that a local, up-to-date copy of our DLL exists on the client side, and serves only to read from that file. As such, it is almost exactly like our previous function, except that it makes no use of our web service, and it uses the `LoadFrom()` method (rather than `Load()`) to read from the file specified in its parameter list:

```
private void ReadLocalDll()
{
    try
    {
        Assembly plugInAssembly = Assembly.LoadFrom
                                        (appPath + "\\TimeSheet.dll");

        Form plugInForm = (Form)plugInAssembly.CreateInstance
                                ("WROXTimeSheetsWinForms.frmTimeSheets");
        plugInForm.Visible = true;
        plugInForm.Activate();
    }
    catch (Exception ex)
    {
        MessageBox.Show("Time for lunch. The following inscrutable error " +
                "occured while attempting the ReadLocalDll() function:\n\n" +
                                        ex.ToString(),"About Face!");
    }
}
```

Our fourth (and final!) method uses the `GetData()` method of our web service, and saves an XML representation of our data to a file on the client for use when the database server is unavailable. Declaring a string (`xmlData`) to hold the output from our web service, we then create a `FileInfo` object, which will act as our XML file. We instantiate a new `StreamWriter` object for writing to this file by calling the `FileInfo`'s `AppendText()` method, and then write the contents of our string to this `StreamWriter` (`sw.Write(XmlData)`). Finally, we call the `StreamWriter`'s `Flush()` method to ensure that all the data is saved to the file:

```
private void SaveData()
{
    try
    {
        this.Cursor = Cursors.WaitCursor;

        localhost.Service1 plugInService = new localhost.Service1();
        string xmlData = plugInService.GetData();
        FileInfo fi = new FileInfo(appPath + "\\TimeSheetData.xml");
        StreamWriter sw = fi.AppendText();
        sw.Write(xmlData);
        sw.Flush();

        this.Cursor = Cursors.Arrow;

        MessageBox.Show("The data has been saved to " + appPath +
                                        "\\Timesheet.xml");

    }
    catch(Exception ex)
    {
        MessageBox.Show("Sorry, the data cannot be saved to disk:\n\n" +
                    ex.ToString(), "No XML Data: Turn on the Server!");
    }
}
```

Lastly, let's add method calls to our four buttons' `Click` events:

```
private void btnInstall_Click(object sender, System.EventArgs e)
{
    GetDll();
    ReadDll();
}

private void btnRun_Click(object sender, System.EventArgs e)
{
    ReadDll();
}

private void btnRunLocal_Click(object sender, System.EventArgs e)
{
    ReadLocalDll();
}

private void btnSaveData_Click(object sender, System.EventArgs e)
{
    SaveData();
}
```

Let's try a test run. Right-click the `PlugInClient` project in the Solution Explorer and select **Set As Startup Project**. Since this is the first time the application has run, `TimeSheet.dll` will not be in the local client's `C:\Program Files\TimeSheet` directory; so our `CheckVersion()` function will ensure that only the **Install and Run New Version** and **Download Data** buttons appear (the same buttons would be provided if the client version happened to be older than that on the network). Click the **Install** button:

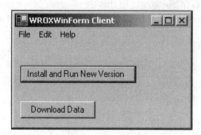

After a few seconds (the time it takes to grab the `byte[]` array and write it out on the client), our application appears in all its glory, indistinguishable from its Windows desktop version:

Now click the **Quit** button and run the client application again. Since the `TimeSheet.dll` is in our `Temp` directory this time, the following form will appear, giving the user the option of loading that DLL from either the network or the local client machine:

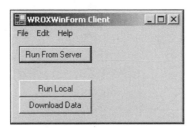

Finally, quit once more and let's try out the **Download Data** button. If all is well, the following friendly message should appear:

And a peek into the `C:\Program Files\TimeSheet` directory should reveal a local copy of our data, named `TimeSheetData.xml`:

Summary

We've covered quite a bit of ground. In addition to the creation of a standard desktop Windows application in the new Visual Studio .NET IDE, we've been able to automate the versioning and distribution concerns that frequently plagued developers in the past with the use of a surprisingly simple web service, and allowed for a local XML copy of our data on the client. There are any number of scenarios one could invent that would require to address the usual issues of application rollout and updating, and the .NET environment is flexible enough to allow you to address just about any one you can concoct with surprising ease and flexibility. With the advent of web services, the most important program logic to facilitate those scenarios can be housed in a single location for access from anywhere, at anytime. As we've seen in this chapter, even traditional Windows desktop application development can benefit.

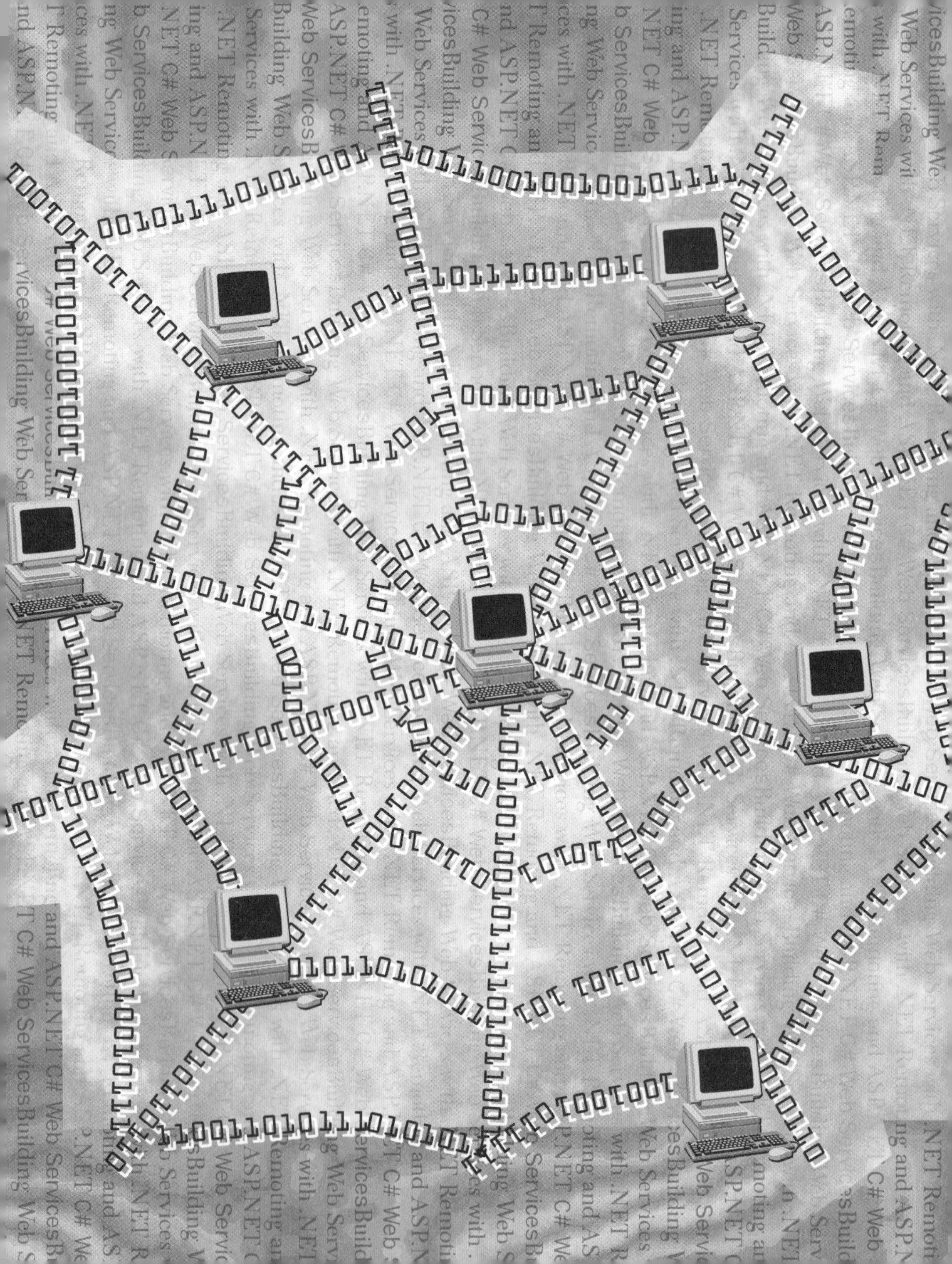

Section Five – Case Studies

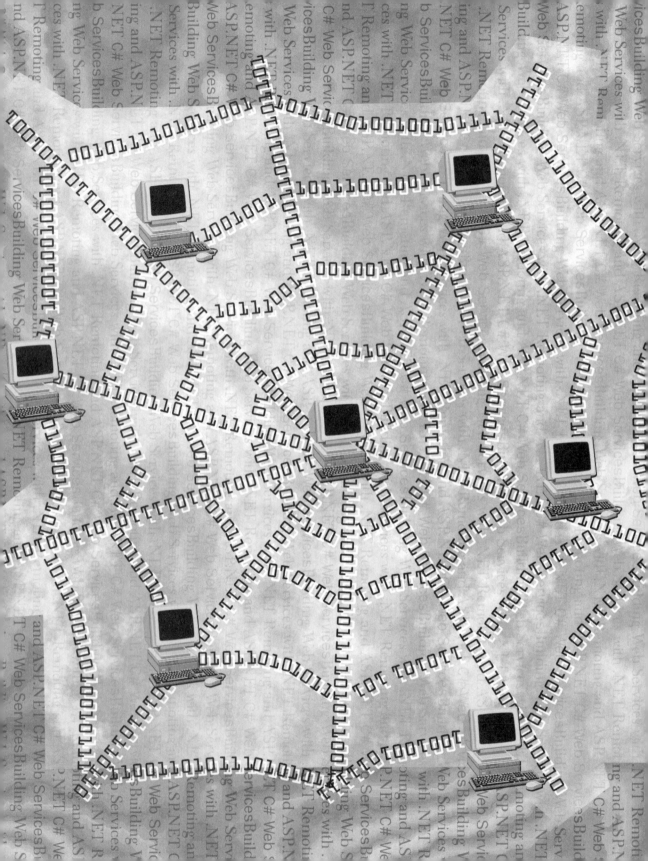

Case Study 1: ASP.NET

Most of today's web sites are designed to work as self-contained units and, if they are to interact with each other, usually require significant additional development effort and investment. The .NET Framework provides a structure for building web sites, services, and intranet-enabled applications that can collaborate seamlessly with each other. ASP.NET is little short of a revolutionary set of web development tools that aim to fulfill Microsoft's goal of producing a system that provides information at any time, for any device. XML-based web services play a major role in Microsoft's dream, because any platform that understands XML can, in theory at least, process web services that communicate with it.

Standardized web services, the topic of this book, address some of the biggest challenges faced by web developers today. Using this model, developers can create programmable, reusable, and intelligent web sites capable of seamlessly integrating with other sites and of providing content for a wide variety of devices.

Up to this point, we have concentrated on what web services are, how they may be built, and so on. This case study aims to highlight the utility and flexibility of web services by putting the knowledge of web services we now have into practice, and to demonstrate how this exciting model can produce scalable, powerful, and flexible web applications. To this end, we will discuss the following tasks:

- ❑ Designing and developing an n-tier web application with the .NET platform. To support this design, we will create reusable components that encapsulate the business logic and data-access logic

- ❑ Creation and consumption of the next generation of web services

- ❑ Creation of a proxy class to bridge the gap between the web service and the consumer

- ❑ Making use of a Windows Service in our application

- ❑ Designing a secured site using HTML form-based authentication technology

- ❑ Designing and consuming reusable user controls

Overview of the Application

For this case study, we shall build a typical online flight reservation application featuring the basic functionality that production systems implement, including:

- Searching for flights based on specific criteria
- Booking tickets for particular flights
- Providing news and information about the latest travel deals
- Allowing customers to register with the site

Business Processes

Since it is not our intention to illustrate general e-commerce development in this case study, we will confine ourselves to discussing only the processes described below. Also note that only the more interesting code sections are reproduced here, although the complete working application is available in the code download. For more information on other issues of e-commerce development, see Matthew Reynolds' *Beginning E-Commerce* from Wrox Press, ISBN 1-861003-98-6.

- Login Process

    The login system allows users to identify themselves to the system. They must provide a valid user ID and password before being able to carry out tasks such as searching for flights, booking tickets, and so on.

- New User Registration

    New users can become a member of the site by filling out an online form with their individual details and preferences. The user is asked to create a unique user ID and choose a password to prevent anyone else using their account. Once all details are entered, the user's profile is stored in the database for later use.

- Search Flights Process

    This process allows the user to search for flights.

- Book Tickets Process

    Unsuprisingly, this process lets the user book tickets for a specified flight.

- News and Deals Process

    Displays the latest travel news and deals.

- Logout Process

    Allows the user to log out of the site, terminating their session.

Limitations

As already mentioned, this case study is not intended to demonstrate how to build and deploy a real-world online reservation system. The real purpose is to show how to tie different features of ASP.NET together. For that reason, many important issues are not addressed here, including:

- ❏ Security. No regard is taken of security in the implementation of the web services in this example.
- ❏ Payment. In this example no real bookings are made, and none of the issues concerned with payment are handled.

Prerequisites

To run all the code for this case study, you will need the following software installed on your machine:

- ❏ Microsoft .NET SDK Beta 2 or above, or Visual Studio .NET Beta 2 or above
- ❏ ASP.NET (Premium edition required for the output caching feature)
- ❏ SQL Server 2000

Architecture of the System

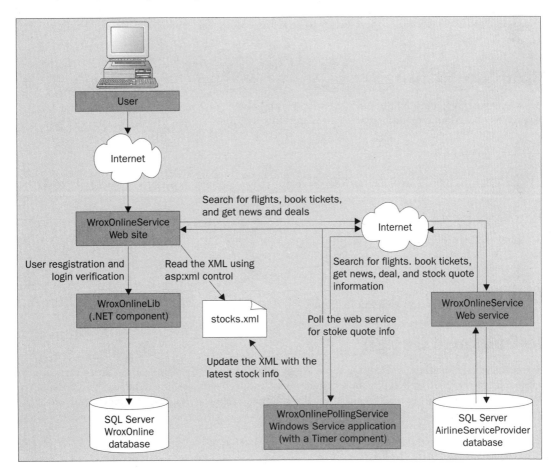

The above diagram illustrates the overall architecture of the solution we shall implement. It can be broken down into the following three parts for our discussion:

1. When the user arrives at the site and performs tasks such as registration and login verification, the WroxOnline web application invokes the methods of the .NET component WroxOnlineLib. Registration details are stored in the WroxOnline database.

2. The WroxOnline web application invokes methods of the remote web service via the Internet to perform the following actions:

   ❑ Searching for flights
   ❑ Booking tickets
   ❑ Requesting the latest travel news and deals

3. At regular intervals, WroxOnlinePollingService, a separate application running as a Windows Service, invokes a stock quote web method of our web service which returns the latest price of Wrox Online Travel Service stock. It stores the price in the stocks.xml XML file of the WroxOnline's virtual root directory to be retrieved and displayed on the site.

Implementation

Now that we have analyzed the business processes involved, we can build the basic building blocks for the application. The remaining discussion is split into six phases:

1. Database Design

2. The WroxOnlineService web service

3. The proxy class library

4. The .NET component WroxOnlineLib

5. The Windows service called WroxOnlinePollingService

6. The WroxOnline web application

The Database Design

From the system diagram, we can see there are two data stores in our application. Since this case study concentrates on .NET web application development and web services, the databases will contain only the minimum number of tables required for the solution, and we will not spend much time on understanding this stage of the design process.

First, we will consider the design of the WroxOnline database.

WroxOnline Database Design

The `WroxOnline` database stores information regarding the users registered to our site. This database contains only the `Users` table, as its entity relationship diagram shows:

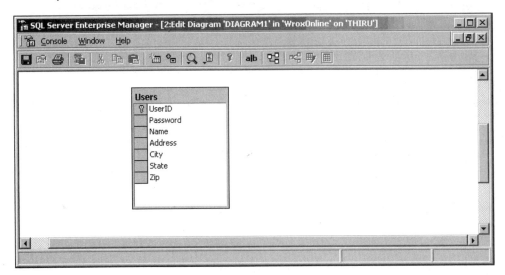

The fields of the `Users` table are described below:

Name	DataType	Length	AllowNull	Description
Userid	varchar	20	No	Represents the user ID
Password	char	10	No	Gives the password for the user
Name	varchar	128	Yes	Name of the user
Address	varchar	128	Yes	Address of the user
City	varchar	50	Yes	City of the user
State	char	2	Yes	State of the customer
Zip	char	9	Yes	Zip code of the user's area

In the above table, we store the password as plain text. In a real-world application of course, it would need to be encrypted before being stored in the database.

This database has two stored procedures. The `UserLogin` stored procedure returns 1 if a record with the supplied user name and password is found in the `Users` table, otherwise it returns –1. It uses an output parameter to pass the result back to the caller:

```
CREATE procedure UserLogin
    (
        @UserID varchar(20),
        @Password char(10),
        @RetValue int OUTPUT
```

```
    )
As
begin
    set nocount on
    SELECT * FROM Users WHERE UserID = @UserID AND Password = @Password
    if @@Rowcount < 1
        select @RetValue = -1
    else
        select @RetValue = 1
end
go
```

As the name suggests, the `InsertUser` procedure simply inserts a record into the `Users` table based on the parameters passed:

```
CREATE procedure InsertUser
    (
        @UserID char(20),
        @Password char(10),
        @Name varchar(128),
        @Address varchar(128),
        @City varchar(50),
        @State char(2),
        @Zip char(9)
    )
As
begin
    set nocount on
    INSERT INTO Users (UserID,Password,Name,Address,City,State,Zip)
    VALUES
    (@UserID,@Password,@Name,@Address,@City,@State,@Zip)
end
go
```

AirlineServiceProvider Database Design

This database holds details related to flight information, ticket availability, and so on:

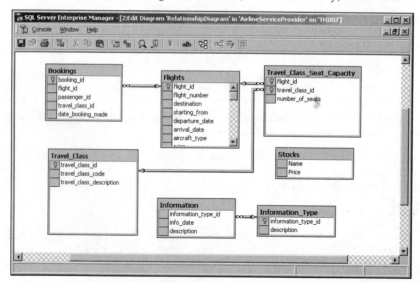

The tables depicted above are described in the tables that follow.

The Flights Table

Name	DataType	Length	AllowNull	Description
flight_ID	int	4	No	Represents the flight ID
flight_number	char	10	No	Indicates the flight number
destination	varchar	50	No	Specifies the destination
starting_from	varchar	50	No	Specifies the starting point
departure_date	datetime	8	No	Gives the departure date
arrival_date	datetime	8	No	Gives the arrival date
aircraft_type	varchar	50	No	Type of aircraft
price	money	8	No	Cost of the ticket

The Travel_Class Table

Name	DataType	Length	AllowNull	Description
travel_class_ID	int	4	No	Represents the travel class ID
travel_class_code	char	1	No	Indicates the travel code
travel_class_description	varchar	50	No	Specifies the description

The Travel_Class_Capacity Table

Name	DataType	Length	AllowNull	Description
flight_ID	int	4	No	Represents the flight ID
travel_class_ID	int	4	No	Indicates the travel class ID
number_of_seats	int	4	No	Specifies the number of seats

The Bookings Table

Name	DataType	Length	AllowNull	Description
booking_ID	int	4	No	Represents the booking ID
flight_ID	int	4	No	Represents the flight ID

Table continued on following page

Name	DataType	Length	AllowNull	Description
passenger_ID	int	4	No	Specifies the passenger ID
travel_class_ID	int	4	No	Specifies the travel class ID
date_booking_made	datetime	8	No	Indicates the date of booking

The Information_Type Table

Name	DataType	Length	AllowNull	Description
information_type_ID	smallint	2	No	Type of the information
description	varchar	100	No	Description of the type

The Information Table

Name	DataType	Length	AllowNull	Description
information_type_ID	smallint	2	No	Type of the information
info_date	datetime	8	No	Date of news or deals
description	varchar	2000	No	Details of news or deals

The Stocks Table

Name	DataType	Length	AllowNull	Description
name	char	4	No	Company symbol
price	varchar	10	No	Stock price

There are three interesting stored procedures for this database. SearchFlight returns flights that match the following parameters: starting location, destination, departure date, arrival date, departure date, and travel class:

```
CREATE procedure dbo.SearchFlight
    @sStartingFrom varchar(50),
    @sDestination varchar(50),
    @dArrivalDate datetime,
    @dDepartureDate datetime,
    @iTravelClassID int
As

begin
    set nocount on

    SELECT F.* FROM flights F
    INNER JOIN travel_class_seat_capacity TCSC
    ON TCSC.flight_id = F.flight_id
```

```
      INNER JOIN travel_class TC
      ON TC.travel_class_id = TCSC.travel_class_id
      WHERE F.starting_from = @sStartingFrom
      AND F.destination = @sDestination
      AND F.arrival_date = @dArrivalDate
      AND F.departure_date = @dDepartureDate
      AND TC.travel_class_id = @iTravelClassID
      AND TCSC.number_of_seats > 0
   end
   go
```

The stored procedure GetInformationByTypeID returns details such as news and deals from the database. The parameter InformationTypeID determines the type of information returned by the stored procedure:

```
CREATE procedure GetInformationByTypeID
@iInformationTypeID smallint
As

begin
   set nocount on

   SELECT convert(varchar(12),info_date) AS info_date,
   description FROM Information
   WHERE information_type_id = @iInformationTypeID
   ORDER BY information_type_id
end
go
```

The AddBooking stored procedure inserts a record into the Bookings table:

```
CREATE procedure dbo.AddBooking
   @iFlightID int,
   @sPassengerID varchar(20),
   @iTravelClassID int,
   @iBookingID int output
As

begin
   set nocount on

   INSERT INTO Bookings
   (flight_id, passenger_id, travel_class_id)
   VALUES
   (@iFlightID,@sPassengerID,@iTravelClassID)
   SELECT @iBookingID = @@identity
end
go
```

Implementing the Web Service

Now that we have set up the databases, let's go ahead and build the web service that access them. Visual Studio .NET will be our primary development tool, but we will also look at the tools that allow us to create and deploy web services using a text editor like Notepad in conjunction with the .NET Framework command-line compilers.

Our web service exposes methods that perform the following operations:

- ❑ Flight search based on parameters such as start date, end date, start place, destination, and travel class
- ❑ Ticket booking for a particular flight
- ❑ Retrieving news stories and the latest deals
- ❑ Returning the latest stock quote for the Wrox Online Travel System (WOTS)

Now, let's create a web service by following the steps below:

1. Select File | New | Project... from the menu. Choose Visual C# Projects in the left-hand pane, and ASP.NET Web Service in the right-hand pane.

2. Name the project WroxOnlineService (by changing the name of the virtual directory for the project) and click OK.

3. Change the name of the default class from Service1 to OnlineService.

The OnlineService web service handles flight-related functions such as searching for flights, booking tickets and so on. Right-click on OnlineService.asmx in Solution Explorer, and choose View Code. You will see that Visual Studio .NET imports the following namespaces by default when we create an ASP.NET web service:

```
using System;
using System.Collections;
using System.ComponentModel;
using System.Data;
using System.Diagnostics;
using System.Web;
using System.Web.Services;
```

To this list, we need to add the following:

```
using System.Data.SqlClient;
using System.Configuration;
```

The System.Data.SqlClient namespace provides access to a set of high-performance data access classes for accessing the SQL database in the managed code environment. The System.Configuration namespace lets us make use of the ConfigurationSettings class to access the connection string stored in the web.config file for our web service.

The SearchFlight Method

As the name suggests, this method searches for flights based on given criteria. We need to begin with the WebMethod attribute to indicate that this is a web-callable method. The ASP.NET runtime can then provide all the plumbing required to enable it to be called over the Internet. Place the code opposite in the OnlineService.asmx.cs code file.

The Description named parameter in this attribute gives a brief description of the web method. Also note the EnableSession property of this attribute – to store session state in the HttpSessionState object, this property needs to be set to true. In our case, we do not want to store session state so we set it to false, eliminating the overhead that session state requires, and significantly improving application performance:

```csharp
[WebMethod (EnableSession=false,Description="This method is used to search for
flights and returns the result as a DataSet")]
public DataSet SearchFlight(string startPlace,
                string destinationPlace,
                DateTime departureDate,
                DateTime arrivalDate,
                int travelClassID)
{
    DataSet flight;

    // Set up the SQL connection
    SqlConnection sqlConnection;
    SqlDataAdapter sqlDataAdapter;
    sqlConnection = new SqlConnection(ConfigurationSettings.AppSettings
      ["connectionString"]);

    try
    {
        sqlDataAdapter = new SqlDataAdapter("SearchFlight", sqlConnection);

        // Indicate that we want to execute a stored procedure
        sqlDataAdapter.SelectCommand.CommandType = CommandType.
         StoredProcedure;

        // Add the Start Place parameter
        SqlParameter paramStartPlace  = new SqlParameter("@sStartingFrom",
         SqlDbType.VarChar, 50);
        paramStartPlace.Value = startPlace;
        sqlDataAdapter.SelectCommand.Parameters.Add(paramStartPlace);

        // Add the Destination Place parameter
        SqlParameter paramDestination  = new SqlParameter("@sDestination",
         SqlDbType.VarChar, 50);
        paramDestination.Value = destinationPlace;
        sqlDataAdapter.SelectCommand.Parameters.Add(paramDestination);

        // Add the Departure Date parameter
        SqlParameter paramDepartureDate  = new SqlParameter("@dDepartureDate",
         SqlDbType.DateTime);
        paramDepartureDate.Value = departureDate;
        sqlDataAdapter.SelectCommand.Parameters.Add(paramDepartureDate);

        // Add the Arrival Date parameter
        SqlParameter paramArrivalDate = new SqlParameter("@dArrivalDate",
         SqlDbType.DateTime);
        paramArrivalDate.Value = arrivalDate;
        sqlDataAdapter.SelectCommand.Parameters.Add(paramArrivalDate);

        // Add the Travel Class ID parameter
        SqlParameter paramTravelClassID  = new SqlParameter("@iTravelClassID",
         SqlDbType.Int);
        paramTravelClassID.Value = travelClassID;
        sqlDataAdapter.SelectCommand.Parameters.Add(paramTravelClassID);

        // Populate the DataSet
        flight = new DataSet();
        sqlDataAdapter.Fill(flight, "Flights");

        // Return the DataSet
        return flight;
```

```
      }
      catch (Exception ex)
      {
         // Throw exceptions back to the client
         throw ex;
      }
      finally
      {
         // Close the connection if it's still open
         if (sqlConnection.State == ConnectionState.Open)
         {
            sqlConnection.Close();
         }
      }
   }
```

The method returns a `DataSet`, an extremely powerful feature that allows us to store complex information and relationships in an intelligent XML structure. The `DataSet` in effect provides a disconnected replica of the database that clients can use, thereby reducing the live database connections the server has to maintain.

Notice the three lines of code near the start of the method that declare objects required for connecting to the database, executing SQL commands, and storing the results. In particular, have another look at this line:

```
sqlConnection = new SqlConnection(ConfigurationSettings.AppSettings
  ["connectionString"]);
```

Here, we get the connection string from the `web.config` file through the `AppSettings` property of the `ConfigurationSettings` class. The connection string appears in the `<appsettings>` element within `web.config`:

```
<appSettings>
   <add key="connectionString" value=
     "server=localhost;uid=sa;pwd=;database=AirlineServiceProvider" />
</appSettings>
```

The `web.config` file stores all the configuration information for an ASP.NET application and it essentially replaces the IIS Metabase used for traditional ASP applications. It is an XML file located in the web application's root directory, and includes information such as authentication type, debugging settings, and session handling. It can also store "special purpose" settings for the application, as above. It gives administrators a way of altering configuration settings without touching the application code or restarting the web server.

The bulk of the method is enclosed within a `try...catch` block to trap any errors that may occur. In this block, we first create a `SqlDataAdapter` instance, passing the name of the stored procedure to execute and the `SqlConnection` object into its constructor:

```
sqlDataAdapter = new SqlDataAdapter("SearchFlight", sqlConnection);
```

Stored procedures are compiled and cached for subsequent executions, so they provide a tremendous performance boost. Next, we set the `SelectCommand.CommandType` property to indicate that we want to execute a stored procedure:

```
// Indicate that we want to execute a stored procedure
sqlDataAdapter.SelectCommand.CommandType = CommandType.StoredProcedure;
```

We can now create the parameter objects, set their `Value` property, and finally add them to the `Command` object by invoking the `Add` method of the `Parameters` collection of `SelectCommand`:

```
// Add the Start Place parameter
SqlParameter paramStartPlace  = new SqlParameter("@sStartingFrom",
 SqlDbType.VarChar, 50);
paramStartPlace.Value = startPlace;
sqlDataAdapter.SelectCommand.Parameters.Add(paramStartPlace);
```

We perform the same steps for all the parameters that we want to pass to our stored procedure, namely `paramStartPlace`, `paramDestination`, `paramDepartureDate`, `paramArrivalDate`, and `paramTravelClassCode`.

When all the parameters are added to the `Parameters` collection, we can create a new `DataSet` object, and use `SqlDataAdapter`'s `Fill` method to populate it by executing the previously assigned stored procedure. The `Fill` method arguments are the `DataSet` to be populated followed by the name of the table to use as the data source:

```
// Populate the DataSet
flight = new DataSet();
sqlDataAdapter.Fill(flight, "Flights");
```

If all goes according to plan, we return the `flight` `DataSet`. If however an error occurs during the execution of the above statements, control passes to the `catch` block, where the error is thrown out to the client to handle as it wishes.

The statements in the `finally` block are performed regardless of whether the `try` block executes successfully or not. If we find that the connection is still open, by checking the `State` property, we close it by calling the `Close` method.

The AddBooking Method

This method adds booking details to the database by running the `AddBooking` stored procedure against the database.

This method bears many similarities to `SearchFlight`. We have a similar `WebMethod` attribute, and we again retrieve the connection string from the `web.config` file. However, this time, we use a `SqlCommand` object and not a `SqlDataAdapter`:

```
[WebMethod (EnableSession=false,Description="This method is used to add a new
 booking for a flight and returns the Booking ID")]
public int AddBooking(int flightID,string passengerID,int travelClassID)

    SqlConnection sqlConnection;
    SqlCommand sqlCommand;

    // Retrieve the connection string from the web.config file
    sqlConnection = new SqlConnection(ConfigurationSettings.AppSettings
     ["connectionString"]);
```

```
    try
    {

        // Establish connection with the database
        sqlConnection.Open();
        sqlCommand = new SqlCommand("AddBooking", sqlConnection);

        // Indicate that we want to execute a stored procedure
        sqlCommand.CommandType = CommandType.StoredProcedure;

        // Add the Flight ID parameter
        SqlParameter paramFlightID = new SqlParameter("@iFlightID",
         SqlDbType.Int);
        paramFlightID.Value = flightID;
        sqlCommand.Parameters.Add(paramFlightID);

        // Add the PassengerID parameter
        SqlParameter paramPassengerID  = new SqlParameter("@sPassengerID",
         SqlDbType.VarChar, 20);
        paramPassengerID.Value = passengerID;
        sqlCommand.Parameters.Add(paramPassengerID);

        // Add the Travel Class ID parameter
        SqlParameter paramTravelClassID = new SqlParameter("@iTravelClassID",
         SqlDbType.Int);
        paramTravelClassID.Value = travelClassID;
        sqlCommand.Parameters.Add(paramTravelClassID);

        // Add the Booking ID parameter as an Output parameter
        SqlParameter paramBookingID = new SqlParameter("@iBookingID",
         SqlDbType.Int);
        paramBookingID.Direction = ParameterDirection.Output;
        sqlCommand.Parameters.Add(paramBookingID);

        // Execute the stored procedure
        sqlCommand.ExecuteNonQuery();

        int bookingID = Convert.ToInt32(sqlCommand.Parameters["@iBookingID"]
         .Value);

        return bookingID;
    }

    catch (Exception ex)
    {
        // Throw exceptions back to the client
        throw ex;
    }

    finally
    {
        // Close the connection if it is still open
        if (sqlConnection.State == ConnectionState.Open)
        {
            sqlConnection.Close();
        }
    }
}
```

Notice that we return the newly created booking ID as an `Output` parameter, by setting the enum constant `ParameterDirection` to `Output`:

```
// Add the Booking ID parameter as an Output parameter
SqlParameter paramBookingID = new SqlParameter("@iBookingID",
 SqlDbType.Int);
paramBookingID.Direction = ParameterDirection.Output;
```

When all the parameters are set up, we invoke `ExecuteNonQuery` to execute the stored procedure. In essence, the `ExecuteNonQuery` method executes a T-SQL statement against the specified connection, and returns the number of rows affected.

If the stored procedure is successful, we retrieve the returned value from the `Parameters` collection of the `SqlCommand` object, passing it through the `ToInt32` method from the `Convert` class to cast the returned value as an integer:

```
int bookingID = Convert.ToInt32(sqlCommand.Parameters["@iBookingID"]
 .Value);
```

The GetInformation Method

This method retrieves information regarding the latest news or travel deals depending on the value of the `informationTypeID` parameter. If this is 1, it returns information about travel deals. If it is 2, it returns travel news.

This method doesn't contain anything we haven't seen in the previous methods, but now we are using a different stored procedure and parameters:

```
[WebMethod (EnableSession=false,Description="This method is used to return
information about either news or deals based on the type id")]

public DataSet GetInformation(int informationTypeID)
{

    DataSet information;

    // Set up the SQL connection
    SqlConnection sqlConnection;
    SqlDataAdapter sqlDataAdapter;
    sqlConnection = new SqlConnection(ConfigurationSettings.AppSettings
     ["connectionString"]);

    try
    {
       sqlDataAdapter = new SqlDataAdapter("GetInformationByTypeID",
        sqlConnection);

       // Indicate that we want to execute a stored procedure
       sqlDataAdapter.SelectCommand.CommandType = CommandType
        .StoredProcedure;

       // Add the Information Type parameter
       SqlParameter paramInformationType  = new SqlParameter(
        "@iInformationTypeID", SqlDbType.SmallInt);
       paramInformationType.Value = informationTypeID;
```

```
        sqlDataAdapter.SelectCommand.Parameters.Add(paramInformationType);

        // Populate the DataSet
        information = new DataSet();
        sqlDataAdapter.Fill(information, "Information");

        // Return the DataSet
        return information;
    }

    catch (Exception ex)
    {
        // Throw exceptions back to the client
        throw ex;
    }

    finally
    {
        // Close the connection if it is still open
        if (sqlConnection.State == ConnectionState.Open)
        {
            sqlConnection.Close();
        }
    }
}
```

We have now implemented the methods for the travel functionality, so let's move on to the web method that returns a stock quote for a given company.

The StockQuoteService Web Service

Add a new web service to our project by right-clicking on **WroxOnlineService** in Solution Explorer, and choosing **Add | Add Web Service....** Call it **StockQuoteService**. View the code for the newly created web service, and again add the `System.Data.SqlClient` and `System.Configuration` namespaces. Insert the `GetQuote` web method shown next:

```
[WebMethod(EnableSession=false,Description="This Method returns the stock quote
based on the name of the company")]

public string GetQuote(string name)
{
    DataSet stocksDataSet;
    DataTable stocksTable;
    string sPrice;

    // Set up the SQL connection
    SqlConnection sqlConnection;
    SqlDataAdapter sqlDataAdapter;
    sqlConnection = new SqlConnection(ConfigurationSettings.AppSettings
      ["connectionString"]);

    try
    {
        sqlDataAdapter = new SqlDataAdapter("StockQuoteGet", sqlConnection);

        // Indicate that we want to execute a stored procedure
        sqlDataAdapter.SelectCommand.CommandType = CommandType
```

```
         .StoredProcedure;

        // Add the Name parameter
        SqlParameter paramName = new SqlParameter("@Name", SqlDbType.Char, 4);
        paramName.Value = name;
        sqlDataAdapter.SelectCommand.Parameters.Add(paramName);

        // Populate the DataSet
        stocksDataSet = new DataSet();
        sqlDataAdapter.Fill(stocksDataSet, "Stocks");

        // Assign the table to the DataTable object variable
        stocksTable = stocksDataSet.Tables["Stocks"];

        // Return the value from the Price column
        sPrice = stocksTable.Rows[0]["Price"].ToString();
        return sPrice;
    }

    catch (Exception ex)
    {
        // Throw exceptions back to the client
        throw ex;
    }

    finally
    {
        // Close the connection if it is still open
        if (sqlConnection.State == ConnectionState.Open)
        {
            sqlConnection.Close();
        }
    }
}
```

This should all be familiar to you from the methods we've already added. Note that we're using the `StockQuoteGet` stored procedure on the `Stocks` table of the database to populate the `stocksDataSet` by calling the `Fill` method of the `SqlDataAdapter`. We then transfer the `Stocks` table in the `DataSet` to the `stocksTable` `DataTable` object:

```
// Assign the table to the DataTable object variable
stocksTable = stocksDataSet.Tables["Stocks"];
```

Once in the `DataTable`, it's easy enough to get the latest price of WOTS stock from the `Price` column of the first row in the table, but we must remember to convert it to a string:

```
// Return the value present in the Price column
sPrice = stocksTable.Rows[0]["Price"].ToString();
```

Now we can create the proxy class library that sits between the web service and its consumers.

Creating the Proxy Class Library

When we invoke a method of a remote web service, it is the proxy that handles the request. It is responsible for sending the request to the remote method, retrieving the results from the remote server, and passing them back to the client in the required form.

The proxy class represents a layer of abstraction that encapsulates the "plumbing" that underlies any communication with the web service. The following diagram shows the role played by a proxy class as the communication mediator between a web service and a consumer application:

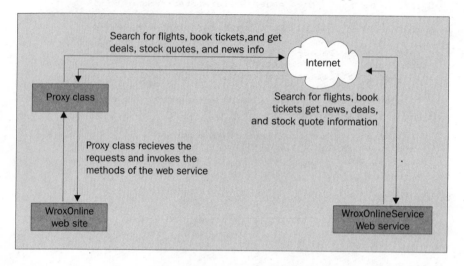

There are three different approaches available to create the proxy class:

❑ Adding a web reference from Visual Studio .NET to create the proxy class for us

❑ Using the Web Services Description Language (WSDL) executable that comes with the .NET Framework SDK

❑ Using the soapsuds utility that also comes with the .NET Framework SDK (see chapter 9 for more information on soapsuds)

We shall discuss the first two approaches in this case study.

Using the WSDL Utility

When we use WSDL.exe to generate the proxy class, a single source file is produced using the specified language. As covered in depth in Chapter 5, the proxy class contains methods for invoking the web methods either synchronously or asynchronously.

To generate a proxy class for the OnlineService web service, enter the following command at a command prompt, noting the path of the OnlineService.cs file it generates:

```
wsdl http://localhost/WroxOnlineService/OnlineService.asmx
    /out:OnlineService.cs
```

For complete information about the usage of the WSDL.exe tool, refer back to Chapter 4.

Once we have the proxy class source code, we can make a class library from it for the web service's consumers to reference. We can use either of the following methods:

- ❑ Using the class library project template supplied by Visual Studio .NET.

- ❑ Using the appropriate command-line compilers. This is really only worth doing if you do not have a copy of Visual Studio .NET and only use the .NET SDK.

We look at both of the above options. First, we'll use Visual Studio .NET, so open it up and create a new Visual C# class library project named WroxOnlineServiceProxy. Right-click on the entry for WroxOnlineServiceProxy that appears in Solution Explorer, select Add | Add Existing Item..., and browse to find the proxy code we just generated. You may want to exclude the default Class1.cs file that appears in Solution Explorer at this point too. Next, select Project | Add Reference..., or use Solution Explorer, and add references to the System.Web.dll and System.Web.Services.dll assemblies. When we now build the project in Visual Studio .NET, a proxy class library is created that lets consumers connect to the web service and invoke its methods.

Now let's try the second method for creating the proxy library: using the command-line compilers supplied with the Microsoft.NET SDK. Open a DOS command prompt, browse to the directory containing the proxy code, and issue the following command:

```
csc /t:library /out:WroxOnlineServiceProxy.dll /r:System.Web.dll
/r:System.Web.Services.dll /r:System.Xml.dll OnlineService.cs
```

Using Visual Studio .NET and the Add Web Reference Option

Visual Studio .NET lets us achieve all this without once having to leave the Windows environment to enter DOS commands. When we add a web reference for a web service in Visual Studio .NET, a proxy class library is created for our project, be the web service local or located anywhere on the Internet.

Later, we'll need to add a web reference to the WroxOnline project. With that project open, select Project | Add Web Reference, and enter the path to the WroxOnlineService web service's .vsdisco file in the dialog box that appears:

http://localhost/WroxOnlineService/WroxOnlineService.vsdisco

The WroxOnlineService.vsdisco file should appear. Visual Studio .NET auto-generated this file when we created the web service project, and it contains all the information a consumer requires to access the exposed web methods:

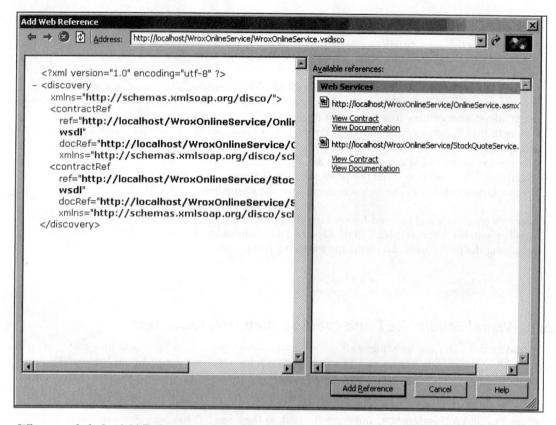

When we click the Add Reference button, Visual Studio .NET creates a folder with the same name as the server hosting that service. The new folder is located directly under the Web References folder within the application's project folder. By default, the name of the server is considered the root namespace for the local proxy class. To assign a different namespace for the proxy, we simply need to rename the server name folder accordingly.

Once we add a reference to a web service in this manner, we can call the web methods it exposes as if they were present on the local machine.

Implementation of the .NET Component

In this section, we implement the .NET component used to handle user data for the WroxOnline application. We start by creating a new Visual C# Class Library project called WroxOnlineLib in the usual manner. Once the project is created, change the name of the default class from Class1.cs to User.cs.

The User class is where we define the class to hold a user's details, which also contains two methods for user-related tasks: CheckLogin and SaveUserInfo. We discuss both of these methods in detail shortly, but first look at the top of the User.cs file. The following namespace has been automatically included:

```
using System;
```

To this, we need to add the following:

```
using System.Data;
using System.Data.SqlClient;
using System.Configuration;
```

The UserInfo Class

Now add the UserInfo class shown next, which provides the data structure we'll use for storing details of specific users:

```
public class UserInfo
{
    protected string userID;
    protected string password;
    protected string name;
    protected string address;
    protected string city;
    protected string state;
    protected string zip;

    public string UserID
    {
        get
        {
            return userID;
        }
        set
        {
            userID = value;
        }
    }

    public string Password
    {
        get
        {
            return password;
        }
        set
        {
            password = value;
        }
    }

    public string Name
    {
        get
        {
            return name;
        }
        set
        {
            name = value;
        }
    }

    public string Address
    {
```

```
        get
        {
            return address;
        }
        set
        {
            address = value;
        }
    }

    public string City
    {
        get
        {
            return city;
        }
        set
        {
            city = value;
        }
    }

    public string State
    {
        get
        {
            return state;
        }
        set
        {
            state = value;
        }
    }

    public string Zip
    {
        get
        {
            return zip;
        }
        set
        {
            zip = value;
        }
    }
}
```

We can represent a user record from our Users table using an instance of this class. As a data storage structure, the class only exposes get and set public properties to allow applications access to its member variables.

The CheckLogin Method

This is the method that authenticates a customer's user name and password against the WroxOnline database, and returns true if the name and password match a record in the Users table. Otherwise it raises an exception of type InvalidLoginException. Inside the CheckLogin method, we invoke the UserLogIn stored procedure, which returns 1 if a record with the specified user name and password is found, or −1 if not:

```
public bool CheckLogin(string userName, string password)
{
    SqlConnection sqlConnection;
    SqlCommand sqlCommand;

    sqlConnection = new SqlConnection(ConfigurationSettings.AppSettings
     ["connectionString"]);

    try
    {
        sqlCommand = new SqlCommand("UserLogIn", sqlConnection);

        // Mark the Command as an SProc
        sqlCommand.CommandType = CommandType.StoredProcedure;

        // Add the User name parameter
        SqlParameter paramUserName = new SqlParameter("@UserID", SqlDbType
         .VarChar, 20);
        paramUserName.Value = userName;
        sqlCommand.Parameters.Add(paramUserName);

        // Add the Password parameter
        SqlParameter paramPassword = new SqlParameter("@Password", SqlDbType
         .VarChar, 10);
        paramPassword.Value = Password;
        sqlCommand.Parameters.Add(paramPassword);

        // Add the return value parameter
        SqlParameter paramRetValue = new SqlParameter("@RetValue", SqlDbType
         .Int, 4);
        paramRetValue.Direction = ParameterDirection.Output;
        sqlCommand.Parameters.Add(paramRetValue);

        // Execute the command
        sqlConnection.Open();
        sqlCommand.ExecuteNonQuery();
        sqlConnection.Close();

        // Copy the return value from the stored procedure into a variable
        int retValue = (int)paramRetValue.Value;

        if (retValue == -1)
        {
            throw new InvalidLoginException("Invalid Login");
        }
        else
        {
            // Return true to indicate that the login is successful
            return true;
        }
    }

    catch (Exception ex)
    {
        throw ex;
    }

    finally
    {
```

```
            if (sqlConnection.State == ConnectionState.Open)
            {
                sqlConnection.Close();
            }
        }
    }
```

Although this is quite a lengthy method, its code follows the pattern set by previous methods. We add input parameters to the SqlCommand object corresponding to those in the stored procedure itself, which here are UserID, Password, and RetValue. This time, the RetValue parameter is an output parameter, that is, one returned by the stored procedure, so we set its Direction property to ParameterDirection.Output. As before, we execute the stored procedure by invoking the ExecuteNonQuery method on the SqlCommand object.

When the stored procedure has completed, we get hold of the result through the Value property of the SqlParameter object that represents the RetValue parameter in the stored procedure:

```
// Copy the return value from the stored procedure into a variable
int retValue = (int)paramRetValue.Value;
```

If the return value is –1, we throw an exception of type InvalidLoginException that will alert the client that the credentials supplied are invalid:

```
if (retValue == -1)
{
    throw new InvalidLoginException("Invalid Login");
}
```

The SaveUserInfo Method

This method saves new user details in the WroxOnline database. It takes the UserInfo object as an argument and returns true or false to indicate the success of the operation:

```
public bool SaveUserInfo(UserInfo userInfo)
{
    SqlConnection sqlConnection;
    SqlCommand sqlCommand;
    sqlConnection = new SqlConnection(ConfigurationSettings.AppSettings
      ["connectionString"]);

    try
    {
        sqlCommand = new SqlCommand("AddUser", sqlConnection);

        // Mark the Command as an SProc
        sqlCommand.CommandType = CommandType.StoredProcedure;

        // Add the User Name parameter
        SqlParameter paramUserName = new SqlParameter("@UserID",
          SqlDbType.VarChar, 20);
        paramUserName.Value = userInfo.UserID;
        sqlCommand.Parameters.Add(paramUserName);

        // Add the Password parameter
        SqlParameter paramPassword  = new SqlParameter("@Password", SqlDbType
```

```
        .VarChar, 10);
    paramPassword.Value = userInfo.Password;
    sqlCommand.Parameters.Add(paramPassword);

    // Add the Name parameter
    SqlParameter paramName = new SqlParameter("@Name", SqlDbType.VarChar,
        128);
    paramName.Value = userInfo.Name;
    sqlCommand.Parameters.Add(paramName);

    // Add the Address parameter
    SqlParameter paramAddress = new SqlParameter("@Address", SqlDbType
        .VarChar, 128);
    paramAddress.Value = userInfo.Address;
    sqlCommand.Parameters.Add(paramAddress);

    // Add the City parameter
    SqlParameter paramCity = new SqlParameter("@City", SqlDbType.VarChar,
        50);
    paramCity.Value = userInfo.City;
    sqlCommand.Parameters.Add(paramCity);

    // Add the State parameter
    SqlParameter paramState = new SqlParameter("@State", SqlDbType.Char,
        2);
    paramState.Value = userInfo.State;
    sqlCommand.Parameters.Add(paramState);

    // Add the Zip parameter
    SqlParameter paramZip = new SqlParameter("@Zip", SqlDbType.Char, 5);
    paramZip.Value = userInfo.Zip;
    sqlCommand.Parameters.Add(paramZip);

    // Execute the command
    sqlConnection.Open();
    sqlCommand.ExecuteNonQuery();
    sqlConnection.Close();
    return true;
}

catch (Exception ex)
{
    throw ex;
}

finally
{
    if (sqlConnection.State == ConnectionState.Open)
    {
        sqlConnection.Close();
    }
}
}
```

This method is very similar to the CheckLogin method, except that here we execute the AddUser stored procedure, which takes parameters related to a new user's details.

The Custom Exception Handler

Before we're done with `WroxOnlineLib`, we must add the `InvalidLoginException` exception class so we can publish to the clients that we will only be raising exceptions of certain types. You can add custom exception processing mechanisms to the exception classes to log errors in the event log, send e-mail alerts to the database administrator, and so on. The constructor for the `InvalidLoginException` class inherits the constructor from the base exception class, and stores the exception message for later retrieval:

```
public class InvalidLoginException : Exception
{
    public InvalidLoginException(string exceptionMessage)
     : base(exceptionMessage)
    {

    }
}
```

Windows Service Applications

There are times when you want a server application to run all the time. If you have ever done any work using Microsoft Message Queuing (MSMQ), you might well have created an application that polls the message queue at predefined intervals to check for new messages. If so, you probably ran the queue checking application as a Windows Service so it could poll the message queue without interruption.

Windows Services do not have a user interface and are outwardly similar to a Unix daemon. They can be set to start whenever the computer boots up, and wait silently in the background for service requests. A Windows Service acts quite independently of its host, and can transparently exchange information with remote clients.

Writing a Windows Service application before Visual Studio .NET was not a simple task. You could use the template provided by ATL, the Active Template Library that exposes a set of classes for COM programming. If you were a Visual Basic programmer, you would have to either embed custom NT Service control code, or access the Win32 API programmatically to achieve the same functionality. But with Visual Studio .NET, it's really not a problem to create an application that can run as a Windows Service. Visual Studio .NET provides a new Windows Service project template that handles much of the tedious work of creating a Windows Service. You can add code to run when the service is started, paused, resumed, or stopped.

Before the Service can be deployed, it has to be installed on the server with the `InstallUtil.exe` command-line utility. You can then start, stop, pause, and resume it using the Service Control Manager found in Administrative Tools.

Implementing the Stock Polling Service

In this case study, we shall use a timer running as a Windows Service to raise events at regular intervals so we can make an asynchronous request to the remote stock quote web service. The frequency of the raised events is determined by the `Interval` property of the `Service` class. Calling the remote web service asynchronously from a Windows Service application avoids the performance hit that would be caused by invoking the web service directly during the page render process.

The Windows Service functions in the following way:

❑ The Timer Windows Service invokes the remote web service asynchronously through the proxy library, passing the name of the callback function, which is initiated when the result from the web service is received

❑ The callback method, defined within the Windows Service, writes the retuned stock information to an XML file in the root virtual directory of the WroxOnline web application

❑ These actions are repeated at the frequency given by the Interval property to ensure that we have up-to-date stock quote information in our local XML file

Our WroxOnline web application (which we come to shortly) can now retrieve stock quote information directly from the local XML file instead of through a remote web service call.

Let's start coding the Windows Service now. Open Visual Studio .NET, and create a new Visual C# Windows Service project. Name it WroxOnlinePollingService. Once the project is created, change the default service name in Solution Explorer from Service1 to QuotePollingService.

The following figure shows a view of the Properties window for QuotePollingService that lets us can set Boolean properties such as CanStop and CanShutdown. These settings determine what features of our service can be controlled with Windows Service Manager:

We need to add installer controls to install our application as a Windows Service. Click on the Add Installer hyperlink at the bottom of the Properties window shown above. This adds the following two classes to our project:

❏ System.ServiceProcess.ServiceProcessInstaller

❏ System.ServiceProcess.ServiceInstaller

Since our Windows Service uses the web methods of StockQuoteService to get stock information, we need to add a web reference to that web service.

Open the Add Web Reference dialog, and enter the path to the web service's .vsdisco file. Visual Studio .NET then generates the proxy class for accessing its web methods.

Now add the following class to the QuotePollingService.cs file:

```csharp
using System;
using System.Collections;
using System.ComponentModel;
using System.Data;
using System.Diagnostics;
using System.ServiceProcess;
using System.Xml;

public class QuotePollingService : System.ServiceProcess.ServiceBase
{

    private localhost.StockQuoteService stockService;
    private System.IAsyncResult asyncResult;
    private System.Timers.Timer timer1;
    private string name;

    private System.ComponentModel.Container components = null;


    static void Main()
    {
        System.ServiceProcess.ServiceBase[] ServicesToRun;
        ServicesToRun = new System.ServiceProcess.ServiceBase[]
        {
            new QuotePollingService()
        };
        System.ServiceProcess.ServiceBase.Run(ServicesToRun);
    }

    protected override void OnStart(string[] args)
    {
        name = "WOTS";
        stockService = new localhost.StockQuoteService();
        timer1.Enabled = true;
    }

    private void WriteResult(IAsyncResult res )
    {
        string result;
        result = stockService.EndGetQuote(res);

        // Set up the XML Writer
        XmlTextWriter writer = new XmlTextWriter ("c:\\Inetpub\\wwwroot\\
          WroxOnline\\stocks.xml", null);
        writer.Formatting = Formatting.Indented;
        writer.WriteStartDocument(false);
```

```
writer.WriteComment("This file represents the stock quote returned
 from the web service");

// Start the element named stockquotes
writer.WriteStartElement("stockquotes");

// Start the element named stockquote
writer.WriteStartElement("stockquote", null);

writer.WriteStartElement(name, null);
writer.WriteElementString("price", result);
writer.WriteEndElement();

// End the element stockquote
writer.WriteEndElement();

// End the element stockquotes
writer.WriteEndElement();

// Write the XML to file and close the writer
writer.Flush();
writer.Close();

}

private void timer1_Elapsed(object sender, System.Timers.ElapsedEventArgs
 e)
{

    // Invoke the GetQuote method asynchronously with the callback method
    asyncResult = stockService.BeginGetQuote(name ,new AsyncCallback(
    WriteResult), null);
}
}
```

Notice that we import the System.Xml namespace to get access to the XML-related classes. We use these to write stock quote information to our XML file, which can then be read by the WroxOnline application.

We start our Main method with the declaration of the ServicesToRun array, which holds a list of the services to run:

```
System.ServiceProcess.ServiceBase[] ServicesToRun;
```

Generally, all the services offered by a Windows Service application are added to a ServiceBase array, and run together. However, we only have the QuotePollingService service in this instance, so we must add that to the array:

```
ServicesToRun = new System.ServiceProcess.ServiceBase[] { new
 QuotePollingService() };
System.ServiceProcess.ServiceBase.Run(ServicesToRun);
```

After Main, we come to the OnStart method, which is executed whenever the service is started from the Service Control Manager, or on boot up when StartType is set to Automatic. In this method, we create an instance of the StockQuoteService and enable the timer component so it can raise the Elapsed event at regular intervals:

```
stockService = new localhost.StockQuoteService();
timer1.Enabled = true;
```

Next is the `WriteResult` method called when the web method has completed and returned the stock price. `WriteResult` takes an object of type `AsycnResult` that encapsulates the results of the asynchronous call, and passes this object to the `EndGetQuote` method to retrieve the stock quote:

```
result = stockService.EndGetQuote(res);
```

In order to update our XML file, the `WriteResult` method creates an `XmlTextWriter` object instance, specifying the path of the XML stocks file:

```
XmlTextWriter writer = new XmlTextWriter ("c:\\Inetpub\\wwwroot\\
WroxOnline\\stocks.xml", null);
```

Note that we assign a value of `Indented` to the `Formatting` property of the `XmlTextWriter`, so that child elements will be indented according to the `Indentation` and `IndentChar` properties. The `IndentChar` property determines the character to use for indenting, while the `Indentation` property determines how many of those characters to write for each level of nesting. We use the default `IndentChar` and `Indentation` values, which are the space character and 2, respectively.

The `WriteStartDocument` method writes out the XML declaration element that should appear at the start of every XML file. The version attribute will be set to `"1.0"`, and the `standalone` attribute will be given the value `"no"` because we use an argument of `false`:

```
writer.WriteStartDocument(false);
```

The `WriteComment` method writes an XML comment to the file, and we use it to insert a comment indicating the purpose of the file:

```
writer.WriteComment("This file represents the stock quote returned
from the web service");
```

Now we're ready to start writing the XML elements. First, we write the `<stockquotes>` start tag:

```
// Start the element named stockquotes
writer.WriteStartElement("stockquotes");
```

We then write out further elements, finishing with the element that contains the actual stock quote information. We need to use the `WriteElementString` method for this:

```
writer.WriteElementString("price", result);
```

We call `WriteEndElement` repeatedly to close the elements in the sequence that they were opened, and finally, we flush the buffer, and close the `XmlTextWriter` object.

The last method in this class is the `timer1_Elapsed` event that is fired off by the timer component at intervals given by its `Interval` property. This should be set to 5000 milliseconds through the Properties window. The `timer1_Elapsed` event calls the web service's `BeginGetQuote` method, passing the company symbol as the first argument. We also pass an `AsyncCallback` delegate object that had the `WriteResult` method name passed to its constructor, setting that method as the callback method to execute when the asynchronous operation completes. The `BeginGetQuote` method returns an object of type `IAsyncResult`, which we can use to check the success of the operation:

```
// Invoke the GetQuote method asynchronously with the callback method
asyncResult = stockService.BeginGetQuote(name ,new AsyncCallback(
  WriteResult), null);
```

A typical XML file generated by the above code is shown in the following screenshot:

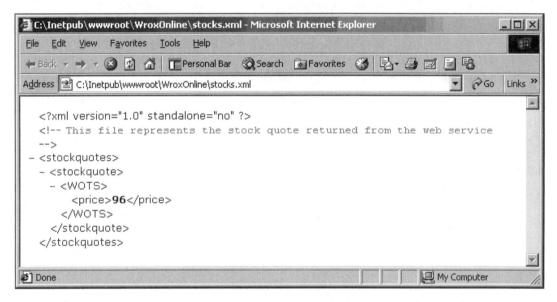

Now we need to install this application using the `InstallUtil` utility. Open a command prompt, navigate to the directory that contains the `WroxOnlinePollingService.exe` file, and execute the following command:

`InstallUtil WroxOnlinePollingService.exe`

This produces output detailing the installation progress and, if all goes well, will finish with a message stating: The transacted install has completed.

Once the service is installed, we manage it through the Windows Service Control Manager in Administrative Tools. Look for the QuotePollingservice entry, and right-click on it to see the list of available commands. Select Start to fire it up.

Our Windows Service now starts polling the web service for stock information every 5000 milliseconds, and updates the `stocks.xml` file accordingly.

Implementing the WroxOnline Web Application

In this section, we discuss the implementation of the main WroxOnline web application. Create a new Visual C# ASP.NET web application, and call it WroxOnline.

The WroxOnline web application uses these building blocks that have now been created:

❑   `WroxOnlineService` – ASP.NET web service

     This carries out tasks such as searching for flights, booking tickets, and retrieving news and travel deals. We add a reference to this web service by the **Add Web Reference** option.

❑   `WroxOnlineLib` – Visual C# .NET class library

     This performs operations such as creating new users and validating the credentials of an existing user against the database. We add a reference to this library using the **Add Reference** option.

❑   `WroxOnlinePollingService` – Visual C# Windows Service Application

     As we have already seen, this application polls the web service `StockQuoteService` at frequent intervals and ensures that the WroxOnline web application has the stock quote information in an XML file for displaying it to the clients.

There are various different processes involved as we implement the WroxOnline web application. Before we look at those, let's go over the code for the user controls that we shall use in our site.

A Look at User Controls

ASP.NET User controls are very powerful and flexible tools that allow us to define our own controls using the same programming techniques that we use for writing web forms. For our application, we are going to create three self-contained reusable user controls:

❑   The Header control (`Header.ascx`) to provide a standard and consistent header for all web pages on our site.

❑   The Left Navigation Bar control (`LeftNavBar.ascx`) to give a standard navigation bar that will appear on the left-hand side of all pages.

❑   The `InformationDisplayControl.ascx` control to display the latest news and travel deals available on our site. Either news or deals information is displayed according to the value assigned to the `InformationTypeID` property. We review the implementation of this control later, when we discuss the web form `InformationDisplay.aspx` that contains this control.

Before discussing the code underlying the header control and the left navigation bar control, I'd just like to outline the general steps for creating a user control:

1. Create a user control and save it with a `.ascx` extension. Any file with this extension is identified as a user control and cannot be executed as a standalone web page.

2. Include the user control in the container web form using the `Register` directive:

```
<%@ Register TagPrefix="WroxOnline" TagName="Header" Src="Header.ascx"%>
```

`TagPrefix` indicates the unique namespace for the user control, and `TagName` gives the control a unique name. The `Src` attribute contains the virtual path to the control.

3. Finally, place the user control in the web form with a tag like this:

```
<WroxOnline:Header id="Header1" runat="server">
</WroxOnline:Header>
```

We can now invoke its properties and methods using the name provided by the `id` attribute in the above line.

Now I think we're ready to create the header user control that we have at the top of all pages in the WroxOnline application. Right-click on **WroxOnline** in Solution Explorer, and select **Add | Add Web User Control....** Give it the name `Header.ascx`, and click on the button labeled **HTML** at the bottom of the Design view for the control. Insert the code below that creates the header from a simple ASP.NET table with three rows:

```
<%@ Control Language="c#" AutoEventWireup="false"
    Codebehind="Header.ascx.cs" Inherits="WroxOnline.Header" %>

<asp:Table id="tblTop"
           BackColor="maroon"
           Style="Z-INDEX: 101; LEFT: 1px; POSITION: absolute; TOP: 3px"
           runat="server"
           Width="819px"
           Height="108px"
           ForeColor="blue">

  <asp:TableRow>

    <asp:TableCell>
       <img src="Images\newwroxlogo.gif">
    </asp:TableCell>

    <asp:TableCell>
       <img align="right" src="Images\newwroxhead.gif">
    </asp:TableCell>

  </asp:TableRow>

  <asp:TableRow HorizontalAlign="Center">

    <asp:TableCell ColumnSpan="2">
       <asp:Label id="Label1"
                  runat="server"
                  ForeColor="White"
                  Font-Size="medium">
          Wrox Online Reservation System
       </asp:Label>
    </asp:TableCell>

  </asp:TableRow>

  <asp:TableRow HorizontalAlign="Center">

    <asp:TableCell ColumnSpan="2" ForeColor="White">

       <asp:xml id="Xml1"
```

```
                        runat="server"
                        TransformSource="stocks.xsl"
                        DocumentSource="stocks.xml">
            </asp:xml>
        </asp:TableCell>

    </asp:TableRow>

</asp:Table>
```

The code involved in the creation of the header control is pretty straightforward, except perhaps for the `<asp:xml>` server control with the ID Xml1 in the last `TableCell`.

The Windows Service that polls `StockQuoteService` stores stock information in the `stocks.xml` XML file. The `<asp:xml>` server control reads this XML file, transforming it to HTML with an XSL stylesheet called `stocks.xsl`. We can display this HTML as part of the header on all pages of our site. The `stocks.xsl` stylesheet that transforms the XML data is shown here:

```
<?xml version="1.0" ?>
<xsl:stylesheet version="1.0" xmlns:xsl="http://www.w3.org/1999/XSL/
  Transform">

    <xsl:template match="stockquotes">
    <b>
        WOTS : <xsl:value-of select="stockquote/WOTS/price" />
    </b>
    </xsl:template>

</xsl:stylesheet>
```

Follow a similar procedure to add the left navigation bar control (`LeftNavBar.ascx`):

```
<%@ Control Language="c#" AutoEventWireup="false"
    Codebehind="LeftNavBar.ascx.cs" Inherits="WroxOnline.LeftNavBar" %>

<asp:table id="Table1"
          Style="Z-INDEX: 101; LEFT: 1px; POSITION: absolute; TOP: 112px"
          ForeColor="White"
          Height="557"
          BackColor="navy"
          Width="191"
          CellPadding="0"
          CellSpacing="0"
          Border="0"
          runat="server">

    <asp:TableRow Height="60px">
        <asp:TableCell RowSpan="1"
                      BackColor="maroon"
                      ColumnSpan="1">
        </asp:TableCell>
    </asp:TableRow>

    <asp:TableRow Height="35px">
        <asp:TableCell RowSpan="1"
                      BackColor="maroon"
                      ColumnSpan="1"
```

```
                    HoziontalAlign="center">

    <asp:HyperLink runat="server"
                    NavigateURL="Registration.aspx"
                    BorderColor="White"
                    ForeColor="White"
                    ID="Hyperlink3"
                    BackColor="Transparent">
        New Member</asp:HyperLink>
    </asp:TableCell>
</asp:TableRow>

<asp:TableRow Height="35px">
    <asp:TableCell RowSpan="1"
                    BackColor="maroon"
                    ColumnSpan="1"
                    HoziontalAlign="center">
    <asp:HyperLink runat="server"
                    ForeColor="White"
                    NavigateURL="SearchFlights.aspx"
                    ID="HyperLink1">
        Search Flights</asp:HyperLink>
    </asp:TableCell>
</asp:TableRow>

<asp:TableRow Height="35px">
    <asp:TableCell RowSpan="1"
                    BackColor="maroon"
                    ColumnSpan="1"
                    HoziontalAlign="center">
    <asp:HyperLink runat="server"
                    ForeColor="White"
                    NavigateURL="SearchFlights.aspx"
                    ID="HyperLink2">
        Book Tickets</asp:HyperLink>
    </asp:TableCell>
</asp:TableRow>

<asp:TableRow Height="35px">
    <asp:TableCell RowSpan="1"
                    BackColor="maroon"
                    ColumnSpan="1"
                    HoziontalAlign="center">
    <asp:HyperLink runat="server"
                    ForeColor="White"
                    NavigateURL="InformationDisplay.aspx?
                     InformationTypeID=1"
                    ID="Hyperlink4">
        Deals</asp:HyperLink>
    </asp:TableCell>
</asp:TableRow>

<asp:TableRow Height="35px">
    <asp:TableCell RowSpan="1"
                    BackColor="maroon"
                    ColumnSpan="1"
                    HoziontalAlign="center">
    <asp:HyperLink runat="server"
                    ForeColor="White"
                    NavigateURL="InformationDisplay.aspx?
```

```
                         InformationTypeID=2"
                         ID="Hyperlink7">
              News</asp:HyperLink>
       </asp:TableCell>
    </asp:TableRow>

    <asp:TableRow Height="35px">
       <asp:TableCell RowSpan="1"
                      BackColor="maroon"
                      ColumnSpan="1"
                      HoziontalAlign="center">
          <asp:HyperLink runat="server"
                      ForeColor="White"
                      NavigateURL="Login.aspx"
                      ID="Hyperlink5">
              Log In</asp:HyperLink>
       </asp:TableCell>
    </asp:TableRow>

    <asp:TableRow Height="35px">
       <asp:TableCell RowSpan="1"
                      BackColor="maroon"
                      ColumnSpan="1"
                      HoziontalAlign="center">
          <asp:HyperLink runat="server"
                      ForeColor="White"
                      NavigateURL="Login.aspx"
                      ID="Hyperlink6">
              Log Out</asp:HyperLink>
       </asp:TableCell>
    </asp:TableRow>

  <asp:TableRow Height="250px">
       <asp:TableCell RowSpan="1"
                      BackColor="maroon"
                      ColumnSpan="1">
       </asp:TableCell>
    </asp:TableRow>
 </asp:table>
```

As you can see, the navigation bar is made up of a table containing hyperlinks for operations such as searching for flights, logging in to or out of the site, creating a new membership, and so on. Note that the **Deals** and **News** hyperlinks point to the same web form (`InformationDisplay.aspx`), but that they pass a different value through the querystring `InformationTypeID` parameter. The `InformationDisplay.aspx` web form uses the value of this querystring parameter to determine which information to display.

Enabling Form-based Authentication

To enable form-based authentication, make the following entry in the `web.config` file for our application:

```
<authentication mode="Forms">
    <forms name="WroxOnlineAuth" loginUrl="Login.aspx" path="/" />
</authentication>
```

The `loginUrl` attribute specifies the login page that users should be redirected to whenever they access a resource that does not allow anonymous access.

Our application does not allow anonymous users to browse the site, so we need to secure the following pages with entries in the web.config file:

❏ Flights Searching page (SearchFlights.aspx)

❏ Flights Search Results page (SearchFlightsResults.aspx)

❏ Book Tickets page (BookTickets.aspx)

❏ Information Display page (InformationDisplay.aspx)

For example, to restrict access for the SearchFlights.aspx page to authenticated users only, add the following entry directly underneath the closing <configuration> tag in the web.config file:

```
<location path="SearchFlights.aspx">
    <system.web>
        <authorization>
            <deny users="?" />
        </authorization>
    </system.web>
</location>
```

Now, when a user attempts to access the SearchFlights.aspx page, ASP.NET's form-based security automatically redirects them to the Login.aspx page, and prevents access to the page until they have successfully validated their credentials. To protect the other pages mentioned above, add the following entries to web.config:

```
<location path="SearchFlightsResults.aspx">
    <system.web>
        <authorization>
            <deny users="?" />
        </authorization>
    </system.web>
</location>
<location path="BookTickets.aspx">
    <system.web>
        <authorization>
            <deny users="?" />
        </authorization>
    </system.web>
</location>
<location path="InformationDisplay.aspx">
    <system.web>
        <authorization>
            <deny users="?" />
        </authorization>
    </system.web>
</location>
```

The Login Page

Add a new Web Form to the WroxOnline application using Solution Explorer, and call it Login.aspx. This page lets users log in so they may search for flights, book tickets, and so on. If the user does not have a valid login, they can create one by clicking the New Users Click here link, taking them to the registration page.

The customer's user name and password are authenticated against the `WroxOnline` database. On validation, the user is redirected to the search flights page. The finished Login screen will look like this:

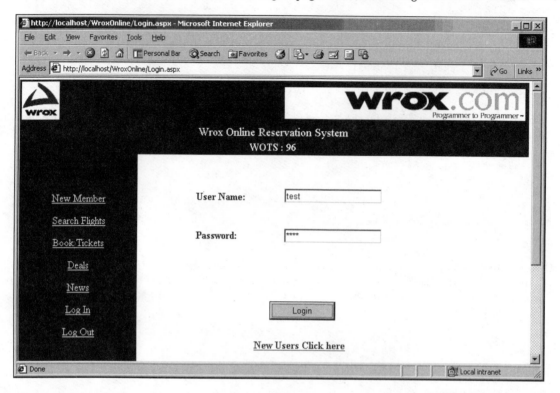

This page provides users with a form-based login mechanism for the WroxOnline application. This form-based authentication uses cookies to store the authentication information for the current user. Once the user is verified against the information in the `Users` table, cookies are used to maintain session information for that user.

The code-behind file for the Login page (`Login.aspx.cs`) implements the process performed when the user clicks the Login button:

```
private void btnLogin_Click(object sender, System.EventArgs e)
{
   try
   {
      WroxOnlineLib.User user = new WroxOnlineLib.User();

      // Validate the user's credentials
      if (user.CheckLogin(txtUserName.Text, txtPassword.Text) == true)
      {
         FormsAuthentication.SetAuthCookie(txtUserName.Text, true);

         // Save the UserID in the Session variable
         Session["UserID"] = txtUserName.Text;
         Response.Redirect("SearchFlights.aspx");
      }
   }
```

```
    catch(InvalidLoginException ex)
    {
        lblMessage.Visible = true;
        lblMessage.Text = ex.Message;;
    }
}
```

The CheckLogin method returns true if the login is successful, otherwise it throws an exception of type InvalidLoginException. If the login is successful, we invoke the SetAuthCookie method to generate an authentication ticket for that user name and password that we attach to the cookies collection of the outgoing response. This cookie will maintain session information for the user while they are at our site:

```
    FormsAuthentication.SetAuthCookie(txtUserName.Text, true);
```

We store the user ID in a session variable for later use, and redirect the user to the SearchFlights.aspx page in the next line so they may search for flights:

```
    // Save the UserID in the Session variable
    Session["UserID"] = txtUserName.Text;
    Response.Redirect("SearchFlights.aspx");
```

The exception handler simply sets the Visible property of the lblMessage label to true and displays the error message:

```
    catch(InvalidLoginException ex)
    {
        lblMessage.Visible = true;
        lblMessage.Text = ex.Message;;
    }
```

The Registration Page

The Registration.aspx page allows users to sign up as members of WroxOnline:

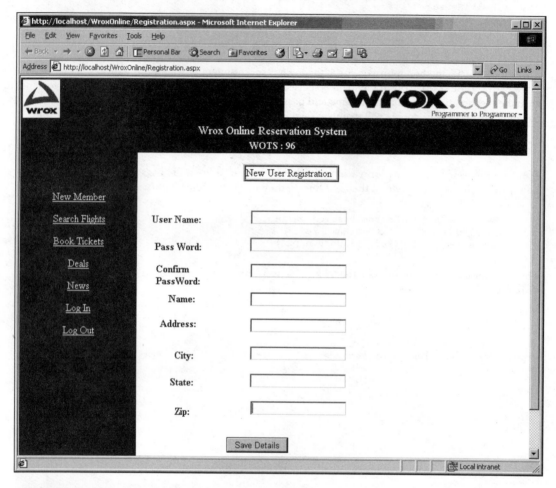

We add ASP.NET's server-side validation controls to the Registration.aspx page to perform validation of certain fields. For example, to ensure that the user provides a value for the txtUserName field, we need to declare a server-side validation control and associate it with the control to be validated by its ControlToValidate property. The ErrorMessage attribute provides the message to display should validation fail:

```
<asp:RequiredFieldValidator id="RequiredFieldValidator1"
        style="Z-INDEX: 103; LEFT: 555px; POSITION: absolute; TOP: 216px"
        runat="server"
        ControlToValidate="txtUserName"
        ErrorMessage="*" />
```

We use the built-in <asp:CompareValidator> validation control to check that the same value is provided in the **Password** and **Confirm password** text boxes. The attributes ControlToValidate and ControlToCompare specify the controls in question:

```
<asp:CompareValidator id="CompareValidator1"
        style="Z-INDEX: 105; LEFT: 578px; POSITION: absolute; TOP: 259px"
        runat="server"
        Height="20px"
        Width="203px"
        ControlToValidate="txtPassWord"
        ErrorMessage="Password does not match! Please reenter!"
        ControlToCompare="txtConfirmPassword" />
```

Now, let's look at the event handler that saves the details entered in the database:

```
// Invokes the WroxOnlineLib methods to save user details in the database
private void btnSave_Click(object sender, System.EventArgs e)
{
    WroxOnlineLib.User userRegister = new WroxOnlineLib.User();
    WroxOnlineLib.UserInfo userInfo = new WroxOnlineLib.UserInfo();

    // Assign values to the UserDetails object
    userInfo.UserID = txtUserName.Text;
    userInfo.PassWord= txtPassWord.Text;
    userInfo.Name = txtName.Text;
    userInfo.Address = txtAddress.Text;
    userInfo.City = txtCity.Text;
    userInfo.State = txtState.Text;
    userInfo.Zip = txtZip.Text;

    // Save the details to the database with the SaveUserInfo method
    userRegister.SaveUserInfo(userInfo);

    // Redirect the user to the Confirmation page
    Server.Transfer("Confirmation.aspx");
}
```

We store the user's details in a UserInfo object and invoke the SaveUserInfo method of the User object to commit to the database. Finally, we direct the user to the confirmation page that informs the user that registration was successful. In this case, the Transfer method is the most efficient, as it carries out the redirection server-side, thereby avoiding the network roundtrip that client-side redirection would require.

Here is the confirmation page that users see when they have registered:

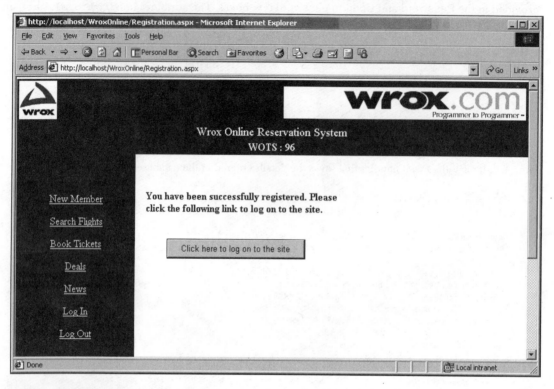

The Click here to log on to the site button simply invokes the `Transfer` method of the `Server` object to redirect the user to the Login page:

```
private void btnLogin_Click(object sender, System.EventArgs e)
{
    Server.Transfer("Login.aspx");
}
```

The Search for Flights Pages

The search page, `SearchFlights.aspx`, lets users look for flights that meet criteria such as start point, arrival date, and destination:

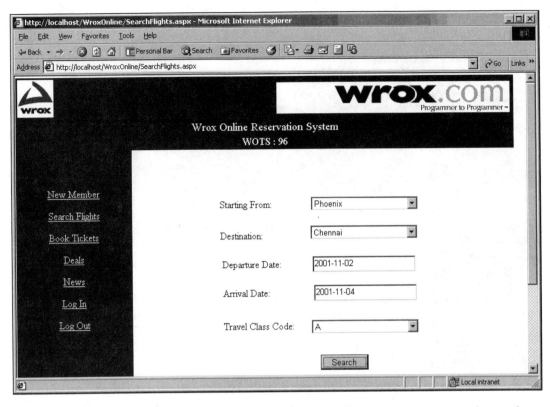

The **Search** button click event handler uses the `Server.Transfer` method to pass control to another page, called `SearchFlightsResults.aspx`, which displays the results of the query. We set the second argument of the `Transfer` method to `true` to preserve the submitted form so the results page can access it:

```
private void btnSearch_Click(object sender, System.EventArgs e)
{
    Server.Transfer("SearchFlightsResults.aspx", true);
}
```

The `SearchFlightsResults.aspx` page looks as shown in the next screenshot:

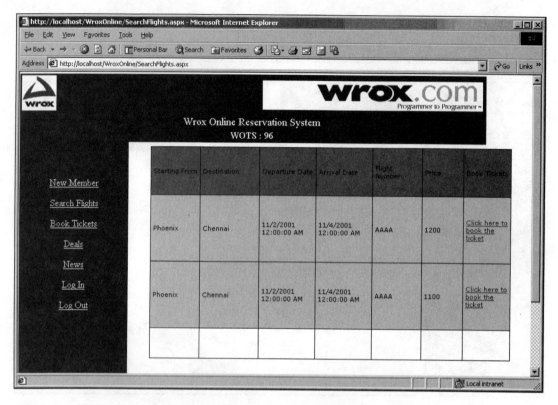

The key to this display is the server-side DataGrid control. We use the Page_Load event to bind a DataGrid directly to the values returned by the web service. The nice thing about the DataGrid is that it lets us set various style properties such as HeaderStyle, FooterStyle, ItemStyle, AlternatingItemStyle, and SelectedItemStyle.

Add the following code to the SearchFlightsResults.aspx file to set up the server-side DataGrid called grdSearchResults:

```
<asp:DataGrid id="grdSearchResults"
            style="Z-INDEX: 101; LEFT: 232px; POSITION: absolute;
                TOP: 127px"
            runat="server"
            Height="363px" Width="633px"
            BorderColor="Black"
            cellpadding="4"
            Font-Name="Verdana" Font-Size="8pt"
            HeaderStyle-CssClass="CartListHead"
            FooterStyle-CssClass="cartlistfooter"
            ShowFooter="True"
            ItemStyle-CssClass="CartListItem"
            AlternatingItemStyle-CssClass="CartListItemAlt"
            AutoGenerateColumns="False"
            Font-Names="Verdana">
```

Next, we set styles for the constituent parts of the `DataGrid`:

```
<FooterStyle ForeColor="Control" CssClass="cartlistfooter"
 BackColor="ActiveCaptionText" />

<HeaderStyle CssClass="CartListHead" BackColor="#00AAAA" />

<AlternatingItemStyle CssClass="CartListItemAlt" />

<ItemStyle CssClass="CartListItem" BackColor="Control" />
```

The columns of the `DataGrid` are defined now, using the `DataField` attribute of `BoundColumn` elements to specify the name of the column in the data view to bind to:

```
<Columns>
   <asp:BoundColumn DataField="starting_from" HeaderText="Starting From">
      <HeaderStyle Width="300px">
      </HeaderStyle>
   </asp:BoundColumn>

   <asp:BoundColumn DataField="destination" HeaderText="Destination">
      <HeaderStyle Width="300px">
      </HeaderStyle>
   </asp:BoundColumn>

   <asp:BoundColumn DataField="departure_date" HeaderText="Departure Date">
      <HeaderStyle Width="300px">
      </HeaderStyle>
   </asp:BoundColumn>

   <asp:BoundColumn DataField="arrival_date" HeaderText="Arrival Date">
      <HeaderStyle Width="300px">
      </HeaderStyle>
   </asp:BoundColumn>

   <asp:BoundColumn DataField="flight_number" HeaderText="Flight Number">
      <HeaderStyle Width="300px">
      </HeaderStyle>
   </asp:BoundColumn>

   <asp:BoundColumn DataField="price" HeaderText="Price">
      <HeaderStyle Width="300px">
      </HeaderStyle>
   </asp:BoundColumn>

   <asp:HyperLinkColumn Text="Click here to book the ticket"
               DataNavigateUrlField="flight_id"
               DataNavigateUrlFormatString="BookTickets.aspx?FlightID={0}"
               HeaderText="Book Tickets">
      <HeaderStyle Width="300px">
      </HeaderStyle>
   </asp:HyperLinkColumn>
</Columns>
</asp:DataGrid>
```

That `<asp:HyperLinkColumn>` control sets up a column in the `DataGrid` as a hyperlink, letting us provide a link for booking a ticket. The `DataNavigateUrlFormatString` attribute provides the URL to use when the link is clicked. The `DataNavigateUrlField` attribute indicates a parameter to pass to the `BookTickets.aspx` page as a querystring.

Now let's work on the code-behind file, `SearchFlightsResults.aspx.cs`, that powers the page. The bulk of the work takes place in the `Page_Load` event:

```
private void Page_Load(object sender, System.EventArgs e)
{
    // Code to initialize the page
    int travelClassID = Convert.ToInt32(Request.Form["lstTravelClassCode"]);

    // Store the TravelClassID in the Session variable for later use
    Session["TravelClassID"] = travelClassID;

    localhost.OnlineService searchService = new localhost.OnlineService();
    DataSet flightsDataSet = searchService.SearchFlight(Request.Form
        ["lstStartingFrom"], Request.Form["lstDestination"], Convert.ToDateTime
        (Request.Form["txtDepartureDate"]), Convert.ToDateTime(Request.Form
        ["txtArrivalDate"]), travelClassID);

    grdSearchResults.DataSource = flightsDataSet.Tables["Flights"]
        .DefaultView;
    grdSearchResults.DataBind();
}
```

The first thing we do in this method is retrieve the `lstTravelClassCode` control from the submitted form collection and place it in a local variable:

```
int travelClassID = Convert.ToInt32(Request.Form["lstTravelClassCode"]);
```

We also store the travel class ID in a session-level variable. This session variable is used in the `BookTickets.aspx` page to book tickets for a particular flight:

```
// Store the TravelClassID in the Session variable for later use
Session["TravelClassID"] = travelClassID;
```

In the next step, we instantiate the web service proxy class:

```
localhost.OnlineService searchService = new localhost.OnlineService();
```

Now, we can invoke the `SearchFlight` web method, passing in all the required parameters. We store the returned value in the `DataSet` named `flightsDataSet`:

```
DataSet flightsDataSet = searchService.SearchFlight(Request.Form
    ["lstStartingFrom"], Request.Form["lstDestination"], Convert.ToDateTime
    (Request.Form["txtDepartureDate"]), Convert.ToDateTime(Request.Form
    ["txtArrivalDate"]), travelClassID);
```

We then bind the results of the flight search held in this `DataSet` to the `DataGrid`:

```
grdSearchResults.DataSource = flightsDataSet.Tables["Flights"]
  .DefaultView;
grdSearchResults.DataBind();
```

The `DataSet` provides links labeled Click here to book the ticket. These transfer control to the `BookTickets.aspx` page, which we look at in the next section.

The Book Tickets Page

Now we shall implement the procedure for booking a ticket using our WroxOnline application. The `BookTickets.aspx` page is responsible for this function. This page's `Page_Load` event retrieves the booking details from the `Session` object and the querystring:

```
private void Page_Load(object sender, System.EventArgs e)
{
    // Code to initialize the page if the page is not posting back to itself
    if (!Page.IsPostBack)
    {
        int flightID = Convert.ToInt32(Request.QueryString["flightid"]);
        string userID = Session["UserID"].ToString();
        int travelClassID = Convert.ToInt32(Session["TravelClassID"]);

        localhost.OnlineService bookingService= new localhost.OnlineService();

        // Call the web method and store the returned booking id
        int bookingID = bookingService.AddBooking(flightID,userID,
          travelClassID);

        // Display the booking confirmation number
        lblConfirmationNumber.Text = bookingID.ToString();
    }
}
```

As long as the page is not posting back to itself, determined by the `IsPostBack` property of the `Page` object, we copy values from the querystring and the `Session` object into local variables. We invoke the `AddBooking` web method to make the booking and save details to the database. We keep the return value representing the booking ID in a local variable:

```
int bookingID = bookingService.AddBooking(flightID,userID,travelClassID);
```

Finally, we display the returned booking ID in the `lblConfrmationNumber` label control, to produce a screen like the following:

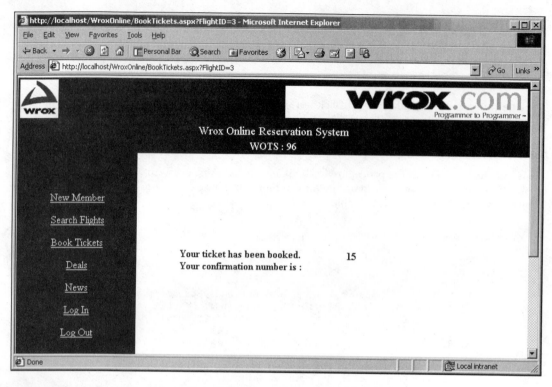

The News and Deals Display Page

The logic to show either the latest news or a list of available deals is encapsulated in the
`InformationDisplay.aspx` web form, and is triggered by the News and Deals links in the left
navigation bar. This web form depends on the user control defined in
`InformationDisplayControl.ascx` to display the appropriate information to users.

We'll start the discussion by considering this user control. It contains code that retrieves either news or
deals according to its `informationTypeID` public property.

When we have implemented this page, clicking on News in the navigation bar will produce the
following output:

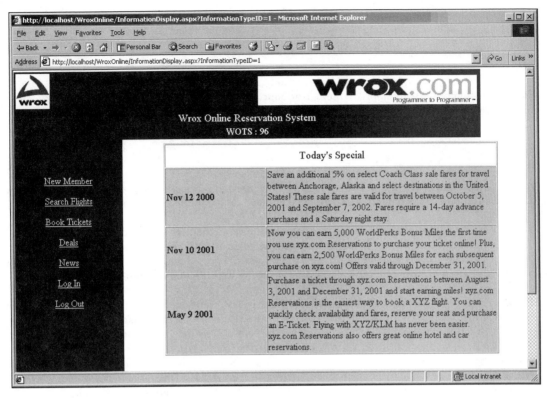

The `InformationDisplay.aspx` page that produces the output depicted in the previous screenshot contains a mix of HTML, server controls, and .NET directives:

```
Inherits="WroxOnline.InformationDisplay" %>
<%@ OutputCache Duration="60" VaryByParam="InformationTypeID" %>
<%@ Register TagPrefix="WroxOnline" TagName="InformationDisplayControl"
    Src="InformationDisplayControl.ascx" %>
<%@ Register TagPrefix="WroxOnline" TagName="LeftNavBar"
    Src="LeftNavBar.ascx" %>
<%@ Register TagPrefix="WroxOnline" TagName="Header" Src="Header.ascx" %>
<!DOCTYPE HTML PUBLIC "-//W3C//DTD HTML 4.0 Transitional//EN" >
<html>
   <head>
      <title>WOTS News and Deals</title>
   </head>

   <body MS_POSITIONING="GridLayout">
      <form id="InformationDisplay" method="post" runat="server">

         <table style="Z-INDEX: 101; LEFT: 264px; WIDTH: 587px; POSITION:
                 absolute; TOP: 127px; HEIGHT: 342px"
                cellSpacing="1" cellPadding="1"
                width="587" border="1">
            <WroxOnline:InformationDisplayControl
              id="InformationDisplayControl1" runat="Server" />
         </table>
```

```
            <WroxOnline:Header id="Header1" runat="Server" />
            <WroxOnline:LeftNavBar id="LeftNavBar1" runat="Server" />
        </form>
    </body>
</html>
```

Output caching can greatly improve the performance of an application especially when invoking a remote web service, and is controlled by the OutputCache directive:

```
<%@ OutputCache Duration="60" VaryByParam="InformationTypeID" %>
```

With output caching, the results of previously served pages are stored in the output cache and if a similar request comes along, the cached pages will be used to service the request instead of recreating the entire response from scratch. This can have a huge impact on the throughput of the application.

The Duration attribute sets how long this page should be cached for – here it is 60 seconds. The VaryByParam attribute allows us to store multiple versions of the cached page for different querystrings. Our page is dependent on the InformationTypeID parameter in the querystring, so we set VaryByParam to store different versions in the cache for different values of this parameter.

Then, we register the user controls we're using on the page, associating a tag name and prefix to the .ascx files that render the news and deals display control, the navigation bar, and the page header. Creating our page is then simply a question of suitably arranging the controls that the .ascx files represent.

The code behind this page, in the InformationDisplayControl.ascx.cs file, is fairly straightforward. We start by declaring a public member called informationTypeID. This variable determines whether the user control is to display news or deals, and must be set by the web form hosting the control.

```
public int informationTypeID;
```

The code to retrieve the information to display is placed in the Page_Load event for the control, and invokes the GetInformation web method using the informationTypeID variable as the argument. We then only have to bind the repeater control to the DefaultView property of the DataSet returned by the web method call:

```
private void Page_Load(object sender, System.EventArgs e)
{
    // Create an instance of the proxy class
    localhost.OnlineService informationService = new localhost
     .OnlineService();

    // Invoke the GetInformation web method, specifying the information type
    DataSet informationDataSet = informationService.GetInformation(
     informationTypeID);
    informationRepeater.DataSource = informationDataSet.Tables["Information"]
     .DefaultView;
    informationRepeater.DataBind();
}
```

We still haven't set the informationTypeID property that we've used above. Open up the InformationDisplay.aspx.cs code-behind file, and add the Page_Load event handler shown next. This code sets the informationTypeID property of the user control to the value passed via the querystring. Note that the user control is identified by the name given when it was defined:

```
private void Page_Load(object sender, System.EventArgs e)
{
    int informationTypeID = Convert.ToInt16(Request.QueryString
    ["InformationTypeID"]);
    InformationDisplayControl1.informationTypeID = informationTypeID;
}
```

Exception Handling

As we write applications that are increasingly complex and depend on a larger number of external resources, there is more opportunity for things to go wrong. An efficient error handling routine is essential to handle errors in an effective and graceful manner. There are some excellent built-in exception handling mechanisms provided by the ASP.NET runtime that we can make use of.

First, we need to add the following entry in the <system.web> element of the configuration section of the web.config file:

```
<customErrors defaultRedirect="ErrorPage.aspx" mode="RemoteOnly" />
```

The defaultRedirect attribute provides a URL to direct the browser to whenever an error occurs on our site. The mode attribute can take any one of the following values:

❑   On – Enables custom errors

❑   Off – Disables custom errors

❑   RemoteOnly – Custom errors are shown only to remote clients

So, users will now be redirected to the `ErrorPage.aspx` page below if an error occurs:

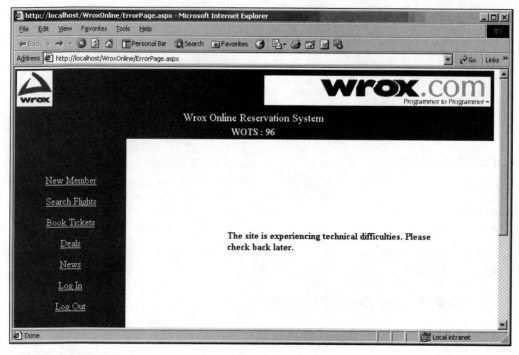

This generic page would probably not be suitable for a real e-commerce site, where you would want to create a more sophisticated and informative exception-handling page. ASP.NET's rich error-handling mechanisms are a great way of trapping errors to prevent the user seeing messy system error messages. However, users are not the only ones who need to be notified should things go wrong. For a start, the database administrator might want to know the circumstances under which an exception occurred.

To address this, we can implement the `Application_Error` event inside the `global.asax.cs` file, which will be called whenever an error occurs on our site. This event gets hold of the exception message with a call to the `GetLastError` method of the `Server` object, and writes it to the event log:

```
protected void Application_Error(Object sender, EventArgs e)
{
    EventLog eventLog;
    String logName;
    String eventSource;

    // Write errors in the system event log
    eventLog = new EventLog();
    logName = "MyLog";
    eventSource = "WroxOnline";
    eventLog.Source = eventSource;
    if (!EventLog.SourceExists(eventSource))
    {
        EventLog.CreateEventSource(eventSource, logName);
    }
    eventLog.WriteEntry(Server.GetLastError().ToString(), EventLogEntryType
      .Error);
}
```

Putting It All Together

We have now constructed the different parts of the application, so let's test it by navigating to the login page of our site. Enter valid user credentials, and click Login. Alternatively, create a new account for yourself, and log in that way. You should be directed to the search flights page to be presented with a web form for searching for flights

Enter some details, and click the Search button to take you to the search results page listing flights that match your search criteria. Click one of the links labeled Click here to book the ticket, and check that you are taken to the confirmation page that shows the booking ID number.

Check that the News and Deals links in the navigation bar work correctly, and display either travel news or deals information respectively.

Summary

This case study has followed the progress of the design and development of an ASP.NET web application using the .NET Framework. The features of ASP.NET that we made use of were:

❑ Exposing a method as a web method. We had a taste of how easy it can be to create and expose web services with .NET.

❑ The proxy class that mediates between web service and its consumer. We had a go at using the WSDL.exe utility to create this class.

❑ The asynchronous web methods automatically generated for a web service. We took advantage of this capability to improve application performance.

❑ User controls that run on the server and can be used in all pages of a client application.

❑ Output caching. We considered how application throughput can be improved by the use of output caching.

We also implemented a .NET component that we could access from our web application.

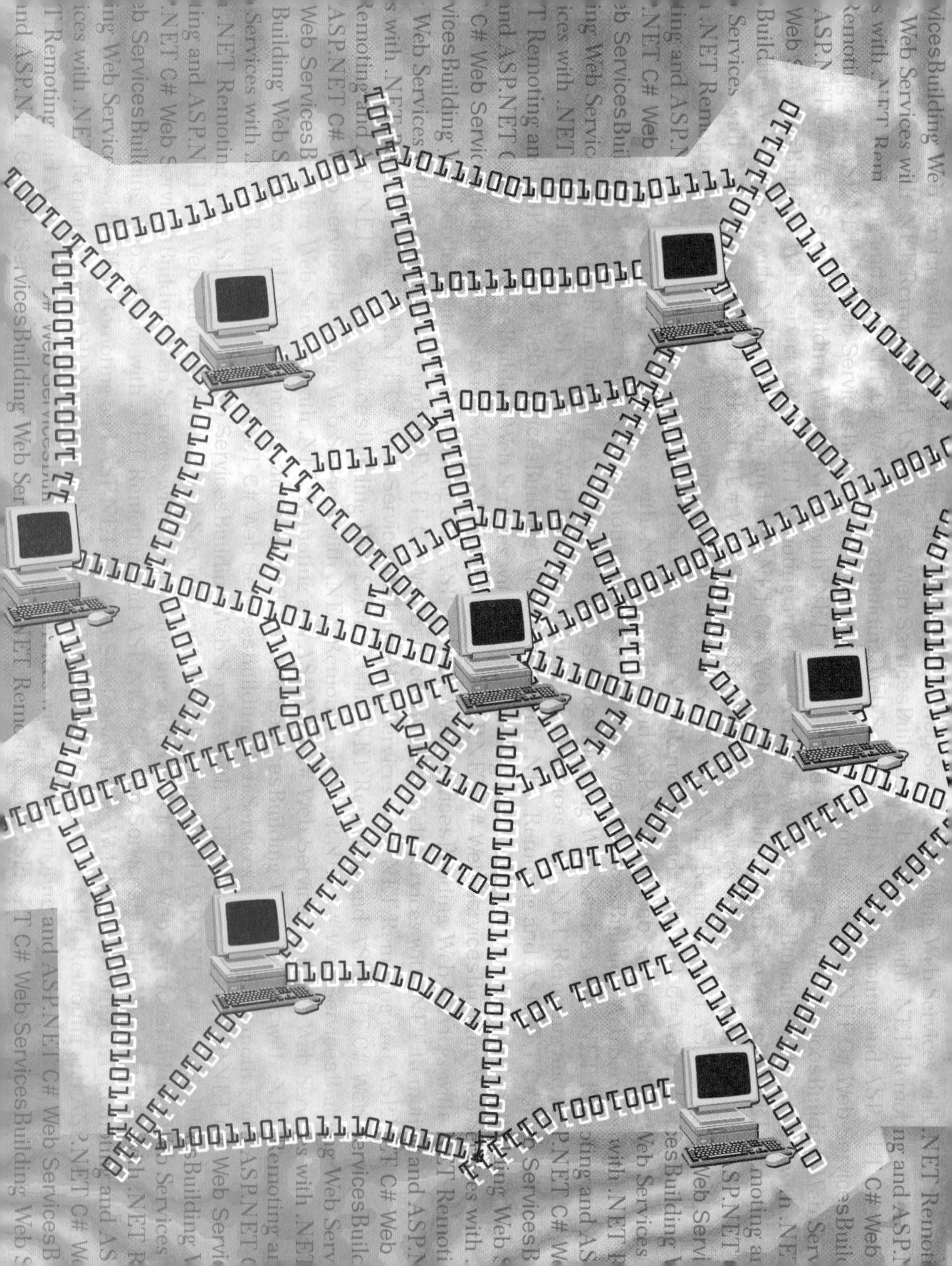

Case Study 2: P2P .NET Remoting

In this chapter, we will look at the design and implementation of a custom security channel sink for secure peer-to-peer (P2P) web services. Using a simple web service, we will build channel sinks to implement security and SOAP formatting, which can be plugged into other web services and reused. As we mentioned in Chapter 6, channel sinks are interception points within the call chain, which the remoting message passes through as it is marshaled from the client to the server. Each sink applies a particular functionality to the message (such as formatting it into SOAP), before passing it on to the next sink. Channels must have both a formatter sink and a transport sink. .NET provides two standard formatters, for serializing the message into SOAP or binary format. Transport sinks are used to pass the message into the channel on the client, and to retrieve the message on the server; .NET provides TCP and HTTP transport sinks.

We will go through the processes of designing and debugging a custom channel sink (both client and server), which will encrypt and digitally sign each message passed between peer web services. All this is achieved without affecting the application-layer design pattern, so an existing web service can be upgraded to use application-layer security simply by plugging in this security channel.

In explaining the object-oriented design that went into the channel sink implementation, I have given snapshots of the iterative refinement process. We will present four stages of refinement (appropriately named Iterations 1 to 4). I have followed this style for two reasons. Firstly, I found this approach very helpful when I first encountered it in the classic book *The Unix Programming Environment* (ISBN 0-13-937681-X) by Brian W. Kernighan (of K & R 'C' fame) and Rob Pike (both of A & T Bell Labs at the time). That book has a case study based on a calculator program that has been incrementally refined from stages 1 to 6. Secondly, I find it much easier to illustrate how a design was arrived at incrementally, and it is easier to explain and comprehend, since each stage has a greater degree of complexity than the preceding stages.

The potential uses for the type of channel sink design and technology demonstrated in this case study range from Peer-to-Peer secure messaging, to micro payments, e-commerce document exchange, and many other distributed applications.

The peer-to-peer (P2P) computing model is rapidly gaining in popularity. The P2P model differs from pure client-server computing in that each peer has both client and server components. Peers communicate directly with each other, rather than through a central server, so dependency on the server is kept to a minimum, if not eliminated altogether:

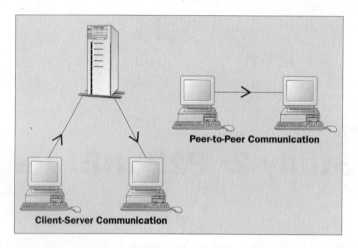

To illustrate our point, let's take the example of an instant messaging service. In today's scenario, a few big instant messenger services such as MSN, AOL, and Yahoo provide centralized logging and instant message exchange to registered users. These services have a very low level of direct interaction between clients (though the situation is changing), and all messages between two users pass through the central web server. The advantage of this arrangement is that users do not need to have a fixed IP address, and they are secure in the knowledge that the central server has authenticated the peer with whom they are communicating and that it really is who it claims to be. However, the downside of this arrangement is the loss of privacy and traffic congestion at the central server, since each message passes from the sender to the server and then back to the receiver. We can add to this another round trip for acknowledgement.

In contrast to the client-server approach, the P2P model eliminates the central server, except perhaps for the initial discovery and lookup to locate the peers, if they are using dynamic IP addresses. For fixed IP services, even this lookup service is not required. Thus, in the P2P paradigm, the sending peer would talk directly to the receiving peer without the arbitration of a Big Brother web service. To achieve this paradigm shift, we need to deal with issues like authentication and discovery.

The software industry (including Sun, Microsoft, and IBM) has built a broad consensus for XML-based peer web services, and issues such as discovery and publishing have been partially resolved with the UDDI (Universal Description, Discovery, and Integration) and WSDL (Web Service Description Language) protocols. See Chapter 2 (Web Service Protocols) and Chapter 10 (UDDI) for more details of these protocols and how to apply them in your web services. However, this is only a *broad* consensus – the messaging protocols, though based on XML, vary from platform to platform and at times implementations of the same protocol have subtle variations, which need additional plumbing to communicate with each other.

A web service programmer would therefore need to cater for a range of competing protocols, till such time as a clear winner emerges and one implementation prevails over its competitors. However, given the wide-ranging and diverse vision of web services, it's entirely possible that a clear winner will never emerge. The name of the game will therefore be to design the service in such a way as to cater for various related, but not identical, XML- and SOAP-based messaging protocols. One of the ways to achieve this goal (without rewriting your application) is to use the .NET Framework and write custom channel sinks.

.NET Remoting has a commendable layered architecture, which we looked at in detail in Section 3 of this book. As an application developer, you design an abstraction layer by defining interfaces. One or more implementations of this service layer abstraction are developed to cater for different deployment scenarios. For cross-platform interoperability, you may need to develop custom channel sinks.

A little math would convince you of the usefulness of this layered technique. Let's say you have n applications and a set of m protocol mutations. Without a pluggable layer approach, you would end up writing $(n \times m)$ applications. Contrast this with the layered approach, where the total components would be $(n + m)$. Thus, for any values greater than two, it makes sense to use a pluggable layer design.

Channel sinks provide a message transformation layer for your web service application.

Aims and Design Goals

The aim in this chapter is to design and implement a secure channel sink that we can use to add security to P2P web services. The design goals for this sink are:

❑　Channel sinks and cryptographic components should be transparent and shouldn't interfere with the application interfaces

❑　Existing web services should upgrade to use this application-layer security

❑　Decentralized and empowered peer cryptography components are desirable

❑　We should have a modular and functionally segregated component design.

❑　The cryptographic components should be reusable and pluggable.

❑　Each component should be testable separately.

❑　We want dynamically traceable logging information to aid debugging.

Planning the Development

As we've seen, our primary aim is to develop a security-based reusable channel sink. It is anticipated that we may need to create many such channel sinks for bridging P2P platforms in the near future. Thus we need a boilerplate design for developing channel sinks in future. Also, the security-layer design should be reusable elsewhere.

The cryptographic sink will be invoked between the SOAP formatter sink and the actual channel – the message will be passed to our custom sink after it has been formatted but before it is passed into the channel. The receiving application processes the message in reverse order – it is decrypted by the security sink before being deserialized by the SOAP formatter. We can represent this process in diagrammatic form as follows:

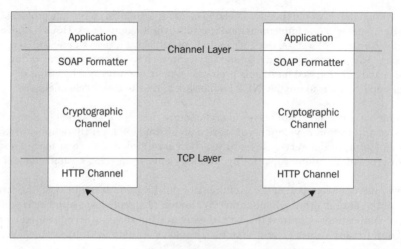

Before we start to implement the channel sink, we'll have a more detailed look at the architecture of our application, and identify the components that we will need to create.

Identifying the Components

The overall P2P application will consist of a web service at each peer machine endpoint. These services will expose an interface, which is used by the peer counterparts to access the actual service. This is fundamentally no different from traditional client-server architecture, except that each application entity that communicates with peers has both client and server components. That is, all application counterparts are symmetrical. P2P computing also accomodates the client-server model, which makes it a superset of client-server.

Although each peer houses both a service and the code to access a similar service, we shall segregate them into client and server components. This arrangement also makes it easy to visualize and discuss the architecture.

The peer web service is defined using a set of interfaces, which provides the abstraction layer. The service will have a set of actual classes implementing those interfaces in our .NET Framework context. These service implementers will extend the `System.MarshalByRefObject` or one of its derivative classes. This type of class provides the main service access point. They will be aided by a set of helper classes; and collectively they will implement the business logic of this service.

Below this layer is another layer that provides formatting and transport support to the application service. This layer interacts with the CLR (Common language Runtime).

Abstracting the Design

I often have to answer a standard question these days: why don't I use UML? My answer is that I like to think in the language of my target platform. And if you can think abstractly, your design will be reusable and portable across languages and platforms.

The design can be visualized in an abstract manner as follows. A general-purpose channel (both server and client side) is created and tested. A cryptographic object is designed with just two entry points, the methods `SignEncrypt()` and `VerifyDecrypt()`. The first method signs the message, thus authenticating the sender. It also encrypts the message to ensure privacy. The second method reverses this process by verifying the signature and decrypting the message:

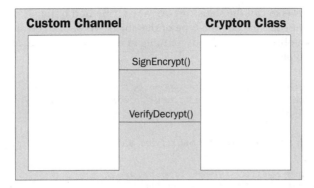

However, it's always important to remember the design rule that to be reusable, your code needs to be usable first! It's also worth remembering that UML diagrams (or similar documentation) can be very important in communicating the application design to clients.

Message Design

Like all design processes, OOD (Object-Oriented Design) is an iterative process. The design is refined as the prototypes are developed – in our case, the messaging design was arrived at only after Iteration 2 of the incremental prototyping stages. The third iteration and the final integration stage deal with the messaging formats as they fold and unfold, while flowing through the channel sinks.

The messaging layer has an onion-peel design. At the core is the SOAP-BOX element which contains the Base64-encoded message. Around this layer is the signature object, which again is an XML-formatted message. The next layer contains the encrypted message, which is itself wrapped in a SOAP message:

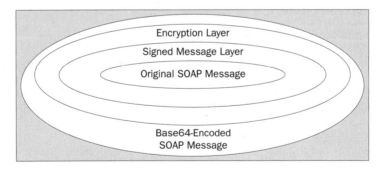

Iteration 1 – A Boilerplate Channel Sink

In the first iteration, we will aim to achieve two intermediate goals:

- ❑ Given only the abstract interfaces, we want the ability to call a remote web service, using a dynamically constructed URL

- ❑ To create a template or a boilerplate model for a channel sink

For P2P computing, we need to be able to call remote web services using only the abstract interface design; that is, with no knowledge of the actual implementing class. We also need to be able to use a dynamically configured URL to make the remote method calls.

One way to achieve this is to call the static `GetObject()` method of the `System.Activator` class, passing in the URL of our service and the type of the object we want to create. This method returns a proxy for a well-known object that is already running at the specified URL, and we can cast this proxy to the actual interface type:

```
string url = "http://localhost:8000/Dude/Talk2Me.soap";
Speak spk = (ISpeak)Activator.GetObject(typeof(Speak),url);
string yo = spk.Hello("Cool");
```

Another way is to design a custom proxy for our service, and to call its `GetTransparentProxy()` method:

```
MyProxy prox = new MyProxy(typeof(ISpeak),url);
Speak spk = (Speak)prox.GetTransparentProxy();
string yo = spk.Hello("Cool");
```

The `GetTransparentProxy()` method is defined in the `RealProxy` class, the base class from which the custom proxy inherits, and which implements much of the functionality for communicating with the remote object. The transparent proxy allows us to make calls on the remote object as though it were running in the same process. Real and transparent proxies are discussed in more detail in Chapter 6.

The ISpeak Interface

The interface we'll use to test our channel sink is called `ISpeak`, and is an equivalent of the classic "Hello World" program so often used for conceptual expositions. This is defined in `speak.cs` in the downloadable source code:

```
namespace Geek
{
    public interface ISpeak
    {
        string Hello(string dude);
    }
}
```

This interface will be used for demonstrating and testing our channel sink throughout this case study, across the four levels. It is implemented by a class named `Talk2Me` (in `Talk2Me.cs`):

```
using System;
using Geek;

namespace Dude
{
    public class Talk2Me : MarshalByRefObject, ISpeak
    {
        public string Hello(string dude)
        {
            Console.WriteLine(dude);
            return ("Yo " + dude + " Wazzup");
        }
    }
}
```

In order to demonstrate what's going on in our application more clearly, we'll use a custom proxy that writes trace information to the console. This allows us to examine the content of the message that is passed to the channel.

The proxy is instantiated and used exactly as above (this code is in `HelloClient.cs`):

```
RemotingConfiguration.Configure("HelloClient.exe.config");
MyProxy prox = new MyProxy(typeof(ISpeak),
                             "http://localhost:8000/Dude/Talk2Me.soap");
ISpeak spk = (ISpeak)prox.GetTransparentProxy();
string yo = spk.Hello("Cool");
Console.WriteLine(yo);
```

To keep the application as simple as possible (so that we can focus on the implementation of the channel sink), we'll host this class in the pre-built `DirectHost.exe` application, which is shipped with the samples for the .NET Framework (as part of the Remoting Hello Technology Sample).

MyProxy.cs

Our first task is therefore to implement the custom proxy, which we will do in a class named `MyProxy`. This class can be found in the file of the same name (`MyProxy.cs`), and should give you an insight into how the channel sink interacts with the CLR:

```
using System;
using System.Collections;
using System.Threading;
using System.Runtime.Remoting;
using System.Runtime.Remoting.Channels;
using System.Runtime.Remoting.Channels.Http;
using System.Runtime.Remoting.Proxies;
using System.Runtime.Remoting.Messaging;

//
// MyProxy extends the CLR Remoting RealProxy.
// This demonstrates the RealProxy extensiblity.
//
namespace Wrox.CSharpWebServices.CaseStudy2
{
    public class MyProxy : RealProxy
    {
        String serviceUrl;
        String objectUri;
        IMessageSink messageSink;
```

The constructor for the class iterates through the registered channels until a sender channel (a client channel that implements the `IChannelSender` interface we met in Chapter 7) is found. If no sender channel can be found, an exception is thrown; otherwise, we call the `CreateMessageSink()` method on the first available sender channel, and store the returned sink in the class's `messageSink` field:

```
        public MyProxy(Type type, string url) : base(type)
        {
            // This constructor forwards the call to base RealProxy.
            // RealProxy uses the Type to generate a transparent proxy
            serviceUrl = url;
```

```
            IChannel[] registeredChannels = ChannelServices.RegisteredChannels;

            foreach (IChannel channel in registeredChannels)
            {
               if (channel is IChannelSender)
               {
                  IChannelSender channelSender = (IChannelSender)channel;

                  messageSink = channelSender.CreateMessageSink(serviceUrl, null,
                                                                out objectUri);
                  if (messageSink != null)
                     break;
               }
            }
            if (messageSink == null)
            {
               throw new Exception("A supported channel could not be found " +
                                                "for url: " + serviceUrl);
            }
         }
}
```

All classes that inherit from `RealProxy` *must* override its `Invoke()` method. This method is called when the transparent proxy transfers the control back to the real proxy, with an `IMessage` instance as a parameter. We'll display the properties of this message object, and then pass it on to the message sink by passing it into the message sink's `SyncProcessMessage()` method. As you'd expect, this method handles the message synchronously, passing it to the next sink in the chain (in this case, the sink we retrieved in the class constructor and stored in the `messageSink` field), and waiting for a return message:

```
      public override IMessage Invoke(IMessage msg)
      {
         Console.WriteLine("MyProxy.Invoke Start\n");

         if (msg is IMethodCallMessage)
            Console.WriteLine("IMethodCallMessage");

         if (msg is IMethodReturnMessage)
            Console.WriteLine("IMethodReturnMessage");

         Type msgType = msg.GetType();
         Console.WriteLine("Message Type: {0}", msgType.ToString());
         Console.WriteLine("Message Properties");
         IDictionary d = msg.Properties;
         IDictionaryEnumerator e = (IDictionaryEnumerator) d.GetEnumerator();

         while (e.MoveNext())
         {
            Object key = e.Key;
            String keyName = key.ToString();
            Object value = e.Value;

            Console.WriteLine("\t{0} : {1}", keyName, e.Value);
            if (keyName == "__Args")
            {
               Object[] args = (Object[])value;
               for (int a = 0; a < args.Length; a++)
                  Console.WriteLine("\t\targ: {0} value: {1}", a, args[a]);
            }
```

```
            if ((keyName == "__MethodSignature") && (null != value))
            {
                Object[] args = (Object[])value;
                for (int a = 0; a < args.Length; a++)
                    Console.WriteLine("\t\targ: {0} value: {1}", a, args[a]);
            }
        }

        Console.WriteLine("url {0} object URI{1}", serviceUrl, objectUri);

        d["__Uri"] = serviceUrl;
        Console.WriteLine("URI {0}", d["__Uri"]);

        IMessage retMsg = messageSink.SyncProcessMessage(msg);

        if (retMsg is IMethodReturnMessage)
        {
            IMethodReturnMessage mrm = (IMethodReturnMessage)retMsg;
        }

        Console.WriteLine("MyProxy.Invoke - Finish");

        return retMsg;
        }
    }
}
```

The Configuration Files

We will develop a pair of client and sever channel sinks, which will serve as our boilerplate – a standard template for creating real-life custom channel sinks. The logger channel sample of the .NET SDK was used as a starting point for our template.

The salient feature of our channel sink is that we can control the level of debugging information dynamically from the configuration file. This is achieved on the client using the highlighted XML tag in the `HelloClient.exe.config` file. This configuration file also specifies the channel sink providers that will be used to process the message (in our case, the provider for the standard SOAP client formatter, and the provider for our custom channel sink). As we saw in Chapter 7, sink providers are factory classes, which we use to create instances of an actual channel sink.

```xml
<configuration>
    <system.runtime.remoting>
        <application>
            <channels>
                <channel type="System.Runtime.Remoting.Channels.Http.HttpChannel,
                                                    System.Runtime.Remoting">
                    <clientProviders>
                        <provider type="System.Runtime.Remoting.Channels.
                        SoapClientFormatterSinkProvider, System.Runtime.Remoting,
                        Version=1.0.3300.0, Culture=neutral,
                        PublicKeyToken=b77a5c5561934e089" />
                        <provider verbose="9" tag="AfterSoap"
                                type="Wrox.CSharpWebServices.CaseStudy2.
                                    TraceClientFormatterSinkProvider, TraceSink" />
                    </clientProviders>
                </channel>
            </channels>
```

```
            </application>
        </system.runtime.remoting>
    </configuration>
```

Each channel has both server- and client-side components, so we will also use the server equivalents of the same providers (these are specified in `DirectHost.exe.config`):

```
<configuration>
    <system.runtime.remoting>
        <application name="Dude">
            <service>
                <wellknown mode="SingleCall" type="Dude.Talk2Me, Talk2Me"
                           objectUri="Talk2Me.soap" />
            </service>
            <channels>
                <channel port="8000" type="System.Runtime.Remoting.Channels.
                                   Http.HttpServerChannel, System.Runtime.Remoting,
                         Version=1.0.3300.0, Culture=neutral,
                         PublicKeyToken=b77a5c5561934e089" >
                    <serverProviders>
                        <provider verbose="9" tag="AfterSoap"
                                  type="Wrox.CSharpWebServices.CaseStudy2.
                                       TracerServerChannelSinkProvider, TraceSink" />
                        <provider type="System.Runtime.Remoting.Channels.
                        SoapServerFormatterSinkProvider, System.Runtime.Remoting,
                        Version=1.0.3300.0, Culture=neutral,
                        PublicKeyToken=b77a5c5561934e089" />
                    </serverProviders>
                </channel>
            </channels>
        </application>
    </system.runtime.remoting>
</configuration>
```

The `verbose` attribute controls the level of the call progress information logged by both client and server. The internal `Logger` class does the job of logging according to the `verbose` level, and provides of lot of useful functionality for displaying messages and headers, which is used by both the client and server channel sink components.

TraceSink.cs

The first sink we pass the message to is the formatter message sink. Here, as in most cases, this is the SOAP formatter sink. The next sink is our custom channel sink; the source for the implementation of this is in the file `TraceSink.cs`.

Our sink consists of six classes: three for the client-side sink, two for the server sink, and a utility class for writing debugging information to the console:

❑   `TraceClientFormatterSinkProvider`. This is the factory class that creates instances of our client sink.

❑   `TraceClientFormatterSink`. A wrapper class around the client-side implementation of our sink. This class is used to indicate to the remoting framework that our sink is a formatter sink and should be the first sink in the chain.

❑   `TraceClientSink`. The actual client-side implementation of our sink.

❑   `TracerServerChannelSinkProvider`. The factory class that creates instances of our server sink.

❑   `TracerServerChannelSink`. The class that implements our server sink.

❑   `Logger`. The utility class for writing debug information.

Since this file contains the boilerplate code for our custom channel sink, we'll go through it in some detail. This should provide good insight into building channel sinks in .NET.

```
using System;
using System.Collections;
using System.IO;
using System.Reflection;
using System.Runtime.Remoting.Channels;
using System.Runtime.Remoting.Channels.Http;
using System.Runtime.Remoting.Messaging;
using System.Runtime.Remoting.Metadata;
using System.Diagnostics;

namespace Wrox.CSharpWebServices.CaseStudy2
{
```

The TraceClientFormatterSinkProvider Class

The first class we'll look at is the `TraceClientFormatterSinkProvider` class; this implements the client side of the sink provider. The class implements the `IClientFormatterSinkProvider` interface, which defines one method, `CreateSink()`, and one property, `Next`. The remoting infrastructure calls the `CreateSink()` method to create the actual message sink when required; the `Next` property sets or returns the next sink in the chain – the sink to which the message will be passed after the current sink.

```
public class TraceClientFormatterSinkProvider :
                                    IClientFormatterSinkProvider
{
    private IClientChannelSinkProvider next = null;
    private Logger logger = new Logger();

    public TraceClientFormatterSinkProvider()
    {
    }
```

As well as the default constructor, we provide a second constructor with two parameters. The first is an implementation of the `IDictionary` interface, containing any attributes supplied. We check for two attributes – the `verbose` attribute we've already discussed, and an attribute named `tag`, which differentiates the output for the purposes of debugging if multiple sinks are used in the same session. The second parameter is a collection containing any data that may need to be passed to the provider; this parameter is required by the framework, but we won't access it in our constructor:

```
public TraceClientFormatterSinkProvider(IDictionary d, ICollection c)
{
    string dbg = (string) d["verbose"];
    if(dbg != null && dbg.Length > 0)
        logger.verbose = int.Parse(dbg);
    Console.WriteLine("verbose = {0}", logger.verbose);

    string tag = (string) d["tag"];
```

```
    if(tag != null && tag.Length > 0)
        logger.tag = tag;
    logger.PrintStackTrace(("ctor" + tag +
                            "@TraceClientFormatterSinkProvider"));
}
```

The `CreateSink()` method is called by the `HttpClientChannel` to create our tracer sink. We also use this method to retrieve the next channel sink in the chain by calling the `CreateSink()` method on the next provider:

```
public IClientChannelSink CreateSink(IChannelSender channel, String url,
                                     Object remoteChannelData)
{
    logger.WriteLine(
            "***TraceClientFormatterSinkProvider.CreateSink() called");
    logger.WriteLine("  url: {0}", url);
    if(channel != null)
        logger.WriteLine("  Type of IChannelSender: {0}",
                                            channel.GetType());
    if(remoteChannelData != null)
        logger.WriteLine("  Type of remoteChannelData: {0}",
                                        remoteChannelData.GetType());

    IClientChannelSink nextSink = null;
    if (next != null)
    {
        logger.WriteLine(" calling next.CreateSink()");

        nextSink = next.CreateSink(channel, url, remoteChannelData);
        if (nextSink == null)
        {
            logger.WriteLine(" nextSink is null");
            return null;
        }
    }

    return new TraceClientFormatterSink(nextSink, logger);
}
```

The `Next` property simply sets or returns the provider for the next channel sink in the chain; this is held in the `next` field of the class. We will use the property `set` to specify that the next channel in the chain is the HTTP client transport sink, as the tracer sink is our only custom sink, and we will pass the message directly to the transport sink afterwards:

```
public IClientChannelSinkProvider Next
{
    get
    {
        logger.PrintStackTrace("get Next@IClientChannelSinkProvider");
        return next;
    }
    set
    {
        next = value;
        logger.PrintStackTrace("set Next@IClientChannelSinkProvider");
    }
}
```

The TraceClientFormatterSink Class

The `TraceClientFormatterSink` class is the custom sink class, but it's really only a wrapper for the actual implementation, which resides in another `internal` class named `TraceClientSink`. As well as inheriting from this class, `TraceClientFormatterSink` also implements the `IClientFormatterSink` interface. This is a marker interface (with no members) that is used as a flag to indicate that `HttpClientSink` should start with it first – the formatter sink is always the first sink in the chain on the client, so implementing this interface lets the .NET Framework know that the message should be passed to this sink before any others:

```
internal class TraceClientFormatterSink :
                           TraceClientSink, IClientFormatterSink

{
    public TraceClientFormatterSink(IClientChannelSink nextSink,
                              Logger logger) : base(nextSink, logger)
    {
    }
}
```

The TraceClientSink Class

The `TraceClientSink` class is the actual client-side sink implementation. The constructor is called in response to the `CreateSink()` method call of the provider by the `HttpClientSink`. The provider also creates a `Logger` instance, sets its `tag` and `verbose` fields and passes it as an argument to the constructor:

```
internal class TraceClientSink : IMessageSink, IClientChannelSink,
                                                 IChannelSinkBase
{
    private IClientChannelSink nextSink;
    protected Logger logger;

    private Hashtable prop = new Hashtable();

    public TraceClientSink(IClientChannelSink nextSink, Logger logger)
    {
        this.logger = logger;
        logger.WriteLine("ctor {0} tag[{1}]", this, logger.tag);
        this.nextSink = nextSink;
        logger.WriteLine("The next IClientChannelSink --> {0}", nextSink);
    }
```

The `AsyncProcessMessage()` method is called only when processing asynchronous requests. We simply pass the message on to the next sink in the chain by calling its `AsyncProcessMessage()` method:

```
public IMessageCtrl AsyncProcessMessage(IMessage msg,
                                        IMessageSink replySink)
    {
        logger.WriteLine(
                "***TraceClientFormatterSink.AsyncProcessMessage() called");
        return NextSink.AsyncProcessMessage(msg, replySink);
    }
```

The `IClientChannelSink` interface also exposes two methods specifically for processing asynchronous requests and responses respectively. To keep track of the order of the sinks in the chain, the remoting infrastructure maintains a sink stack. When processing a request, we push the current sink onto the stack and pass the message to the next sink (by calling its `AsyncProcessRequest()` method). When processing the responses, we simply pass the message on to the next sink in the chain:

```
            public void AsyncProcessRequest(IClientChannelSinkStack sinkStack,
                                            IMessage msg,
                                            ITransportHeaders headers,
                                            Stream stream)
            {
                logger.WriteLine("***{0}@AsyncProcessRequest() called", logger.tag);

                sinkStack.Push(this, null);
                nextSink.AsyncProcessRequest(sinkStack, msg, headers, stream);
            }

            public void AsyncProcessResponse(
                                    IClientResponseChannelSinkStack sinkStack,
                                    object state,
                                    ITransportHeaders headers,
                                    Stream stream)
            {
                logger.WriteLine("***{0}@AsyncProcessResponse() called", logger.tag);
                nextSink.AsyncProcessResponse(sinkStack, state, headers, stream);
            }
```

As well as the `AsyncProcessMessage()` method, the `IClientChannelSink` interface also defines a `SyncProcessMessage()` method. This is the first method called on our custom sink by the previous sink in the chain, the `SoapClientFormatterSink`. In this method, we simply print out some debugging information, and then pass the message on to the next sink in the chain:

```
            public IMessage SyncProcessMessage(IMessage msg)
            {
                logger.PrintStackTrace(("SyncProcessMessage@"+logger.tag));
                logger.WriteLine("*** Input Message ***");
                logger.PrintMessage(msg);

                logger.WriteLine("BEFORE calling nextSink<{0}>.SyncProcessMessage " +
                                                "@{1}", nextSink, logger.tag);

                IMessage rmsg = NextSink.SyncProcessMessage(msg);

                logger.WriteLine("AFTER calling nextSink<{0}>.SyncProcessMessage " +
                                                "@{1}", nextSink, logger.tag);
                logger.WriteLine("*** Output Message ***");
                logger.PrintMessage(msg);

                return msg;
            }
```

The `GetRequestStream()` method is called by the `SoapClientFormatterSink` to get a stream for the message. We simply forward the call on to the next sink, by calling its `GetRequestStream()` method. If our method returns `null`, the `SoapClientFormatterSink` will create its own stream:

```
            public Stream GetRequestStream(IMessage msg, ITransportHeaders headers)
            {
                logger.PrintStackTrace(("GetRequestStream@" + logger.tag));
                Stream ret = null;

                if(nextSink != null)
                    ret = nextSink.GetRequestStream(msg, headers);

                logger.WriteLine("return Stream@{0} type -> {1}", logger.tag, ret);
```

```
            return ret;
      }
```

Once a message stream has been retrieved from the `GetRequestStream()` and the message has been serialized, the `ProcessMessage()` method is called by the `SoapClientFormatterSink`. Here we simply print out the request, pass the call on to the next sink in the chain, and finally print the response:

```
        public void ProcessMessage(IMessage msg,
                                   ITransportHeaders requestHeaders,
                                   Stream requestStream,
                                   out ITransportHeaders responseHeaders,
                                   out Stream responseStream)
    {
        logger.PrintStackTrace(("ProcessMessage@" + logger.tag));
        logger.PrintRequest(requestHeaders, ref requestStream);
        logger.PrintMessage(msg);

        nextSink.ProcessMessage(msg, requestHeaders, requestStream,
                                out responseHeaders, out responseStream);

        logger.WriteLine("After calling nextSink<{0}>.ProcessMessage @{1}",
                                            nextSink, logger.tag);
        logger.PrintResponse(responseHeaders, ref responseStream);
    }
```

The `TraceClientSink` class also has three read-only properties: `Properties`, `NextChannelSink`, and `NextSink`.

The `Properties` property is the only member defined by the `IChannelSinkBase` interface, and references an `IDictionary` object, which holds the properties for the sink. In our class, this is implemented as a private `Hashtable` field; however, this property is never accessed:

```
        public IDictionary Properties
        {
           get
           {
              logger.PrintStackTrace((logger.tag + "@Properties"));
              return prop;
           }
        }
```

The `NextChannelSink` property is defined by the `IClientChannelSink` interface and returns the next channel sink in the chain. However, since our custom sink is the last client sink in the chain, this property is never called.

```
        public IClientChannelSink NextChannelSink
        {
           get { return nextSink; }
        }
```

The last property, `NextSink`, returns the next message sink in the chain. This property is defined by the `IMessageSink` interface. In the property `get`, we iterate through all the remaining channel sinks in the chain until we find one that implements the `IMessageSink` interface. If we do, we cast it to the `IMessageSink` type, and return it. Again, this property is never called.

```
    public IMessageSink NextSink
    {
      get
      {
        IMessageSink ret = null;
        for (IClientChannelSink nxt = nextSink; nxt != null;
                                    nxt = nxt.NextChannelSink)
        {
          if(nxt is IMessageSink)
          {
            ret = (IMessageSink)nxt;
            break;
          }
        }
        return ret;
      }
    }
  }
}
```

The TracerServerChannelSinkProvider Class

The next class brings us to the server side of things. Here again, the first class we'll implement is the sink provider – the factory class for our `TracerServerChannelSink`. As with the client sink provider, we have two constructors – the default parameterless constructor, and a constructor that takes two parameters, a dictionary and a collection. This second constructor sets the `verbose` and `tag` fields of the class's private `Logger` field:

```
public class TracerServerChannelSinkProvider : IServerChannelSinkProvider
{
    private IServerChannelSinkProvider next = null;
    private Logger logger = new Logger();

    public TracerServerChannelSinkProvider()
    {
    }

    public TracerServerChannelSinkProvider(IDictionary d,
                                            ICollection providerData)
    {
      string dbg = (string) d["verbose"];
      if(dbg != null && dbg.Length > 0)
        logger.verbose = int.Parse(dbg);
      Console.WriteLine("verbose = {0}", logger.verbose);

      string tag = (string) d["tag"];
      if(tag != null && tag.Length > 0)
        logger.tag = tag;

      logger.PrintStackTrace(("ctor of " + tag +
                              "@TracerServerChannelSinkProvider"));
    }
```

As well as the `CreateSink()` method and `Next` property similar to the ones for the client sink provider, the `IServerChannelSinkProvider` interface also defines a `GetChannelData()` method, which is used to retrieve the data for the message (passed into the method as an `IChannelDataStore` object). In our implementation, we simply iterate through the URIs for the channel and display those using our `Logger` class:

```
public void GetChannelData(IChannelDataStore channelData)
{
    logger.WriteLine("{0}@GetChannelData({1})", logger.tag, channelData);
    if(channelData != null)
    {
        string [] uris = channelData.ChannelUris;
        if(uris != null)
            for(int i=0; i < uris.Length; i++)
                logger.WriteLine("uri[{0}] = {1}", i, uris[i]);
    }
    logger.PrintStackTrace((logger.tag + "@GetChannelData"));
}
```

The implementations of the CreateSink() method and Next property are very similar to the equivalent members of the TraceClientSink:

```
public IServerChannelSink CreateSink(IChannelReceiver channel)
{
    logger.WriteLine("{0}@CreateSink({1})", logger.tag,channel);
    logger.PrintStackTrace((logger.tag + "@CreateSink"));

    IServerChannelSink nextSink = null;
    if (next != null)
    {
        logger.WriteLine("calling {0}@CreateSink({1})", next,channel);
        nextSink = next.CreateSink(channel);
    }
    return new TracerServerChannelSink(nextSink, logger);
}

public IServerChannelSinkProvider Next
{
    get
    {
        logger.PrintStackTrace((logger.tag + "@Next being called"));
        return next;
    }
    set
    {
        next = value;
    }
}
}
```

The TracerServerChannelSink Class

The next class, TracerServerChannelSink, is the server-side implementation of our channel sink. This sink is invoked after the message is retrieved from the channel, but before the server-side SOAP formatter.

The constructor simply sets the class's nextSink field to the server channel sink passed in as a parameter, and prints out debugging information using the Logger class:

```
internal class TracerServerChannelSink : IServerChannelSink
{
    private IServerChannelSink nextSink = null;
    private Logger logger;

    private Hashtable prop = new Hashtable();
```

```
       public TracerServerChannelSink(IServerChannelSink nextSink,
                                                   Logger logger) : base()
       {
          this.nextSink = nextSink;
          this.logger = logger;
          logger.WriteLine("ctor {0}@TracerServerChannelSink({1})", logger.tag,
                                                                  nextSink);
       }
```

Like the client-side sink, our server sink implements a `ProcessMessage()` method. This returns a `ServerProcessing` enumeration member. This can be one of:

❑   `Async`. The message is being processed asynchronously. In this case, we will need to store the message data on the sink stack so that it can be processed later.

❑   `Complete`. The server-side processing for the message has been completed.

❑   `OneWay`. No response message is required.

Within this method, we push the current sink on to the sink stack, and then pass the `ProcessMessage()` call on to the next sink in the chain. This method call also returns a `ServerProcessing` enum member, so what action we take next depends on the result we get back. If the message processing is `OneWay` or `Complete`, we just pop the current sink off the stack and write some debugging information to the console (if the processing is complete, we display the entire response). If `ServerProcessing.Async` is returned, we store the sink on the sink stack. Finally, we return the same `ServerProcessing` member that we received from the next sink:

```
       public ServerProcessing ProcessMessage(
                             IServerChannelSinkStack sinkStack,
                             IMessage requestMsg,
                             ITransportHeaders requestHeaders,
                             Stream requestStream,
                             out IMessage msg,
                             out ITransportHeaders responseHeaders,
                             out Stream responseStream)
       {
          logger.PrintStackTrace((logger.tag + "@ProcessMessage"));
          logger.PrintRequest(requestHeaders, ref requestStream);

          sinkStack.Push(this, null);

          logger.WriteLine("before calling {0}@ProcessMessage", nextSink);
          ServerProcessing processing = nextSink.ProcessMessage(sinkStack,
                                               requestMsg,
                                               requestHeaders,
                                               requestStream,
                                               out msg,
                                               out responseHeaders,
                                               out responseStream);

          switch (processing)
          {
             case ServerProcessing.Complete:
             {
                sinkStack.Pop(this);
                logger.WriteLine("Got ServerProcessing.Complete " +
                                    "{0}@ProcessMessage", logger.tag);
```

```
                    logger.PrintResponse(responseHeaders, ref responseStream);
                    logger.PrintMessage(msg);
                    break;
            }
            case ServerProcessing.OneWay:
            {
                    logger.WriteLine("Got ServerProcessing.OneWay " +
                                        "{0}@ProcessMessage", logger.tag);
                    sinkStack.Pop(this);
                    break;
            }
            case ServerProcessing.Async:
            {
                    logger.WriteLine("Got ServerProcessing.Async " +
                                        "{0}@ProcessMessage", logger.tag);
                    sinkStack.Store(this, null);
                    break;
            }
        }
        return processing;
}
```

The `IServerChannelSink` interface also defines an `AsyncProcessResponse()` method, which allows a response message to be processed asynchronously. Again, we simply output some debugging information and pass the call on to the next sink:

```
public void AsyncProcessResponse(
                            IServerResponseChannelSinkStack sinkStack,
                            Object state,
                            IMessage msg,
                            ITransportHeaders headers,
                            Stream stream)
{
    logger.PrintStackTrace((logger.tag + "@AsyncProcessResponse"));
    logger.PrintMessage(msg);
    logger.PrintResponse(headers, ref stream);

    sinkStack.AsyncProcessResponse(msg, headers, stream);
}
```

The last method exposed by our `TracerServerChannelSink` class is the server equivalent of the client sink's `GetRequestStream()` method. Here we simply return `null`, so that the SOAP formatter will be forced to create a stream:

```
public Stream GetResponseStream(
                            IServerResponseChannelSinkStack sinkStack,
                            Object state,
                            IMessage msg,
                            ITransportHeaders headers)
{
    logger.PrintStackTrace((logger.tag + "@GetResponseStream"));
    logger.PrintMessage(msg);

    return null; // The SOAP formatter creates a mem chunk stream on null
}
```

Finally, we have two properties, NextChannelSink and Properties. The NextChannelSink property is used by the HttpChannelSink to iterate through the sink chain; the next sink in the chain is stored in our private nextSink field.

As with the client sink, the Properties property is a Hashtable object, which is used to store the properties of the sink:

```
public IServerChannelSink NextChannelSink
{
    get
    {
        logger.PrintStackTrace(logger.tag + "@NextChannelSink");
        logger.WriteLine("nextSink --> {0}", nextSink);
        return nextSink;
    }
}

public IDictionary Properties { get { return prop; } }
}
```

The Logger Class

The last class in our tracer sink code is Logger; this is a helper class, accessed by both the server and client sinks, which prints the request and response details, as well as a stack trace. The level of detail depends on the verbose level, which is set in the client- and server-side configuration files. The Logger class has two constructors; the first sets the verbose level to zero, and the second takes the verbose level as a parameter:

```
internal class Logger
{
    public TextWriter output = Console.Out;
    public int verbose = 0;
    public string tag = "";

    public Logger()
    {
        verbose = 0;
    }
    public Logger(int verbose)
    {
        this.verbose = verbose;
    }
```

Next, we define a method for printing to the console window. This will have two overloads; the first takes a format string and an array of arguments and passes these directly to the Console.Out.WriteLine() method (output is an instance of Console.Out).

The second takes a single string parameter and passes it to our Display() method, which we'll define next, together with a parameter indicating a verbose level of one:

```
public void WriteLine(string fmt, params object[] args)
{
    if(verbose >= 1)
        output.WriteLine(fmt, args);
}

public void WriteLine(string msg)
{
```

```
            Display(msg, 1);
    }
```

The `Display()` method writes a string to the console window, but also takes the verbose level for the message as a parameter. It will only display the message if the application verbose level is greater than this:

```
public void Display(string msg, int level)
{
    if(verbose >= level)
        output.WriteLine(msg);
}
```

The `PrintRequest()` method is called from the `ProcessMessage()` methods of both our client and server channels, and writes a request message to the console. This takes two parameters – the headers of the message (in our case, the HTTP headers), and a stream representing the message. If the verbose level is greater than or equal to two, we print out both the headers and the stream using custom `PrintHeaders()` and `PrintStream()` methods:

```
public void PrintRequest(ITransportHeaders requestHeaders,
                                            ref Stream requestStream)
{
    if(verbose < 2)
        return;
    output.WriteLine("----------Request Headers-----------");
    PrintHeaders(requestHeaders);

    // Print request message
    string contentType = requestHeaders["Content-Type"] as string;
    if ((contentType != null) && contentType.StartsWith("text"))
    {
        output.WriteLine("----------Request Message-----------");
        PrintStream(ref requestStream);
        output.WriteLine("------End of Request Message--------");
    }
    output.Flush();
}
```

The `PrintResponse()` method is identical, except that it prints a response rather than a request:

```
public void PrintResponse(ITransportHeaders responseHeaders,
                                            ref Stream responseStream)
{
    if(verbose < 2)
        return;
    output.WriteLine("----------Response Headers----------");
    PrintHeaders(responseHeaders);

    // Print response message
    String contentType = responseHeaders["Content-Type"] as String;
    if ((contentType != null) && contentType.StartsWith("text"))
    {
        output.WriteLine("----------Response Message----------");
        PrintStream(ref responseStream);
        output.WriteLine("------End of Response Message-------");
    }
    output.Flush();
}
```

The `PrintHeaders()` method iterates through all the headers of a message and displays the key-value pair for each entry:

```
private void PrintHeaders(ITransportHeaders headers)
{
    foreach (DictionaryEntry header in headers)
    {
        output.WriteLine(header.Key + ": " + header.Value);
    }
}
```

The `PrintStream()` method reads through the supplied stream, one line at a time, and writes it to the console. We store the current stream position in a `long` variable, so that we can return to this position when we've finished reading the stream. However, if the stream doesn't support seeking, it won't allow us to access its `Position` property. We get round this by making a copy of the stream:

```
public void PrintStream(ref Stream stream)
{
    if(verbose < 2)
        return;
    output.WriteLine("---------- Stream START ---------");
    output.WriteLine("Type {0}", stream.GetType());

    // If the stream isn't seekable, make a copy
    if (!stream.CanSeek)
        stream = CopyStream(stream);

    long startPosition = stream.Position;
    StreamReader sr = new StreamReader(stream);
    string line;
    while ((line = sr.ReadLine()) != null)
    {
        output.WriteLine(line);
    }
    output.WriteLine("---------- Stream END ---------");
    stream.Position = startPosition;
}
```

The reason why we need to make a copy of the stream is that the default stream supplied by the `HttpChannel` can only be read once. The `CopyStream()` method simply creates a new `MemoryStream` and copies the data from the original stream into it via a `byte` array:

```
public Stream CopyStream(Stream stream)
{
    Stream streamCopy = new MemoryStream();

    const int bufferSize = 1024;
    byte[] buffer = new byte[bufferSize];

    int readCount;
    do
    {
        readCount = stream.Read(buffer, 0, bufferSize);
        if (readCount > 0)
            streamCopy.Write(buffer, 0, readCount);
    } while (readCount > 0);
```

```
                    // Close original stream
                    stream.Close();

                    streamCopy.Position = 0;
                    return streamCopy;
    }
```

We also provide a `PrintMessage()` method, which takes an entire message object (rather than separate objects for the header and the stream), and displays its properties. We iterate through each of the properties in turn, displaying them as key-value pairs. The "`__Args`" and "`__MethodSignature`" properties have multiple values (that is, the value is an object array), so we iterate through each of these values:

```
public void PrintMessage(IMessage msg)
{
    if(verbose < 3)
        return;

    IDictionary d = msg.Properties;
    IDictionaryEnumerator e = (IDictionaryEnumerator)d.GetEnumerator();
    output.WriteLine("---------- IMessage START ---------");
    output.WriteLine("Type {0}", msg.GetType());
    while (e.MoveNext())
    {
        Object key = e.Key;
        string keyName = key.ToString();
        Object value = e.Value;

        output.WriteLine("\t{0} : {1}", keyName, e.Value);
        if (keyName == "__Args")
        {
            Object[] args = (Object[])value;
            for (int a = 0; a < args.Length; a++)
                output.WriteLine("\t\targ: {0} value: {1}", a, args[a]);
        }

        if ((keyName == "__MethodSignature") && (null != value))
        {
            Object[] args = (Object[])value;
            for (int a = 0; a < args.Length; a++)
                output.WriteLine("\t\targ: {0} value: {1}", a, args[a]);
        }
    }

    output.WriteLine("URI {0}", d["__Uri"]);
    output.WriteLine("---------- IMessage END ---------");
}
```

The last method allows us to print out a stack trace of the current position in the call stack:

```
public void PrintStackTrace(string msgTag)
{
    if(verbose < 5)
        return;
    StackTrace trace = new StackTrace();
    output.WriteLine("---- START Trace {0} ----", msgTag);
    output.WriteLine(trace);
    output.WriteLine("---- END Trace ----");
```

```
        }
    }        // End of the Logger class
}            // End of the Namespace
```

This code is used as a template for a secure P2P channel sink, which we will create by plugging in a cryptography layer. We will develop this in Iteration 3 of our application.

Running the Example

The source for this iteration is found in a subdirectory named lev1. This contains the DirectHost application from the .NET examples, and the MyProxy.cs and TraceSink.cs files we've just looked at. We've already looked briefly at the other source files: Talk2Me.cs is the sample service; speak.cs contains the interface that defines the service; and HelloClient.cs is the client that calls this service, using only the ISpeak interface and the service URL.

The comp_all.bat batch file compiles all the assemblies required to run this iteration:

```
csc DirectHost.cs
csc /t:library Speak.cs
csc /t:library TraceSink.cs
csc /t:library /r:Speak.dll Talk2Me.cs
csc /t:library MyProxy.cs
csc /r:Speak.dll /r:MyProxy.dll HelloClient.cs
```

The console host can be started using the command below:

```
DirectHost -cfg DirectHost.exe.config
```

Type the following at another console to run the client:

```
HelloClient
```

Depending on the verbose level set in the configuration file, you will see the trace logs and finally the client returns the server response string.

A verbose level of zero provides no logging, and nine has the highest response level. The standard output may be redirected for a detailed analysis.

An edited snapshot of the stack trace gives the real picture:

```
Tracer.TraceClientSink.ProcessMessage(IMessage, ... )
Channels.SoapClientFormatterSink.SyncProcessMessage(IMessage)
RemotingProxy.CallProcessMessage(IMessageSink, Message, ... )
RemotingProxy.InternalInvoke(Message, Boolean)
RemotingProxy.Invoke(IMessage)
RealProxy.PrivateInvoke(MessageData&, Int32)
Geek.ISpeak.Hello(String)
HelloClient.Main(String[])
```

This stack snapshot highlights the call propagation from the Hello() method to our custom channel sink. I will defer an analysis of the stack trace until Iteration 4. However, I do encourage you to play around and tinker with the channel sink and analyze the client and server trace log.

Iteration 2 – Serialization and SOAP Boxing

In the second level of this incremental refinement model, we will test out SOAP serialization and packaging. This is really a validation stage for the messaging model. Here we try to reconcile the W3C encryption and digital signature model with the classes supported by the .NET Framework, such as `XmlSerializer` and `SoapFormatter`.

It was at this stage that we first tested and refined `XorCrypt.cs`, a symmetrical encryption helper class. However, since we will look at it in later sections with further refinements, we will forego the discussion at this level.

I also experimented with an encryption model using the interface given below:

```
public interface ISignedEnvelope
{
    string      KeyId { get; set; }
    RSA         RSAPublicKey { get; set; }
    byte[]      Data { get; set;}
    byte[]      Signature { get; set;}
}
```

The full source is available in the file `TestSig.cs`. We do not list it here, since I refined it later to reflect the W3C model. As a stepping-stone, and for understanding the design evolution, we have included it in the sourcecode.

The signature XML format is listed in Iteration 3 after due refinement, so again, we won't list it in this section. However, I do encourage you to go through the sourcecode of the `TestSoap.cs` and `TestVerify.cs` files before proceeding to the next iteration.

These two files may be compiled using the following console commands:

```
csc /t:library X.cs
csc TestSoap.cs /r:X.dll /r:System.Runtime.Serialization.Formatters.Soap.dll
csc TestVerify.cs /r:X.dll
```

This produces two executable files, `TestSoap.exe` and `TestVerify.exe`. Executing the first file produces an XML-formatted signed object in the file `delme-sig.xml`. `TestVerify.exe` loads and verifies this file.

`X.cs` just contains a serializable test class with a couple of public fields that we use to test the formatter:

```
[Serializable]
public class X
{
 public string hi = "Moe";
 public int counts = 1;
}
```

We will conclude this short and sweet level, by looking quickly at two code fragments. The first method uses the SOAP formatter to serialize an object and convert it to a byte array:

```
public static byte[] Obj2Bytes(Object obj)
{
    MemoryStream ms = new MemoryStream();
    SoapFormatter soap = new SoapFormatter();
    soap.Serialize(ms,obj);
    ms.Position = 0;

    return ms.ToArray();
}
```

The next code fragment instantiates an object of class X, serializes it by passing it into the `Obj2Bytes()` method, before encoding it into Base64 format and wrapping it in a `<SOAP-BOX>` element:

```
X x = new X();
x.hi = "Its Me!";
byte[] dat = Obj2Bytes(x);
XmlDocument xdox = new XmlDocument();
xdox.LoadXml("<SOAP-BOX>" + Convert.ToBase64String(dat) + "</SOAP-BOX>");
```

Iteration 3 – Cryptographic Modeling

Iteration 3 is devoted to cryptography. In the following sections, we assume that you have already read Chapter 11 (*.NET Security and Cryptography*), which discusses the .NET cryptographic API.

In this iteration, we develop an encryption and signing model for P2P computing. It does not depend on a CA (Certificate Authority); the rationale of this approach is discussed in the following section.

Eliminating the Certificate Authority

The one of the two principal goals of this case study was to introduce the concept of applying cryptography for P2P computing, in absence of a central certificate authority. This is apparently an unworkable proposition; but not really! The PGP (Pretty Good Privacy) model has been flourishing for more than a decade. The trick is to communicate the public key of the known peer "out-of-band". This is analogous to an e-mail address: you need to know the e-mail addresses of your friends in order to communicate with them.

So, in a P2P context, the public key of an individual may be viewed just like an e-mail address or an unlisted telephone number. I need to tell you my phone number before you can talk to me. Alternatively, a mutual friend of ours may be able to tell you my number. But to talk to him, I need to know his phone number!

Similarly, in P2P as well as in PGP, we can communicate the public key out-of-band, or alternatively a mutually known peer entity may introduce two peers, by digitally signing both their Public Keys and sending back each other's copy in a X.509 certificate.

This process is very similar to the Certificate Authority (CA) procedure, except that any peer can act as a temporary CA to others, if they trust it.

Signing and Encrypting Data

Having made a case for abolishing the CA, we will now implement an object model for P2P cryptography. This is represented by the following classes and structs contained in the `PeerCrypt.cs` file in the `lev3` subdirectory:

❑ Crypton: The class encapsulating the processes for signing and encrypting files and for decrypting and verifying encrypted files

❑ EncryptedData: A struct with two fields to represent the encrypted data (CipherData) and information about the key (KeyInfo)

❑ CipherData: A simple struct that uses two raw byte arrays to represent the encrypted data

❑ XorRand: A class for handling secret key encryption; this has been adapted from an example in Chapter 11

In the next level, however, these classes will be further enhanced. To test this object model, we have created a file encryption utility called EncrDox.cs.

Even before we start to design the Crypton class, we will first test the encryption process; this is a combination of Public Key and Secret Key encryption. The FileCrypt.cs file in the lev3 directory provides a testbed for proving this subprocess.

We need a private key and a public key to decrypt and encrypt files respectively. Here is a tiny program to achieve this:

```
using System.Security.Cryptography.Xml;
public class MakeRSAKey
{
    public static void Main(string [] args)
    {
        RSAKeyValue rsa = new RSAKeyValue();
        string pub = rsa.Key.ToXmlString(false);
        string prv = rsa.Key.ToXmlString(true);
        FileUtil.SaveString("PubKey.xml", pub);
        FileUtil.SaveString("PrvKey.xml", prv);
        System.Console.WriteLine("PubKey.xml and PrvKey.xml generated");
    }
}
```

This program appears in the lev3 source code as MakeRSAKey.cs, and can be compiled using the following console command:

csc MakeRSAKey.cs FileUtil.cs

Our FileUtil.cs utility and the RSAKeyValue .NET class were described in Chapter 11. This program produces two XML files containing public and private keys in XML format. The file PrvKey.xml looks like this:

```
<RSAKeyValue>
<Modulus>2qFL3aSPlp ... iJyR3OlvSM= </Modulus>
<Exponent>AQAB </Exponent>
<P>91ONfviduF2SG1P  ... NxvV/5BLQ== </P>
<Q>4kwdIj1WYoPWGpYMz ... F+Qx/Jjw==</Q>
<DP>375eizcut9MukjpV4 ... eRaRmIQ==</DP>
<DQ>OLVIK7dhOWi5/eHPXF ... Nr95g0ow==</DQ>
<InverseQ>odxub0Pvvyx+7 ... PiQkgVAw==</InverseQ>
<D>zpIMPpVX3irKdCU2+kXEO ... qqtOn7uZ9E=</D>
</RSAKeyValue>
```

The PubKey.xml file contains only the public key parts of the private key – the <Modulus> and <Exponent> elements.

FileCrypt.cs

Having generated the keys, let us now return to `FileCrypt.cs`. This file is very similar to `TestCrypt.cs`, which we saw in Chapter 11, but here we use a secret key for the actual encryption, and use the public and private keys to encrypt the secret key. We will employ .NET's `RSAPKCS1KeyExchangeFormatter` class for this purpose:

```
using System;
using System.IO;
using System.Security.Cryptography.Xml;
using System.Security.Cryptography;
using System.Text;
using System.Xml.Serialization;

public class FileCrypt
{
```

The `Encrypt()` method loads the public key file and the input file to be encrypted. We then generate a secret key and encrypt the input file using an XOR operation. We then use the `RSAPKCS1KeyExchangeFormatter` class to encrypt the secret key. It can only be decrypted using the corresponding private key. The output file is encapsulated in an instance of the `CipherData` class. This class is found at the end of `FileCrypt.cs`.

```
public static void Encrypt(string keyFile, string inFile, string outFile)
{
    RSACryptoServiceProvider rsa = File2Key(keyFile);
    FileStream fis = new FileStream(inFile, FileMode.Open);

    RSAPKCS1KeyExchangeFormatter fmt = new
                                        RSAPKCS1KeyExchangeFormatter(rsa);

    byte[] tmp = MakeSecret();
    FileUtil.SaveString("1.txt", Convert.ToBase64String(tmp));
    byte[] secret = fmt.CreateKeyExchange(tmp);

    MemoryStream ms = new MemoryStream();
    XorRand xoro = new XorRand(tmp);
    xoro.XorStream(fis, ms);
    ms.Close();
    fis.Close();

    byte[] encr = ms.ToArray();

    CipherData dat = new CipherData(encr, secret);
    XmlSerializer xml = new XmlSerializer(typeof(CipherData));
    FileStream fos = new FileStream(outFile, FileMode.Create);
    xml.Serialize(fos, dat);
    fos.Close();

    Console.Write("generated XML Encrypted {0} file", outFile);
}
```

To decrypt the encrypted file, we use the `Decrypt()` method. First, we need to de-serialize `CipherData`, and read the private key from the file. We then use the `RSAPKCS1KeyExchangeDeformatter` class to find out the secret key. Finally, we repeat the XOR process; since this is a symmetrical process, it will yield the original clear text file:

```
public static void Decrypt(string keyFile, string inFile, string outFile)
{
    RSACryptoServiceProvider rsa = File2Key(keyFile);

    FileStream fis = new FileStream(inFile, FileMode.Open);
    XmlSerializer xml = new XmlSerializer(typeof(CipherData));
    CipherData dat = (CipherData)xml.Deserialize(fis);
    fis.Close();

    RSAPKCS1KeyExchangeDeformatter dfmt = new
                                RSAPKCS1KeyExchangeDeformatter(rsa);
    byte[] secret = dfmt.DecryptKeyExchange(dat.cipherSecret);

    MemoryStream ms = new MemoryStream(dat.cipherValue);
    XorRand xoro = new XorRand(secret);
    FileStream fos = new FileStream(outFile, FileMode.Create);
    xoro.XorStream(ms, fos);
    fos.Close();

    Console.Write("Generated DECRYPTED {0} file", outFile);
}
```

A secret key is generated using the MakeSecret() method:

```
private static byte[] MakeSecret()
{
    return BitConverter.GetBytes(((long)(new Random()).Next()));
}
```

We also need a method for loading an XML file into a key:

```
public static RSACryptoServiceProvider File2Key(string keyFile)
{
    string xstr = FileUtil.LoadString(keyFile);
    RSACryptoServiceProvider rsa = new RSACryptoServiceProvider();
    rsa.FromXmlString(xstr);

    return rsa;
}
```

The Main() method is the entry point of this console utility; from here, we simply call the Encrypt() and Decrypt() methods:

```
public static void Main(string [] args)
{

    if(args.Length != 4)
    {
        Console.WriteLine("Usage: FileCrypt <E|D> <key xml> <in> <out>");
        Console.WriteLine(" E= Encrypt, D= Decrypt (needs private key)");
        Environment.Exit(1);
    }

    if(args[0].ToUpper().StartsWith("E"))
        Encrypt(args[1], args[2], args[3]);
    else
        Decrypt(args[1], args[2], args[3]);
}
} // End of the FileCrypt class
```

Next we provide the `EncryptedData` and `CipherData` structs used to represent the encrypted data:

```
[XmlRootAttribute(Namespace="http://www.w3.org/2001/04/xmlenc#",
                  ElementName = "EncryptedData",
                  IsNullable = false)]
public struct EncryptedData
{
    public KeyInfo    keyInfo;
    public CipherData data;    // encrypted signed XML
}
```

```
[XmlRootAttribute(ElementName = "CipherData")]
public struct CipherData
{
    public CipherData(byte[] val, byte[] sec)
    {
        cipherValue = val;
        cipherSecret = sec;
    }
    [XmlElementAttribute(ElementName = "CipherSecret")]
    public byte[] cipherSecret;

    [XmlElementAttribute(ElementName = "CipherValue")]
    public byte[] cipherValue;
}
```

Finally, we define an `XorRand` class to provide an XOR-based encryption and decryption utility.

```
public class XorRand
{
    public XorRand(byte[] secret)
    {
        string passwd = Convert.ToBase64String(secret);
        rand = new PasswordDeriveBytes(passwd,SALT);

        xorBuf = rand.GetBytes(LEN);
        count = 0;
    }

    public void XorStream(Stream inx, Stream outx)
    {
        int b;
        while((b = inx.ReadByte()) != -1)
            outx.WriteByte(crypt((byte)b));
    }

    public byte crypt(byte b)
    {
        byte by = b;
        by ^= xorBuf[count++];
        if(count >= xorBuf.Length)
        {
            xorBuf = rand.GetBytes(LEN);
            count = 0;
        }
        return by;
    }
}
```

```
        private byte [] xorBuf;
        private static byte[] SALT = {0xC0,0xFF,0xE};
        private const int LEN = 128;
        private int count;
        private PasswordDeriveBytes rand;
}
```

This code instantiates three objects – XorRand, EncryptedData, and CipherData. These objects will be refined and incorporated in the next phase. We have also deduced the encryption and decryption methods, which we will incorporate in our Crypton class.

The core encryption algorithm is contained in the code repeated below. This has been extracted from the Encrypt() method of the FileCrypt class:

```
RSAPKCS1KeyExchangeFormatter fmt = new RSAPKCS1KeyExchangeFormatter(rsa);
byte[] tmp = MakeSecret();
byte[] secret = fmt.CreateKeyExchange(tmp);
MemoryStream ms = new MemoryStream();
XorRand xoro = new XorRand(tmp);
xoro.XorStream(fis, ms);
```

First, we obtain a randomly-generated secret key by calling our MakeSecret() method. This is then encrypted using the RSAPKCS1KeyExchangeFormatter class of the .NET cryptographic API. This class applies the standard key exchange technique using the Public and Private Key Cryptography System (PKCS). We use the public key of the target web service for this purpose. For decryption, however, we need to know the private key.

Decryption is achieved using the following code snippet from the FileCrypt.cs file. This can be found in the Decrypt() method of the FileCrypt class:

```
RSAPKCS1KeyExchangeDeformatter
dfmt = new RSAPKCS1KeyExchangeDeformatter(rsa);
byte[] secret = dfmt.DecryptKeyExchange(dat.cipherSecret);
MemoryStream ms = new MemoryStream(dat.cipherValue);
XorRand xoro = new XorRand(secret);
FileStream fos = new FileStream(outFile, FileMode.Create);
xoro.XorStream(ms, fos);
```

FileCrypt.cs is compiled using the following command:

csc FileCrypt.cs FileUtil.cs

To encrypt a file (for example, the FileUtil.cs file itself), we use the public key:

FileCrypt E PubKey.xml FileUtil.cs delme.xml

This produces an XML-formatted file similar to this (the encrypted data is abridged here):

```
<?xml version="1.0"?>
<CipherData xmlns:xsi="http://www.w3.org/2001/XMLSchema-instance"
            xmlns:xsd="http://www.w3.org/2001/XMLSchema">
```

```
        <CipherSecret>Gx3CEpBAJstX ... ZzYY=</CipherSecret>
        <CipherValue>eNXTvT9RZtahc ... FAPH4=</CipherValue>
    </CipherData>
```

The `<CipherSecret>` element contains the Base64-encoded secret key, encrypted using the target public key. Thus, only the person who holds the private key can know the secret key. The secret key is used to encrypt the actual content, using a simple XOR operation. The `XorRand` class does the job of generating a pseudo-random sequence and performs an XOR operation on this and the original data stream. XOR is symmetrical, so we can decrypt the file using the same operation.

To decrypt the encrypted file, we use the command given below. Notice that we will to use the private key for decryption, and the public key to encrypt the file:

`FileCrypt D PrvKey.xml delme.xml delme.txt`

The `delme.txt` file will now contain the original content of the file we encrypted.

The Crypton Class

On the basis of this command-line utility, we will now design a class called `Crypton`. This class will be responsible for the signing and encryption process, and the reverse process of decryption and verification of the digital signature. The signing code has been imported from Iteration 2. This class (along with `XorRand` and `EncryptedData`) is packaged into a file called `PeerCrypt.cs` in the `lev3` subdirectory. These classes will ultimate find their way into Iteration 4, with minor modifications and a few enhancements.

```
public class Crypton
{
    public Crypton(RSACryptoServiceProvider myKey)
    {
        this.myKey = myKey;
    }
```

The first method we define, `SignEncrypt()`, is used for signing and encryption. This method is the top-level method, which serves as a convenient point for accessing this class. This method in turn calls separate `Sign()` and `Encrypt()` methods:

```
public MemoryStream SignEncrypt(Stream soapMsg,
                                RSACryptoServiceProvider targ)
{
    byte[] rawIn = Stream2Bytes(soapMsg);
    XmlElement ele = Sign(rawIn);
    FileUtil.SaveString("delme-sign.xml",ele.OuterXml);
    Console.WriteLine("___ delme-sign.xml ___ created");
    return Encrypt(ele, targ );
}
```

The next method, `DecryptVerfiy()`, is complementary to the `SignEncrypt()` method. It reverses the process, by decrypting the message and verifying the signature:

```
public MemoryStream DecryptVerify(Stream encod,
                                out RSACryptoServiceProvider targ)
{
    MemoryStream ret = null;
```

```
        XmlElement ele = Decrypt(encod);
        ret = Verify(ele, out targ);
        return ret;
    }
```

To sign the data, we first convert it into Base64-encoded format and put into a `<SOAP-BOX>` XML element. This is then signed using the sender's private key. This signed object is encrypted using the receiver's public key, so that no one other than the intended receiver can decrypt it:

```
    private XmlElement Sign(byte[] rawIn)
    {
        // 1st: box the SOAP message into a signable entity.
        XmlDocument xdox = new XmlDocument();
        xdox.LoadXml("<SOAP-BOX>" + Convert.ToBase64String(rawIn) +
                                                    "</SOAP-BOX>");

        // 2nd: prepare to sign
        DataObject datObj = new DataObject();
        datObj.Data = xdox.ChildNodes;
        datObj.Id = "soap-msg";

        SHA1 sha1 = SHA1.Create("SHA1");
        byte[] hash = sha1.ComputeHash(rawIn);

        Signature sig = new Signature();
        sig.ObjectList = new Object[] { datObj };
        sig.SignatureValue = myKey.SignData(rawIn,"SHA1");

        sig.SignedInfo = new SignedInfo();
        //sig.SignedInfo.Id = "AAA";
        sig.SignedInfo.SignatureMethod = myKey.SignatureAlgorithm ;

        // 2.5: Add the public key derived from my private key to signature.
        RSACryptoServiceProvider myPubKey = new RSACryptoServiceProvider();
        myPubKey.FromXmlString(myKey.ToXmlString(false));
        RSAKeyValue rsaKey = new RSAKeyValue(myPubKey);

        sig.KeyInfo = new KeyInfo();
        sig.KeyInfo.AddClause(rsaKey);

        Reference refx = new Reference();
        refx.Uri = "#"+ datObj.Id;
        refx.DigestMethod = "SHA1";
        refx.DigestValue = hash;

        refx.AddTransform(new XmlDsigXPathTransform());
        refx.AddTransform(new XmlDsigBase64Transform());
        sig.SignedInfo.AddReference(refx);

        return sig.GetXml();
    }
```

To encrypt the data, we generate a secret key, and then use our `XorRand` class to XOR the message with the secret key. The secret key itself is encrypted using the public key, so it can be known to the program that has access to the private key of the pair. We use `RSAPKCS1KeyExchangeFormatter` to send the secret key:

```
private MemoryStream Encrypt(XmlElement ele, RSACryptoServiceProvider targ)
{
    // 3rd: Convert signed XML to encrypted XML object
    MemoryStream msx = new MemoryStream();
    string xstr = ele.OuterXml;
    StreamWriter stw = new StreamWriter(msx);
    stw.Write(xstr);
    stw.Flush();

    FileUtil.SaveBytes("Delme-PRE-ENC.xml", msx.ToArray());
    Console.WriteLine("GENERATED Delme-PRE-ENC.xml");

    byte[] tmp = XorRand.MakeSecret();
    RSAPKCS1KeyExchangeFormatter fmt = new
                                       RSAPKCS1KeyExchangeFormatter(targ);
    byte[] secret = fmt.CreateKeyExchange(tmp);
    XorRand xoro = new XorRand(tmp);

    msx.Position = 0;
    MemoryStream msOut = new MemoryStream();
    xoro.XorStream(msx, msOut);
    byte[] encr = msOut.ToArray();

    Console.WriteLine("byte[] {0}",encr.Length);

    // 4th: created encrypted XML
    CipherData cyph = new CipherData(encr,secret);
    EncryptedData encDat = new EncryptedData();
    encDat.Data = cyph;

    if(targ == null)
        throw new Exception("ERROR: Target Public Key is null");

    Console.WriteLine(targ);

    RSAKeyValue rsaKey =  new RSAKeyValue(targ);
    encDat.keyInfo = new KeyInfo();
    encDat.keyInfo.AddClause(rsaKey);

    MemoryStream ret = new MemoryStream();
    Console.WriteLine("Enc: {0}",typeof(EncryptedData));
    XmlSerializer xml = new XmlSerializer(typeof(EncryptedData));
    xml.Serialize(ret,encDat);

    ret.Position =0;

    return ret;
}
```

The Decrypt() method, as the name suggests, is used for decryption. We use the private key and the RSAPKCS1KeyExchangeDeformatter class to decrypt the secret key. Using the the XorRand class, we XOR the secret key with the encrypted data to decrypt the message:

```
private XmlElement Decrypt(Stream encod)
{
    Console.WriteLine("Decrypt 1");
    // 1st: Deserialize the EncryptedData & Dencrypt
    XmlSerializer xml = new XmlSerializer(typeof(EncryptedData));
    XmlSerializer xml = new XmlSerializer(typeof(encryptedData));
    encod.Position = 0;
```

```
        EncryptedData encDat = (EncryptedData)xml.Deserialize(encod);
        RSAPKCS1KeyExchangeDeformatter dfmt = new
                                    RSAPKCS1KeyExchangeDeformatter(myKey);
        byte[] secret = dfmt.DecryptKeyExchange(encDat.Data.cipherSecret);
        MemoryStream msIn = new MemoryStream(encDat.Data.cipherValue);
        MemoryStream msOut = new MemoryStream();
        XorRand xoro = new XorRand(secret);
        xoro.XorStream(msIn, msOut);
        msOut.Position = 0;

        FileUtil.SaveBytes("111.txt", msOut.ToArray());
        Console.WriteLine("Decrypt 2 Generated 111.txt");
        XmlTextReader xtr = new XmlTextReader(msOut);
        XmlDocument xdox = new XmlDocument();
        xdox.Load(xtr);

        return xdox.DocumentElement;
    }
```

When it is received, the encrypted and signed document must first be decrypted using the receiver's private key, and then the signature must be verified using the sender's public key. Both the sending and receiving peers must know each other's public key, just as they must know each other's e-mail addresses to send a document:

```
    private MemoryStream Verify(XmlElement ele,
                            out RSACryptoServiceProvider targ)
    {
        Signature sig = new Signature();
        sig.LoadXml(ele);
        DataObject datObj = (DataObject)sig.ObjectList[0];
        XmlNodeList soapBox = datObj.Data;

        byte[] dat = Convert.FromBase64String(soapBox.InnerText);

        IEnumerator enu = sig.KeyInfo.GetEnumerator(typeof(RSAKeyValue));
        enu.MoveNext();
        RSAKeyValue rsaKey = (RSAKeyValue) enu.Current;
        string xs = rsaKey.Key.ToXmlString(false);
        targ = new RSACryptoServiceProvider();
        targ.FromXmlString(xs);

        byte[] sigValue = sig.SignatureValue;
        MemoryStream ret = null;

        if(targ.VerifyData(dat, "SHA1",sigValue))
            ret = new MemoryStream(dat);

        return ret;
    }
```

The next two methods are utility methods for manipulating streams, which are used internally. The first copies the stream into a byte array:

```
    protected byte[] Stream2Bytes(Stream stream)
    {
        return CopyStream(stream).ToArray();
    }
```

The second copies a stream into a new `MemoryStream`; this is similar to the `CopyStream()` method of our `Logger` class from Iteration 1:

```
    protected MemoryStream CopyStream(Stream stream)
    {
        MemoryStream streamCopy = new MemoryStream();

        const int bufferSize = 1024;
        byte[] buffer = new byte[bufferSize];

        int readCount;
        do
        {
            readCount = stream.Read(buffer, 0, bufferSize);
            if (readCount > 0)
                streamCopy.Write(buffer, 0, readCount);
        } while (readCount > 0);

        // Close original stream
        stream.Close();

        streamCopy.Position = 0;
        return streamCopy;
    }

    protected RSACryptoServiceProvider myKey;
} // End of the Crypton class
```

This class forms the core engine for the encryption, signing, decryption, and verification of our data. This design could not have been achieved without the prior prototypes.

At this point, let me highlight a minor refinement – the static method for generating the secret key is now moved to the `XorRand` class:

```
    public static byte[] MakeSecret()
    {
        return BitConverter.GetBytes(((long)(new Random()).Next()));
    }
```

EncrDox.cs

We now need to test the `Crypton` class. To do so, we have devised another console utility, similar to `FileCrypt.cs`, except that this utility also signs the document. This program is called `EncrDox.cs`, and we can use it to encrypt and sign a document and send it to a friend. We must supply the public key of the receiver to encrypt the document, and our own private key to sign it. The receiver, who has sole access to their private key, can only decrypt the document. The receiver then verifies the signature, using the public key of the sender.

To sign and encrypt the document, we call the `SignEncrypt()` method of the `Crypton` class:

```
    public static byte[] Encrypt()
    {
        Crypton cryp = new Crypton(prvKey);
        FileStream fs = new FileStream(inFile, FileMode.Open);
        MemoryStream ms = cryp.SignEncrypt(fs, targKey);
        fs.Close();

        return ms.ToArray();
    }
```

The process is reversed at the receiving end:

```
public static byte[] Decrypt()
{
    Crypton cryp = new Crypton(prvKey);
    FileStream fs = new FileStream(inFile, FileMode.Open);
    Console.WriteLine("DECRYPT-->{0}, ", inFile);
    MemoryStream ms = cryp.DecryptVerify(fs, out targKey);
    fs.Close();
    byte[] ret = null;
    if(ms != null)
        ret = ms.ToArray();

    return ret;
}
```

Note that during the signature verification, we also get back the signer's public key. This key can be compared with the receiver's record to verify that this key is indeed the authenticated one, sent out of band (the phrase "out of band" is used in security parlance to indicate information that is pre-communicated using a different channel of communication).

The full code for the `EncrDox.cs` utility is listed below:

```
using System;
using System.IO;
using System.Security.Cryptography;
using System.Security.Cryptography.Xml;
using System.Runtime.Serialization.Formatters.Soap;
using System.Xml.Serialization;
using System.Xml;
using System.Text;
using System.Collections;
using PeerCrypt;

public class EncrDox
{
    public  static RSACryptoServiceProvider prvKey;
    public  static RSACryptoServiceProvider targKey;
    public  static string inFile;
    public  static string outFile;

    public static void Main(string [] args)
    {
        if(args.Length != 5)
        {
            Console.WriteLine("To Encrypt: TestEnc <E|D> <my key xml> " +
                                            "<target key> <in> <out>");
            Console.WriteLine(" E = Encrypt, D= Decrypt");
            Environment.Exit(1);
        }
        bool toEncr = args[0].ToUpper().StartsWith("E");

        string xstr = FileUtil.LoadString(args[1]);

        prvKey = new RSACryptoServiceProvider();
        prvKey.FromXmlString(xstr);
        Console.WriteLine("my Key File: " + args[1]);
```

```
        inFile = args[3];
        outFile = args[4];

        string op = "Encrypted";

        byte[] outbuf = null;

        if(!toEncr)
        {
            op = "Decrypted";
            try
            {
                outbuf = Decrypt();
                // Save the target public key of the sender
                if(outbuf != null)
                {
                    string trgx = targKey.ToXmlString(false);
                    FileUtil.SaveString(args[2], trgx);
                    Console.WriteLine("Target key file save as {0}",args[2]);
                }
                else
                    Console.WriteLine("Decryption Failed ");
            }
            catch(Exception x)
            {
                Console.WriteLine(x.StackTrace);
                Console.WriteLine("***\nERROR: Decrypting\n{0}\n***",x.Message);
            }
        }
        else
        {
            // Load the target public key
            xstr = FileUtil.LoadString(args[2]);
            targKey = new RSACryptoServiceProvider();
            targKey.FromXmlString(xstr);
            Console.WriteLine("Target public key file: " + args[2]);
            try
            {
                outbuf = Encrypt();
            }
            catch(Exception x)
            {
                Console.WriteLine(x.StackTrace);
                Console.WriteLine("***\nERROR: Encrypting\n{0}\n***", x.Message);
            }
        }

        /* Write back to output file */
        if(outFile != null)
        {
            FileUtil.SaveBytes(outFile, outbuf);
            Console.WriteLine(op + " input [" + inFile + "] to output [" +
                                                        outFile + "]");
        }
        else
            Console.WriteLine("Output files not created");
}

public static byte[] Encrypt()
{
```

```
            Crypton cryp = new Crypton(prvKey);
            FileStream fs = new FileStream(inFile, FileMode.Open);
            MemoryStream ms = cryp.SignEncrypt(fs, targKey);
            fs.Close();

            return ms.ToArray();
        }

        public static byte[] Decrypt()
        {
            Crypton cryp = new Crypton(prvKey);
            FileStream fs = new FileStream(inFile, FileMode.Open);
            Console.WriteLine("DECRYPT-->{0},", inFile);
            MemoryStream ms = cryp.DecryptVerify(fs, out targKey);
            fs.Close();
            byte[] ret = null;
            if(ms != null)
                ret = ms.ToArray();

            return ret;
        }
    }
```

To compile this file, type the following command at the console:

```
csc EncrDox.cs FileUtil.cs PeerCrypt.
cs /r:System.Runtime.Serialization.Formation.Formatters.Soap.dll
```

You will need a couple of key pairs to test this utility; these can be generated using the MakeRSAKey.cs program discussed earlier. To test the EncrDox.cs program, I created two pairs of keys called PrvKey1.xml and PubKey1.xml, and PrvKey2.xml and PubKey2.xml. I also copied the content of FileUtil.cs into another file called input.txt, to use it as the target document.

Assuming that the sender's private key is PrvKey1.xml, and the receiver has access to PrvKey2.xml, the sender would use PrvKey1.xml to sign the document and PubKey2.xml to encrypt it. The resulting document, called encr.xml, is to be transported over an unsecured channel. The command to generate this is:

```
EncrDox E PrvKey1.xml PubKey2.xml input.txt encr.xml
```

An abridged version of the encrypted and signed document is listed below. Notice that it is an XML-formatted document containing Base64-encoded binary data:

```
<?xml version="1.0"?>
<EncryptedData xmlns:xsi="http://www.w3.org/2001/XMLSchema-instance"
               xmlns:xsd="http://www.w3.org/2001/XMLSchema"
               xmlns="http://www.w3.org/2001/04/xmlenc#">
    <KeyInfo xmlns="http://www.w3.org/2000/09/xmldsig#">
        <KeyValue xmlns="http://www.w3.org/2000/09/xmldsig#">
            <RSAKeyValue>
                <Modulus>wnG3HszU1fqu/axyaM11YtFr ... LinfeuZhITMtlM=</Modulus>
                <Exponent>AQAB</Exponent>
            </RSAKeyValue>
        </KeyValue>
    </KeyInfo>
```

```
        <CipherData xmlns="http://www.w3.org/2001/04/xmlenc#2">
            <CipherSecret>AQjXombTpKnpvDlulp4cmA ... vSG8pKw=</CipherSecret>
            <CipherValue>KL1dHvFOF1U4HYiIGUdl5M ... de/ST4P8HCE</CipherValue>
        </CipherData>
    </EncryptedData>
```

The `<CipherValue>` XML element contains the Base64-encoded signature, which is XOR-encrypted using the secret key. This secret key is itself encrypted using the receiver's public key, and this Base64-encoded, encrypted secret key is contained in the `<CipherSecret>` element.

The signature is also contained in an XML document (encr-sign.xml):

```
<Signature xmlns="http://www.w3.org/2000/09/xmldsig#">
    <SignedInfo>
        <CanonicalizationMethod
                Algorithm="http://www.w3.org/TR/2001/REC-xml-c14n-20010315" />
        <SignatureMethod
                Algorithm="http://www.w3.org/2000/09/xmldsig#rsa-sha1" />
        <Reference URI="#soap-msg">
            <Transforms>
                <Transform
                    Algorithm="http://www.w3.org/TR/1999/REC-xpath-19991116">
                    <XPath></XPath>
                </Transform>
                <Transform Algorithm="http://www.w3.org/2000/09/xmldsig#base64" />
            </Transforms>
            <DigestMethod Algorithm="SHA1" />
            <DigestValue>xCvUEIHTc5n+pjL+mH8j3twmzvg=</DigestValue>
        </Reference>
    </SignedInfo>
    <SignatureValue>MPnK7RxxrtGH9 ... SDGZvEgWc=</SignatureValue>
    <KeyInfo>
        <KeyValue xmlns="http://www.w3.org/2000/09/xmldsig#">
            <RSAKeyValue>
                <Modulus>vehnUHf7Fw6+l ... xw2SuTyzDZ29xE5U=</Modulus>
                <Exponent>AQAB</Exponent>
            </RSAKeyValue>
        </KeyValue>
    </KeyInfo>
    <Object Id="soap-msg">
        <SOAP-BOX xmlns="">dXNpbmcg ... Ow0KICAgIH0NCn0=</SOAP-BOX>
    </Object>
</Signature>
```

The public key of the signer is contained in the `<KeyInfo>` element. The `<SOAP-BOX>` element contains the Base64-encoded original document.

On receiving the encrypted and signed document, the receiver needs to supply their private key to decrypt the document:

```
EncrDox D PrvKey2.xml senders_pub.xml encr.xml decr.txt
```

The RSAComparer Class

The signature is verified using the key supplied with this document and extracted to senders_pub.xml. This file is same as the public key PubKey1.xml. The public key supplied and used for signing needs to be compared with the key file that we know belongs to the sender. The RSA object's Equals() method does not compare the keys, so we will need to write a custom class to do it:

```
public class RSAComparer : IComparer
{
    public RSAComparer() {}

    public int Compare(Object r1, Object r2)
    {
        bool ret = false;
        if((r1 != null) && (r2 != null) && (r1 is RSA) && (r2 is RSA))
            ret = Equals((RSA)r1, (RSA)r2);

        return ((ret) ? 0 : -1);
    }

    public static bool Equals(byte[] b1, byte[] b2)
    {
        if((b1 == null) || (b2 == null) || (b1.Length != b1.Length))
            return false;

        bool ret=true;
        for(int i=0; (ret) && (i < b1.Length); i++)
            ret = (b1[i] == b2[i]);

        return ret;
    }

    public static bool Equals(RSA r1, RSA r2)
    {
        if(r1 == null || r2 == null)
            return false;

        RSAParameters p1 = r1.ExportParameters(false);
        RSAParameters p2 = r2.ExportParameters(false);
        bool eqMod = Equals(p1.Modulus, p2.Modulus);
        bool eqExp = Equals(p1.Exponent, p2.Exponent);

        return (eqMod && eqExp);
    }
}
```

The RSAComparer class implements the IComparer interface, so we can pass it in Hashtables or other .NET Framework classes. The class has two overloads of the Equals() methods. The simpler takes two byte arrays; if one of these is null, or if the lengths of the arrays are different, we return false. Otherwise, we iterate through the arrays, checking that each byte matches.

The second overload takes two RSA objects. We call the ExportParameters() methods on both of these, passing in false, since we only want to compare the public key information. We then make two calls to the first overload of our Equals() method, passing in the Modul and Exponent of each RSA object as byte arrays.

This completes our look at Iteration 3, so we can now move on to Iteration 4, where we will integrate our cryptography class with the channel sink, to create a P2P application-layer security channel.

Iteration 4 – Plugging Cryptography into the Channel Sink

Iteration 4 is an integration stage, where we will combine the functionality of Iterations 1 and 3. Iteration 2 was primarily devoted to refining the message design.

In this stage, we will plug the cryptographic model developed in Iteration 3 into the boilerplate channel sink developed in Iteration 1.

Consolidating the Cryptography Classes

The first step is to consolidate the utility and helper classes into a namespace called `Peer.Crypt`. This namespace is contained in the file `lev4\PeerCryptUtil.cs`. We will look quickly at the main points of this file.

```
namespace Peer.Crypt
{
using System;
using System.IO;
using System.Security.Cryptography;
using System.Security.Cryptography.Xml;
using System.Runtime.Serialization.Formatters.Soap;
using System.Xml.Serialization;
using System.Xml;
using System.Text;
using System.Collections;
```

Mapping Public Keys to Web Services

If our web service clients are to be able to decrypt the data received from the web service, they will need access to the public key of that web service (given prior knowledge of its URL). We'll give them this by creating an object that contains the services' URLs and the keys as key-value pairs. The client will be able to look up the URL in this object, and retrieve the associated public key.

To achieve this, our `Peer.Crypt` namespace has a new interface called `IKeyStore`, which contains methods for retrieving the key for a given URL, and for adding and deleting entries in the store. We'll also provide methods for loading and saving a store. This interface is the abstract model that we will use to represent a public key store:

```
public interface IKeyStore
{
    ICollection Uris { get; }
    RSA  GetPublicKey(string uri);
    void RegisterUri(string uri, RSA pubKey);

    bool IsRegistered(string uri);
    void Deregister(string uri);
    void Load(string fileName);
    void Save(string fileName);
}
```

We also have a `Hashtable`-based implementation of this interface. For most methods, this simply maps calls to the `Hashkeystore` directly to the `Hashtable`'s methods, but we also provide a `GetPublicKey()` method to retrieve the public key of a web service from its URI by loading the XML-formatted key into an `RSA` object using its `FromXmlString()` method. Finally, we also provide `Save()` and `Load()` methods, which respectively save the `Hashtable` in SOAP format to a file and populate the `Hashtable` from a saved file:

```
public class HashKeyStore : IKeyStore
{
    public HashKeyStore() {}

    public HashKeyStore(string fileName)
    {
        Load(fileName);
    }

    public ICollection Uris { get { return tab.Keys; } }

    public RSA GetPublicKey(string uri)
    {
        string xtr = (string)tab[uri];
        RSA pubKey = null;
        if(xtr != null)
        {
            pubKey = new RSACryptoServiceProvider();
            pubKey.FromXmlString(xtr);
        }

        return pubKey;
    }

    public void RegisterUri(string uri, RSA pubKey)
    {
        tab.Add(uri, pubKey.ToXmlString(false));
    }

    public bool IsRegistered(string uri)
    {
        return tab.Contains(uri);
    }

    public void Deregister(string uri)
    {
        tab.Remove(uri);
    }

    public void Load(string fileName)
    {
        FileStream fs = new FileStream(fileName, FileMode.Open);
        SoapFormatter soap = new SoapFormatter();
        tab = (Hashtable)soap.Deserialize(fs);
        fs.Close();
    }

    public void Save(string fileName)
    {
        FileStream fs = new FileStream(fileName, FileMode.Create);
        SoapFormatter soap = new SoapFormatter();
        soap.Serialize(fs, tab);
```

465

```
        fs.Close();
    }

    protected Hashtable tab = new Hashtable();
}
```

We have already walked through the code of the Crypton class in the previous iteration, so we won't repeat the code here. As we saw, this class encapsulates the process of signature and encryption at one end and decryption and verification at the other. The two methods are SignEncrypt and VerifyDecrypt respectively. We also need the RSAComparer helper class and the EncryptedData and CipherData structs used by Crypton. Finally, we also include our FileUtil class from Chapter 11. Again, we won't repeat the code for these here.

Let's pack this up into a DLL assembly:

```
csc /t:library PeerCryptUtil.cs /r:System.Runtime.Serialization.Formatters.Soap.dll
```

This generates a DLL file called PeerCryptUtil.dll.

Managing the Key Store Manually

We now need a utility to maintain this key store. As discussed earlier, the public keys are communicated out of band. Associating the URL with the public key and appending them to the key storage can be automated by a discovery-based component in the peer application.

For our proof-of-concept implementation, we have developed a command-line utility that allows us to maintain the key store manually (ManageKeyStore.cs). This utility provides methods to add, delete, replace, and list entries in our Hashkeystore class:

```
using System;
using System.IO;
using System.Security.Cryptography;
using System.Security.Cryptography.Xml;
using System.Runtime.Serialization.Formatters.Soap;
using System.Xml.Serialization;
using System.Xml;
using System.Text;
using System.Collections;
using System.Reflection;
using Peer.Crypt;

public class ManageKeyStore
{
    public static void Main(string[] args)
    {
        if(args.Length > 5 || args.Length < 2)
        {
            Console.WriteLine("Invalid params");
            UsageAndExit();
        }

        Type myType = typeof(ManageKeyStore);
        MethodInfo cmd = myType.GetMethod(args[0].ToUpper());

        if(cmd == null)
            UsageAndExit();
```

```
      else
      {
         ParameterInfo[] pars = cmd.GetParameters();
         if(pars.Length != args.Length)
         {
            Console.WriteLine("Invalid number of params");
            UsageAndExit();
         }
         try
         {
            cmd.Invoke(null,args);
         }
         catch(Exception ex)
         {
            Console.WriteLine(ex.StackTrace);
            Console.WriteLine(ex.Message);
         }
      }
   }

public static void INIT(string ignore, string fileName)
{
   HashKeyStore keyStore = new HashKeyStore();
   RSACryptoServiceProvider prvKey = new RSACryptoServiceProvider();
   keyStore.RegisterUri("localhost", prvKey);

   Save(keyStore, fileName);

   Console.WriteLine("Initialized Hash Key Store [{0}]", fileName);
}

public static void DELETE(string ignore, string fileName, string uri)
{
   HashKeyStore keyStore = Load(fileName);

   if(!keyStore.IsRegistered(uri))
   {
      Console.WriteLine("uri[{0}] NOT present! Remember Uri has case",
                                                             uri);
   }
   else
   {
      keyStore.Deregister(uri);
      Save(keyStore, fileName);
      Console.WriteLine("REMOVED uri[{0}] From file {1}", uri, fileName);
   }
}

public static void LIST(string ignore, string fileName)
{
   HashKeyStore keyStore = Load(fileName);
   foreach(string uri in keyStore.Uris)
   {
      Console.WriteLine(uri);
   }
}

public static void ADD(string ignore, string fileName, string uri,
                                                  string xmlKeyFile)
{
```

467

```
         HashKeyStore keyStore = Load(fileName);
         if(keyStore.IsRegistered(uri))
         {
            Console.WriteLine("uri[{0}] already register use REPLACE option",
                                                              uri);
         }
         else
         {
            AddToStore(keyStore,uri,xmlKeyFile);
            Save(keyStore, fileName);
            Console.WriteLine("ADDed uri[{0}] with key[{1}] to key store {2}",
                                       uri, xmlKeyFile, fileName);
         }
      }

      public static void REPLACE(string ignore, string fileName, string uri,
                                                     string xmlKeyFile)
      {
         HashKeyStore keyStore = Load(fileName);

         if(!keyStore.IsRegistered(uri))
         {
            Console.WriteLine("uri[{0}] NOT present, but does not matter", uri);
         }
         AddToStore(keyStore,uri,xmlKeyFile);
         Save(keyStore, fileName);
         Console.WriteLine("ADDed uri[{0}] with key[{1}] to key store {2}",
                                       uri, xmlKeyFile, fileName);
      }

      protected static HashKeyStore Load(string fileName)
      {
         HashKeyStore keyStore = new HashKeyStore();
         try
         {
            keyStore.Load(fileName);
         }
         catch(Exception x)
         {
            Console.WriteLine("Error in loading key store, because:");
            Console.WriteLine(x.Message);
            Environment.Exit(1);
         }

         return keyStore;
      }

      protected static void Save(HashKeyStore keyStore, string fileName)
      {
         try
         {
            keyStore.Save(fileName);
         }
         catch(Exception x)
         {
            Console.WriteLine("Error in saving key store, because:");
            Console.WriteLine(x.Message);
            Environment.Exit(1);
         }
      }
```

```
    protected static void AddToStore(HashKeyStore keyStore, string uri,
                                                     string xmlKeyFile)
    {
        RSACryptoServiceProvider pubKey = new RSACryptoServiceProvider();
        string xstr = FileUtil.LoadString(xmlKeyFile);
        pubKey.FromXmlString(xstr);

        keyStore.RegisterUri(uri, pubKey);
    }

    public static void UsageAndExit()
    {
        Console.WriteLine("ManageKeyStore <options> <serialized Hashtable> " +
                                                 "[<parameters>]*");
        foreach(string op in options)
            Console.WriteLine(op);
        Environment.Exit(1);
    }

    public static string [] options =
    {
        "Initialize: ManageKeyStore INIT <hash store file name>",
        "Add: ManageKeyStore ADD <hash store file> <uri> <pub key xml>",
        "Replace: ManageKeyStore REPLACE <hash store file> <uri> <pub key xml>",
        "List: ManageKeyStore LIST <hash store file>",
        "Delete: ManageKeyStore DELETE <hash store file> <uri>",
    };
}
```

To compile this utility, we use the command:

```
csc /r:PeerCryptUtil.dll /r:System.Runtime.Serialization.Formatters.Soap.dll
ManageKeyStore.cs
```

This utility uses a saved key store, so we need to initialize the key store before manipulating entries in it:

```
ManageKeyStore INIT KeyStore.xml
```

The above command creates and saves a new key store. An empty Hashtable cannot be deserialized, so we add a dummy entry for the localhost, with a new private key.

Now let us add a URL with a public key into the store:

```
ManageKeyStore ADD KeyStore.xml "http://localhost:8000/Dude/Talk2Me.soap"
PubKey1.xml
```

We are using here the PubKey1.xml file that we introduced and used in Iteration 3. This file has to be present in the same folder as ManageKeyStore.exe.

After this entry has been added, we can list the URL using the following command:

```
ManageKeyStore LIST KeyStore.xml
```

The KeyStore.xml file has a SOAP-serialized Hashtable. You might find it interesting to open it with IE 5.5 or above:

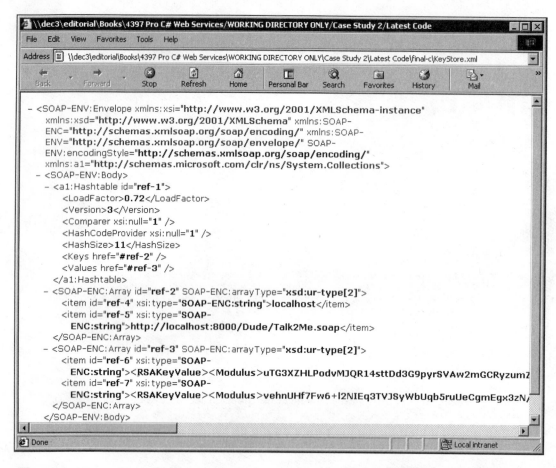

The `ManageKeyStore` utility has an innovative command parser, which uses reflection. This technique avoids a mile-long `switch...case` statement, such as plagues most command-line utilities. The pseudo-code for this is:

```
Type myType = typeof (ManageKeyStore);
...
MethodInfo cmd = myType.GetMethod(commandName);
...
ParameterInfo[] pars = cmd.GetParameters();
...
cmd.Invoke(null, args);
...
```

This technique allows commands to be added like methods, without disturbing the main routing code. For example, see the `INIT` command's method signature:

```
public static void INIT(string ignore, string fileName);
```

Putting it Together – A Security Channel Sink

We're now ready to put all the parts together by plugging in our `Crypton` class to the boilerplate channel sink in order to create our security channel sink. The code for this sink is contained in a file named `PeerSink.cs` in the `lev4` subdirectory:

```
using System;
using System.Collections;
using System.IO;
using System.Reflection;
using System.Runtime.Remoting.Channels;
using System.Runtime.Remoting.Channels.Http;
using System.Runtime.Remoting.Messaging;
using System.Runtime.Remoting.Metadata;
using System.Diagnostics;

using System.Security;
using System.Security.Cryptography;
using System.Security.Cryptography.Xml;

using Peer.Crypt;

namespace Peer.Channel
{
```

The PeerClientSinkProvider Class

Again, the first class that we implement will be the client sink provider:

```
public class PeerClientSinkProvider : IClientChannelSinkProvider
{
    private IClientChannelSinkProvider next = null;
    private Logger logger = new Logger();
    private RSACryptoServiceProvider prvKey = null;
    private HashKeyStore keyStore = null;

    public PeerClientSinkProvider()
    {
    }
```

As with `TraceClientSinkProvider`, this class has a second constructor beside the parameterless default constructor. In this constructor, we use the first argument (of type `IDictionary`), to collect the attributes provided in the configuration file. Again, we use the `verbose` attribute to control the level of debugging information displayed. However, we now also specify the client's private key file and the key storage file in the client-side configuration file (`HelloClient.exe.config`, in the `final-c` subdirectory):

```
<provider verbose="9" PrivateKeyFile="PrvKey2.xml" KeyStoreFile="KeyStore.xml"
          type="Peer.Channel.PeerClientSinkProvider, PeerSink" />
```

The `PrivateKeyFile` attribute contains the private key file for the sender; this key will be used to sign the sender's data and decrypt the response from the server. As well as loading the private key, we also load the key store:

```
        public PeerClientSinkProvider(IDictionary d, ICollection c)
        {
            string dbg = (string)d["verbose"];
            if(dbg != null && dbg.Length > 0)
                logger.verbose = int.Parse(dbg);
            Console.WriteLine("verbose = {0}", logger.verbose);

            logger.tag = "PeerClient";
            string prvKeyFile = (string)d["PrivateKeyFile"];
            if(prvKeyFile == null)
                throw new SecurityException("[PrivateKeyFile] attribute undefined");

            string keyStoreFile = (string) d["KeyStoreFile"];
            if(keyStoreFile == null)
                throw new SecurityException("[KeyStoreFile] attribute undefined");

            try
            {
                prvKey = new RSACryptoServiceProvider();
                string xstr = FileUtil.LoadString(prvKeyFile);
                prvKey.FromXmlString(xstr);
            }
            catch(Exception ex)
            {
                logger.Display(ex);
                throw new SecurityException("Error Loading Private Key");
            }

            try
            {
                keyStore = new HashKeyStore();
                keyStore.Load(keyStoreFile);
            }
            catch(Exception ex)
            {
                logger.Display(ex);
                throw new SecurityException("Error Loading Private Key");
            }

            logger.PrintStackPeer(("ctor of " + logger.tag +
                                              "@PeerClientSinkProvider"));
        }

        public IKeyStore KeyStore
        {
            get { return keyStore; }
        }
```

The CreateSink() method is again called by the HttpClientSink. The URL of the service is passed as one of the parameters to this method, and we pass it into the key store's GetPublicKey() method to retrieve the public key associated with the service:

```
        public IClientChannelSink CreateSink(IChannelSender channel, String url,
                                       Object remoteChannelData)
        {
            logger.WriteLine("***PeerClientSinkProvider.CreateSink() called");
            logger.WriteLine("   url: {0}", url);
            if(channel != null)
                logger.WriteLine("   Type of IChannelSender: {0}",channel.GetType());
```

```
        if(remoteChannelData != null)
            logger.WriteLine("   Type of remoteChannelData: {0}",
                                        remoteChannelData.GetType());

        IClientChannelSink nextSink = null;
        if (next != null)
        {
            logger.WriteLine(" calling next.CreateSink()");
            nextSink = next.CreateSink(channel, url, remoteChannelData);
            if (nextSink == null)
            {
                logger.WriteLine(" nextSink is null");
                return null;
            }
            else
                logger.WriteLine("After next.CreateSink() type is[{0}]",
                                        nextSink);
        }
        RSACryptoServiceProvider targetRsa = null;
        try
        {
            targetRsa = (RSACryptoServiceProvider)keyStore.GetPublicKey(url);
        }
        catch(Exception ex)
        {
            logger.Display(ex);
            throw new SecurityException("Error getting public key [" + url +
                                        "]", ex);
        }
        if(targetRsa == null)
        {
            throw new SecurityException(("No Public Key for [" + url + "]"));
        }

        return new PeerClientSink(nextSink, prvKey, targetRsa, logger);
    }
```

The Next property is very similar to that for the `TraceClientFormatterSinkProvider`:

```
    public IClientChannelSinkProvider Next
    {
        get
        {
            logger.WriteLine(" Property get Next of PeerClientSinkProvider");
            logger.PrintStackPeer("get Next@IClientChannelSinkProvider");
            return next;
        }
        set
        {
            next = value;
            logger.WriteLine(" Property set Next of " +
                    PeerClientFormatterSinkProvider called with [{0}]", value);
            logger.PrintStackPeer("set Next@IClientChannelSinkProvider");
        }
    }
}
```

The PeerClientSink Class

The actual channel sink is implemented in the internal `PeerClientSink` class. The constructor for this class differs from our previous sink in that it takes the client's private key and the server's public key as parameters, as well as the next sink in the chain and an instance of our `Logger` class. These keys are simply stored in protected fields of our class:

```
internal class PeerClientSink :
                        IMessageSink, IClientChannelSink, IChannelSinkBase
{
    private IClientChannelSink nextSink;
    protected Logger logger;
    protected RSACryptoServiceProvider prvKey;
    protected RSACryptoServiceProvider targetKey;

    public PeerClientSink(IClientChannelSink nextSink,
                        RSACryptoServiceProvider prvKey,
                        RSACryptoServiceProvider targetKey,
                        Logger logger)
    {
        this.logger = logger;
        this.prvKey = prvKey;
        this.targetKey = targetKey;

        logger.WriteLine("ctor {0} tag[{1}]", this, logger.tag);

        this.nextSink = nextSink;

        logger.WriteLine("The next IClientChannelSink --> {0}", nextSink);
    }
```

The asynchronous processing methods and the `GetRequestStream()` method of this sink don't use cryptography and are very similar to those of our `TraceClientSink` from Iteration 1:

```
    public IMessageCtrl AsyncProcessMessage(IMessage msg,
                                                IMessageSink replySink)
    {
        logger.WriteLine("***PeerClientFormatterSink.AsyncProcessMessage() " +
                                                "called");
        return NextSink.AsyncProcessMessage(msg, replySink);
    }

    public void AsyncProcessRequest(IClientChannelSinkStack sinkStack,
                                IMessage msg,
                                ITransportHeaders headers,
                                Stream stream)
    {
        logger.WriteLine("***{0}@AsyncProcessRequest() called", logger.tag);
        sinkStack.Push(this, null);
        nextSink.AsyncProcessRequest(sinkStack, msg, headers, stream);
    }

    public void AsyncProcessResponse(IClientResponseChannelSinkStack sinkStack,
                                object state,
                                ITransportHeaders headers,
                                Stream stream)
    {
```

```
      logger.WriteLine("***{0}@AsyncProcessResponse() called", logger.tag);
      nextSink.AsyncProcessResponse(sinkStack, state, headers, stream);
   }

   public Stream GetRequestStream(IMessage msg, ITransportHeaders headers)
   {
      logger.PrintStackPeer(("GetRequestStream@" + logger.tag));
      Stream ret = null;

      if(nextSink != null)
         ret = nextSink.GetRequestStream(msg, headers);

      logger.WriteLine("return Stream@{0} type -> {1}", logger.tag,ret);

      return ret;
   }
```

The `ProcessMessage()` method is the most important method of this class, since it is the focal point where both synchronous and asynchronous calls converge. This is the method we use to hook in our cryptographic manipulations. Using the `Crypton` class's `SignEncrypt()` method, we sign and encrypt the request and pass it to the next sink, and, on receiving the response, we verify and decrypt the response stream using the `VerifyDecrypt()` method:

```
   public void ProcessMessage(IMessage msg,ITransportHeaders requestHeaders,
                        Stream requestStream,
                        out ITransportHeaders responseHeaders,
                        out Stream responseStream )
   {
      logger.PrintStackPeer(("ProcessMessage@"+logger.tag));
      logger.PrintRequest(requestHeaders, ref requestStream);
      logger.PrintMessage(msg);

      Crypton crypt = new Crypton(prvKey);
      Stream sigEncStream = null;

      try
      {
         sigEncStream = crypt.SignEncrypt(requestStream, targetKey);
      }
      catch(Exception ex)
      {
         logger.Display(ex);
         throw new SecurityException("Error Signing & Encrypting ",ex);
      }

      logger.WriteLine("After SignEncrypt @"+logger.tag);
      logger.PrintStream(sigEncStream);
      sigEncStream.Position =0;

      //********* next sink *********
      nextSink.ProcessMessage(msg,requestHeaders, sigEncStream,
                                out responseHeaders, out responseStream);

      MemoryStream resStream = SafeCopy(ref responseStream);

      logger.WriteLine("After calling nextSink<{0}>.ProcessMessage @{1}",
                                            nextSink, logger.tag);

      Stream t = resStream;
      logger.PrintResponse(responseHeaders, ref t);
```

```
        RSACryptoServiceProvider retTargKey = null;

        MemoryStream decryptOut = null;
        try
        {
           decryptOut = crypt.DecryptVerify(resStream, out retTargKey);
        }
        catch(Exception ex)
        {
           logger.Display(ex);
           throw new SecurityException("Error Decrypting ",ex);
        }

        // TODO: To stop PLAY BACK attack, enforce a timestamp in encrypt
        // packet, or make the secret key to be encrypted & sent back.

        if((decryptOut == null) || !RSAComparer.Equals(targetKey,retTargKey))
        {
           throw new SecurityException(
                            "Decryption Error OR Under Intercept Attack");
        }

        logger.WriteLine("Post Decrypt ");
        logger.PrintStream(decryptOut);

        responseStream = decryptOut;
        TransportHeaders resHdr = new TransportHeaders();
        foreach (DictionaryEntry header in responseHeaders)
        {
           if(((string)header.Key) != "Content-Length")
              resHdr[header.Key] = header.Value;
        }
        responseHeaders = resHdr;
}
```

The remaining methods and properties of this class don't need to be plugged into our `Crypton` class:

```
public IMessage SyncProcessMessage(IMessage msg)
{
   logger.PrintStackPeer(("SyncProcessMessage@"+logger.tag));
   logger.WriteLine("*** Input Message ***");
   logger.PrintMessage(msg);

   logger.WriteLine("BEFORE calling nextSink<{0}>.SyncProcessMessage @{1}",
                                            nextSink, logger.tag);

   IMessage rmsg = NextSink.SyncProcessMessage(msg);

   logger.WriteLine("AFTER calling nextSink<{0}>.SyncProcessMessage @{1}",
                                            nextSink, logger.tag);
   logger.WriteLine("*** Output Message ***");
   logger.PrintMessage(msg);

   return msg;
}

public IDictionary Properties
{
```

```
            get
            {
                logger.PrintStackPeer((logger.tag+"@Properties"));
                return prop;
            }
        }

        private Hashtable prop = new Hashtable();

        public IClientChannelSink NextChannelSink
        {
            get { return nextSink;}
        }
        public IMessageSink NextSink
        {
            get
            {
                IMessageSink ret = null;
                for(IClientChannelSink nxt = nextSink; nxt != null;
                                        nxt = nxt.NextChannelSink)
                {
                    if(nxt is IMessageSink)
                    {
                        ret = (IMessageSink) nxt;
                        break;
                    }
                }

                return ret;
            }
        }
```

This class has one method that didn't exist for the tracer sink – `SafeCopy()`. We use this method to copy the response stream into a `MemoryStream` object, because the stream provided by the HTTP channel can only be read once:

```
    protected MemoryStream SafeCopy(ref Stream responseStream)
    {
        MemoryStream resStream = new MemoryStream();
        StreamWriter sw = new StreamWriter(resStream);
        StreamReader sr = new StreamReader(responseStream);
        string line;
        while ((line = sr.ReadLine()) != null)
        {
            sw.WriteLine(line);
        }
        sw.Flush();
        resStream.Position = 0;

        return resStream;
    }
}
```

The PeerServerChannelSinkProvider Class

We now move to the server side. Again, our first class will be the sink provider, which creates instances of our sink. As with the client sink provider, the server-side provider extracts the `verbose` level and the private key file from the configuration file:

```
<provider verbose="9" PrivateKeyFile="PrvKey1.xml"
        type="Peer.Channel.PeerServerChannelSinkProvider, PeerSink" />
```

Apart from loading this private key and storing it in a private field, the constructor for the server channel sink isn't much changed from our first iteration:

```
public class PeerServerChannelSinkProvider : IServerChannelSinkProvider
{
    private IServerChannelSinkProvider next = null;
    private Logger logger = new Logger();
    private RSACryptoServiceProvider prvKey = null;

    public PeerServerChannelSinkProvider()
    {
    }

    public PeerServerChannelSinkProvider(IDictionary d,
                                            ICollection providerData)
    {
        string dbg = (string)d["verbose"];
        if(dbg != null && dbg.Length > 0)
            logger.verbose = int.Parse(dbg);
        Console.WriteLine("verbose = {0}", logger.verbose);

        logger.tag = "PeerServer";

        string prvKeyFile = (string)d["PrivateKeyFile"];
        if(prvKeyFile == null)
            throw new SecurityException("[PrivateKeyFile] attribute undefined");

        try
        {
            prvKey = new RSACryptoServiceProvider();
            string xstr = FileUtil.LoadString(prvKeyFile);
            prvKey.FromXmlString(xstr);
        }
        catch(Exception ex)
        {
            logger.Display(ex);
            throw new SecurityException("Error Loading Private Key");
        }

        logger.PrintStackPeer(("ctor of " + logger.tag +
                                    "@PeerServerChannelSinkProvider"));
    }
```

The remaining methods and the Next property are also largely unchanged, except that in the CreateSink() method, we need to pass the private key into the constructor for the server sink:

```
public void GetChannelData(IChannelDataStore channelData)
{
    logger.WriteLine("{0}@GetChannelData({1})", logger.tag, channelData);
    if(channelData != null)
    {
        string [] uris = channelData.ChannelUris;
        if(uris != null)
            for(int i=0; i < uris.Length; i++)
```

```
                         logger.WriteLine("uri[{0}] = {1}", i, uris[i]);
            }
        logger.PrintStackPeer((logger.tag + "@GetChannelData"));
    }

    public IServerChannelSink CreateSink(IChannelReceiver channel)
    {
        logger.WriteLine("{0}@CreateSink({1})", logger.tag, channel);
        logger.PrintStackPeer((logger.tag + "@CreateSink"));

        IServerChannelSink nextSink = null;
        if (next != null)
        {
            logger.WriteLine("calling {0}@CreateSink({1})", next, channel);
            nextSink = next.CreateSink(channel);
        }
        return new PeerServerChannelSink(nextSink, prvKey, logger);
    }

    public IServerChannelSinkProvider Next
    {
        get
        {
            logger.PrintStackPeer((logger.tag + "@Next being called"));
            return next;
        }
        set
        {
            next = value;
        }
    }
}
```

The PeerServerChannelSink Class

The PeerServerChannelSink class is where we actually implement the server side of our cryptography sink. The constructor for the class (called by the provider's CreateSink() method) simply stores the private key, the next sink in the chain, and an instance of our Logger class in private fields:

```
internal class PeerServerChannelSink : IServerChannelSink
{
    private IServerChannelSink nextSink = null;
    private Logger logger;
    private RSACryptoServiceProvider prvKey = null;

    public PeerServerChannelSink(IServerChannelSink nextSink,
                  RSACryptoServiceProvider prvKey, Logger logger) : base()
    {
        this.nextSink = nextSink;
        this.logger = logger;
        this.prvKey = prvKey;

        logger.WriteLine("ctor {0}@PeerServerChannelSink({1})", logger.tag,
                                                    nextSink);
    }
```

The key work on the server side is again performed by the `ProcessMessage()` method. Here we decrypt and verify the incoming message, and extract the original SOAP message representing the method call. This message is passed on to the next message sink for the actual method call. The return values that are marshaled and repackaged into the returned SOAP message are encrypted using the client's public key and signed by the server's private key:

```
public ServerProcessing ProcessMessage(IServerChannelSinkStack sinkStack,
                                       IMessage requestMsg,
                                       ITransportHeaders requestHeaders,
                                       Stream requestStream,
                                       out IMessage msg,
                                       out ITransportHeaders responseHeaders,
                                       out Stream responseStream)
{

    MemoryStream reqCopyStream =
                        (MemoryStream)logger.CopyStream(requestStream);

    logger.WriteLine("Type of request stream {0}", requestStream.GetType());
    logger.PrintStackPeer((logger.tag + "@ProcessMessage"));

    byte[] bx = reqCopyStream.ToArray();
    logger.WriteLine(" --ProcessMessage-- {0}", bx.Length);
    Stream t = (Stream)reqCopyStream;
    logger.PrintRequest(requestHeaders, ref t);

    RSACryptoServiceProvider clntPubKey = null;

    Crypton crypt = new Crypton(prvKey);
    MemoryStream decryptOut = null;

    FileUtil.SaveBytes("AAA.xml", bx);
    logger.WriteLine("AAA.xml saved {0}", bx.Length);

    reqCopyStream.Position =0;
    try
    {
        logger.WriteLine("typeof request stream 1: {0}",
                                         requestStream.GetType());
        decryptOut = crypt.DecryptVerify(reqCopyStream, out clntPubKey);
    }
    catch(Exception ex)
    {
        logger.WriteLine("ERROR: Decrypt Verify Failed");
        logger.Display(ex);
        throw new SecurityException("Error Decrypting ",ex);
    }
    if((decryptOut==null) || (clntPubKey == null))
    {
        logger.WriteLine("ERROR: {0}@ProcessMessage --> decryptOut or " +
                                  "clntPubKey is null", logger.tag);
        throw new SecurityException("Decryption got null key or stream");
    }

    decryptOut.Position = 0;
    logger.WriteLine("After Decrypt and verify -- dumping stream--");
    logger.PrintStream(decryptOut);

    decryptOut.Position = 0;
```

```
TransportHeaders reqHdr = new TransportHeaders();
foreach (DictionaryEntry header in requestHeaders)
{
   if(((string)header.Key) != "Content-Length")
      reqHdr[header.Key] = header.Value;
}
logger.WriteLine("Printing Request hdr {0}", decryptOut.Length);
logger.PrintHeaders(reqHdr);
logger.WriteLine("---- end Printing Request hdr----");

sinkStack.Push(this, clntPubKey);

logger.WriteLine("before calling {0}@ProcessMessage",nextSink);
ServerProcessing processing = nextSink.ProcessMessage(sinkStack, requestMsg,
reqHdr, decryptOut, out msg, out responseHeaders, out responseStream);

switch (processing)
{
   case ServerProcessing.Complete:
   {
      sinkStack.Pop(this);
      logger.WriteLine("Got ServerProcessing.Complete {0}" +
                                       "@ProcessMessage", logger.tag);
      logger.PrintResponse(responseHeaders, ref responseStream);
      logger.PrintMessage(msg);
      Stream sigEncStream = null;
      try
      {
         sigEncStream = crypt.SignEncrypt(responseStream, clntPubKey);
      }
      catch(Exception ex)
      {
         logger.Display(ex);
         throw new SecurityException("Error Signing & Encrypting ",ex);
      }
      if(sigEncStream == null)
         throw new SecurityException("Sign Encrypt stream is null");

      logger.WriteLine("After SignEncrypt @"+logger.tag);
      logger.PrintStream(sigEncStream);

      responseStream = sigEncStream;
      break;
   }
   case ServerProcessing.OneWay:
   {
      logger.WriteLine("Got ServerProcessing.OneWay {0}@ProcessMessage",
                                                      logger.tag);
      sinkStack.Pop(this);
      break;
   }
   case ServerProcessing.Async:
   {
      logger.WriteLine("Got ServerProcessing.Async {0}@ProcessMessage",
                                                      logger.tag);
      sinkStack.Store(this, clntPubKey);
      break;
   }
} // End of switch statement
```

```
        return processing;
    }
```

The remaining methods and properties don't differ significantly from our boilerplate code:

```
public void AsyncProcessResponse(IServerResponseChannelSinkStack sinkStack,
        Object state, IMessage msg, ITransportHeaders headers, Stream stream)
{
    logger.PrintStackPeer((logger.tag+"@AsyncProcessResponse"));
    logger.PrintMessage(msg);
    logger.PrintResponse(headers, ref stream);

    sinkStack.AsyncProcessResponse(msg, headers, stream);
}

public Stream GetResponseStream(IServerResponseChannelSinkStack sinkStack,
                    Object state, IMessage msg, ITransportHeaders headers)
{
    logger.PrintStackPeer((logger.tag + "@GetResponseStream"));
    logger.PrintMessage(msg);

    return null; // the SOAP formatter creates a mem chunk stream on null
}

public IServerChannelSink NextChannelSink
{
    get
    {
        logger.PrintStackPeer((logger.tag + "@NextChannelSink"));
        logger.WriteLine("nextSink --> {0}", nextSink);
        return nextSink;
    }
}

public IDictionary Properties { get { return prop; } }
private Hashtable prop = new Hashtable();
}
```

The namespace also contains the `Logger` helper class we use for emitting debug information; however this is the same as the `Logger` class in Iteration 1 of our code (except that we have appropriately renamed the `PrintStackTrace()` method to `PrintStackPeer()`), so we won't reprint it here.

Overview of the Cryptography Sink

Because the implementation of our cryptography sink is easily lost in all the boilerplate channel sink code, it's useful to spend a moment looking at what's happening using pseudo-code to highlight the important method calls.

The salient features of the server-side processing can be represented as below:

```
public ServerProcessing ProcessMessage(...)
{
    ...
    Crypton crypt = new Crypton(prvKey);
    ...
    decryptOut = crypt.DecryptVerify(reqCopyStream, out clntPubKey);
    ...
    ServerProcessing processing = nextSink.ProcessMessage(sinkStack, reqHdr,
                decryptOut, out msg, out responseHeaders, out responseStream);
```

```
    ...
    sigEncStream = crypt.SignEncrypt(responseStream, clntPubKey);
}
```

After creating an instance of our `Crypton` class, we call its `DecryptVerify()` method to decrypt the request message; we then pass this down the sink stack by calling the next sink's `ProcessMessage()` method, and finally call `Crypton's` `SignEncrypt()` method to sign the response with the receiver's private key, and encrypt it with the sender's private key.

The client-side counterpart is as follows:

```
public void ProcessMessage(...)
{
    Crypton crypt = new Crypton(prvKey);
    ...
    sigEncStream = crypt.SignEncrypt(requestStream, targetKey);
    ...
    nextSink.ProcessMessage(msg,requestHeaders, sigEncStream,
                                    out responseHeaders, out responseStream);

    ...
    decryptOut = crypt.DecryptVerify(resStream, out retTargKey);
    ...
    if((decryptOut == null) || !RSAComparer.Equals(targetKey, retTargKey))
    {
        throw new SecurityException("...Under Intercept Attack");
    }
}
```

This is pretty well the reverse of the server process – we instantiate our `Crypton` object, and call its `SignEncrypt()` method to sign the message with the sender's private key and encrypt it using the server's public key. Then we call `ProcessMessage()` for the next sink to propagate the message down the chain; when this call returns, we decrypt the response and verify its signature. Finally, we use the `RSAComparer` class to compare the server's public key with the key used to encrypt the response. If they don't match, we throw a new `SecurityException`.

To compile `PeerSink.cs`, use the command given below:

csc /t:library /r:PeerCryptUtil.dll PeerSink.cs

Iteration 4 was a bit like *The Merchant of Venice*. This phase apparently passed off peacefully. However, later (during the final integration stage), it demanded and extracted its pound of flesh.

Final Integration – Walking the Talk

Now comes the big test – the final integration stage, where we test the channel sink.

Here we create two subdirectories (called `final-c` for the client side and `final-s` for the server side). The "`Hello`" sample described in Iteration 1 will serve to illustrate the use of our secured channel sink.

The following assemblies are required at the client side.

❑ `HelloClient.exe`

- ❑   ManageKeyStore.exe
- ❑   PeerCryptUtil.dll
- ❑   PeerSink.dll
- ❑   Speak.dll
- ❑   TraceSink.dll

The server side needs the following assemblies:

- ❑   DirectHost.exe
- ❑   PeerCryptUtil.dll
- ❑   PeerSink.dll
- ❑   Speak.dll
- ❑   Talk2Me.dll
- ❑   TraceSink.dll

These are created and copied by the batch file called `copy_final.bat`, provided for your convenience in the download code.

The test procedure is similar to that of Iteration 1, except that, as we've seen, the configuration files have an additional entry for our security channel sink.

To test the secured P2P channel sink, type the following command at the console to start the server:

```
DirectHost -cfg DirectHost.exe.config
```

The client is simply executed using the command:

```
HelloClient
```

The result externally achieved is apparently the same as in Iteration 1. However, let us trace the stack to see how the encryption and signature of the message followed by its decryption and verification take place transparently, both at client and server ends.

Analyzing the Stack Trace

The stack trace and message logging can be achieved by setting the `verbose` level to 9 and redirecting the standard output of both the client and server ends to a file.

The following line in `DirectHost.cs` sets the ball rolling at the server end:

```
RemotingConfiguration.Configure(args[i+1]);
```

The `PeerServerChannelSinkProvider` constructor is called with the values of the `verbose` and `PrivateKeyFile` attributes contained in the `IDictionary` parameter:

```
Peer.Channel.PeerServerChannelSinkProvider..ctor(IDictionary, ICollection)
Reflection.RuntimeConstructorInfo.InternalInvoke(BindingFlags, ...
    Reflection.RuntimeConstructorInfo.Invoke(BindingFlags, Binder, Object[] ...
    RuntimeType.CreateInstanceImpl(BindingFlags, Binder, Object[], ...
```

```
Activator.CreateInstance(Type, BindingFlags, Binder, Object[], ...
RemotingConfigHandler.CreateChannelSinkProvider(SinkProviderEntry, Boolean)
RemotingConfigHandler.CreateServerChannelSinkProviderChain(ArrayList)
RemotingConfigHandler.CreateChannelFromConfigEntry(ChannelEntry)
RemotingConfigHandler.ConfigureChannels(RemotingXmlConfigFileData)
RemotingConfigHandler.ConfigureRemoting(RemotingXmlConfigFileData)
RemotingConfiguration.Configure(String)
DirectHost.Initialize(String[])
DirectHost.Main(String[])
```

This is followed by a call to the method:

```
Peer.Channel.PeerServerChannelSinkProvider.get_Next()
```

Next, the CreateSink() method of the PeerServerChannelSinkProvider is called by the SetupChannel() method of the HttpServerChannel class:

```
Peer.Channel.PeerServerChannelSinkProvider.CreateSink(IChannelReceiver)
Channels.Http.HttpServerChannel.SetupChannel()
Channels.Http.HttpServerChannel..ctor(IDictionary, IServerChannelSinkProvider)
Reflection.RuntimeConstructorInfo.InternalInvoke(BindingFlags, Binder, ...
Reflection.RuntimeConstructorInfo.Invoke(BindingFlags, Binder, Object[], ...
RuntimeType.CreateInstanceImpl(BindingFlags, Binder, Object[], ...
Activator.CreateInstance(Type, BindingFlags, Binder, Object[], ...
RemotingConfigHandler.CreateChannelFromConfigEntry(ChannelEntry)
RemotingConfigHandler.ConfigureChannels(RemotingXmlConfigFileData)
RemotingConfigHandler.ConfigureRemoting(RemotingXmlConfigFileData)
RemotingConfiguration.Configure(String)
DirectHost.Initialize(String[])
DirectHost.Main(String[])
```

All this happens during the initialization stage, at the server side. Now that the server is waiting for a service request, let's get back to the client end.

When the client starts, the following code is executed:

```
RemotingConfiguration.Configure("HelloClient.exe.config");
```

This triggers a chain reaction, which results in the construction of our client channel sink provider, PeerClientSinkProvider:

```
Peer.Channel.PeerClientSinkProvider..ctor(IDictionary, ICollection)
Reflection.RuntimeConstructorInfo.InternalInvoke(BindingFlags, ...
Reflection.RuntimeConstructorInfo.Invoke(BindingFlags, ...
RuntimeType.CreateInstanceImpl(BindingFlags, Binder, Object[] ...
Activator.CreateInstance(Type, BindingFlags, Binder, Object[] ...
RemotingConfigHandler.CreateChannelSinkProvider(SinkProviderEntry ...
RemotingConfigHandler.CreateClientChannelSinkProviderChain(ArrayList)
RemotingConfigHandler.CreateChannelFromConfigEntry(ChannelEntry)
RemotingConfigHandler.ConfigureChannels(RemotingXmlConfigFileData)
RemotingConfigHandler.ConfigureRemoting(RemotingXmlConfigFileData)
RemotingConfiguration.Configure(String)
HelloClient.Main(String[])
```

Then the Next property of the PeerClientSinkProvider is set by the AppendProviderToClient
ProviderChain() method of the Remoting.Channels.CoreChannel class:

```
Peer.Channel.PeerClientSinkProvider.set_Next(IClientChannelSinkProvider)
CoreChannel.AppendProviderToClientProviderChain(IclientChannelSinkProvider ...
Remoting.Channels.Http.HttpClientChannel.SetupChannel()
Remoting.Channels.Http.HttpClientChannel..ctor(IDictionary,
IClientChannelSinkProvider)
Remoting.Channels.Http.HttpChannel..ctor(IDictionary, IClientChannelSinkProvider,
...
Reflection.RuntimeConstructorInfo.InternalInvoke(BindingFlags, ...
Reflection.RuntimeConstructorInfo.Invoke(BindingFlags, ...
RuntimeType.CreateInstanceImpl(BindingFlags, ...
Activator.CreateInstance(Type, BindingFlags, ...
Remoting.RemotingConfigHandler.CreateChannelFromConfigEntry(ChannelEntry)
Remoting.RemotingConfigHandler.ConfigureChannels(RemotingXmlConfigFileData)
Remoting.RemotingConfigHandler.ConfigureRemoting(RemotingXmlConfigFileData)
Remoting.RemotingConfiguration.Configure(String)
HelloClient.Main(String[])
```

The peer web service is invoked using a URL and the interface type of the service:

```
Speak spk = (Speak)Activator.GetObject(typeof(Speak),
                          "http://localhost:8000/Dude/Talk2Me.soap");
```

This causes the CreateSink() method of the PeerClientSinkProvider class instance to be called,
with the web service URL as a parameter. Using this URL, the public key of the web service is retrieved
from the key storage.

Next, a transparent proxy is requested by the client. When a method call is made on this proxy, it is
marshaled and converted into a message and passed to the RealProxy through the Invoke() method
(we saw what is happening here when we built the custom proxy in Iteration 1).

Finally, the SOAP formatter calls our ProcessMessage() method, after serializing the message into a
SOAP-formatted stream:

```
Peer.Channel.PeerClientSink.ProcessMessage(IMessage, ITransportHeaders, Stream,
ITransportHeaders&, Stream&)
Tracer.TraceClientSink.ProcessMessage(IMessage, ITransportHeaders, Stream,
ITransportHeaders&, Stream&)
System.Runtime.Remoting.Channels.SoapClientFormatterSink.SyncProcessMessage(
IMessage)
System.Runtime.Remoting.Proxies.RemotingProxy.CallProcessMessage(IMessageSink,
Message
System.Runtime.Remoting.Proxies.RemotingProxy.InternalInvoke(Message, Boolean)
System.Runtime.Remoting.Proxies.RemotingProxy.Invoke(IMessage)
System.Runtime.Remoting.Proxies.RealProxy.PrivateInvoke(MessageData&, Int32)
Geek.Speak.Hello(String)
HelloClient.Main(String[])
```

The request header contains the target URL in the SOAPAction directive:

```
SOAPAction: "http://schemas.microsoft.com/clr/nsassem/Geek.Speak/Speak#Hello"
Content-Type: text/xml; charset="utf-8"
```

The SOAP-formatted serialized message is passed in the request stream parameter:

```
<SOAP-ENV:Envelope xmlns:xsi="http://www.w3.org/2001/XMLSchema-instance"
        xmlns:xsd="http://www.w3.org/2001/XMLSchema"
        xmlns:SOAP-ENC="http://schemas.xmlsoap.org/soap/encoding/"
        xmlns:SOAP-ENV="http://schemas.xmlsoap.org/soap/envelope/"
        SOAP-ENV:encodingStyle="http://schemas.xmlsoap.org/soap/encoding/"
        xmlns:i2="http://schemas.microsoft.com/clr/nsassem/Geek.Speak/Speak">
    <SOAP-ENV:Body>
        <i2:Hello id="ref-1">
            <dude id="ref-3">Cool</dude>
        </i2:Hello>
    </SOAP-ENV:Body>
</SOAP-ENV:Envelope>
```

The message is signed and encrypted using the public key of the web service:

```
<?xml version="1.0"?>
<EncryptedData xmlns:xsi="http://www.w3.org/2001/XMLSchema-instance"
               xmlns:xsd="http://www.w3.org/2001/XMLSchema"
               xmlns="http://www.w3.org/2001/04/xmlenc#">
    <KeyInfo xmlns="http://www.w3.org/2000/09/xmldsig#">
        <KeyValue xmlns="http://www.w3.org/2000/09/xmldsig#">
            <RSAKeyValue>
                <Modulus>vehnUHf7Fw6+l2NIEq3TVJSyWb ... yzDZ29xE5U=</Modulus>
                <Exponent>AQAB</Exponent>
            </RSAKeyValue>
        </KeyValue>
    </KeyInfo>
    <CipherData xmlns="http://www.w3.org/2001/04/xmlenc#2">
        <CipherSecret>KAu8/CviJfyY8mifD1/ ... 9TVQwU=</CipherSecret>
        <CipherValue>AVuBt2LLgud1QyeZM5vNK ... mSyxHG4=</CipherValue>
    </CipherData>
</EncryptedData>
```

This message is passed to the `ProcessMessage()` method of the next channel sink in the chain. In this case, this is the `HttpClientTransportSink`.

On the server side, the `ProcessMessage()` method of our `PeerServerChannelSink` instance is called by the `ServiceRequest()` method of the `HttpServerTransportSink`:

```
Peer.Channel.PeerServerChannelSink.ProcessMessage
System.Runtime.Remoting.Channels.Http.HttpServerTransportSink.ServiceRequest
System.Runtime.Remoting.Channels.SocketHandler.BeginReadMessageCallback
System.NET.Sockets.OverlappedAsyncResult.OverlappedCallback(Object, Boolean)
```

The `ProcessMessage()` method receives the encrypted and signed message. This is the same message sent by the client channel sink.

After decryption using the server-side private key and verification of the signature, the original message looks like this, ready for consumption by the SOAP deserializer:

```
<SOAP-ENV:Envelope xmlns:xsi="http://www.w3.org/2001/XMLSchema-instance"
        xmlns:xsd="http://www.w3.org/2001/XMLSchema"
        xmlns:SOAP-ENC="http://schemas.xmlsoap.org/soap/encoding/"
```

```
            xmlns:SOAP-ENV="http://schemas.xmlsoap.org/soap/envelope/"
            SOAP-ENV:encodingStyle="http://schemas.xmlsoap.org/soap/encoding/"
            xmlns:i2="http://schemas.microsoft.com/clr/nsassem/Geek.Speak/Speak">
    <SOAP-ENV:Body>
        <i2:Hello id="ref-1">
            <dude id="ref-3">Cool</dude>
        </i2:Hello>
    </SOAP-ENV:Body>
</SOAP-ENV:Envelope>
```

This decrypted message is passed to the next server channel sink, and after the target method is invoked, we get back the marshaled return value:

```
<SOAP-ENV:Envelope xmlns:xsi="http://www.w3.org/2001/XMLSchema-instance"
        xmlns:xsd="http://www.w3.org/2001/XMLSchema"
        xmlns:SOAP-ENC="http://schemas.xmlsoap.org/soap/encoding/"
        xmlns:SOAP-ENV="http://schemas.xmlsoap.org/soap/envelope/"
        SOAP-ENV:encodingStyle="http://schemas.xmlsoap.org/soap/encoding/"
        xmlns:i2="http://schemas.microsoft.com/clr/nsassem/Geek.Speak/Speak">
    <SOAP-ENV:Body>
        <i2:HelloResponse id="ref-1">
            <return id="ref-3">Yo Cool Wazzup</return>
        </i2:HelloResponse>
    </SOAP-ENV:Body>
</SOAP-ENV:Envelope>
```

This SOAP message is SOAP-boxed, signed using the server's private key, and then encrypted using the client's public key; see Iteration 3 for a detailed discussion.

```
<?xml version="1.0"?>
<EncryptedData xmlns:xsi="http://www.w3.org/2001/XMLSchema-instance"
               xmlns:xsd="http://www.w3.org/2001/XMLSchema"
               xmlns="http://www.w3.org/2001/04/xmlenc#">
    <KeyInfo xmlns="http://www.w3.org/2000/09/xmldsig#">
        <KeyValue xmlns="http://www.w3.org/2000/09/xmldsig#">
            <RSAKeyValue>
                <Modulus>wnG3HszU ... LinfeuZhITMtlM=</Modulus>
                <Exponent>AQAB</Exponent>
            </RSAKeyValue>
        </KeyValue>
    </KeyInfo>
    <CipherData xmlns="http://www.w3.org/2001/04/xmlenc#2">
        <CipherSecret>vUyUv5Ru6Mpn ... KedV6ulCeHEA=</CipherSecret>
        <CipherValue>czRa8Y0kNsX60 ... 74tEJ/lX+3rZR</CipherValue>
    </CipherData>
</EncryptedData>
```

This message is decrypted at the client side, and the signature is verified, to produce the same message as the original response before encryption.

This concludes our tight-rope stack walking.

Contrary to my belief that it would be a cakewalk, the final integration has been indisputably the most tortuous development stage. In spite of the fact that all the components used had already been tested, certain issues came up that sent me reeling back to the previous iterations.

To-Do List

There are still quite a few improvements that we could make, and I would encourage you to try to resolve some of these issues. This will give you first-hand experience of working on a channel sink design, before you develop and deploy your own components:

❑ Implementing the asynchronous call model

❑ Adding `CallContext` hooks into the channel sink, to store the digitally signed objects

❑ Enhancing the `ManageKeyStore.cs` utility to accept Public Key from X.509 certificates

❑ Adding digital signature for version control of the assembly files.

❑ Complying fully with W3C XML encryption formats

❑ Implementing dynamic peer lookup for web services with dynamic IP addresses

Application Scenarios

In this section, we'll look quickly at a few application scenarios where our secure channel sink will find ready use:

❑ Peer-to-Peer Instant Messaging

❑ Anonymous Payment System

❑ P2P Invoice and Ordering System

❑ Supply Chain Management

Characteristics of Peer to Peer Applications

In P2P computing, the all-encompassing characteristic is the absence of the centralized server role; all peers host both client and server objects. Although conceptually the client and service objects still exist, the machines hosting the peer web service don't need to have a higher configuration than the conventional high-end workstation.

There is an apparent contradiction – why do today's applications need a high-end server when in P2P computing we claim that a workstation will do the job?

Consider the fact that for each client there also exists a server within the same computing domain. Thus the load is architecturally balanced in P2P, while in the conventional scenario the load balancing has to be engineered.

To abolish the central server, we will need a different cryptographic model, based on peer trust rather than a central certificate authority.

Peer-to-Peer Instant Messaging

Peer-to-Peer Instant Messaging will be the next killer application on the Internet, the one the world is waiting for! And I am willing to stick my neck out on this one.

The catch, however, will be that more than a few islands of standards and de facto protocols will co-exist. The .NET SDK would be an ideal platform to provide access to multiple-protocol peers, without changing the higher layers of application business logic encapsulation objects.

A fixed IP is easier to get these days, thanks to XDSL and broadband technologies. Peer web services can therefore be devised that do not need a central server to route every message or to act as an intermediary. Our channel sink could provide an application security layer, with minimal plumbing.

For dynamic IP clients, a lookup service will be required. However, this service would not be overloaded since the peers would need to come here to get a fix on their counterpart's current IP; after that, they would communicate directly with each other without any intermediary.

Anonymous Payment Systems

Anonymous payment systems are the Holy Grail of the e-commerce world. Many have thought or claimed to have got it, but none could deliver it to the world – at least not yet!

Here is another idea for an anonymous payment system, based on P2P computing concept. Suppose a service provider sets up an anonymous payment gateway; just like long-distance calling cards, you could buy a scratchcard by paying cash in the real world, or buy the tokens (randomly regenerated numbers) online using a credit card from a third party, unrelated to the anonymous payment gateway.

The anonymous gateway keeps track of the random numbers sold to the third parties for final sales to the end user. Soon after buying a token of a predefined value, the token owner generates or uses an existing public and private key pair. The token is signed using the private key and sent to the anonymous payment gateway, which checks if this random number is vacant and unclaimed. If so, it blocks it and associates it with the signer's public key, without knowing the signer's identity.

The anonymous payment is now ready to accept any cheque signed using the private key corresponding to the public key associated with the random token, so long as the total value of the cheques disbursed against the token does not exceed the cash value minus the commission for which it was sold.

The token owner can write the electronic equivalent of a cheque by authorizing the gateway to pay the presenter the sum promised. The owner of the token effectively writes a promissory note by supplying the token, the promised amount, and a unique reference ID to tag the transaction. The first person to present this promissory note is given the payment, by way of crediting an account. This itself could be another anonymous account.

P2P Invoice and Ordering System

Much of the P2P model is already being put into practice in the B2B world. Business-to-Business applications are ideal for peer computing, since a lot of pre-negotiations take place before a document exchange mechanism is set up. This provides a good opportunity to exchange public keys out of band.

A few competing standards exist for ordering and invoicing, many of which are XML-encoded. OFX, Visa Invoice, and EDI-XML are a few such standards. These diverse standards provide an opportunity to the programmer community to write custom channel sinks.

Supply Chain Management

This is another B2B application that could also be usefully adapted to the P2P model. Supply chain management is about maintaining a transparent inventory status with downstream suppliers; and ordering items just in time, yet providing an adequate advanced warning system.

The .NET Framework provides a flexible way of bridging existing and new applications through remoting. Cryptography provides signing for authorization and encryption for keeping away snooping competition.

Conclusion

In this case study, we've looked at some of the advantages and possibilities of the P2P model, and we've discussed how web services fit into this model. In particular, we've seen how we can extend .NET Remoting by creating a custom channel sink to implement cryptography. This can be plugged into our web services as an abstraction layer, without rewriting our existing code.

To achieve this, we first developed the boilerplate design for a custom channel sink, and then plugged our cryptography class into it. The .NET Framework has made it easier to separate the communication nuances from the application logic.

As the .NET Framework evolves along with P2P computing, you will find many opportunities to implement channel sinks for dealing with application-specific needs and interoperating with existing or competing frameworks. I hope that this case study will be a positive contribution to your web service designs.

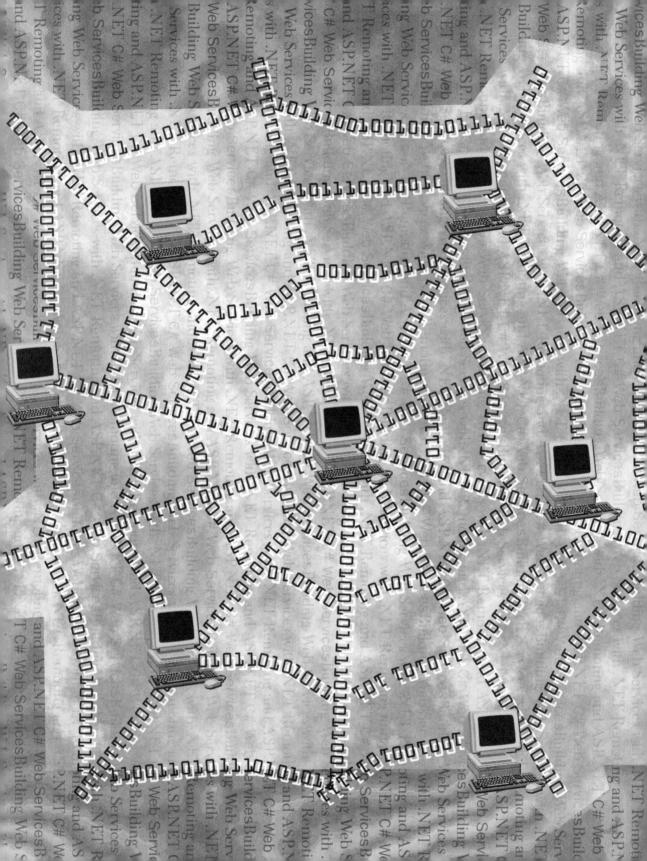

Section Six – Appendix

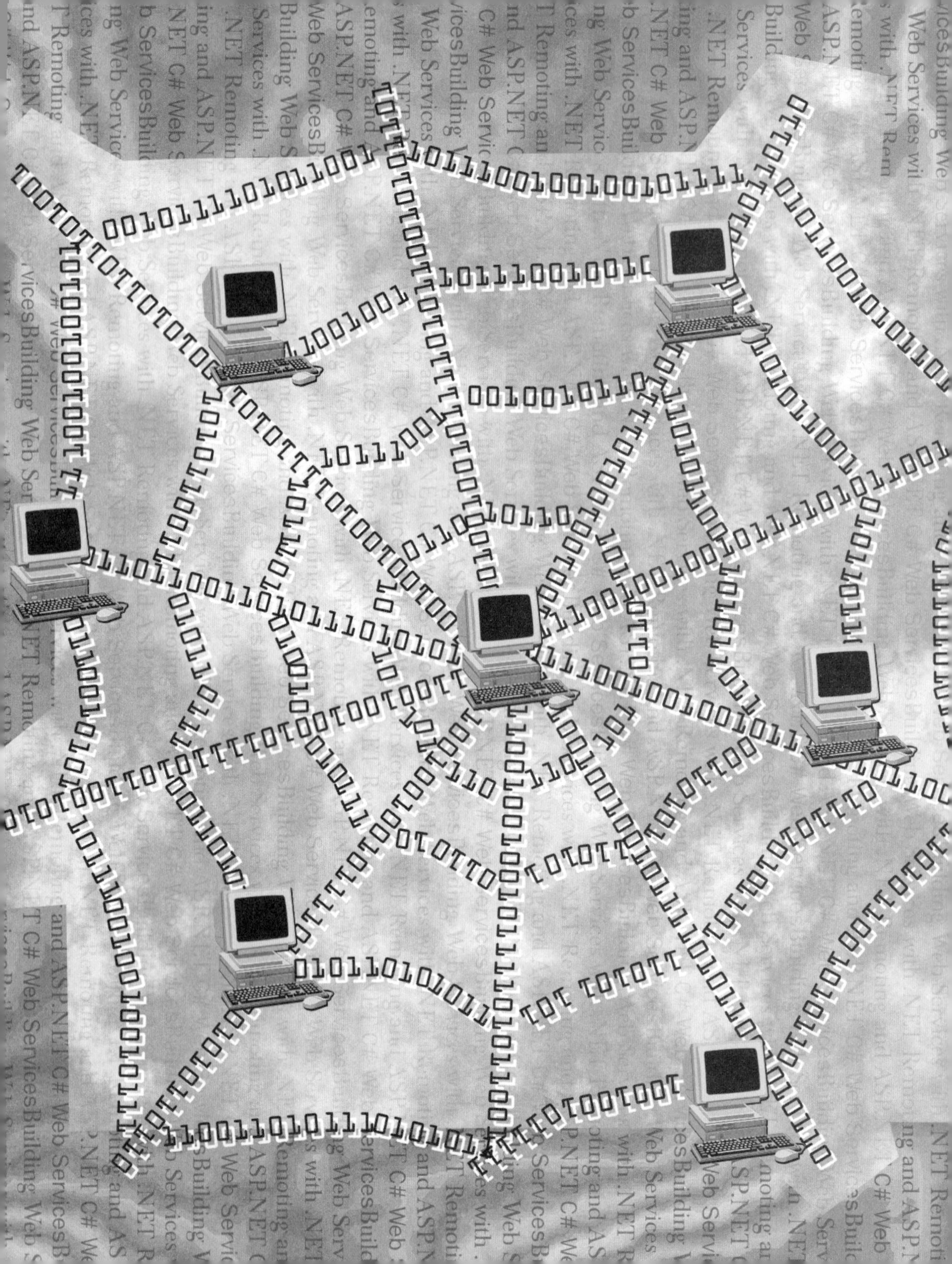

.NET Remoting Object Model

Objects are classified according to their affinity for cross-context calls, and in order to understand what this really means, we need to clarify two key terms – **AppDomain** and **Context**.

An **AppDomain** (Application Domain) is a *light-weight* process hosted by the Common Language Runtime (CLR). The term *light-weight* essentially means that an AppDomain is not a true physical OS process and can thus dispense with much of the baggage associated with true OS processes. Essentially, AppDomains are granular fault-isolation boundaries hosted under the aegis of the CLR, which itself runs within a true OS process such as the Windows Shell, the ASP.NET runtime, or Internet Explorer (IE). A default AppDomain is always created with every process, and every individual AppDomain has its own security principles. AppDomains can be created and destroyed programmatically in a process, and any process can host multiple AppDomains. Like a Win32 process, an AppDomain is free to create secondary threads as and when required. A thread's execution path can flow across AppDomain boundaries when invoking remote objects.

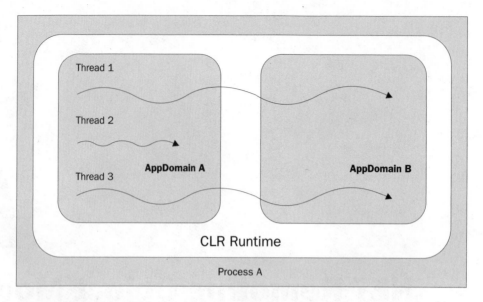

An AppDomain is itself divided by logical environment boundaries to form **Contexts** in which .NET objects reside. Contexts group together .NET objects that require similar services such as synchronization, transactions, JIT activation, object pooling, security, and so on. When new objects get created, the runtime places the object in a compatible context if one already exists, otherwise it creates a suitable context for the purpose. Once assigned to a context, a .NET object stays there for its entire lifetime, that is, until it has been destroyed and garbage-collected. When an AppDomain is first created, a default context is also created and associated with it. Other contexts are created in the AppDomain when new objects require specific interception services that an existing context cannot provide. Just as threads can cross AppDomain boundaries, they can flow into other contexts as well, including contexts in other AppDomains:

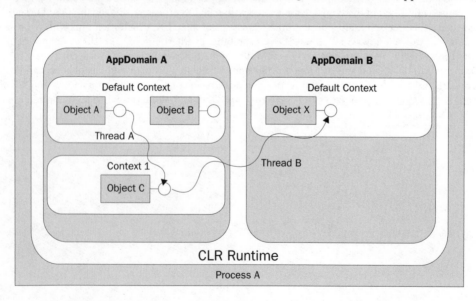

.NET objects are classified according to the **cross-context** interaction that they require. In the managed .NET world, method calls to objects that cross AppDomain boundaries are called **remote method calls**. The target AppDomain could be in the same process, in a different process, or even in a process running on another machine. It is the remoting runtime infrastructure that takes care of dispatching the call to the remote AppDomain that hosts the object so it can service the method call.

According to their need for cross-context calls, objects exposed via .NET remoting are classified as either **context-agile** objects, or **context-bound** objects.

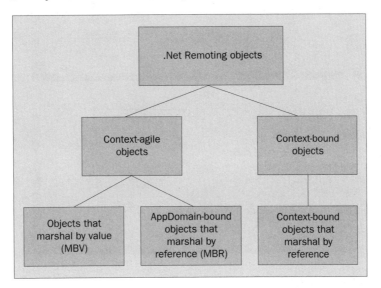

Context-Agile Objects

Context-agile objects are not bound to any specific context within the AppDomain that hosts them. They can be accessed without proxy indirection for cross-context calls within the same AppDomain. Calls across AppDomain boundaries are either **marshaled by value** (**MBV**) or **marshaled by reference** (**MBR**) to the caller's AppDomain.

Context-Agile Marshal-by-Value Objects

Context-agile MBV objects can be accessed directly from contexts within the same AppDomain. Across AppDomain boundaries, a copy of the complete state of the object is passed to the target AppDomain. These classes are marked with the [Serializable] attribute indicating that the entire object must be copied verbatim to the target AppDomain. This holds true whether the target AppDomain is in the same process, a different process, or even in a process running on a separate machine. There is no proxy indirection required whatsoever when accessing these objects.

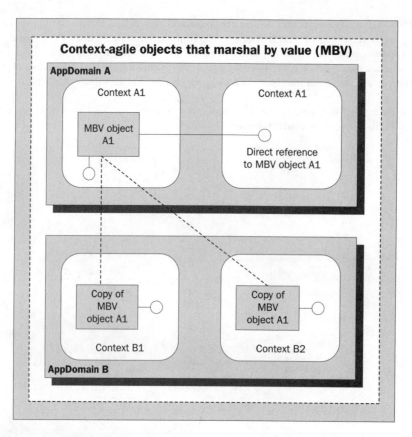

Context-agile objects that marshal by value (MBV)

Once the object is copied over to the target AppDomain, all calls are made on the copy of the object. This avoids roundtrips and reduces performance overhead, especially if the object comes from an AppDomain hosted in a process running on a remote machine.

You can control the fields to serialize by implementing the `ISerializable` interface in your MBV object, and providing custom serialization through its `GetObjectData()` method:

```
[Serializable]
public class Temperature : ISerializable
{
    public void GetObjectData(SerializationInfo info,
                              StreamingContext context)
    {
        // Perform custom serialization here
    }
}
```

AppDomain-Bound Context-Agile MBR Objects

```
System.Object
    System.MarshalByRefObject
```

AppDomain-bound MBR objects inherit from `System.MarshalByRefObject`. Callers in the same AppDomain can directly reference the object, but if the caller is in another AppDomain, a reference to the object is marshaled to the calling AppDomain. The calling AppDomain then uses the type information in the object reference to manufacture a proxy, which is then used to access the remote object. The state of the object is confined to its home AppDomain (the AppDomain in which it is created), and only object references are handed over to the calling AppDomain:

```
class WeatherService : MarshalByRefObject
{
    // Class implementation goes here
}
```

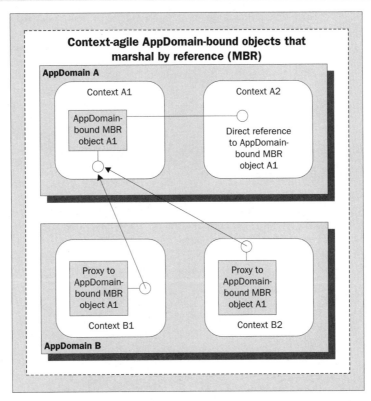

Methods of the MarshalByRefObject Class

Method	Returns	Description
CreateObjRef	ObjRef	Creates an object reference (ObjRef) for the specified object type. An object reference is a serialized representation of an MBR object that can be marshaled across AppDomain boundaries. The object reference is used by the target AppDomain to manufacture a proxy, which allows methods on the object to be invoked.

Table continued on following page

499

Method	Returns	Description
GetLifetime Service	ILease interface of the lease object containing the lease lifetime policy settings for this object	Returns an object that handles the lease lifetime policy for this remote object instance. Lease objects are created for objects that are marshaled across AppDomain boundaries (**remoted**). The lease manager holds a list of such lease lifetime policy objects (see *Remoting Lifetime Management with Leases* in the *.NET Remoting Building Blocks* section of this appendix).
Initialize Lifetime Service	ILease interface of the lease object containing the lease lifetime policy settings for this object	Overridden by remoted MBR objects to initialize the lease properties and control their lifetime. You can initialize lease properties only when the lease object is in its initial state. Attempts to initialize lease properties of a lease object that has already been activated will result in an exception. You can examine the lease state by the ILease.CurrentState of the object. If the lease has just been created but is not yet activated, the CurrentState property has a LeaseState enumeration value of Initial.

An MBR object can override the InitializeLifetimeService() method if it needs to control its own lifetime. In the overridden implementation, the object can return a lease object with the appropriate lease lifetime policy settings. To make the object persist indefinitely, set the InitializeLifetimeService() method to return null, as shown:

```
class WeatherServiceAlwaysAlive : MarshalByRefObject
{
    public override Object InitializeLifetimeService()
    {
        return null;
    }
}
```

Context-Bound Marshal-by-Reference Objects

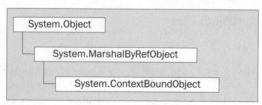

Context-bound objects inherit from `System.ContextBoundObject`. They are strongly bound to their home context (the context in which they were created). A context-bound object can be accessed directly by calls made from its home context alone. From any other context, access is only available via a proxy. A context-bound object can be tagged with context attributes to indicate any special interception services that it needs from its context, such as synchronization, JIT activation, and so on. If no existing context is able to provide the required services, a new context is created and the object is placed there. See the section on the `System.Runtime.Remoting.Contexts.Context` class, and the following section on the `System.Runtime.Remoting.Contexts.ContextAttribute` class, in the *.NET Remoting Framework Classes* section of this appendix for more details on contexts, context bound objects, and context attributes.

```
[SomeContextAttribute()]
class WeatherService : ContextBoundObject
{
    // Rest of the class implementation goes here
}
```

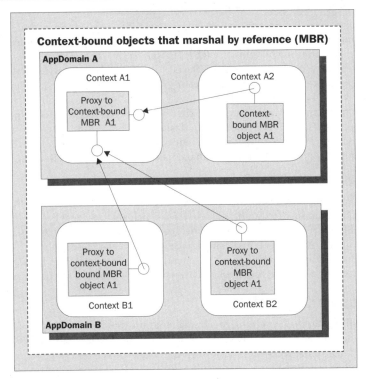

.NET Remoting Building Blocks

The .NET Remoting framework provides an infrastructure geared towards creating scalable, powerful, robust, and reliable web services. It offers a variety of hosting options, transport channels, message formatters, lifetime management, and activation policies, which act as the building blocks for the assembly of web services capable of meeting the needs of many business processes. Let's take a dip into the remoting framework now, to see the part that each of these pieces plays in the grand scheme of things in the .NET world.

Remoting Hosting Options

The .NET Remoting infrastructure has a variety of hosting environments to choose from when deploying objects that will be exposed to remote clients. The most useful of these are discussed here.

IIS Hosting

The IIS hosting option is very convenient and allows you to expose your objects to remote clients with very little effort. It's as simple as creating a virtual directory through the IIS Administration snap-in, and copying the object's assembly to a `bin` subdirectory of the corresponding physical folder for your IIS application. You also need to specify the object's type, activation mode, and the URI endpoint in the `web.config` file found in the root physical folder of the application. The *Remoting Configuration File Format Reference* section towards the end of this appendix details the format of this configuration information for the `web.config` file when hosting objects in IIS. The other plus point with IIS is that it doesn't require channels to be registered explicitly as it listens for HTTP requests on port 80 by default.

Managed .NET Executable and Windows NT Services Hosting

When hosting your objects within a managed .NET executable application, you do need to register and configure one or more transport channels to listen for incoming requests. You must also register the object types on the server as a well-known URI endpoint (in the case of well-known objects), or as an activated type (in the case of client-activated objects). The differences between well-known objects and client-activated objects are described in the *Remoting Activation Policies* topic later in this section. The activation mode and URI endpoint registration are specific to well-known objects only and do not apply to client-activated objects. Once a transport channel is configured to listen for requests, and has registered the object types, and the activation modes and URI endpoints they require, you need to leave the managed application running so that clients can connect to it. Hosting objects in a managed NT Service is very similar to hosting them in a managed .NET executable application.

COM+ Services Hosting

Hosting your objects from COM+ allows you to leverage the rich set of services that COM+ provides, such as object pooling, automatic transaction services, synchronization, JIT activation, and so on. You could create an ASP.NET web service as a 'façade' for an object hosted in COM+. The ASP.NET web service could call the COM+ object, and return its response to the client. With **COM+ 1.5** (available with Windows XP at the time of writing), all you need do is select an option from the COM+ Component Services snap-in, and voilà, your COM+ object is exposed to clients as a web service.

Remoting Transport Channels

Channels are an abstraction representing the actual conduits that carry messages to the remote object across AppDomain boundaries, possibly crossing machine boundaries. The **HTTP**, **TCP**, and **SMTP** channels are provided by the remoting framework out-of-the-box. The HTTP channel is your best bet if the consumers of your remote objects are outside your firewall because most firewalls are configured to allow HTTP traffic only. The HTTP channel carries messages to remote objects as **SOAP** payloads by default. For more information on SOAP, refer to Chapter 2.

The TCP channel offers improved performance compated to HTTP. By default, it uses a binary payload to carry messages to remote objects and uses raw sockets-based communication. If the consumers of your service are located on your corporate network, where the deployment environment can be controlled and there are no problems opening additional ports on the server hosting the remote objects, the TCP channel is an option. If however the clients of your remote objects are spread far and wide throughout the internet cloud beyond your corporate firewall, then you will probably have to use the HTTP channel.

The SMTP channel also uses SOAP-based serialization by default. In the end, it's a matter of weighing up the tradeoffs between performance and interoperability. The good thing about the remoting architecture is that it *does not* mandate a specific message serialization formatter (which we examine next) for a given transport channel. You are free to use the binary message formatter with the HTTP channel, or the SOAP message formatter with the TCP channel. The 'pluggable channel' and 'pluggable formatter' architecture of the remoting infrastructure allows you to mix-and-match channels and message formatters according to your application's requirements. This table summarizes the key issues in transport channels decisions:

HTTP channel	TCP channel
Uses the SOAP serialization formatter by default.	Uses the binary serialization formatter by default.
Suited for remote clients on the Internet beyond the corporate firewall.	More suited for deployment of remote objects within a controlled and secure environment such as a corporate LAN.
Performance is fairly good.	Excellent performance since it uses raw sockets-based communication and a binary payload by default.
High interoperability. Can be used to communicate with web services deployed on disparate platforms, which usually respond only to SOAP requests over HTTP.	Not as platform-agnostic as the HTTP channel.

Remoting Message Serialization and Deserialization Formatters

Before a method can be invoked on an object, the method information and the parameter stack need to be packaged for transport across the wire. At the other end of the transport channel, the message is deserialized to recreate the call stack before the method can be invoked.

A message formatter is responsible for serializing and deserializing messages that flow over a channel. Two message serialization formatters are provided out-of-the-box by the .NET Framework – the binary formatter that converts messages to a binary stream, and a SOAP formatter that serializes messages as the XML payload of a SOAP message. More information on SOAP is given in Chapter 2. The SOAP serialization formatter is the way to go when talking to web services deployed on other platforms that generally only accept and respond to SOAP-conformant requests.

There's no need for us to worry about how exactly the remoting infrastructure serializes and deserializes remote method invocation requests and object references for sending across the channel. The message formatter associated with the channel automatically handles all this for us. If you are curious, try applications such as the **Trace utility** from the MS SOAP Toolkit 2.0, or **TcpTrace** (for information on TcpTrace, see http://www.pocketsoap.com/tcptrace/) to sneak peeks inside the SOAP packets sent over the HTTP channel. Similarly, tools like **Microsoft Network Monitor** (Netmon.exe) let you monitor messages that flow through the TCP channel.

Remoting Lifetime Management with Leases

In traditional distributed object models such as DCOM, object lifetime is managed using reference counting. Such protocols need to ping server objects at predefined intervals to check if they are still servicing clients, and stop the server from keeping 'zombie' objects alive after the client dies unexpectedly. If an object has not received an invocation request from the client for a long enough time period, the protocol assumes that the client is dead and destroys the object that is servicing that client. For example, DCOM's resolver process pings server objects every 2 minutes to check if they have received any client invocations. If 6 minutes pass without any client invocations, it destroys the corresponding object (by calling the Release() method on the object's IUnknown interface).

Though this model usually works acceptably, it doesn't scale well for scenarios where huge numbers of clients are hitting the same remoting service at the same time. To address this failing, the .NET Remoting infrastructure provides a lease-based lifetime management policy for remote objects. In a nutshell, this policy assigns every object a lease period that determines how long the object will live. When the lease period expires, a check is made to see if there are any **sponsors** that can renew that object's lease period. If there are none, the object is marked for garbage collection.

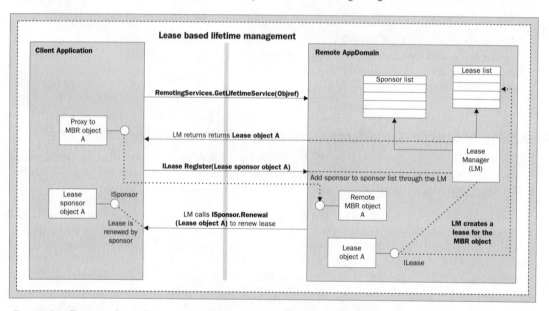

Every AppDomain has a **lease manager** to manage the lease lifetime policy settings for remote objects. Whenever an object reference (ObjRef) for an MBR object is passed across an AppDomain boundary, the lease manager associates a lease with the object. The lease settings that define a lease policy are provided through a lease object that implements the ILease interface. This interface exposes properties that define the lease policy settings as described in the following table:

Property	Description
CurrentLeaseTime	Represents the lease time period remaining for the object.
InitialLeaseTime	Represents the initial lease time period. The default period is 5 minutes.

Property	Description
RenewOnCallTime	Represents the time increment applied to the lease time period when a method call is made on the object. The default increment is 2 minutes.
SponsorshipTimeout	Specifies how long the lease manager should wait for a sponsor to return with a lease renewal time before removing that sponsor from the sponsor list, and attempting to contact the next sponsor in the list. The default time is 2 minutes.
CurrentState	Represents the current state of the lease. This is one of the System.Runtime.Remoting.Lifetime.LeaseState enumeration values shown in the table below.

Members of the LeaseState Enumeration	Description
Active	Lease is active.
Expired	Lease has expired and cannot be renewed. When the lease manager finds that the lease on an object has expired, it contacts the lease sponsors in its sponsor list to determine whether to renew its lease. If the response from a sponsor times out, it tries to contact the next sponsor in the list. If the lease manager has no success in getting a lease renewal from any of the sponsors, it sets the lease object to the Expired state. Once this is set, the object cannot be resurrected, and the object will be garbage-collected.
Initial	Lease has been created, but is still inactive.
Null	Lease has not been initialized.
Renewing	Lease has expired and the lease manager is looking for sponsors. This state indicates the lease manager is trying to contact the lease sponsors that have registered for lease renewal for this object.

The lease manager maintains all its lease objects in a lease list. It continuously monitors these lease objects to check for expired leases. When it finds that a lease has expired, it checks to see if there are any sponsors registered to renew it. Lease sponsors are essentially objects that implement the ISponsor interface. The client application can register a lease sponsor for a remote object by calling the GetLifetimeServices static method of the RemotingServices class. When the client calls this method, the remote object's home domain's lease manager returns the corresponding lease object from its internal lease list. The client uses the lease object to register itself as a lease sponsor by calling the Register method of the ILease interface, passing it a lease sponsor object (implementing the ISponsor interface). The lease manager then squirrels away this sponsor object in its internal list of lease sponsors.

When a lease period expires for an object, the lease manager checks if any registered lease sponsors wish to renew the object's lease by calling the Renewal method on the sponsor object's ISponsor interface. If there are multiple sponsors for the object in the lease manager's sponsor list, they are called in order of the highest lease renewal time returned from previous lease renewal attempts. If the lease sponsor does not get back within the time span dictated by the lease's SponsorshipTimeout property, the lease manager removes that sponsor from the sponsor list. It then tries the next sponsor in the sponsor list. If no lease sponsors successfully return a lease renewal time, the lease's CurrentState property is set to Expired, removing the lease from the lease list. Once Expired is set for the lease object, the object is doomed to garbage collection, and no new sponsors can register themselves for lease renewal to resurrect the object.

Remoting Activation Policies

Remote objects are classified as either **well-known objects** (also known as **server-activated objects**) or **client-activated objects** (**CAO**), depending on how they are activated by the remoting infrastructure.

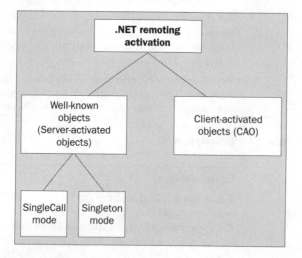

Well-known objects are registered at URI endpoints that clients use to connect. Since the remoting infrastructure directly controls the creation of well-known objects, constructor arguments cannot be used. When the client creates an instance of the object, all that really happens is the client generates a proxy based on the remote object's reference. The object is not created on the server and there are no calls across the wire. The object is activated on the server only when the client makes a method call via the proxy. There are two modes that apply to **well-known objects**, namely **Singleton** and **SingleCall**.

In the **Singleton** activation mode, the same object instance services all client requests. In reality, `Singleton` objects do get regenerated on the server depending on the lease lifetime policies. However, you can enforce a lease policy that keeps the object alive indefinitely. This mode is good when you need to maintain shared data or resources between all clients that use an object, such as for a hit counter that tracks the hits on a server resource.

The **SingleCall** activation mode, on the other hand, is essentially a stateless model where a new object instance is created for every client request. The object is destroyed as soon as the method call exits, and a new object is created to service any subsequent request. This model scales well and can be used in deployment environments such as server farms, where load balancing is required.

Client-activated objects (**CAO**) use an activation model analogous to the classic COM activation model. Client-activated objects are activated on the server when the client creates a new instance of the object, and they allow clients to maintain state between method calls on a per-client basis. They are destroyed when a client releases the proxy to the object, or when the lease lifetime period expires for the object. Since CAO objects are activated on the server as soon as the client creates a new instance (unlike well-known objects, which get created only on the first method call), clients can pass arguments to CAO constructors. Here's a summary of the various activation models:

Well-known Singleton	Well-known SingleCall	Client-activated objects
Same object instance services all client requests.	For every method call, a new object instance is created on the server to service the call.	Very similar to the classic COM activation model. Every method call on the object is serviced by the same server object instance created by the client. This allows you to maintain state between method calls in the object on a per-client basis.
Will not scale in a server farm.	Will scale extremely well when deployed in a server farm.	Will not scale as well as the well-known `SingleCall` activation model.
The client manufactures a proxy to the remote object. The object is activated on the server only when the first method call is made on the proxy. The same instance is used to service all subsequent client requests. The object instance may be recycled depending on lease lifetime policies.	The client manufactures a proxy to the remote object. The object is created and activated only when the first method call is made on the proxy. It is deactivated and destroyed when the method call completes.	A CAO object is created and activated on the server when the client creates the object using `new` or `Activator.CreateInstance()`. The object is destroyed when the client releases the object's proxy or when the lease lifetime period expires for the object.
No arguments can be passed to constructors.	No arguments can be passed to constructors.	Arguments can be passed to constructors. Overloaded constructors can also be used.
Stateful model.	Stateless model.	Stateful model.

.NET Remoting Framework Classes

In the previous section, we took a bird's-eye survey of the building blocks that make up the .NET Remoting framework. The remoting classes in the .NET Framework class library provide all the functionality to configure, manage, and customize these building blocks based on the requirements of your application.

It's beyond the scope of this appendix to look at all the remoting classes in this section, and instead we'll focus on the important classes in the `System.Runtime.Remoting` namespace (the parent namespace for the remoting classes), and its child namespaces. If you're developing pluggable interception sinks, custom message formatters, custom channels, or other infrastructure that needs an in-depth understanding of the remoting framework, then the documentation and samples provided with the .NET Framework SDK should be of help. This section aims to illuminate the usage and purpose of the remoting classes that developers are most likely to run into when developing applications with .NET remoting.

The System.Runtime.Remoting.RemotingConfiguration Class

The RemotingConfiguration class is perhaps the most useful of the System.Runtime.Remoting namespace classes. Server applications use its methods to register object types that they expose, while client applications use its methods to register the remote object types that they consume. Object types are registered with the remoting infrastructure using the RegisterWellKnownServiceType() and RegisterActivatedServiceType() methods. The Configure() method allows you to use a configuration file to specify configuration and registration information for the remoting infrastructure, rather than performing the configuration programmatically.

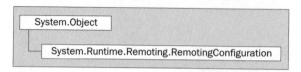

Property	Property type	Description
ApplicationName *(Static property)*	String	Gets or sets the name of the remoting application. Remote application hosts can provide a name that can be used along with the URL of the remote object. For example, if a well-known object is hosted in a managed application, which sets the ApplicationName property to PizzaParlor, and the URI endpoint of the object is PizzaOrder.soap, then the fully qualified URL is: http://remotemachine:8080/PizzaParlor/PizzaOrder.soap. This assumes that the application host has registered an HTTP channel for requests listening on port 8080. For IIS hosting, this is the name of the IIS application's virtual root, which need not be specified explicitly using this property.

Method	Returns	Description
Configure *(Static Method)*	–	Configures the remoting framework using the specified configuration file. IIS hosting requires you to specify configuration information through the web.config file. For more details of the format of a remoting configuration file, refer to the *Remoting Configuration File Format Reference* section at the end of this appendix.
RegisterWellKnown ClientType *(Static Method)*	–	Registers a well-known object type at the client end so that method calls execute in the remote well-known object (SingleCall or Singleton) on the server.
RegisterWellKnown ServiceType *(Static Method)*	–	Registers a well-known object type (SingleCall or Singleton) at the service end so remote clients can connect to it.

Method	Returns	Description
RegisterActivated ClientType *(Static Method)*	–	Registers a CAO object type at the client end so that it is activated in a remote application on the server.
RegisterActivated ServiceType *(Static Method)*	–	Registers a CAO object type at the service end so that remote clients can activate it.
GetRegistered WellKnownClient Types *(Static Method)*	WellKnown Client TypeEntry[]	Returns an array of well-known object types that are registered at the client end.
GetRegistered WellKnownService Types *(Static Method)*	WellKnown Service TypeEntry[]	Returns an array of well-known (`SingleCall` or `Singleton`) object types that are registered at the service end.
GetRegistered ActivatedClient Types *(Static Method)*	Activated Client TypeEntry[]	Returns an array of CAO object types that are registered at the client end.
GetRegistered ActivatedService Types *(Static Method)*	Activated Service TypeEntry[]	Returns an array of CAO object types that are registered at the service end.
IsActivation Allowed *(Static Method)*	bool	This method is used at the service end and returns a Boolean flag indicating whether the remote application allows the specified object type to be activated as a CAO.
IsRemotely ActivatedClient Type *(Static Method)*	Activated Client TypeEntry	Checks if the specified object type is registered at the client end as a CAO so that it may be activated in a remote server application.
IsWellKnownClient Type *(Static Method)*	WellKnown Client TypeEntry	Checks if the specified object type is registered at the client end as a well-known object so that method calls execute in the remote well-known object (`SingleCall` or `Singleton`) on the server.

For illustration, take a look at the PizzaOrder class shown overleaf. The class is scoped under a namespace called PizzaOrderNS and exposes a public method called OrderPizza, which places a pizza order at your favorite pizza joint:

```
namespace PizzaOrderNS
{
    public class PizzaOrder : MarshalByRefObject
    {
        public PizzaOrder() { }

        public String OrderPizza(String strOrderDetailsXML)
        {
            // Do some pizza order processing here
            String strOrderStatusXML =
                    OrderHelperClass.processOrder(strOrderDetailsXML);

            return strOrderStatusXML;
        }
    }
}
```

Let's assume that this class is compiled into the `PizzaOrder.dll` assembly. To register the `PizzaOrder` class as a well-known object on the server, we'd need to use the static method called `RegisterWellKnownServiceType()` shown below:

```
Type typePizzaOrder = Type.GetType("PizzaOrderNS.PizzaOrder,PizzaOrder");

RemotingConfiguration.RegisterWellKnownServiceType(typePizzaOrder,
                                "PizzaOrder.soap",
                                WellKnownObjectMode.Singleton);
```

This code snippet registers the `PizzaOrder` object as a well-known object in the `Singleton` activation mode at an URI endpoint named `PizzaOrder.soap`. The object's type name should take the format *Qualified type name, Assembly Name*. This is `PizzaOrderNS.PizzaOrder, PizzaOrder` in our example.

To register the `PizzaOrder` class as a CAO, use the `RegisterActivatedServiceType()` method as shown:

```
Type typePizzaOrder = Type.GetType("PizzaOrderNS.PizzaOrder,PizzaOrder");

RemotingConfiguration.RegisterActivatedServiceType(typePizzaOrder);
```

The `RegisterActivatedServiceType()` method does not require details such as the URI endpoint and the activation mode because CAO objects are activated by the remoting activator registered by their host application and do not need a well-known URI endpoint to expose themselves to remote clients. The CAO client only needs to have knowledge of the object's type information, the machine on which it is hosted, the channel to use, and the port number on which the CAO application host is listening for activation requests. Armed with that information, the client can instantiate the remote `PizzaOrder` object using the new keyword as if it were creating a local object. Here's an example of how a client could instantiate and invoke a method of the `PizzaOrder` object exposed as a CAO:

```
Type typePizzaOrder = Type.GetType("PizzaOrderNS.PizzaOrder,PizzaOrder");

RemotingConfiguration.RegisterActivatedClientType(typePizzaOrder,
  "tcp://bingo:8080");

PizzaOrder objOrder = new PizzaOrder();

if(objOrder != null)
{
    String strOrderStatus = objOrder.OrderPizza(OrderInfoXML);
}
```

As we can see, the `RegisterActivatedClientType` can register CAO types at the client end so that they can be remotely activated at the specified URL. The above example assumes that the `PizzaOrder` object is hosted in a managed application using a TCP channel to listen on port 8080, on the machine called `bingo`.

You could register your remote object types, configure channels, and specify lease lifetime policies either programmatically or through a configuration file that contains all this information. To use a configuration file, you have to use the `Configure` method, passing it a file path to the configuration file. For more information on remoting configuration files and their format, refer to the *Remoting Configuration File Format Reference* section towards the end of this appendix. Consider the configuration file shown below, called `PizzaOrderClient.exe.config`:

```
<configuration>
    <system.runtime.remoting>
        <application name="PizzOrderClient">
            <client url="tcp://bingo:8080">
                <activated type="PizzaOrderNS.PizzaOrder,PizzaOrder"/>
            </client>
            <channels>
                <channel type="System.Runtime.Remoting.Channels.Tcp.TcpChannel,
                                System.Runtime.Remoting,
                                Version=1.0.3300.0,Culture=neutral,
                                PublicKeyToken=677a561934e089" port="8081" />
            </channels>
        </application>
    </system.runtime.remoting>
</configuration>
```

This file registers the `PizzaOrder` object as a CAO type in the client to be activated at the `tcp://bingo:8080` remote URL. Here's how you would configure remoting based on the information provided in this configuration file:

```
RemotingConfiguration.Configure("C:\\AppCfgs\\PizzaOrderClient.exe.config");

PizzaOrder objOrder = new PizzaOrder();
```

The System.Runtime.Remoting.TypeEntry Class

The `TypeEntry` class is the base class for classes that hold configuration and registration information for well-known objects and client-activated objects whose types need to be registered at the client or service-end of a remoting application. We'll examine each of these classes in the following sections:

❑ `ActivatedClientTypeEntry`

❑ `ActivatedServiceTypeEntry`

❑ `WellKnownClientTypeEntry`

❑ `WellKnownServiceTypeEntry`

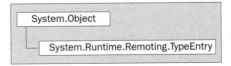

511

Property	Property type	Description
AssemblyName	String	Gets or sets the assembly name containing the object's type. If the object type you are registering is present in an assembly called PizzaOrder.dll, then the AssemblyName is PizzaOrder.
TypeName	String	Gets or sets the fully qualified type name of the object of the form *Qualified type name, Assembly Name*. If your object is called WimpyNS.Wimpy, present in an assembly named Popeye.dll, then the fully qualified name is: WimpyNS.Wimpy, Popeye.

The System.Runtime.Remoting.ActivatedClientTypeEntry Class

The ActivatedClientTypeEntry class holds configuration information to register a CAO's type in the client so that the object can be activated at a remote URL. CAO object types are registered in the client by the RegisterActivatedClientType() static method of the RemotingConfiguration class. An ActivatedClientTypeEntry object can be passed to this method to perform the registration.

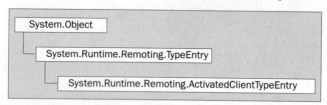

Property	Property type	Description
ApplicationUrl	String	Gets the URL of the remote application hosting the CAO. For example, if your CAO's application host has registered a HTTP channel to listen on port 8080, then the ApplicationUrl would be http://remotemachine:8080. For IIS hosting, the ApplicationUrl includes the name of the application's virtual root. For example, if MyIISAppName is the name of the IIS application's virtual root configured to host the CAO, and if MyIISServer Name is the name of the machine in which IIS is running, then the ApplicationUrl is http://MyIISServer Name:80/MyIISAppName.
ObjectType	Type	Gets type information for the CAO object.
Context Attributes	IContext Attribute[]	Gets or sets the context attributes associated with this CAO object's type to enforce policies such as synchronization, JIT activation, transactions, etc. For more information on context attributes and how to use them to demand special interception services for objects from their context, refer to the section of this appendix headed *The System.Runtime.Remoting.Contexts.ContextAttribute Class*.

To register the `PizzaOrder` CAO's type at the client end, we would need to create an `ActivatedClientTypeEntry` object, and populate it with the CAO's type information and the remote URL location of its activator. We then pass this object to the `RegisterActivatedClientType()` static method of the `RemotingConfiguration` class to perform the registration, as shown:

```
Type typePizzaOrder = Type.GetType("PizzaOrderNS.PizzaOrder,PizzaOrder");

ActivatedClientTypeEntry entryCAOClient = new
    ActivatedClientTypeEntry(typePizzaOrder, "tcp://bingo:8080");

RemotingConfiguration.RegisterActivatedClientType(entryCAOClient);

PizzaOrder objOrder = new PizzaOrder();
```

The System.Runtime.Remoting.ActivatedServiceTypeEntry Class

The `ActivatedServiceTypeEntry` class holds configuration information to register a CAO's type in the server so that remote clients can activate the object. CAO object types are registered in the server by the `RegisterActivatedServiceType()` static method of the `RemotingConfiguration` class. An `ActivatedServiceTypeEntry` object can be passed to this method to perform the registration. This is the server-side counterpart of the `ActivatedClientTypeEntry` class.

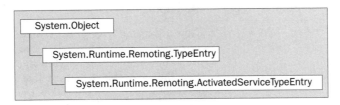

Property	Property type	Description
ObjectType	Type	Gets type information for the CAO object.
ContextAttributes	IContextAttribute[]	Gets or sets the context attributes associated with this CAO object's type, thus enforcing policies such as synchronization, JIT activation, transactions, etc. For information on context attributes and how to use them to demand special interception services for objects from their context, refer to *The System.Runtime.Remoting.Contexts. ContextAttribute Class* section of this appendix.

To register the `PizzaOrder` CAO's type at the service end, create an `ActivatedServiceTypeEntry` object and populate it with the CAO's type information. We would then pass this object to the `RegisterActivatedServiceType()` static method of the `RemotingConfiguration` class to perform the registration as shown:

```
Type typePizzaOrder = Type.GetType("PizzaOrderNS.PizzaOrder,PizzaOrder");

ActivatedServiceTypeEntry entryCAOService =
```

```
                               new ActivatedServiceTypeEntry(typePizzaOrder);

RemotingConfiguration.RegisterActivatedServiceType(entryCAOService);
```

The System.Runtime.Remoting.WellKnownClientTypeEntry Class

The `WellKnownClientTypeEntry` class holds configuration information to register a well-known (`SingleCall` or `Singleton`) object's type on the client so that any method calls made on objects of this type are directed to the object exposed at the specified remote URI endpoint. Well-known object types are registered in the client by calling the `RegisterWellKnownClientType()` static method of the `RemotingConfiguration` class. A `WellKnownClientTypeEntry` object can be passed to this method to perform the registration.

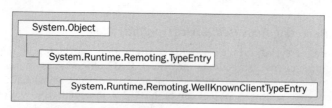

Property	Property type	Description
ApplicationUrl	String	Gets or sets the URL of the remote application that is hosting the well-known object. For example, if your well-known object is hosted in a managed application with the name `WeatherHost` that has registered a TCP channel listening on port 8090, the `ApplicationUrl` would be `tcp://WeatherMachine:8090/WeatherHost`, where `WeatherMachine` is the name of the machine in which the application host is running.
ObjectType	Type	Gets type information for the `well-known object`.
ObjectUrl	String	Gets the URL at which the well-known object type is exposed in the server. This URL includes the URI endpoint of the object in addition to the application host's URL path. For example, if your well-known object is exposed at an URI endpoint called `WeatherLookup.soap` in a managed application named `WeatherHost` that has registered a TCP channel listening on port 8090, the `ObjectUrl` would be `tcp://WeatherMachine:8090/WeatherHost/WeatherLookup.soap`, where `WeatherMachine` is the name of the machine in which the application host is running.

To register the `PizzaOrder` well-known object type at the service end, create a `WellKknownServiceTypeEntry` object and populate it with the well-known object's type information and the URL at which it is exposed. This object can be passed to the `RegisterWellKnownClientType` static method of the `RemotingConfiguration` class to perform the registration as shown below:

```
Type typePizzaOrder = Type.GetType("PizzaOrderNS.PizzaOrder,PizzaOrder");

WellKnownClientTypeEntry entryWKOClient =
    new  WellKnownClientTypeEntry(typePizzaOrder,
                    "tcp://bingo:8080/PizzaHost/PizzaOrder.soap");

RemotingConfiguration.RegisterWellKnownClientType(entryWKOClient);
```

The System.Runtime.Remoting.WellKnownServiceTypeEntry Class

The `WellKnownServiceTypeEntry` class holds configuration information to register a well-known (`SingleCall` or `Singleton`) object's type in the server at a specified URI endpoint so that remote clients can connect to the object and invoke its methods. Well-known object types are registered in the server by the `RegisterWellKnownServiceType()` static method of the `RemotingConfiguration` class. A `WellKnownServiceTypeEntry` object can be passed to this method to perform the registration. This class is the server-side counterpart of `WellKnownClientTypeEntry`.

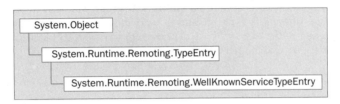

Property	Property type	Description
ObjectType	Type	Gets type information for the well-known object.
ObjectUri	String	Gets the URI endpoint of the well-known object. This name can be any valid URI name. However, if your well-known object is hosted in IIS, the URI's extension should either be .rem or .soap so that remote calls can be intercepted by the ASP.NET ISAPI extension (aspnet_isapi.dll).
Mode	WellKnownObjectMode enumeration value that specifies the activation mode for a well-known object. Refer to the table below for possible values.	Gets the activation mode (SingleCall or Singleton) for the well-known object.
ContextAttributes	IContextAttribute[]	Gets or sets the context attributes associated with this well-known object's type, enforcing policies such as synchronization, JIT activation, transactions, etc. For information on context attributes and how objects can use them to specify special interception services from their context, refer to the section headed *The System.Runtime.Remoting.Contexts. ContextAttribute Class* in this appendix.

WellKnownObjectMode enum members	Description
SingleCall	In SingleCall mode, a new object instance is created to service every client request. Since the object is destroyed when the method call completes, this activation mode doesn't allow you to maintain state in an object between method calls, unless you explicitly maintain state in a persistent store, and restore that state whenever your object is activated.
Singleton	In Singleton mode, the same object instance services all client requests. This allows you to maintain state in the object between method calls.

To register the PizzaOrder well-known object's type at the service end, we would need to create a WellKnownServiceTypeEntry object and populate it with the well-known object's type information, the URI endpoint name where it is exposed, and its activation mode (SingleCall or Singleton). This object can be passed to the RegisterWellKnownServiceType() static method of the RemotingConfiguration class to perform the registration as shown:

```
Type typePizzaOrder = Type.GetType("PizzaOrderNS.PizzaOrder,PizzaOrder");
WellKnownServiceTypeEntry entryWKOService =
        new WellKnownServiceTypeEntry(typePizzaOrder, "PizzaOrder.soap",
                                    WellKnownObjectMode.SingleCall);
RemotingConfiguration.RegisterWellKnownServiceType(entryWKOService);
```

The System.Runtime.Remoting.ObjectHandle Class

The ObjectHandle class wraps object references and allows the client to control when the remote object's type is loaded into its AppDomain. This means that the type information of the underlying object that it wraps need not be loaded into every AppDomain through which an ObjectHandle passes. The object wrapped by the ObjectHandle can be unwrapped when required by the target AppDomain. Since an ObjectHandle object is an MBR object, the lease manager associates a lease object with it whenever it is marshaled across AppDomain boundaries. After the ObjectHandle's lease expires and it has been marked for garbage collection, any attempt to unwrap the wrapped object or invoke a method on the wrapped object will fail.

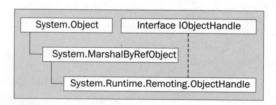

Method	Returns	Description
Unwrap	Object that was wrapped by the ObjectHandle	Returns the object that was wrapped by the ObjectHandle. If the lease has expired on an ObjectHandle, then any attempt to unwrap the wrapped object will result in an exception.

Method	Returns	Description
Initialize Lifetime Service	ILease interface of the lease object containing the lease lifetime policy settings for this object	Overridden by MBR objects to control their lifetime by initializing the lease properties. You can initialize lease properties only when the lease object is in its initial state. Any attempt to initialize the lease properties of a lease object that has already been activated results in an exception. You can examine the lease state by calling ILease.CurrentState on the lease object. If the lease has just been created but not yet activated, the CurrentState property will be set to Initial.

Earlier, we used the new keyword to create a PizzaOrder object whose CAO types were registered in the client so that it could be activated at a remote URL. Alternatively, the CreateInstance static method of the System.Activator class could be used by passing it the assembly name, type name, and the activator's URL for the PizzaOrder object. This method marshals the PizzaOrder object wrapped in an ObjectHandle instance from the remote AppDomain into the client's AppDomain. Once the ObjectHandle is obtained, you can use its Unwrap() method to retrieve the PizzaOrder object that was squirreled away in the ObjectHandle.

```
UrlAttribute attrURL = new UrlAttribute("tcp://bingo:8080");
ObjectHandle objHandle = Activator.CreateInstance("PizzaOrder",
        "PizzaOrderNS.PizzaOrder", new object[] {attrURL} );
PizzaOrder objOrder = (PizzaOrder)objHandle.Unwrap();
if(objOrder != null)
{
    String strOrderStatus = objOrder.OrderPizza(OrderInfoXML);
}
```

The System.Runtime.Remoting.ObjRef Class

An object reference is a serialized representation of an MBR object that can be marshaled across the wire. This serialized representation contains, among other things, information on the object's type structure, its assembly name, the URI endpoint at which it is exposed, and information on the transport channel used.

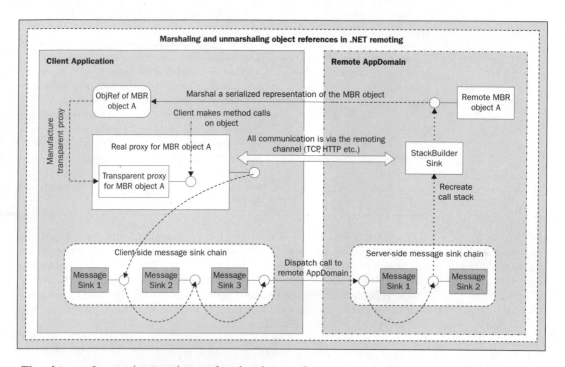

The object reference (ObjRef) is used at the client end to create two proxies – a **transparent proxy** and a **real proxy**. The transparent proxy is a mirror image of the remote object's type structure recreated in the client's AppDomain. The transparent proxy is itself is ensconced in a managed class instance of another proxy called the real proxy. When the client makes a method call, it invokes the method on the transparent proxy object. The remoting runtime intercepts calls made to the transparent proxy to determine if the target object exists in the same AppDomain as the proxy – you can use the ObjRef's IsFromThisAppDomain() method if you need to determine this. If the object resides in the same AppDomain as the proxy, a local method call is made on the object. However, if the target object is located in another AppDomain, the transparent proxy serializes the call-stack that applies to the method call into an IMethodMessage-based message object, and forwards the call to the real proxy.

The real proxy is responsible for dispatching calls to remote objects. It passes the message through a client-side message sink chain, in which each message sink intercepts the message and performs any necessary tasks. For example, a message formatter sink could serialize the message into a format that can be transported across the channel. A message formatter sink is usually the first sink, and the channel sink is usually the last sink in the client-side message sink chain. The channel sink at the end of the sink chain uses a transport channel (such as HTTP or TCP) to send the message to the target object's AppDomain, possibly crossing machine boundaries.

The transport channel of the server-side receives the message and passes it through a server-side message sink chain. At the server end, the first message sink is the channel sink and the last sink is the message formatter sink. The message formatter sink deserializes the message into an IMethodMessage-based object, which is then passed to a StackBuilder sink. This sink recreates the call-stack for the method call from the information in the message object so it can then invoke the method on the target object.

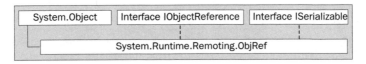

Property	Property type	Description
ChannelInfo	IChannelInfo	Gets or sets transport channel specific data associated with the AppDomain hosting the remote object. When the remote object is marshaled to produce an ObjRef, information on each registered channel is serialized with it. This property can be used by the client's AppDomain to retrieve channel data for the channels registered in a remote object's AppDomain.
TypeInfo	IRemotingTypeInfo	Gets or sets type information for the remote object. The client uses this type information to manufacture a transparent proxy representing the remote object's type structure. You can also use this property to tweak the type information to control how the transparent proxy is generated.
EnvoyInfo	IEnvoyInfo	Gets or sets the information needed to create an envoy message sink chain in the client's AppDomain. Envoy sinks can provide the interception services that context-bound objects require. Information on these envoy sinks is serialized into the ObjRef when context-bound objects are passed across AppDomain boundaries.
URI	String	Gets or sets the URI endpoint of the object.

Method	Returns	Description
GetObjectData	–	Called by the message serialization formatter to get information on the ObjRef, prior to serializing the ObjRef to a message stream. You can use this opportunity to populate the SerializationInfo object that is passed in with custom data (in the form of *name, type, value* triads) to be serialized along with the ObjRef. This custom data would then be available in the client's AppDomain when the ObjRef is received.

Table continued on following page

Method	Returns	Description
GetRealObject	Object	Used to get a reference to the remote object that this ObjRef represents. When the ObjRef is unmarshaled, this method is called to construct a proxy representing the type structure of the remote object.
IsFromThisApp Domain	bool	Returns a Boolean flag indicating whether the ObjRef represents an object within the current AppDomain.
IsFromThis Process	bool	Returns a Boolean indicating whether the ObjRef represents an object within the current process.

A remote MBR object is marshaled and serialized to its ObjRef representation whenever you register well-known or CAO objects at the service end (using methods like RegisterActivatedServiceType() or RegisterWellKnownServiceType() from the RemotingConfiguration class). An ObjRef is also implicitly created whenever an MBR object is passed a parameter to a remote method call. We can also use the Marshal() static method of the RemotingServices class to explicitly create an ObjRef representation for a MBR object, as shown below:

```
// Example of how to explicitly create an ObjRef
// Following code is at the service end (in a managed application host)

// Create a TCPChannel (Listen at port 8080)
TcpChannel chan = new TcpChannel(8080);

// Register the channel
ChannelServices.RegisterChannel(chan);

// Create the PizzaOrder object
PizzaOrder orderPizza = new PizzaOrder();

// Marshal the PizzaOrder object to get back a serialized ObjRef
ObjRef objref = RemotingServices.Marshal(orderPizza,"PizzaOrder.soap");

// Check the URI end point and the Type name persisted in the ObjRef
Console.WriteLine("URI endpoint of the object is: {0}", objref.URI);
Console.WriteLine("Type name of the object is: {0}", objref.TypeInfo.TypeName);

// Check if channel information for the channels registered in this
// AppDomain are persisted in the ObjRef, too
IEnumerator enumChannels = objref.ChannelInfo.ChannelData.GetEnumerator();
enumChannels.MoveNext();
ChannelDataStore channelDS = (ChannelDataStore)enumChannels.Current;
Console.WriteLine("Channel Registered is: {0}", channelDS.ChannelUris);

Console.WriteLine ("Press any key to shut me down....");
Console.ReadLine ();

// Disconnect the object from the channel
RemotingServices.Disconnect(orderPizza);

// Unregister the TCP Channel
ChannelServices.UnregisterChannel(chan);
```

The output of this code snippet would be something like this:

```
URI endpoint of the object is:
/e9369e85_bae3_4e4f_927e_4b2499d21f6e/PizzaOrder.soap
Type name of the object is: PizzaOrderNS.PizzaOrder, PizzaOrder,
Version=1.0.673.300, Culture=neutral, PublicKeyToken=null
Channel Registered is: tcp://167.254.34.107:8080
```

The System.Runtime.Remoting.RemotingServices Class

The `RemotingServices` class provides several helper methods to expose and consume remote objects. The `Marshal()` method can serialize an MBR object to its `ObjRef` representation, while the `Unmarshal` method can be used in the client's AppDomain to create a proxy to the MBR object from its `ObjRef`.

Consumers of remote MBR objects can use the `Connect()` method to connect to a well-known object registered in the server at a specified URL and obtain a transparent proxy for it. If you want the `ObjRef` representation from a transparent proxy returned by `Connect()`, use the `GetObjRefForProxy()` method.

The `Disconnect()` method can be useful when you wish to prevent the remote object receiving any further messages from its transport channel. We used this method in the previous section to disconnect the `PizzaOrder` object from the TCP channel. The `RemotingServices` class is sealed and therefore cannot be inherited by other classes.

Method	Returns	Description
Marshal *(Static Method)*	ObjRef	Marshals a remote MBR object into a serialized `ObjRef` representation that can be transferred across AppDomain boundaries.
Unmarshal *(Static Method)*	Object	Unmarshals the `ObjRef` into a transparent proxy representing the remote MBR object. This method is the inverse of the `GetObjRefForProxy()` method.
GetObjRefForProxy *(Static Method)*	ObjRef	Gets the `ObjRef` representation from the specified transparent proxy representing an MBR object. This method is the inverse of the `Unmarshal()` method.
GetRealProxy *(Static Method)*	RealProxy	Gets the `RealProxy` object associated with a specified transparent proxy. While a transparent proxy object is a recreation in the client's AppDomain of a remote object's type structure, the real proxy is responsible for dispatching the request to the remote AppDomain.

Table continued on following page

Method	Returns	Description
Connect *(Static Method)*	Object	Connects to a remote well-known object using its type and remote URL location, and returns a transparent proxy to the object. The transparent proxy can be used to invoke methods on the remote object.
Disconnect *(Static Method)*	bool	Disconnects the remote object from its transport channel thus preventing the object from any processing any further messages.
ExecuteMessage *(Static Method)*	IMethodReturn Message	Connects to the specified MBR object, executes a method call on it, and gets back the response message. This method is rarely used, and is used only on occasions when the method calls dispatched to an object need to be redirected to other remote objects, such as in a scenario where load balancing is required.
GetEnvoyChainFor Proxy *(Static Method)*	IMessageSink	This method returns the envoy message sink chain associated with a remote object. Objects that maintain context information usually serialize an envoy message sink chain to their ObjRef representation when they are marshaled outside AppDomain boundaries. This envoy message sink chain can be obtained from the ObjRef at the client end using its EnvoyInfo property. The real proxy dispatches messages to the remote object through this envoy sink chain.
GetLifetime Service *(Static Method)*	Ilease	Returns an object that handles the lease lifetime policy for this remote object. Client sponsors can use this method to get the lease object associated with a remote object to register themselves as sponsors for lease renewal.
GetObjectData *(Static Method)*	–	Serializes the specified MBR object into the provided SerializationInfo object.
GetObjectUri *(Static Method)*	String	Returns the URI endpoint that uniquely identifies the specified well-known MBR object.
SetObjectUriFor Marshal *(Static Method)*	–	Sets the URI endpoint for the specified well-known MBR object. You must set the URI endpoint for well-known objects prior to marshaling. Any attempt to call this method after marshaling throws a RemoteException.

Method	Returns	Description
GetServerType ForUri *(Static Method)*	Type	Returns the object type for a well-known object exposed at the specified URI endpoint. Since an URI endpoint can uniquely identify a well-known MBR object that has been marshaled outside its AppDomain, this method can be useful when you need the type information for a well-known object but you only know its URI endpoint at the server.
GetMethodBaseFrom MethodMessage *(Static Method)*	MethodBase	Returns type information for a method message as a MethodBase object.
GetSessionIdFor MethodMessage *(Static Method)*	String	Returns the session ID string for the current session associated with a method message being sent to the remote object. The session IDs are 120-bit strings to ensure uniqueness when tracking multiple sessions.
IsTransparent Proxy *(Static Method)*	bool	Returns a Boolean flag indicating if the specified object is a transparent proxy to the object, or the actual object itself.
IsObjectOutOf AppDomain *(Static Method)*	bool	Returns a Boolean flag indicating if the object that represents the specified transparent proxy is in the same AppDomain as the object invoking this method.
IsObjectOutOf Context *(Static Method)*	bool	Returns a Boolean flag indicating if the object that represents the specified transparent proxy is in the same context as the object invoking this method.
IsOneWay *(Static Method)*	bool	Returns a Boolean flag indicating if the client is waiting for the specified method in the server to complete, before it resumes its thread execution. For more information on the related topic of OneWay attributes, refer to the *System.Runtime.Remoting.Messaging.AsyncResult Class* section of this appendix.
IsMethod Overloaded *(Static Method)*	bool	Returns a Boolean indicating if the method represented by the specified method message is overloaded.

Let's see yet another way of invoking remote MBR objects – using the `Connect()` method. This method is very important from the perspective of a remoting client that connects to a well-known object. As a matter of fact, the `Activator.GetObject()` method used by remoting clients to consume well-known objects is a wrapper for a call to the `Connect()` method. Under the hood, the `Connect` method uses the type information and the URL location to connect to the well-known object and retrieve a serialized representation of the MBR object. It then calls the `Unmarshal()` method to deserialize the `ObjRef` to construct a transparent proxy for the remote object. Since the transparent proxy's type structure is a replica of the remote object, it can be cast to the actual type of the remote object and method calls can be made on it. The following code snippet shows how the `Connect()` method is used to obtain a transparent proxy for a well-known object registered in the server:

```
// Create and register a TCP channel
TcpChannel chan = new TcpChannel(8081);
ChannelServices.RegisterChannel(chan);

// Connect to the well-known object and obtain a proxy to the object
Object objTransparentProxy = RemotingServices.Connect(typePizzaOrder,
                            "tcp://bingo:8080/PizzaOrder.soap");

// Cast the proxy to the actual object's type
PizzaOrder objPizzaOrder = (PizzaOrder)objTransparentProxy;

if(objPizzaOrder != null)
{
    String strOrderStatus = objPizzaOrder.OrderPizza(OrderInfoXML);
}

// Unregister the channel
ChannelServices.UnregisterChannel(chan);
```

The above example assumes that the `PizzaOrder` object is exposed as a well-known object at a URI endpoint with the name `PizzaOrder.soap` and hosted in a managed application that has registered a TCP channel to listen on port 8080.

To obtain the `RealProxy` object associated with the transparent proxy, you can use the `GetRealProxy()` static method of the `RemotingServices` class as shown:

```
// Get the Real proxy that backs this transparent proxy
RealProxy realProxy = RemotingServices.GetRealProxy(objTransparentProxy);

// Get the full type name of the object that this real proxy represents
Console.WriteLine(realProxy.GetProxiedType().FullName);
```

The above code snippet displays **PizzaOrderNS.PizzaOrder**, if the `RealProxy` object represents the `PizzaOrder` object used in the earlier example.

Exception Classes of the System.Runtime.Remoting Namespace

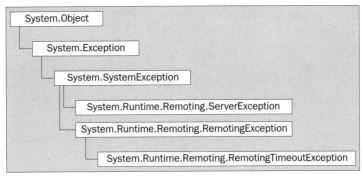

Exception class	Description
RemotingException	A RemotingException exception is thrown if an error occurs during a remoting operation. The standard HRESULT value associated with this exception is COR_E_REMOTING.
ServerException	A ServerException exception is thrown if communication errors occur when trying to contact applications that cannot throw exceptions (such as applications not based on the .NET Framework). The standard HRESULT value associated with this exception is COR_E_SERVER.
RemotingTimeoutException	The RemotingTimeoutException exception is thrown if the client end or the service end fails to respond within a specified time interval when contacted by the other end. The standard HRESULT value associated with this exception is COR_E_REMOTING.

The System.Runtime.Remoting.SoapServices Class

The SoapServices class allows you to serialize CLR types to SOAP-based XML schema types. Conversely, it allows you to deserialize an XML schema type to retrieve the corresponding CLR type that it represents. Tools like soapsuds.exe use this class extensively for converting XML schema types to CLR types and vice-versa.

Property	Property type	Description
XmlNsForClrType *(Static Property)*	String	Gets the XML namespace prefix for the XML encoding of CLR types
XmlNsForClrTypeWithNs *(Static Property)*	String	Returns the XML namespace prefix for the XML encoding of a CLR class present in mscorlib.dll

Table continued on following page

Property	Property type	Description
XmlNsForClrType WithAssembly *(Static Property)*	String	Gets the XML namespace prefix for XML encoding of a CLR class that has an assembly, but no native namespace
XmlNsForClrTypeWith NsAndAssembly *(Static Property)*	String	Returns the XML namespace prefix for the XML encoding of a CLR class that has an assembly as well as its own native namespace

We can quite easily put together some code to display the default XML namespace prefixes for CLR types when they are serialized to the XML type system:

```
Console.WriteLine("DEFAULT XML NAMESPACE PREFIX VALUES FOR CLR TYPES");
Console.WriteLine(SoapServices.XmlNsForClrType);
Console.WriteLine(SoapServices.XmlNsForClrTypeWithNs);
Console.WriteLine(SoapServices.XmlNsForClrTypeWithAssembly);
Console.WriteLine(SoapServices.XmlNsForClrTypeWithNsAndAssembly);
```

This code will produce the following output:

```
DEFAULT XML NAMESPACE PREFIX VALUES FOR CLR TYPES
http://schemas.microsoft.com/clr/
http://schemas.microsoft.com/clr/ns/
http://schemas.microsoft.com/clr/assem/
http://schemas.microsoft.com/clr/nsassem/
```

Methods for Serializing CLR Types to XML Schema Types

Method	Returns	Description
CodeXmlNamespaceForClr Type Namespace *(Static Method)*	String	Returns the XML namespace from a given CLR object's type name and assembly name
GetXmlElementFor InteropType *(Static Method)*	bool	Gets the XML element name and the XML namespace for the specified CLR type
GetXmlTypeForInterop Type *(Static Method)*	bool	Returns the XML type name and the XML namespace for the specified CLR type
GetXmlNamespaceFor MethodCall *(Static Method)*	String	Gets the XML namespace for the method call associated with the specified `MethodBase`
GetXmlNamespaceFor Method Response *(Static Method)*	String	Returns the XML namespace for the method response of the method associated with the specified `MethodBase`

Let's take a look at the XML namespaces generated for the `PizzaOrder` class when it is flattened to an XML schema. You can use the `CodeXmlNamespaceForClrTypeNamespace()` method to obtain this value as shown here:

```
// Get the XML namespace for the PizzaOrder class
Console.WriteLine(SoapServices.CodeXmlNamespaceForClrTypeNamespace
  ("PizzaOrderNS.PizzaOrder", "PizzaOrder"));
```

This code outputs the following line:

```
http://schemas.microsoft.com/clr/nsassem/PizzaOrderNS.PizzaOrder/PizzaOrder
```

On a similar note, let's check out the XML namespaces under which the `OrderPizza()` method and its method response are scoped. We can use the `GetXMLNamespaceForMethodCall()` and the `GetXMLNamespaceForMethodResponse()` methods for this. Both accept a `MethodBase` object. We need to obtain a `MethodInfo` array from the object's type, and enumerate it to find the `MethodInfo` object associated with the `OrderPizza()` method. Once we have that, we can pass the `MethodInfo` object to these XML namespace methods:

```
// Get the XML namespace for the OrderPizza method and its response
MethodInfo[] mInfoArray = typeof(PizzaOrderNS.PizzaOrder).GetMethods();
foreach(MethodInfo mInfo in mInfoArray)
{
  if(mInfo.Name == "OrderPizza")
  {
    Console.WriteLine(SoapServices.GetXmlNamespaceForMethodCall(mInfo));
    Console.WriteLine(SoapServices.GetXmlNamespaceForMethodResponse(mInfo));
  }
}
```

The output that you get back looks something like this:

```
http://schemas.microsoft.com/clr/nsassem/PizzaOrderNS.PizzaOrder/PizzaOrder
http://schemas.microsoft.com/clr/nsassem/PizzaOrderNS.PizzaOrder/PizzaOrder
```

Notice that both the `OrderPizza` method and its response are scoped under the same XML namespace.

Methods for Deserializing XML Schema Types to CLR Types

Method	Returns	Description
`DecodeXmlNamespaceForClr Type() Namespace` *(Static Method)*	`bool`	Gets the CLR type name and the assembly name from the specified XML namespace.
`GetInteropFieldTypeAnd NameFromXmlAttribute` *(Static Method)*	–	Gets the field name and the field type from the specified XML attribute name. (The containing object's type and field type's XML namespace also need to be specified.)

Table continued on following page

Method	Returns	Description
GetInteropFieldTypeAnd NameFromXmlElement *(Static Method)*	–	Gets the field name and the field type from the specified XML element name. (The containing object's type and field type's XML namespace also needs to be specified.)
GetInteropTypeFromXml Element *(Static Method)*	Type	Given an XML element name and XML namespace, this method returns the CLR type that was registered to be returned while deserializing an unrecognized object. Associations between XML element names and the corresponding CLR types to which they are deserialized can be made by the RegisterInteropXmlElement method.
GetInteropTypeFromXmlType *(Static Method)*	Type	Given an XML type name and XML namespace, this method returns the CLR type that was registered to be returned while deserializing an unrecognized object. Associations between XML type names and the corresponding CLR types to which they are deserialized can be made with the RegisterInteropXmlType() method.
IsClrTypeNamespace *(Static Method)*	bool	A Boolean specifying whether the given namespace represents a CLR type namespace.
RegisterInteropXmlElement *(Static Method)*	–	Registers a XML element name and XML namespace to a particular CLR type to use during deserialization.
RegisterInteropXmlType *(Static Method)*	–	Registers a given XML type name and XML namespace to a specified CLR type to use during deserialization.
PreLoad *(Static Method)*	–	Registers a specific type or all types in the assembly based on the properties set in the SoapType attribute tagged to the type.

During deserialization, given an XML namespace, you can recover the CLR type name along with the name of the assembly that houses that CLR type as shown here:

```
String strCLRNamespace;
String strAssemblyName;

// Get the CLR type namespace and the assembly name
SoapServices.DecodeXmlNamespaceForClrTypeNamespace(
"http://schemas.microsoft.com/clr/nsassem/PizzaOrderNS.PizzaOrder/PizzaOrder", out
strCLRNamespace, out strAssemblyName);

Console.WriteLine("Namespace is: {0}",strCLRNamespace);
Console.WriteLine("Assembly Name is: {0}",strAssemblyName);
```

As shown above, the `DecodeXmlNamespaceForClrTypeNamespace()` method acts as the inverse of the `CodeXmlNamespaceForClrTypeNamespace()` method. The output should be as follows:

```
Namespace is: PizzaOrderNS.PizzaOrder
Assembly Name is: PizzaOrder
```

Methods Specific to the SoapAction Attribute

Method	Returns	Description
RegisterSoapActionFor Method Base *(Static Method)*	–	Associates a `SOAPAction` value with the specified `MethodBase`.
GetSoapActionFromMethod Base *(Static Method)*	String	Gets the `SOAPAction` value associated with the specified `MethodBase`.
GetTypeAndMethodName From SoapAction *(Static Method)*	bool	Gets the type and method name associated with the specified `SOAPAction`.
IsSoapActionValidFor MethodBase *(Static Method)*	bool	Checks to see if the `SOAPAction` is valid for a specified `MethodBase`.

The XML fragment below is taken from the WSDL description of the methods exposed by the `PizzaOrder` object. You can generate similar XML schemas for types in a CLR assembly using the `soapsuds.exe` tool that ships with the .NET Framework. The fragment below details the `OrderPizza()` method. In WSDL parlance, methods are called **operations**. More information on WSDL can be found in Chapter 2. You will notice that a `SoapAction` attribute is associated with the `<soap:operation>` element that maps the `SoapAction` attribute's value to a specific method or operation:

```xml
<operation name="OrderPizza">
  <soap:operation  soapAction="http://schemas.microsoft.com/
      clr/nsassem/PizzaOrderNS.PizzaOrder/PizzaOrder#OrderPizza"/>
        <input name="OrderPizzaRequest">
          <soap:body use="encoded"
            encodingStyle="http://schemas.xmlsoap.org/soap/encoding/"
            namespace="http://schemas.microsoft.com/clr/nsassem/
                       PizzaOrderNS.PizzaOrder/PizzaOrder" />
        </input>
        <output name="OrderPizzaResponse">
          <soap:body use="encoded"
             encodingStyle="http://schemas.xmlsoap.org/soap/encoding/"
             namespace="http://schemas.microsoft.com/clr/nsassem/
                        PizzaOrderNS.PizzaOrder/PizzaOrder" />
        </output>
  </operation>
```

The `SoapServices` class provides methods to determine the value of the `SoapAction` attribute in the WSDL definition generated for a specific method exposed by a CLR type. Conversely, given the value of the `SoapAction` attribute in a WSDL schema, it can provide you with the CLR object's fully qualified type name and the method name:

```
MethodInfo[] mInfoArray = typeof(PizzaOrderNS.PizzaOrder).GetMethods();

foreach(MethodInfo mInfo in mInfoArray)
{
    if(mInfo.Name == "OrderPizza")
    {
        // Get the SOAPAction attribute's value for the OrderPizza method
        Console.WriteLine(SoapServices.GetSoapActionFromMethodBase(mInfo));
    }
}
```

As shown above, the GetSoapActionFromMethodBase() method gets the SoapAction attribute's value for the specified method exposed by a CLR type. The SoapAction value associated with the OrderPizza() method would look something like this:

```
http://schemas.microsoft.com/clr/nsassem/PizzaOrderNS.PizzaOrder
        /PizzaOrder#OrderPizza
```

To extract the CLR type name and the method name from the SoapAction attribute, use the GetTypeAndMethodNameFromSoapAction() method as shown:

```
String strTypeName;
String strMethodName;

// Get the CLR object's type name and method name from the SoapAction value
SoapServices.GetTypeAndMethodNameFromSoapAction(
    "http://schemas.microsoft.com/clr/nsassem/PizzaOrderNS.PizzaOrder
    /PizzaOrder#OrderPizza", out strTypeName, out strMethodName);

Console.WriteLine("Type name is: {0}",strTypeName);
Console.WriteLine("Method name is: {0}",strMethodName);
```

The output would be:

```
Type name is: PizzaOrderNS.PizzaOrder, PizzaOrder
Method name is: OrderPizza
```

The System.Runtime.Remoting.Contexts.Context Class

In first section of this appendix, we saw how a context can group together .NET objects that require comparable interception services from their home context (services like synchronization, automatic transactions, etc.). Contexts play a very important role in the .NET Remoting paradigm, and issues such as marshaling requirements and proxy creation semantics are decided according to context and AppDomain boundaries. Once an object is assigned to a context, it stays in that context for the rest of its life. The Context class allows you to manage contexts and their associated properties. It provides methods to associate data with local memory slots that can be shared between objects in the same context. Take a look at the AllocateNamedDataSlot(), GetNamedDataSlot(), FreeNamedDataSlot(), GetData(), and SetData() family of methods for how to share data between objects housed within the same context.

```
System.Object
    System.Runtime.Remoting.Contexts.Context
```

Property	Property type	Description
DefaultContext *(Static Property)*	Context	Gets the Context object associated with the current AppDomain's default context. When an AppDomain is created, a default context is created along with it. Objects that do not need any context interception services such as synchronization, JIT activation, etc., are assigned to the default context.
ContextID	int	Gets the current context's ID, which can uniquely identify a context within an AppDomain.
ContextProperties	IContextProperty[]	Returns the current context's properties.

Method	Returns	Description
AllocateDataSlot *(Static Method)*	LocalDataStoreSlot	Allocates an unnamed local memory slot to store data that can be shared between objects in this context.
AllocateNamedData Slot *(Static Method)*	LocalDataStoreSlot	Allocates a publicly named local memory slot using the specified name to store data that can be shared between objects in this context.
FreeNamedDataSlot *(Static Method)*	–	Frees the specified publicly named local memory slot.
GetNamedDataSlot *(Static Method)*	LocalDataStoreSlot	Returns the named local memory slot with the specified name.
GetData *(Static Method)*	Object	Returns the data associated with the specified local memory slot.
SetData *(Static Method)*	Object	Associates data with the specified local memory slot.
GetProperty	IContextProperty	Gets the context property with the specified name from the current context.
SetProperty	–	Associates a context property with the current context. You cannot set context properties on an AppDomain's default context.
RegisterDynamic Property *(Static Method)*	bool	This method is used to register a sink for proxy or context interception services. Once a sink is registered, the sink can intercept any remoting calls entering a proxy, or entering or leaving a context.

Table continued on following page

Method	Returns	Description
UnregisterDynamic Property *(Static Method)*	bool	This method is used to unregister a sink that has registered itself for proxy or context interception services.
DoCallBack	–	Executes code in another context with provision for callbacks through a `CrossContext` delegate.
Freeze	–	Freezes the context. No further context properties can be added to a context once it's been frozen.

The example below shows how objects are assigned to contexts based on metadata properties that indicate their requirements for interception services from their home context:

```
class Sleepy
{
    static void Main(string[] args)
    {
        Console.WriteLine ("Default Context ID is: {0}", Thread.CurrentContext
         .ContextID);

        Grumpy grumpy = new Grumpy();
        grumpy.DisplayContextInfo();
    }
}

class Grumpy
{
    public void DisplayContextInfo()
    {
        Console.WriteLine ("Grumpy's Context ID is: {0}", Thread
         .CurrentContext.ContextID);
    }
}
```

In the example above, the `Main` entry point displays the context ID of the default context in the AppDomain. It then creates an object called `Grumpy` and asks it to display the context ID of the context in which it's created. It turns out that `Grumpy` is also created in the AppDomain's default context, as shown by the identical context IDs in the output produced:

```
Default Context ID is: 0
Grumpy's Context ID is: 0
```

Now we'll make `Grumpy` grumpy, and insist on a context that can provide synchronization services. So we make `Grumpy` inherit from the `System.ContextBoundObject` class, which must be inherited by any object that requires context based interception services. `SynchronizationAttribute` is set to indicate that all calls to objects in this context should be serialized. See the section later in this appendix headed *The System.Runtime.Remoting.Contexts.SynchronizationAttribute Class* for more details on how to use this.

Here's the modified class for Grumpy:

```
[Synchronization(SynchronizationAttribute.REQUIRES_NEW)]
class Grumpy : ContextBoundObject
{
    public void DisplayContextInfo()
    {
        Console.WriteLine ("Grumpy's Context ID is: {0}",
                            Thread.CurrentContext.ContextID);
    }
}
```

This time the output that you would see is as follows:

```
Default Context ID is: 0
Grumpy's Context ID is: 1
```

Grumpy has now been assigned a new context indicated by a differing context ID because of the requirement for context synchronization, which the default context was not able to provide.

A handy feature to note is the ability to share state between objects within a single context using **named local memory slots**, which allow us to store per-context state in named variables that can be accessed by all objects in a given context. We create a named local memory slot by the AllocateNamedDataSlot static method of the Context class, which returns a LocalDataStoreSlot instance. The SetData() static method can then assign a value to the new data slot. Other objects living in the same context can use the GetNamedDataSlot() static method to retrieve the LocalDataStoreSlot object, and read the value that it contains using the GetData() static method.

```
class Sleepy
{
    static void Main(string[] args)
    {
        // Create a new memory slot called Dwarf that can be shared
        // by objects in this context
        LocalDataStoreSlot lds = Context.AllocateNamedDataSlot("Dwarf");
        Context.SetData(lds,"Sneezy");

        // Ask Grumpy if he can read the value in the local memory slot
        Grumpy grumpy = new Grumpy();
        grumpy.AskGrumpy();

        // Get the modified value that Grumpy set in the local memory slot
        Console.WriteLine ("Sleepy says: {0}",Context.GetData(lds));
    }
}

class Grumpy
{
    public void AskGrumpy()
    {
        // Get the current value of the local memory slot named Dwarf
        LocalDataStoreSlot lds = Context.GetNamedDataSlot("Dwarf");
        Console.WriteLine ("Grumpy says: {0}",Context.GetData(lds));

        // Modify the value in the local memory slot named Dwarf
        Context.SetData(lds,"Bashful");
    }
}
```

Here's the output of the above code snippet:

```
Grumpy says: Sneezy
Sleepy says: Bashful
```

Every context has context properties associated with it. You can obtain the context properties for a context using the `ContextProperties` property. The code below obtains the context properties of a context-bound object:

```
[Synchronization(SynchronizationAttribute.REQUIRES_NEW)]
class Dopey : ContextBoundObject
{
    public void DisplayContextProperties()
    {
        IContextProperty[] ctxPropArray =
                        Thread.CurrentContext.ContextProperties;

        foreach(IContextProperty ctxProp in ctxPropArray)
        {
            Console.WriteLine(ctxProp.Name);
        }
    }
}
```

Calling the `DisplayContextProperties()` method on `Dopey` will result in the following output, indicating that the context in which `Dopey` lives has two properties – one associated with lease lifetime services and the other associated with synchronization:

```
LeaseLifeTimeServiceProperty
Synchronization
```

The System.Runtime.Remoting.Contexts.ContextAttribute Class

The `ContextAttribute` class is the base class for all context attributes. Typically, classes that inherit from `System.ContextBoundObject` are tagged with context attributes to indicate specific interception services that they require from their home context. For example, the `SynchronizationAttribute`, which we examine in the next section, can be applied to context-bound objects to declaratively indicate that they require synchronization services from their context. Developers can write home-grown context attributes by deriving from this class and providing the appropriate context properties and interception sinks. The `ThreadAffinity` and `Synchronization` context attributes are two such attributes provided by the .NET Framework.

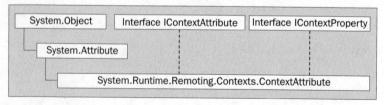

Property	Property type	Description
Name	String	Gets the name of the context attribute

Field	Field Type	Description
AttributeName *(Protected Field)*	String	Gets the name of the context attribute.

Method	Returns	Description
Freeze	–	This method is called by the runtime to indicate that all context properties have been finalized for the context, and that no more may be added.
GetPropertiesForNew Context	–	This method is called by the runtime to ask the context attribute to add its context properties to the ContextProperties property of the object that represents a construction call message. These context properties can then be used to set up the required context environment.
IsContextOK	bool	This method is called by the runtime to determine if the current context meets the context attribute's requirements. If all such context attributes return true, the creator's context will house the object. Otherwise, a new context is created and the object is placed there.
IsNewContextOK	bool	This method is called by the runtime to determine if the context properties in the context attribute have any issues with the new context. Context properties can check if they can co-exist with the context properties of other context attributes by checking the ContextProperties property of the Context object passed in.

The System.Runtime.Remoting.Contexts.SynchronizationAttribute Class

The SynchronizationAttribute is applied to an object to indicate that its home context should serialize access to all objects when multiple threads call into that context. This attribute installs a server-context interception sink that actively tracks incoming calls to the context and serializes concurrent access to the objects within the context. To improve throughput, the IsReEntrant property can be set to true. This has the effect that any calls made by the currently executing thread outside the current context are intercepted too, and one of the waiting threads may resume its execution path in the synchronized context while the call-out is performed.

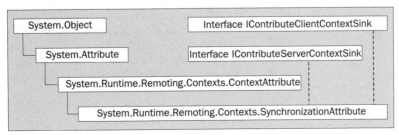

Field	Field Type	Description
NOT_SUPPORTED *(Static Field)*	const int	Indicates that the class to which this attribute is applied should **not** be created in a synchronized context
REQUIRED *(Static Field)*	const int	Indicates that the class to which this attribute is applied should **only** be created in a synchronized context
REQUIRES_NEW *(Static Field)*	const int	Indicates that the class to which this attribute is applied should be created in a **new** synchronized context
SUPPORTED *(Static Field)*	const int	Indicates that the class to which this attribute is applied can be created either in a synchronized context or in a context that does not provide synchronization

Property	Property type	Description
IsReEntrant	bool	A Boolean value indicating if reentrancy is required, which enables waiting threads to enter a synchronized context when the currently executing thread makes a call outside the current context
Locked	bool	Gets or sets a Boolean value indicating if the context to which this attribute is applied is locked

Method	Returns	Description
GetClient ContextSink	IMessageSink	Creates a call-out sink, and links it to the front of an existing message sink chain at the context boundary in the client end.
GetServer ContextSink	IMessageSink	Creates a synchronized dispatch sink, and links it to the front of an existing message sink chain at the context boundary in the server end.
GetProperties ForNew Context	–	This method is called by the runtime to ask this attribute to add its synchronization context properties to the ContextProperties property of the object that represents a construction call message. These context properties can then be used when setting up the required synchronized context.
IsContextOK	bool	This method is called by the runtime to determine if the current context meets the Synchronization attribute's requirements. If all such context attributes return true, the creator's context will house the object. Otherwise, a new context is created and the object is placed there.

Let's see how we can apply the `SynchronizationAttribute` to a context-bound object:

```
class Sleepy
{
    static void Main(string[] args)
    {
        Console.WriteLine ("Sleepy's Context ID is: {0}",
                            Thread.CurrentContext.ContextID);

        Grumpy grumpy = new Grumpy();
        grumpy.StartComplaining();
    }
}

[Synchronization(SynchronizationAttribute.REQUIRES_NEW)]
class Grumpy : ContextBoundObject
{
    public void StartComplaining()
    {
        Console.WriteLine("Grumpy's Context ID is: {0}",
                            Thread.CurrentContext.ContextID);

        Sneezy sneezy = new Sneezy();
        sneezy.HearComplains();
    }
}

[Synchronization(SynchronizationAttribute.REQUIRED)]
class Sneezy : ContextBoundObject
{
    public void HearComplains()
    {
        Console.WriteLine("Sneezy's Context ID is: {0}",
                            Thread.CurrentContext.ContextID);
    }
}
```

The output from this code is shown below:

```
Sleepy's Context ID is: 0
Grumpy's Context ID is: 1
Sneezy's Context ID is: 1
```

Notice in the code that `Grumpy` and `Sneezy` inherit from `System.ContextBoundObject`. This is a requirement for all objects that require special interception services from their home context.

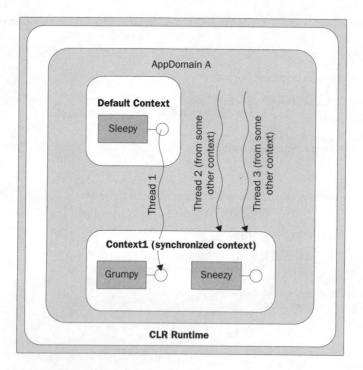

`Sleepy` can live in the AppDomain's default context because it does not have any special requirements. It creates `Grumpy`, which states that it needs a synchronized home context. However, the default context does not support synchronization, and the `SynchronizationAttribute.REQUIRES_NEW` value of `Grumpy`'s `Synchronization` attribute indicates that it is to be created *only* in a *new* context that provides synchronization services. So `Grumpy` moves into a new context, and goes on to create `Sneezy`. `Sneezy` indicates that it requires synchronization services from the context in which it lives. However, `Sneezy` does not demand to be created in a new context and is willing to reside in a compatible context if one exists, as indicated by the `SynchronizationAttribute.REQUIRED` value of its `Synchronization` attribute. It is therefore housed in its creator's context (`Grumpy`'s context) since this context provides synchronization and is compatible with the requirements of `Sneezy`'s context. Since `Grumpy` and `Sneezy` live in a synchronized context, access to these objects from multiple threads will be serialized at context-level granularity.

The System.Runtime.Remoting.Activation.UrlAttribute Class

The `UrlAttribute` specifies the URL where a client-activated object is to be activated. Consumers of a CAO object can use the `CreateInstance()` static method of the `Activator` class and pass a `UrlAttribute` object containing the URL of the CAO's activator. This class is sealed and therefore cannot be inherited by other classes.

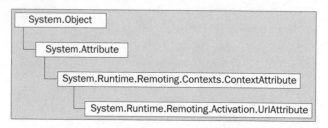

Property	Property type	Description
UrlValue	String	Gets the URL where a client-activated object will be activated. The UrlValue of the activator needs to be set before a call is made to the CreateInstance() static method of the Activator class to create the CAO.

Method	Returns	Description
Equals	bool	Returns a Boolean indicating if the CAO activator's URL for the specified object matches the URL of the CAO activator for this instance. Overrides the Equals() method provided by System.Object.
GetHashCode	int	Returns the hash code associated with this URLAttribute object. Overrides the GetHashCode() method provided by System.Object.
GetProperties ForNewContext	–	Called by the remoting runtime to create the context at the specified URL location, and to activate the CAO inside it. The runtime does not expect this attribute to contribute any context properties. Context properties are typically provided by context attributes to set up the context environment.
IsContextOK	bool	This method is called by the runtime to determine if the current context meets the URL attribute's requirements. The URL attribute makes this decision by examining the ContextProperties property of the Context object.

Let's see how we can use the UrlAttribute class to specify the URL of the activator for a CAO:

```
UrlAttribute attrURL = new UrlAttribute("tcp://popeye:8080");

ObjectHandle objHandle = Activator.CreateInstance(
        typeof(PizzaOrderNS.PizzaOrder), new object[] {attrURL} );
```

This code tells the remoting runtime to activate the PizzaOrder object at the tcp://popeye:8080 URL. We're assuming that an application host has registered the PizzaOrderNS.PizzaOrder CAO type for remote activation at the service end and is using a TCP channel to listen on port 8080 for requests, in a machine named popeye.

The System.Runtime.Remoting.Channels.ChannelDataStore Class

The ChannelDataStore class stores data associated with the transport channel such as the URI endpoints that the channel is currently servicing. Transport channels such as the HTTP and TCP channels store channel-specific information, which can be accessed through their ChannelData property, which returns a ChannelDataStore object, or more accurately, an object that implements the IChannelDataStore interface. When an MBR object is marshaled across an AppDomain boundary, the channel data of the transport channels servicing the MBR object's AppDomain is also serialized into the ObjRef so that the client AppDomain can access its properties.

539

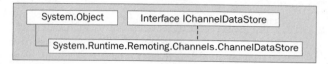

Property	Property type	Description
ChannelUris	String[]	Gets or sets the URI endpoints that the current channel is servicing
Item	Object	Indexer property that gets or sets the value associated with the specified key

The code below demonstrates how the ChannelDataStore class can retrieve URI details for a transport channel:

```
HttpChannel chan = new HttpChannel(8080);

// Get the channel data associated with this channel
ChannelDataStore channelData = (ChannelDataStore)chan.ChannelData;

// Display the URI endpoint associated with this channel
Console.WriteLine("Channel URI is: {0}",channelData.ChannelUris[0]);
```

The output looks something like this:

```
Channel URI is: http://167.254.34.107:8080
```

The System.Runtime.Remoting.Channels.ChannelServices Class

The ChannelServices class contains static methods for channel registration, unregistration, and message dispatching. This class is sealed and therefore cannot be inherited by other classes.

Property	Property type	Description
RegisteredChannels *(Static Property)*	IChannel[]	Returns a list of the currently registered channels

Method	Returns	Description
RegisterChannel *(Static Method)*	–	Registers a channel with the remoting services infrastructure. Channels are registered on a per-AppDomain basis.
UnregisterChannel *(Static Method)*	–	Unregisters a channel that was registered with the remoting services infrastructure.

540

Method	Returns	Description
GetChannel *(Static Method)*	IChannel	Returns a registered channel object with the specified name.
GetUrlsForObject *(Static Method)*	String[]	Returns an array of URL strings followed by generated GUIDs that can be used to uniquely identify a remote MBR object.
SyncDispatchMessage *(Static Method)*	IMessage	Synchronously dispatches the specified message to the server-side message sink chain installed at the URI endpoint specified in the message. This method doesn't return until the server has processed the message and returned a response. Returns the reply message returned by the server-side sink chain.
AsyncDispatchMessage *(Static Method)*	IMessageCtrl	Asynchronously dispatches the specified message to the server-side message sink chain installed at the URI endpoint specified in the message. This method returns immediately without waiting for the server to respond to the message. Returns an interface that allows you to exercise control over asynchronously dispatched messages.
DispatchMessage *(Static Method)*	Server Processing	Dispatches the specified message through a chain of server channel sinks specified through the IServerChannelSinkStack interface, which provides stack-based behavior for the server-side channel sinks while processing asynchronous message responses. Returns an enumeration value that indicates the status of the message processing on the server (see the table below)
GetChannelSink Properties *(Static Method)*	IDictionary	Returns an IDictionary of properties for the specified channel sink.

ServerProcessing enum members	Description
Async	The message is being processed asynchronously. Channel sinks should store response data for later processing.
Complete	The message was processed synchronously.
OneWay	The message was dispatched and the caller does not require a response.

The `RegisterChannel()` and `UnregisterChannel()` methods register and unregister transport channels with the remoting services framework respectively. Channels are registered on a per-AppDomain basis. Also, only one channel may listen on the same port, so watch out for registering channels on ports that other channels are currently listening on. Conflicting ports are checked on a machine-wide basis, and have little to do with the fact that transport channels are registered on a per-AppDomain basis. When a process terminates, all channels that it registered with the remoting services infrastructure are removed as well.

```
HttpChannel channelHTTP = new HttpChannel(8080);

// Register a HTTP channel
ChannelServices.RegisterChannel(channelHTTP);

// Register remote object types (well-known/CAO types) here...

// Listen for requests here by keeping the application host running

// Unregister the HTTP channel
ChannelServices.UnregisterChannel(channelHTTP);
```

Once you've registered multiple channels with remoting, you can use the `RegisteredChannels()` method to find the registered channel objects as shown here:

```
HttpChannel channelHTTP = new HttpChannel(8080);
TcpChannel  channelTCP = new TcpChannel(8095);
ChannelServices.RegisterChannel(channelHTTP);
ChannelServices.RegisterChannel(channelTCP);

// Get the list of registered channels
IChannel[] channelArray = ChannelServices.RegisteredChannels;

// Enumerate through the array and display the channel name
foreach(IChannel channel in channelArray)
{
    Console.WriteLine(channel.ChannelName);
}
```

Here's the output:

```
http
tcp
```

As shown above, the names that are returned for both channels are default names assigned by the system when a channel is not explicitly named. We'll see how to give a channel a specified name when we examine the `HttpChannel` and `TcpChannel` classes. Once we have the name of a channel, we can retrieve the channel object from the list of registered channels using the `GetChannel()` method:

```
IChannel chan = ChannelServices.GetChannel("http");
if (chan is HttpChannel)
{
    HttpChannel channelHttp = (HttpChannel)chan;

    // Party with the channel...
}
```

The System.Runtime.Remoting.Channels.Http.HttpChannel Class

The HttpChannel class provides a transport channel implementation that sends and receives messages across remoting boundaries using the HTTP protocol. This class is a convenience class that combines both the client-side and the server-side implementations of the HTTP transport channel, provided by the HttpClientChannel and HttpServerChannel classes respectively. By default, the HTTP channel carries messages to the remote object in SOAP format, because the default message formatter for the HttpChannel is the SOAP message serialization formatter, SoapFormatter. However, it's quite possible to send binary payloads using this channel. The pluggable channel and pluggable formatter architecture in the .NET remoting framework lets us replace the SOAP formatter sink provider in the message sink chain with a binary formatter sink provider that serializes messages to the object as a binary stream before being sent across the transport channel.

The HTTP channel is the preferred method of communication with remote objects and services spread disparately throughout the Internet, beyond the confines of corporate firewalls. It becomes all the more compelling to use SOAP over HTTP when your application needs to interact with web services deployed on platforms that typically only respond to HTTP requests that carry SOAP messages. Your system administrator is also freed from the rigmarole of having to open additional ports for clients outside your firewall, as we can use good old port 80 to service HTTP requests.

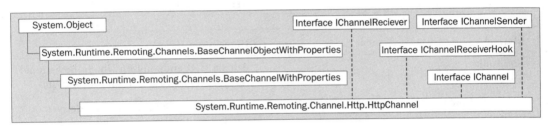

Property	Property type	Description
ChannelData	Object	Returns information on the URI endpoints serviced by this channel. The returned object can be cast to a ChannelDataStore object to retrieve the channel's URI details.
ChannelName	String	Returns the name of the channel. The default HTTP channel name is http.
ChannelPriority	int	Gets the priority of the channel. The default priority value is 1. The remoting runtime prioritizes connection for channels with higher priority values over those with lower values.
ChannelScheme	String	Gets the listener type.
ChannelSinkChain	IServerChannelSink	Gets the chain of channel sink providers through which the messages pass before being sent out on the transport channel. Returns the interface of the channel sink object at the strat of the chain

Table continued on following page

Property	Property type	Description
Keys	ICollection	Gets an ICollection of keys representing various channel properties associated with the client-side channel implementation (HttpClientChannel) and the server-side channel implementation (HttpServerChannel). The most important property keys are name, port, priority, proxyName, proxyPort, and clientConnectionLimit.
Properties	IDictionary	Gets an IDictionary interface to the list of properties associated with the channel.
Item	Object	Indexer property that gets or sets a channel property associated with a specified key.
WantsToListen	bool	Gets or sets a Boolean flag to indicate whether the channel is using a channel receiver hook.

Method	Returns	Description
AddHook ChannelUri	–	Adds a URI endpoint on which the channel receiver hook should listen for requests.
CreateMessage Sink	IMessageSink	Creates a channel sink that can deliver messages either to a specified URL location or to a channel data object.
GetUrlsForUri	String[]	Returns an array of URL strings for the specified well-known object's URI endpoint. The URLs are fully qualified with the channel URI and the well-known object's URI endpoint.
Parse	String	Given a fully qualified URL (like those returned by the GetUrlsForUri() method), this method parses it into the channel URI and the well-known object's URI endpoint.
StartListening	–	Starts listening for channel requests.
StopListening	–	Stops listening for channel requests.

The default name assigned to an HTTP channel is http, and is stored as one of the channel's properties. The HttpChannel and TcpChannel objects allow you to pass a 'dictionary' of named properties to their constructors for initializing the channel's properties. For example, you can use the name property to explicitly assign a user-defined name to the channel:

```
// Initialize the channel properties for the HTTP Channel
IDictionary channelProps = new Hashtable();
channelProps["name"] = "SneezyHTTP";
channelProps["priority"] = "1";
channelProps["port"] = "8080";

HttpChannel channelHTTP = new HttpChannel(channelProps, new
 SoapClientFormatterSinkProvider(), new SoapServerFormatterSinkProvider());

// Display the channel's name
Console.WriteLine(channelHTTP.ChannelName);

// Display the channel's priority
Console.WriteLine(channelHTTP.ChannelPriority);

// Display the listener type
Console.WriteLine(channelHTTP.ChannelScheme);

// Get the channel data containing URI specific information
ChannelDataStore cds = (ChannelDataStore)channelHTTP.ChannelData;
```

Here's the output:

```
SneezyHTTP
1
http
```

In the code above, the `HttpChannel` constructor is passed an `IDictionary` interface to an object containing name-value pairs for certain channel properties. The second and third parameters of the constructor represent the message formatter sink providers to use on the client and server side respectively. The above code uses the SOAP formatter sink provider.

The pluggable channel and pluggable formatter architecture allows channels and formatters to matched to best suit an application's requirements and its deployment environment. To use the binary formatter instead of the default SOAP formatter, install binary formatter sinks at either end of the message sink chain as shown below:

```
HttpChannel channelHTTP = new HttpChannel(channelProps, new
  BinaryClientFormatterSinkProvider(), new
  BinaryServerFormatterSinkProvider());
```

Every time we register a channel to listen on a specific port, the remoting runtime spawns a separate thread that monitors that port for incoming requests. To terminate the listener thread and stop the channel listening for requests, use the `StopListening` method of the `IChannelReceiver` interface implemented by `HttpChannel`:

```
// Get the list of registered channels
IChannel[] channelArray = ChannelServices.RegisteredChannels;

// Enumerate through the array
foreach(IChannel channel in channelArray)
{
    // Check for our HTTP channel's name
    if(channel.ChannelName == "SneezyHTTP")
    {
```

```
        // Cast to the IChannelReceiver interface
        IChannelReceiver channelReceiver = (IChannelReceiver)channel;

        // Ask the HTTP Channel to stop listening for requests
        channelReceiver.StopListening(null);
    }
}
```

Be aware that, although the channel stops listening for requests, it remains present in the list of registered channels. The channel is removed from the list only when we call the `Unregister` static method of the `ChannelServices` class.

The System.Runtime.Remoting.Channels.Tcp.TcpChannel Class

The `TcpChannel` class provides a transport channel implementation that sends and receives messages across remoting boundaries using the TCP protocol. This class is a convenience class combining the functionality of the client-side and the server-side implementations of the TCP transport channel, as provided by the `TcpClientChannel` and `TcpServerChannel` classes respectively. By default, the TCP channel serializes messages sent to the remote object as binary streams using the binary message serialization formatter, `BinaryFormatter`. As with the HTTP channel, you can plug in a different message formatter, such as the SOAP formatter, to use in place of the binary formatter.

Since the TCP channel uses raw sockets to communicate between the client and server, it's much faster than its HTTP counterpart. If you have a controlled deployment environment within a corporate LAN or intranet, then you might be able to cash in on the improved performance of the TCP channel. If, however, your remote objects are going to be accessed by clients beyond a firewall, then the HTTP channel is likely to be the preferred choice for the reasons described in the previous section.

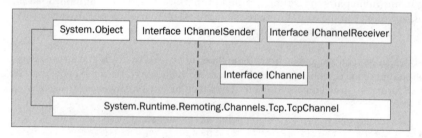

Property	Property type	Description
ChannelData	Object	Returns information on the URI endpoints serviced by this channel. The returned object can be cast to a `ChannelDataStore` object to retrieve the channel's URI details.
ChannelName	String	Returns the name of the channel. The default TCP channel name is `tcp`.
ChannelPriority	int	Gets the priority of the channel. The default priority value is 1. The remoting runtime prioritizes connection for channels with higher priority values over those with lower values.

Method	Returns	Description
CreateMessageSink	IMessageSink	Creates a channel sink that can deliver messages either to a specified URL location or to a channel data object.
GetUrlsForUri	String[]	Returns an array of URL strings for the specified well-known object's URI endpoint. The URL values are fully qualified with the channel's URI and the well-known object's URI endpoint.
Parse	String	Given a fully qualified URL (like those returned by the GetUrlsForUri method), this method parses it to obtain the channel's URI and the well-known object's URI endpoint.
StartListening	–	Starts listening for channel requests.
StopListening	–	Stops listening for channel requests.

The following snippet of code creates, registers, and unregisters a TCP channel:

```
// Create a TCP channel
TcpChannel channelTCP = new TcpChannel(8085);

// Register the channel
ChannelServices.RegisterChannel(channelTCP);

// Register remote object types in the server here
// Keep the application host running...

// Unregister the TCP channel
ChannelServices.UnregisterChannel(channelTCP);
```

To replace the default binary message formatter of the TCP channel with the SOAP formatter, substitute the client-side and server-side binary message sink providers with their respective SOAP counterparts:

```
// Set the channel properties for the TCP Channel
IDictionary channelProps = new Hashtable();
channelProps["name"] = "ExpressTCP";
channelProps["priority"] = "1";
channelProps["port"] = "8085";

// Ask the TCP channel to use SOAP formatter
TcpChannel channelTCP = new TcpChannel(channelProps, new
SoapClientFormatterSinkProvider(), new SoapServerFormatterSinkProvider());
```

The System.Runtime.Remoting.Lifetime.ClientSponsor Class

The ClientSponsor class provides a default implementation for a lease lifetime sponsor, which can be used to renew leases for client-activated objects and well-known Singleton objects whose lifetime is managed by lease lifetime policies. For information on how lease sponsors register with the lease lifetime manager, refer to the *Remoting Lifetime Management with Leases* topic in the *.NET Remoting Building Blocks* section earlier in this appendix.

Lease lifetime management does not apply to well-known SingleCall objects because they are destroyed after every method call.

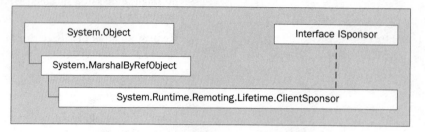

Property	Property type	Description
RenewalTime	TimeSpan	Gets or sets the time period by which the lease lifetime should be increased when the lease manager contacts the sponsor for lease renewal

Method	Returns	Description
Register	bool	Registers this object as a lease lifetime sponsor for the specified MBR object. When a ClientSponsor object registers itself with the lease manager, it is added to the lease manager's list of sponsors for the lease object associated with the specified MBR object. The sponsors are contacted when the lease lifetime of the MBR object expires.
Unregister	–	Unregisters the object as a lease lifetime sponsor for the specified MBR object.
Renewal	TimeSpan	The lease manager calls this method when the lease expires on an MBR object for which this object is a registered lease lifetime sponsor. This method is passed a lease object which can be used to set various lease options such as the lease time, lease renewal time for every method call, and sponsorship timeout settings. The return value is the additional lease time granted to the MBR object.
Close	–	Revokes itself as a lease lifetime sponsor for all MBR objects for which it has registered itself as a lease lifetime sponsor.
InitializeLife timeService	ILease	Overridden by MBR objects to control their lifetime by initializing the lease properties. ClientSponsor objects override this method to return null, granting them indefinite lease lifetime. (The examples in this section show how to exercise control over the lifetime of your lease sponsor objects.)

Registering a `ClientSponsor` object as a lease lifetime sponsor is quite straightforward. Just call the object's `Register` method, passing in the MBR object for which it is to sponsor the lease lifetime:

```
// Create a ClientSponsor that specifies infinite lease
ClientSponsor sponsor = new ClientSponsor(TimeSpan.Zero);

// Register this as a sponsor for the remote object
sponsor.Register(objRemote);
```

Since a lifetime sponsor is itself an MBR object whose lifetime is controlled by the lease lifetime manager on the client's AppDomain, it is possible to manage the lifetime of the lease sponsor itself. For example, you might want the lease sponsor to provide its lease renewal services for only 30 minutes. A `ClientSponsor` object has infinite lease because it overrides its `MarshalByRefObject` base class's `InitializeLifetimeService()` method to return `null`, thus registering a permanent lease sponsor. To exercise finer control over the lifetime of a lease sponsor, create a lease lifetime sponsor class that inherits from `MarshalByRefObject` and implements the `ISponsor` interface. We can override the `InitializeLifetimeService()` method in this class to set its lease lifetime. In the implementation of the `ISponsor` interface's `Renewal()` method, we can set the various lease properties for the lease object passed in by the lease manager:

```
class MyObjectResurrector : MarshalByRefObject, ISponsor
{
    public TimeSpan Renewal(ILease lease)
    {
        lease.InitialLeaseTime = TimeSpan.FromHours(3);
        lease.RenewOnCallTime = TimeSpan.FromMinutes(5);
        lease.SponsorshipTimeout = TimeSpan.FromSeconds(20);
        return TimeSpan.FromHours(24);
    }

    public override object InitializeLifetimeService()
    {
        ILease lease = (ILease)base.InitializeLifetimeService();
        lease.InitialLeaseTime = TimeSpan.FromMinutes(30);
        return(lease);
    }
}
```

To register a lease lifetime sponsor with the lease manager, we need to obtain the lease object associated with the MBR object whose lease lifetime is being sponsored. Then, we call the `Register()` method on the lease object to register the sponsor:

```
// Create a lease lifetime sponsor object
MyObjectResurrector leaseSponsor = new MyObjectResurrector();

// Get the lease object associated with the remote object whose lease
// lifetime is being sponsored
ILease lease = (ILease)RemotingServices.GetLifetimeService(objRemoteMBR);

// Register this sponsor with the lease manager
lease.Register(leaseSponsor);
```

The System.Runtime.Remoting.Messaging.CallContext Class

We saw earlier that the System.Runtime.Remoting.Contexts.Context class provides methods that use named local memory slots to share data between objects in a single context. However, in order to propagate data along the logical execution path of a thread that crosses context and AppDomain boundaries, we need something analogous to the Thread Local Storage (TLS). Win32 threads use TLS to associate data with a thread that can be accessed by any object in the thread's execution path. The CallContext class stores data in named data slots, which can be propagated along the logical execution path of a thread regardless of context and AppDomain boundaries. Sharing objects through CallContext is not too difficult when they are accessed across context boundaries within the *same* AppDomain. However, to share objects through CallContext across AppDomain boundaries, the shared object needs to implement the ILogicalThreadAffinative interface. Named data slots associated with a CallContext are available when callbacks are received through asynchronous delegate invocations too. Even security policies such as code access security use the CallContext to propagate Windows principals across AppDomain boundaries.

Method	Returns	Description
SetData *(Static Method)*	–	Stores the specified object in a named data slot in the CallContext. The object stored in a CallContext's named data slot needs to implement the ILogicalThreadAffinative interface to be accessible through CallContext to objects in other AppDomains through which the current logical execution thread passes.
GetData *(Static Method)*	Object	Returns the object associated with the specified CallContext's data slot name. Data can be stored in a CallContext's data slot using the SetData method.
FreeNamedDataSlot *(Static Method)*	–	Frees the data slot with the specified name from the CallContext. The object in the named slot is no longer accessible to objects in other contexts and AppDomains.
GetHeaders *(Static Method)*	Header[]	Returns headers sent as out-of-band data along with the method call.
SetHeaders *(Static Method)*	–	Sets headers that are sent as out-of-band data with the method call.

To associate data with a named data slot in a CallContext, use the SetData static method. The example below associates the string Abaracadabra.NET with a named data slot called MagicWord:

```
CallContext.SetData("MagicWord", "Abracadabra.NET");
```

Other objects in the context through which this logical execution thread passes can use the GetData() static method to retrieve the data from a specific data slot:

```
String strMagicWord = (String) CallContext.GetData("MagicWord")
```

Let's take a quick look at how we can use named data slots to pass data between contexts and AppDomains using the `CallContext` class. Let's say we have three objects – `Sleepy`, `Grumpy`, and `Sneezy`. `Sleepy` is created in the default context in the default AppDomain. `Sleepy` creates `Grumpy`, which is a context-bound object that requires a synchronized context and so must be placed in a new context within the default AppDomain. `Grumpy` creates a new AppDomain called `SneezyLand` and creates an instance of `Sneezy` in `SneezyLand`'s default context. Each of the trio lives in a different context, with `Sneezy` living in an AppDomain of its own. In the following code, `Sleepy` uses `CallContext` to share data with `Grumpy` and `Sneezy`:

```
using System;
using System.Threading;
using System.Runtime.Remoting;
using System.Runtime.Remoting.Contexts;
using System.Runtime.Remoting.Messaging;

class Sleepy
{
    static void Main(string[] args)
    {
        Console.WriteLine("Sleepy's AppDomain: {0}, Context ID: {1}",
                          AppDomain.CurrentDomain.FriendlyName,
                          Thread.CurrentContext.ContextID);

        CallContext.SetData("DwarfComm", "Snow White's turn to cook today");

        // Create Grumpy
        Grumpy grumpy = new Grumpy();
        grumpy.SayHello();

        // Free the slot from the CallContext
        CallContext.FreeNamedDataSlot("DwarfComm");

    }
}

[Synchronization(SynchronizationAttribute.REQUIRES_NEW)]
class Grumpy : ContextBoundObject
{
    public void SayHello()
    {
        Console.WriteLine ("Grumpy's AppDomain: {0}, Context ID: {1}",
                          AppDomain.CurrentDomain.FriendlyName,
                          Thread.CurrentContext.ContextID);

        Console.WriteLine ("Grumpy received the message: {0}",
                          CallContext.GetData("DwarfComm"));

        // Create Sneezy in another AppDomain
        AppDomain sneezyLand = AppDomain.CreateDomain("SneezyLand",null,null);
        ObjectHandle objHandle =
                          sneezyLand.CreateInstance("DwarfApp","Sneezy");
        Sneezy sneezy = (Sneezy)objHandle.Unwrap();
        sneezy.SayHello();
    }
}
```

```
class Sneezy : MarshalByRefObject
{
    public void SayHello()
    {
        Console.WriteLine ("Sneezy's AppDomain: {0}, Context ID: {1}",
                           AppDomain.CurrentDomain.FriendlyName,
                           Thread.CurrentContext.ContextID);

        Console.WriteLine ("Sneezy received the message: {0}",
                           CallContext.GetData("DwarfComm"));
    }
}
```

Here's the output of this short program:

```
Sleepy's AppDomain: DwarfApp.exe, Context ID: 0
Grumpy's AppDomain: DwarfApp.exe, Context ID: 1
Grumpy received the message: Snow White's turn to cook today
Sneezy's AppDomain: SneezyLand, Context ID: 0
Sneezy received the message:
```

Notice that `Sleepy`'s message reached only `Grumpy`, and not `Sneezy`. Certainly some kind of lapse in communication – but where's the glitch? It's because `Sneezy` lives in a different AppDomain, and any data passed across AppDomain boundaries through the logical thread's `CallContext` must implement the `ILogicalThreadAffinative` interface in order to be accessible to the objects that live there.

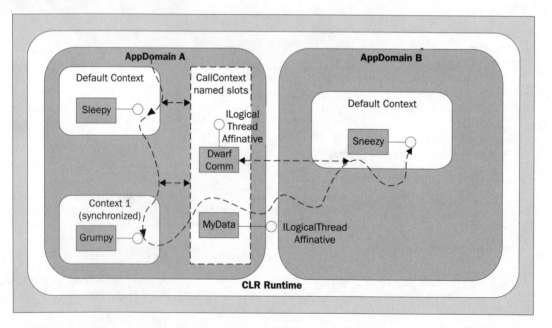

Let's quickly create a new class that implements the `ILogicalThreadAffinative` interface to wrap the data that `Sleepy` intends to share with `Grumpy` and `Sneezy`:

```
[Serializable]
class DwarfMessageComm : ILogicalThreadAffinative
{
    public DwarfMessageComm(String strMessage)
    {
        DwarfMessage = strMessage;
    }
    public String DwarfMessage;
}
```

The DwarfMessageComm class shown above implements the ILogicalThreadAffinative interface. Sleepy can now pack data into a DwarfMessageComm object and set this data to the DwarfComm named data slot in CallContext:

```
// Set the data for the DwarfComm named slot in the CallContext
CallContext.SetData("DwarfComm",
                new DwarfMessageComm("Snow White's turn to cook today"));
```

This ensures that the data associated with this named slot is persisted within CallContext when the execution thread crosses AppDomain boundaries. Here's how Sneezy would get this data from the DwarfComm named data slot of CallContext:

```
// Retrieve the data from the DwarfComm named slot in the CallContext
DwarfMessageComm message =
                (DwarfMessageComm)CallContext.GetData("DwarfComm");

Console.WriteLine ("Sneezy received the message: {0}",message.DwarfMessage);
```

After making these changes, the program now allows Sneezy, sole resident of the SneezyLand AppDomain, to partake in dwarf gossip:

```
Sleepy's AppDomain: DwarfApp.exe, Context ID: 0
Grumpy's AppDomain: DwarfApp.exe, Context ID: 1
Grumpy received the message: Snow White's turn to cook today
Sneezy's AppDomain: SneezyLand, Context ID: 0
Sneezy received the message: Snow White's turn to cook today
```

The System.Runtime.Remoting.Messaging.Header Class

The Header class can carry out-of-band data along with a message. Headers provide additional instructions to a message processor to tell it how to process the data in the message. The **SOAP 1.1** protocol defines such an extensibility mechanism through SOAP headers. These headers can use the mustUnderstand attribute to tell the message processor whether it's mandatory for it to understand what the message means and to process it accordingly. If this attribute is set to true, message processors that cannot handle the message are expected to throw exceptions (SOAP faults. You can piggyback headers on a CallContext so that they are available across context and AppDomain boundaries, along the execution path of the thread. Message sinks in the message sink chain can examine these CallContext headers to find out if they contain any instructions for them to act on.

Field	Field Type	Description
HeaderNamespace	String	Represents the XML namespace under which the header is scoped
MustUnderstand	bool	A Boolean indicating whether it is mandatory for the message processor to understand and process this header
Name	String	Represents the name of the header
Value	Object	Represents the value associated with the header

A typical SOAP envelope contains instructions for its message processor within the SOAP headers. The `<authdwarf:enter>` element shown below is one such instruction. The `mustUnderstand` attribute of this element is set to `true`, indicating that the message processor should understand this header and process it accordingly. If the processor does not understand the header, it is expected to throw a SOAP fault.

```
<soap:Envelope xmlns:soap='http://www.w3.org/2001/10/soap-envelope'>

  <soap:Header>
    <authdwarf:enter
          xmlns:authdwarf='http://snowwhitesdwarfs.net/authentication/sec'
                  soap:mustUnderstand='true'>
      <dwarfuser>bashful@snowwhitesdwarfs.net</dwarfuser>
    </authdwarf:enter>
  </soap:Header>

  <soap:Body>
    <m:EnterCaves xmlns:m='http://snowwhitesdwarfs.net/authentication'>
      <dwarfname>Bashful</dwarfname>
    </m:EnterCaves>
  </soap:Body>

</soap:Envelope>
```

We can associate header information with a `CallContext` so that it can travel along the execution path of the thread over context and AppDomain boundaries. We add headers to a `CallContext` using the `SetHeaders()` static method:

```
Header header = new Header("dwarfuser","bashful@snowwhitesdwarfs.net");
header.HeaderNamespace = "http://snowwhitesdwarfs.net/authentication/sec";
header.MustUnderstand = true;
CallContext.SetHeaders(new Header [] { header });
```

When the headers are associated with the `CallContext`, other objects and message sinks along the execution path of that thread can examine these headers and process them accordingly:

```
// Enumerate the headers to check if they need to be processed
Header[] hdrs = CallContext.GetHeaders();
foreach(Header header in hdrs)
{
    if(header.MustUnderstand)
    {
```

```
                    Console.WriteLine(header.Name);
                    Console.WriteLine(header.Value);

            // Process the header...
            // Probably to check if Bashful is authorized to enter the cave
        }
    }
```

The System.Runtime.Remoting.Messaging.AsyncResult Class

This class can track the status of execution of an asynchronous method call on a remote object and can retrieve the results when the method call completes. Essentially, .NET clients invoke remote services asynchronously using delegates. The compiler generates the BeginInvoke() and EndInvoke() methods for the delegate for making asynchronous remote method calls. Calls to BeginInvoke() return an AsyncResult object immediately, and the client thread is free to continue with other chores while the remote method continues execution on the server. The AsyncResult object returned from the BeginInvoke call exposes the IsCompleted property that we can use to track when the method call completes on the server. Generally, we'll set up some sort of while loop to detect when this property becomes true indicating that the results of the method call are ready. The AsyncWaitHandle property provides a WaitHandle synchronization primitive, which gets signaled when the method call completes on the server. This allows client applications to use blocking or timeout semantics provided by the synchronization primitive while waiting for the method call to complete. To get the result returned by the asynchronous method, call the delegate's EndInvoke() method passing in the AsyncResult object returned by BeginInvoke(). Calling EndInvoke() before the method call has finished executing on the server will result in the client thread being blocked until the asynchronous method call finishes. Alternatively, you can register a callback handler that is called when the asynchronous method call completes.

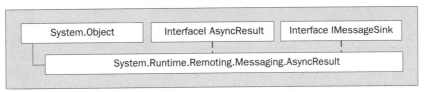

Property	Property type	Description
AsyncDelegate	Object	Gets the delegate object on which the asynchronous method call was made. The delegate's BeginInvoke() method is called to start asynchronous method execution. When the method call completes, the delegate's EndInvoke() method can be called to retrieve the results of the method call.
AsyncState	Object	The AsyncState property allows you to maintain state between the start and end of execution of an asynchronous method call on the server. The value passed to the last parameter of the BeginInvoke() method call can be accessed through this property.

Table continued on following page

Property	Property type	Description
AsyncWaitHandle	WaitHandle	Gets a `WaitHandle` synchronization primitive, which is alerted when the server completes the aynchronous method call. Clients can use this property to perform one of the various blocking semantics (block till completion of the asynchronous method call, block with timeouts, etc.).
CompletedSynchronously	bool	Gets a Boolean indicating if the method completed its execution synchronously. The current implementation of the method returns `false`.
EndInvokeCalled	bool	Gets or sets a Boolean indicating if the `EndInvoke()` method has been called on the delegate.
IsCompleted	bool	Gets a Boolean value indicating if the asynchronous method call has completed. Ideally, you would call this method in some sort of a `while` loop that checks if the asynchronous method call has completed, allowing us to perform other operations in the client thread inside the loop. When this property is `true`, you can call `EndInvoke` on the delegate to get the results of the asynchronous method.

For an example to illustrate these concepts, let's assume that we have a well-known object called `BankTeller`, which exposes a method called `GetBankBalance()`. Let's say that this method performs some long-winded operation (such as `MakeCoffee()`, or `ChatToColleague()`) and hence takes a while to return, thus becoming a perfect candidate for asynchronous execution. The `BankTeller` class is no different from any of the other MBR classes that we've seen so far – it has no specific keyword to indicate that the `GetBankBalance()` method can execute asynchronously. A remote method does not decide itself whether to execute synchronously or asynchronously. The client makes this decision and uses synchronous or asynchronous calls to invoke the remote method accordingly.

```
public class BankTeller : MarshalByRefObject
{

    public void GetBankBalance(String AccountNumber, String PinNumber,
                            ref double dBalanceRet)
    {
        // Some long-winded operation, such as having a chin wag
        Thread.Sleep(10000);

        // Return the account balance (assume the balance is $650)
        dBalanceRet = 650.00;
    }
}
```

It's in the client code where we see the asynchronous invocation pattern in use. Our first order of business is to declare a delegate for the GetBankBalance method:

```
public delegate void BankBalanceCallback(String AccountNumber,
                              String PinNumber, ref double dBalanceRet);
```

Next, register the object types and the channels with the remoting services infrastructure. For the sake of brevity, we'll use a remoting configuration file to do this. For more information on remoting configuration files, see the *Remoting Configuration File Format Reference* section of this appendix. Create an instance of the BankBalanceCallback delegate that references the GetBankBalance() method of the BankTeller object:

```
RemotingConfiguration.Configure("BankCustomer.exe.config");
BankTeller bankTeller = new BankTeller();

BankBalanceCallback bankDelegate =
                new BankBalanceCallback(bankTeller.GetBankBalance);
```

The delegate declaration makes the compiler generate a BeginInvoke() and EndInvoke() method for the delegate, which let us execute the method asynchronously. Take a look at the signature of the BeginInvoke() method as generated by the compiler:

```
instance class [mscorlib]System.IAsyncResult
BeginInvoke(string AccountNumber,string PinNumber,
            float64& dBalanceRet,
            class [mscorlib]System.AsyncCallback callback,
            object 'object')
```

The first three parameters of the BankBalanceCallback delegate's BeginInvoke() method are the parameters associated with the GetBankBalance() method. The fourth parameter is a parameter to an asynchronous callback handler, which can be registered to receive a notification when the asynchronous method call completes. For now, ignore this parameter. We'll look at an example of registering a callback handler for asynchronous invocations later in this section. The last parameter allows you to manage state between the start and the end of an asynchronous method call, which can be accessed through the AsyncResult object's AsyncState property. To start execution of an asynchronous method, use the BeginInvoke() method call, which returns immediately without waiting to complete. It returns an AsyncResult object, which will be our object of focus from now on, and which we'll use to track the progress of the method call:

```
String AccountNumber = "7738323";
String PinNumber = "1234";
double dBalanceRet = 0.0;

AsyncResult balanceAsyncResult = (AsyncResult)bankDelegate.BeginInvoke(
  AccountNumber, PinNumber, ref dBalanceRet, null, null);
```

To check if the asynchronous method call has completed, use the IsCompleted property as shown below. This property is set to true when the method call completes:

```
while (!balanceAsyncResult.IsCompleted)
{
    // Do something in the client thread, while the async method
    // is cranking away on the server
}
```

Finally, to pick up the results that the method has returned, use the `EndInvoke()` method. Let's take a look at the signature for the `BankBalanceCallback` delegates's `EndInvoke()` method that the compiler has generated for us:

```
instance void  EndInvoke(float64& dBalanceRet,
                        class [mscorlib]System.IAsyncResult result)
```

The first parameter of this call is a reference to the bank balance parameter returned by the `GetBankBalance()` method. The second parameter is of type `IAsyncResult`, for which you need to pass the `AsyncResult` object returned by the `BeginInvoke()` method. Calling `EndInvoke()` on the delegate before the asynchronous method call completes will result in blocking the client thread until the asynchronous method returns with the results. For this reason, it's prudent to first check if the method call has completed using the `AsyncResult` object's `IsCompleted` property:

```
bankDelegate.EndInvoke(ref dBalanceRet, balanceAsyncResult);
Console.WriteLine("Your balance is : ${0}", dBalanceRet);
```

The sourcecode for a client application that executes the `GetBankBalance` method asynchronously is shown below:

```
using System;
using System.Runtime.Remoting.Messaging;
using System.Runtime.Remoting;
using System.Threading;

// Declare a delegate for the GetBankBalance method
public delegate void BankBalanceCallback(String AccountNumber,
                    String PinNumber, ref double dBalanceRet);

class BankCustomer
{
    static void Main(string[] args)
    {
        // Configure remoting
        RemotingConfiguration.Configure("BankCustomer.exe.config");

        // Create a new BankTeller instance
        BankTeller bankTeller = new BankTeller();

        // Create a delegate instance for asynchronous
        // invocation of the  GetBankBalance method
        BankBalanceCallback bankDelegate =
                new BankBalanceCallback(bankTeller.GetBankBalance);

        String AccountNumber = "7738323";
        String PinNumber = "1234";
        double dBalanceRet = 0.0;

        // Invoke the remote method asynchronously using the delegate
        AsyncResult balanceAsyncResult =
            (AsyncResult)bankDelegate.BeginInvoke(AccountNumber, PinNumber,
                                        ref dBalanceRet, null,null);

        // Make customers lose their nerve - Time for some blatant advertising
        // while the ATM calculates the balance on the server
```

```
            while (!balanceAsyncResult.IsCompleted)
            {
                Thread.Sleep(1000);
                Console.WriteLine("Please wait. Processing request...");
                Console.WriteLine("And while you are waiting, would you like to try
                    our new WAP based internet banking acct. blah, blah, blah...");
            }

            // The remote object has finally returned with the result
            // Get the out/ref parameters through the EndInvoke call
            bankDelegate.EndInvoke(ref dBalanceRet, balanceAsyncResult);
            Console.WriteLine("Your balance is : ${0}", dBalanceRet);
        }
    }
```

As mentioned earlier, we can register a callback handler to be called when the asynchronous method completes. We do this by declaring a function that has an identical signature to that of the `BankBalanceCallbackHandler()` method below:

```
[OneWay()]
static void BankBalanceCallbackHandler(IAsyncResult asyncResult)
{
    // Get the AsyncResult associated with this call
    AsyncResult balanceAsyncResult = (AsyncResult)asyncResult;

    // Get the delegate associated with the asynchronous invocation
    BankBalanceCallback bankDelegate = (BankBalanceCallback)
                                        balanceAsyncResult.AsyncDelegate;

    // Get the out/ref parameters through the EndInvoke call
    double dBalanceRet = 0.0;
    bankDelegate.EndInvoke(ref dBalanceRet, balanceAsyncResult);
    Console.WriteLine("Your balance is : ${0}", dBalanceRet);
}
```

Notice that the handler function is tagged with the `OneWayAttribute`. This attribute lets the caller know that no assumptions should be made as to whether the method call executed successfully or not. In other words, it instructs the caller not to worry about the outcome of the method call (**fire-and-forget semantics**). The method itself could be executing either synchronously or asynchronously.

It makes sense to use the `OneWay` attribute for the callback handler above as the thread calling the handler function with the results from the asynchronous method invocation need not be concerned whether the client will process the results or not. Methods marked with the `OneWay` attribute cannot have any return values. Also, `out` or `ref` directional types for parameters are *not* permitted for such methods.

The callback handler function is invoked when the asynchronous method execution completes. The `AsyncResult` object is passed to the handler function, which can use it to get the delegate instance associated with the asynchronous invocation by the `AsyncDelegate` property. To obtain the results of the asynchronous method, call the `EndInvoke()` method on the delegate, just as we did earlier.

To register this asynchronous callback handler, create an `AsyncCallback` delegate instance that refers to the `BankBalanceCallbackHandler`, and pass this `AsyncCallback` delegate instance to the `BankBalanceCallback` delegate's `BeginInvoke()` method:

```
AsyncResult balanceAsyncResult = (AsyncResult)bankDelegate.BeginInvoke(
    AccountNumber, PinNumber, ref dBalanceRet, new AsyncCallback(
    BankBalanceCallbackHandler), null);
```

Registering a callback handler function to receive the results of an asynchronous method invocation avoids the need for additional code in the client to check for completion of the asynchronous method call, and removes the risk of blocking the client thread while the asynchronous method call completes.

The System.Runtime.Remoting.Proxies.RealProxy Class

The `RealProxy` class is responsible for directing method calls made on the transparent proxy to the remote object. Like the transparent proxy, the real proxy is manufactured by the runtime using information taken from the remote object's `ObjRef`. While the transparent proxy is simply a recreation of the remote object's type structure on the client, the `RealProxy` dispatches method calls to the actual object itself, after passing it through a message sink chain, and finally out through the transport channel to the remote object's URL. The message sink chain comprises a series of message sinks, which include formatter sinks (which provide message serialization), envoy sinks (which provide context interception services), user sinks (which provide custom features such as call logging, etc.), and channel sinks (which send messages to the remote object using the transport channel).

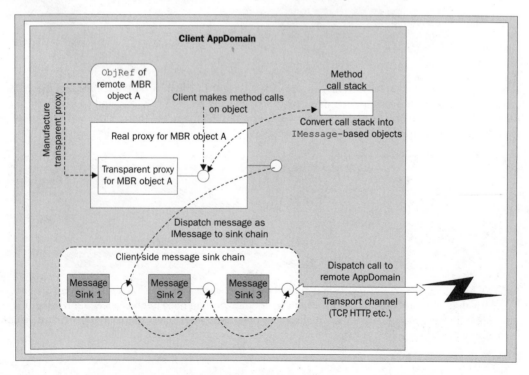

While the transparent proxy cannot be extended, the `RealProxy` is a managed class that can have custom interception features added to it, for instance to perform logging, load balancing, call redirection, user authentication, and so on before and after a method is invoked on the remote object.

Listed below are the most commonly used methods in the `RealProxy` class. The .NET Framework class library documentation contains a complete list of methods should you require one.

Method	Return Value	Description
CreateObjRef	ObjRef	Creates an `ObjRef` for the specified object's type. An `ObjRef` is a serialized representation of an MBR object that can be marshaled across AppDomain boundaries. In the target AppDomain, the `ObjRef` is used to manufacture a real proxy and transparent proxy, so that objects in that AppDomain may invoke the methods of the MBR object.
GetProxiedType	Type	Returns the object type of the remote MBR object that this `RealProxy` instance represents.
GetTransparentProxy	Object	Returns the transparent proxy object associated with this `RealProxy` instance. For every `RealProxy`, there is an underlying transparent proxy that models the remote object's type structure. Both proxies are manufactured from the remote object's `ObjRef`.
Invoke	IMessage	Implementers of custom proxies need to override this method to invoke the method on the remote object. The transparent proxy calls this method, passing a message object that implements the `IMethodCallMessage` interface to it, which contains information on the method to be invoked on the remote object.
GetObjectData	–	This method serializes the transparent proxy object associated with this `RealProxy` instance into the specified `SerializationInfo` object.

Table continued on following page

Method	Return Value	Description
`InitializeServerObject`	`IConstruction ReturnMessage object`	This method is used to activate client-activated objects on the server. Typically, when you call `new` or `Activator.CreateInstance()` on the remote object, the `RealProxy` sends an activation request in the form of an `IConstructionCallMessage`, which contains parameter values for the CAO constructor. On the server side, the object's activator creates the CAO and returns its `ObjRef` in an object that implements the `IConstructionReturnMessage`.

The following code snippet obtains the `RealProxy` object associated with a remote MBR object:

```
// Get the transparent proxy representing the remote object
Object objTransparentProxy = RemotingServices.Connect(typeof(
 PizzaOrderNS.PizzaOrder), "tcp://bingo:8080/PizzaOrder.soap");

// Get the RealProxy associated with this transparent proxy
RealProxy realProxy = RemotingServices.GetRealProxy(objTransparentProxy);

// Get the type name of the object that the RealProxy represents
Console.WriteLine(realProxy.GetProxiedType().FullName);
```

To extend the functionality provided by a `RealProxy`, we inherit from the `RealProxy` class and override its `Invoke` method to provide custom interception services prior to dispatching a method message (as represented by an object implementing `IMethodMessage`) to the remote object, or after receiving a method return message (an object implementing `IMethodReturnMessage`) from the remote object. The following code extends the `RealProxy()` class to enforce a business rule that prevents user `Sneezy()` invoking the `OrderPizza()` method:

```
class PizzaOrderDietAuthProxy : RealProxy
{
    Object m_objPizzaOrder = null;
    Type m_objType = null;
    String m_strUserName = "";

    public PizzaOrderDietAuthProxy(Type objType, String strUserName)
                                                    : base(objType)
    {
        m_objType = objType;
        m_strUserName = strUserName;

        // Activate the CAO at its remote URL location
        m_objPizzaOrder= Activator.CreateInstance(m_objType);
    }

    public override IMessage Invoke(IMessage objMessage)
    {
        // Cast to an IMethodMessage based object
```

```
        IMethodMessage objMethodMessage = (IMethodMessage) objMessage;

        // Enforce business rules
        String strMethodName = objMethodMessage.MethodName;
        if(strMethodName == "OrderPizza")
        {
            // Check if Sneezy, who is on a diet, is trying to order pizzas
            if(m_strUserName == "Sneezy")
            {
                throw new Exception("Alert !. Sneezy's trying to order pizzas");
            }
        }

        // Invoke the method on the remote object
        Object objReturn = m_objType.InvokeMember(strMethodName,
         BindingFlags.Default | BindingFlags.InvokeMethod, null,
         m_objPizzaOrder, objMethodMessage.Args);

        // Get the return message as an IMethodReturnMessage based object
        Object [] argsResult = null;
        ReturnMessage objReturnMessage = new ReturnMessage(objReturn,
         argsResult, 1, null, (IMethodCallMessage) objMessage);

        return objReturnMessage;
    }
}
```

To route remote method calls through the `PizzaOrderDietAuthProxy`, method invocations on the `PizzaOrder` object need to be made on the transparent proxy object associated with the `PizzaOrder DietAuthProxy`. This calls the `PizzaOrderDietAuthProxy` class's overridden `Invoke()` implementation, which we use to provide user-defined interception services that could include logging, authentication, role-based security checks on method calls, and the like:

```
String strCurrentDwarfUserName = "Sneezy";
HttpChannel chan = new HttpChannel(8081);
try
{
    ChannelServices.RegisterChannel(chan);
    ActivatedClientTypeEntry entryCAO = new
            ActivatedClientTypeEntry(typeof(PizzaOrderNS.PizzaOrder),
                                "http://bingo:8080");
    RemotingConfiguration.RegisterActivatedClientType(entryCAO);

    // Create an instance of our home-grown custom authentication RealProxy
    PizzaOrderDietAuthProxy PizzaOrderAuthProxy = new PizzaOrderDietAuthProxy
     (typeof(PizzaOrderNS.PizzaOrder), strCurrentDwarfUserName);

    // Get the transparent proxy associated with PizzaOrderDietAuthProxy
    PizzaOrder objPizza = (PizzaOrder)PizzaOrderAuthProxy
     .GetTransparentProxy();

    // Invoke the method on the object routed through PizzaOrderDietAuthProxy
    String strReultXML = objPizza.OrderPizza(strPizzaOrderXML);

}
catch(Exception ex)
{
```

```
    Console.WriteLine(ex.Message);
}
finally
{
    ChannelServices.UnregisterChannel(chan);
}
```

Remoting Configuration File Format Reference

The previous sections of this appendix have looked at that the classes of the remoting framework for exposing and consuming remote objects (both well-known and client-activated objects), for managing their lifetime and activation policies, and for configuring transport channels that carry messages to and from objects across remoting boundaries. While this configuration can all be done programmatically, real-world enterprise applications typically have very complex configuration requirements that usually change constantly according to the deployment environment. For example, a remote application host might use a TCP channel listening on port 8080 for remote requests. The changing needs at the deployment site could require that no ports other than port 80 be open on the deployment machine. In such a scenario, it may not be desirable to change all the configuration settings programmatically and rebuild the application to suit the deployment environment. Furthermore, another deployment environment for the same application may have a totally different set of configuration requirements. What we really need is to be able to declaratively specify these configuration settings in such a way that the application administrator can modify them as and when required. This is what the configuration files provided by the remoting framework aim to do.

Remoting configuration files are XML files that contain configuration information for object types, the URI endpoints where the objects are exposed, their activation mode, the URLs for remote applications and activators, channels and their properties, lease lifetime policy settings, and so on. This saves the programmer (that's us) the rigmarole of having to explicitly change registration and configuration settings programmatically every time the deployment requirements change. Configuration files help immensely in this regard. We can specify all the remoting configuration settings in the standard XML format defined by the remoting framework, and tell the remoting infrastructure to use that file for configuration information. To do this, we call the Configure method of the RemotingConfiguration() class, passing in the file path for the configuration file. The preferred naming convention for configuration files is ApplicationName.Extension.config, although the remoting framework will accept any other convention we may prefer. So, if we have a remote object hosted in a managed executable called PizzaOrderHost.exe, the recommended naming for its configuration file would be PizzaOrderHost.exe.config, and we would register this configuration file like this:

```
RemotingConfiguration.Configure("PizzaOrderHost.exe.config")
```

If we are hosting an application in IIS, then we have to add the remoting configuration information to the web.config file that maintains ASP.NET configuration details. The web.config file needs to be present in the physical directory pointed to by the application's virtual root. Remoting configuration files are not restricted to the server end of the remoting application, and they can be used client-side to register remote object types, channel properties, URLs for remote objects, and such like.

Server-Side Registration

At the server end of a remoting application, the following configuration and registration information can be specified to the remoting services infrastructure:

- ❑ The fully qualified type name of the object being exposed as a service
- ❑ The URI endpoint at which the object is exposed
- ❑ Whether the object needs to be exposed as a well-known object or as a client-activated object
- ❑ The activation mode for well-known objects (`SingleCall` or `Singleton`)
- ❑ The lease lifetime policy to be used (applies to client-activated objects and `Singleton` well-known objects only)
- ❑ The type of transport channels to be used, and the port number on which to listen for requests

Below is a skeleton XML hierarchy for a remoting configuration file for the server end of a remoting application. The table that appears after it details what each of its elements and attributes mean:

```xml
<configuration>
  <system.runtime.remoting>

    <application name="Specify the name of your application here">

      <!-- Register well-known or CAO object types and object URIs -->
      <service>

        <!-- Here's how you register a well-known object type -->
        <wellknown mode="Specify activation mode (Singleton or SingleCall)"
            type="Qualified type name of object, assembly name"
            objectUri="Specify the URI endpoint of the object" />

        <!-- Here's how you register a client activated object type -->
        <activated type="Qualified type name of object, assembly name" />

      </service>

      <!-- Lifetime management policies for CAO and well-known Singletons-->
      <lifetime leaseTime="Specify initial duration of lease"
          sponsorshipTimeOut="Specify time to wait for sponsor to respond"
          renewOnCallTime="Specify lease renewal time on method call"
          leaseManagerPollTime="Specify the poll time for the lease manager">
      </lifetime>

      <!--Configure one or more channels used by the service -->
      <channels>

        <!-- This is just one way of configuring a channel-->
        <!-- Simply point to a channel that is predefined in the template -->
        <channel ref="Specify channel id as defined in the channel template"
            port="Specify a port number that the channel will listen on" />

        <!-- This is yet another way to configure the channel -->
        <!-- This channel specifies its type explicitly -->
        <channel type="Qualified type name of the channel, channel assembly"
            port="Specify a port number that the channel will listen on" />

      </channels>
```

```
    </application>

    <!-- These are channel templates -->
    <!-- Use the channels tag at this level only if defining new channels-->
    <channels>
      <channel id="Specify the channel ID by which it will be referenced"
        type="Qualified type name of the channel, channel assembly" />
    </channels>

  </system.runtime.remoting>
  </configuration>
```

Name	Type	Parent Element	Description
configuration	Element	–	The root element for the remoting configuration file.
system.runtime . remoting	Element	configuration	The parent element for remoting configuration-related information.
application	Element	system.runtime. remoting	The parent element for application-specific remoting configuration.
name	Attribute (optional)	application	Indicates the name of the remoting application. This name plays an important role in how clients connect to well-known objects. For example, if the name specified is PizzaOrderHost and the URI endpoint is PizzaOrder.soap, then clients can connect to it using the URL http://bingo:8080/ PizzaOrderHost/PizzaOrder.soap. If the application name is not specified, then clients can connect to the object using a URL such as http://bingo:8080/ PizzaOrder.soap.
service	Element	application	The parent element for registration of well-known and client-activated object types in the server.
wellknown	Element	service	The parent element for registering well-known object types in the server. It contains attributes that also provide details such as the well-known object's activation mode and its URI endpoint in the server.
mode	Attribute	wellknown	Specifies the activation mode of the well-known object. Either Singleton or SingleCall.

Name	Type	Parent Element	Description
type	Attribute	wellknown	Specifies the fully qualified type name for the well-known object. The fully qualified type name is of the form *Qualified type name, assembly name*. For example, if `PizzaOrderNS.PizzaOrder` is the qualified type name of the object, which is present in an assembly called `PizzaOrderAssem.dll`, then the type attribute would have the value `PizzaOrderNS.PizzaOrder, PizzaOrderAssem`.
objectUri	Attribute	wellknown	Specifies the URI endpoint of the well-known object in the server. This can be any valid URI. However, for IIS hosting, the URI's extension should either be `.rem` or `.soap` so that remote calls can be intercepted by the ASP.NET ISAPI extension (`aspnet_isapi.dll`). For example, the `PizzaOrder` object could be exposed at an URI endpoint called `PizzaOrder.soap`.
activated	Element	service	The parent element for registering client-activated object types in the server.
type	Attribute	activated	Specifies the fully qualified type name for the client-activated object The fully qualified type name is of the form *Qualified type name, assembly name*.
lifetime	Element	application	The parent element for specifying lease lifetime policy settings for client activated objects and well-known `Singleton` objects. (Note that since `SingleCall` objects are destroyed after every call, lease lifetime policy settings have no effect on well-known `SingleCall` objects.)
leaseTime	Attribute (optional)	lifetime	Specifies the initially allotted lease time for an object. The default value is **five minutes**. You have to append an appropriate suffix to indicate the time units that this value represents. *(For more information on these suffixes, refer to the table below.)*

Table continued on following page

Name	Type	Parent Element	Description
sponsorship Time out	Attribute (optional)	lifetime	Specifies the time to wait for a lease sponsor to respond before setting the lease state to Expired, which subsequently marks the object for garbage collection. The default is **two minutes**. You have to append an appropriate suffix to indicate the time units that this value represents. *(For more information on these suffixes, refer to the table below.)*
renewOnCall Time	Attribute (optional)	lifetime	Specifies the amount of time by which an object's lease lifetime is extended for every method call that is made on the object. The default value is **2 minutes**. You have to append an appropriate suffix to indicate the time units that this value represents. *(For more information on these suffixes, refer to the table below.)*
leaseManager PollTime	Attribute (optional)	lifetime	Specifies how often the lease manager should wakeup to check if the lease has expired for the object. The default value is **ten seconds**. You have to append an appropriate suffix to indicate the time units that this value represents. *(For more information on these suffixes, refer to the table below.)*
channels	Element	application	The parent element for configuring transport channels associated with the remoting application. Do not confuse this element and the similarly named <channels> element that appears directly under the <system.runtime.remoting> element. While this element (a direct child of the <application> element) contains a list of channels configured for a specified remoting application, the latter contains a list of predefined channel templates that can be referred from configured channels such as this one.
channel	Element	channels	The parent element associated with a channel's configuration details. The channel can either refer to one of the predefined channels in a channel template or can specify a channel's fully qualified type name. There is also a set of predefined HTTP and TCP channel templates defined in the machine.config file to which a channel can point to using its ref attribute.

Name	Type	Parent Element	Description
ref	Attribute (optional)	channel	Refers to one of the predefined channel templates that have been specified in the `machine.config` file or through the `<channels>` element directly under the `<system.runtime.remoting>` element. The standard HTTP and TCP transport channels are predefined in `machine.config` using the `http` and `tcp` identifiers respectively. If you need to use the HTTP or TCP channel implementation provided by the `HttpChannel` and `TcpChannel` classes, all you need to do is set `ref="http"` or `ref="tcp"` respectively.
port	Attribute	channel	Specifies the port number on which the channel will listen for incoming requests.
type	Attribute (optional)	channel	Specifies the fully qualified type name for the channel. The fully qualified type name is of the form *Qualified type name of channel, channel's assembly name*. From the RC onwards, if the assembly is signed, we need to provide full versioning and key information (Version, Culture, and PublicKeyToken).

Time span suffixes for lease lifetime policy related attributes	Duration
D	Days
H	Hours
M	Minutes
S	Seconds
MS	Milliseconds

The following example shows how we can use a remoting configuration file to register object types and configure channels. We're assuming that we already have a class named `ZipCode` in an assembly named `ZipCode.dll` that we wish to expose to remoting clients. We'll begin by seeing how to expose this class as a well-known object to remote clients using a remoting configuration file:

```
using System;

namespace ZipCodeNS
{
    public class ZipCode : MarshalByRefObject
    {
        public String GetZipCodeForCity(String strCity, String strState)
        {
```

```
            // Perform some kind of Zipcode look up operation here...

            return strZipCode;
        }
    }
}
```

We host this class within a managed application host that loads a remoting configuration file containing the information to register and configure the `ZipCode` object types and channels. The host application code shown below simply loads the configuration file using the `RemotingServices.Configure()` method, and then listens for requests until it's shut down:

```
using System;
using System.Runtime.Remoting;

class ZipCodeLookupHost
{
    static void Main(string[] args)
    {
        RemotingConfiguration.Configure("ZipCodeLookupHost.exe.config");
        System.Console.WriteLine("Zipcode lookup host is up and running");
        System.Console.WriteLine("Press any key to shut me down...");
        System.Console.ReadLine();
    }
}
```

And now to the heart of the matter: the configuration file itself. First, we define the elements and attributes to register the `ZipCode` object as a well-known object:

```
<service>
  <wellknown mode="SingleCall"
             type="ZipCodeNS.ZipCode,ZipCode"
             objectUri="ZipCodeLookup.soap" />
</service>
```

Notice that the activation mode for the object is set to `SingleCall` using the `mode` attribute, so the object will be destroyed after every method call. The fully qualified type name of the `ZipCode` class happens to be `ZipCodeNS.ZipCode, ZipCode`, where `ZipCodeNS.ZipCode` is the qualified type name, and `ZipCode` the name of its assembly. The URI endpoint for the object is set to `ZipCodeLookup.soap` using the `objectUri` attribute. Now let's register a couple of channels to listen for incoming requests from clients:

```
<channels>
  <channel ref="http" port="8080" />
  <channel ref="tcp" port="9095"  />
</channels>
```

If your object is hosted in IIS, do not use the `port` attribute with the `<channel>` element in the configuration file. The port number should not be specified explicitly because IIS will automatically listen on the default HTTP port (port 80) for requests. Any changes to this port number should be made through **Internet Services Manager** and not through the `port` attribute in the configuration file.

We'll register a TCP channel to listen on port 9095, and an HTTP channel to listen on port 8080, both of which refer to predefined channel templates for the HTTP and TCP channels. You'll find these templates in the `machine.config` file, where machine-wide configuration settings are stored.

> You'll find the `machine.config` file in the `Microsoft.NET\Framework\` `v1.0.2914\CONFIG` subdirectory of your Windows installation. Please note that you may need to substitute the `v1.0.2914` in the above path with the current version of your .NET Framework installation.

Here is the section of the `machine.config` file that pertains to channel templates:

```
<!-- This is a part of the machine.config file -->
<!-- This file maintains machine wide configuration settings -->

<system.runtime.remoting>

<!-- Rest of the stuff omitted for brevity   -->

  <channels>
    <channel id="http"
            type="System.Runtime.Remoting.Channels.Http.HttpChannel,
                System.Runtime.Remoting,
                Version=1.0.3300.0,Culture=neutral,PublicKeyToken=b77a5c561934e089" />
    <channel id="http client"
            type="System.Runtime.Remoting.Channels.Http.HttpClientChannel,
                System.Runtime.Remoting,
                Version=1.0.3300.0,Culture=neutral,PublicKeyToken=b77a5c561934e089" />
    <channel id="http server"
            type="System.Runtime.Remoting.Channels.Http.HttpServerChannel,
                System.Runtime.Remoting" />
    <channel id="tcp"
            type="System.Runtime.Remoting.Channels.Tcp.TcpChannel,
                System.Runtime.Remoting,
                Version=1.0.3300.0,Culture=neutral,PublicKeyToken=b77a5c561934e089" />
    <channel id="tcp client"
            type="System.Runtime.Remoting.Channels.Tcp.TcpClientChannel,
                System.Runtime.Remoting,
                Version=1.0.3300.0,Culture=neutral,PublicKeyToken=b77a5c561934e089" />
    <channel id="tcp server"
            type="System.Runtime.Remoting.Channels.Tcp.TcpServerChannel,
                System.Runtime.Remoting,
                Version=1.0.3300.0,Culture=neutral,PublicKeyToken=b77a5c561934e089" />
  </channels>

<!-- Rest of the stuff omitted for brevity   -->

</system.runtime.remoting>
```

As seen above, there are standard channel templates defined for the TCP and HTTP channels based on the `HttpChannel` and `TcpChannel` classes. Also notice that there are templates predefined for the client-side only and server-side only implementations of the channels. For example, the `HttpClientChannel` and `HttpServerChannel` class implementations are available through the `http client` and `http server` identifiers. We'll use the channel configuration settings in the `ZipCodeLookupHost` application's configuration file to refer to the `http` and `tcp` templates, which combine the client- and server-side implementation of the channels through the `HttpChannel` and `TcpChannel` classes respectively.

You can also configure a channel explicitly by specifying the fully qualified type name of the channel, instead of referring to a predefined channel template:

```
<channel type="System.Runtime.Remoting.Channels.Tcp.TcpChannel,
                System.Runtime.Remoting,
                Version=1.0.3300.0,Culture=neutral,PublicKeyToken=677a5c561934e089" />
" port="8076"/>
```

With the channel configuration done, there's just one little thing left to do, although not strictly necessary. We can provide a name for the application through the configuration file, so that clients can use the application's host name in the URL when connecting to the application. The application's name is specified using the name attribute of the <application> element:

```
<application name="ZipCodeLookupHost">
```

Since the ZipCode object is exposed at an URI endpoint called ZipCodeLookup.soap, the client would use the following URLs to connect to the service:

- ❑ Clients using the HTTP channel would use the following URL:
  http://machinename:8080/ZipCodeLookupHost/ZipCodeLookup.soap
- ❑ Clients using the TCP channel would use the following URL:
  tcp://machinename:9095/ZipCodeLookupHost/ZipCodeLookup.soap

Sandwich the XML elements that we created so far between the standard XML remoting configuration element tags – <configuration> and <system.runtime.remoting> – and save it to a file called ZipCodeLookupHost.exe.config. Here's the completed ZipCodeLookupHost.exe.config file:

```
<configuration>
  <system.runtime.remoting>
    <application name="ZipCodeLookupHost">
<service>
      <wellknown mode="SingleCall"
                 type="ZipCodeNS.ZipCode,ZipCode"
                 objectUri="ZipCodeLookup.soap" />
    </service>
<channels>
      <channel ref="http" port="8080" />
      <channel ref="tcp" port="9095"  />
    </channels>
</application>
  </system.runtime.remoting>
</configuration>
```

Next, we'll expose the ZipCode object as a client-activated object instead of a well-known object through the configuration file. If we'd used the programmatic approach for registering this object as a well-known object, we'd have to rewrite the application code in order to change how the ZipCode object is registered. The configuration file approach means that all we have to change is a simple XML tag, from <wellknown> to <activated>:

```
<service>
  <activated type="ZipCodeNS.ZipCode,ZipCode" />
</service>
```

Note that the type attribute of the <activated> element provides the fully qualified type name of the ZipCode object.

We can also play around with the lease lifetime policy settings for the ZipCode object using the <lifetime> element and its attributes:

```
<lifetime leaseTime="10M"
          sponsorshipTimeout="10S"
          renewOnCallTime="3M"
          leaseManagerPollTime="5S" />
```

The `leaseTime` attribute indicates that an initial lease time of 10 minutes will be assigned to the object. The `leaseManagerPollTime` attribute instructs the lease manager to wake up every 5 seconds and check for expired leases. The `renewOnCallTime` attribute specifies that any incoming method call on the object increments the lease period by 3 minutes. If the object is still alive when the lease period elapses, the lease manager tries to contact a lease sponsor registered in its lease sponsor list, to see if they wish to renew the lease. If the sponsor does not respond within 10 seconds, specified by the `sponsorshipTimeout` attribute, the lease manager tries to contact the next sponsor in the list. If none of the sponsors respond, the lease state is set to `Expired` and the object is marked for garbage collection. Here's the modified `ZipCodeLookupHost.exe.config` file for exposing the `ZipCode` object as a client-activated object:

```
<configuration>
  <system.runtime.remoting>
    <application name="ZipCodeLookupHost">

      <lifetime leaseTime="10M" sponsorshipTimeout="10S"
                renewOnCallTime="3M" leaseManagerPollTime="5S" />

      <service>
        <activated type="ZipCodeNS.ZipCode,ZipCode" />
      </service>

      <channels>
        <channel ref="http" port="8080" />
        <channel ref="tcp" port="9095"  />
      </channels>

    </application>
  </system.runtime.remoting>
</configuration>
```

Client-Side Registration

Consumers of remoting applications can dynamically change configuration settings on the fly using a configuration file at the client end, for example to switch between remote server locations during server downtimes and so on. We can specify the following configuration and registration information at the client end of a remoting application:

- ❑ The fully qualified type name of the object being consumed

- ❑ The URL location of the activator for the client activated object

- ❑ The URL location of the well-known object

- ❑ The type of transport channels to use for the dispatch of message requests to the remote object, and the port number on which to listen for callback requests

Here is a skeletal XML hierarchy for a client-end remoting configuration file, followed by a table describing each of its elements and attributes:

```xml
<configuration>
  <system.runtime.remoting>

    <application>

        <!-- Register well-known or CAO object types on the client -->
        <client url="Specify the URL of the activator for the CAO">

          <!-- Here's how to register a well-known object type(client-side)-->
          <wellknown type="Qualified type name of object, assembly name"
               url="Specify the URL location of the well-known object " />

          <!-- Here's how you register a CAO type (client-side) -->
          <activated type="Qualified type name of object, assembly name" />

        </client>

        <!--Configure one or more channels to send messages to the objects -->
        <channels>

        <!-- This is just one way of configuring a channel-->
        <!-- Simply point to a channel that is predefined in the template -->
        <channel ref="Specify channel id as defined in the channel template"
            port="Specify a port number on which to listen for callbacks" />

         <!-- This is yet another way to configure the channel -->
         <!-- This channel specifies its type explicitly -->
         <channel type="Qualified type name of the channel, channel assembly"
           port=" Specify a port number on which to listen for callbacks" />

        </channels>

    </application>

    <!-- These are channel templates -->
    <!-- Use the channels tag at this level only if defining new channels-->
    <channels>
      <channel id="Specify the channel ID by which it will be referenced"
        type="Qualified type name of the channel, channel assembly" />
    </channels>

  </system.runtime.remoting>
</configuration>
```

Name	Type	Parent Element Name	Description
configuration	Element	–	The root element for the remoting configuration file.
system. runtime. remoting	Element	configuration	The parent element for remoting configuration-related information.
application	Element	system.runtime. remoting	The parent element for application-specific remoting configuration.
client	Element	application	The parent element for registration of well-known and client-activated object types in the client.

Name	Type	Parent Element Name	Description
url	Attribute	client	Only used with client-activated objects to specify the URL of the activator for a client-activated object. If the client activated object type is registered by a managed application host that has configured an HTTP channel to listen for requests on port 8090 in a machine named SkyWalker, then the URL of the CAO activator would be http://SkyWalker:8090
wellknown	Element	client	The parent element for registering well-known object types in the client.
type	Attribute	wellknown	Specifies the fully qualified type name for the well-known object. The fully qualified type name is of the form *Qualified type name, assembly name.* For example, if StockQuoteNS.StockQuote is the qualified type name of the object, which is present in an assembly called StockQuoteClientProxy.dll, then the type attribute would be StockQuoteNS.StockQuote, StockQuoteClientProxy.
url	Attribute	wellknown	Specifies the URL of the well-known object on the server. The URL is fully qualified with the URI endpoint information. For example, if a StockQuote object is deployed at a URI endpoint called StockQuote.soap in an IIS application whose virtual root alias is StockQuoteApp, and is running on a machine called *SkyWalker*, then the URL would be something like http://SkyWalker:80/StockQuoteApp/StockQuote.soap.
activated	Element	client	The parent element for registering client-activated object types in the client.
type	Attribute	activated	Specifies the fully qualified type name for the client activated object, of the form: *qualified type name, assembly name.*

Table continued on following page

Name	Type	Parent Element Name	Description
channels	Element	application	The parent element for configuring transport channels used by the client to dispatch messages to the server across remoting boundaries. Do not confuse this element and the similarly named `<channels>` element that appears directly under the `<system.runtime.remoting>` element. While this element (a direct child of the `<application>` element) contains a list of channels configured for a specified client wanting to transport messages to the server, the latter contains a list of predefined channel templates that can be referred to from configured channels such as this one.
channel	Element	channels	The parent element associated with channel's configuration details. The channel can either refer to one of the predefined channels in a channel template, or specify a channel's fully qualified type name. There is also a set of predefined HTTP and TCP channel templates defined in the `machine.config` file to which a channel can point to using its `ref` attribute.
ref	Attribute (optional)	channel	Refers to one of the predefined channel templates specified in the machine.config file or through the `<channels>` element directly under the `<system.runtime.remoting>` element. The standard HTTP and TCP transport channel are predefined in the `machine.config` using the `http` and `tcp` identifiers, respectively. If you need to use the HTTP or TCP channel implementation provided by the `HttpChannel` and `TcpChannel` classes, all you need to do is set `ref="http"` or `ref="tcp"` respectively.
port	Attribute	channel	Specifies the port number on which the transport channel listens for callbacks from the remote object.

Name	Type	Parent Element Name	Description
type	Attribute (optional)	channel	Specifies the fully qualified type name for the channel. The fully qualified type name is of the form *Qualified type name of channel, channel's assembly name.*

A quick bird's eye view of the client-end remoting configuration file format shows that it is not too different from its server-side counterpart. Essentially, the object types registered at the client end are used by the application consuming the remote object to find type information for the objects. The client application also needs to be told the URL of the remote object if it is consuming a well-known object, or the URL of the activator if it is consuming a client-activated object.

Let's create a remoting configuration file for a client that wishes to consume the ZipCode object. On the client side, the <client> element is the parent element for details such as the remote types registered on the client and the URL where these object types should be created or activated. If the ZipCode object is exposed as a well-known object in the server, we use the <wellknown> element in the client to specify the object type and its URL. The type attribute specifies the fully qualified type name of the object to be created at that URL. The url attribute specifies the URL where the well-known object should be created, and includes the URI endpoint information as well. Below is the complete client-side configuration file for consuming the ZipCode well-known object:

```
<configuration>
  <system.runtime.remoting>
    <application>

      <client>
        <wellknown type="ZipCodeNS.ZipCode,ZipCode"
               url="http://bingo:80/ZipCodeLookupApp/ZipCodeLookup.soap" />
      </client>

      <channels>
        <channel ref="http" port="8085" />
        <channel ref="tcp" port="8181"  />
      </channels>

    </application>
  </system.runtime.remoting>
</configuration>
```

This configuration file assumes that the ZipCode object is deployed in an IIS application with the name ZipCodeLookupApp that is registered at an URI endpoint called ZipCodeLookup.soap. In this example, IIS is assumed to be running on a machine called bingo.

If the ZipCode object is exposed as a client-activated object on the server, we need to specify the URL of the activator in the <client> element's url attribute within the configuration file (this attribute does not apply to well-known objects). The <activated> element's type attribute specifies the fully qualified type name of the object that this client application should activate remotely. Below is the equivalent client side configuration file for consuming the ZipCode object exposed as a client-activated object:

```
<configuration>
  <system.runtime.remoting>
    <application>

      <client url="http://SkyWalker:8080">
        <activated type="ZipCodeNS.ZipCode,ZipCode"/>
      </client>

      <channels>
        <channel ref="http" port="8085" />
        <channel ref="tcp" port="8181"  />
      </channels>

    </application>
  </system.runtime.remoting>
</configuration>
```

The above configuration file assumes that the ZipCode object is deployed in a managed application host, which has registered the ZipCode object as a CAO and is using the HTTP channel to listen on port 8080 for requests in a machine named SkyWalker. A client application can then use this configuration file when it wishes to consume the ZipCode object as shown:

```
using System;
using System.Runtime.Remoting;
using ZipCodeNS;

class ZipClient
{
    static void Main(string[] args)
    {
        RemotingConfiguration.Configure("C:\\Cfgs\\ZipCodeClient.exe.config");
        ZipCode zipObj = new ZipCode();
        Console.WriteLine(zipObj.GetZipCodeForCity("Orlando","Florida"));
    }
}
```

This example assumes that the client-side configuration file is ZipCodeClient.exe.config, and is present in the C:\Cfgs folder. Notice that the client application instantiates the ZipCode object as if it were a local object. The configuration file contains all information required to instruct the remoting infrastructure to create or activate the registered types at the specified remote URL.

Using configuration files to expose and consume objects through .NET remoting is as easy as pie. Configuration files separate the application development cycle from the deployment cycle, thus giving application administrators greater control over configuring, maintaining, and fine-tuning applications running at the deployment site.

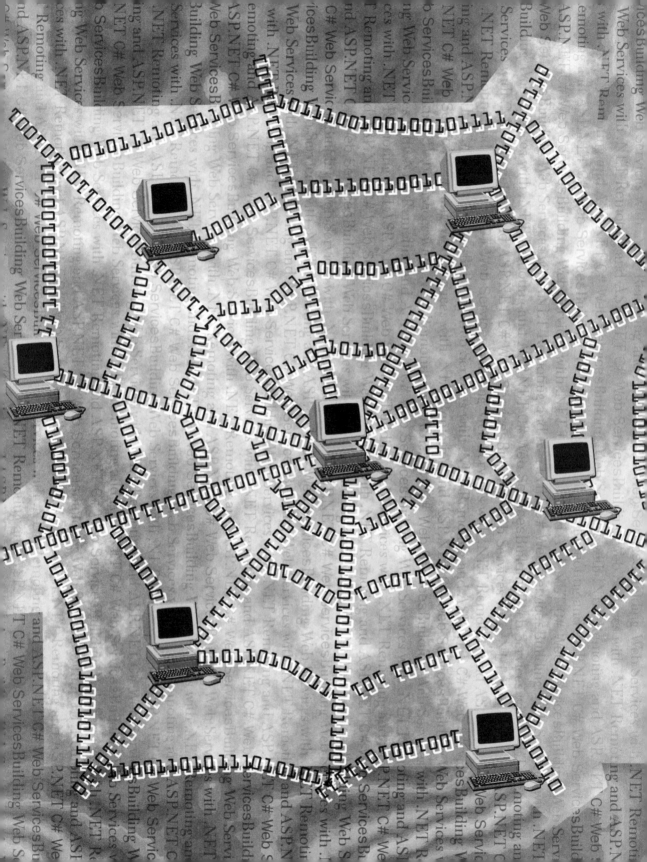

Index

A Guide to the Index

The index covers the numbered chapters but not the Introduction or Appendix. It is arranged alphabetically in word-by-word order (that is, New York would be listed before Newark). Angle-brackets and hyphens have been ignored in the alphabetization, and .NET appears under NET. Acronyms have been preferred to their expansions as main entries, on the grounds that unfamiliar acronyms are easier to construct than to expand.

A

T

U

V

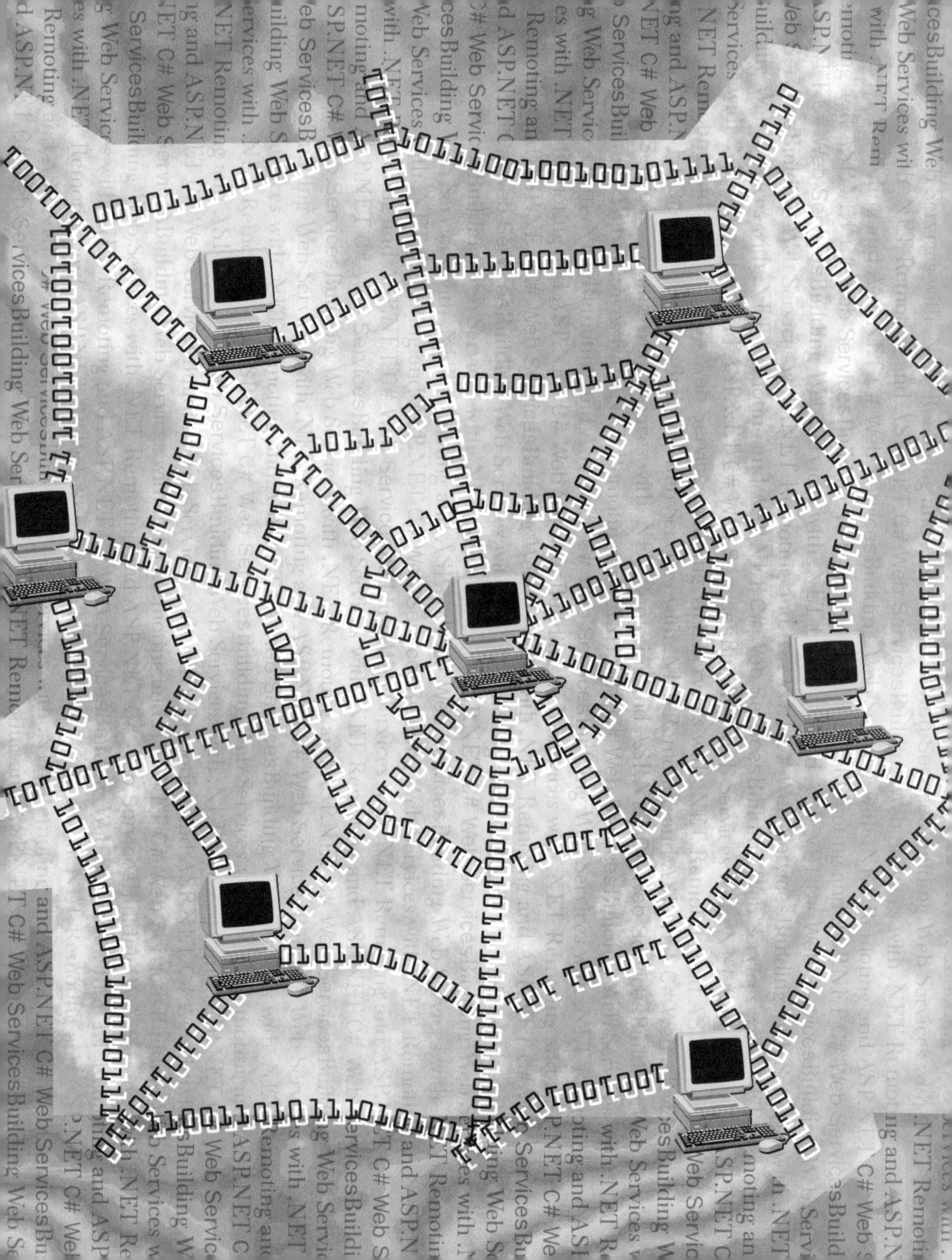

C#Today -
Your Just in Time C# Code Center

www.csharptoday.com

C#Today is an exciting new site set to provide just in time solutions to busy programmers just like its sister site ASPToday. C#Today will offer you:

- New articles every week
- Articles written by programmers for programmers
- A constantly growing archive of relevant technical articles
- The most advanced search facilities available, enabling you to track down specific areas quickly and efficiently.

Featured articles include:

Advanced Techniques for InterThread Communication By Kaushal Sanghavi

In Kaushal Sanghavi's previous article on interthread communication, he discussed some of the common and traditional ways of communication in a multithreaded system - methods which suffice for most situations. However, under certain conditions, we might want to use special techniques to allow threads within a process or across processes to communicate. In this article, Kaushal discusses some advanced techniques for inter-thread communication. Some of these techniques are not currently supported in the .NET framework natively, and we will use C#'s ability to call unmanaged code to achieve this.

.NET Metadata and Custom Attributes in C# By Aravind Corera

Attributes allow you to declaratively inject metadata information into types such as assemblies, classes, interfaces, and methods etc. At runtime, they allow you to elicit the values of these declarative properties through Reflection. In this article, Aravind Corera shows you how to define custom attributes, use them in your applications, and glean out the metadata properties from these attributes at runtime using reflection. And finally, to see how all this fits in, we see how to build a Project Status tracking system based on custom attributes.

People choose C#Today because of Wrox's proven track record of publishing expert content, and our experience of knowing the solutions you will want and need. You will find solutions that will improve your C# skills, enabling you to better serve your customers and enhance your company's knowledge base.

Welcome to the Wrox Developer Community. Through your purchase of this book, we'd like to offer you a substantial discount off your C#Today subscription. Simply go to:

http://www.csharptoday.com/special-offers/

If you have any questions please contact **customersupport@wrox.com**

wrox
Programmer to Programmer™

p2p.wrox.com
The programmer's resource centre

A unique free service from Wrox Press
With the aim of helping programmers to help each other

Wrox Press aims to provide timely and practical information to today's programmer. P2P is a list server offering a host of targeted mailing lists where you can share knowledge with four fellow programmers and find solutions to your problems. Whatever the level of your programming knowledge, and whatever technology you use P2P can provide you with the information you need.

ASP Support for beginners and professionals, including a resource page with hundreds of links, and a popular ASP.NET mailing list.

DATABASES For database programmers, offering support on SQL Server, mySQL, and Oracle.

MOBILE Software development for the mobile market is growing rapidly. We provide lists for the several current standards, including WAP, Windows CE, and Symbian.

JAVA A complete set of Java lists, covering beginners, professionals, and server-side programmers (including JSP, servlets and EJBs)

.NET Microsoft's new OS platform, covering topics such as ASP.NET, C#, and general .NET discussion.

VISUAL BASIC Covers all aspects of VB programming, from programming Office macros to creating components for the .NET platform.

WEB DESIGN As web page requirements become more complex, programmer's are taking a more important role in creating web sites. For these programmers, we offer lists covering technologies such as Flash, Coldfusion, and JavaScript.

XML Covering all aspects of XML, including XSLT and schemas.

OPEN SOURCE Many Open Source topics covered including PHP, Apache, Perl, Linux, Python and more.

FOREIGN LANGUAGE Several lists dedicated to Spanish and German speaking programmers, categories include. NET, Java, XML, PHP and XML

How to subscribe
Simply visit the P2P site, at http://p2p.wrox.com/

wrox

Programmer to Programmer™

Wrox writes books for you. Any suggestions, or ideas about how you want information given in your ideal book will be studied by our team.
Your comments are always valued at Wrox.

Free phone in USA 800-USE-WROX
Fax (312) 893 8001

UK Tel.: (0121) 687 4100   Fax: (0121) 687 4101

C# Web Services Building Web Services with .NET Remoting and ASP.NET – Registration Card

Name _____

Address _____

_____

_____

City _____ State/Region _____

Country _____ Postcode/Zip _____

E-Mail _____

Occupation _____

How did you hear about this book?

☐ Book review (name) _____

☐ Advertisement (name) _____

☐ Recommendation _____

☐ Catalog _____

☐ Other _____

Where did you buy this book?

☐ Bookstore (name) _____ City_____

☐ Computer store (name) _____

☐ Mail order _____

☐ Other _____

What influenced you in the purchase of this book?

☐ Cover Design ☐ Contents ☐ Other (please specify):

How did you rate the overall content of this book?

☐ Excellent ☐ Good ☐ Average ☐ Poor

What did you find most useful about this book? _____

_____

What did you find least useful about this book? _____

_____

Please add any additional comments. _____

_____

What other subjects will you buy a computer book on soon?

_____

What is the best computer book you have used this year?

_____

wrox

Programmer to Programmer™

Note: If you post the bounce back card below in the UK, please send it to:

Wrox Press Limited, Arden House, 1102 Warwick Road,
Acocks Green, Birmingham B27 6HB. UK.

Computer Book Publishers